CRACK OF NOON

Also by Jerry Scott and Jim Borgman

Zits: Sketchbook 1
Growth Spurt: Zits Sketchbook 2
Don't Roll Your Eyes at Me, Young Man!: Zits Sketchbook 3
Are We an "Us"?: Zits Sketchbook 4
Zits Unzipped: Zits Sketchbook 5
Busted!: Zits Sketchbook 6
Road Trip: Zits Sketchbook 7
Teenage Tales: Zits Sketchbook 8
Thrashed: Zits Sketchbook No. 9
Pimp My Lunch: Zits Sketchbook No. 10

Treasuries
Humongous Zits
Big Honkin' Zits
Zits: Supersized
Random Zits

CRACK OF NOON

A *Zits*® Treasury
by Jerry Scott and Jim Borgman

**Andrews McMeel
Publishing**

Kansas City

Zits® is syndicated internationally by King Features Syndicate, Inc. For information, write King Features Syndicate, Inc., 888 Seventh Avenue, New York, New York 10019.

06 07 08 09 10 BAM 10 9 8 7 6 5 4 3 2 1

ISBN-13: 978-0-7407-5684-9
ISBN-10: 0-7407-5684-2

Library of Congress Control Number: 2005936145

Zits® may be viewed online at
www.kingfeatures.com.

www.andrewsmcmeel.com

――――――― **ATTENTION: SCHOOLS AND BUSINESSES** ―――――――

Andrews McMeel books are available at quantity discounts with bulk purchase for educational, business, or sales promotional use. For information, please write to: Special Sales Department, Andrews McMeel Publishing, LLC, 4520 Main Street, Kansas City, Missouri 64111.

To Mark and Meryl Goldman,
heartfelt thanks.
—J.B.

To Abbey, cool chick.

—J.S.

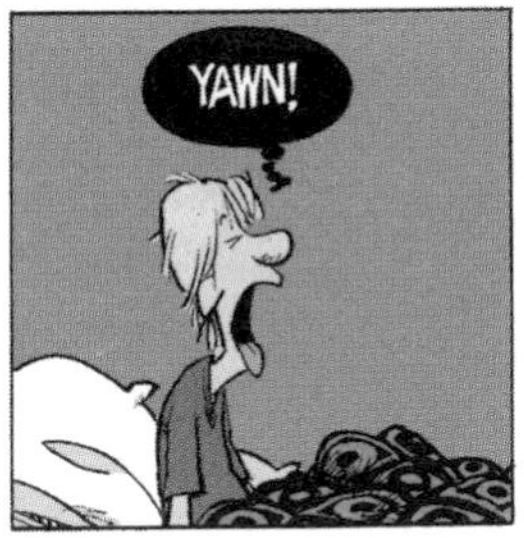
YAWN!

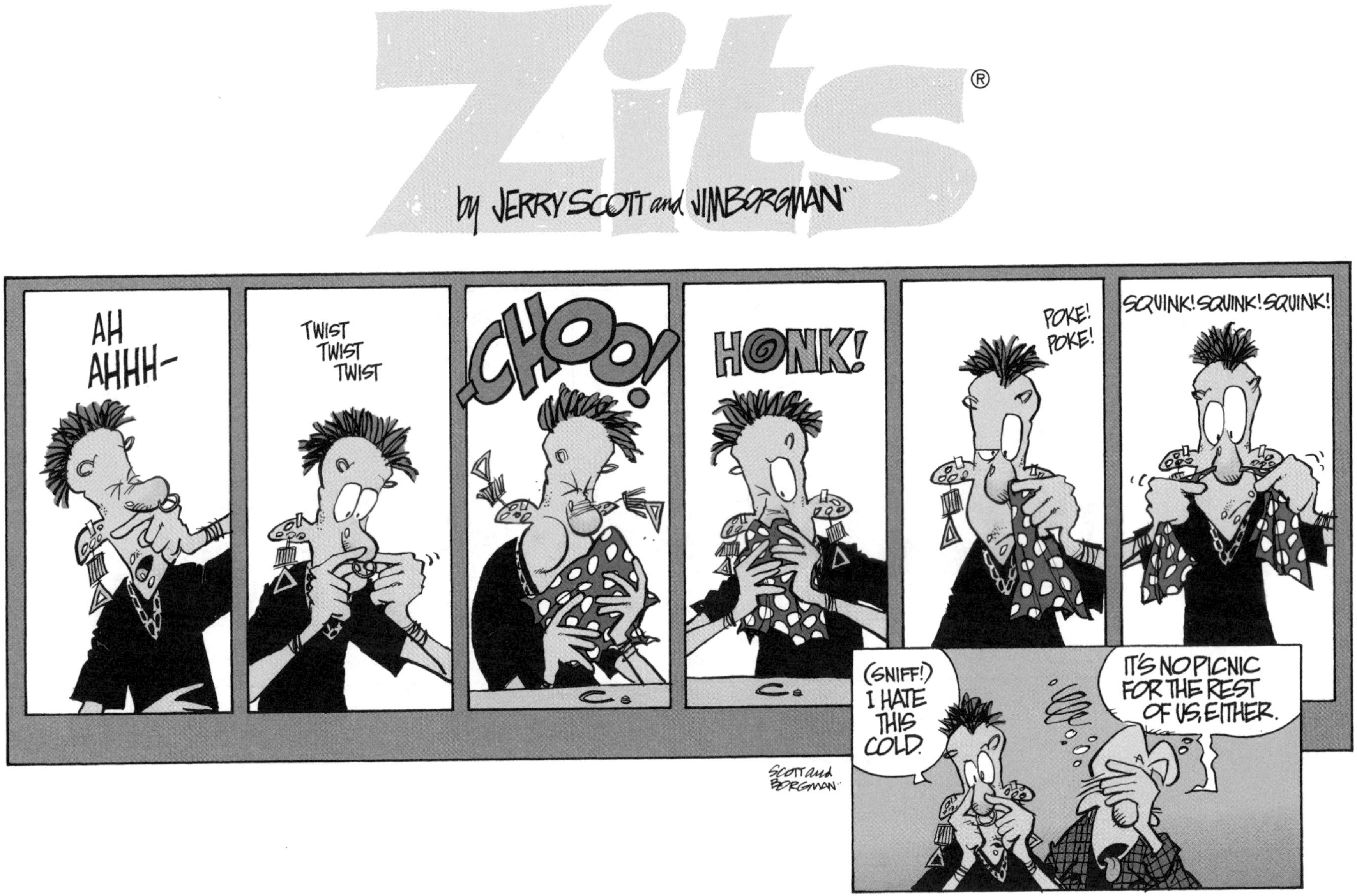
Zits®
by JERRY SCOTT and JIM BORGMAN
AH AHHH-
TWIST TWIST TWIST
-CHOO!
HONK!
POKE! POKE!
SQUINK! SQUINK! SQUINK!
(SNIFF!) I HATE THIS COLD.
IT'S NO PICNIC FOR THE REST OF US, EITHER.
SCOTT and BORGMAN

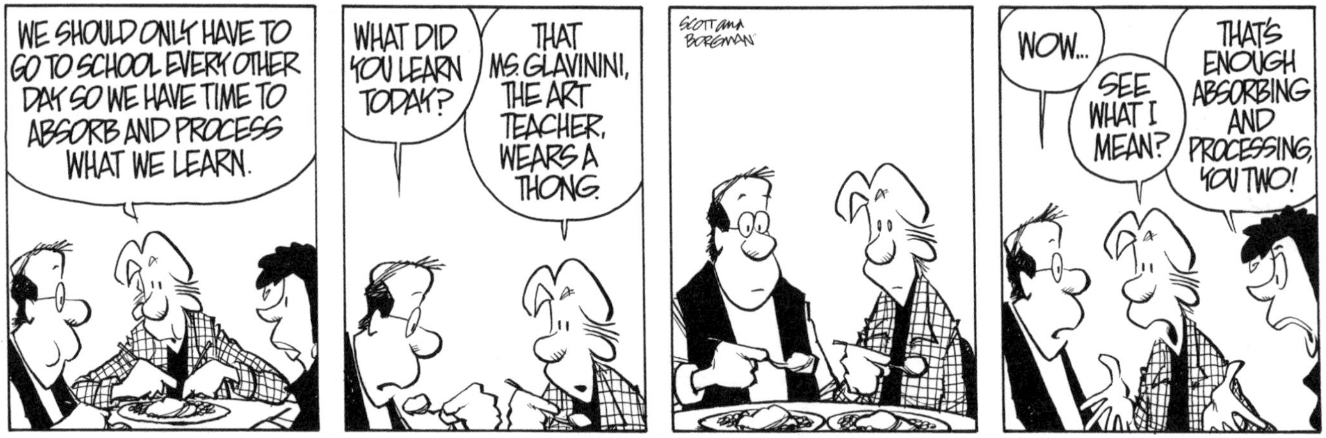
WE SHOULD ONLY HAVE TO GO TO SCHOOL EVERY OTHER DAY SO WE HAVE TIME TO ABSORB AND PROCESS WHAT WE LEARN.
WHAT DID YOU LEARN TODAY?
THAT MS. GLAVININI, THE ART TEACHER, WEARS A THONG.
SCOTT and BORGMAN
WOW...
SEE WHAT I MEAN?
THAT'S ENOUGH ABSORBING AND PROCESSING, YOU TWO!

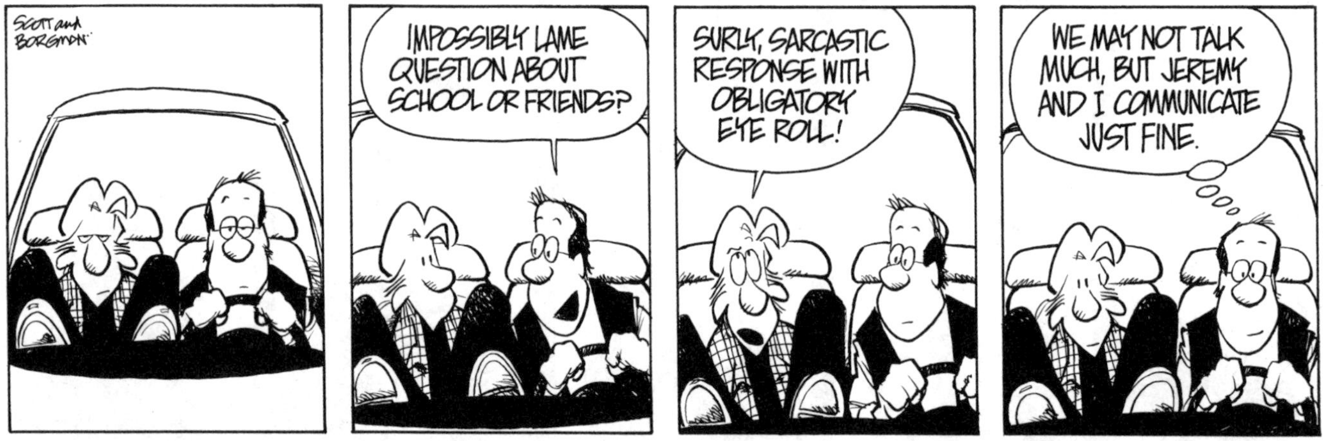
SCOTT and BORGMAN
IMPOSSIBLY LAME QUESTION ABOUT SCHOOL OR FRIENDS?
SURLY, SARCASTIC RESPONSE WITH OBLIGATORY EYE ROLL!
WE MAY NOT TALK MUCH, BUT JEREMY AND I COMMUNICATE JUST FINE.

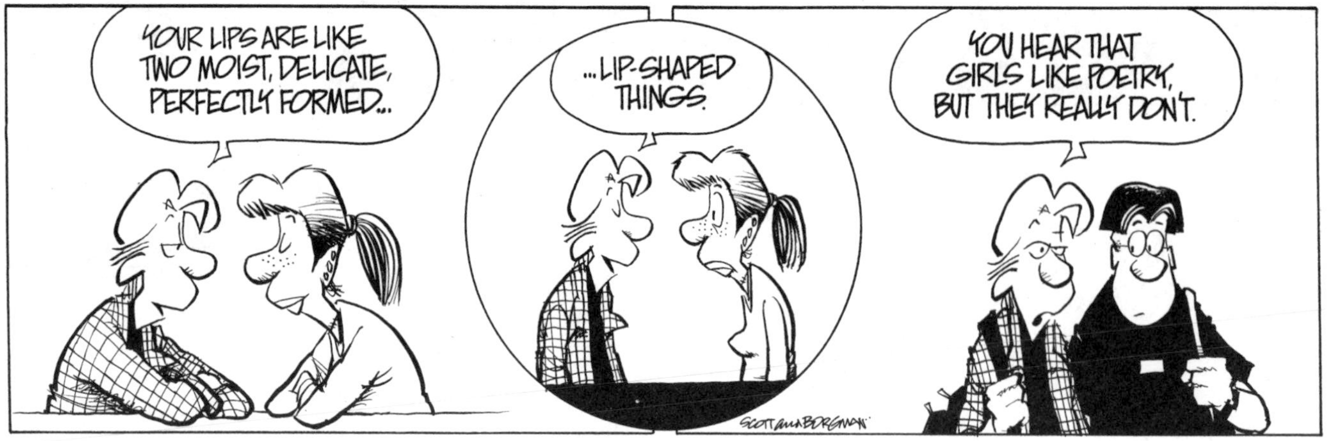
YOUR LIPS ARE LIKE TWO MOIST, DELICATE, PERFECTLY FORMED...
...LIP-SHAPED THINGS.
SCOTT and BORGMAN
YOU HEAR THAT GIRLS LIKE POETRY, BUT THEY REALLY DON'T.

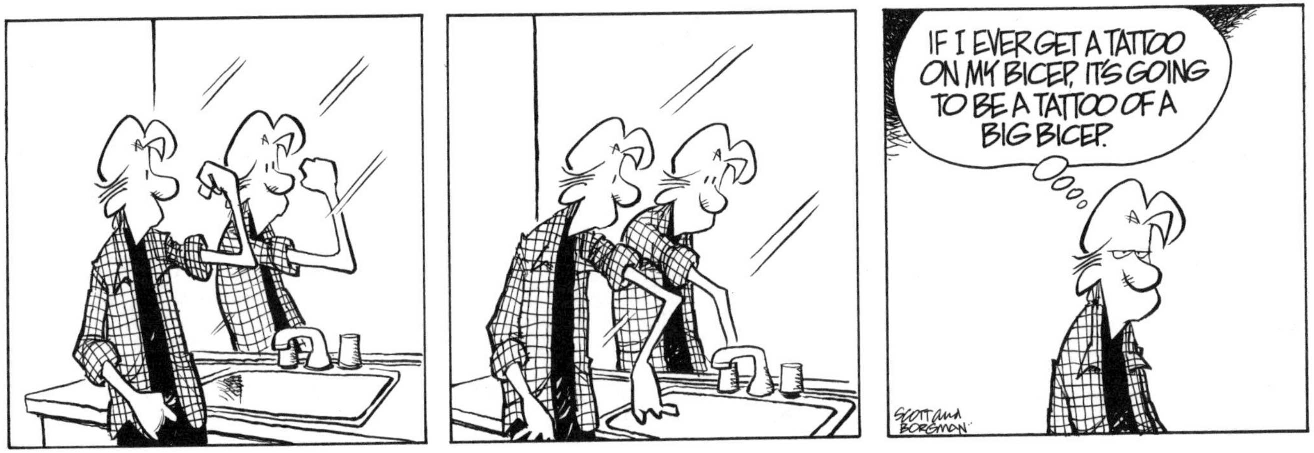
IF I EVER GET A TATTOO ON MY BICEP, IT'S GOING TO BE A TATTOO OF A BIG BICEP.
SCOTT and BORGMAN

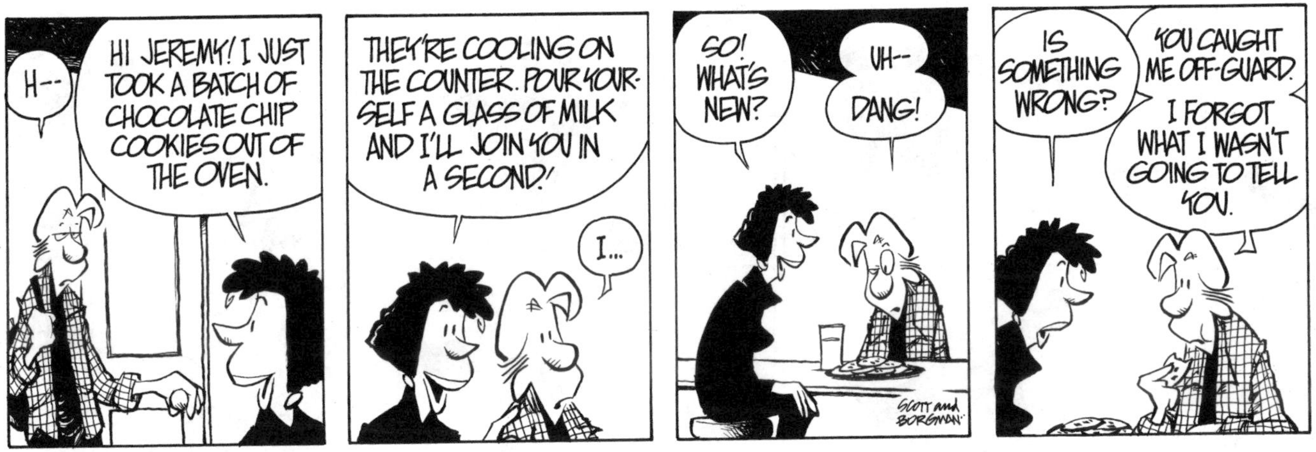
H--
HI JEREMY! I JUST TOOK A BATCH OF CHOCOLATE CHIP COOKIES OUT OF THE OVEN.
THEY'RE COOLING ON THE COUNTER. POUR YOURSELF A GLASS OF MILK AND I'LL JOIN YOU IN A SECOND!
I...
SO! WHAT'S NEW?
UH--
DANG!
SCOTT and BORGMAN
IS SOMETHING WRONG?
YOU CAUGHT ME OFF-GUARD.
I FORGOT WHAT I WASN'T GOING TO TELL YOU.

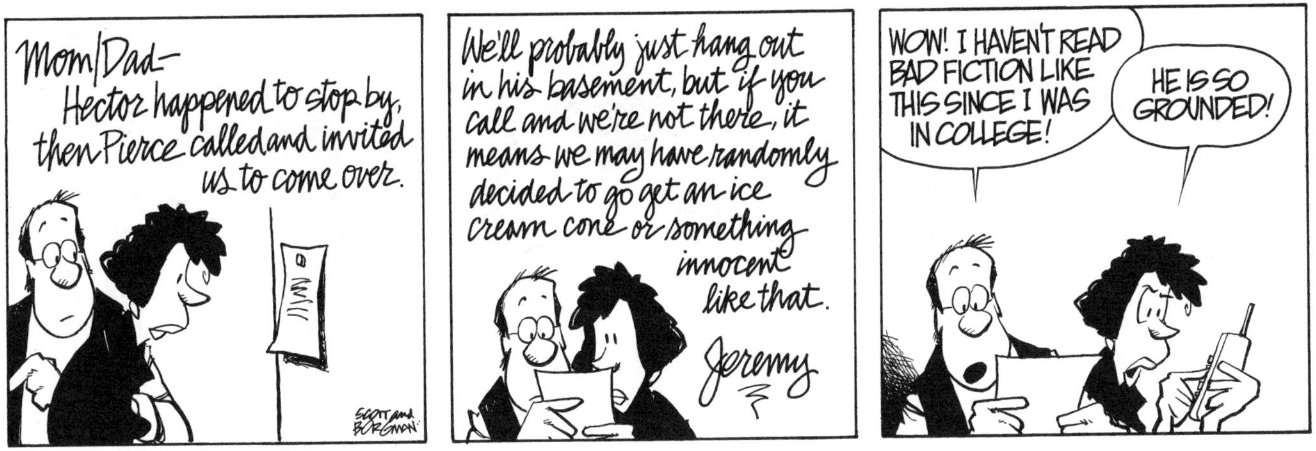
Mom/Dad-
Hector happened to stop by, then Pierce called and invited us to come over.
SCOTT and BORGMAN
We'll probably just hang out in his basement, but if you call and we're not there, it means we may have randomly decided to go get an ice cream cone or something innocent like that.
Jeremy
WOW! I HAVEN'T READ BAD FICTION LIKE THIS SINCE I WAS IN COLLEGE!
HE IS SO GROUNDED!

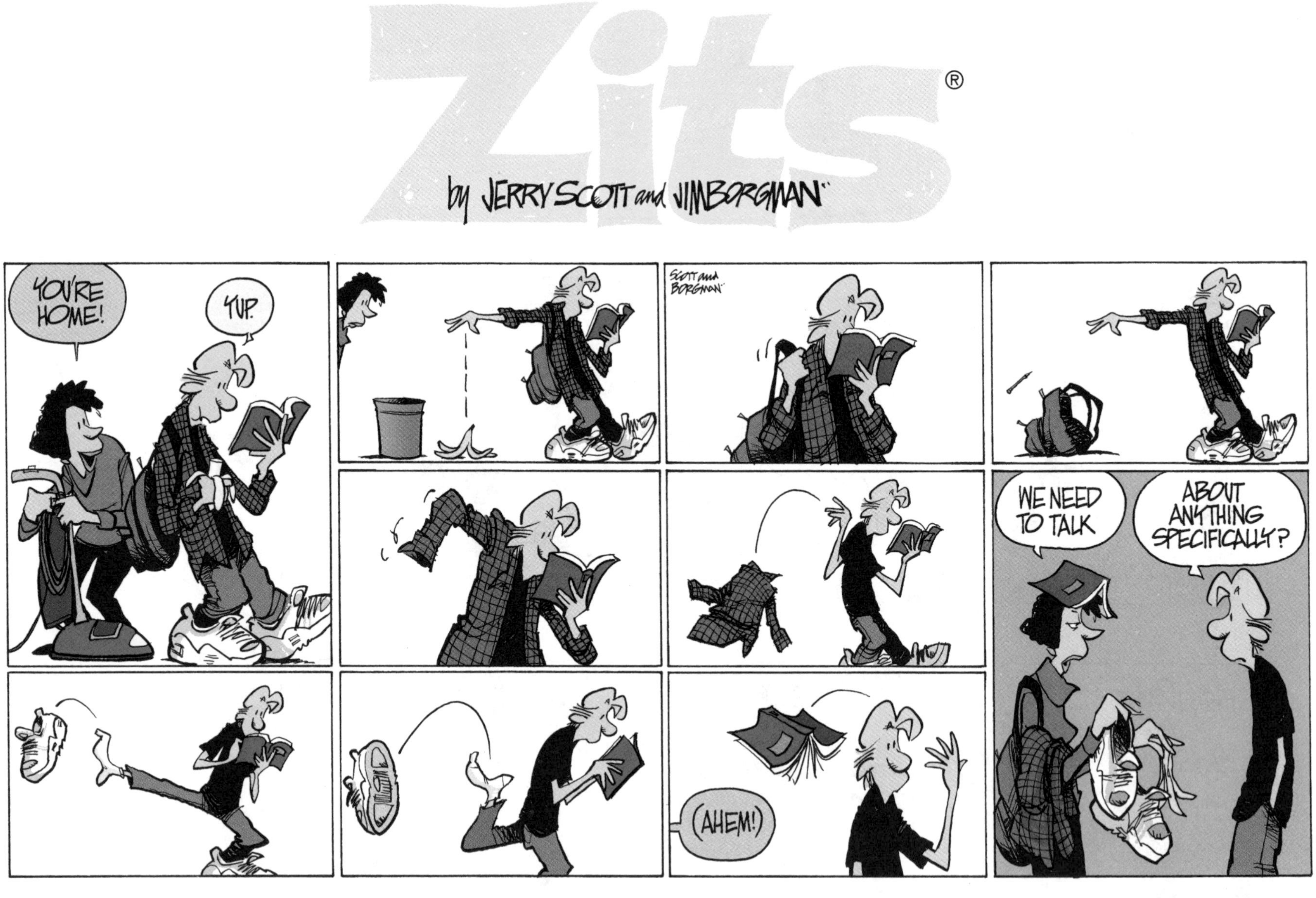
Zits®
by JERRY SCOTT and JIM BORGMAN
YOU'RE HOME!
YUP.
SCOTT AND BORGMAN
(AHEM!)
WE NEED TO TALK
ABOUT ANYTHING SPECIFICALLY?

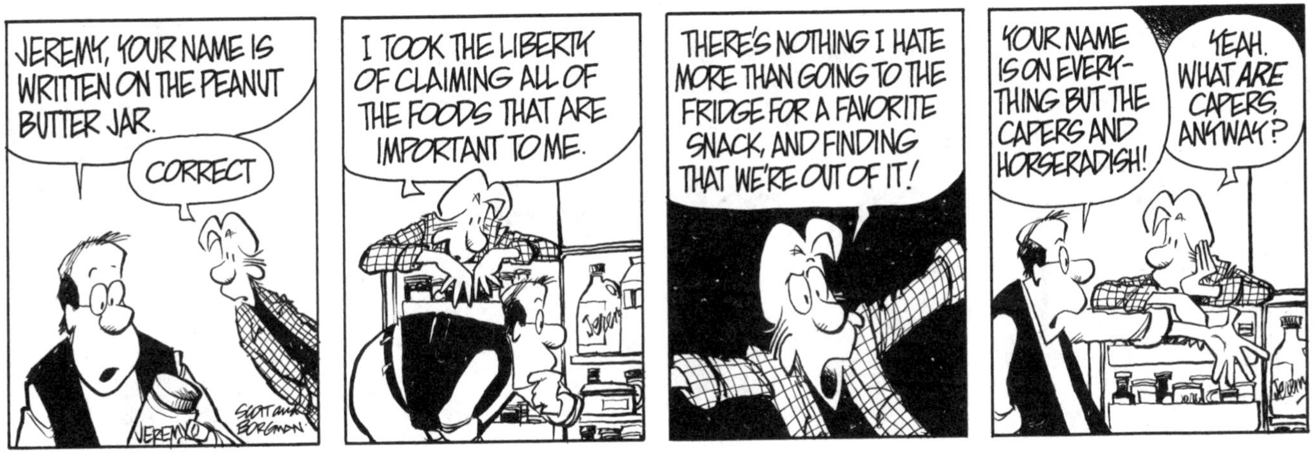
JEREMY, YOUR NAME IS WRITTEN ON THE PEANUT BUTTER JAR.
CORRECT
JEREMY
SCOTT and BORGMAN
I TOOK THE LIBERTY OF CLAIMING ALL OF THE FOODS THAT ARE IMPORTANT TO ME.
THERE'S NOTHING I HATE MORE THAN GOING TO THE FRIDGE FOR A FAVORITE SNACK, AND FINDING THAT WE'RE OUT OF IT!
YOUR NAME IS ON EVERYTHING BUT THE CAPERS AND HORSERADISH!
YEAH. WHAT ARE CAPERS, ANYWAY?

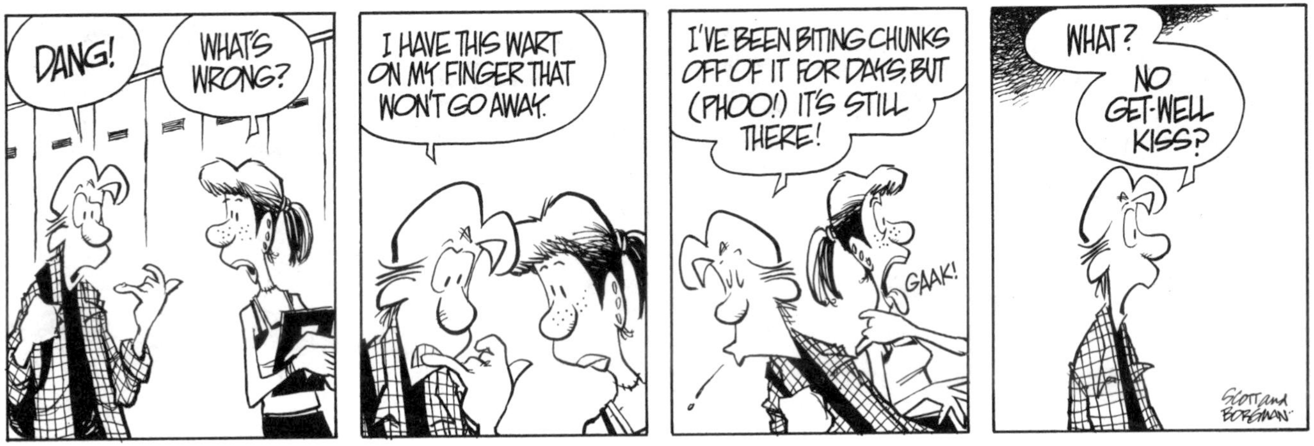
DANG!
WHAT'S WRONG?
I HAVE THIS WART ON MY FINGER THAT WON'T GO AWAY.
I'VE BEEN BITING CHUNKS OFF OF IT FOR DAYS, BUT (PHOO!) IT'S STILL THERE!
GAAK!
WHAT?
NO GET-WELL KISS?
SCOTT and BORGMAN

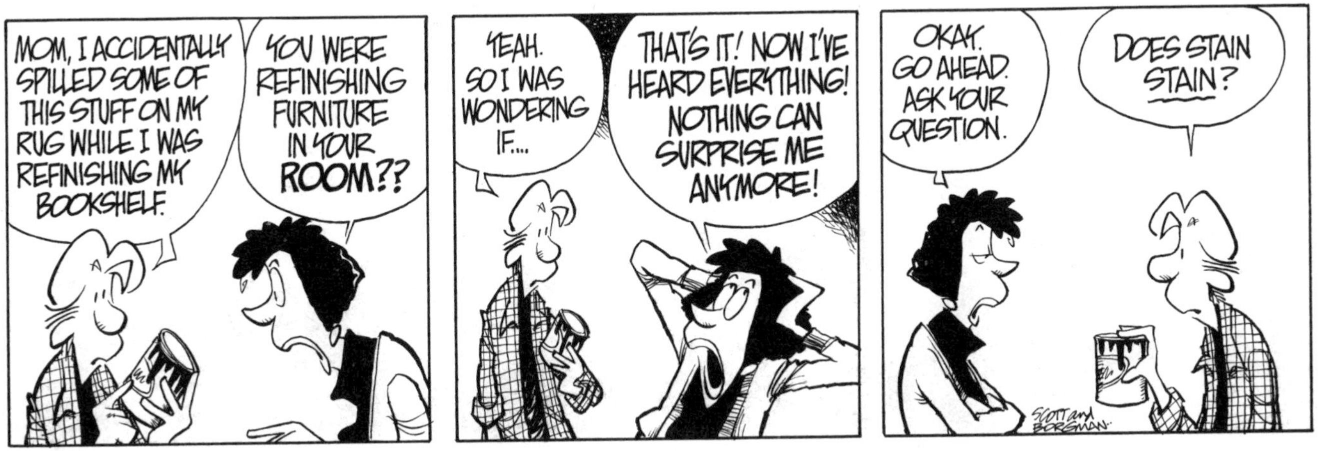
MOM, I ACCIDENTALLY SPILLED SOME OF THIS STUFF ON MY RUG WHILE I WAS REFINISHING MY BOOKSHELF.
YOU WERE REFINISHING FURNITURE IN YOUR ROOM??
YEAH. SO I WAS WONDERING IF....
THAT'S IT! NOW I'VE HEARD EVERYTHING! NOTHING CAN SURPRISE ME ANYMORE!
OKAY. GO AHEAD. ASK YOUR QUESTION.
DOES STAIN STAIN?
SCOTT and BORGMAN

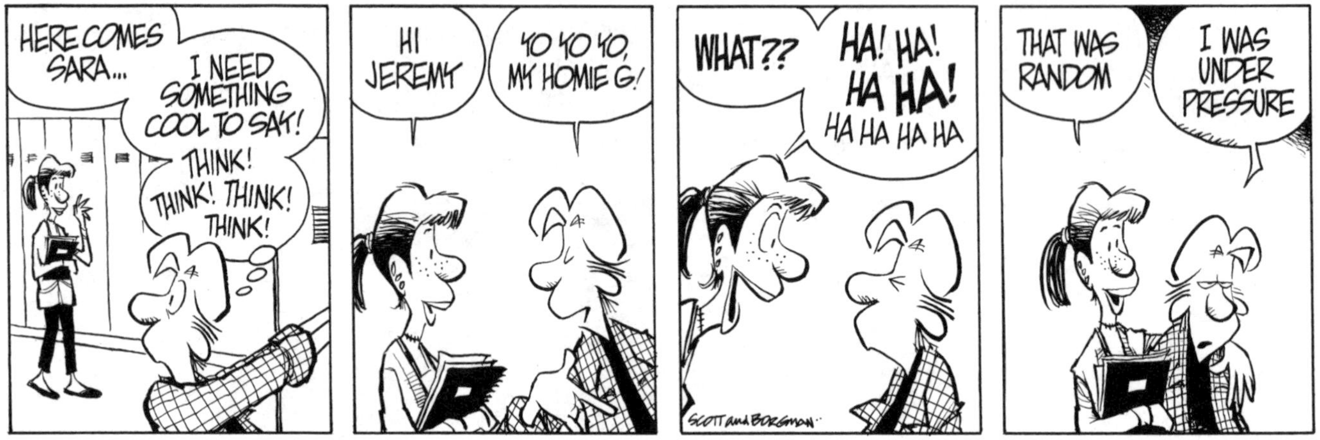
HERE COMES SARA...
I NEED SOMETHING COOL TO SAY!
THINK! THINK! THINK! THINK!
HI JEREMY
YO YO YO, MY HOMIE G!
WHAT??
HA! HA! HA HA! HA HA HA HA
THAT WAS RANDOM
I WAS UNDER PRESSURE
SCOTT AND BORGMAN

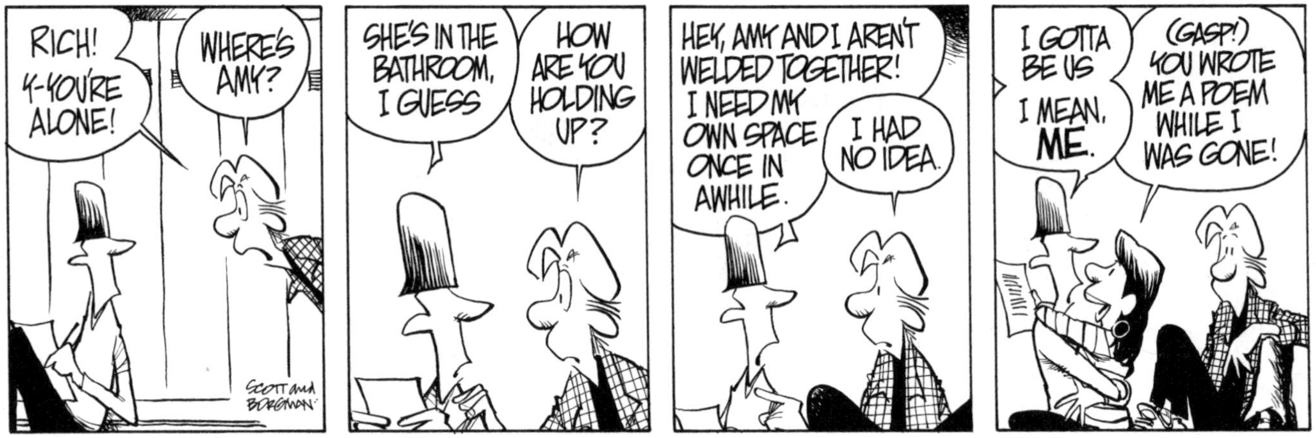
RICH! Y-YOU'RE ALONE!
WHERE'S AMY?
SHE'S IN THE BATHROOM, I GUESS
HOW ARE YOU HOLDING UP?
HEY, AMY AND I AREN'T WELDED TOGETHER! I NEED MY OWN SPACE ONCE IN AWHILE.
I HAD NO IDEA.
I GOTTA BE US
I MEAN, ME.
(GASP!) YOU WROTE ME A POEM WHILE I WAS GONE!
SCOTT AND BORGMAN

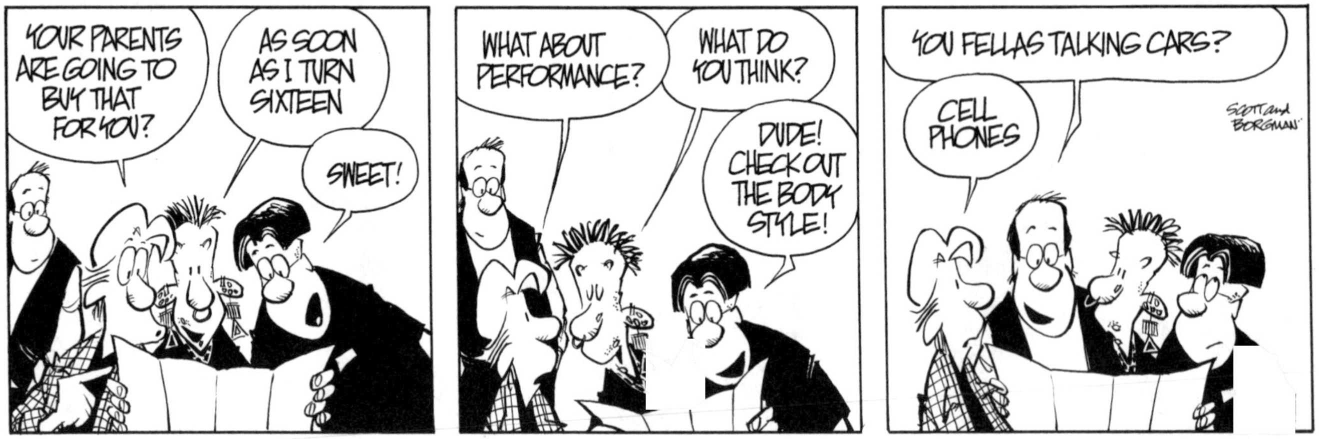
YOUR PARENTS ARE GOING TO BUY THAT FOR YOU?
AS SOON AS I TURN SIXTEEN
SWEET!
WHAT ABOUT PERFORMANCE?
WHAT DO YOU THINK?
DUDE! CHECK OUT THE BODY STYLE!
YOU FELLAS TALKING CARS?
CELL PHONES
SCOTT AND BORGMAN

Zits®

by JERRY SCOTT and JIM BORGMAN

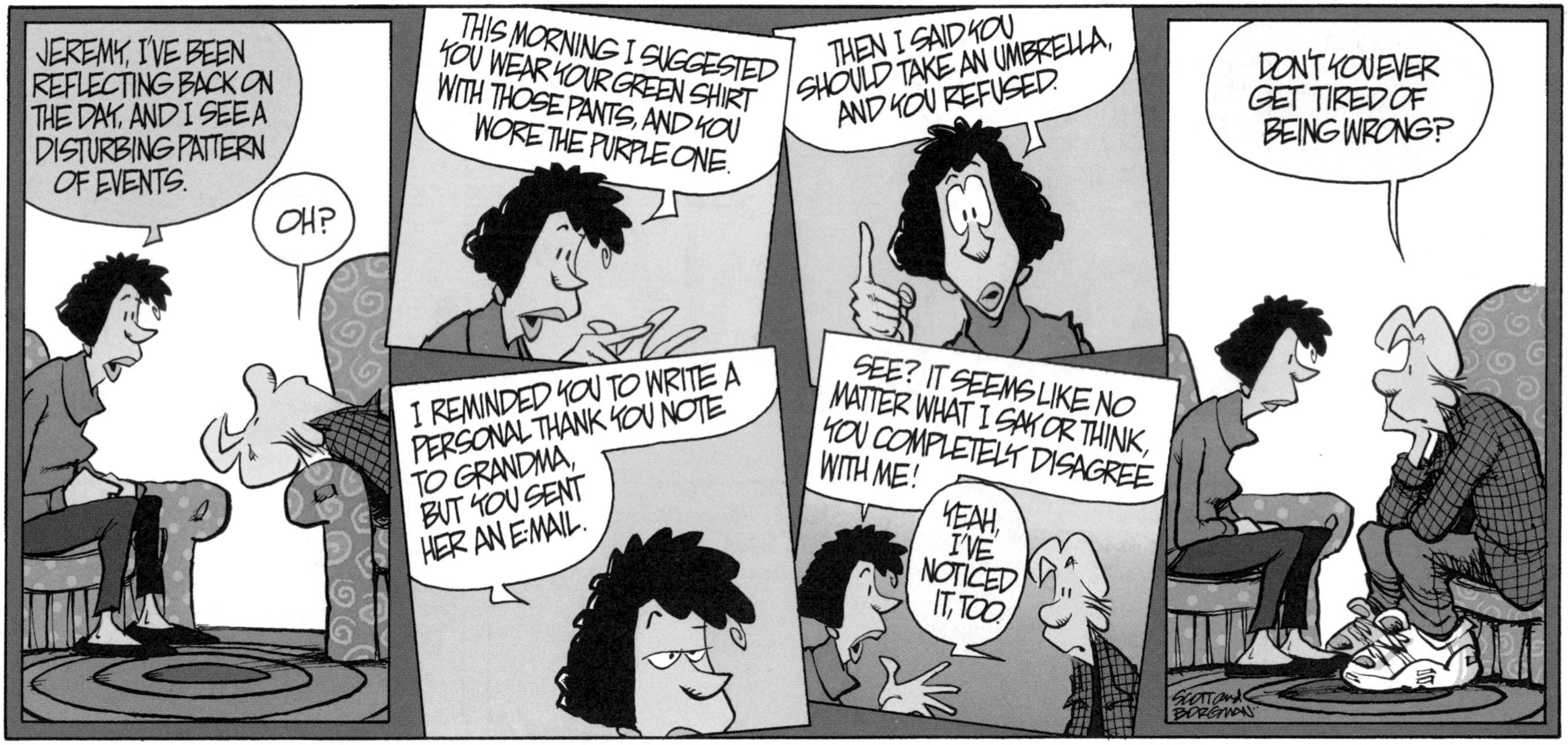
JEREMY, I'VE BEEN REFLECTING BACK ON THE DAY, AND I SEE A DISTURBING PATTERN OF EVENTS.
OH?
THIS MORNING I SUGGESTED YOU WEAR YOUR GREEN SHIRT WITH THOSE PANTS, AND YOU WORE THE PURPLE ONE.
THEN I SAID YOU SHOULD TAKE AN UMBRELLA, AND YOU REFUSED.
I REMINDED YOU TO WRITE A PERSONAL THANK YOU NOTE TO GRANDMA, BUT YOU SENT HER AN E-MAIL.
SEE? IT SEEMS LIKE NO MATTER WHAT I SAY OR THINK, YOU COMPLETELY DISAGREE WITH ME!
YEAH, I'VE NOTICED IT, TOO.
DON'T YOU EVER GET TIRED OF BEING WRONG?
SCOTT and BORGMAN

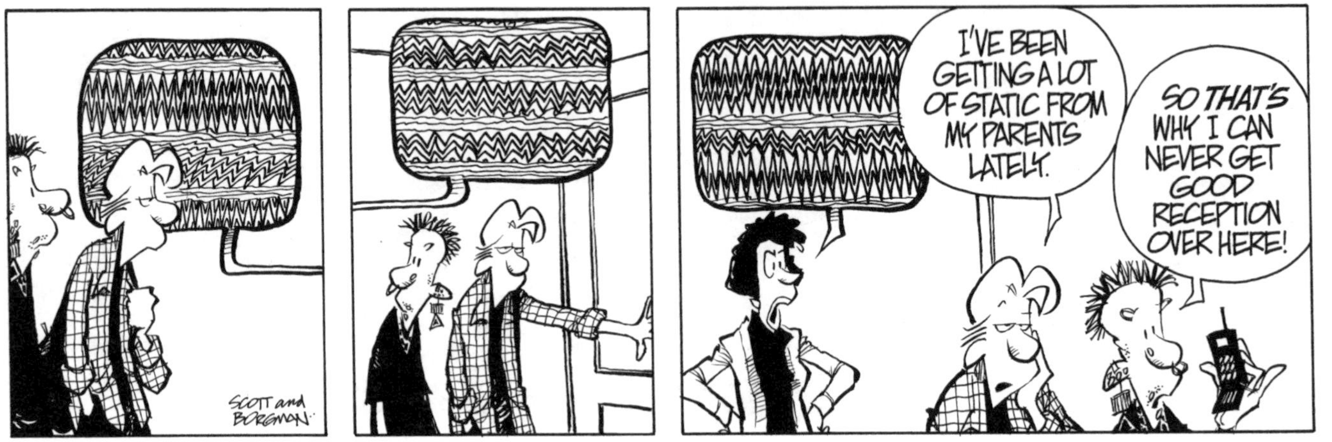
SCOTT and BORGMAN
I'VE BEEN GETTING A LOT OF STATIC FROM MY PARENTS LATELY.
SO THAT'S WHY I CAN NEVER GET GOOD RECEPTION OVER HERE!

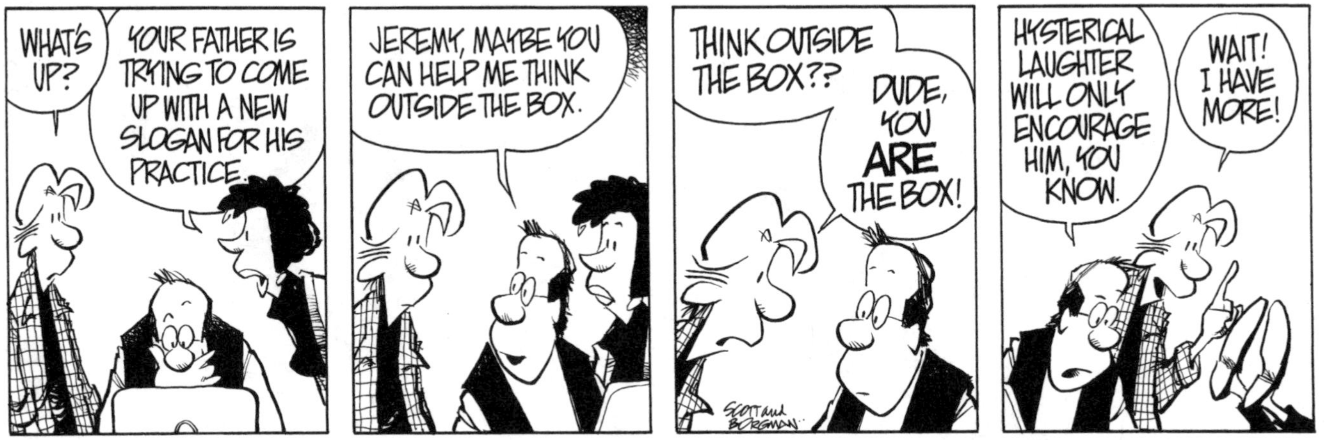
WHAT'S UP?
YOUR FATHER IS TRYING TO COME UP WITH A NEW SLOGAN FOR HIS PRACTICE.
JEREMY, MAYBE YOU CAN HELP ME THINK OUTSIDE THE BOX.
THINK OUTSIDE THE BOX??
DUDE, YOU ARE THE BOX!
SCOTT and BORGMAN
HYSTERICAL LAUGHTER WILL ONLY ENCOURAGE HIM, YOU KNOW.
WAIT! I HAVE MORE!

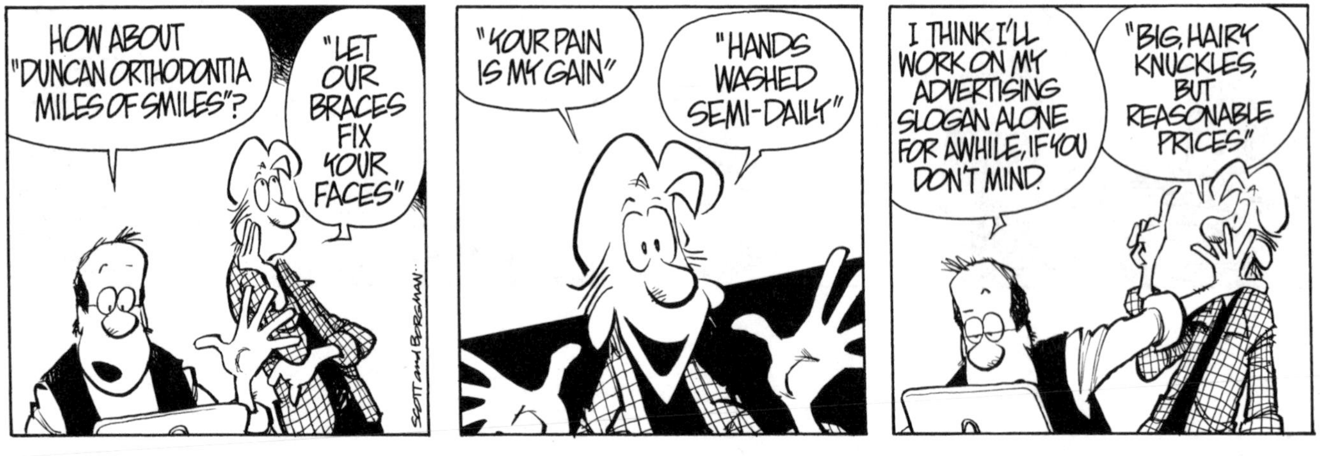
HOW ABOUT "DUNCAN ORTHODONTIA MILES OF SMILES"?
"LET OUR BRACES FIX YOUR FACES"
SCOTT and BORGMAN
"YOUR PAIN IS MY GAIN"
"HANDS WASHED SEMI-DAILY"
I THINK I'LL WORK ON MY ADVERTISING SLOGAN ALONE FOR AWHILE, IF YOU DON'T MIND.
"BIG, HAIRY KNUCKLES, BUT REASONABLE PRICES"

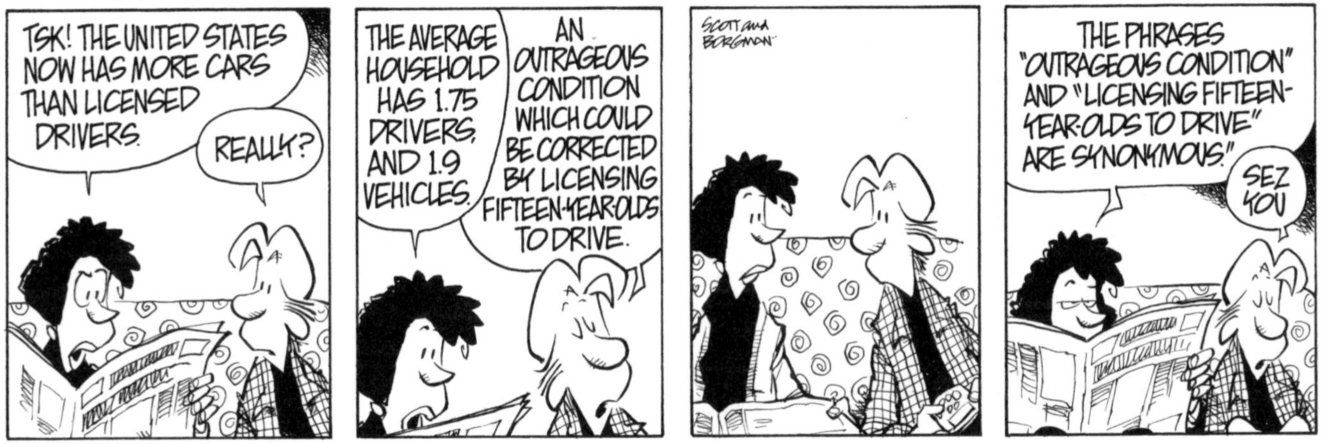
TSK! THE UNITED STATES NOW HAS MORE CARS THAN LICENSED DRIVERS.
REALLY?
THE AVERAGE HOUSEHOLD HAS 1.75 DRIVERS, AND 1.9 VEHICLES.
AN OUTRAGEOUS CONDITION WHICH COULD BE CORRECTED BY LICENSING FIFTEEN-YEAR-OLDS TO DRIVE.
SCOTT and BORGMAN
THE PHRASES "OUTRAGEOUS CONDITION" AND "LICENSING FIFTEEN-YEAR-OLDS TO DRIVE" ARE SYNONYMOUS.
SEZ YOU

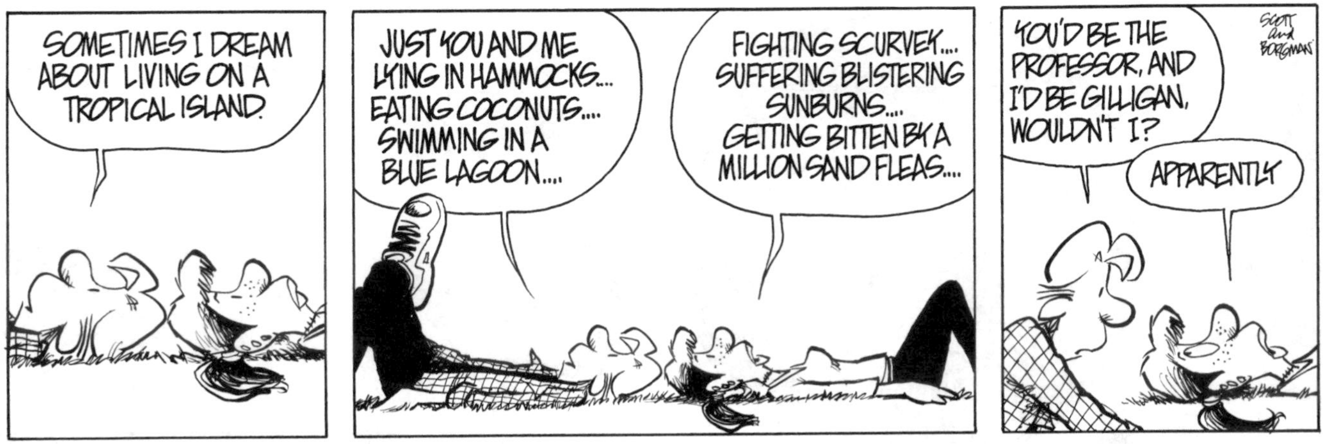
SOMETIMES I DREAM ABOUT LIVING ON A TROPICAL ISLAND.
JUST YOU AND ME LYING IN HAMMOCKS... EATING COCONUTS.... SWIMMING IN A BLUE LAGOON....
FIGHTING SCURVEY.... SUFFERING BLISTERING SUNBURNS.... GETTING BITTEN BY A MILLION SAND FLEAS....
YOU'D BE THE PROFESSOR, AND I'D BE GILLIGAN, WOULDN'T I?
APPARENTLY
SCOTT and BORGMAN

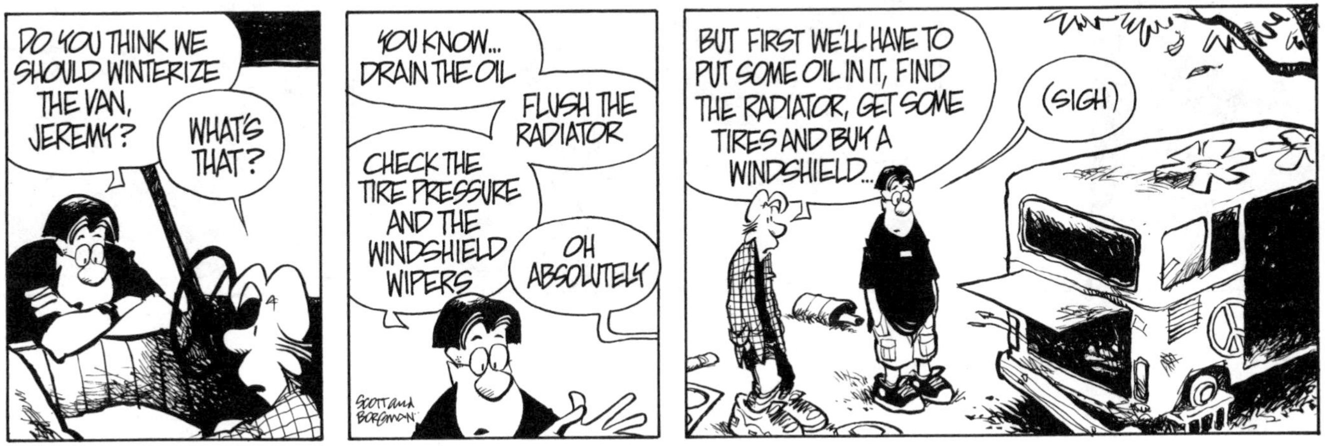
DO YOU THINK WE SHOULD WINTERIZE THE VAN, JEREMY?
WHAT'S THAT?
YOU KNOW... DRAIN THE OIL
FLUSH THE RADIATOR
CHECK THE TIRE PRESSURE AND THE WINDSHIELD WIPERS
OH ABSOLUTELY
SCOTT and BORGMAN
BUT FIRST WE'LL HAVE TO PUT SOME OIL IN IT, FIND THE RADIATOR, GET SOME TIRES AND BUY A WINDSHIELD...
(SIGH)

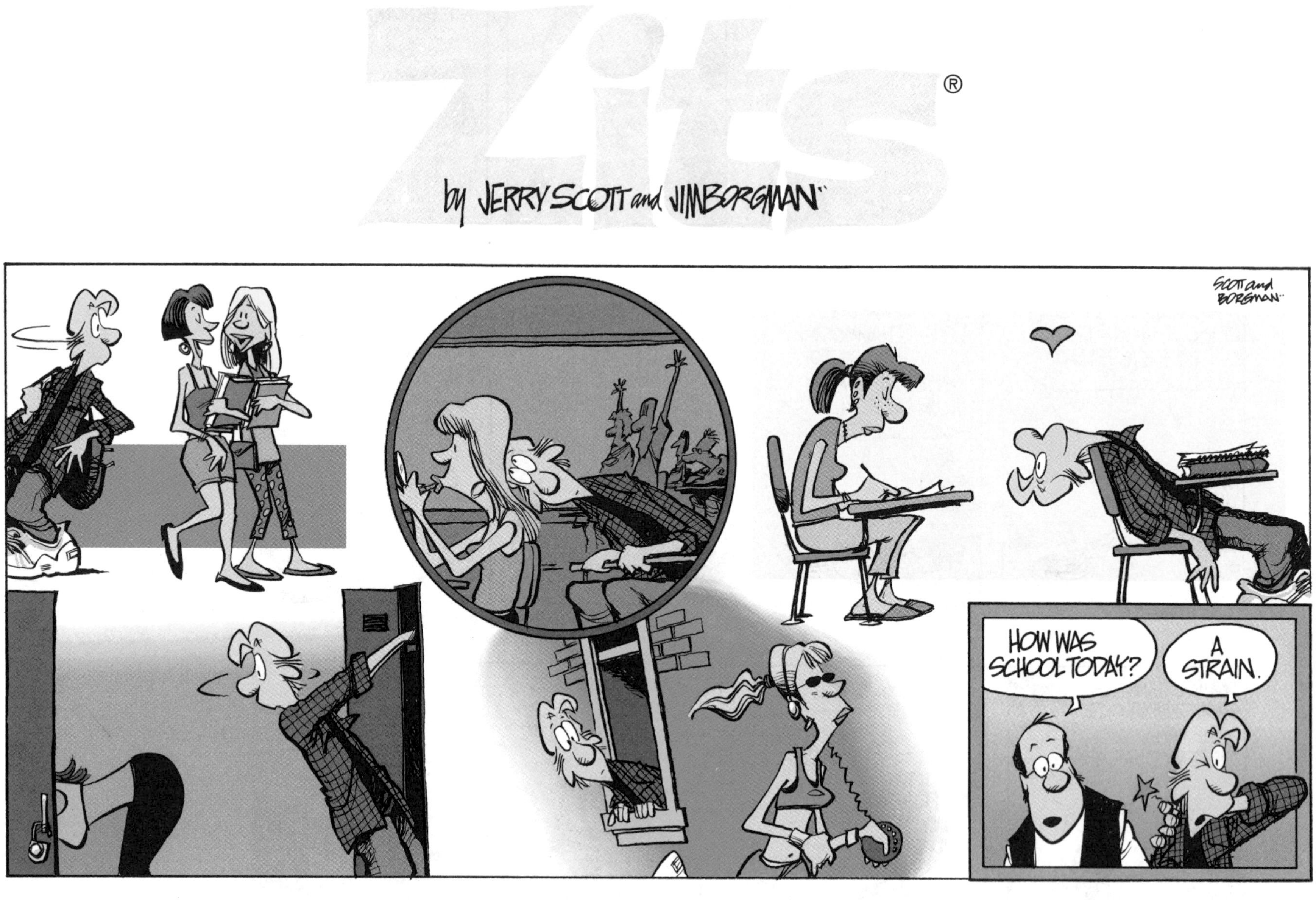
Zits®
by JERRY SCOTT and JIM BORGMAN
SCOTT and BORGMAN
HOW WAS SCHOOL TODAY?
A STRAIN.

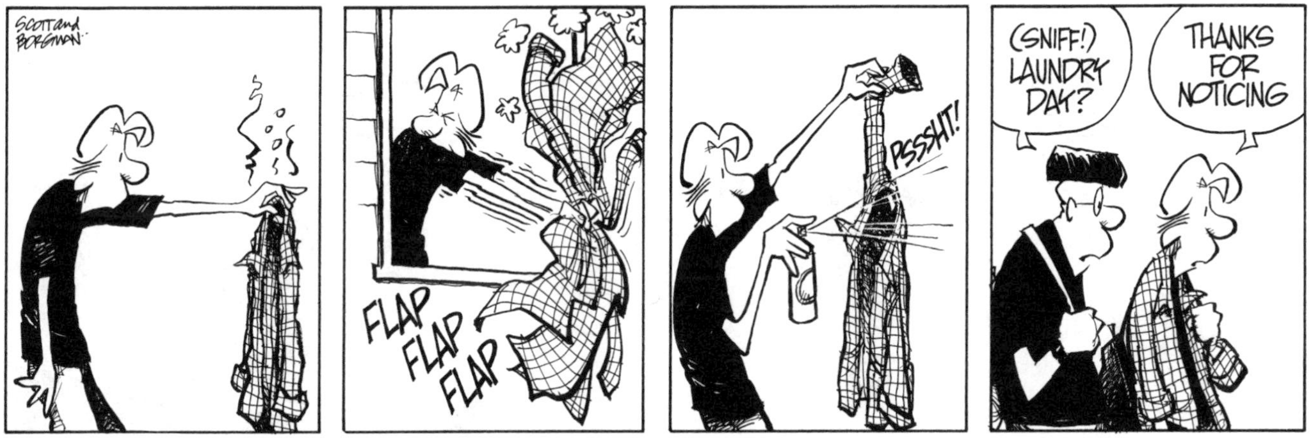
SCOTT and BORGMAN
FLAP FLAP FLAP
PSSSHT!
(SNIFF!) LAUNDRY DAY?
THANKS FOR NOTICING

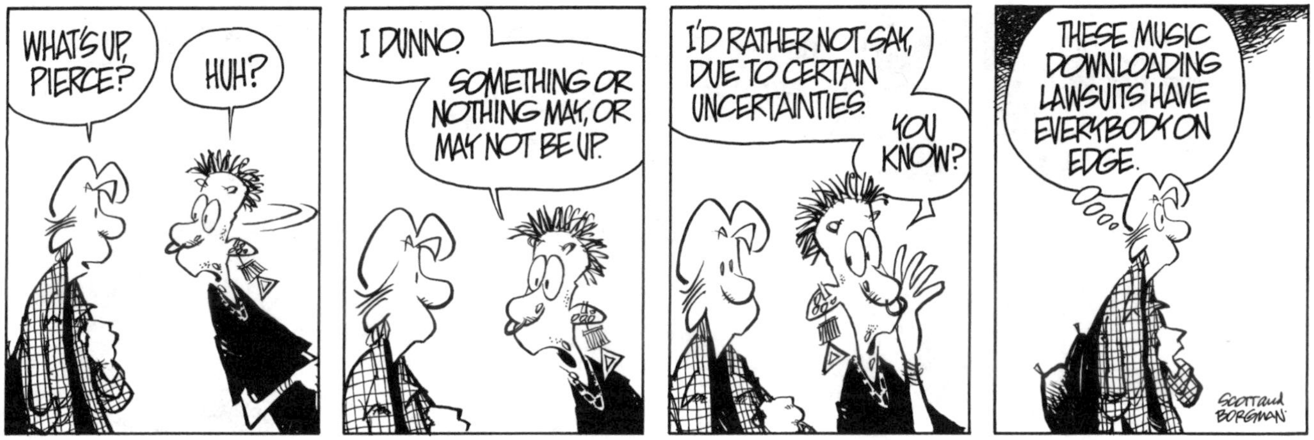
WHAT'S UP, PIERCE?
HUH?
I DUNNO.
SOMETHING OR NOTHING MAY, OR MAY NOT BE UP.
I'D RATHER NOT SAY, DUE TO CERTAIN UNCERTAINTIES.
YOU KNOW?
THESE MUSIC DOWNLOADING LAWSUITS HAVE EVERYBODY ON EDGE.
SCOTT and BORGMAN

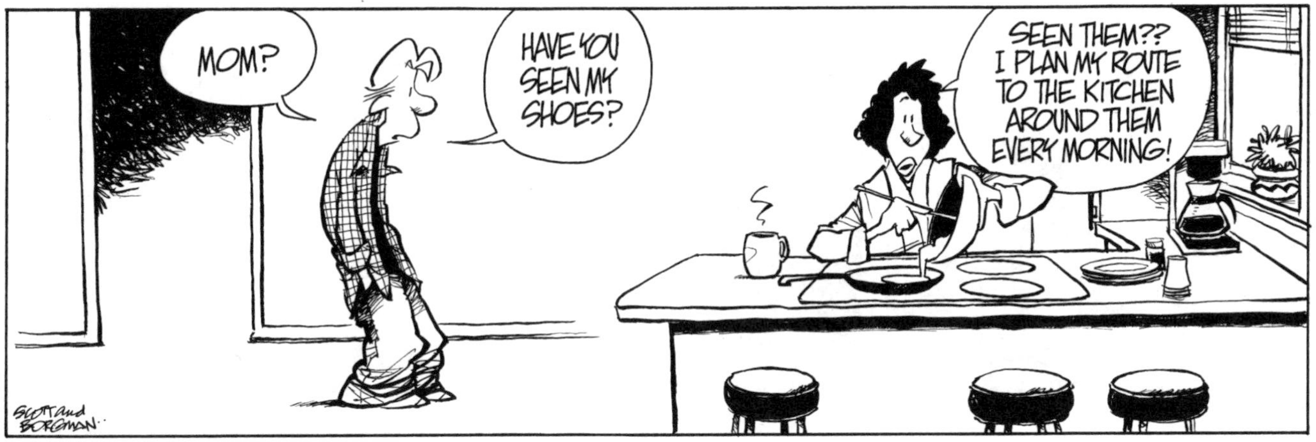
MOM?
HAVE YOU SEEN MY SHOES?
SEEN THEM?? I PLAN MY ROUTE TO THE KITCHEN AROUND THEM EVERY MORNING!
SCOTT and BORGMAN

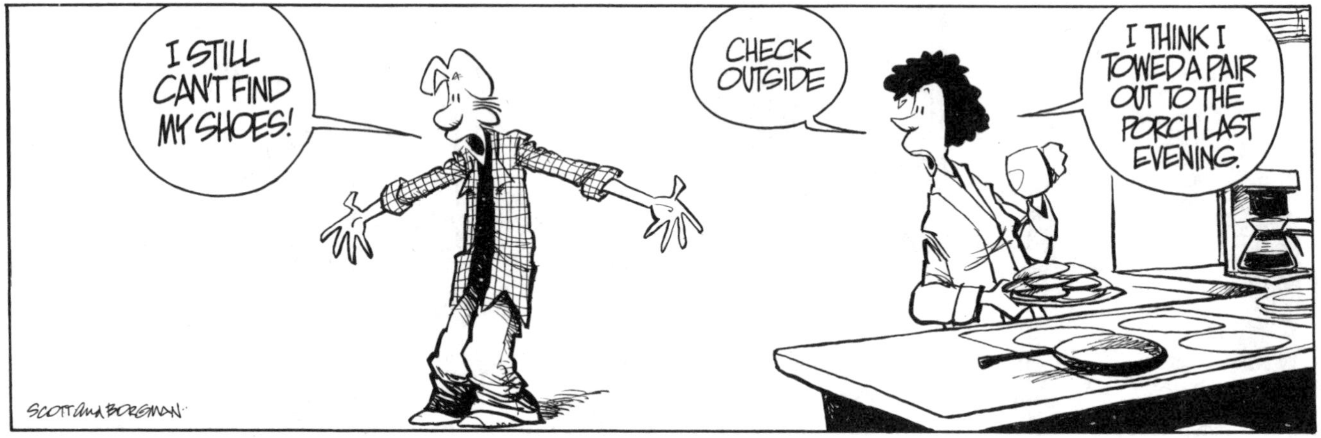
I STILL CAN'T FIND MY SHOES!
CHECK OUTSIDE
I THINK I TOWED A PAIR OUT TO THE PORCH LAST EVENING.
SCOTT and BORGMAN

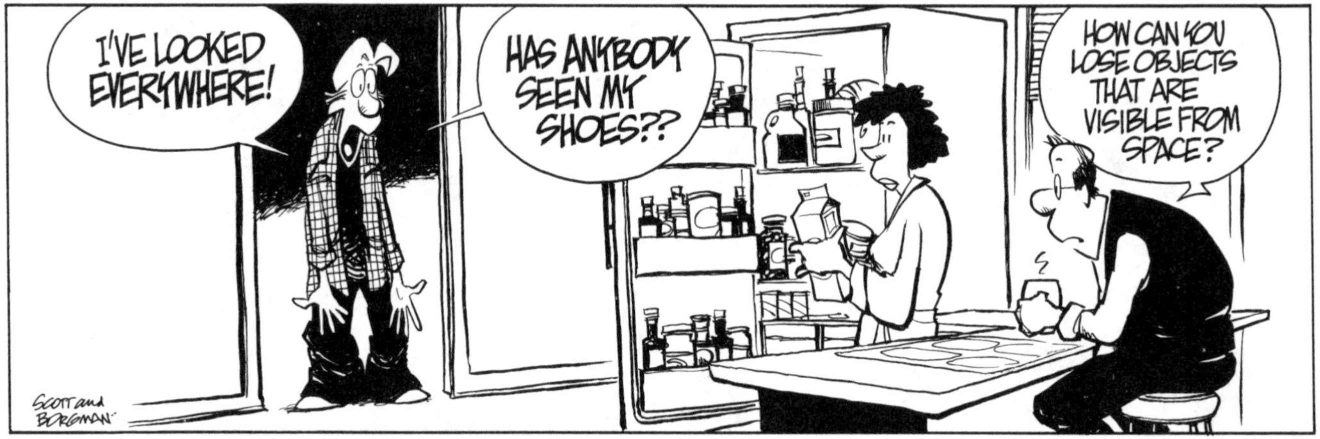
I'VE LOOKED EVERYWHERE!
HAS ANYBODY SEEN MY SHOES??
HOW CAN YOU LOSE OBJECTS THAT ARE VISIBLE FROM SPACE?
SCOTT and BORGMAN

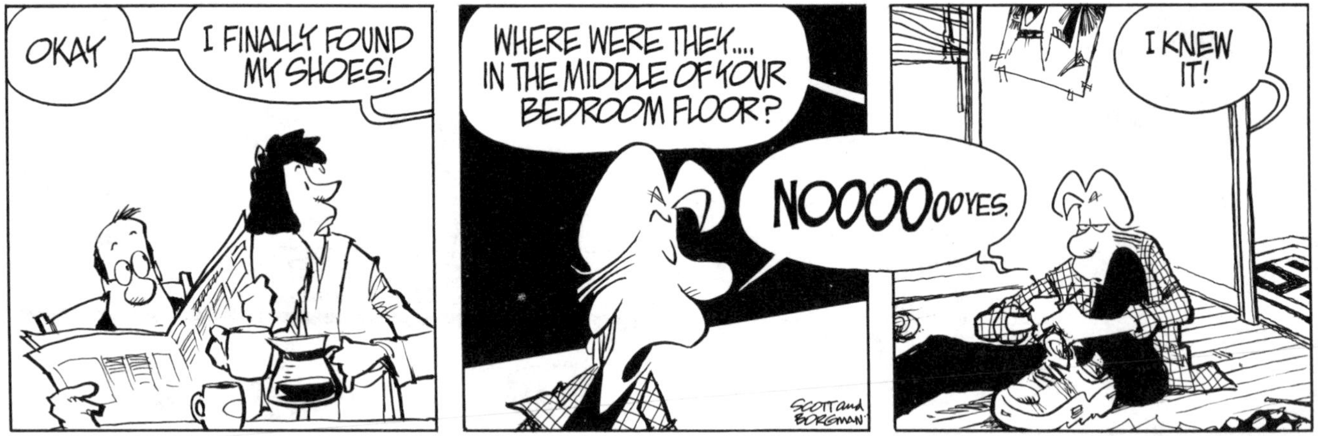
OKAY
I FINALLY FOUND MY SHOES!
WHERE WERE THEY.... IN THE MIDDLE OF YOUR BEDROOM FLOOR?
NOOOOOOYES.
I KNEW IT!
SCOTT and BORGMAN

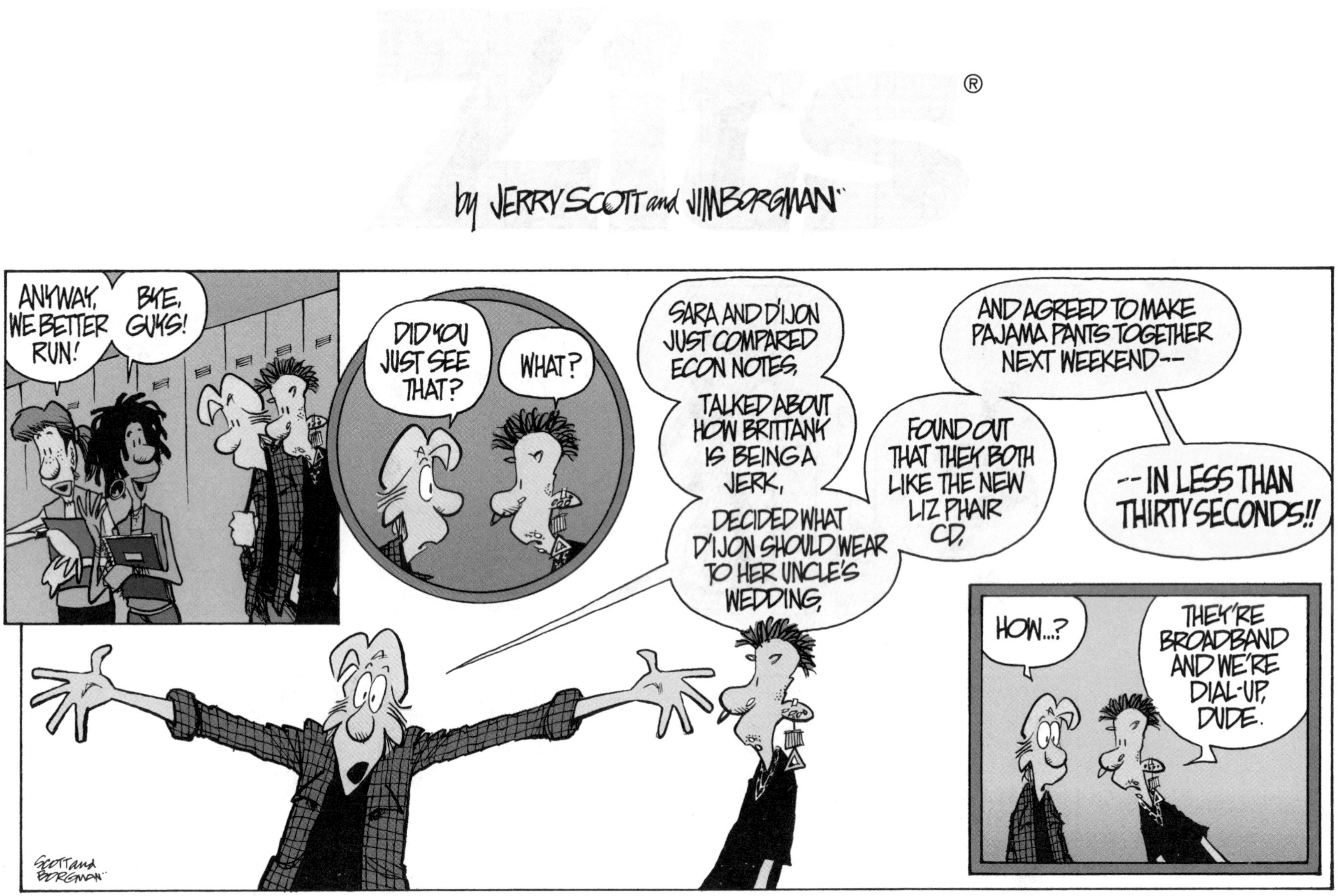
Zits®
by JERRY SCOTT and JIM BORGMAN
ANYWAY, WE BETTER RUN!
BYE, GUYS!
DID YOU JUST SEE THAT?
WHAT?
SARA AND D'IJON JUST COMPARED ECON NOTES,
TALKED ABOUT HOW BRITTANY IS BEING A JERK,
DECIDED WHAT D'IJON SHOULD WEAR TO HER UNCLE'S WEDDING,
FOUND OUT THAT THEY BOTH LIKE THE NEW LIZ PHAIR CD,
AND AGREED TO MAKE PAJAMA PANTS TOGETHER NEXT WEEKEND--
--IN LESS THAN THIRTY SECONDS!!
HOW...?
THEY'RE BROADBAND AND WE'RE DIAL-UP, DUDE.
SCOTT and BORGMAN

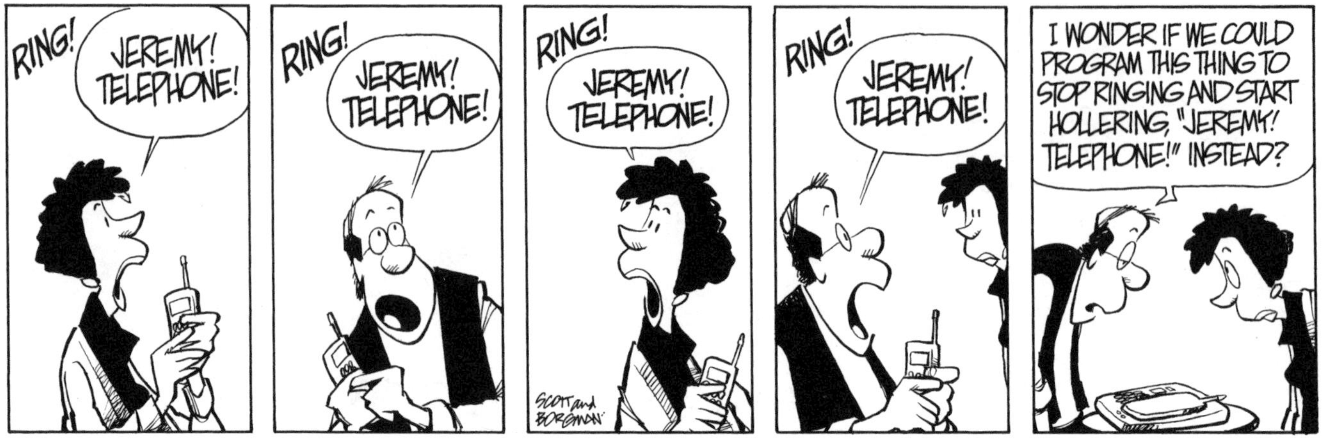
RING!
JEREMY! TELEPHONE!
RING!
JEREMY! TELEPHONE!
RING!
JEREMY! TELEPHONE!
RING!
JEREMY! TELEPHONE!
I WONDER IF WE COULD PROGRAM THIS THING TO STOP RINGING AND START HOLLERING, "JEREMY! TELEPHONE!" INSTEAD?
SCOTT and BORGMAN

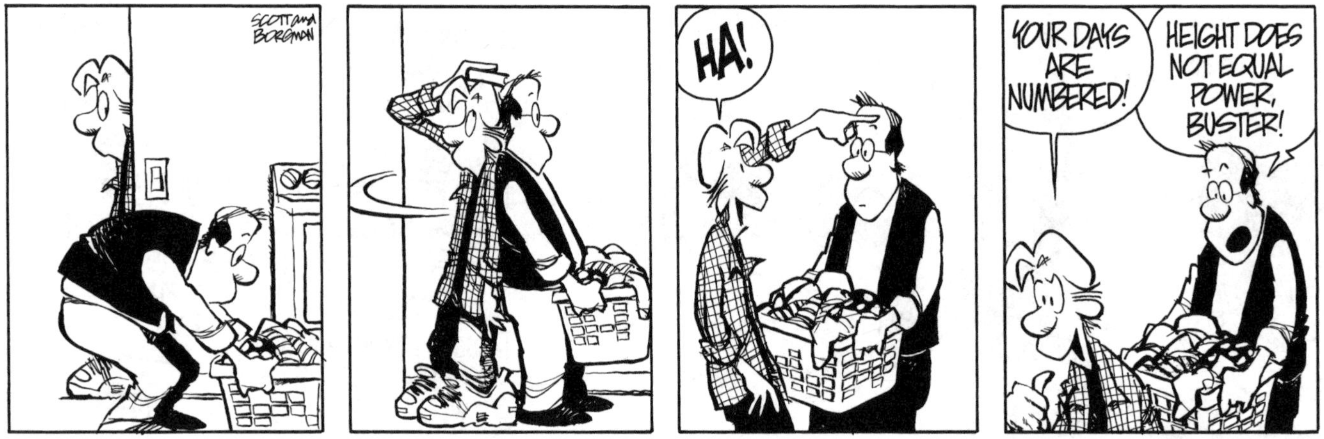
SCOTT and BORGMAN
HA!
YOUR DAYS ARE NUMBERED!
HEIGHT DOES NOT EQUAL POWER, BUSTER!

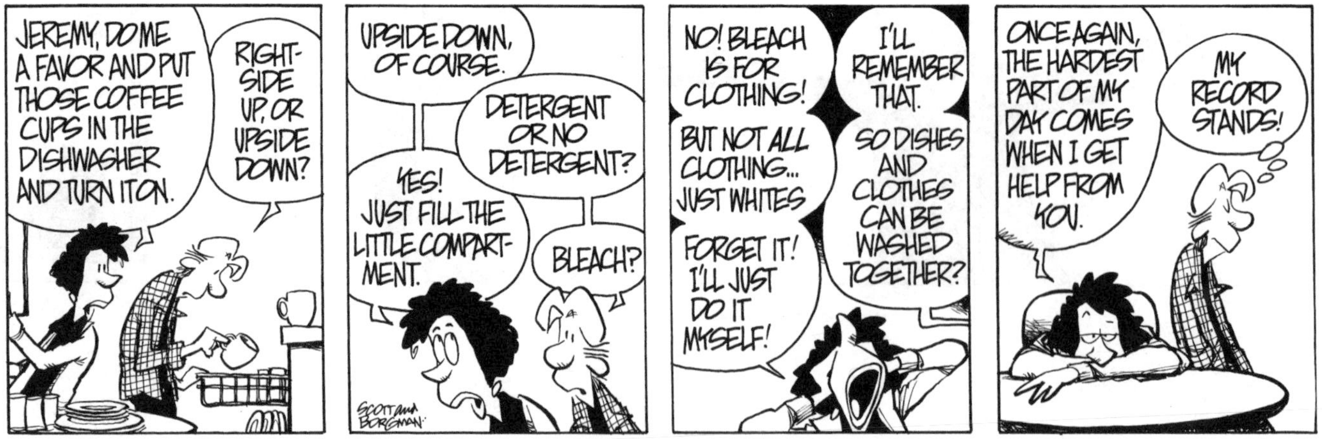
JEREMY, DO ME A FAVOR AND PUT THOSE COFFEE CUPS IN THE DISHWASHER AND TURN IT ON.
RIGHT-SIDE UP, OR UPSIDE DOWN?
UPSIDE DOWN, OF COURSE.
DETERGENT OR NO DETERGENT?
YES! JUST FILL THE LITTLE COMPART-MENT.
BLEACH?
SCOTT and BORGMAN
NO! BLEACH IS FOR CLOTHING!
I'LL REMEMBER THAT.
BUT NOT ALL CLOTHING... JUST WHITES
SO DISHES AND CLOTHES CAN BE WASHED TOGETHER?
FORGET IT! I'LL JUST DO IT MYSELF!
ONCE AGAIN, THE HARDEST PART OF MY DAY COMES WHEN I GET HELP FROM YOU.
MY RECORD STANDS!

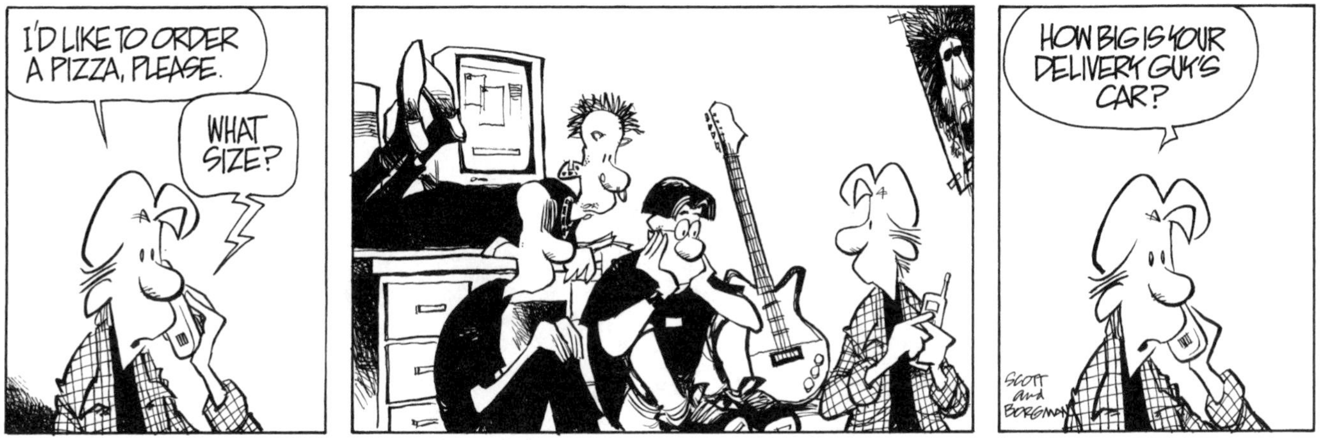
I'D LIKE TO ORDER A PIZZA, PLEASE.
WHAT SIZE?
HOW BIG IS YOUR DELIVERY GUY'S CAR?
SCOTT and BORGMAN

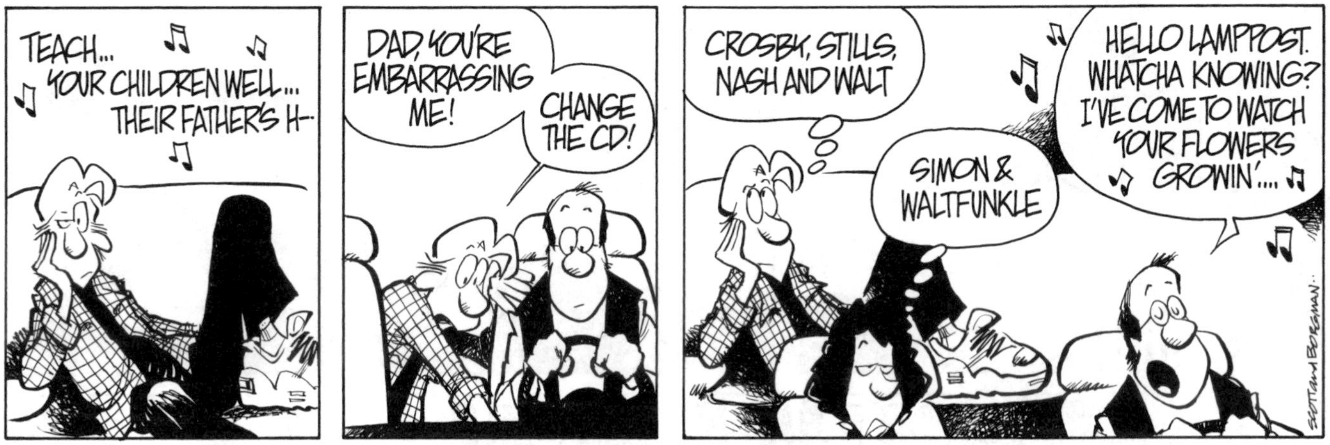
TEACH... YOUR CHILDREN WELL... THEIR FATHER'S H--
DAD, YOU'RE EMBARRASSING ME!
CHANGE THE CD!
CROSBY, STILLS, NASH AND WALT
SIMON & WALTFUNKLE
HELLO LAMPPOST. WHATCHA KNOWING? I'VE COME TO WATCH YOUR FLOWERS GROWIN'....
SCOTT and BORGMAN

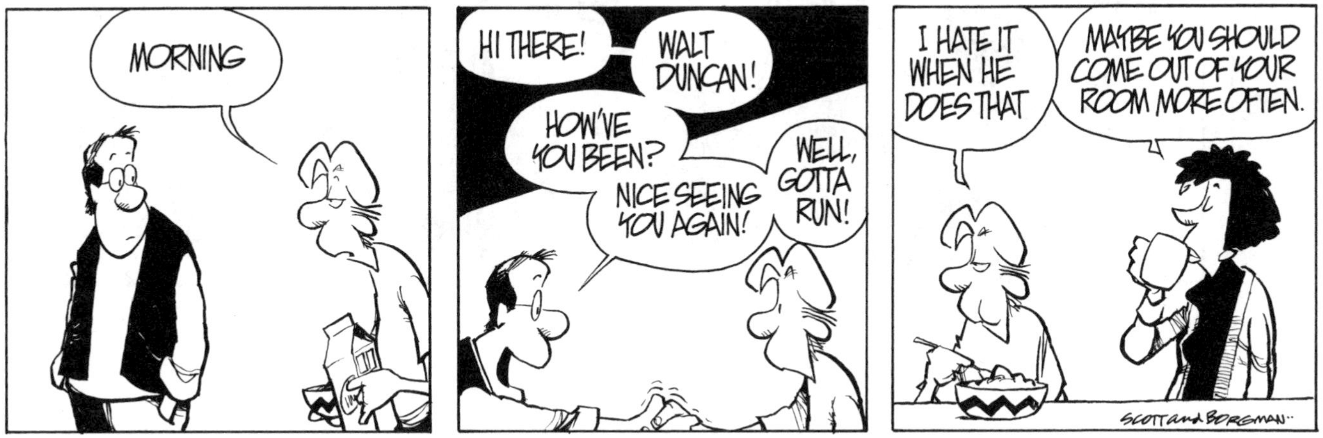
MORNING
HI THERE!
WALT DUNCAN!
HOW'VE YOU BEEN?
NICE SEEING YOU AGAIN!
WELL, GOTTA RUN!
I HATE IT WHEN HE DOES THAT
MAYBE YOU SHOULD COME OUT OF YOUR ROOM MORE OFTEN.
SCOTT and BORGMAN

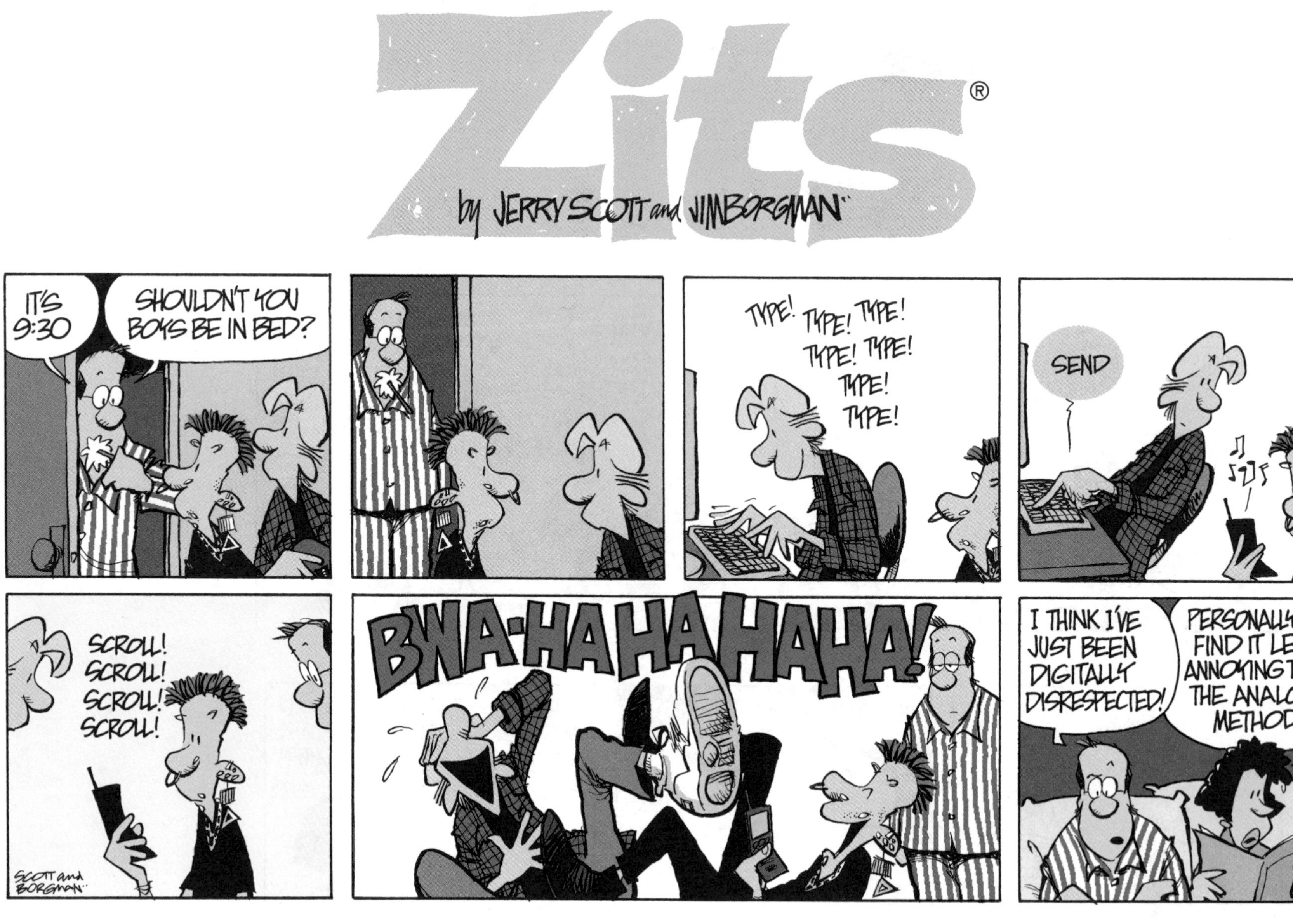
Zits®
by JERRY SCOTT and JIM BORGMAN
IT'S 9:30
SHOULDN'T YOU BOYS BE IN BED?
TYPE! TYPE! TYPE! TYPE! TYPE! TYPE! TYPE!
SEND
SCROLL! SCROLL! SCROLL! SCROLL!
SCOTT and BORGMAN
BWA-HA HA HA HA HA!
I THINK I'VE JUST BEEN DIGITALLY DISRESPECTED!
PERSONALLY, I FIND IT LESS ANNOYING THAN THE ANALOG METHOD.

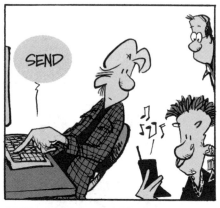

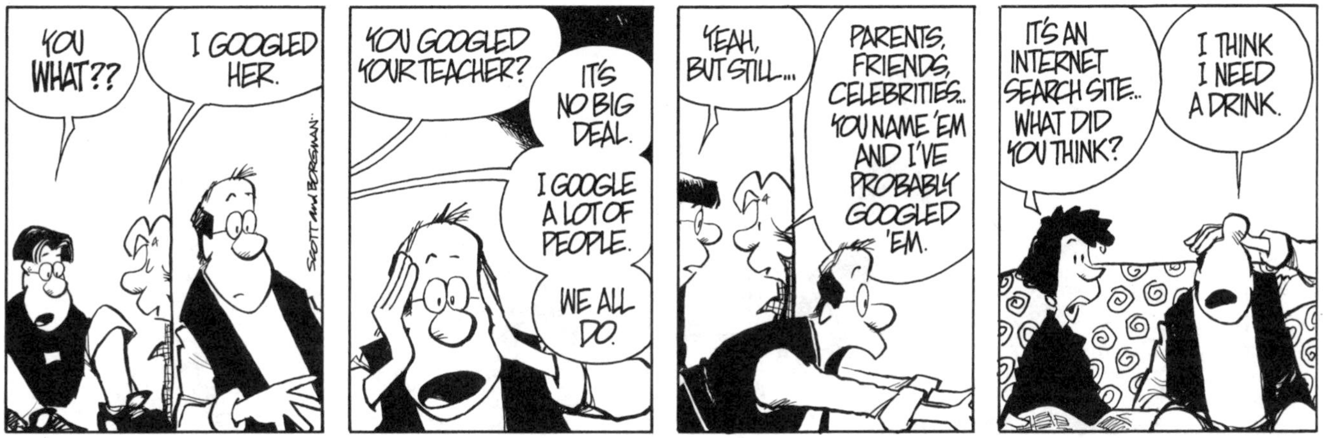
YOU WHAT??
I GOOGLED HER.
YOU GOOGLED YOUR TEACHER?
IT'S NO BIG DEAL.
I GOOGLE A LOT OF PEOPLE.
WE ALL DO.
YEAH, BUT STILL....
PARENTS, FRIENDS, CELEBRITIES... YOU NAME 'EM AND I'VE PROBABLY GOOGLED 'EM.
IT'S AN INTERNET SEARCH SITE... WHAT DID YOU THINK?
I THINK I NEED A DRINK.

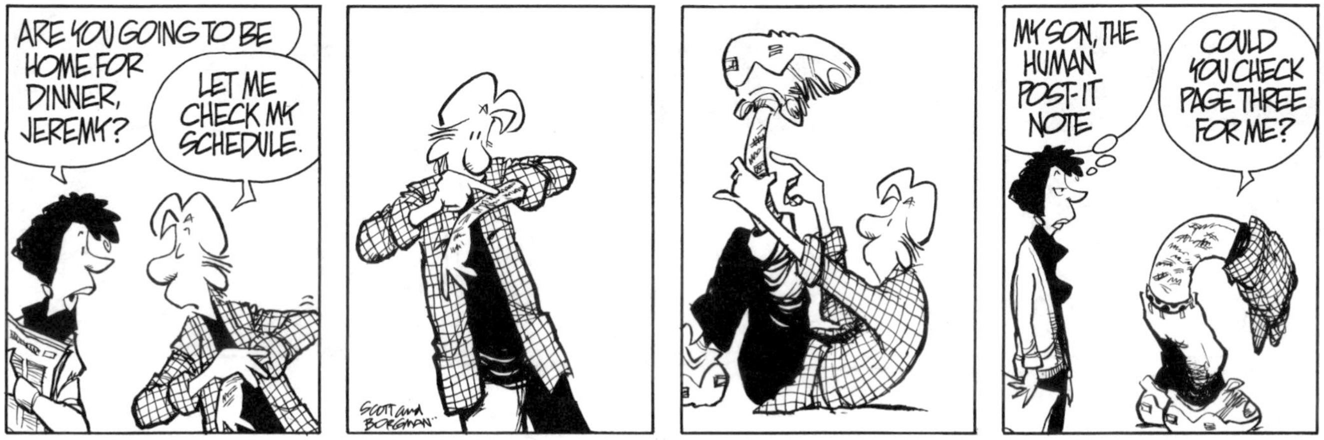
ARE YOU GOING TO BE HOME FOR DINNER, JEREMY?
LET ME CHECK MY SCHEDULE.
MY SON, THE HUMAN POST-IT NOTE
COULD YOU CHECK PAGE THREE FOR ME?

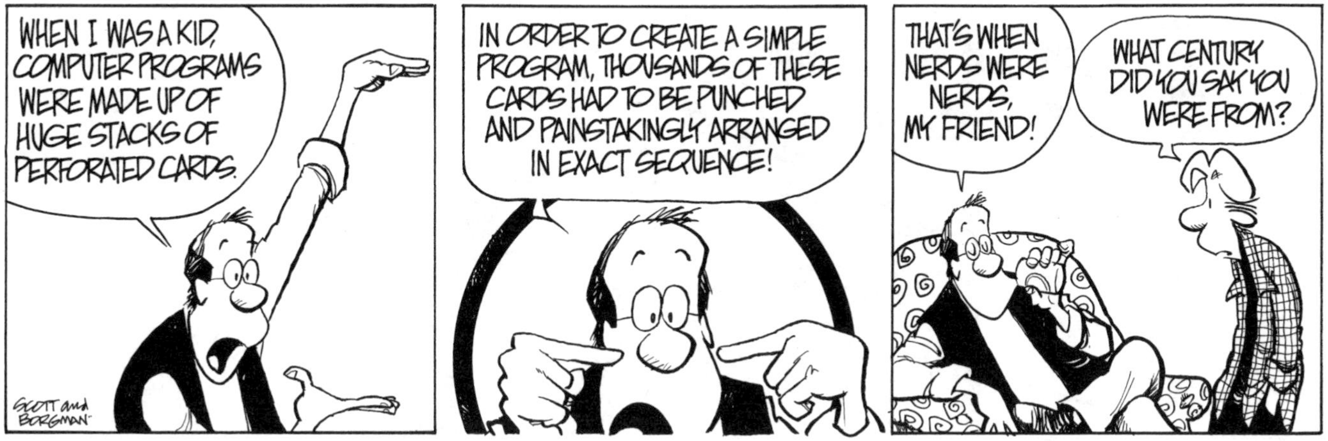
WHEN I WAS A KID, COMPUTER PROGRAMS WERE MADE UP OF HUGE STACKS OF PERFORATED CARDS.
IN ORDER TO CREATE A SIMPLE PROGRAM, THOUSANDS OF THESE CARDS HAD TO BE PUNCHED AND PAINSTAKINGLY ARRANGED IN EXACT SEQUENCE!
THAT'S WHEN NERDS WERE NERDS, MY FRIEND!
WHAT CENTURY DID YOU SAY YOU WERE FROM?

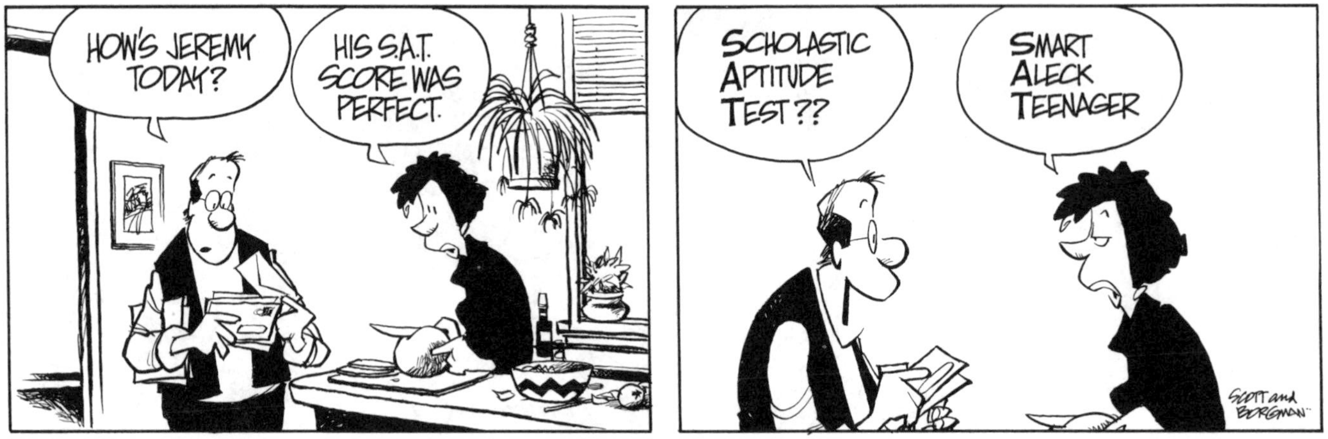
HOW'S JEREMY TODAY?
HIS S.A.T. SCORE WAS PERFECT.
SCHOLASTIC APTITUDE TEST??
SMART ALECK TEENAGER
SCOTT and BORGMAN

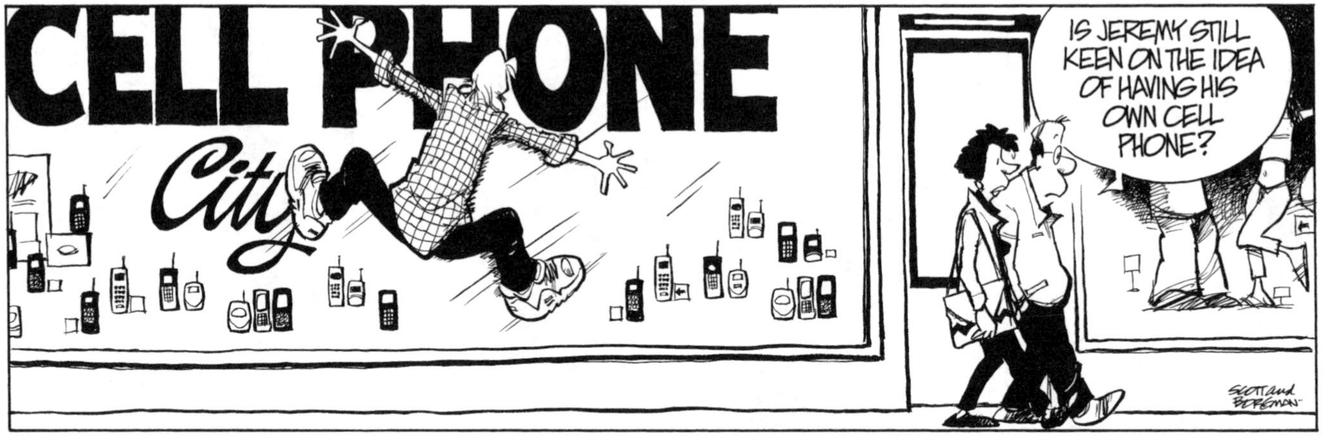
CELL PHONE
City
IS JEREMY STILL KEEN ON THE IDEA OF HAVING HIS OWN CELL PHONE?
SCOTT and BORGMAN

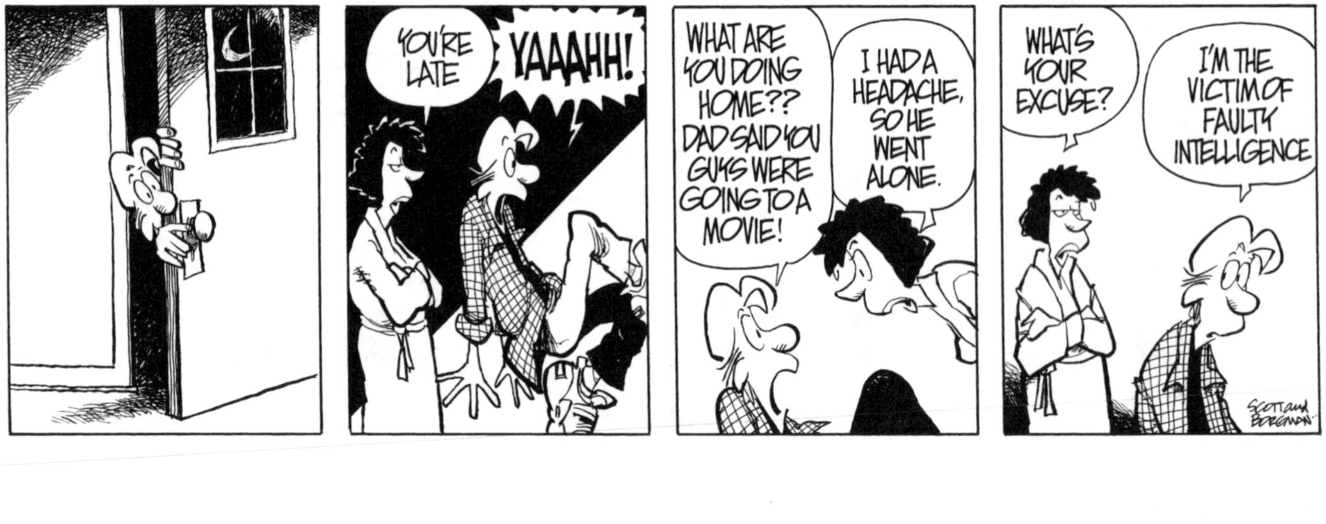
YOU'RE LATE
YAAAHH!
WHAT ARE YOU DOING HOME?? DAD SAID YOU GUYS WERE GOING TO A MOVIE!
I HAD A HEADACHE, SO HE WENT ALONE.
WHAT'S YOUR EXCUSE?
I'M THE VICTIM OF FAULTY INTELLIGENCE
SCOTT and BORGMAN

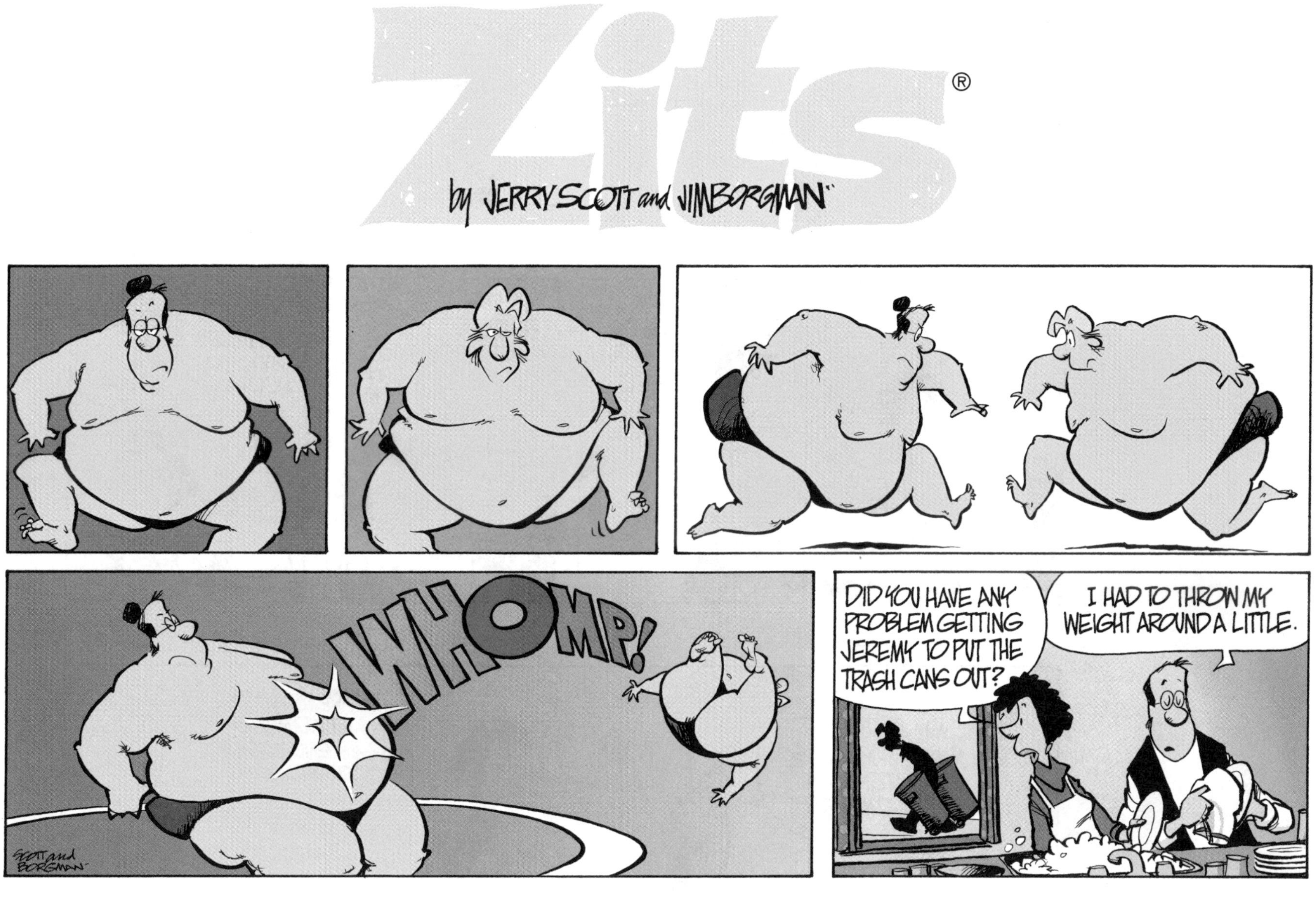
Zits®
by JERRY SCOTT and JIM BORGMAN
WHOMP!
SCOTT and BORGMAN
DID YOU HAVE ANY PROBLEM GETTING JEREMY TO PUT THE TRASH CANS OUT?
I HAD TO THROW MY WEIGHT AROUND A LITTLE.

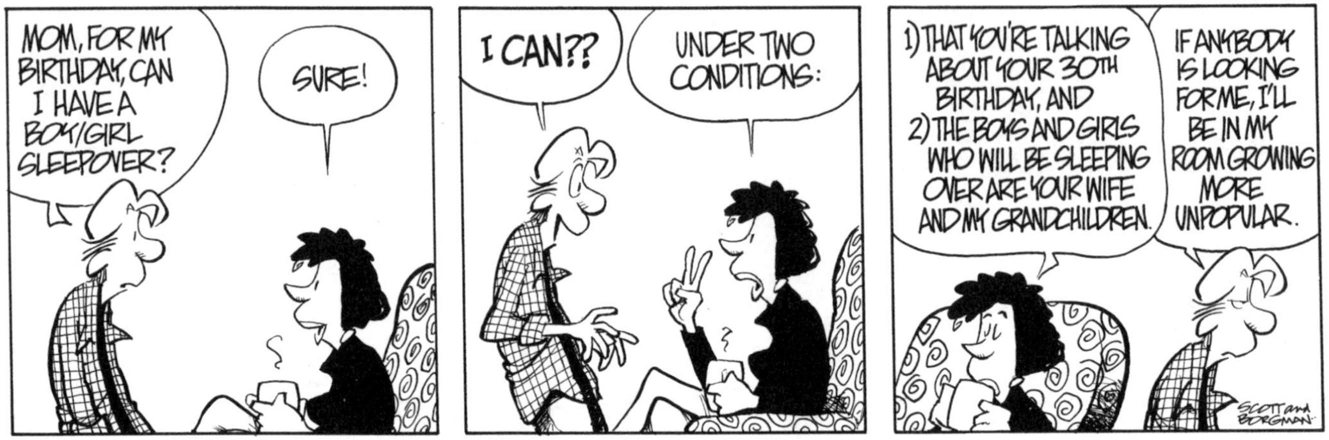
MOM, FOR MY BIRTHDAY, CAN I HAVE A BOY/GIRL SLEEPOVER?
SURE!
I CAN??
UNDER TWO CONDITIONS:
1) THAT YOU'RE TALKING ABOUT YOUR 30TH BIRTHDAY, AND
2) THE BOYS AND GIRLS WHO WILL BE SLEEPING OVER ARE YOUR WIFE AND MY GRANDCHILDREN.
IF ANYBODY IS LOOKING FOR ME, I'LL BE IN MY ROOM GROWING MORE UNPOPULAR.
SCOTT and BORGMAN

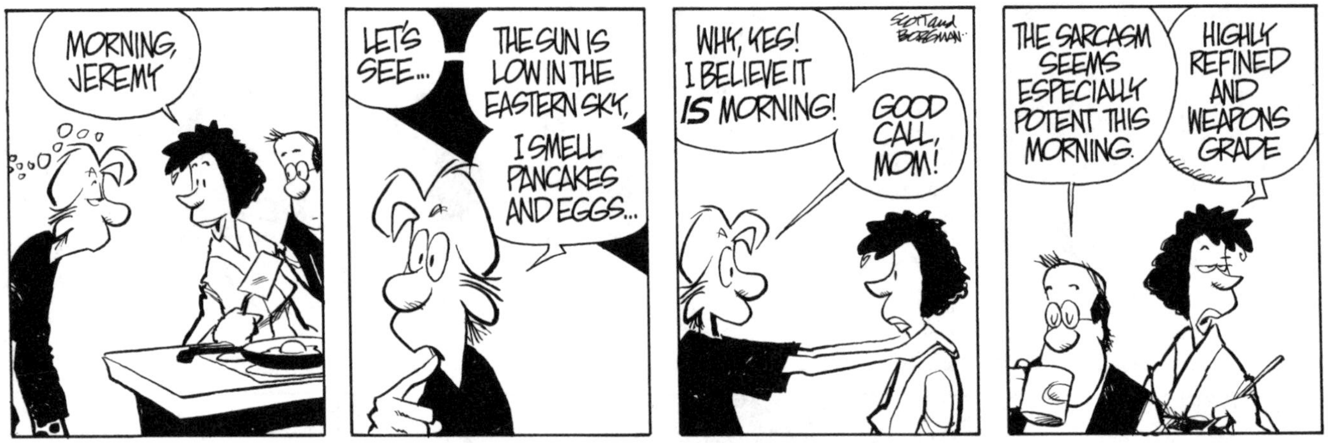
MORNING, JEREMY
LET'S SEE...
THE SUN IS LOW IN THE EASTERN SKY,
I SMELL PANCAKES AND EGGS...
WHY, YES! I BELIEVE IT IS MORNING!
GOOD CALL, MOM!
SCOTT and BORGMAN
THE SARCASM SEEMS ESPECIALLY POTENT THIS MORNING.
HIGHLY REFINED AND WEAPONS GRADE

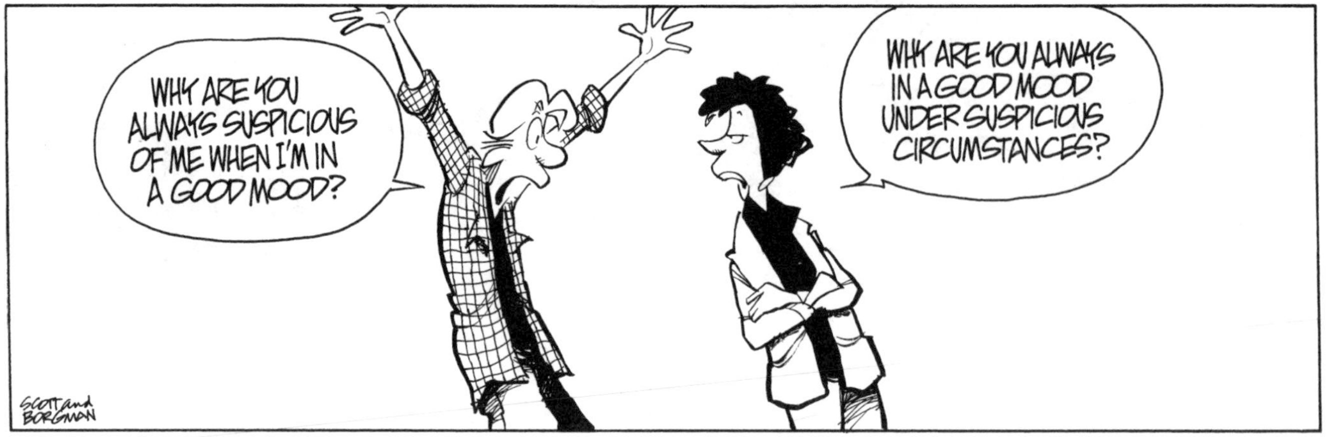
WHY ARE YOU ALWAYS SUSPICIOUS OF ME WHEN I'M IN A GOOD MOOD?
WHY ARE YOU ALWAYS IN A GOOD MOOD UNDER SUSPICIOUS CIRCUMSTANCES?
SCOTT and BORGMAN

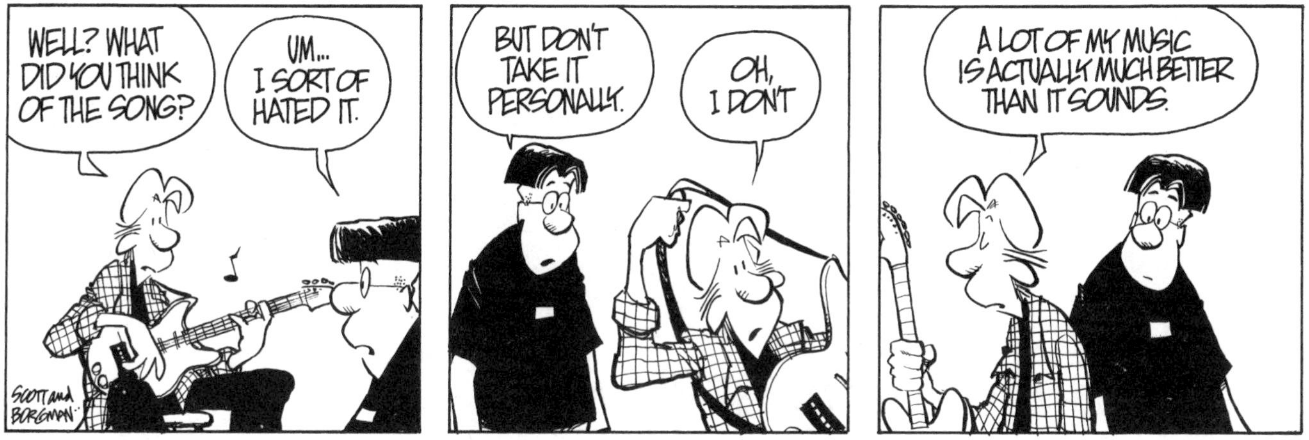
WELL? WHAT DID YOU THINK OF THE SONG?
UM... I SORT OF HATED IT.
SCOTT and BORGMAN
BUT DON'T TAKE IT PERSONALLY.
OH, I DON'T
A LOT OF MY MUSIC IS ACTUALLY MUCH BETTER THAN IT SOUNDS.

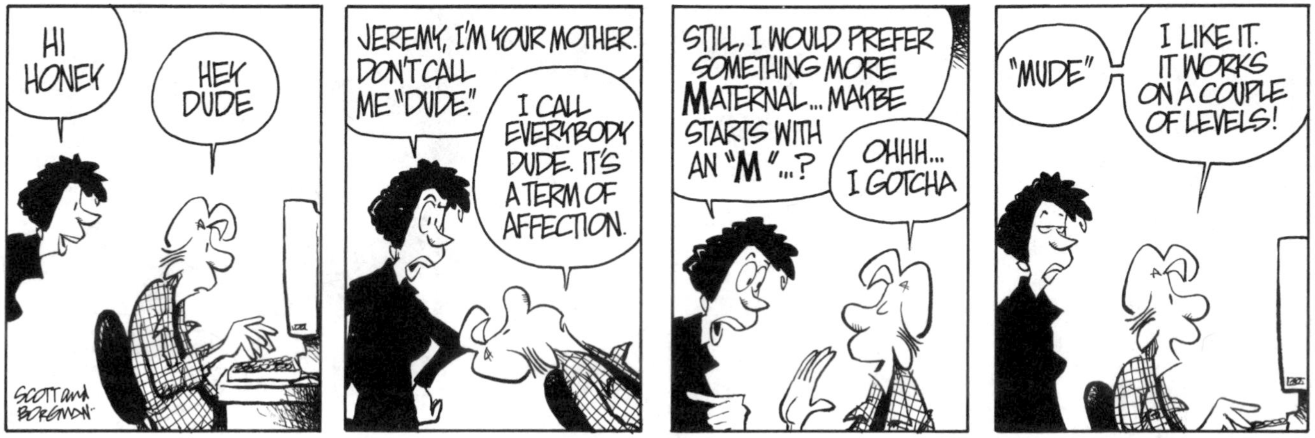
HI HONEY
HEY DUDE
SCOTT and BORGMAN
JEREMY, I'M YOUR MOTHER. DON'T CALL ME "DUDE."
I CALL EVERYBODY DUDE. IT'S A TERM OF AFFECTION.
STILL, I WOULD PREFER SOMETHING MORE MATERNAL... MAYBE STARTS WITH AN "M"...?
OHHH... I GOTCHA
"MUDE"
I LIKE IT. IT WORKS ON A COUPLE OF LEVELS!

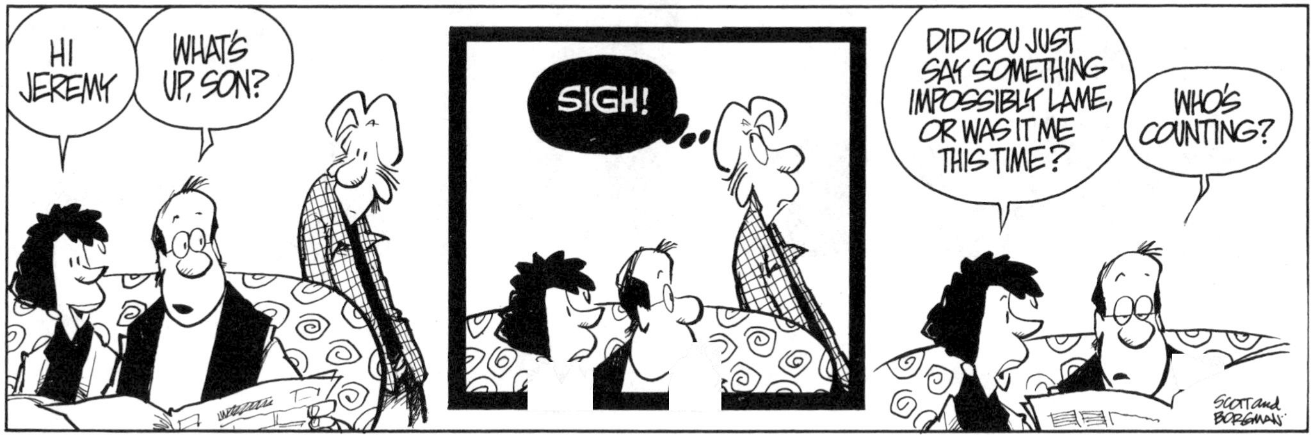
HI JEREMY
WHAT'S UP, SON?
SIGH!
DID YOU JUST SAY SOMETHING IMPOSSIBLY LAME, OR WAS IT ME THIS TIME?
WHO'S COUNTING?
SCOTT and BORGMAN

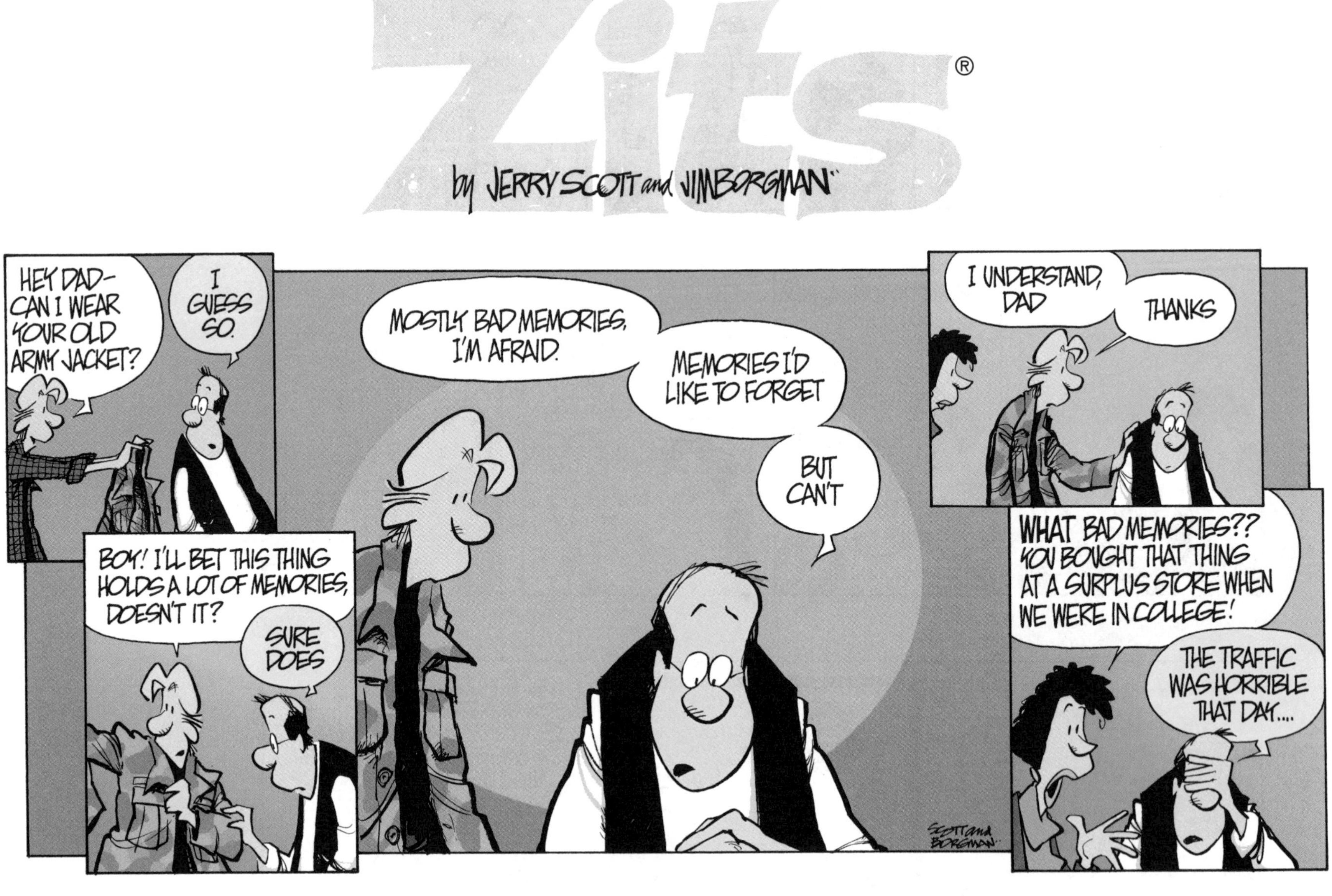
Zits®
by JERRY SCOTT and JIM BORGMAN
HEY DAD- CAN I WEAR YOUR OLD ARMY JACKET?
I GUESS SO.
BOY! I'LL BET THIS THING HOLDS A LOT OF MEMORIES, DOESN'T IT?
SURE DOES
MOSTLY BAD MEMORIES, I'M AFRAID.
MEMORIES I'D LIKE TO FORGET
BUT CAN'T
I UNDERSTAND, DAD
THANKS
WHAT BAD MEMORIES?? YOU BOUGHT THAT THING AT A SURPLUS STORE WHEN WE WERE IN COLLEGE!
THE TRAFFIC WAS HORRIBLE THAT DAY....
SCOTT and BORGMAN

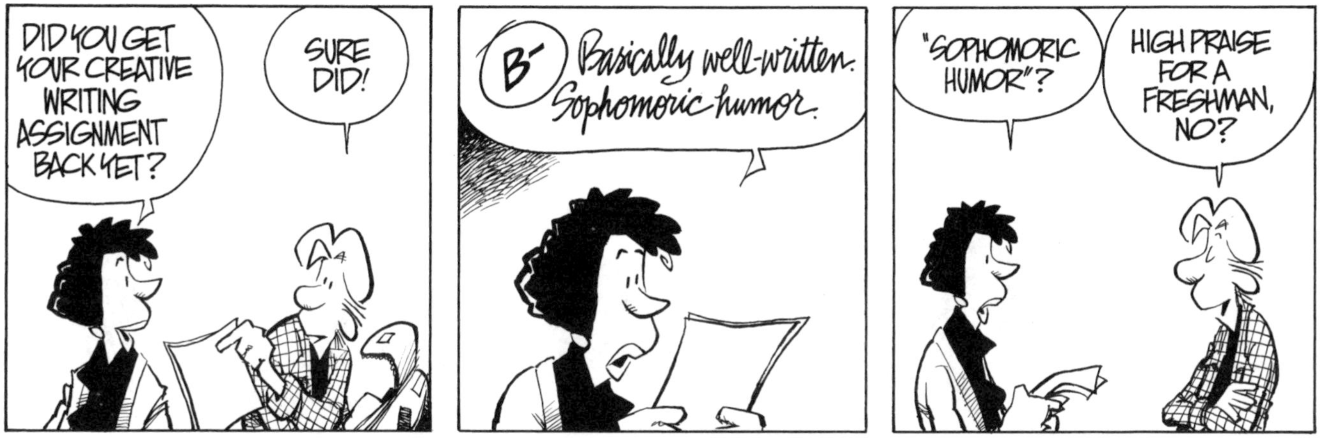
DID YOU GET YOUR CREATIVE WRITING ASSIGNMENT BACK YET?
SURE DID!
B-
Basically well-written. Sophomoric humor.
"SOPHOMORIC HUMOR"?
HIGH PRAISE FOR A FRESHMAN, NO?

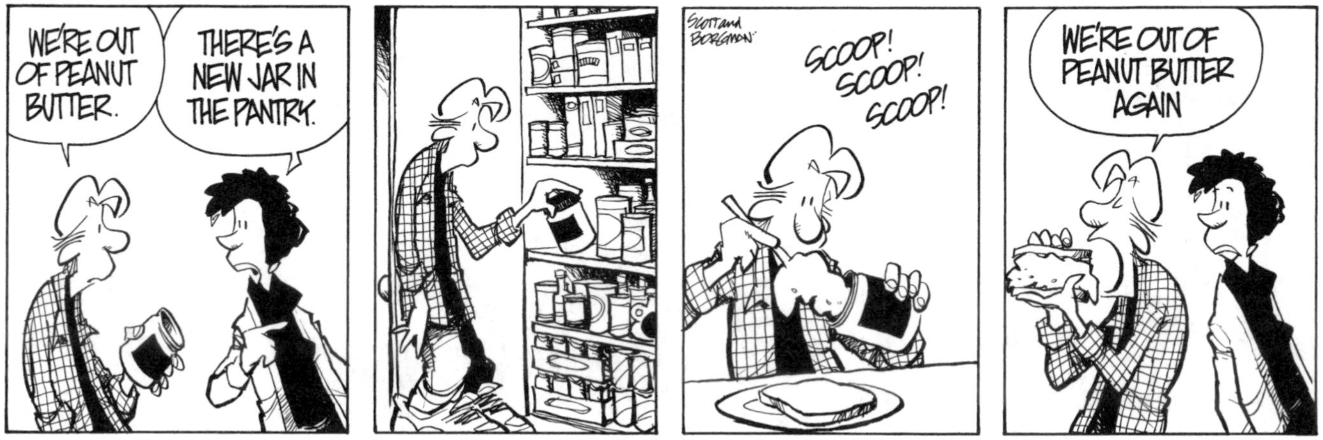
WE'RE OUT OF PEANUT BUTTER.
THERE'S A NEW JAR IN THE PANTRY.
SCOTT AND BORGMAN
SCOOP! SCOOP! SCOOP!
WE'RE OUT OF PEANUT BUTTER AGAIN

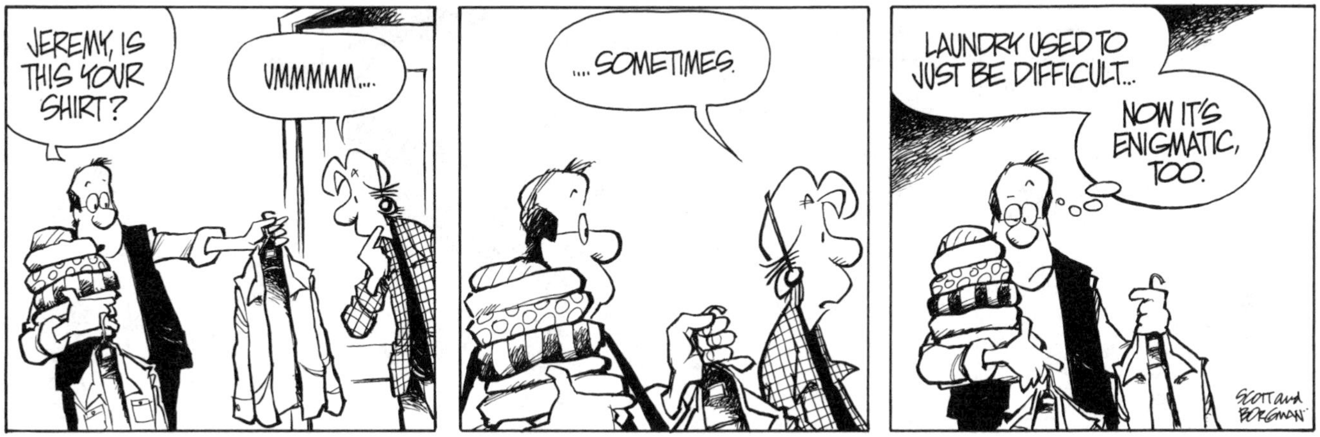
JEREMY, IS THIS YOUR SHIRT?
UMMMMM....
....SOMETIMES.
LAUNDRY USED TO JUST BE DIFFICULT...
NOW IT'S ENIGMATIC, TOO.
SCOTT AND BORGMAN

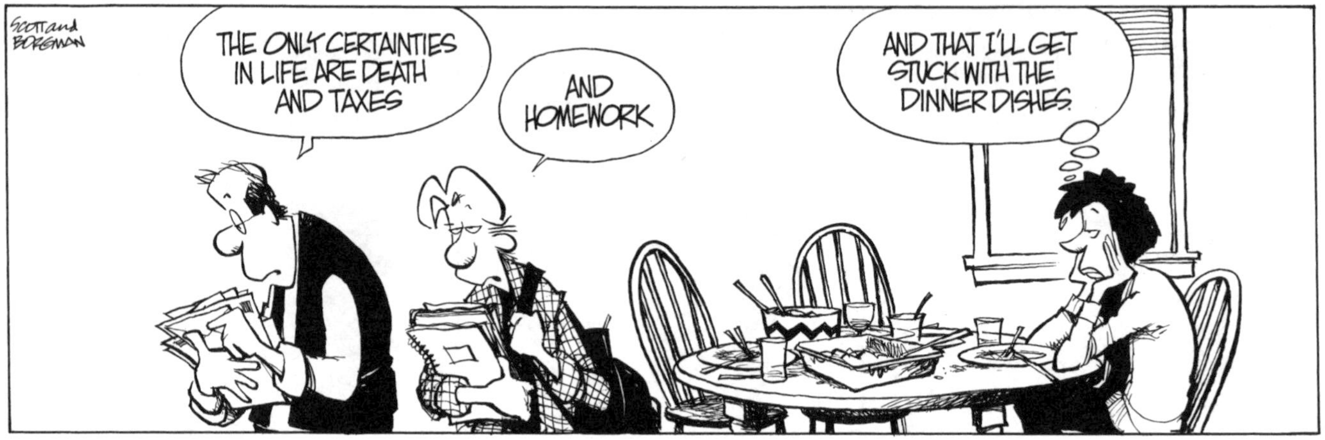
SCOTT and BORGMAN
THE ONLY CERTAINTIES IN LIFE ARE DEATH AND TAXES
AND HOMEWORK
AND THAT I'LL GET STUCK WITH THE DINNER DISHES.

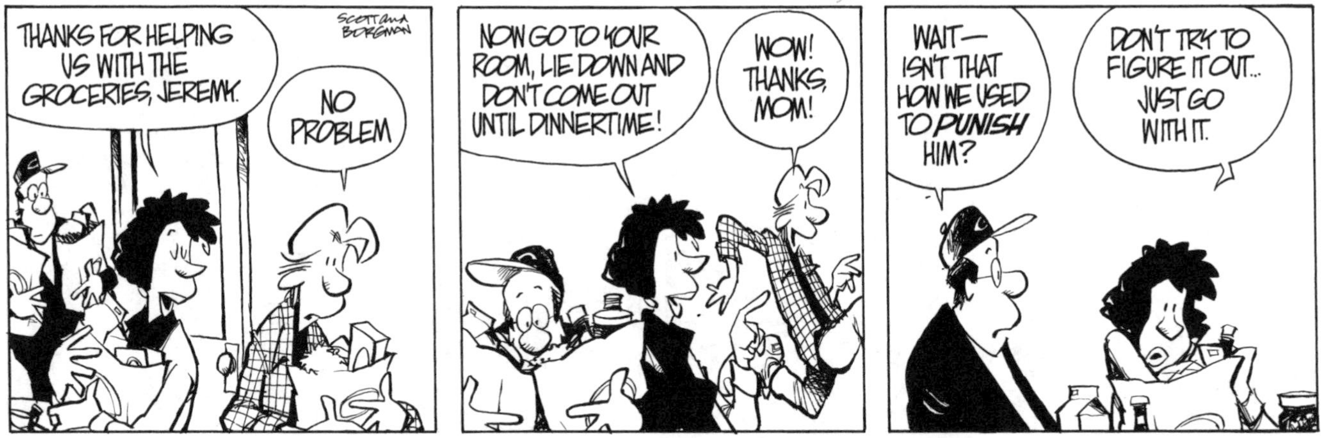
SCOTT and BORGMAN
THANKS FOR HELPING US WITH THE GROCERIES, JEREMY.
NO PROBLEM
NOW GO TO YOUR ROOM, LIE DOWN AND DON'T COME OUT UNTIL DINNERTIME!
WOW! THANKS, MOM!
WAIT— ISN'T THAT HOW WE USED TO **PUNISH** HIM?
DON'T TRY TO FIGURE IT OUT... JUST GO WITH IT.

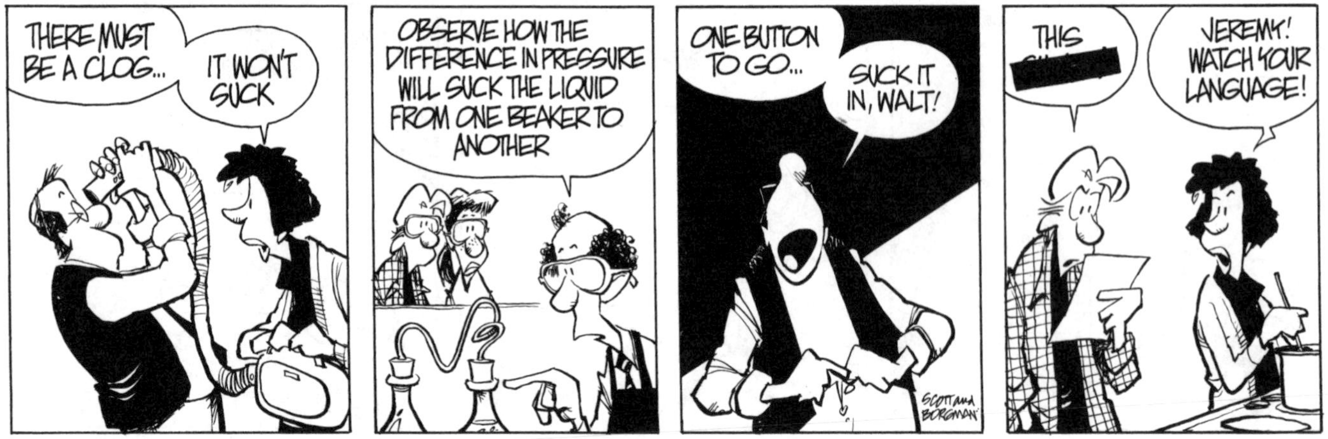
THERE MUST BE A CLOG...
IT WON'T SUCK
OBSERVE HOW THE DIFFERENCE IN PRESSURE WILL SUCK THE LIQUID FROM ONE BEAKER TO ANOTHER
ONE BUTTON TO GO...
SUCK IT IN, WALT!
SCOTT and BORGMAN
THIS [redacted]
JEREMY! WATCH YOUR LANGUAGE!

Zits®

by JERRY SCOTT and JIM BORGMAN

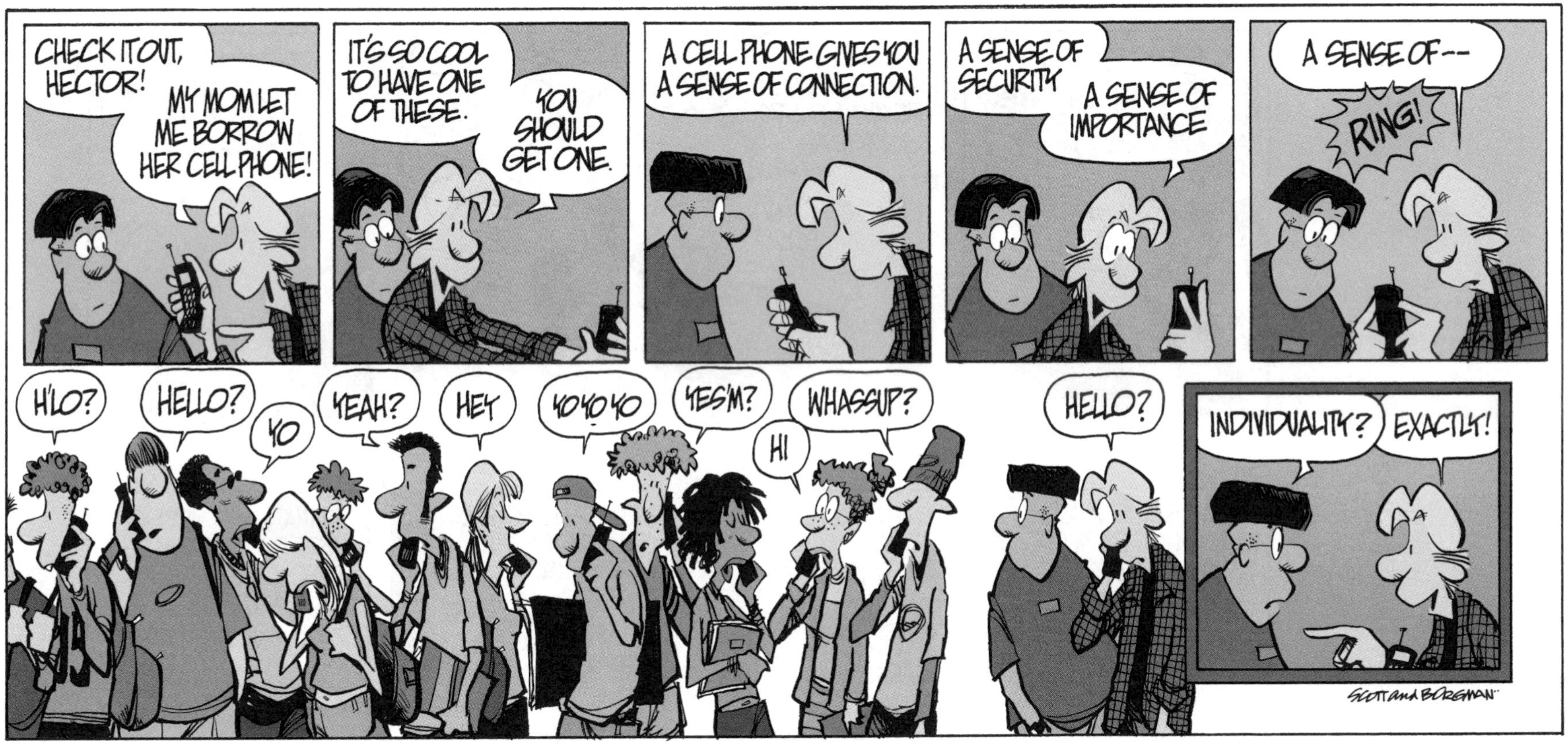
CHECK IT OUT, HECTOR!
MY MOM LET ME BORROW HER CELL PHONE!
IT'S SO COOL TO HAVE ONE OF THESE.
YOU SHOULD GET ONE.
A CELL PHONE GIVES YOU A SENSE OF CONNECTION.
A SENSE OF SECURITY
A SENSE OF IMPORTANCE
A SENSE OF--
RING!
H'LO?
HELLO?
YO
YEAH?
HEY
YO YO YO
YES'M?
HI
WHASSUP?
HELLO?
INDIVIDUALITY?
EXACTLY!
SCOTT and BORGMAN

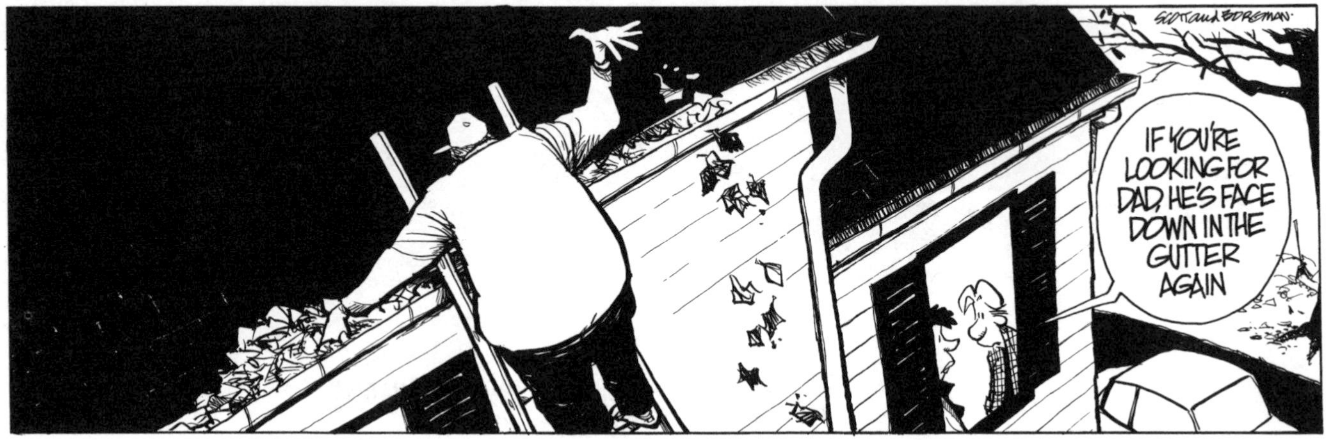
SCOTT and BORGMAN
IF YOU'RE LOOKING FOR DAD, HE'S FACE DOWN IN THE GUTTER AGAIN

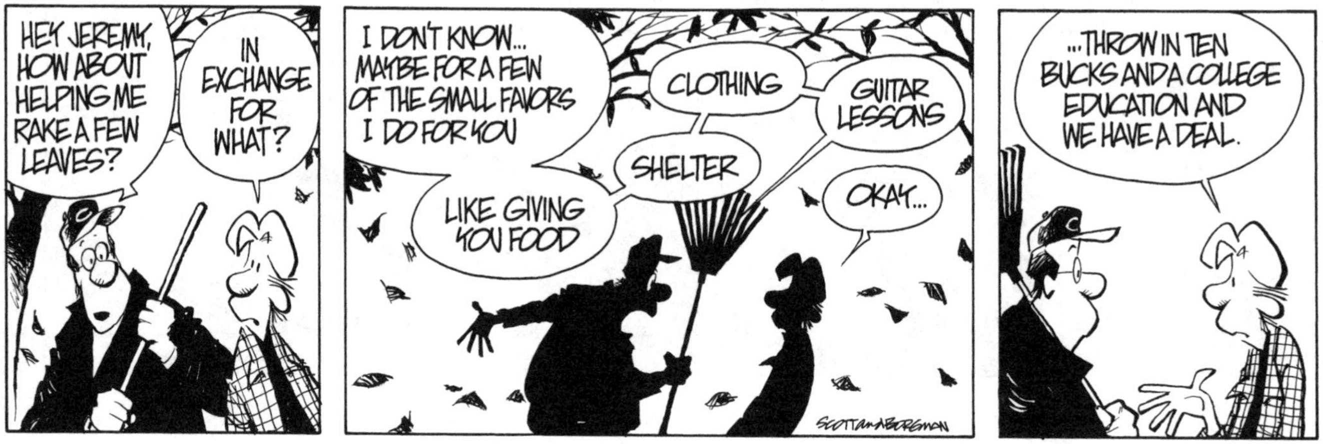
HEY JEREMY, HOW ABOUT HELPING ME RAKE A FEW LEAVES?
IN EXCHANGE FOR WHAT?
I DON'T KNOW... MAYBE FOR A FEW OF THE SMALL FAVORS I DO FOR YOU
LIKE GIVING YOU FOOD
SHELTER
CLOTHING
GUITAR LESSONS
OKAY...
SCOTT and BORGMAN
...THROW IN TEN BUCKS AND A COLLEGE EDUCATION AND WE HAVE A DEAL.

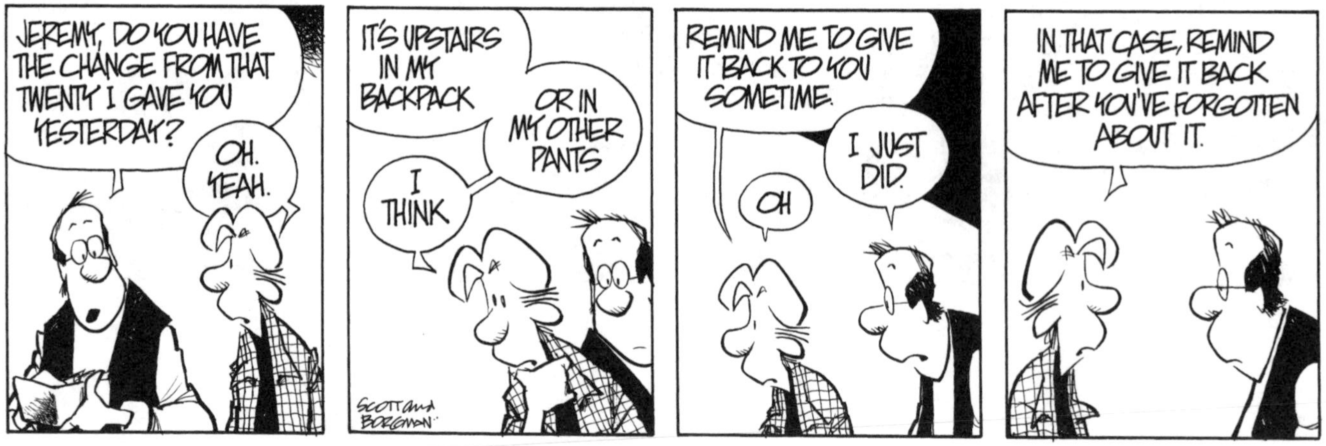
JEREMY, DO YOU HAVE THE CHANGE FROM THAT TWENTY I GAVE YOU YESTERDAY?
OH. YEAH.
IT'S UPSTAIRS IN MY BACKPACK
OR IN MY OTHER PANTS
I THINK
SCOTT and BORGMAN
REMIND ME TO GIVE IT BACK TO YOU SOMETIME.
OH
I JUST DID.
IN THAT CASE, REMIND ME TO GIVE IT BACK AFTER YOU'VE FORGOTTEN ABOUT IT.

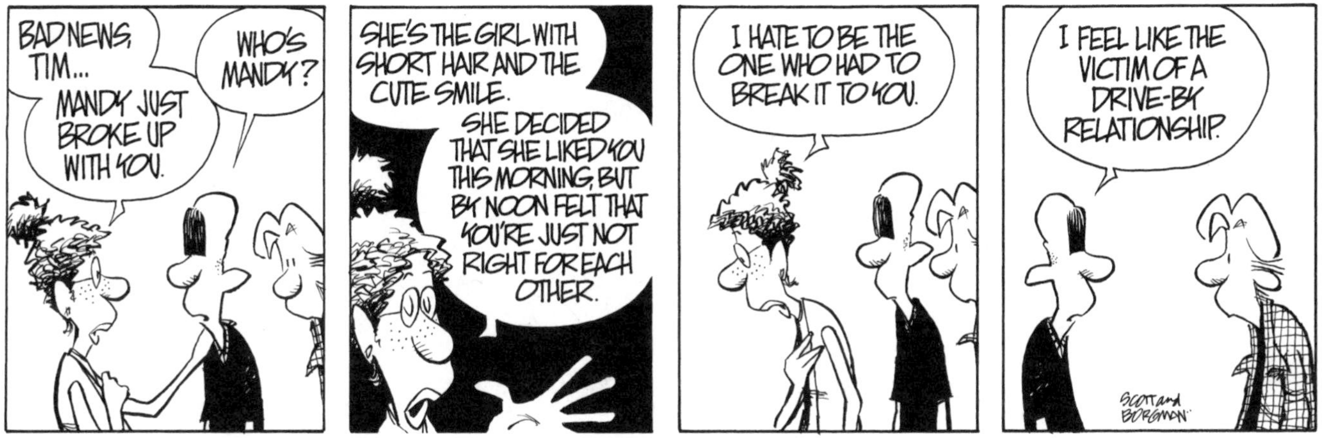
BAD NEWS, TIM... MANDY JUST BROKE UP WITH YOU.
WHO'S MANDY?
SHE'S THE GIRL WITH SHORT HAIR AND THE CUTE SMILE.
SHE DECIDED THAT SHE LIKED YOU THIS MORNING, BUT BY NOON FELT THAT YOU'RE JUST NOT RIGHT FOR EACH OTHER.
I HATE TO BE THE ONE WHO HAD TO BREAK IT TO YOU.
I FEEL LIKE THE VICTIM OF A DRIVE-BY RELATIONSHIP.
SCOTT and BORGMAN

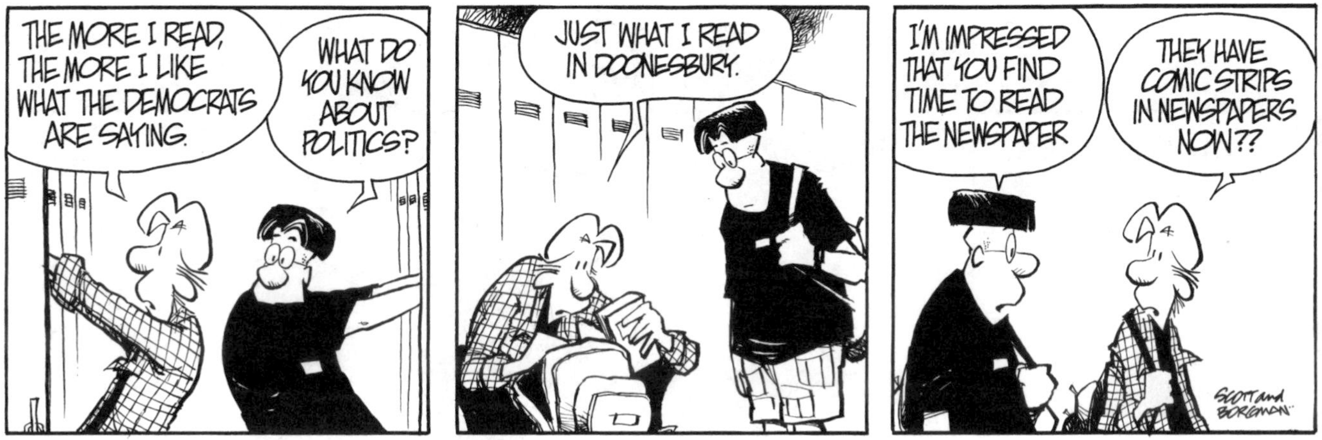
THE MORE I READ, THE MORE I LIKE WHAT THE DEMOCRATS ARE SAYING.
WHAT DO YOU KNOW ABOUT POLITICS?
JUST WHAT I READ IN DOONESBURY.
I'M IMPRESSED THAT YOU FIND TIME TO READ THE NEWSPAPER
THEY HAVE COMIC STRIPS IN NEWSPAPERS NOW??
SCOTT and BORGMAN

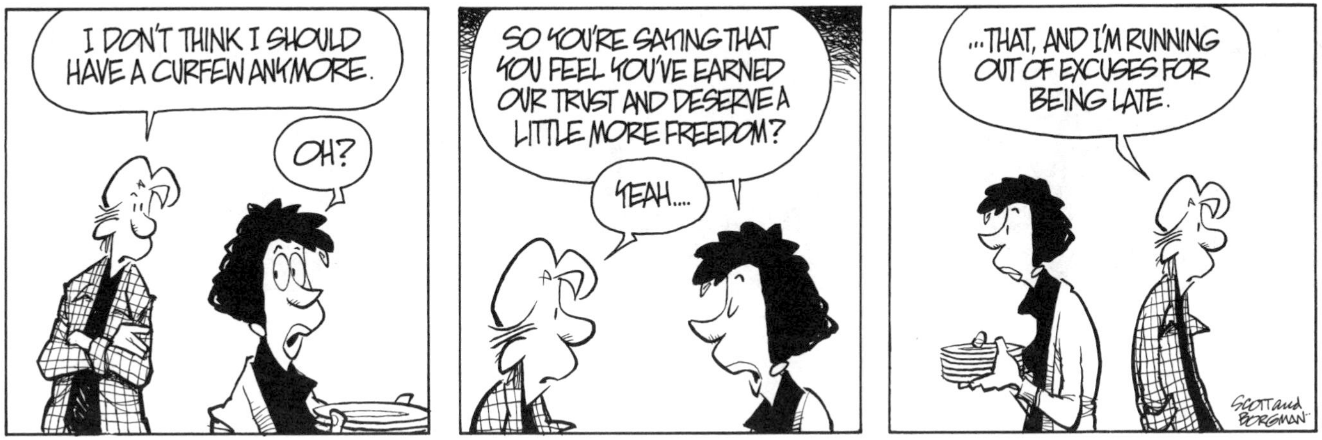
I DON'T THINK I SHOULD HAVE A CURFEW ANYMORE.
OH?
SO YOU'RE SAYING THAT YOU FEEL YOU'VE EARNED OUR TRUST AND DESERVE A LITTLE MORE FREEDOM?
YEAH....
...THAT, AND I'M RUNNING OUT OF EXCUSES FOR BEING LATE.
SCOTT and BORGMAN

Zits®

by JERRY SCOTT and JIM BORGMAN

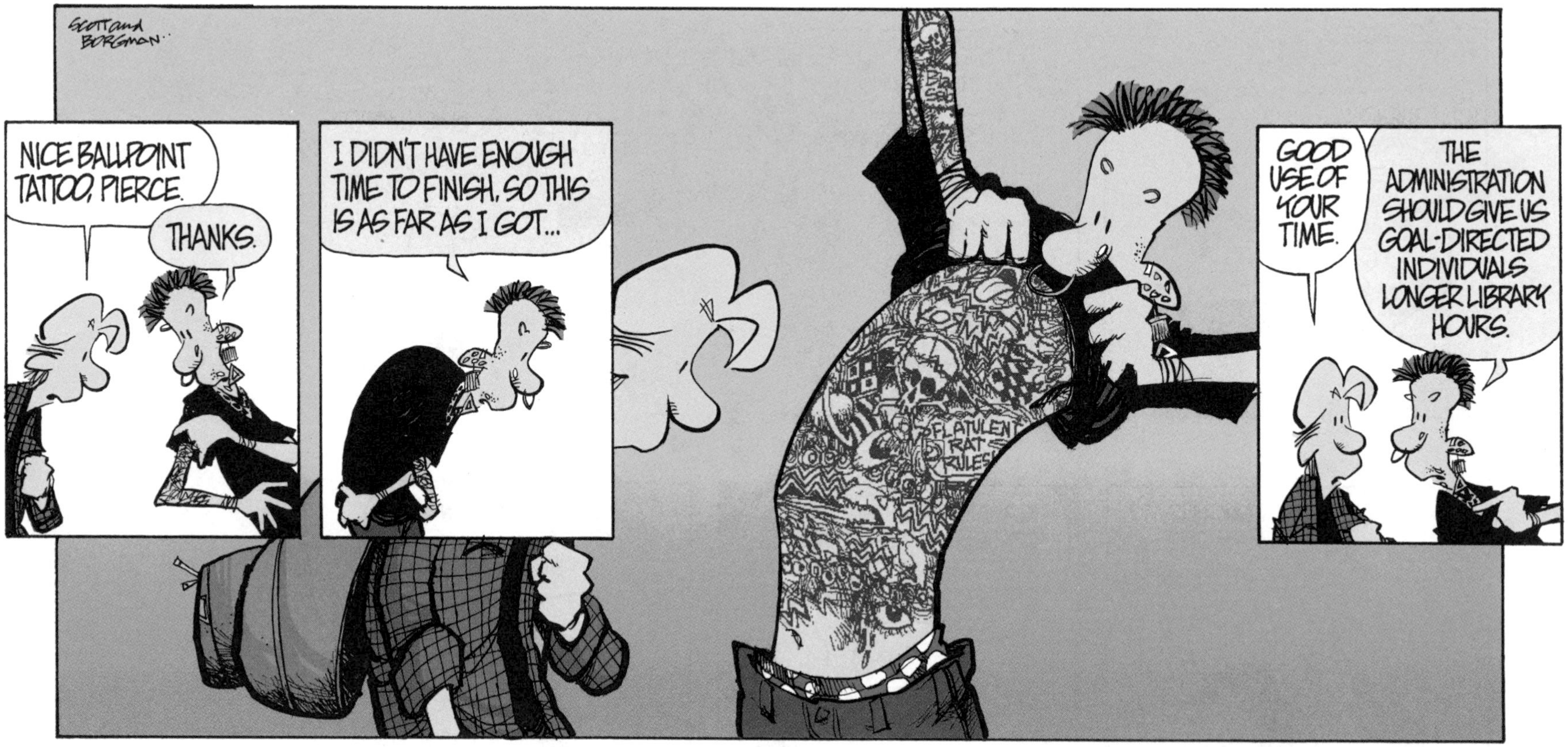

SCOTT and BORGMAN
NICE BALLPOINT TATTOO, PIERCE.
THANKS.
I DIDN'T HAVE ENOUGH TIME TO FINISH, SO THIS IS AS FAR AS I GOT...
FLATULENT RAT RULES!
GOOD USE OF YOUR TIME.
THE ADMINISTRATION SHOULD GIVE US GOAL-DIRECTED INDIVIDUALS LONGER LIBRARY HOURS.

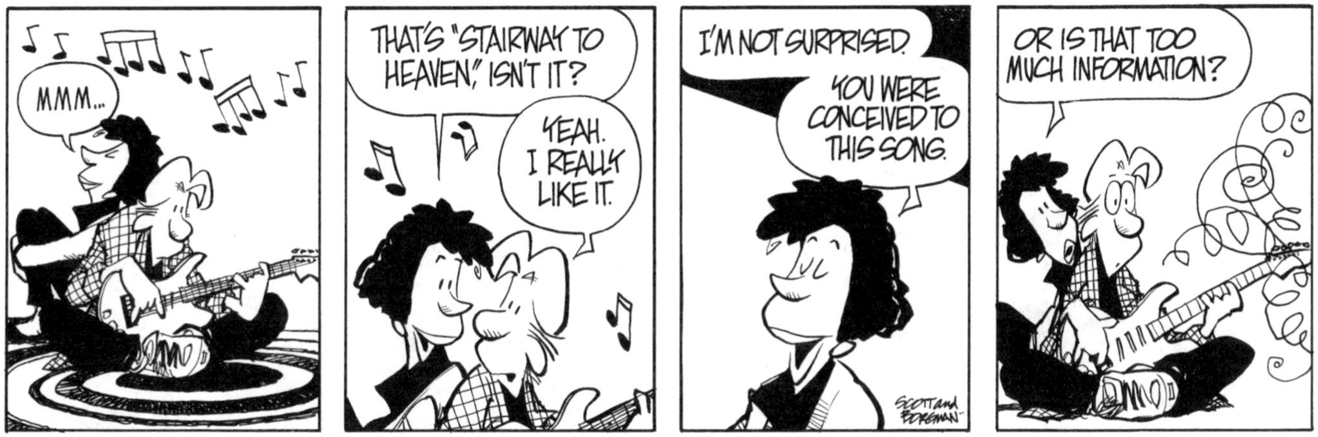
MMM...
THAT'S "STAIRWAY TO HEAVEN," ISN'T IT?
YEAH. I REALLY LIKE IT.
I'M NOT SURPRISED.
YOU WERE CONCEIVED TO THIS SONG.
OR IS THAT TOO MUCH INFORMATION?

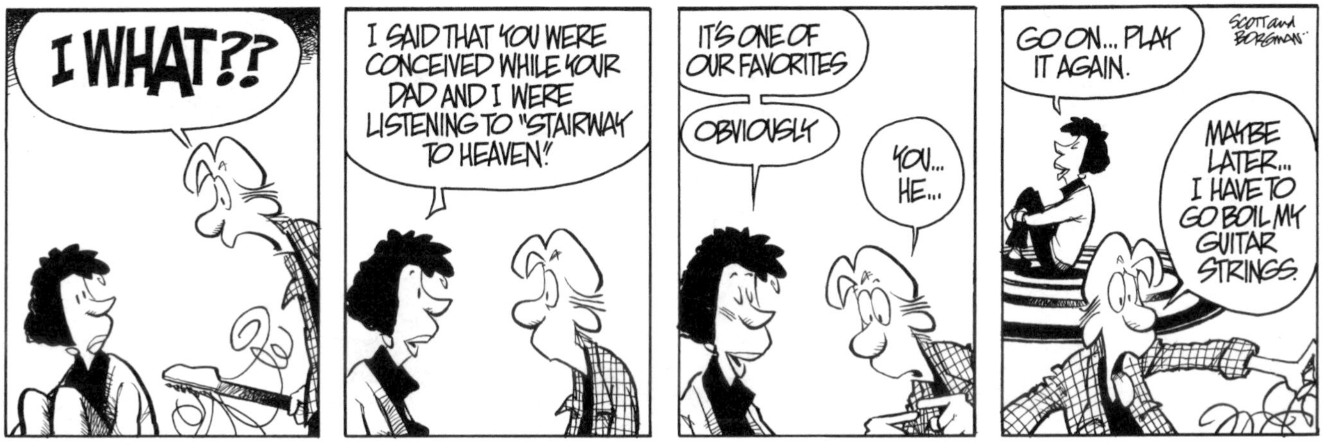
I WHAT??
I SAID THAT YOU WERE CONCEIVED WHILE YOUR DAD AND I WERE LISTENING TO "STAIRWAY TO HEAVEN."
IT'S ONE OF OUR FAVORITES
OBVIOUSLY
YOU... HE...
GO ON... PLAY IT AGAIN.
MAYBE LATER... I HAVE TO GO BOIL MY GUITAR STRINGS.

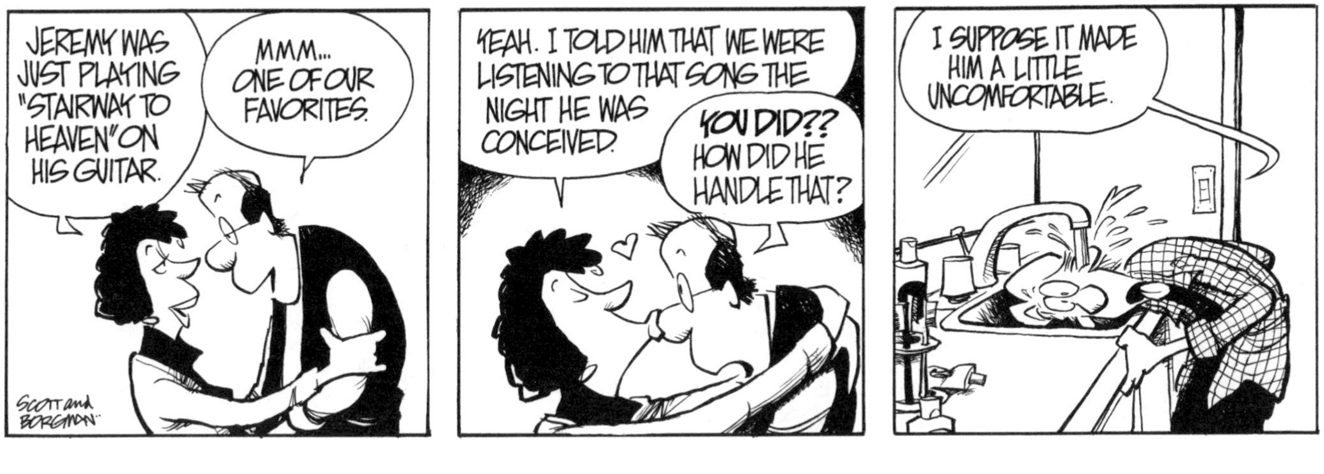
JEREMY WAS JUST PLAYING "STAIRWAY TO HEAVEN" ON HIS GUITAR.
MMM... ONE OF OUR FAVORITES.
YEAH. I TOLD HIM THAT WE WERE LISTENING TO THAT SONG THE NIGHT HE WAS CONCEIVED.
YOU DID?? HOW DID HE HANDLE THAT?
I SUPPOSE IT MADE HIM A LITTLE UNCOMFORTABLE.

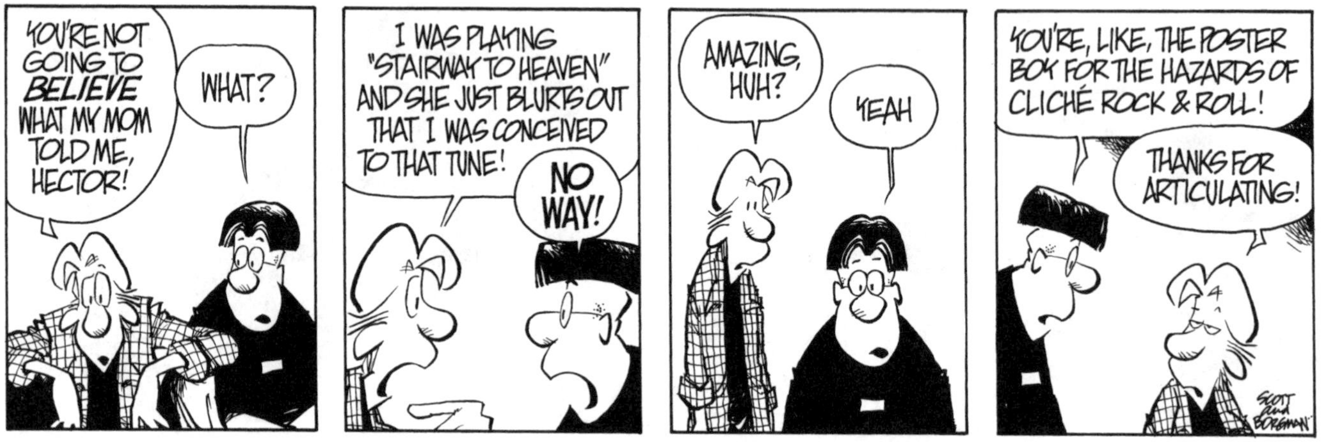
YOU'RE NOT GOING TO BELIEVE WHAT MY MOM TOLD ME, HECTOR!
WHAT?
I WAS PLAYING "STAIRWAY TO HEAVEN" AND SHE JUST BLURTS OUT THAT I WAS CONCEIVED TO THAT TUNE!
NO WAY!
AMAZING, HUH?
YEAH
YOU'RE, LIKE, THE POSTER BOY FOR THE HAZARDS OF CLICHÉ ROCK & ROLL!
THANKS FOR ARTICULATING!
SCOTT and BORGMAN

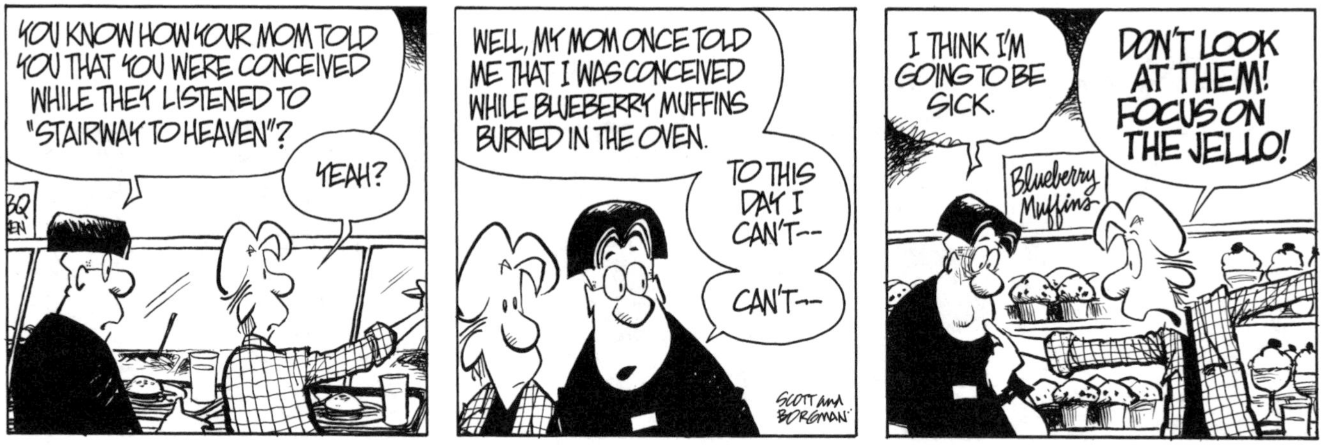
YOU KNOW HOW YOUR MOM TOLD YOU THAT YOU WERE CONCEIVED WHILE THEY LISTENED TO "STAIRWAY TO HEAVEN"?
YEAH?
WELL, MY MOM ONCE TOLD ME THAT I WAS CONCEIVED WHILE BLUEBERRY MUFFINS BURNED IN THE OVEN.
TO THIS DAY I CAN'T--
CAN'T--
SCOTT and BORGMAN
I THINK I'M GOING TO BE SICK.
DON'T LOOK AT THEM! FOCUS ON THE JELLO!
Blueberry Muffins

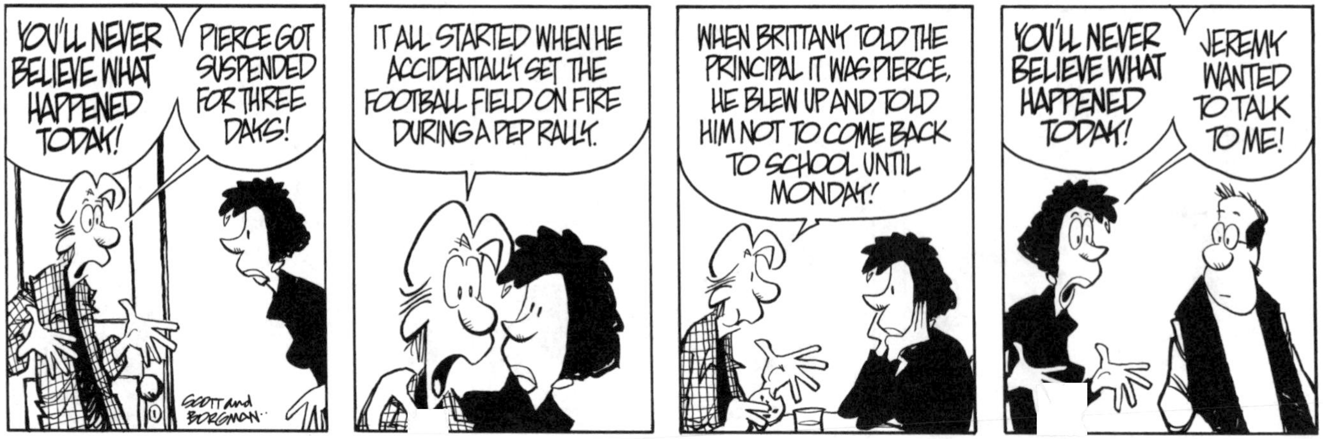
YOU'LL NEVER BELIEVE WHAT HAPPENED TODAY!
PIERCE GOT SUSPENDED FOR THREE DAYS!
SCOTT and BORGMAN
IT ALL STARTED WHEN HE ACCIDENTALLY SET THE FOOTBALL FIELD ON FIRE DURING A PEP RALLY.
WHEN BRITTANY TOLD THE PRINCIPAL IT WAS PIERCE, HE BLEW UP AND TOLD HIM NOT TO COME BACK TO SCHOOL UNTIL MONDAY!
YOU'LL NEVER BELIEVE WHAT HAPPENED TODAY!
JEREMY WANTED TO TALK TO ME!

Zits®

by JERRY SCOTT and JIM BORGMAN

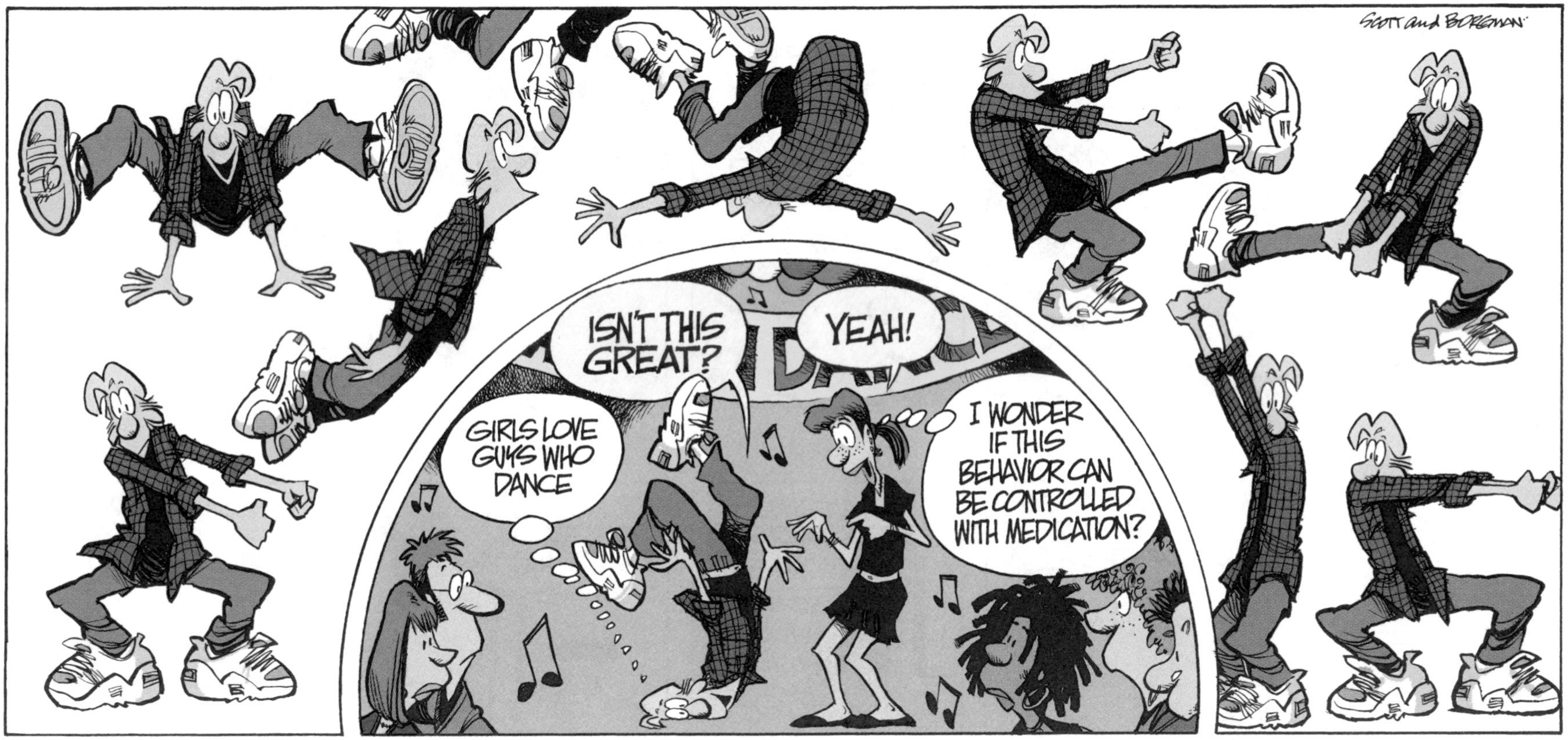

SCOTT and BORGMAN
ISN'T THIS GREAT?
YEAH!
GIRLS LOVE GUYS WHO DANCE
I WONDER IF THIS BEHAVIOR CAN BE CONTROLLED WITH MEDICATION?

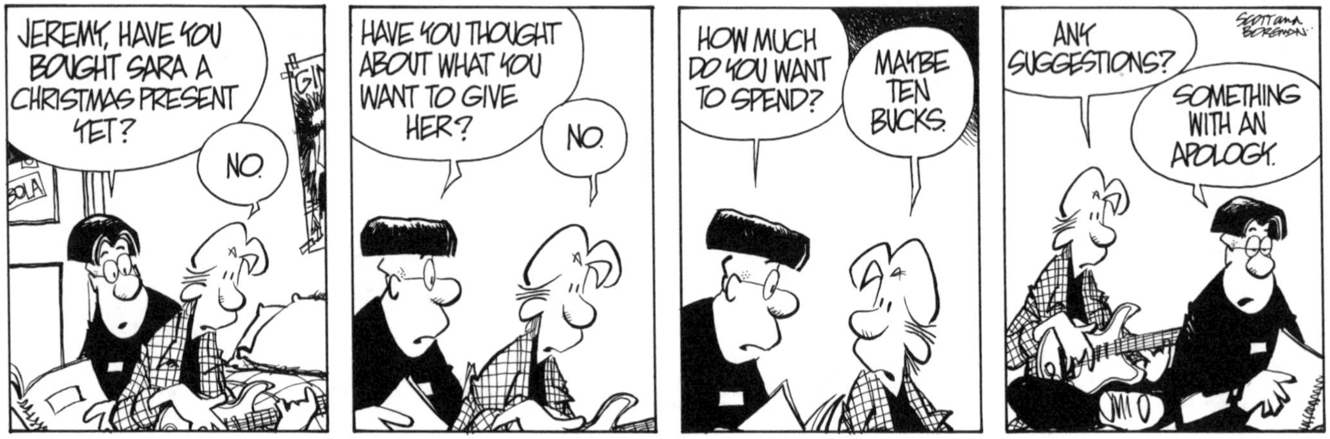
JEREMY, HAVE YOU BOUGHT SARA A CHRISTMAS PRESENT YET?
NO.
HAVE YOU THOUGHT ABOUT WHAT YOU WANT TO GIVE HER?
NO.
HOW MUCH DO YOU WANT TO SPEND?
MAYBE TEN BUCKS.
ANY SUGGESTIONS?
SOMETHING WITH AN APOLOGY.
SCOTT and BORGMAN

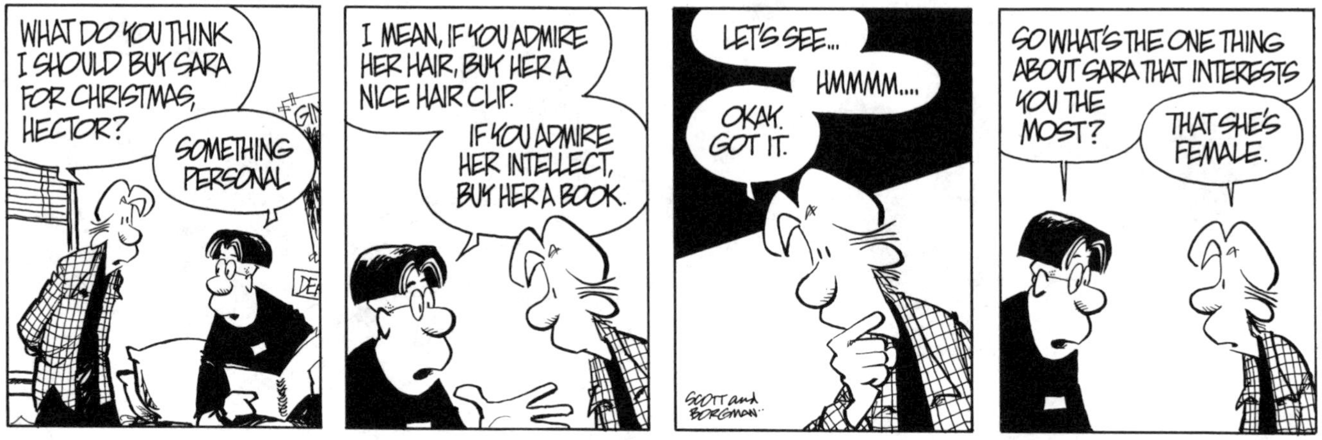
WHAT DO YOU THINK I SHOULD BUY SARA FOR CHRISTMAS, HECTOR?
SOMETHING PERSONAL
I MEAN, IF YOU ADMIRE HER HAIR, BUY HER A NICE HAIR CLIP.
IF YOU ADMIRE HER INTELLECT, BUY HER A BOOK.
LET'S SEE...
HMMMM....
OKAY. GOT IT.
SCOTT and BORGMAN
SO WHAT'S THE ONE THING ABOUT SARA THAT INTERESTS YOU THE MOST?
THAT SHE'S FEMALE.

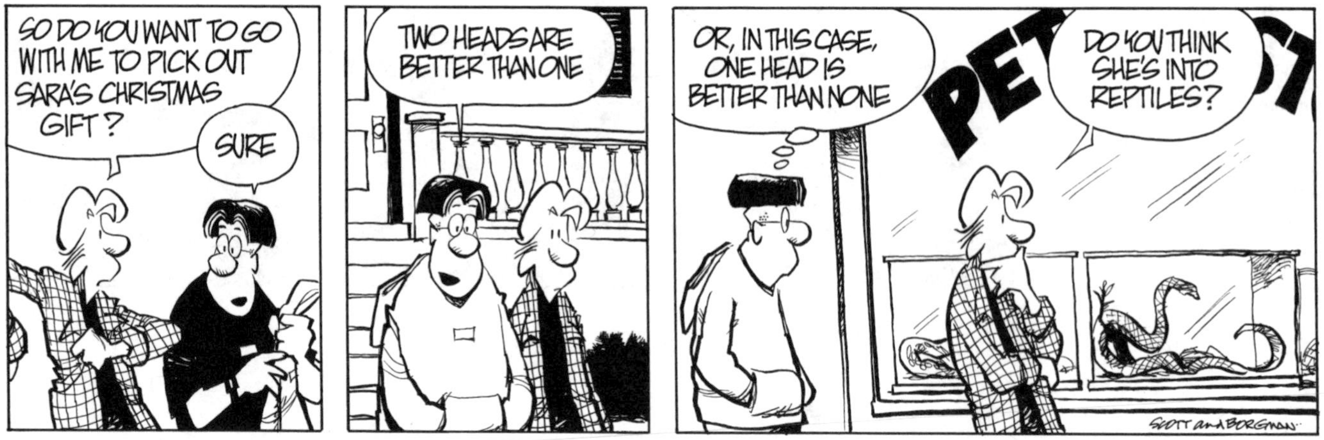
SO DO YOU WANT TO GO WITH ME TO PICK OUT SARA'S CHRISTMAS GIFT?
SURE
TWO HEADS ARE BETTER THAN ONE
OR, IN THIS CASE, ONE HEAD IS BETTER THAN NONE
DO YOU THINK SHE'S INTO REPTILES?
SCOTT and BORGMAN

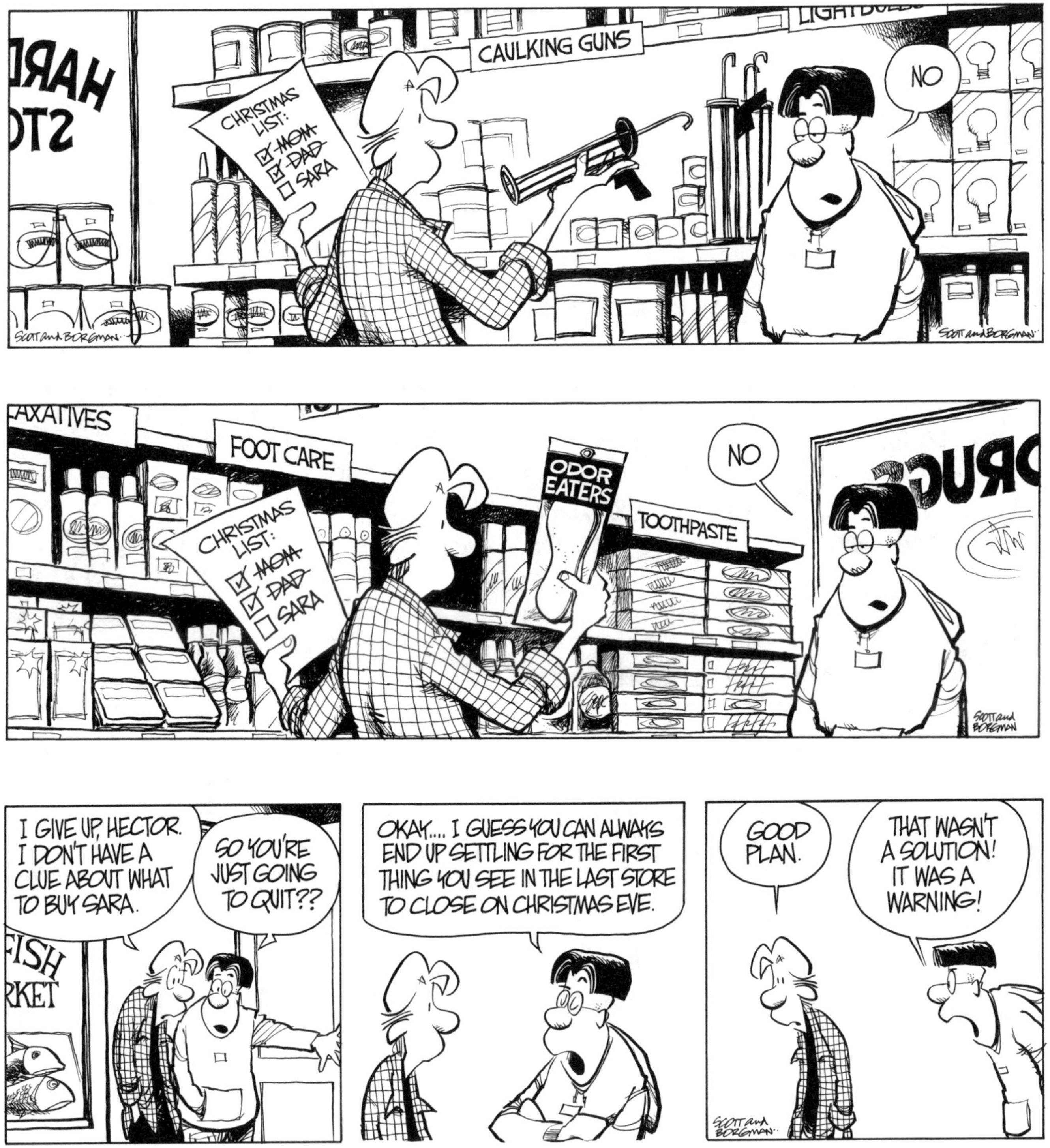
CAULKING GUNS
CHRISTMAS LIST:
MOM
DAD
SARA
NO
LAXATIVES
FOOT CARE
ODOR EATERS
TOOTHPASTE
CHRISTMAS LIST:
MOM
DAD
SARA
NO
I GIVE UP, HECTOR. I DON'T HAVE A CLUE ABOUT WHAT TO BUY SARA.
SO YOU'RE JUST GOING TO QUIT??
FISH
OKAY.... I GUESS YOU CAN ALWAYS END UP SETTLING FOR THE FIRST THING YOU SEE IN THE LAST STORE TO CLOSE ON CHRISTMAS EVE.
GOOD PLAN.
THAT WASN'T A SOLUTION! IT WAS A WARNING!
SCOTT and BORGMAN

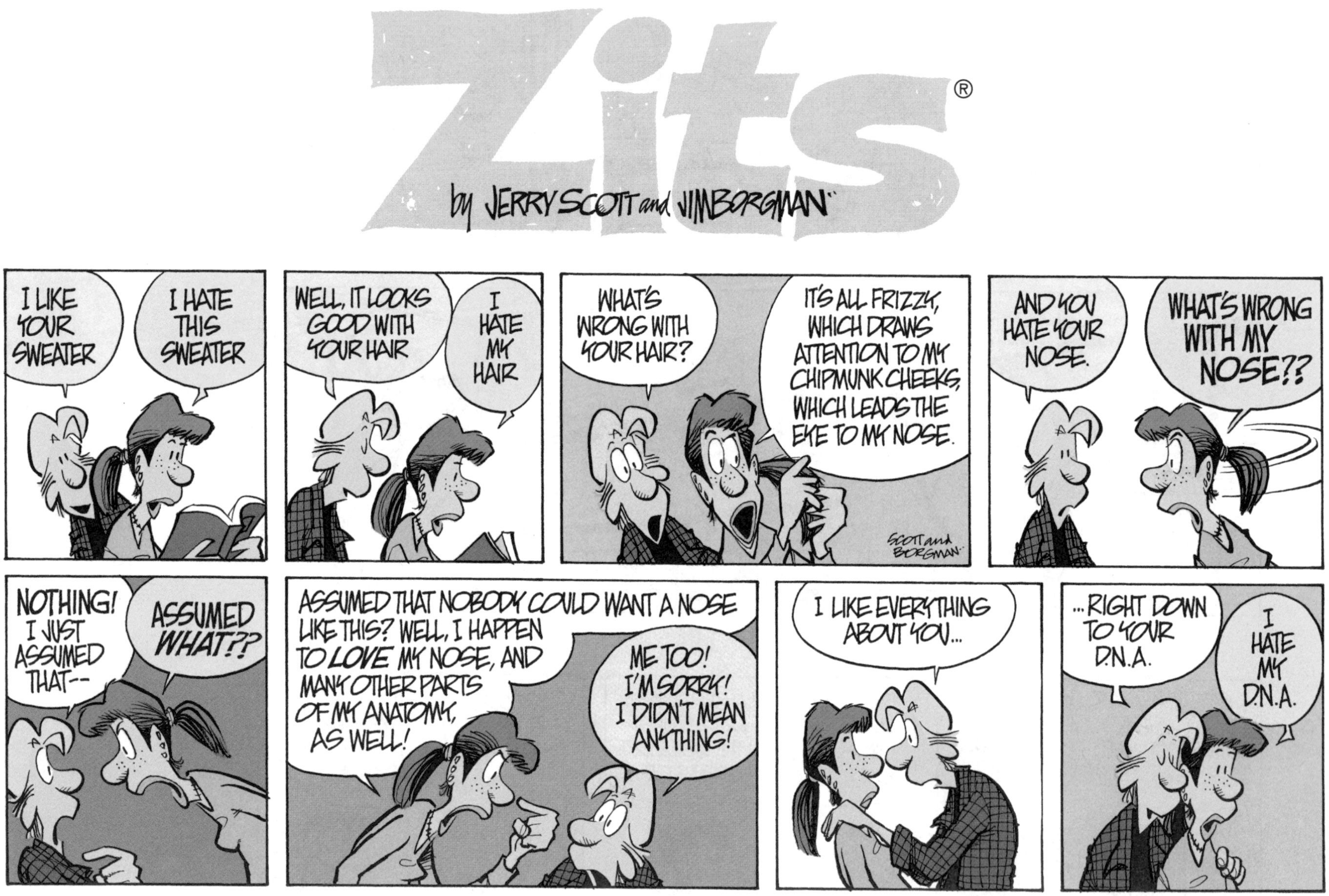
Zits®
by JERRY SCOTT and JIM BORGMAN
I LIKE YOUR SWEATER
I HATE THIS SWEATER
WELL, IT LOOKS GOOD WITH YOUR HAIR
I HATE MY HAIR
WHAT'S WRONG WITH YOUR HAIR?
IT'S ALL FRIZZY, WHICH DRAWS ATTENTION TO MY CHIPMUNK CHEEKS, WHICH LEADS THE EYE TO MY NOSE.
SCOTT and BORGMAN
AND YOU HATE YOUR NOSE.
WHAT'S WRONG WITH MY NOSE??
NOTHING! I JUST ASSUMED THAT--
ASSUMED WHAT??
ASSUMED THAT NOBODY COULD WANT A NOSE LIKE THIS? WELL, I HAPPEN TO LOVE MY NOSE, AND MANY OTHER PARTS OF MY ANATOMY, AS WELL!
ME TOO! I'M SORRY! I DIDN'T MEAN ANYTHING!
I LIKE EVERYTHING ABOUT YOU...
...RIGHT DOWN TO YOUR D.N.A.
I HATE MY D.N.A.

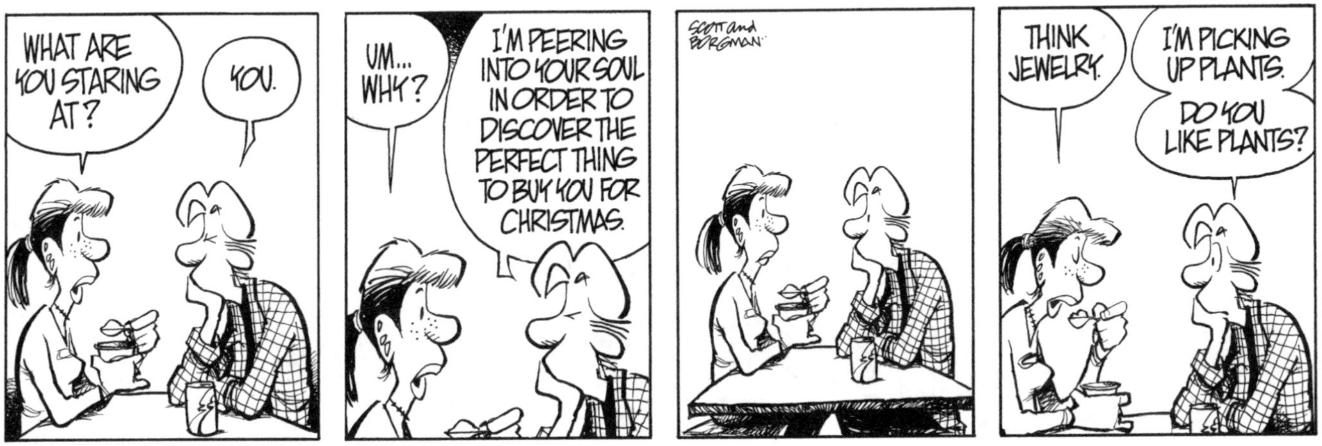
WHAT ARE YOU STARING AT?
YOU.
UM... WHY?
I'M PEERING INTO YOUR SOUL IN ORDER TO DISCOVER THE PERFECT THING TO BUY YOU FOR CHRISTMAS.
SCOTT and BORGMAN
THINK JEWELRY.
I'M PICKING UP PLANTS.
DO YOU LIKE PLANTS?

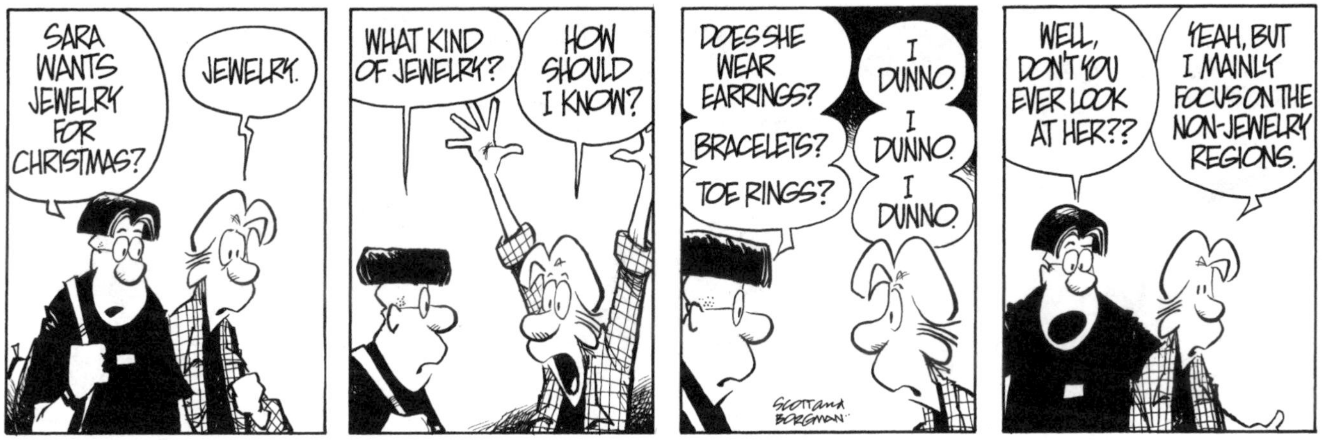
SARA WANTS JEWELRY FOR CHRISTMAS?
JEWELRY.
WHAT KIND OF JEWELRY?
HOW SHOULD I KNOW?
DOES SHE WEAR EARRINGS?
I DUNNO.
BRACELETS?
I DUNNO.
TOE RINGS?
I DUNNO.
SCOTT and BORGMAN
WELL, DON'T YOU EVER LOOK AT HER??
YEAH, BUT I MAINLY FOCUS ON THE NON-JEWELRY REGIONS.

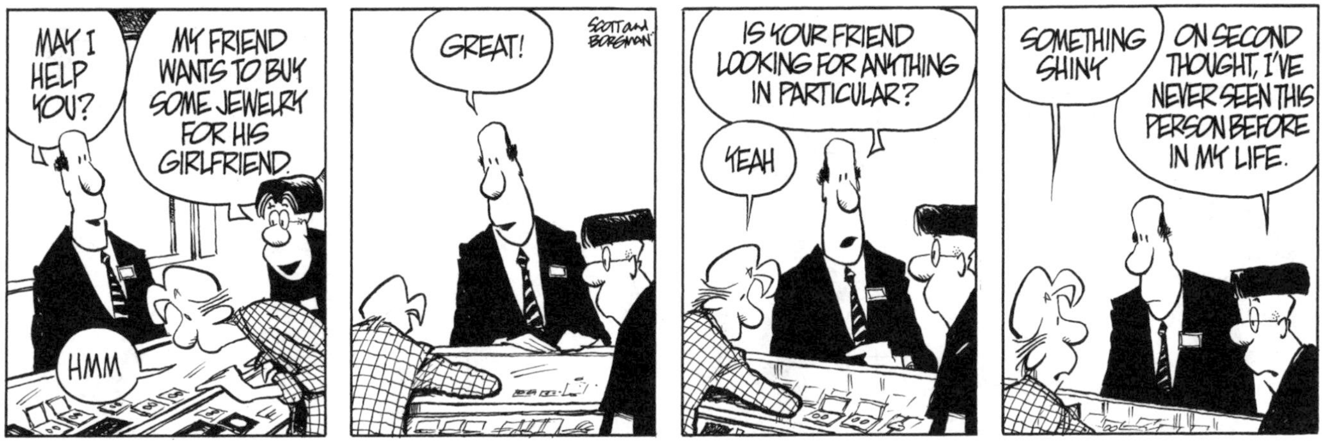
MAY I HELP YOU?
MY FRIEND WANTS TO BUY SOME JEWELRY FOR HIS GIRLFRIEND.
HMM
GREAT!
SCOTT and BORGMAN
IS YOUR FRIEND LOOKING FOR ANYTHING IN PARTICULAR?
YEAH
SOMETHING SHINY
ON SECOND THOUGHT, I'VE NEVER SEEN THIS PERSON BEFORE IN MY LIFE.

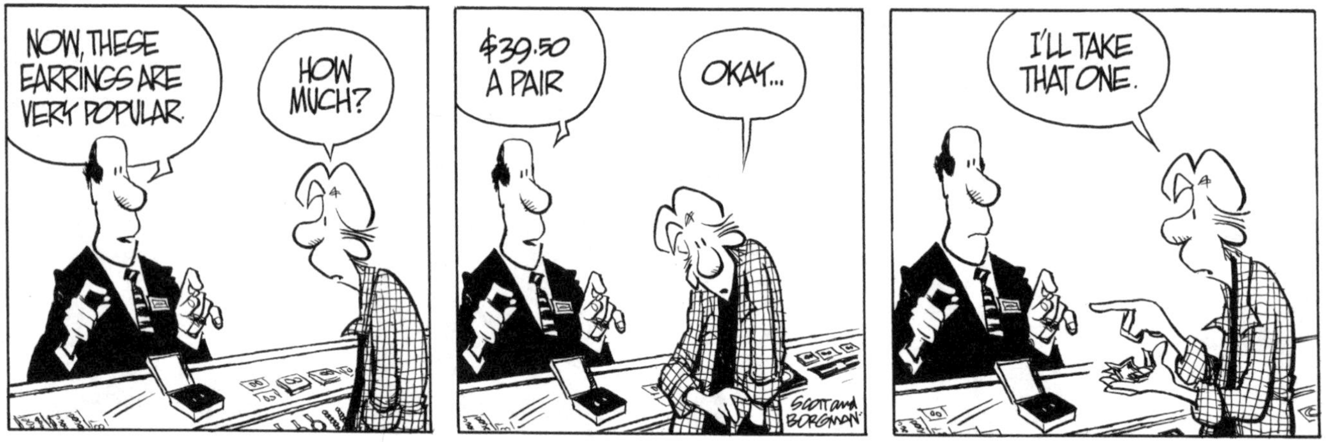
NOW, THESE EARRINGS ARE VERY POPULAR.
HOW MUCH?
$39.50 A PAIR
OKAY...
I'LL TAKE THAT ONE.

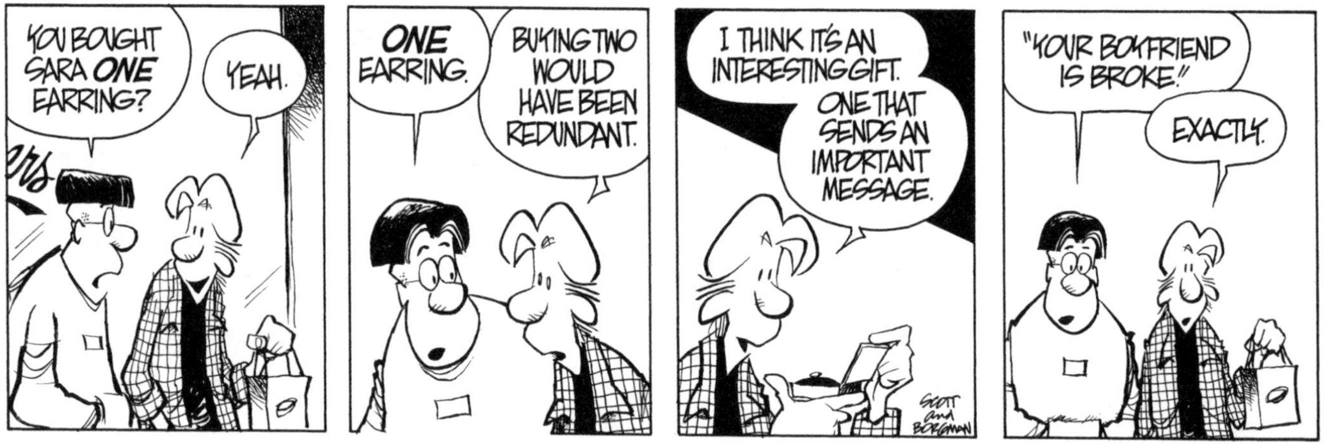
YOU BOUGHT SARA **ONE** EARRING?
YEAH.
ONE EARRING.
BUYING TWO WOULD HAVE BEEN REDUNDANT.
I THINK IT'S AN INTERESTING GIFT.
ONE THAT SENDS AN IMPORTANT MESSAGE.
"YOUR BOYFRIEND IS BROKE."
EXACTLY.

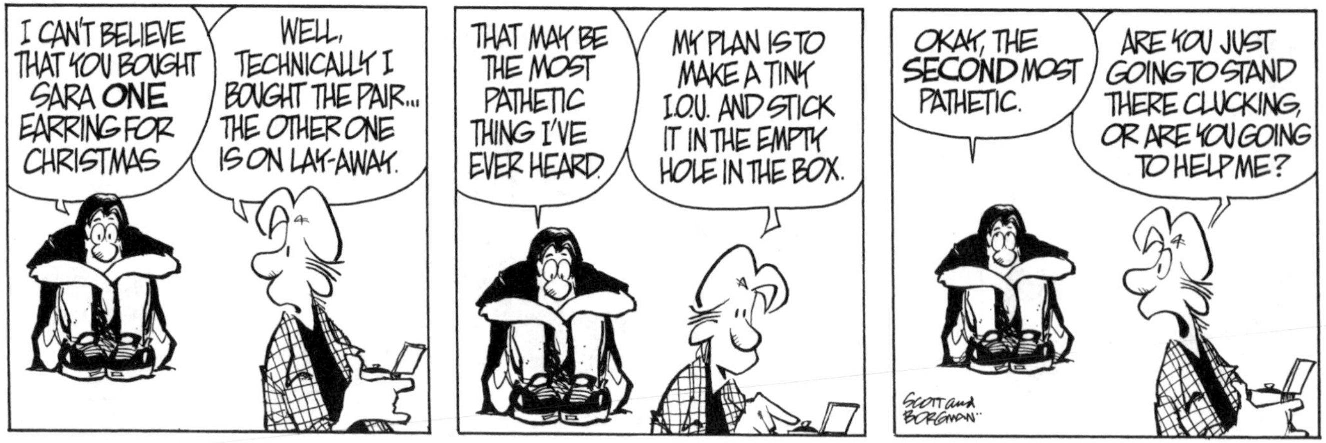
I CAN'T BELIEVE THAT YOU BOUGHT SARA **ONE** EARRING FOR CHRISTMAS
WELL, TECHNICALLY I BOUGHT THE PAIR... THE OTHER ONE IS ON LAY-AWAY.
THAT MAY BE THE MOST PATHETIC THING I'VE EVER HEARD.
MY PLAN IS TO MAKE A TINY I.O.U. AND STICK IT IN THE EMPTY HOLE IN THE BOX.
OKAY, THE **SECOND** MOST PATHETIC.
ARE YOU JUST GOING TO STAND THERE CLUCKING, OR ARE YOU GOING TO HELP ME?

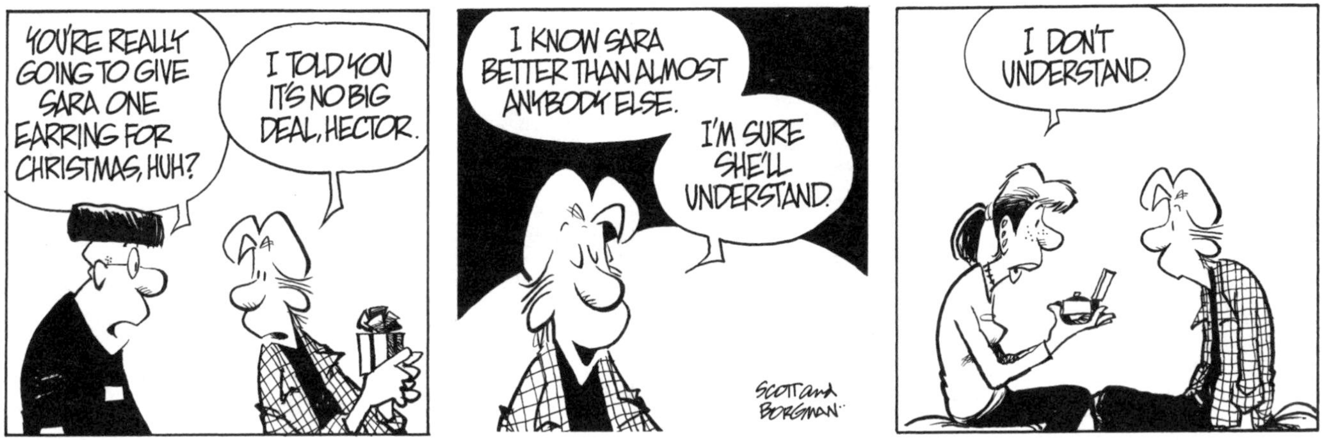
YOU'RE REALLY GOING TO GIVE SARA ONE EARRING FOR CHRISTMAS, HUH?
I TOLD YOU IT'S NO BIG DEAL, HECTOR.
I KNOW SARA BETTER THAN ALMOST ANYBODY ELSE.
I'M SURE SHE'LL UNDERSTAND.
SCOTT and BORGMAN
I DON'T UNDERSTAND.

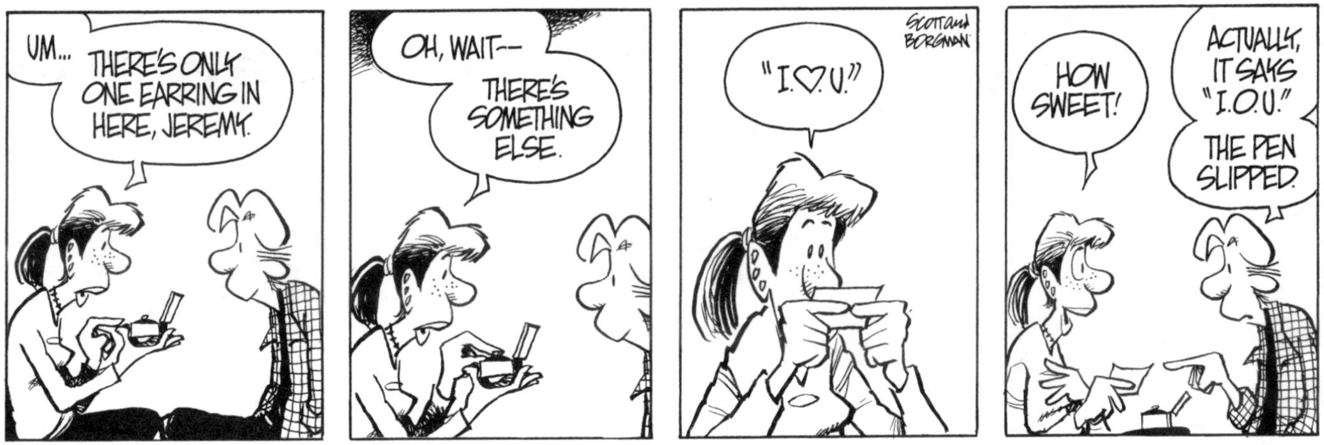
UM...
THERE'S ONLY ONE EARRING IN HERE, JEREMY.
OH, WAIT--
THERE'S SOMETHING ELSE.
SCOTT and BORGMAN
"I.♡.U."
HOW SWEET!
ACTUALLY, IT SAYS "I.O.U."
THE PEN SLIPPED.

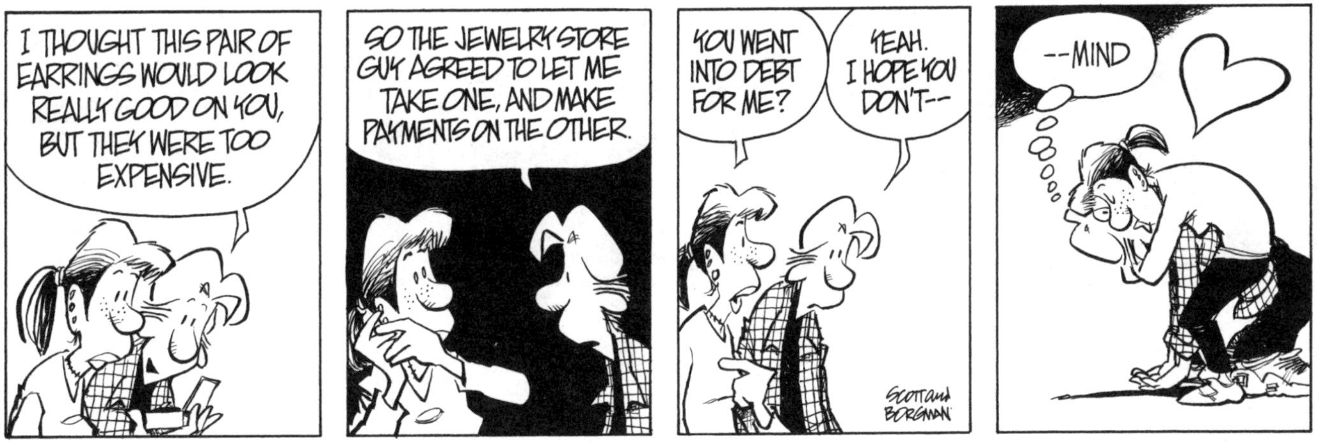
I THOUGHT THIS PAIR OF EARRINGS WOULD LOOK REALLY GOOD ON YOU, BUT THEY WERE TOO EXPENSIVE.
SO THE JEWELRY STORE GUY AGREED TO LET ME TAKE ONE, AND MAKE PAYMENTS ON THE OTHER.
YOU WENT INTO DEBT FOR ME?
YEAH. I HOPE YOU DON'T--
SCOTT and BORGMAN
--MIND

Zits®

by JERRY SCOTT and JIM BORGMAN

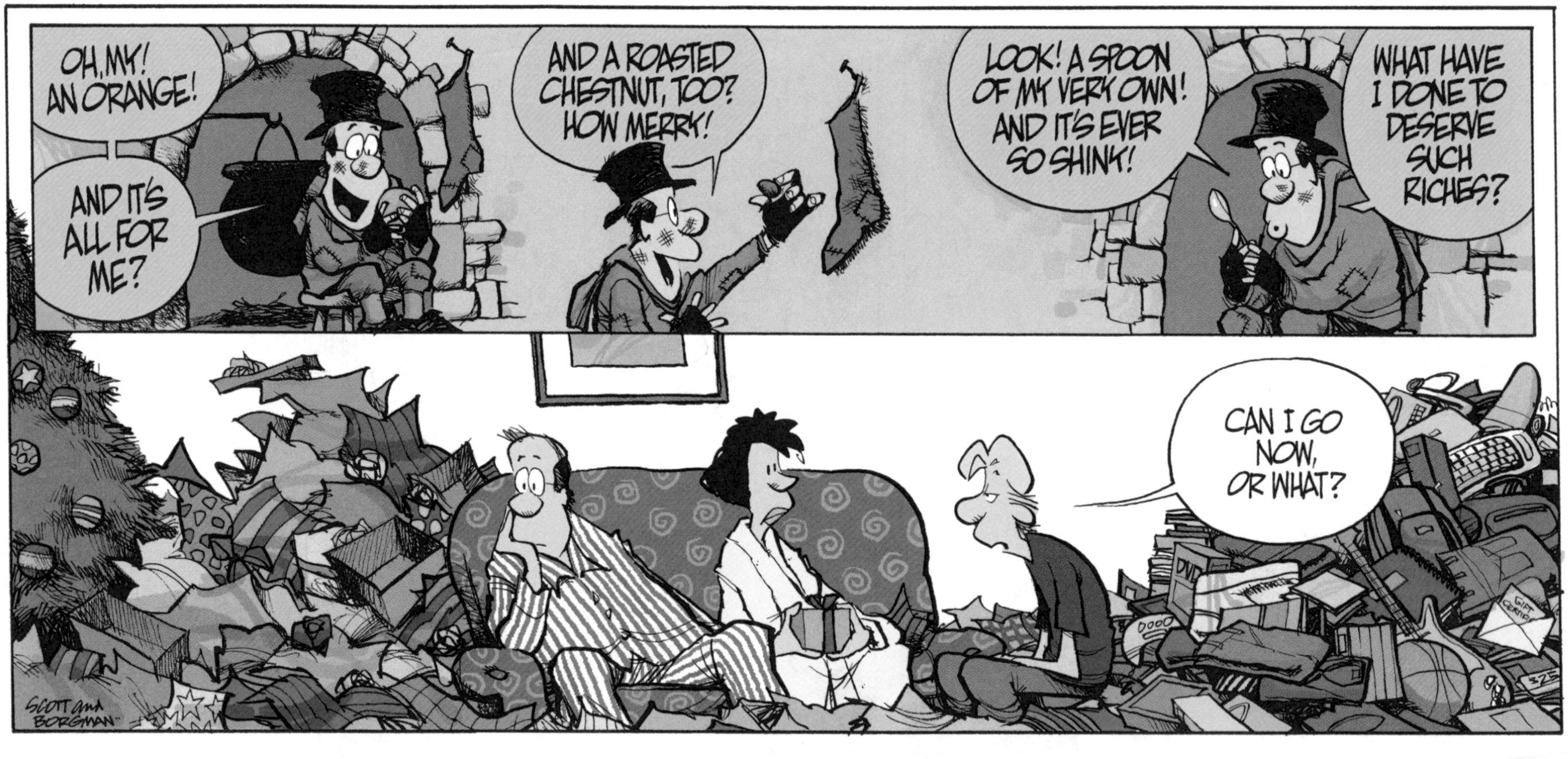
OH, MY! AN ORANGE!
AND IT'S ALL FOR ME?
AND A ROASTED CHESTNUT, TOO? HOW MERRY!
LOOK! A SPOON OF MY VERY OWN! AND IT'S EVER SO SHINY!
WHAT HAVE I DONE TO DESERVE SUCH RICHES?
CAN I GO NOW, OR WHAT?
SCOTT and BORGMAN

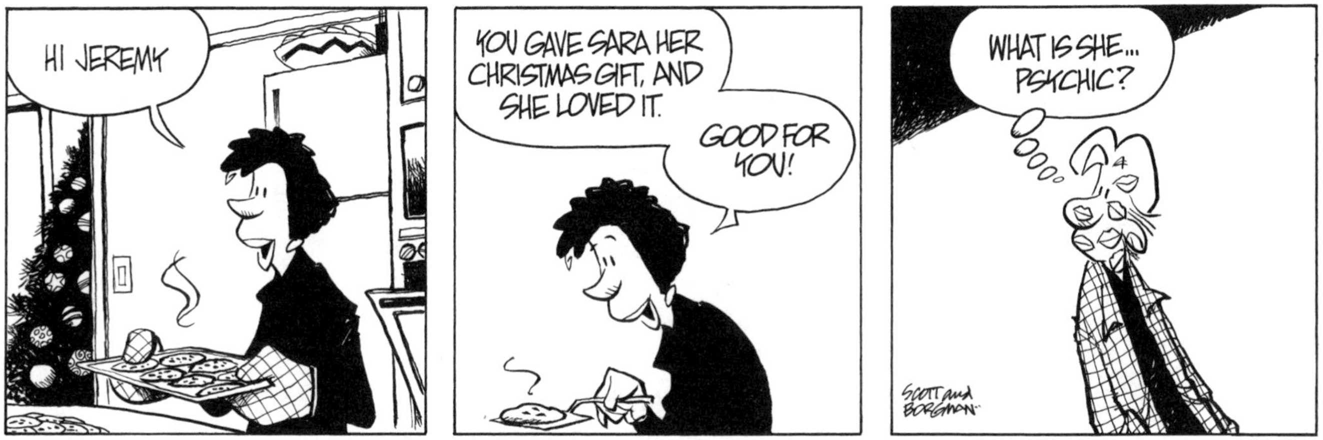
HI JEREMY
YOU GAVE SARA HER CHRISTMAS GIFT, AND SHE LOVED IT.
GOOD FOR YOU!
WHAT IS SHE... PSYCHIC?
SCOTT and BORGMAN

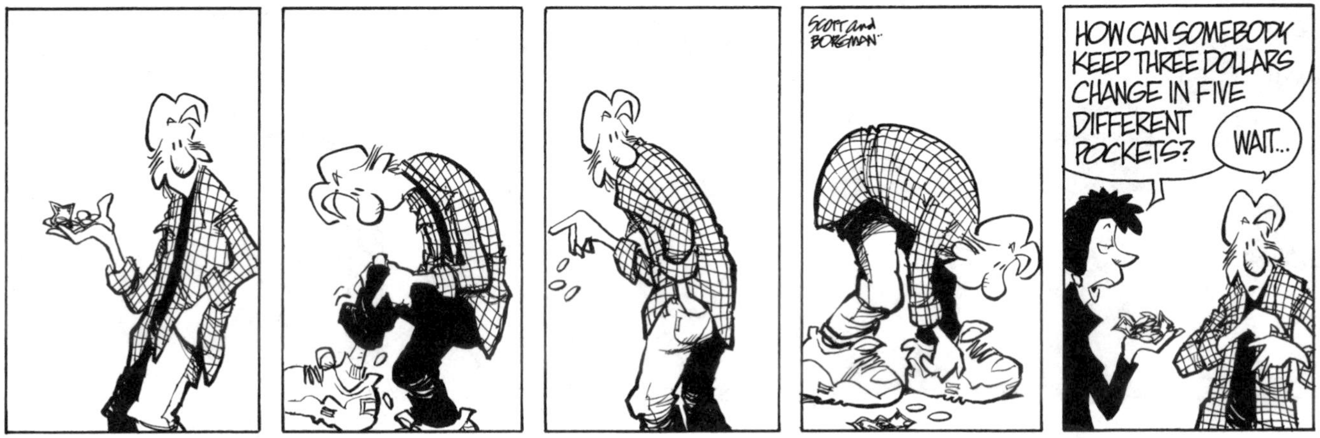
SCOTT and BORGMAN
HOW CAN SOMEBODY KEEP THREE DOLLARS CHANGE IN FIVE DIFFERENT POCKETS?
WAIT...

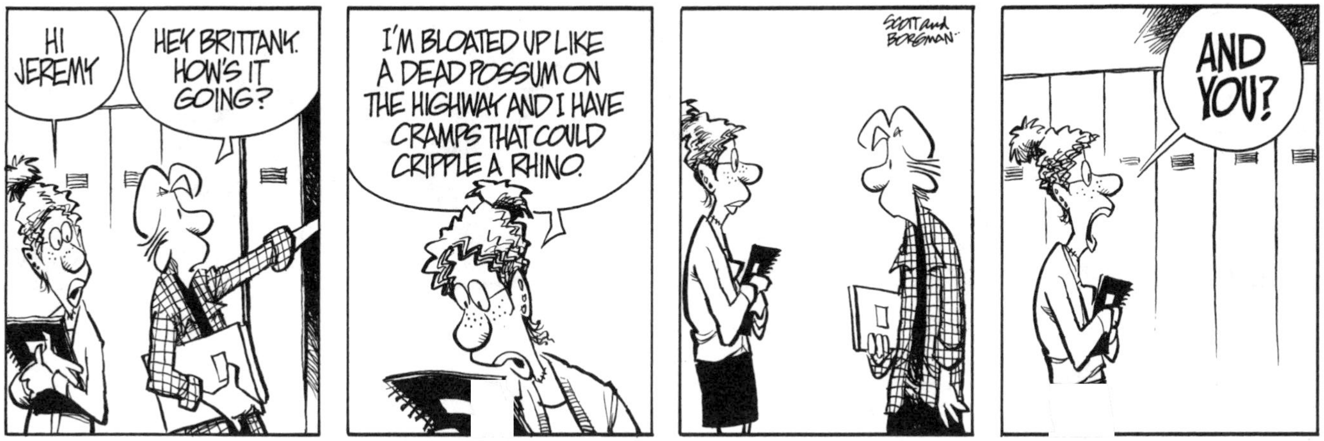
HI JEREMY
HEY BRITTANY. HOW'S IT GOING?
I'M BLOATED UP LIKE A DEAD POSSUM ON THE HIGHWAY AND I HAVE CRAMPS THAT COULD CRIPPLE A RHINO.
SCOTT and BORGMAN
AND YOU?

Zits®

by JERRY SCOTT and JIM BORGMAN

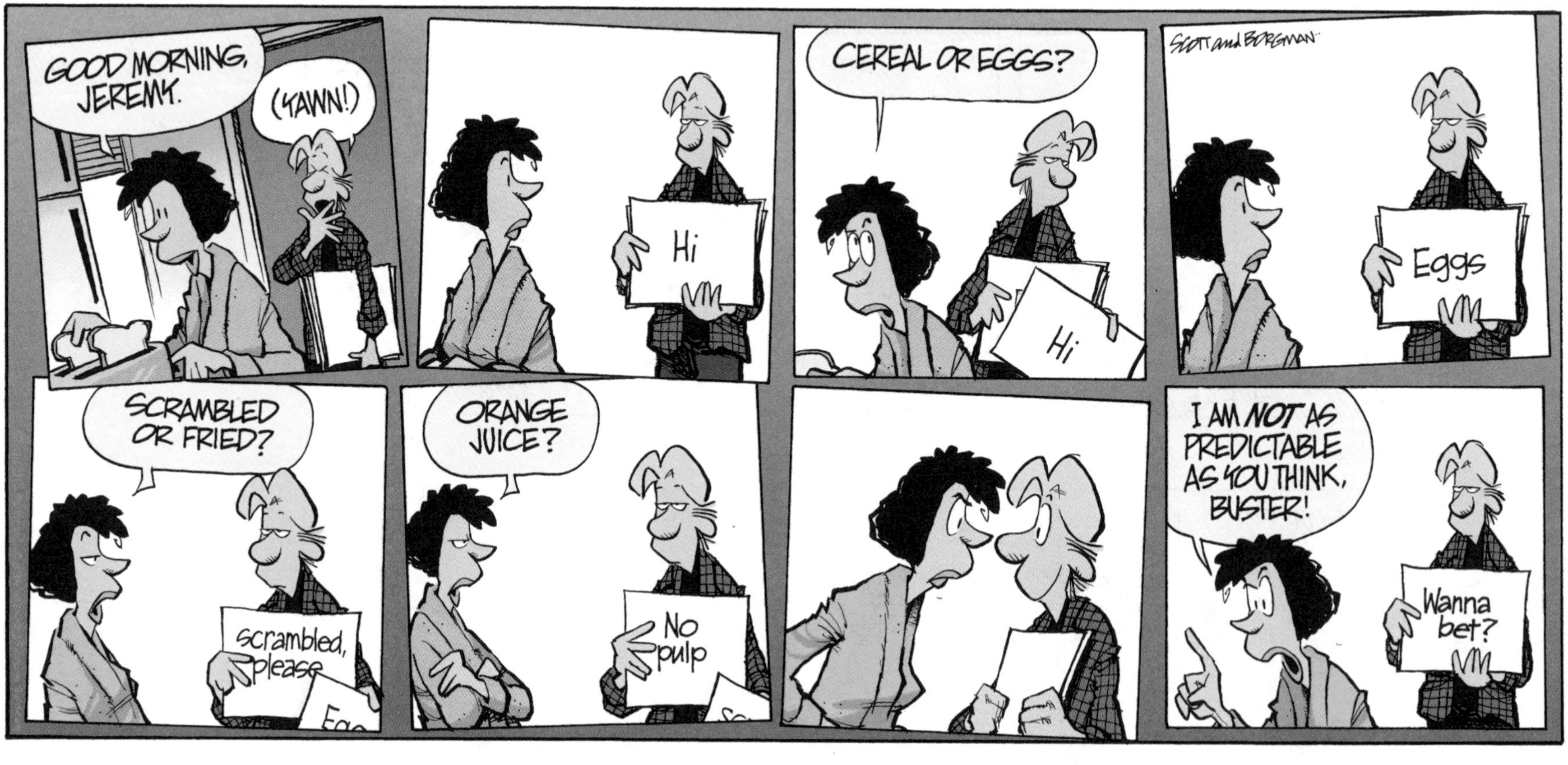

GOOD MORNING, JEREMY.
(YAWN!)
Hi
CEREAL OR EGGS?
Hi
SCOTT and BORGMAN
Eggs
SCRAMBLED OR FRIED?
scrambled, please
ORANGE JUICE?
No pulp
I AM NOT AS PREDICTABLE AS YOU THINK, BUSTER!
Wanna bet?

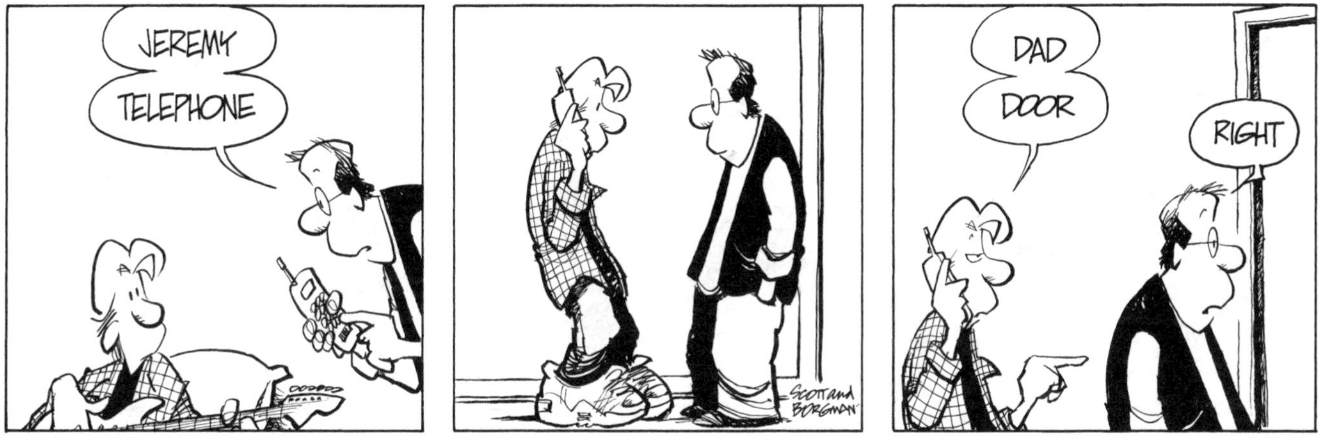
JEREMY
TELEPHONE
SCOTT AND BORGMAN
DAD
DOOR
RIGHT

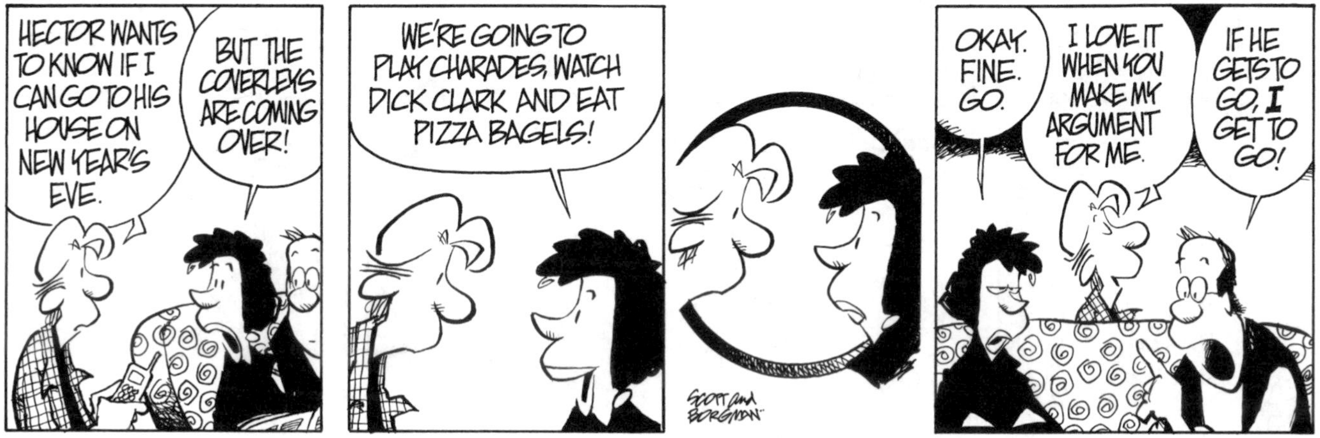
HECTOR WANTS TO KNOW IF I CAN GO TO HIS HOUSE ON NEW YEAR'S EVE.
BUT THE COVERLEYS ARE COMING OVER!
WE'RE GOING TO PLAY CHARADES, WATCH DICK CLARK AND EAT PIZZA BAGELS!
SCOTT AND BORGMAN
OKAY. FINE. GO.
I LOVE IT WHEN YOU MAKE MY ARGUMENT FOR ME.
IF HE GETS TO GO, **I** GET TO GO!

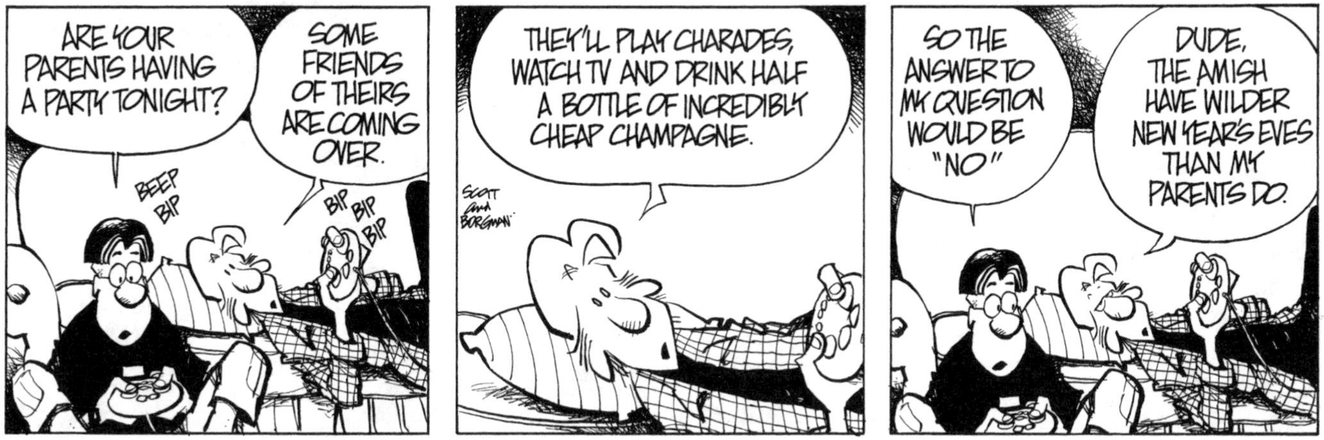
ARE YOUR PARENTS HAVING A PARTY TONIGHT?
BEEP BIP
SOME FRIENDS OF THEIRS ARE COMING OVER.
BIP BIP BIP
SCOTT AND BORGMAN
THEY'LL PLAY CHARADES, WATCH TV AND DRINK HALF A BOTTLE OF INCREDIBLY CHEAP CHAMPAGNE.
SO THE ANSWER TO MY QUESTION WOULD BE "NO"
DUDE, THE AMISH HAVE WILDER NEW YEAR'S EVES THAN MY PARENTS DO.

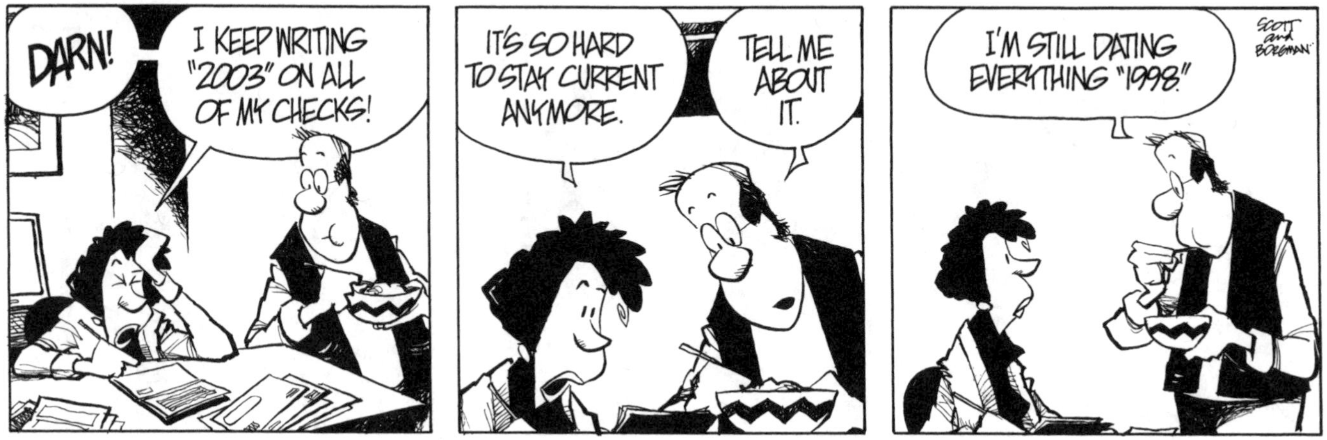
DARN!
I KEEP WRITING "2003" ON ALL OF MY CHECKS!
IT'S SO HARD TO STAY CURRENT ANYMORE.
TELL ME ABOUT IT.
I'M STILL DATING EVERYTHING "1998."
SCOTT and BORGMAN

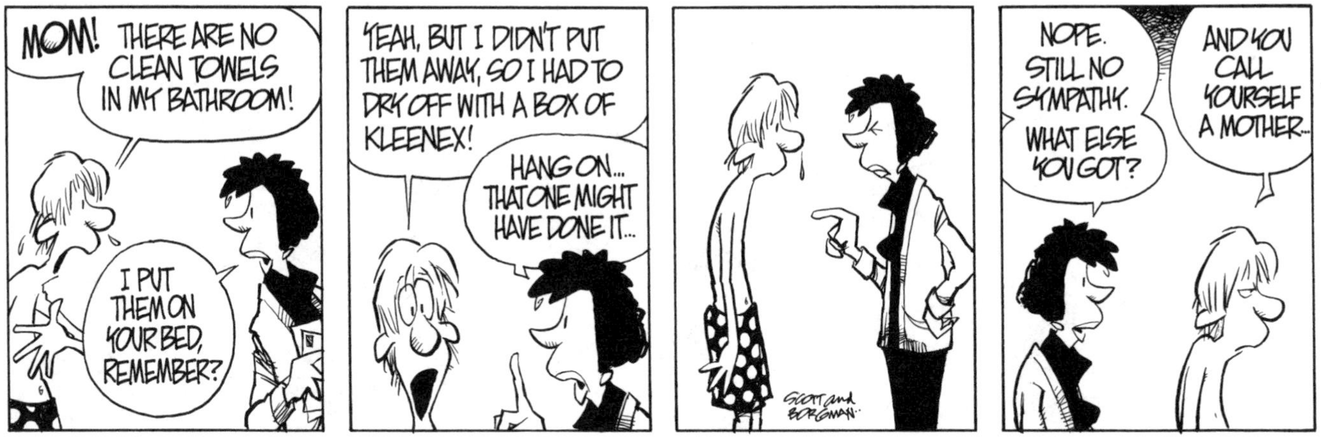
MOM! THERE ARE NO CLEAN TOWELS IN MY BATHROOM!
I PUT THEM ON YOUR BED, REMEMBER?
YEAH, BUT I DIDN'T PUT THEM AWAY, SO I HAD TO DRY OFF WITH A BOX OF KLEENEX!
HANG ON... THAT ONE MIGHT HAVE DONE IT...
SCOTT and BORGMAN
NOPE. STILL NO SYMPATHY. WHAT ELSE YOU GOT?
AND YOU CALL YOURSELF A MOTHER...

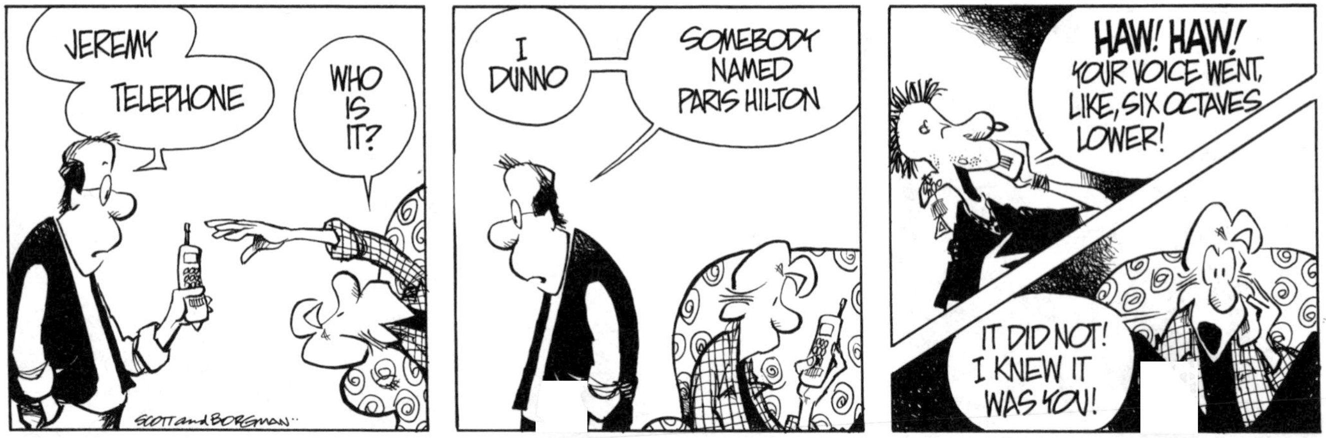
JEREMY
TELEPHONE
WHO IS IT?
SCOTT and BORGMAN
I DUNNO
SOMEBODY NAMED PARIS HILTON
HAW! HAW! YOUR VOICE WENT, LIKE, SIX OCTAVES LOWER!
IT DID NOT! I KNEW IT WAS YOU!

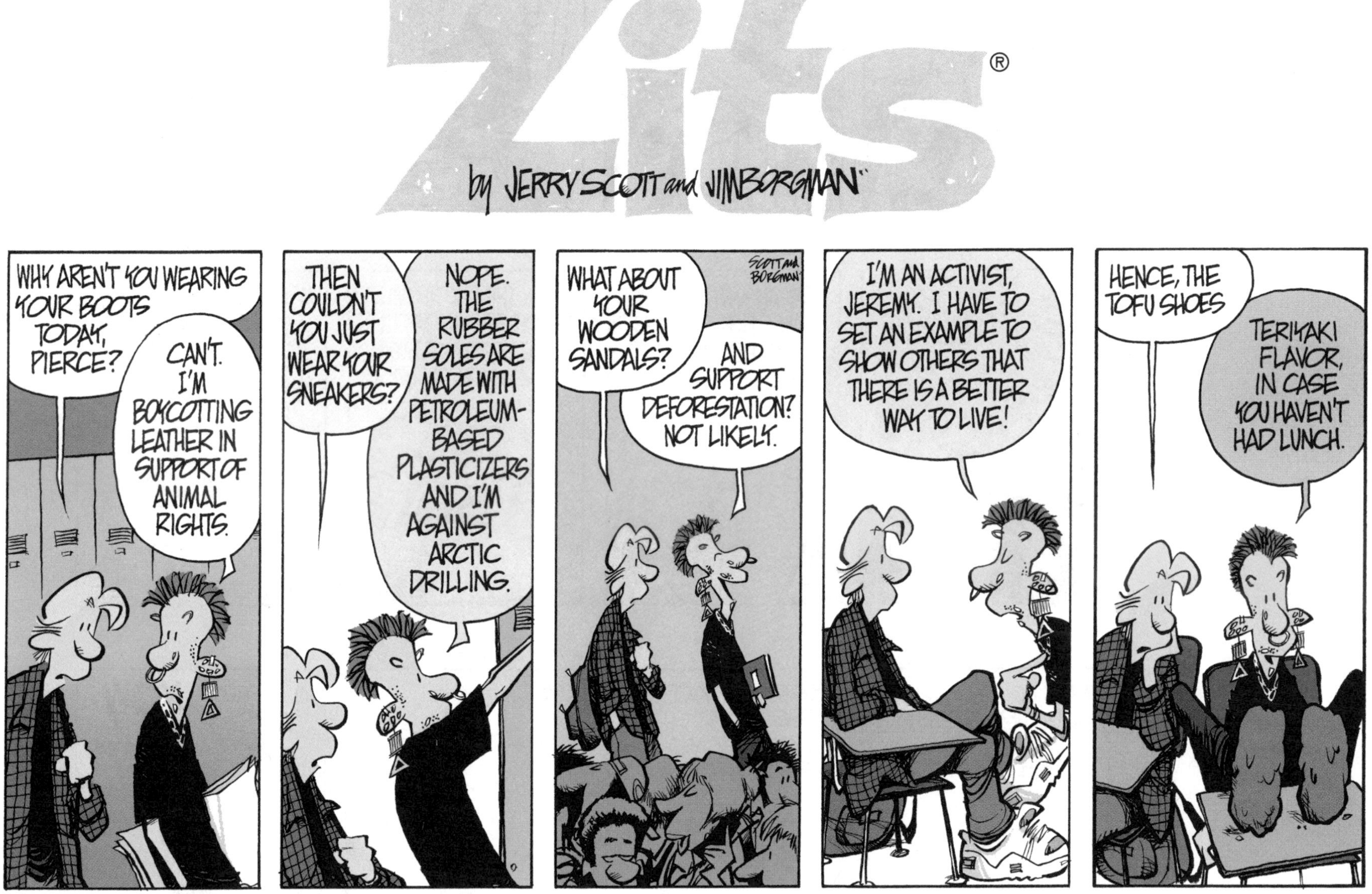
Zits®
by JERRY SCOTT and JIM BORGMAN
WHY AREN'T YOU WEARING YOUR BOOTS TODAY, PIERCE?
CAN'T. I'M BOYCOTTING LEATHER IN SUPPORT OF ANIMAL RIGHTS.
THEN COULDN'T YOU JUST WEAR YOUR SNEAKERS?
NOPE. THE RUBBER SOLES ARE MADE WITH PETROLEUM-BASED PLASTICIZERS AND I'M AGAINST ARCTIC DRILLING.
WHAT ABOUT YOUR WOODEN SANDALS?
AND SUPPORT DEFORESTATION? NOT LIKELY.
I'M AN ACTIVIST, JEREMY. I HAVE TO SET AN EXAMPLE TO SHOW OTHERS THAT THERE IS A BETTER WAY TO LIVE!
HENCE, THE TOFU SHOES
TERIYAKI FLAVOR, IN CASE YOU HAVEN'T HAD LUNCH.

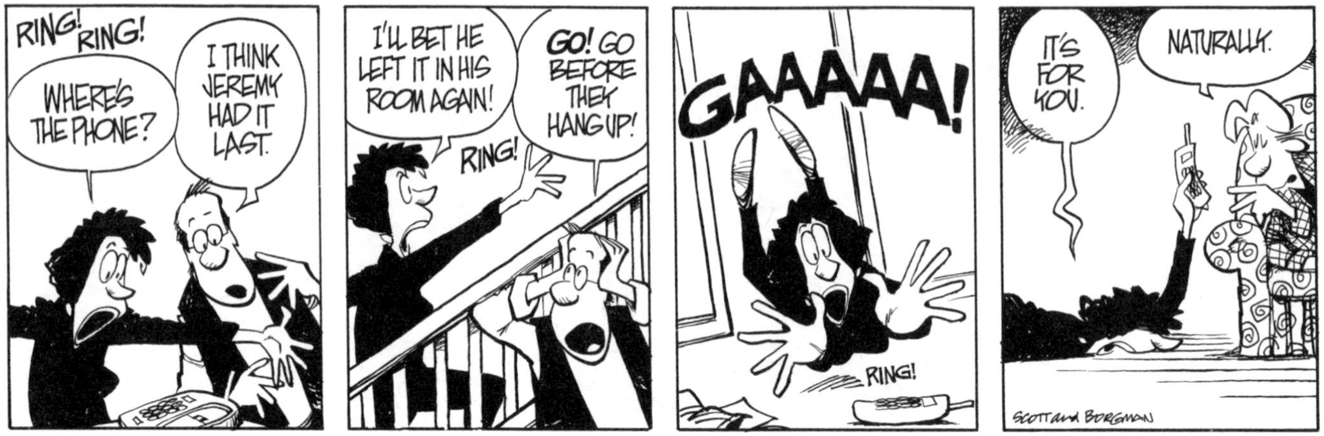
RING! RING!
WHERE'S THE PHONE?
I THINK JEREMY HAD IT LAST.
I'LL BET HE LEFT IT IN HIS ROOM AGAIN!
RING!
GO! GO BEFORE THEY HANG UP!
GAAAAA!
RING!
IT'S FOR YOU.
NATURALLY.
SCOTT and BORGMAN

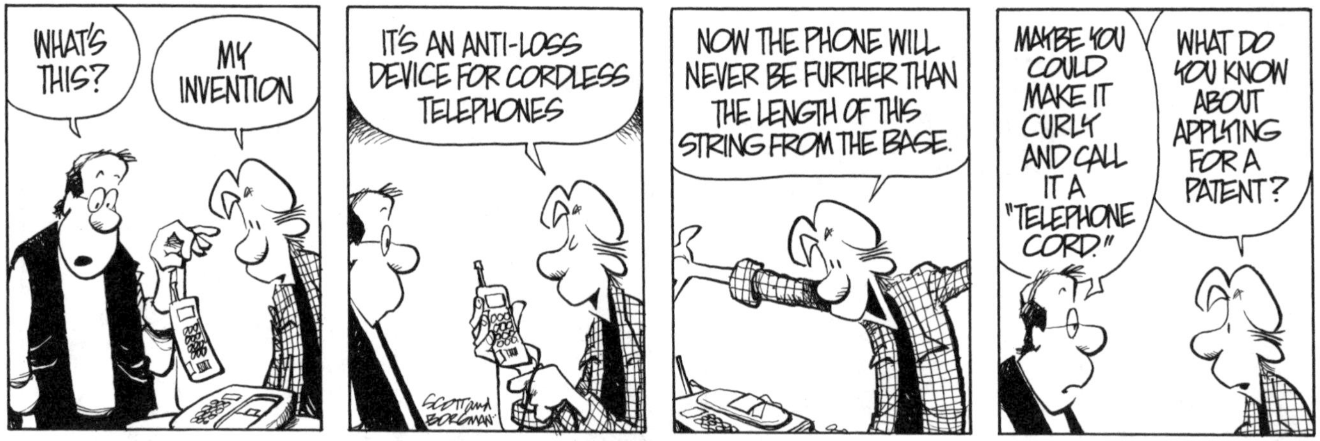
WHAT'S THIS?
MY INVENTION
IT'S AN ANTI-LOSS DEVICE FOR CORDLESS TELEPHONES
SCOTT and BORGMAN
NOW THE PHONE WILL NEVER BE FURTHER THAN THE LENGTH OF THIS STRING FROM THE BASE.
MAYBE YOU COULD MAKE IT CURLY AND CALL IT A "TELEPHONE CORD."
WHAT DO YOU KNOW ABOUT APPLYING FOR A PATENT?

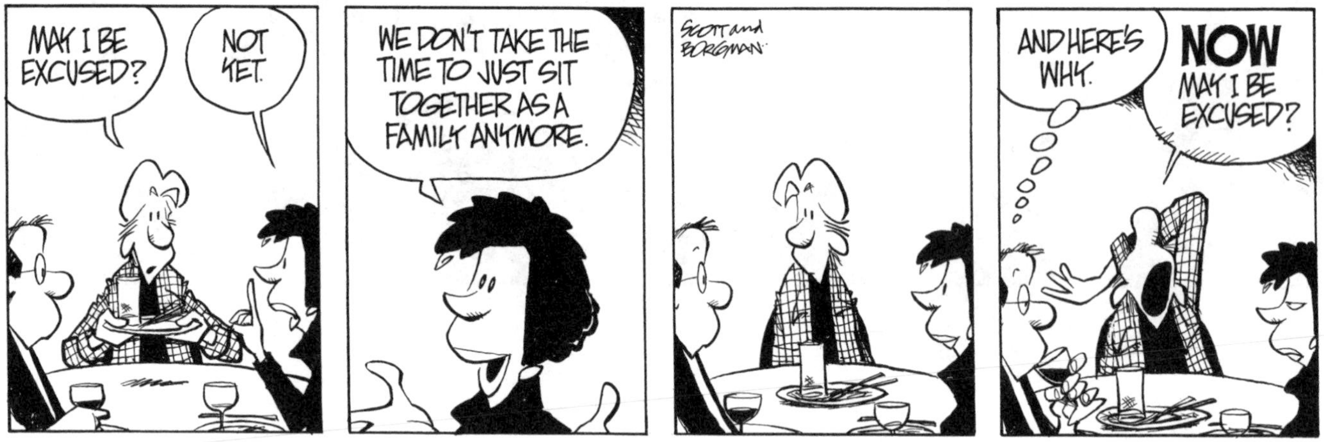
MAY I BE EXCUSED?
NOT YET.
WE DON'T TAKE THE TIME TO JUST SIT TOGETHER AS A FAMILY ANYMORE.
SCOTT and BORGMAN
AND HERE'S WHY.
NOW MAY I BE EXCUSED?

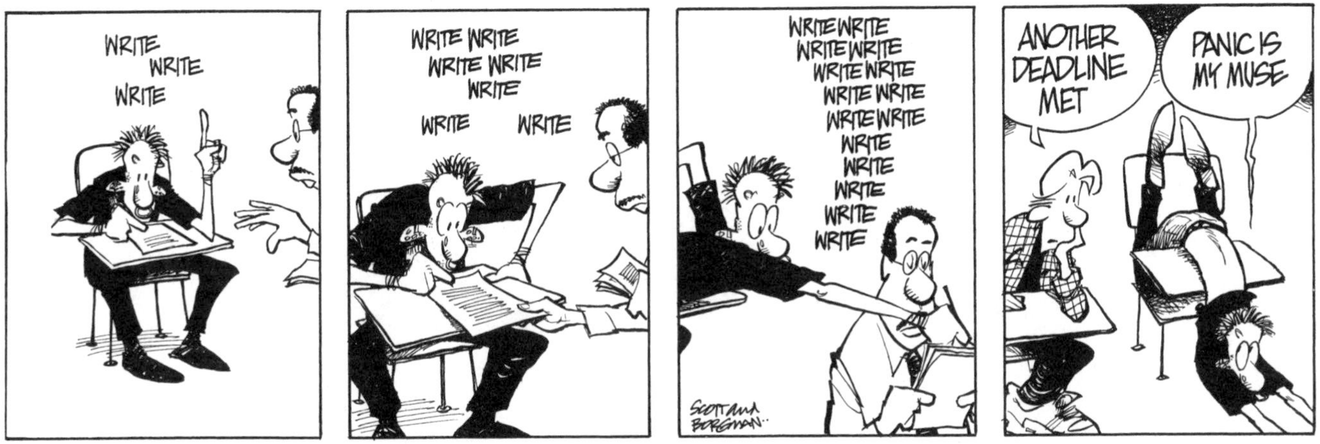
WRITE WRITE WRITE
WRITE WRITE WRITE WRITE WRITE WRITE WRITE
WRITE WRITE WRITE WRITE WRITE WRITE WRITE WRITE WRITE WRITE WRITE WRITE WRITE WRITE
SCOTT AND BORGMAN
ANOTHER DEADLINE MET
PANIC IS MY MUSE

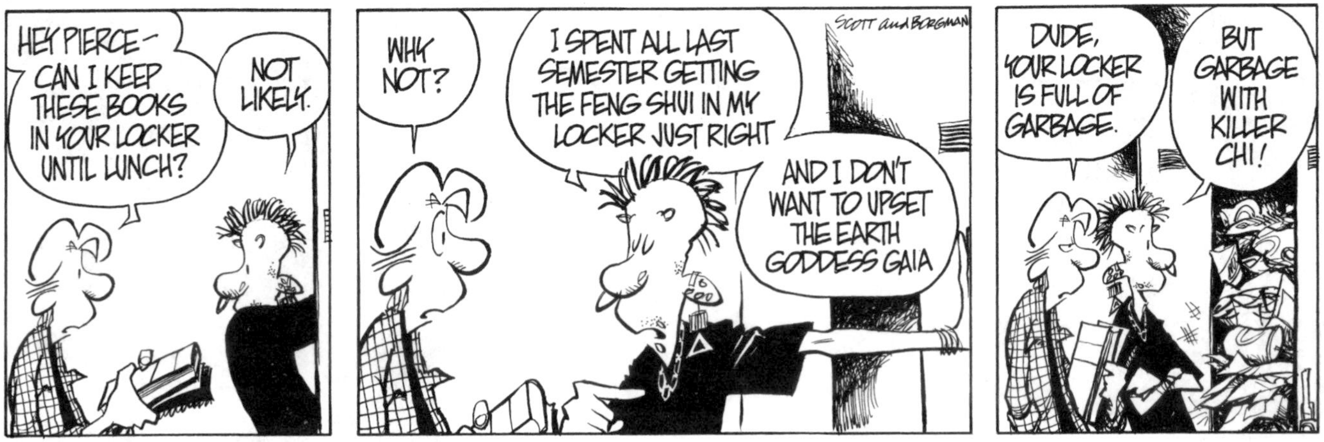
HEY PIERCE - CAN I KEEP THESE BOOKS IN YOUR LOCKER UNTIL LUNCH?
NOT LIKELY.
WHY NOT?
I SPENT ALL LAST SEMESTER GETTING THE FENG SHUI IN MY LOCKER JUST RIGHT
AND I DON'T WANT TO UPSET THE EARTH GODDESS GAIA
SCOTT AND BORGMAN
DUDE, YOUR LOCKER IS FULL OF GARBAGE.
BUT GARBAGE WITH KILLER CHI!

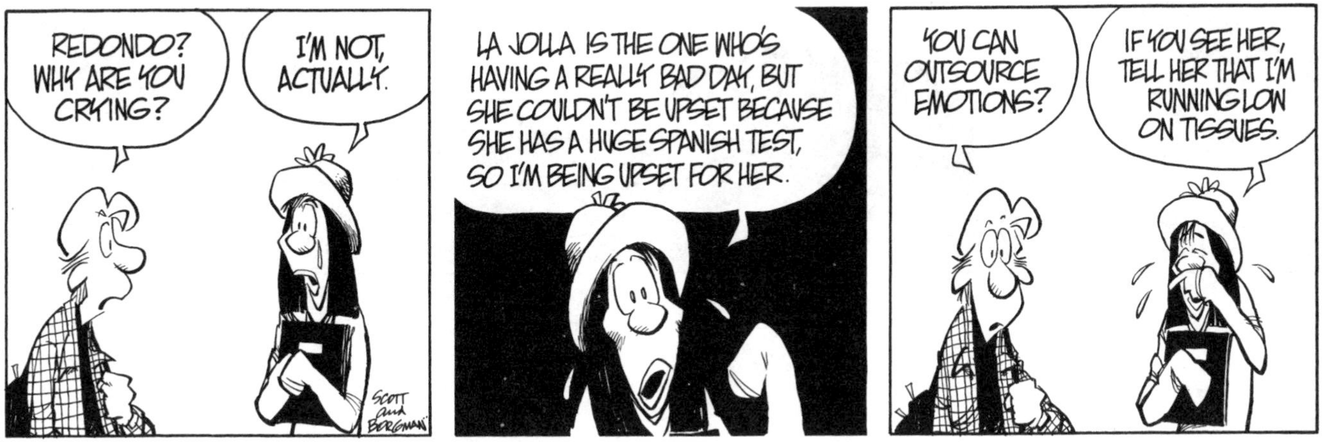
REDONDO? WHY ARE YOU CRYING?
I'M NOT, ACTUALLY.
SCOTT AND BORGMAN
LA JOLLA IS THE ONE WHO'S HAVING A REALLY BAD DAY, BUT SHE COULDN'T BE UPSET BECAUSE SHE HAS A HUGE SPANISH TEST, SO I'M BEING UPSET FOR HER.
YOU CAN OUTSOURCE EMOTIONS?
IF YOU SEE HER, TELL HER THAT I'M RUNNING LOW ON TISSUES.

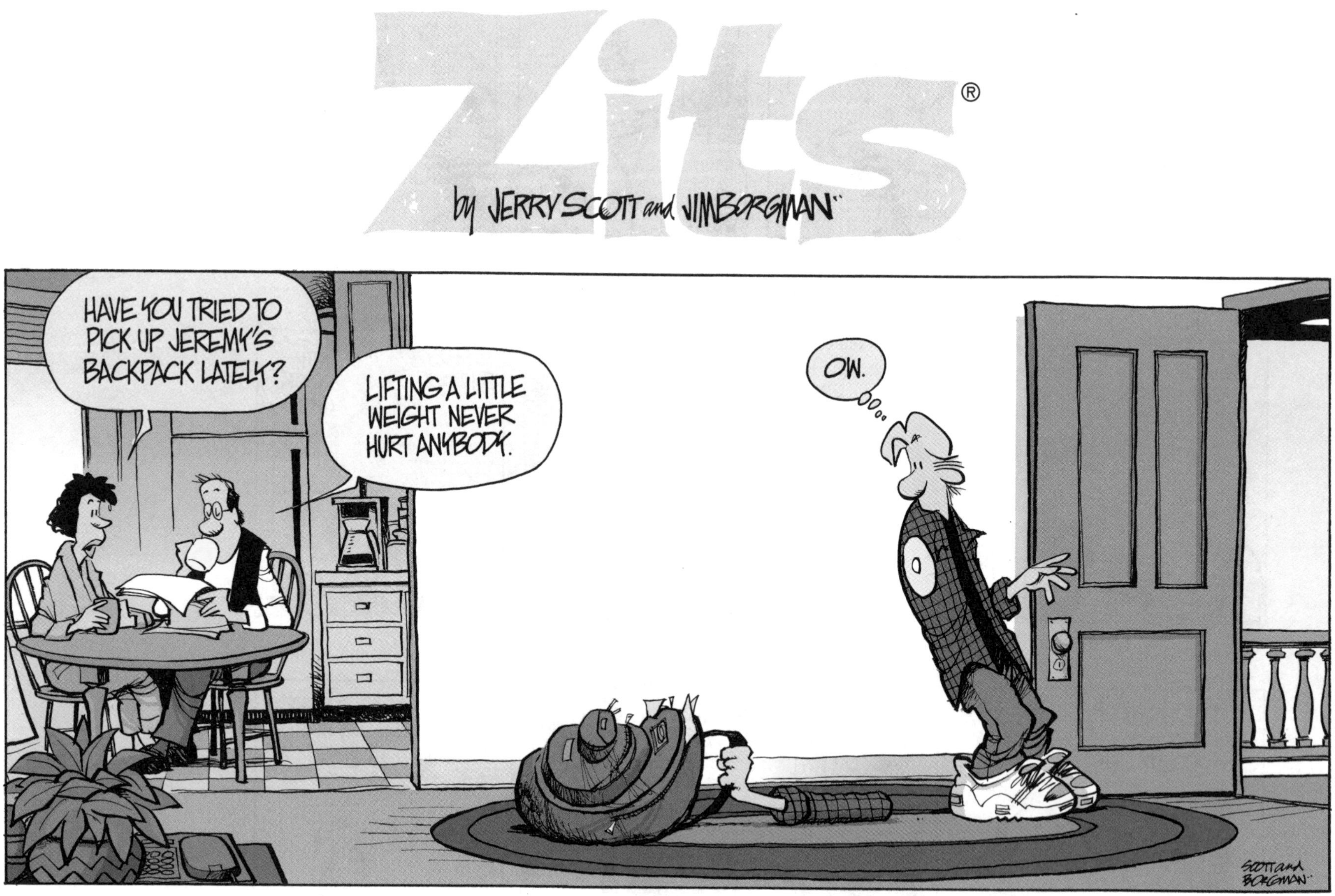
Zits®
by JERRY SCOTT and JIM BORGMAN
HAVE YOU TRIED TO PICK UP JEREMY'S BACKPACK LATELY?
LIFTING A LITTLE WEIGHT NEVER HURT ANYBODY.
OW.
SCOTT and BORGMAN

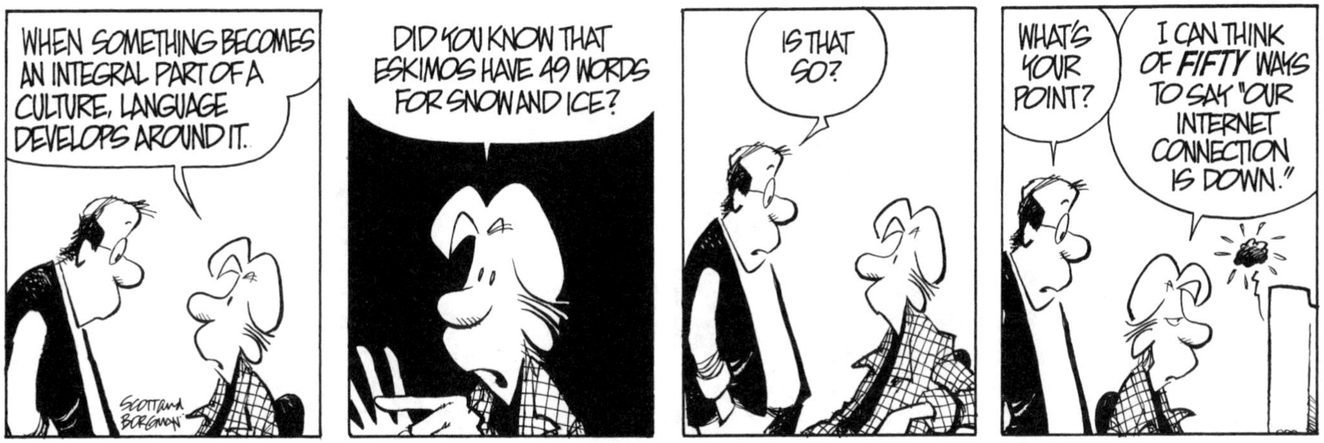
WHEN SOMETHING BECOMES AN INTEGRAL PART OF A CULTURE, LANGUAGE DEVELOPS AROUND IT..
DID YOU KNOW THAT ESKIMOS HAVE 49 WORDS FOR SNOW AND ICE?
IS THAT SO?
WHAT'S YOUR POINT?
I CAN THINK OF **FIFTY** WAYS TO SAY "OUR INTERNET CONNECTION IS DOWN."
SCOTT and BORGMAN

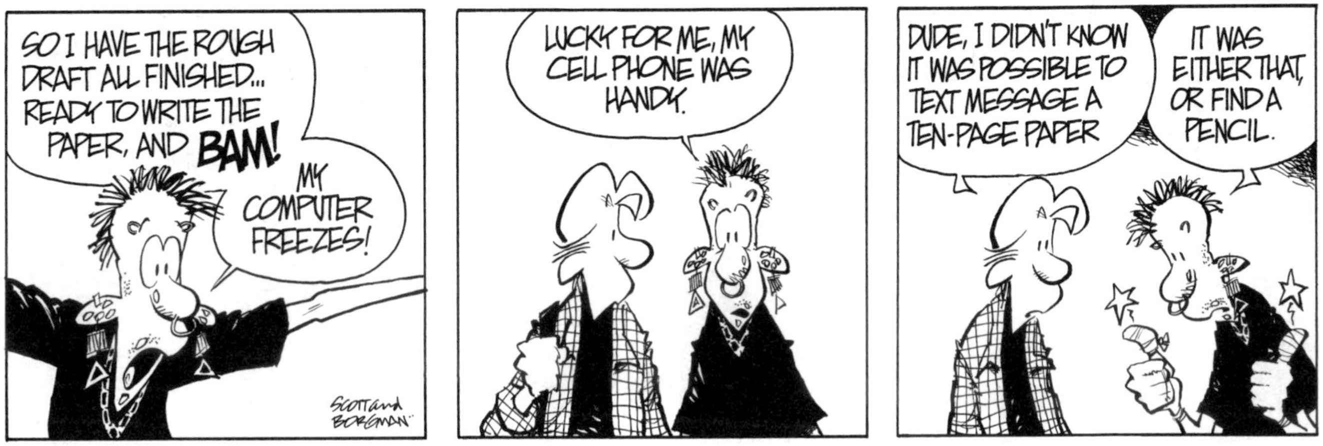
SO I HAVE THE ROUGH DRAFT ALL FINISHED... READY TO WRITE THE PAPER, AND **BAM!**
MY COMPUTER FREEZES!
SCOTT and BORGMAN
LUCKY FOR ME, MY CELL PHONE WAS HANDY.
DUDE, I DIDN'T KNOW IT WAS POSSIBLE TO TEXT MESSAGE A TEN-PAGE PAPER
IT WAS EITHER THAT, OR FIND A PENCIL.

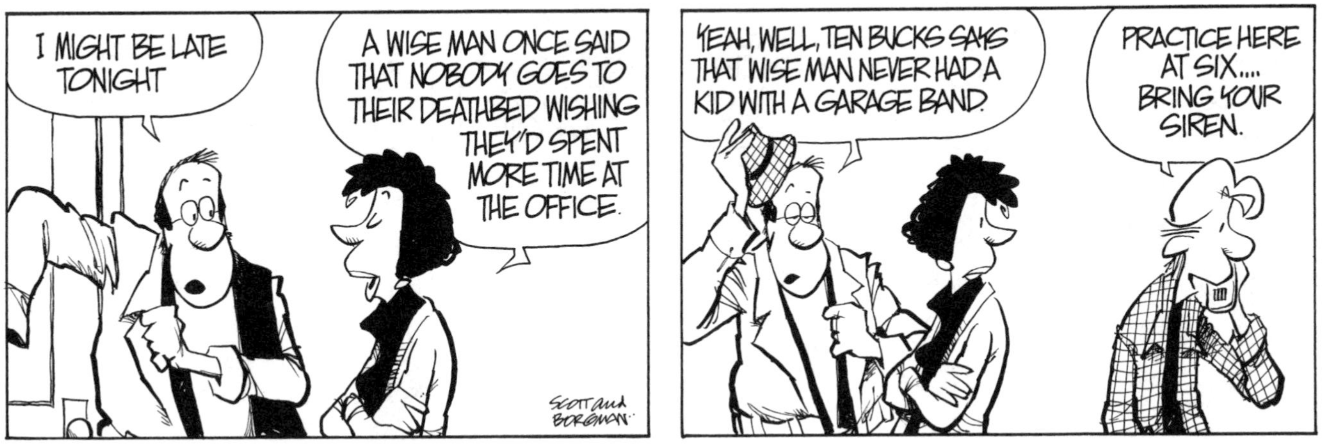
I MIGHT BE LATE TONIGHT
A WISE MAN ONCE SAID THAT NOBODY GOES TO THEIR DEATHBED WISHING THEY'D SPENT MORE TIME AT THE OFFICE.
SCOTT and BORGMAN
YEAH, WELL, TEN BUCKS SAYS THAT WISE MAN NEVER HAD A KID WITH A GARAGE BAND.
PRACTICE HERE AT SIX.... BRING YOUR SIREN.

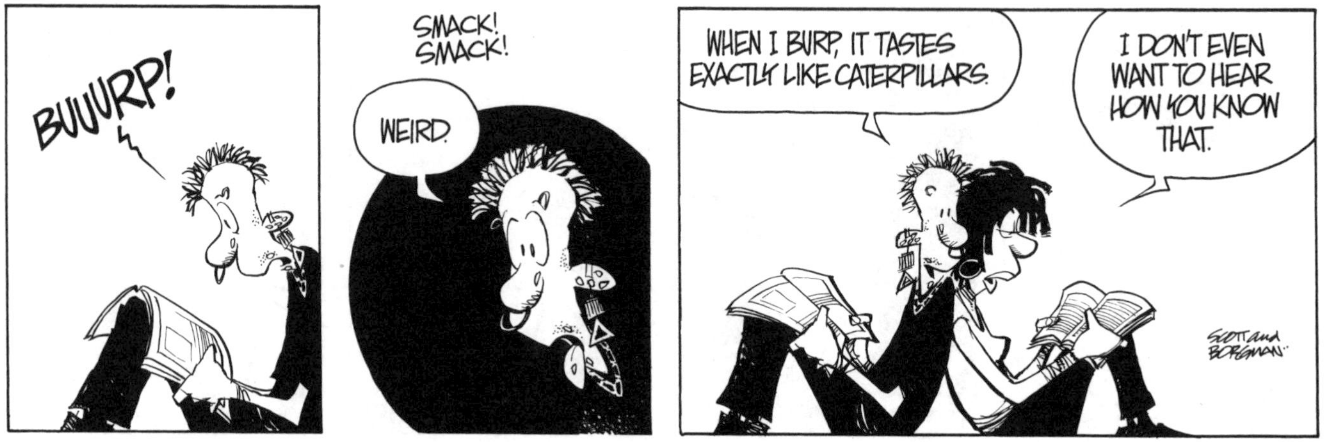
BUUURP!
SMACK! SMACK!
WEIRD.
WHEN I BURP, IT TASTES EXACTLY LIKE CATERPILLARS.
I DON'T EVEN WANT TO HEAR HOW YOU KNOW THAT.
SCOTT and BORGMAN

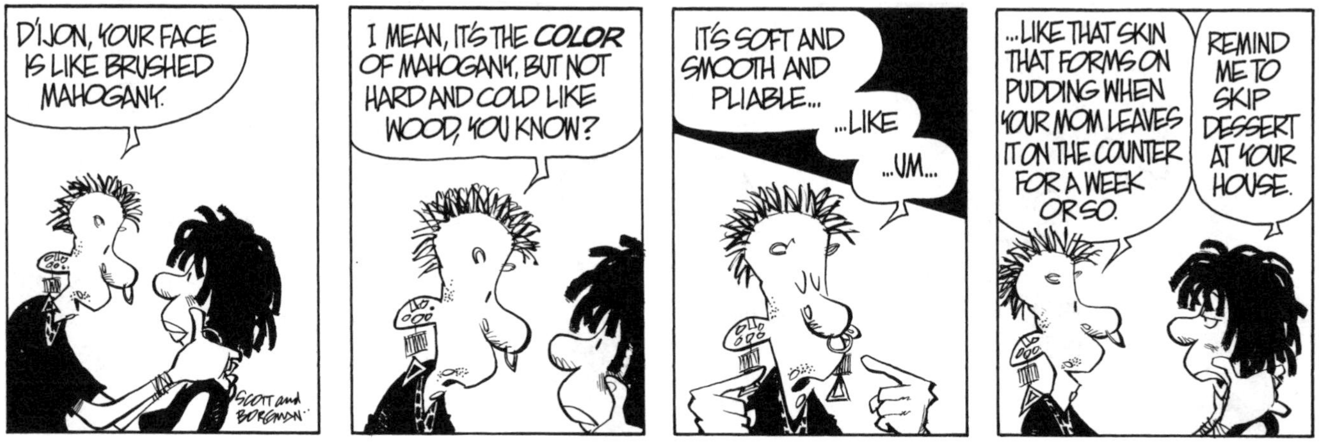
D'JON, YOUR FACE IS LIKE BRUSHED MAHOGANY.
I MEAN, IT'S THE COLOR OF MAHOGANY, BUT NOT HARD AND COLD LIKE WOOD, YOU KNOW?
IT'S SOFT AND SMOOTH AND PLIABLE...
...LIKE
...UM...
...LIKE THAT SKIN THAT FORMS ON PUDDING WHEN YOUR MOM LEAVES IT ON THE COUNTER FOR A WEEK OR SO.
REMIND ME TO SKIP DESSERT AT YOUR HOUSE.
SCOTT and BORGMAN

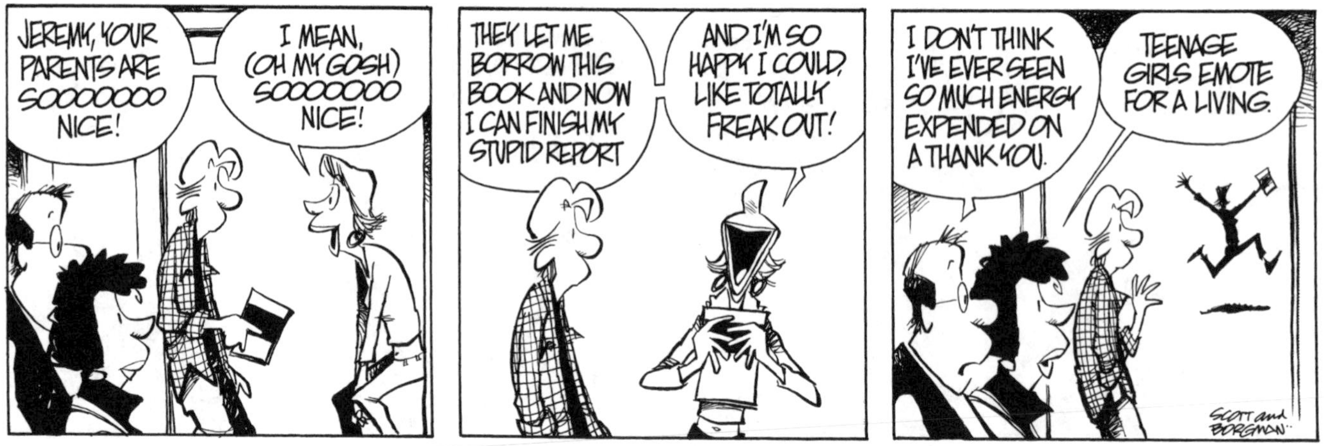
JEREMY, YOUR PARENTS ARE SOOOOOOO NICE!
I MEAN, (OH MY GOSH) SOOOOOOO NICE!
THEY LET ME BORROW THIS BOOK AND NOW I CAN FINISH MY STUPID REPORT
AND I'M SO HAPPY I COULD, LIKE TOTALLY FREAK OUT!
I DON'T THINK I'VE EVER SEEN SO MUCH ENERGY EXPENDED ON A THANK YOU.
TEENAGE GIRLS EMOTE FOR A LIVING.
SCOTT and BORGMAN

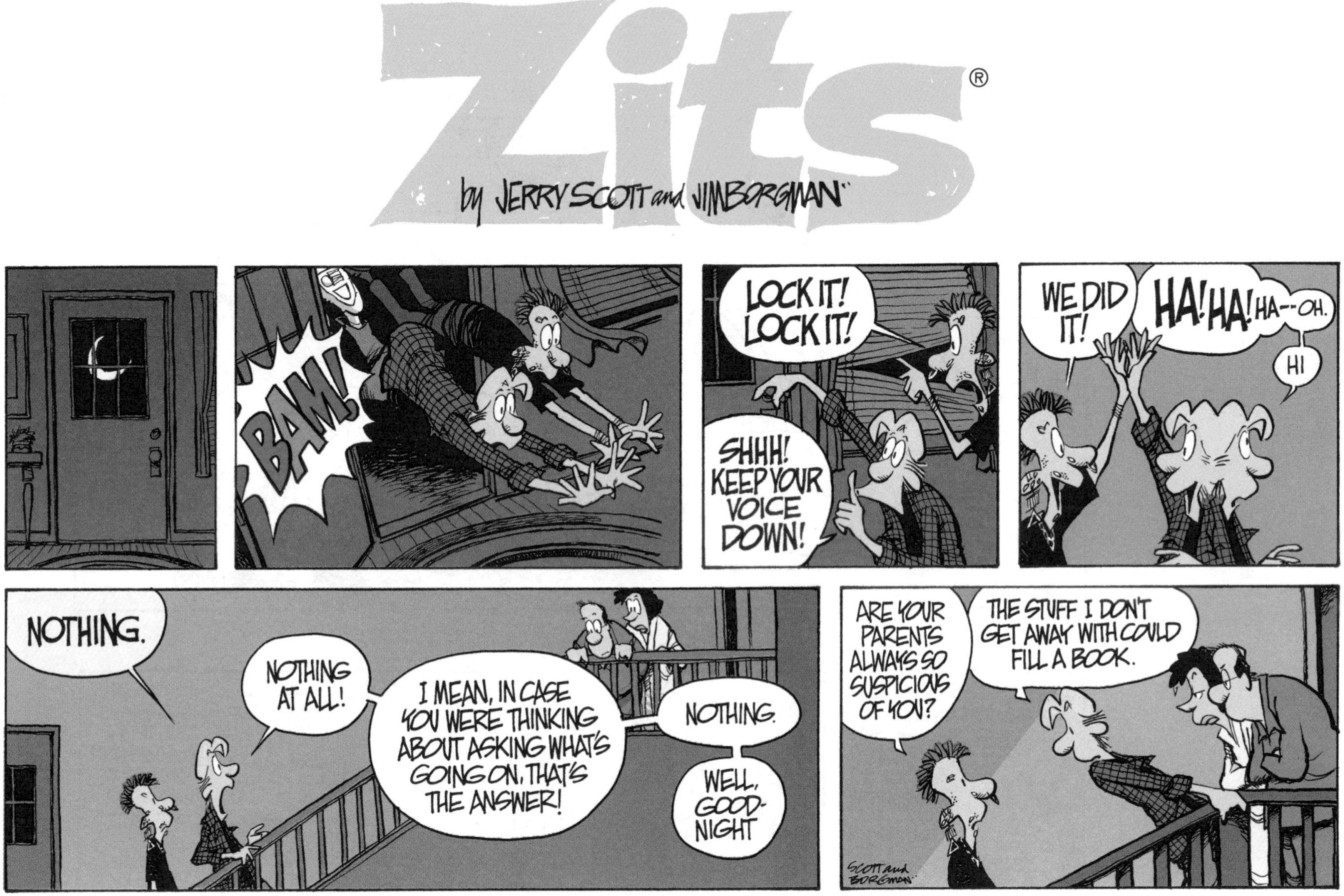
Zits®
by JERRY SCOTT and JIM BORGMAN
BAM!
LOCK IT! LOCK IT!
SHHH! KEEP YOUR VOICE DOWN!
WE DID IT!
HA! HA! HA--OH.
HI
NOTHING.
NOTHING AT ALL!
I MEAN, IN CASE YOU WERE THINKING ABOUT ASKING WHAT'S GOING ON, THAT'S THE ANSWER!
NOTHING.
WELL, GOOD-NIGHT
ARE YOUR PARENTS ALWAYS SO SUSPICIOUS OF YOU?
THE STUFF I DON'T GET AWAY WITH COULD FILL A BOOK.
SCOTT and BORGMAN

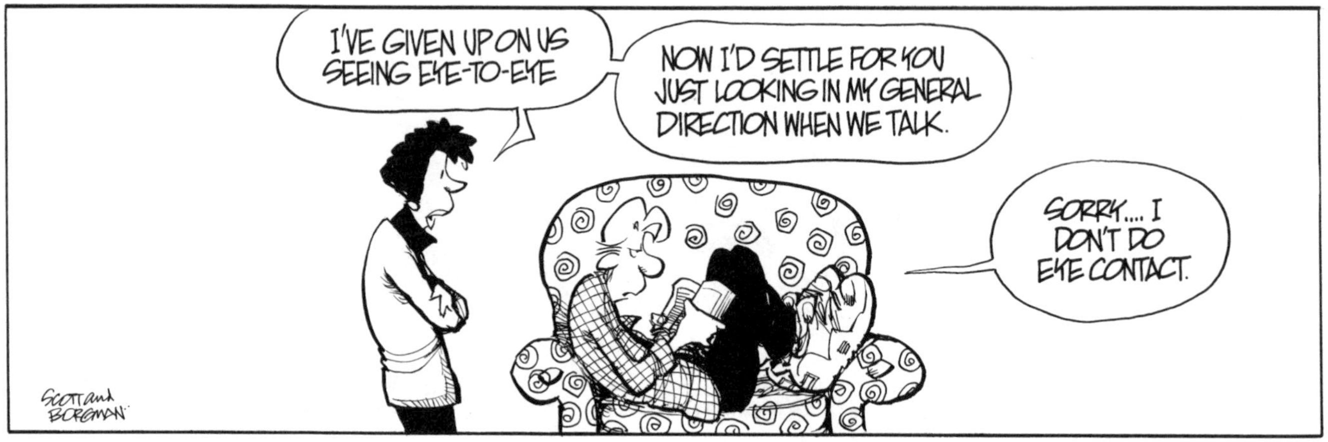
I'VE GIVEN UP ON US SEEING EYE-TO-EYE
NOW I'D SETTLE FOR YOU JUST LOOKING IN MY GENERAL DIRECTION WHEN WE TALK.
SORRY.... I DON'T DO EYE CONTACT.
SCOTT and BORGMAN

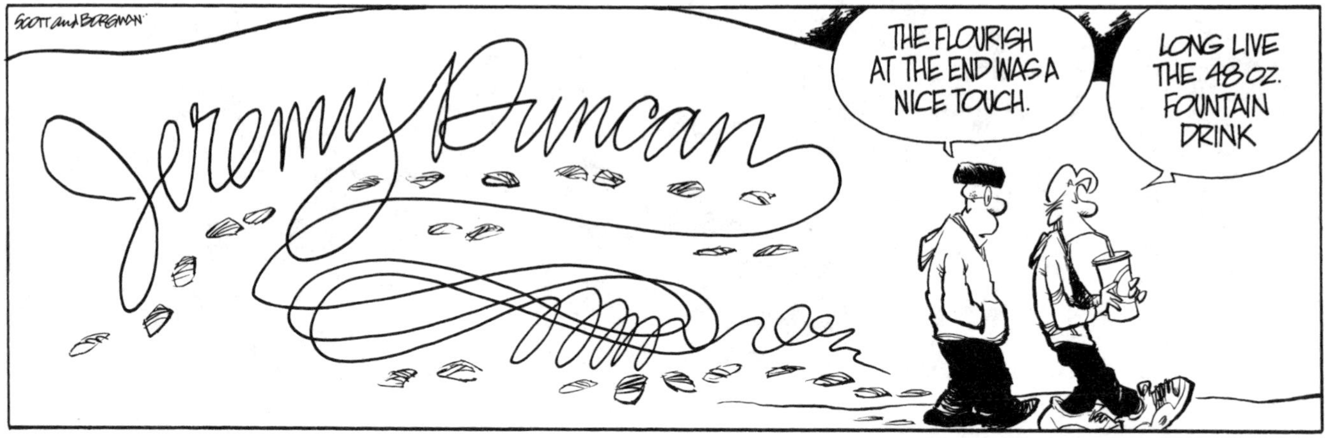
SCOTT and BORGMAN
Jeremy Duncan
THE FLOURISH AT THE END WAS A NICE TOUCH.
LONG LIVE THE 48 OZ. FOUNTAIN DRINK

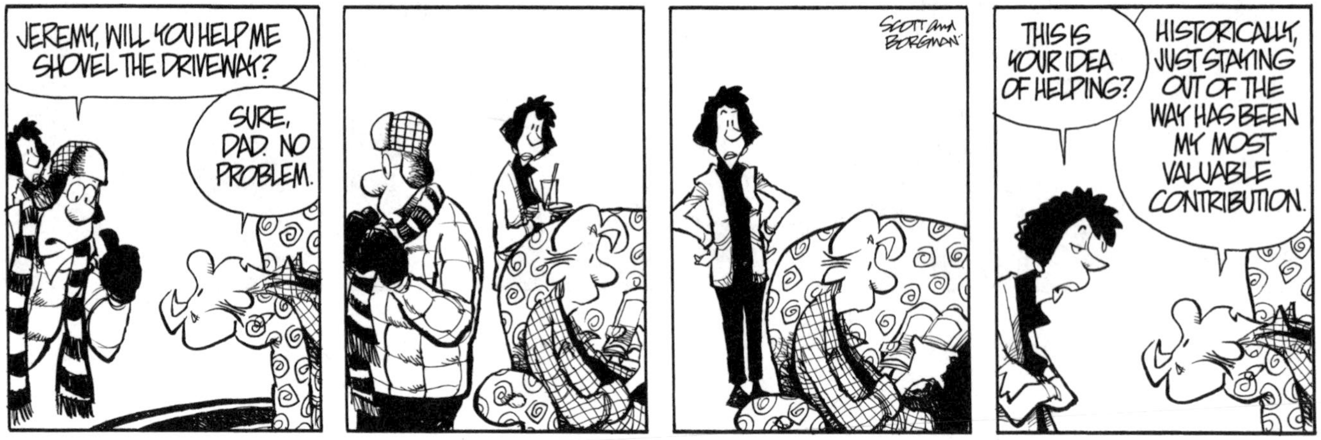
JEREMY, WILL YOU HELP ME SHOVEL THE DRIVEWAY?
SURE, DAD. NO PROBLEM.
SCOTT and BORGMAN
THIS IS YOUR IDEA OF HELPING?
HISTORICALLY, JUST STAYING OUT OF THE WAY HAS BEEN MY MOST VALUABLE CONTRIBUTION.

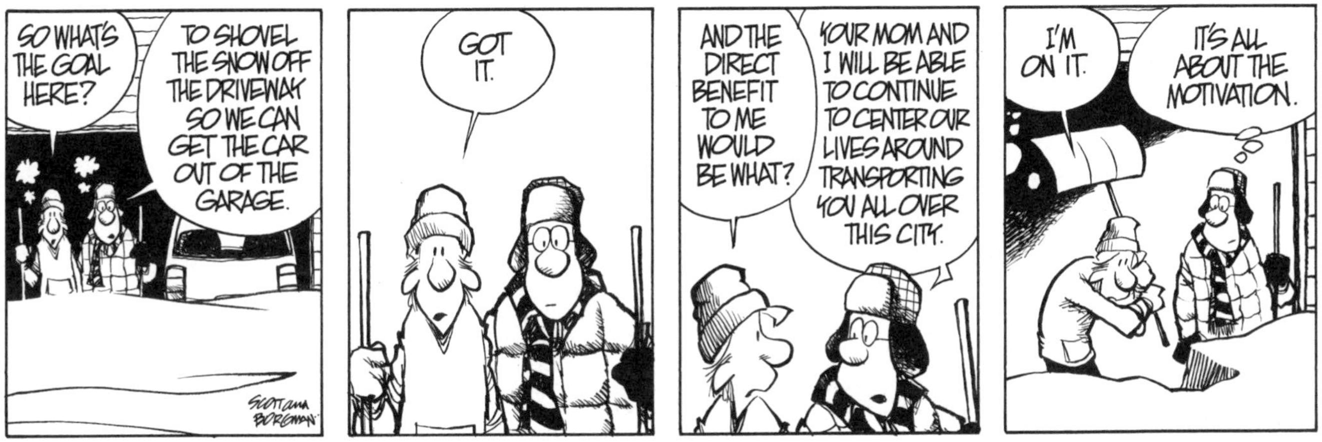
SO WHAT'S THE GOAL HERE?
TO SHOVEL THE SNOW OFF THE DRIVEWAY SO WE CAN GET THE CAR OUT OF THE GARAGE.
SCOTT and BORGMAN
GOT IT.
AND THE DIRECT BENEFIT TO ME WOULD BE WHAT?
YOUR MOM AND I WILL BE ABLE TO CONTINUE TO CENTER OUR LIVES AROUND TRANSPORTING YOU ALL OVER THIS CITY.
I'M ON IT.
IT'S ALL ABOUT THE MOTIVATION.

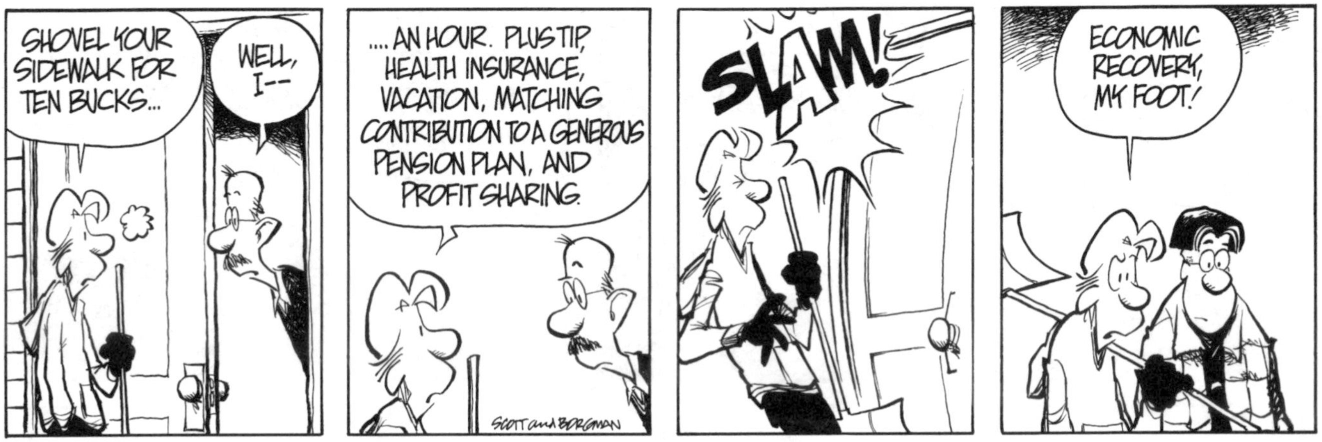
SHOVEL YOUR SIDEWALK FOR TEN BUCKS...
WELL, I--
.... AN HOUR. PLUS TIP, HEALTH INSURANCE, VACATION, MATCHING CONTRIBUTION TO A GENEROUS PENSION PLAN, AND PROFIT SHARING.
SCOTT and BORGMAN
SLAM!
ECONOMIC RECOVERY, MY FOOT!

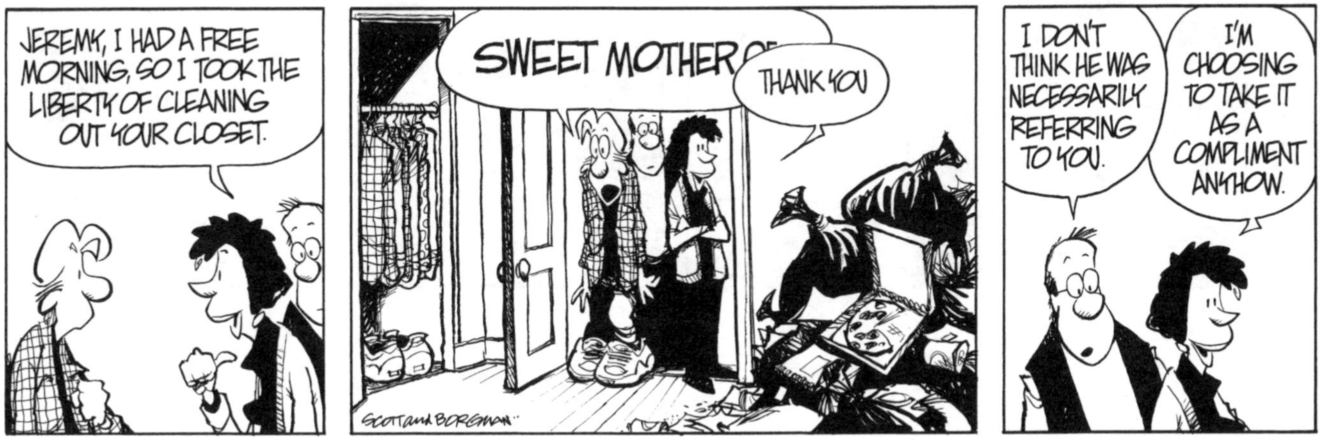
JEREMY, I HAD A FREE MORNING, SO I TOOK THE LIBERTY OF CLEANING OUT YOUR CLOSET.
SWEET MOTHER OF
THANK YOU
SCOTT and BORGMAN
I DON'T THINK HE WAS NECESSARILY REFERRING TO YOU.
I'M CHOOSING TO TAKE IT AS A COMPLIMENT ANYHOW.

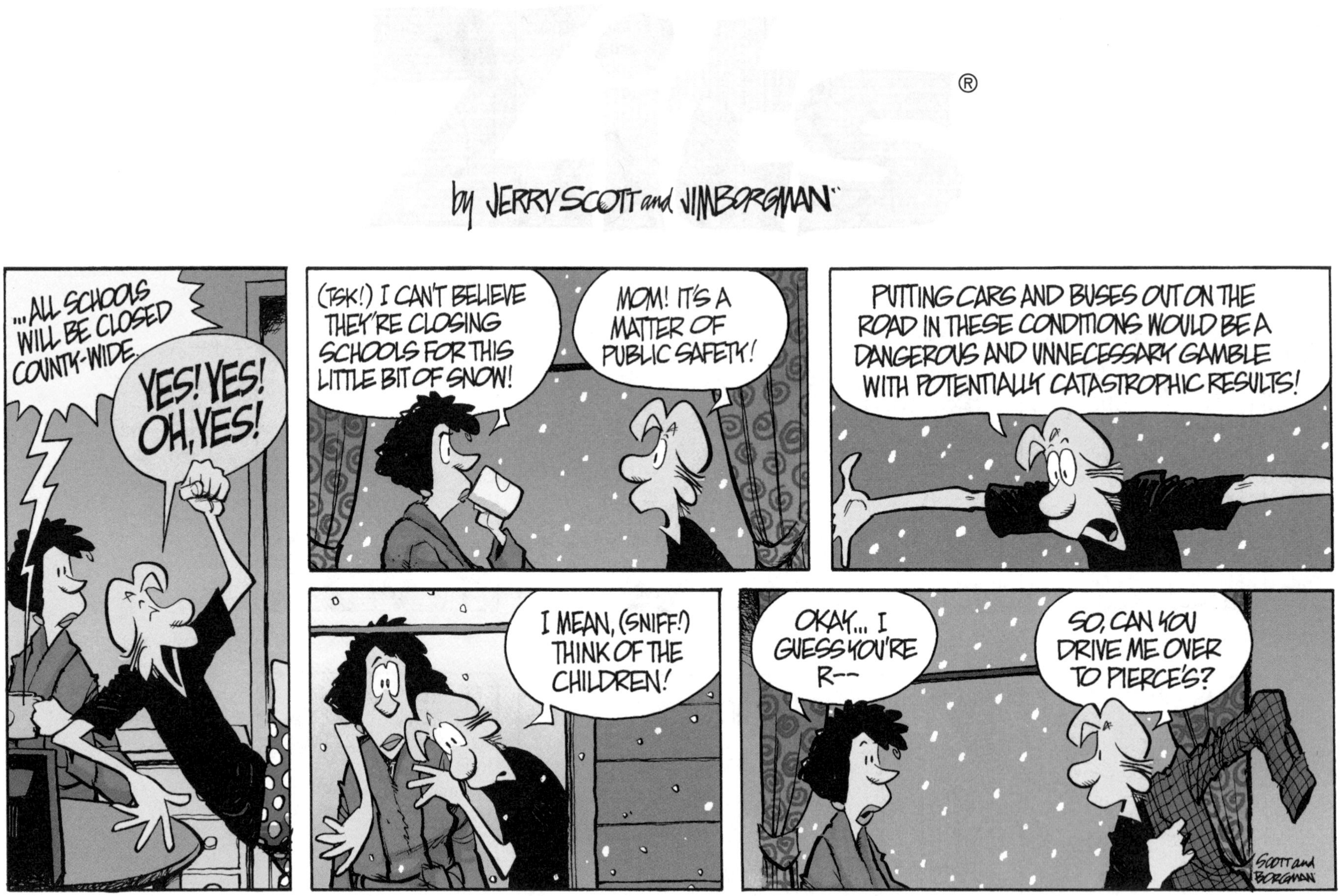
Zits®
by JERRY SCOTT and JIM BORGMAN
...ALL SCHOOLS WILL BE CLOSED COUNTY-WIDE.
YES! YES! OH, YES!
(TSK!) I CAN'T BELIEVE THEY'RE CLOSING SCHOOLS FOR THIS LITTLE BIT OF SNOW!
MOM! IT'S A MATTER OF PUBLIC SAFETY!
PUTTING CARS AND BUSES OUT ON THE ROAD IN THESE CONDITIONS WOULD BE A DANGEROUS AND UNNECESSARY GAMBLE WITH POTENTIALLY CATASTROPHIC RESULTS!
I MEAN, (SNIFF!) THINK OF THE CHILDREN!
OKAY... I GUESS YOU'RE R--
SO, CAN YOU DRIVE ME OVER TO PIERCE'S?
SCOTT and BORGMAN

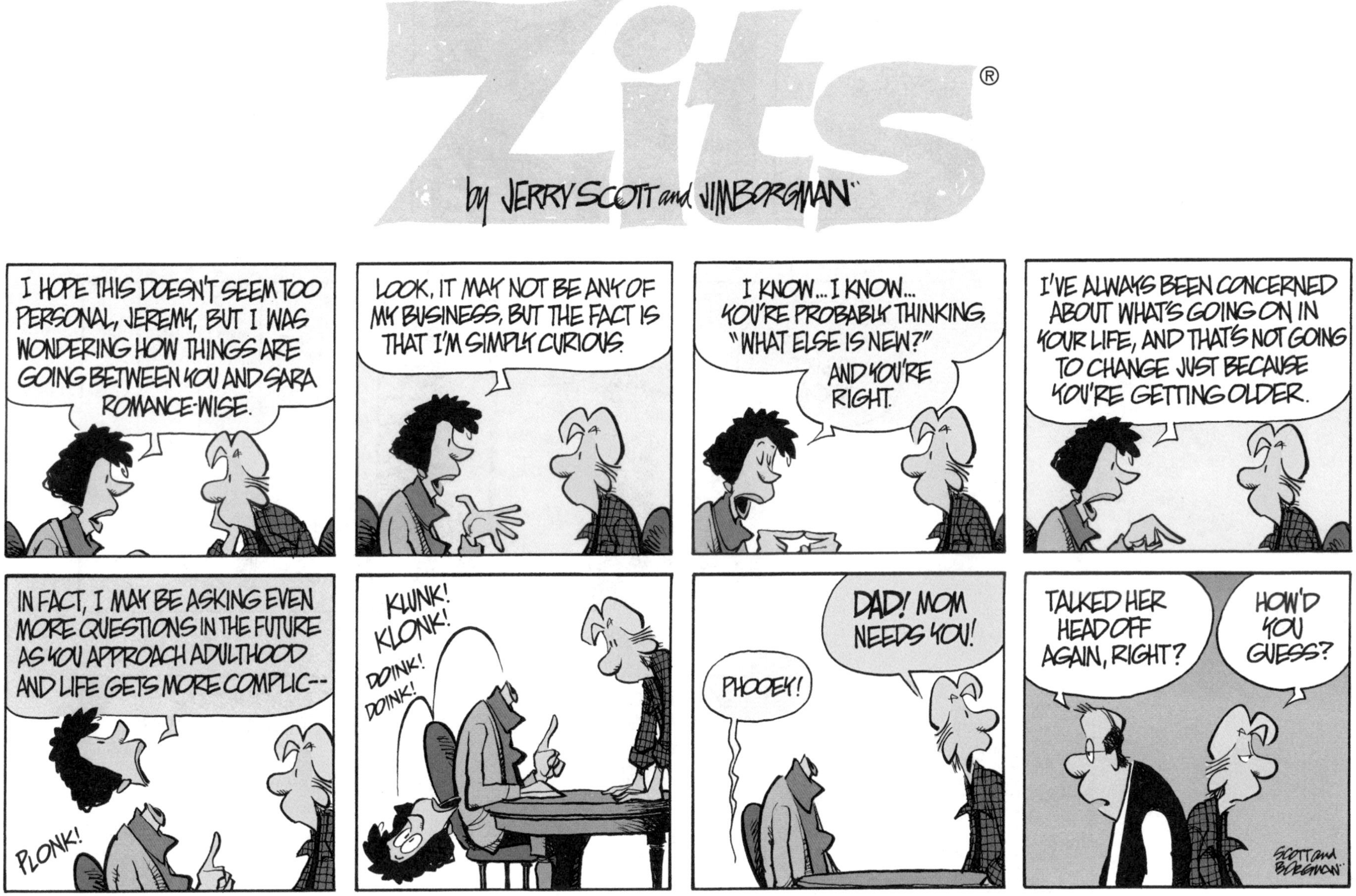
Zits®
by JERRY SCOTT and JIM BORGMAN
I HOPE THIS DOESN'T SEEM TOO PERSONAL, JEREMY, BUT I WAS WONDERING HOW THINGS ARE GOING BETWEEN YOU AND SARA ROMANCE-WISE.
LOOK, IT MAY NOT BE ANY OF MY BUSINESS, BUT THE FACT IS THAT I'M SIMPLY CURIOUS.
I KNOW... I KNOW... YOU'RE PROBABLY THINKING, "WHAT ELSE IS NEW?"
AND YOU'RE RIGHT.
I'VE ALWAYS BEEN CONCERNED ABOUT WHAT'S GOING ON IN YOUR LIFE, AND THAT'S NOT GOING TO CHANGE JUST BECAUSE YOU'RE GETTING OLDER.
IN FACT, I MAY BE ASKING EVEN MORE QUESTIONS IN THE FUTURE AS YOU APPROACH ADULTHOOD AND LIFE GETS MORE COMPLIC--
PLONK!
KLUNK! KLONK!
DOINK! DOINK!
DAD! MOM NEEDS YOU!
PHOOEY!
TALKED HER HEAD OFF AGAIN, RIGHT?
HOW'D YOU GUESS?
SCOTT and BORGMAN

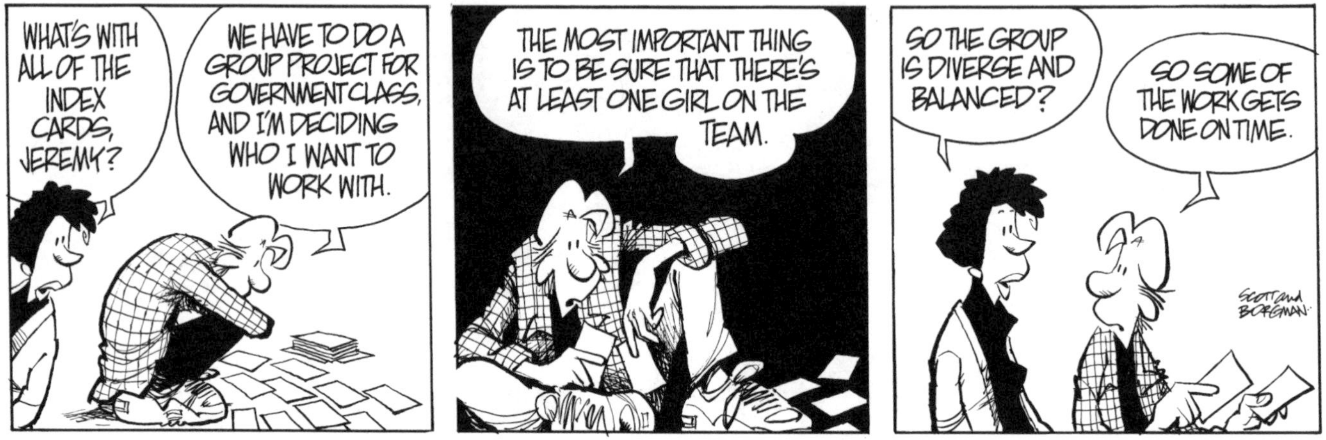
WHAT'S WITH ALL OF THE INDEX CARDS, JEREMY?
WE HAVE TO DO A GROUP PROJECT FOR GOVERNMENT CLASS, AND I'M DECIDING WHO I WANT TO WORK WITH.
THE MOST IMPORTANT THING IS TO BE SURE THAT THERE'S AT LEAST ONE GIRL ON THE TEAM.
SO THE GROUP IS DIVERSE AND BALANCED?
SO SOME OF THE WORK GETS DONE ON TIME.

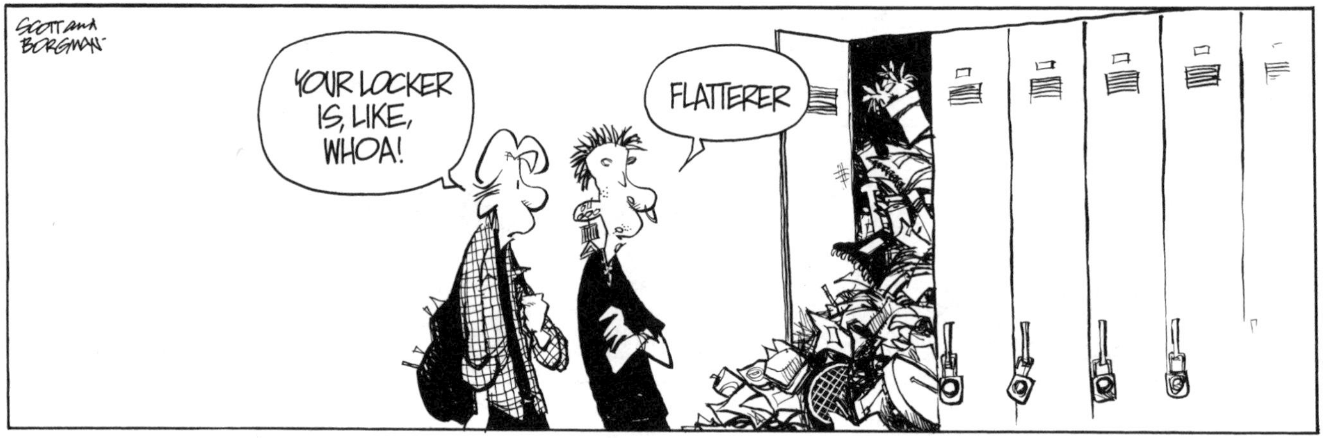
YOUR LOCKER IS, LIKE, WHOA!
FLATTERER

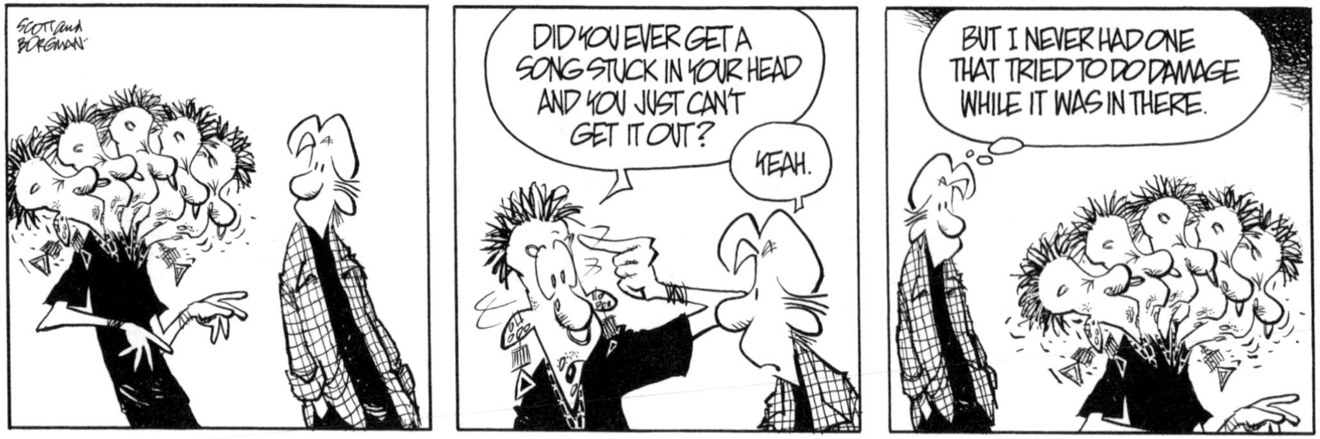
DID YOU EVER GET A SONG STUCK IN YOUR HEAD AND YOU JUST CAN'T GET IT OUT?
YEAH.
BUT I NEVER HAD ONE THAT TRIED TO DO DAMAGE WHILE IT WAS IN THERE.

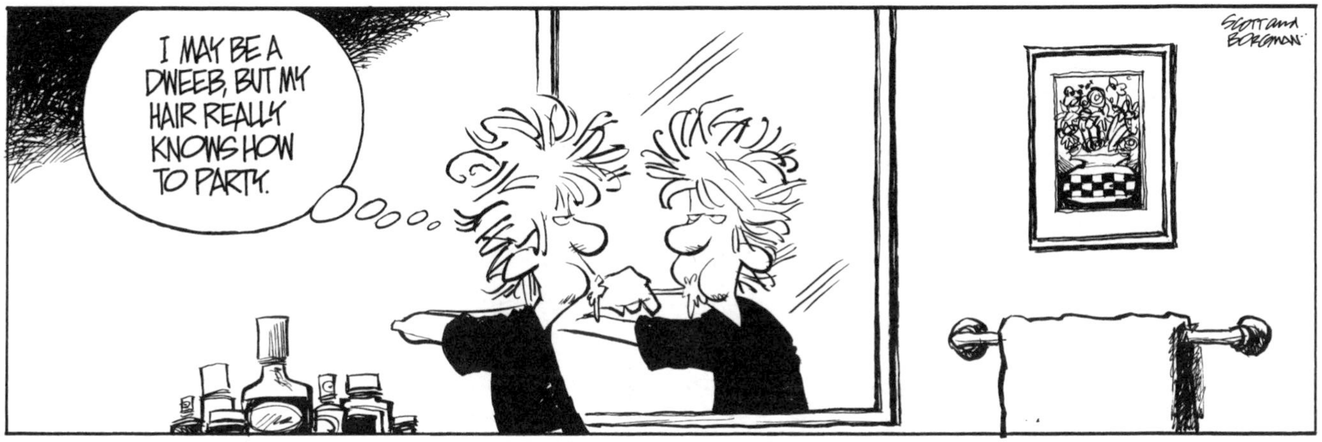
I MAY BE A DWEEB, BUT MY HAIR REALLY KNOWS HOW TO PARTY.
SCOTT and BORGMAN

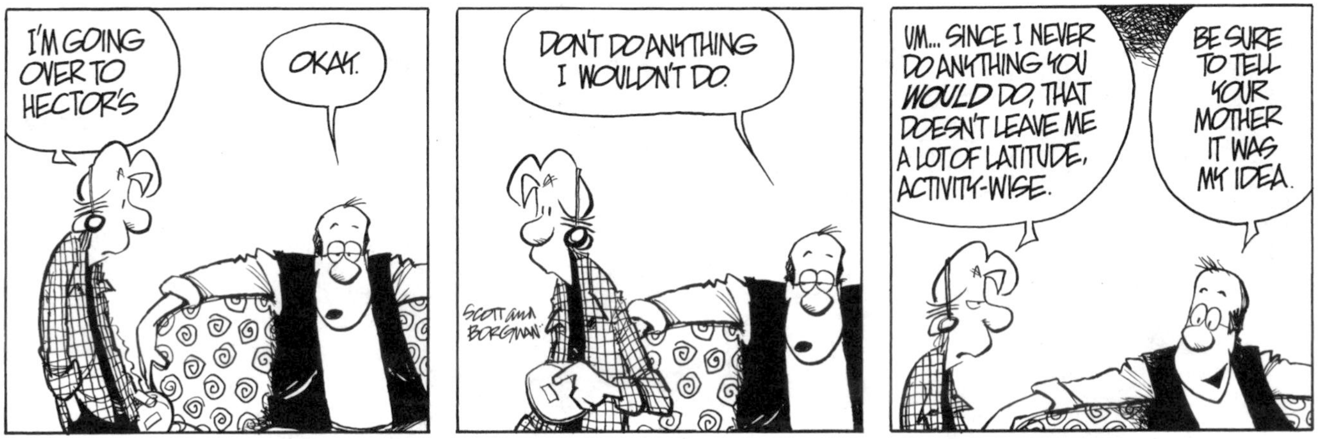
I'M GOING OVER TO HECTOR'S
OKAY.
DON'T DO ANYTHING I WOULDN'T DO.
SCOTT and BORGMAN
UM... SINCE I NEVER DO ANYTHING YOU **WOULD** DO, THAT DOESN'T LEAVE ME A LOT OF LATITUDE, ACTIVITY-WISE.
BE SURE TO TELL YOUR MOTHER IT WAS MY IDEA.

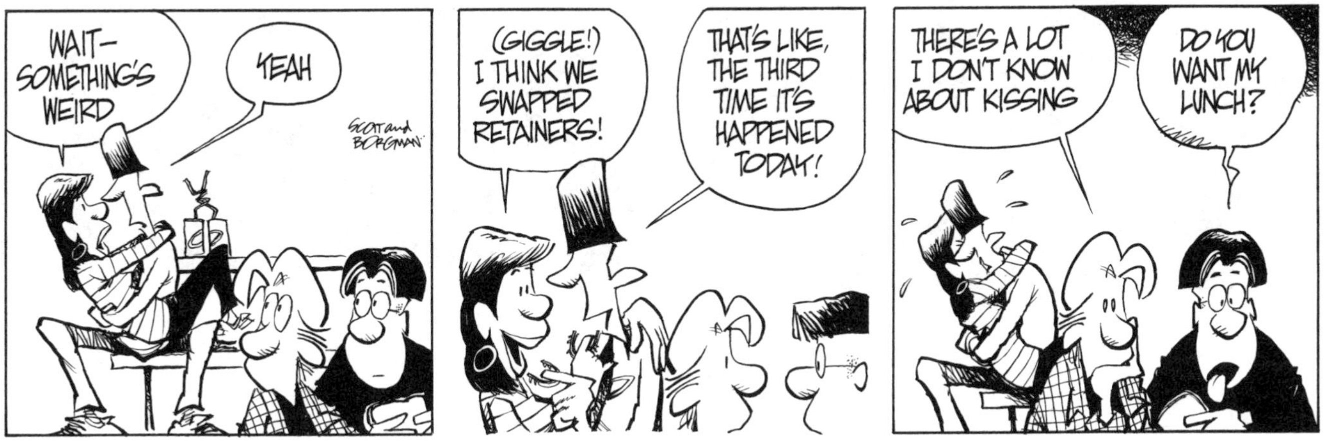
WAIT- SOMETHING'S WEIRD
YEAH
SCOTT and BORGMAN
(GIGGLE!) I THINK WE SWAPPED RETAINERS!
THAT'S LIKE, THE THIRD TIME IT'S HAPPENED TODAY!
THERE'S A LOT I DON'T KNOW ABOUT KISSING
DO YOU WANT MY LUNCH?

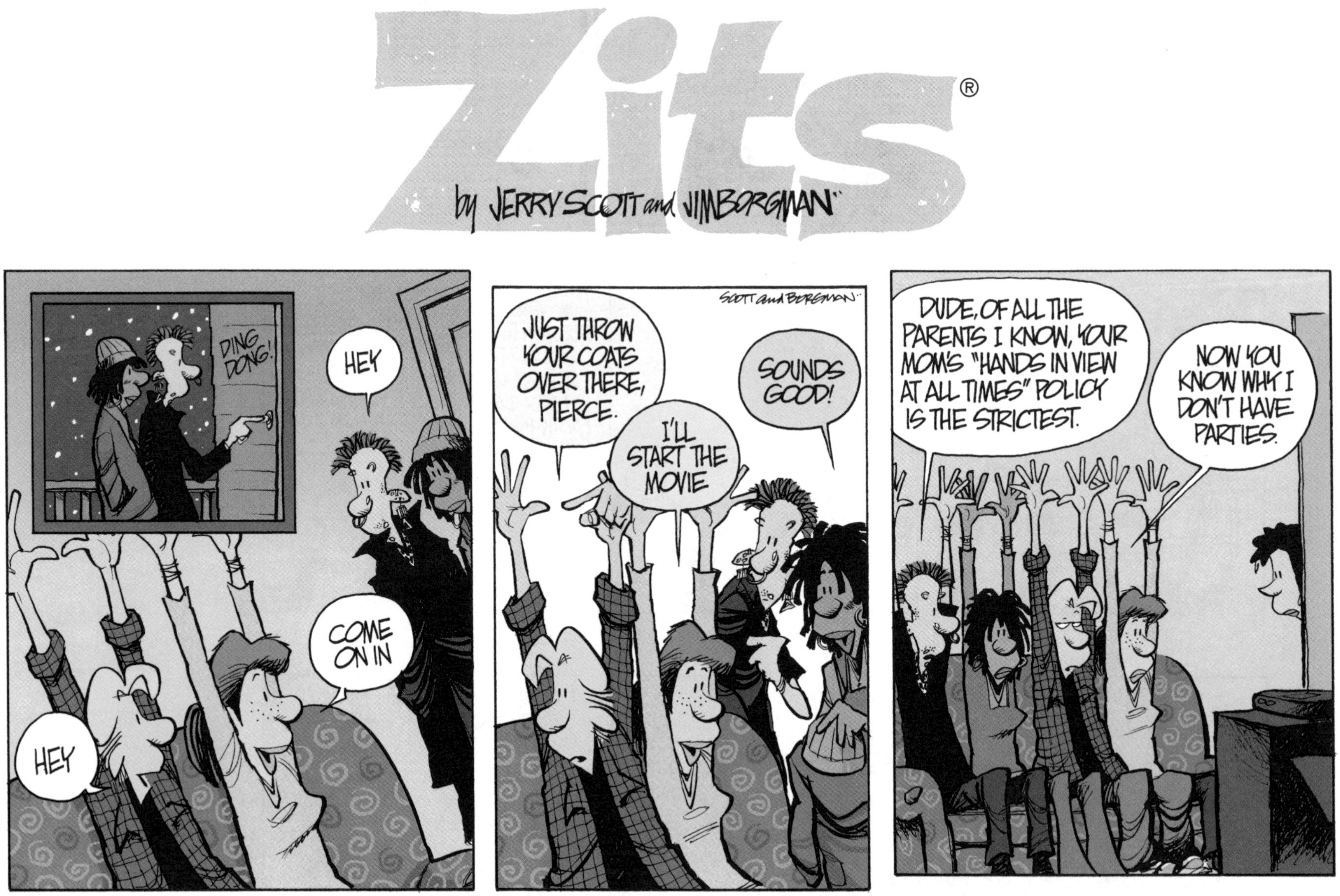
Zits®
by JERRY SCOTT and JIM BORGMAN
DING DONG!
HEY
COME ON IN
HEY
SCOTT and BORGMAN
JUST THROW YOUR COATS OVER THERE, PIERCE.
I'LL START THE MOVIE
SOUNDS GOOD!
DUDE, OF ALL THE PARENTS I KNOW, YOUR MOM'S "HANDS IN VIEW AT ALL TIMES" POLICY IS THE STRICTEST.
NOW YOU KNOW WHY I DON'T HAVE PARTIES.

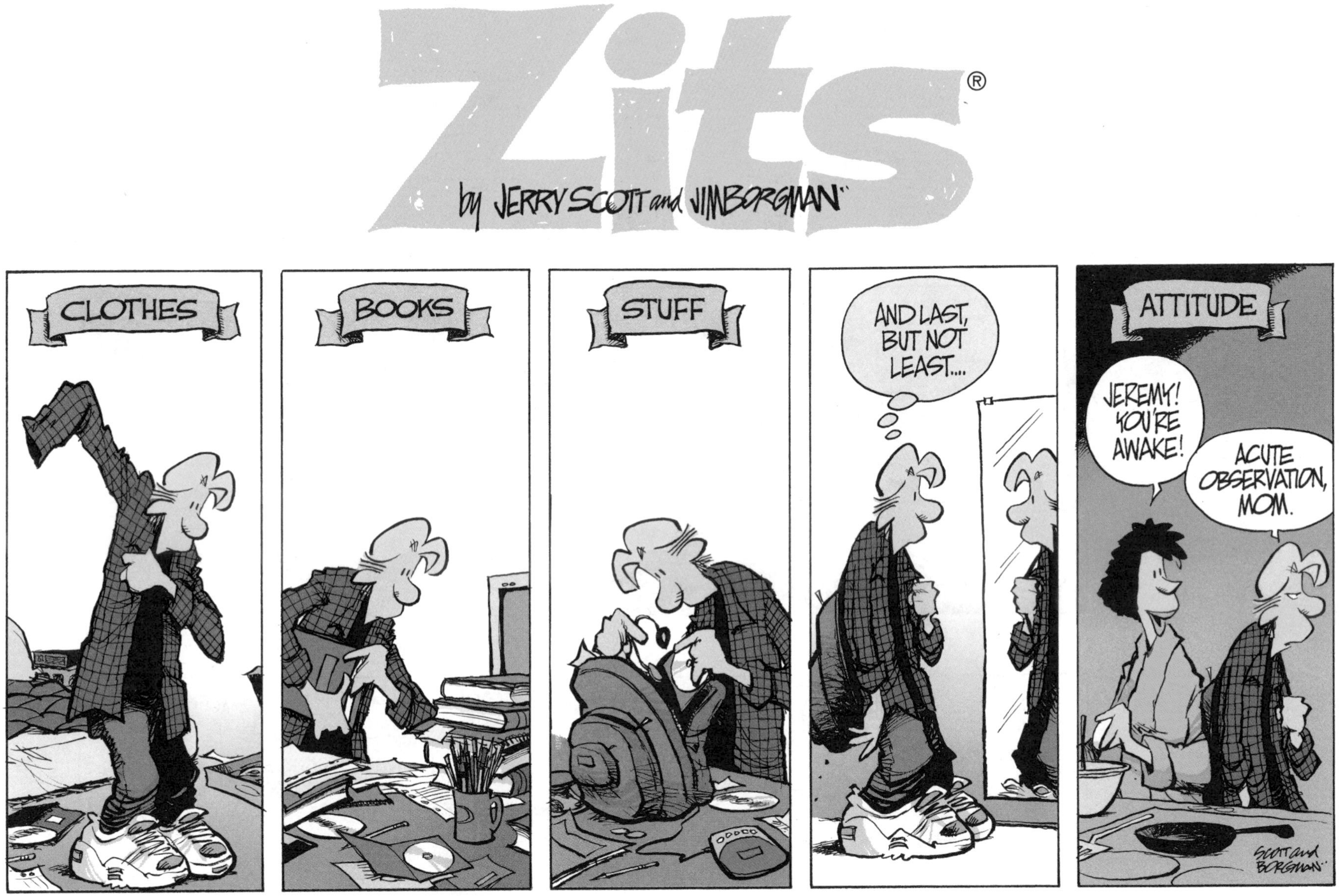
Zits®
by JERRY SCOTT and JIM BORGMAN
CLOTHES
BOOKS
STUFF
AND LAST, BUT NOT LEAST....
ATTITUDE
JEREMY! YOU'RE AWAKE!
ACUTE OBSERVATION, MOM.
SCOTT and BORGMAN

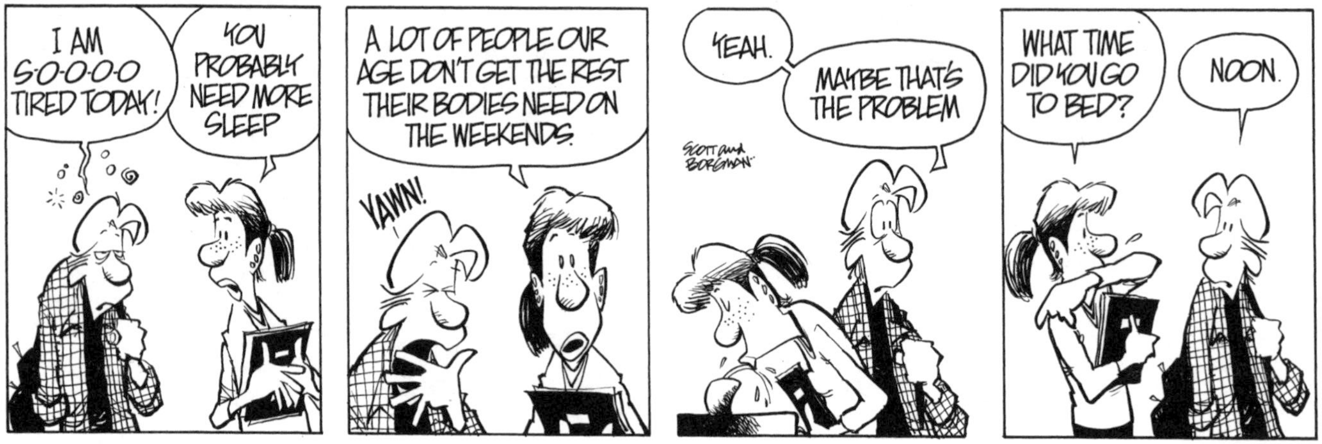
I AM S-O-O-O-O TIRED TODAY!
YOU PROBABLY NEED MORE SLEEP
YAWN!
A LOT OF PEOPLE OUR AGE DON'T GET THE REST THEIR BODIES NEED ON THE WEEKENDS.
YEAH.
MAYBE THAT'S THE PROBLEM
WHAT TIME DID YOU GO TO BED?
NOON.

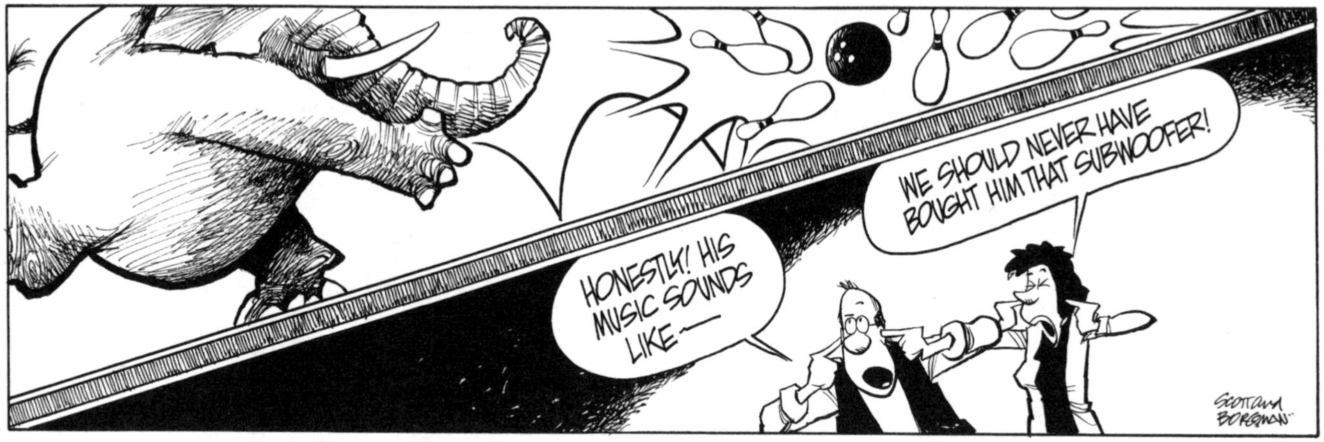
WE SHOULD NEVER HAVE BOUGHT HIM THAT SUBWOOFER!
HONESTLY! HIS MUSIC SOUNDS LIKE—

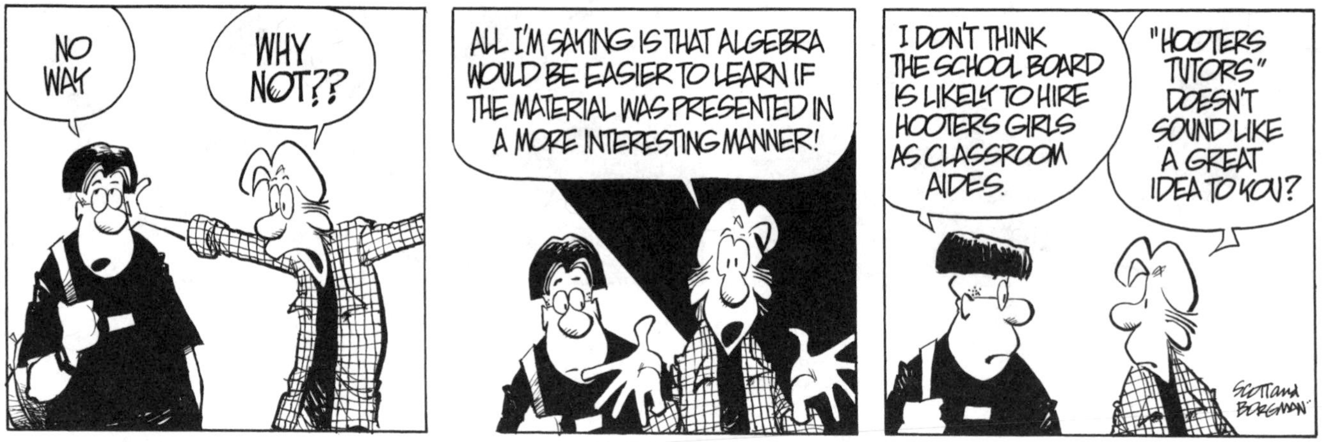
NO WAY
WHY NOT??
ALL I'M SAYING IS THAT ALGEBRA WOULD BE EASIER TO LEARN IF THE MATERIAL WAS PRESENTED IN A MORE INTERESTING MANNER!
I DON'T THINK THE SCHOOL BOARD IS LIKELY TO HIRE HOOTERS GIRLS AS CLASSROOM AIDES.
"HOOTERS TUTORS" DOESN'T SOUND LIKE A GREAT IDEA TO YOU?

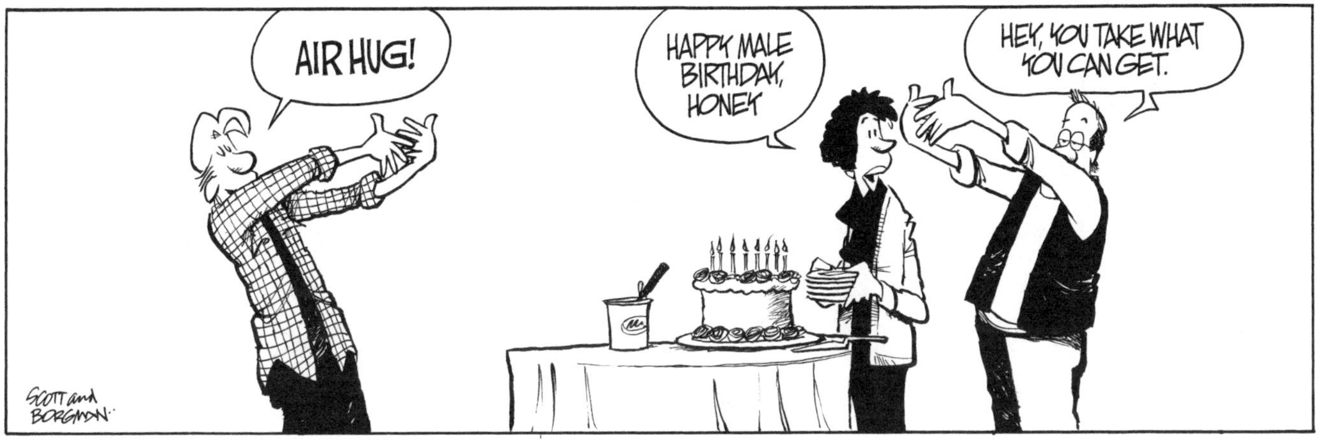
AIR HUG!
HAPPY MALE BIRTHDAY, HONEY
HEY, YOU TAKE WHAT YOU CAN GET.
SCOTT and BORGMAN

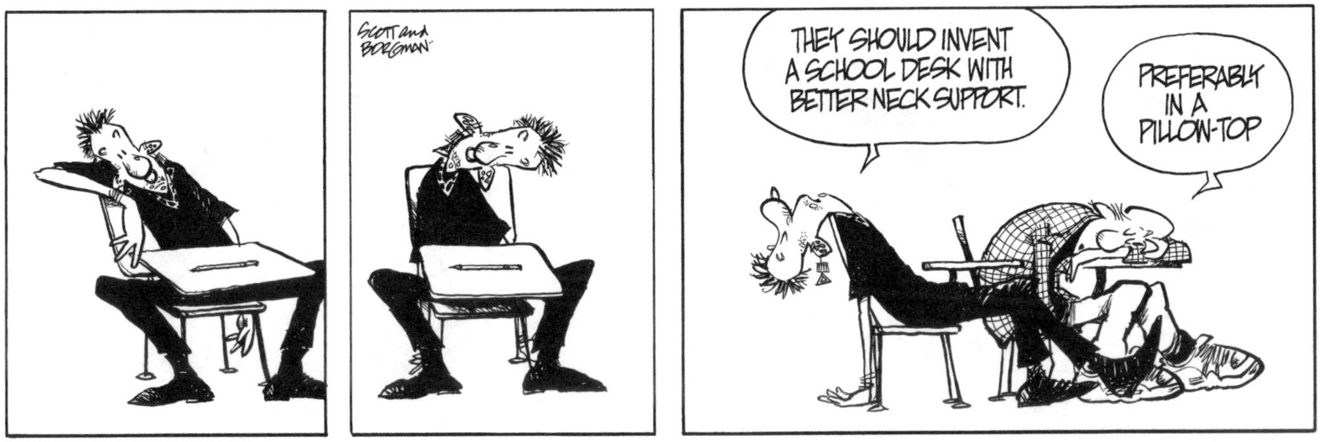
SCOTT and BORGMAN
THEY SHOULD INVENT A SCHOOL DESK WITH BETTER NECK SUPPORT.
PREFERABLY IN A PILLOW-TOP

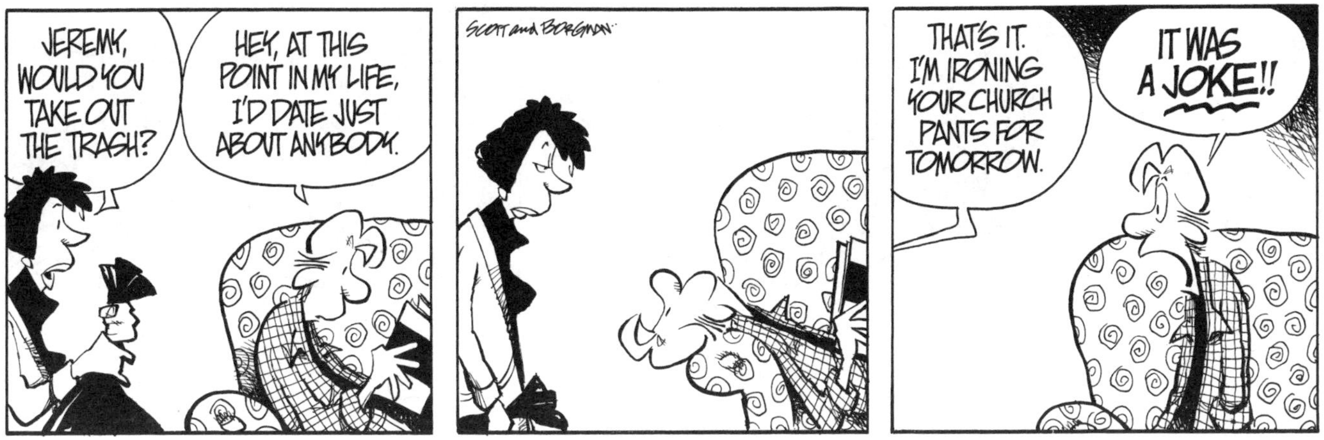
JEREMY, WOULD YOU TAKE OUT THE TRASH?
HEY, AT THIS POINT IN MY LIFE, I'D DATE JUST ABOUT ANYBODY.
SCOTT and BORGMAN
THAT'S IT. I'M IRONING YOUR CHURCH PANTS FOR TOMORROW.
IT WAS A JOKE!!

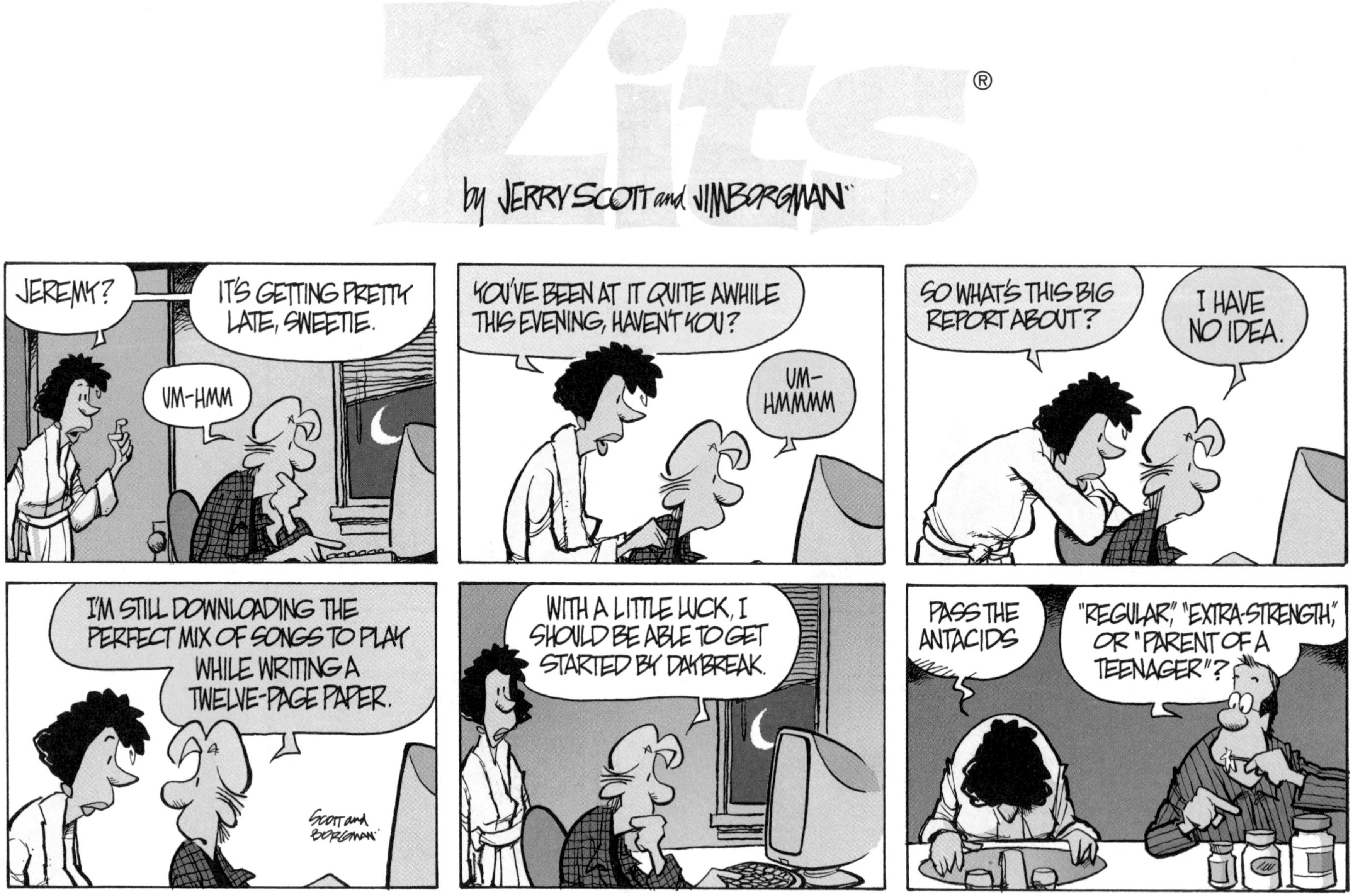
Zits®
by JERRY SCOTT and JIM BORGMAN
JEREMY?
IT'S GETTING PRETTY LATE, SWEETIE.
UM-HMM
YOU'VE BEEN AT IT QUITE AWHILE THIS EVENING, HAVEN'T YOU?
UM-HMMMM
SO WHAT'S THIS BIG REPORT ABOUT?
I HAVE NO IDEA.
I'M STILL DOWNLOADING THE PERFECT MIX OF SONGS TO PLAY WHILE WRITING A TWELVE-PAGE PAPER.
SCOTT and BORGMAN
WITH A LITTLE LUCK, I SHOULD BE ABLE TO GET STARTED BY DAYBREAK.
PASS THE ANTACIDS
"REGULAR," "EXTRA-STRENGTH," OR "PARENT OF A TEENAGER"?

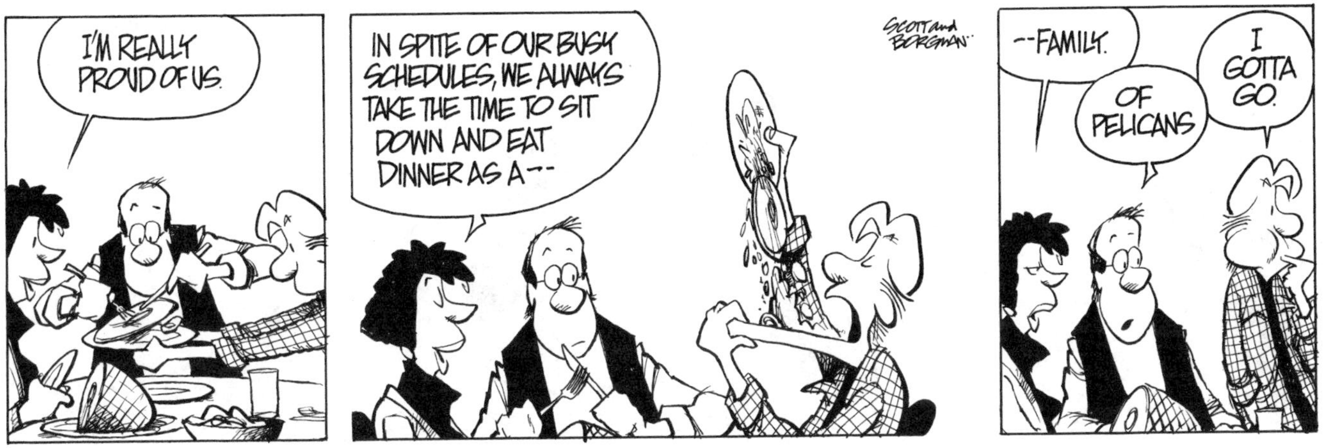
I'M REALLY PROUD OF US.
IN SPITE OF OUR BUSY SCHEDULES, WE ALWAYS TAKE THE TIME TO SIT DOWN AND EAT DINNER AS A--
SCOTT and BORGMAN
--FAMILY.
OF PELICANS
I GOTTA GO.

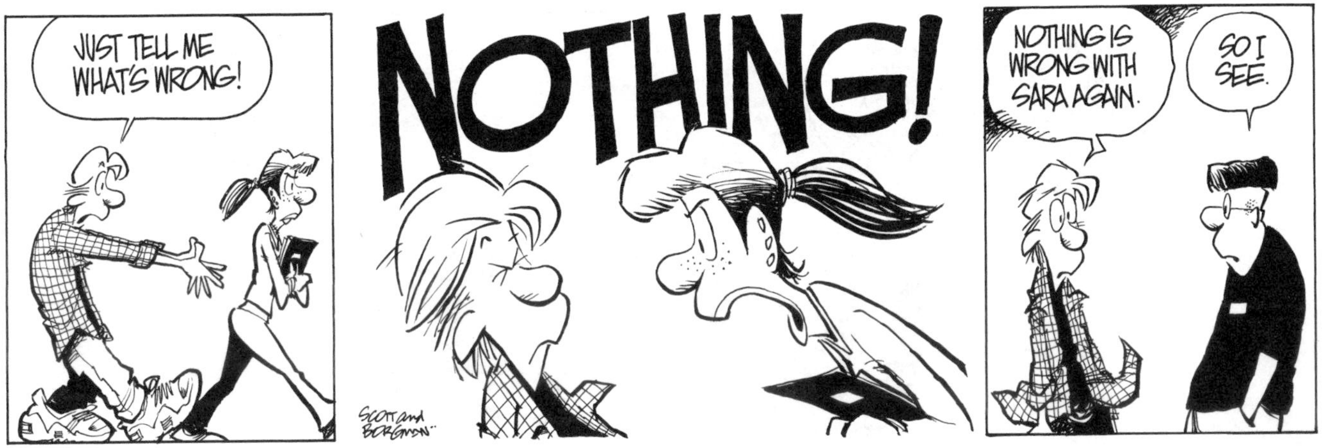
JUST TELL ME WHAT'S WRONG!
SCOTT and BORGMAN
NOTHING!
NOTHING IS WRONG WITH SARA AGAIN.
SO I SEE.

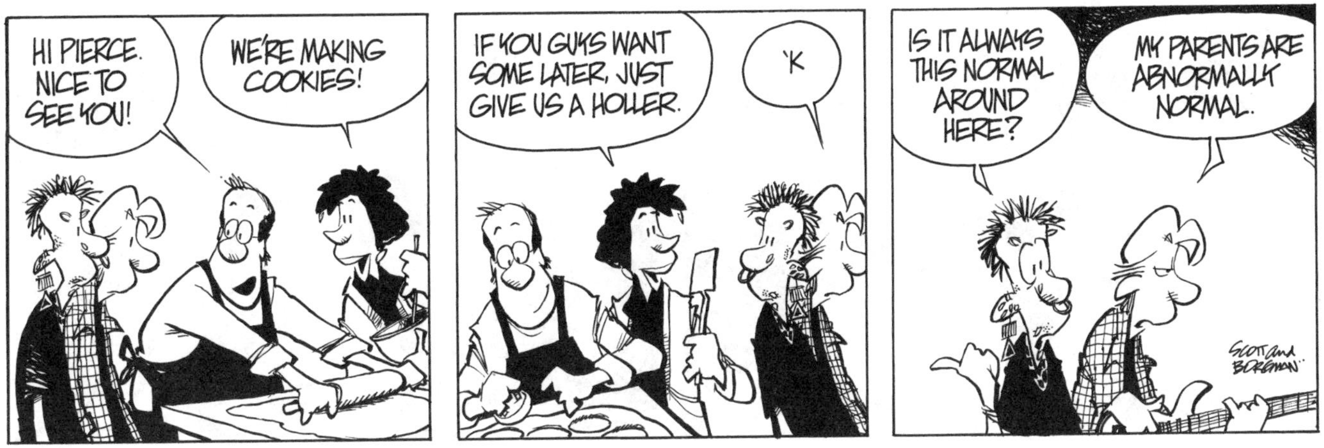
HI PIERCE. NICE TO SEE YOU!
WE'RE MAKING COOKIES!
IF YOU GUYS WANT SOME LATER, JUST GIVE US A HOLLER.
'K
IS IT ALWAYS THIS NORMAL AROUND HERE?
MY PARENTS ARE ABNORMALLY NORMAL.
SCOTT and BORGMAN

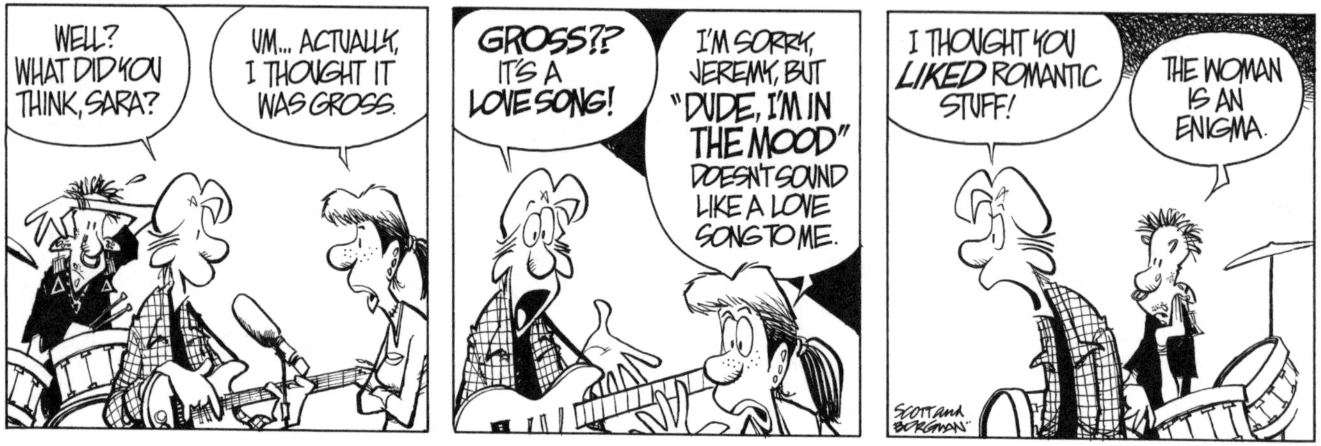
WELL? WHAT DID YOU THINK, SARA?
UM... ACTUALLY, I THOUGHT IT WAS GROSS.
GROSS?? IT'S A LOVE SONG!
I'M SORRY, JEREMY, BUT "DUDE, I'M IN THE MOOD" DOESN'T SOUND LIKE A LOVE SONG TO ME.
I THOUGHT YOU LIKED ROMANTIC STUFF!
THE WOMAN IS AN ENIGMA.
SCOTT AND BORGMAN

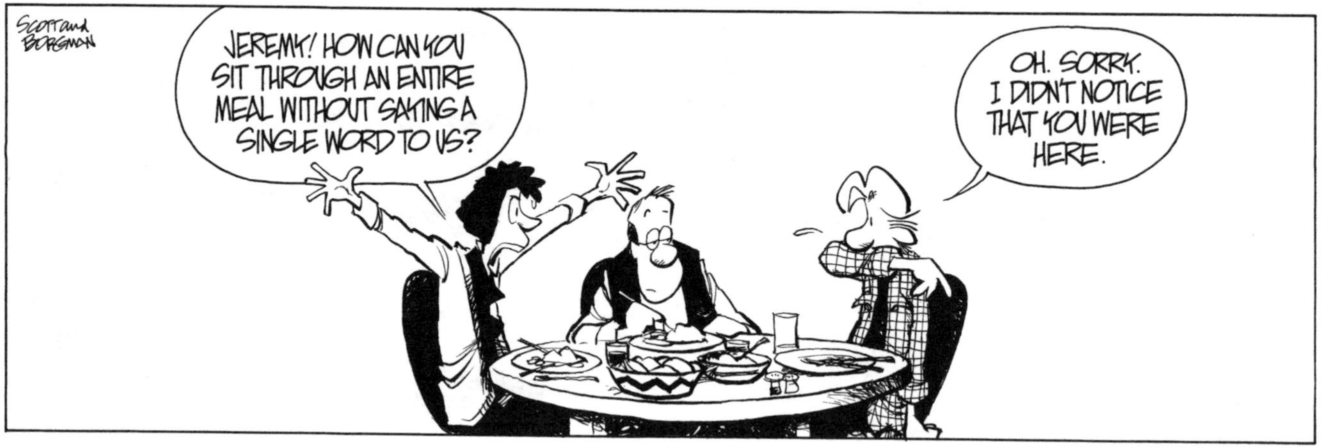
SCOTT AND BORGMAN
JEREMY! HOW CAN YOU SIT THROUGH AN ENTIRE MEAL WITHOUT SAYING A SINGLE WORD TO US?
OH. SORRY. I DIDN'T NOTICE THAT YOU WERE HERE.

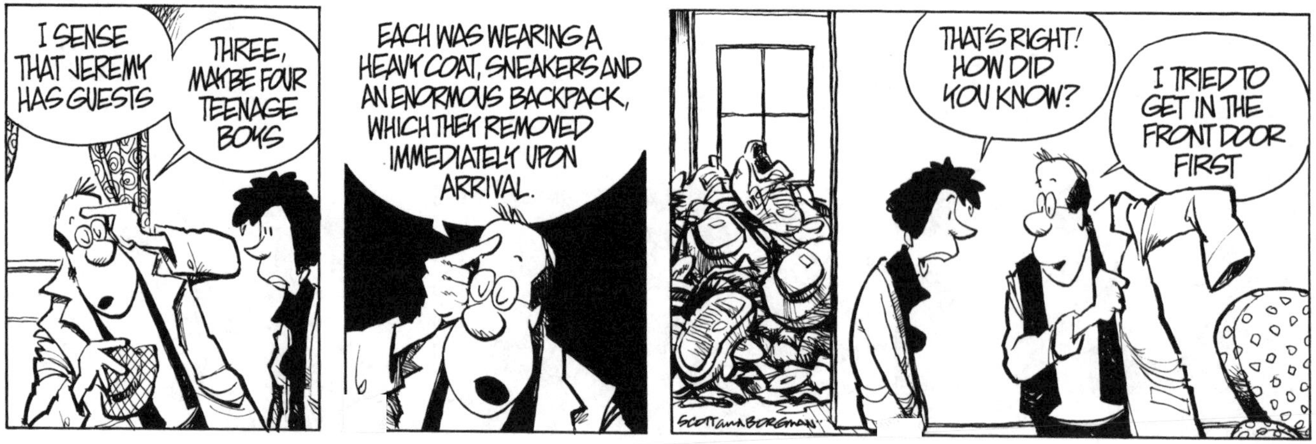
I SENSE THAT JEREMY HAS GUESTS
THREE, MAYBE FOUR TEENAGE BOYS
EACH WAS WEARING A HEAVY COAT, SNEAKERS AND AN ENORMOUS BACKPACK, WHICH THEY REMOVED IMMEDIATELY UPON ARRIVAL.
THAT'S RIGHT! HOW DID YOU KNOW?
I TRIED TO GET IN THE FRONT DOOR FIRST
SCOTT AND BORGMAN

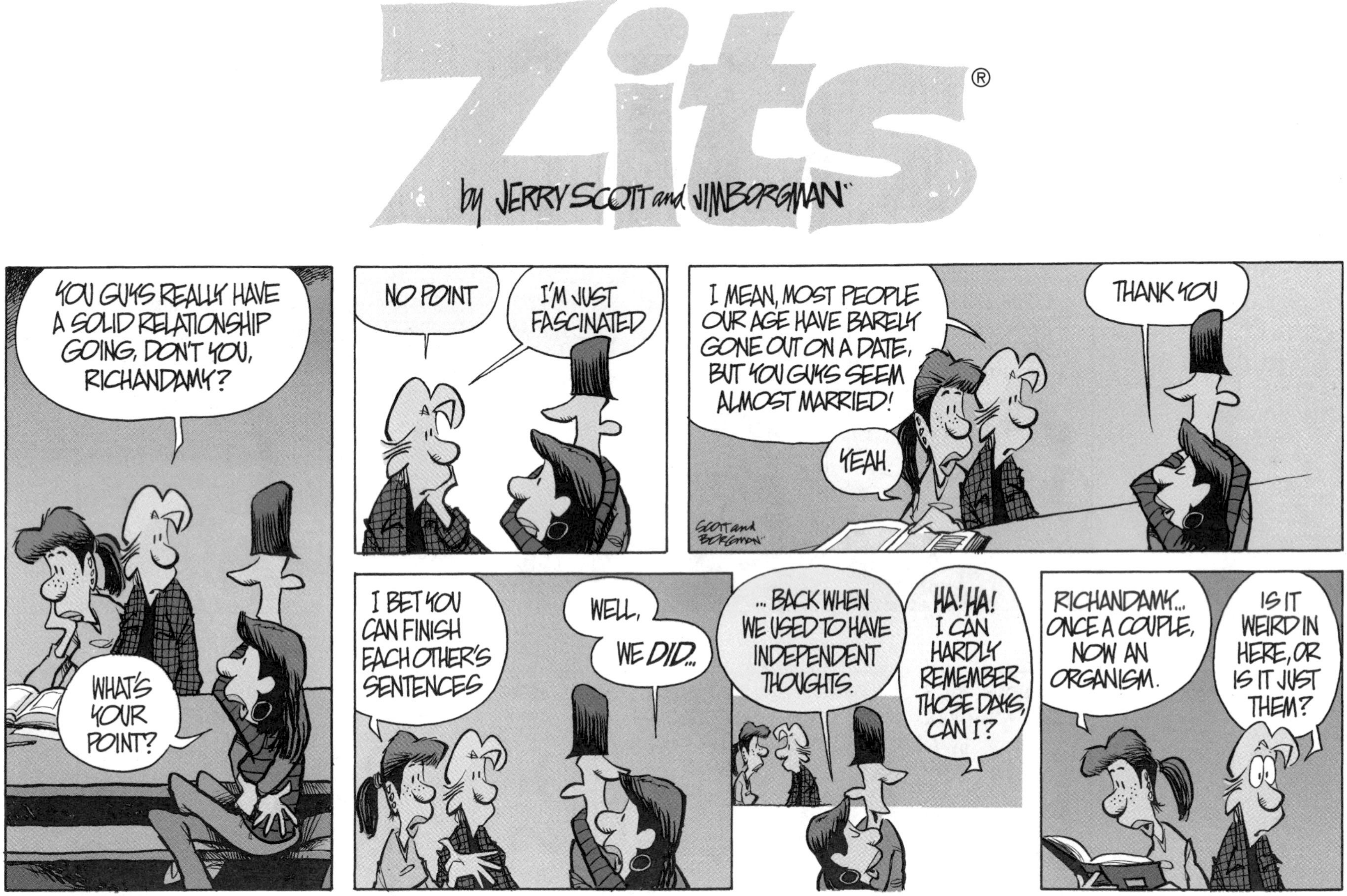

Zits®
by JERRY SCOTT and JIM BORGMAN
YOU GUYS REALLY HAVE A SOLID RELATIONSHIP GOING, DON'T YOU, RICHANDAMY?
WHAT'S YOUR POINT?
NO POINT
I'M JUST FASCINATED
I MEAN, MOST PEOPLE OUR AGE HAVE BARELY GONE OUT ON A DATE, BUT YOU GUYS SEEM ALMOST MARRIED!
YEAH.
THANK YOU
SCOTT and BORGMAN
I BET YOU CAN FINISH EACH OTHER'S SENTENCES
WELL,
WE DID...
... BACK WHEN WE USED TO HAVE INDEPENDENT THOUGHTS.
HA! HA! I CAN HARDLY REMEMBER THOSE DAYS, CAN I?
RICHANDAMY... ONCE A COUPLE, NOW AN ORGANISM.
IS IT WEIRD IN HERE, OR IS IT JUST THEM?

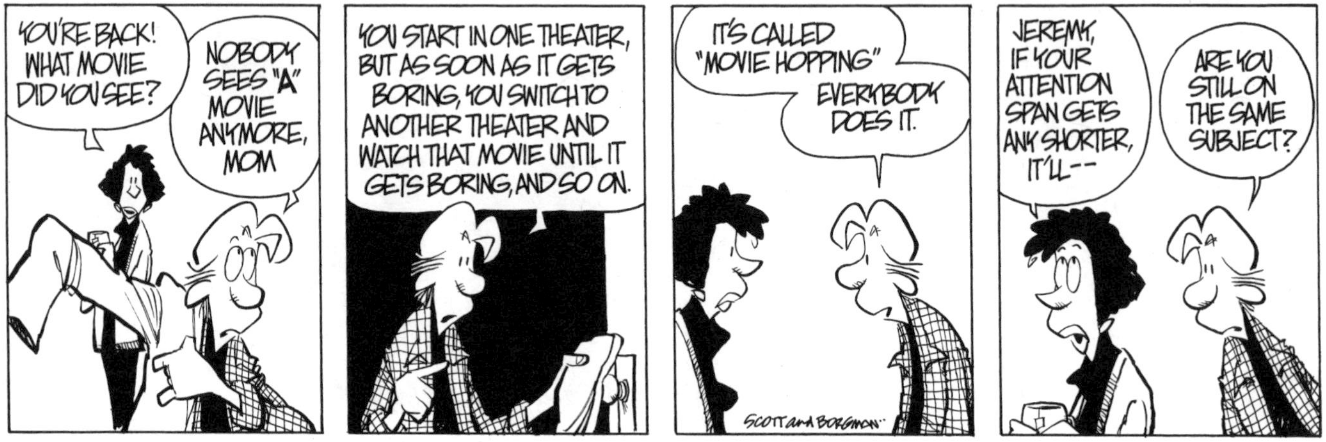
YOU'RE BACK! WHAT MOVIE DID YOU SEE?
NOBODY SEES "A" MOVIE ANYMORE, MOM
YOU START IN ONE THEATER, BUT AS SOON AS IT GETS BORING, YOU SWITCH TO ANOTHER THEATER AND WATCH THAT MOVIE UNTIL IT GETS BORING, AND SO ON.
IT'S CALLED "MOVIE HOPPING"
EVERYBODY DOES IT.
JEREMY, IF YOUR ATTENTION SPAN GETS ANY SHORTER, IT'LL--
ARE YOU STILL ON THE SAME SUBJECT?

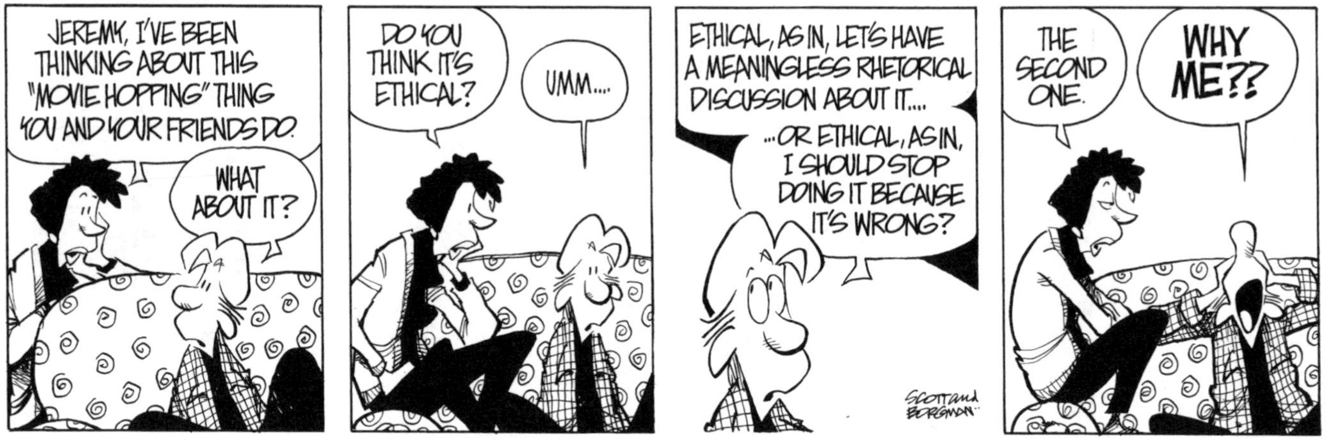
JEREMY, I'VE BEEN THINKING ABOUT THIS "MOVIE HOPPING" THING YOU AND YOUR FRIENDS DO.
WHAT ABOUT IT?
DO YOU THINK IT'S ETHICAL?
UMM....
ETHICAL, AS IN, LET'S HAVE A MEANINGLESS RHETORICAL DISCUSSION ABOUT IT....
...OR ETHICAL, AS IN, I SHOULD STOP DOING IT BECAUSE IT'S WRONG?
THE SECOND ONE.
WHY ME??

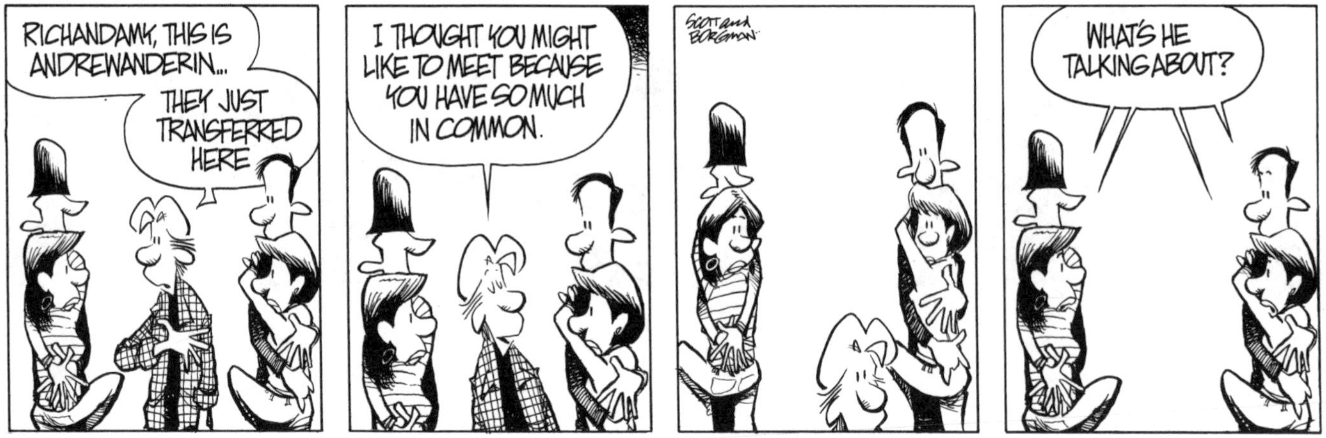
RICHANDAMY, THIS IS ANDREWANDERIN...
THEY JUST TRANSFERRED HERE
I THOUGHT YOU MIGHT LIKE TO MEET BECAUSE YOU HAVE SO MUCH IN COMMON.
WHAT'S HE TALKING ABOUT?

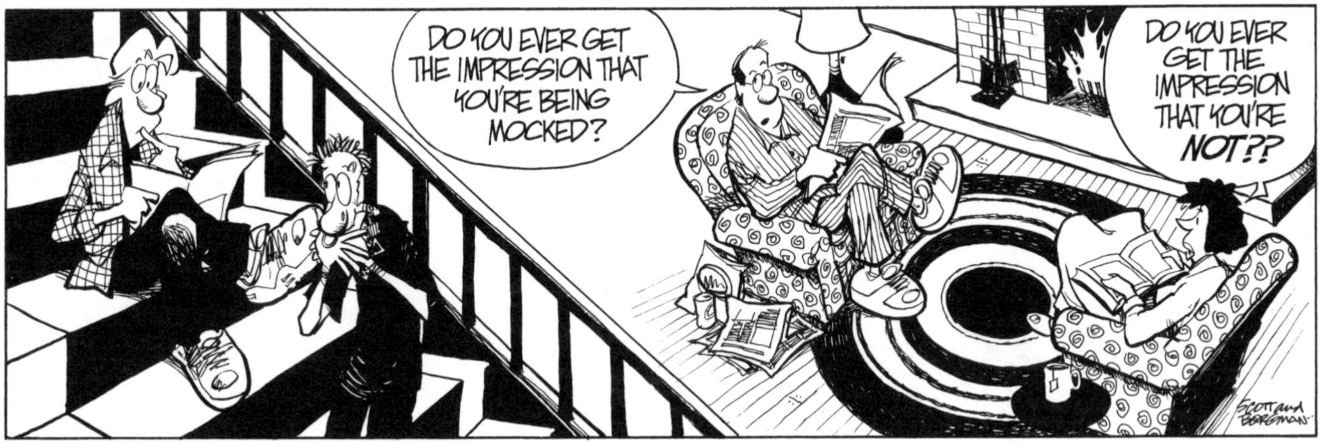
DO YOU EVER GET THE IMPRESSION THAT YOU'RE BEING MOCKED?
DO YOU EVER GET THE IMPRESSION THAT YOU'RE NOT??

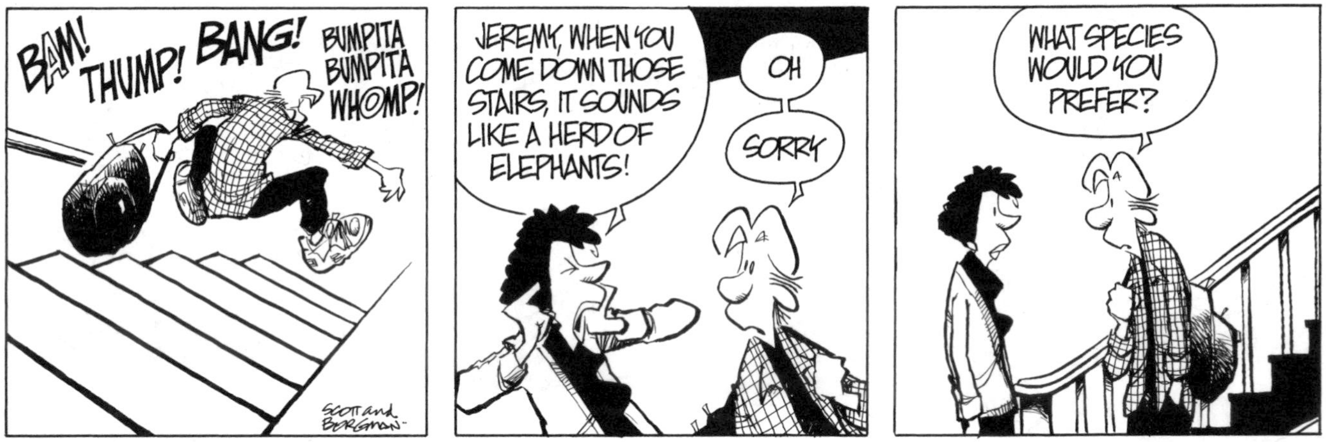
BAM! THUMP! BANG! BUMPITA BUMPITA WHOMP!
JEREMY, WHEN YOU COME DOWN THOSE STAIRS, IT SOUNDS LIKE A HERD OF ELEPHANTS!
OH
SORRY
WHAT SPECIES WOULD YOU PREFER?

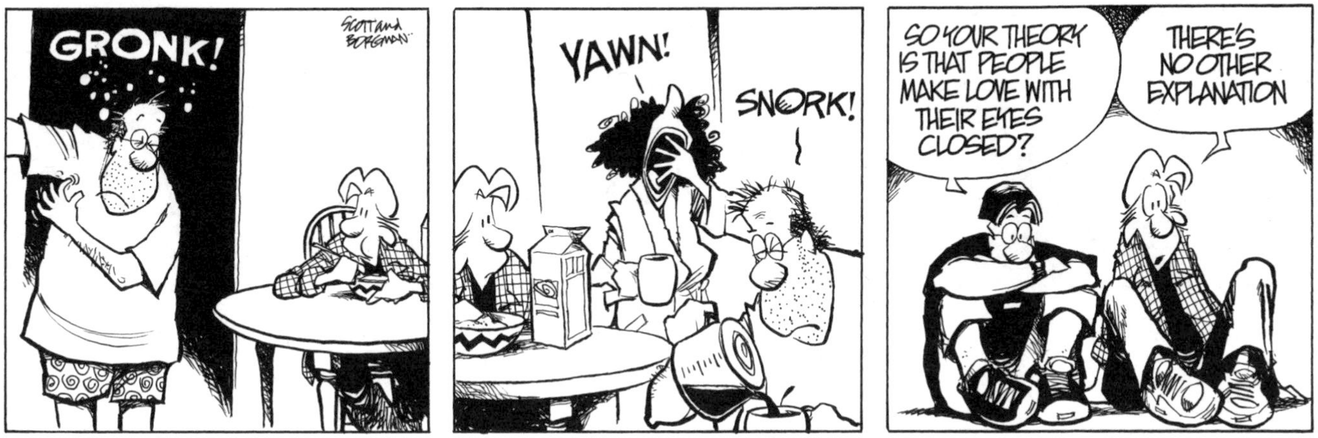
GRONK!
YAWN!
SNORK!
SO YOUR THEORY IS THAT PEOPLE MAKE LOVE WITH THEIR EYES CLOSED?
THERE'S NO OTHER EXPLANATION

Zits®

by JERRY SCOTT and JIM BORGMAN

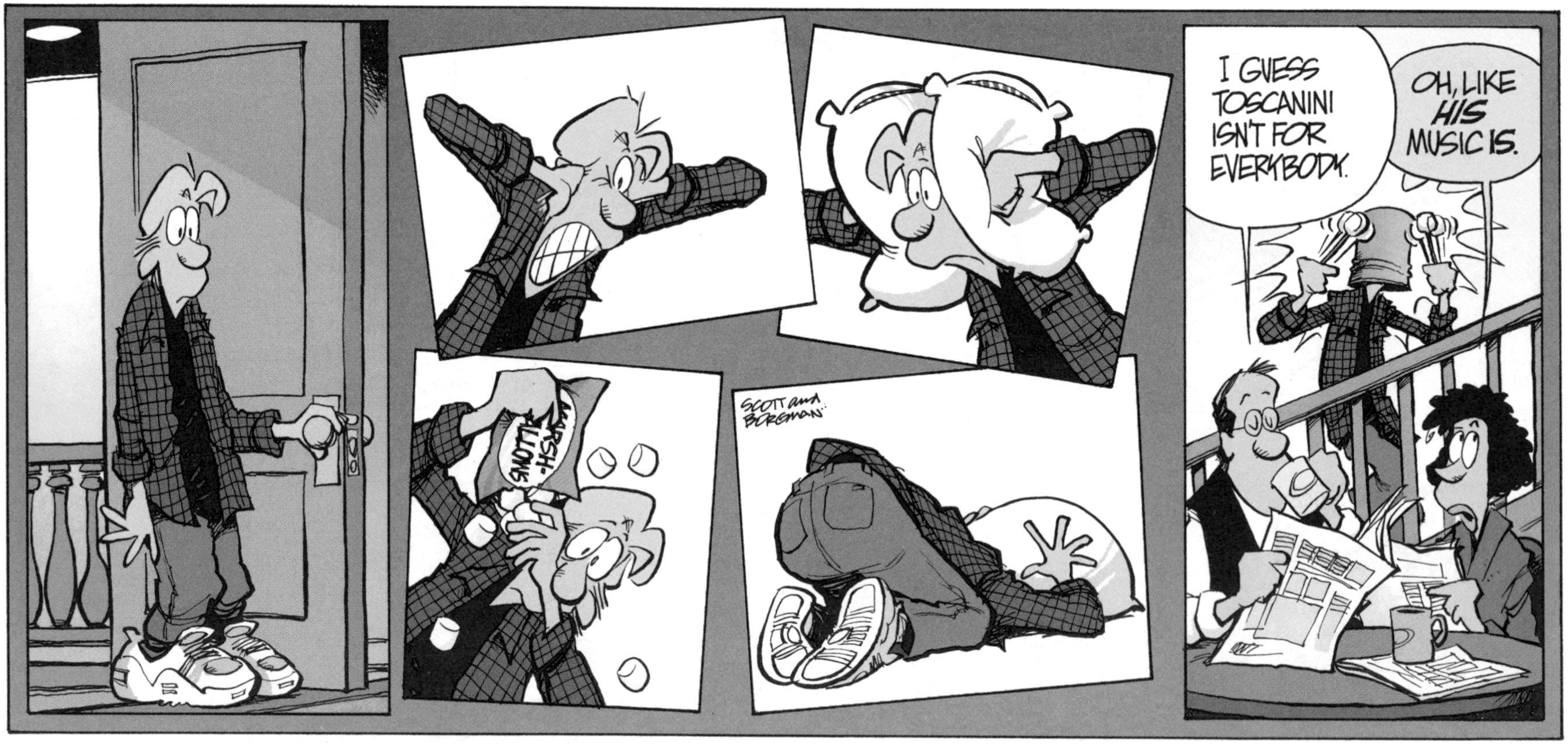
MARSH-MALLOWS
SCOTT and BORGMAN
I GUESS TOSCANINI ISN'T FOR EVERYBODY.
OH, LIKE *HIS* MUSIC IS.

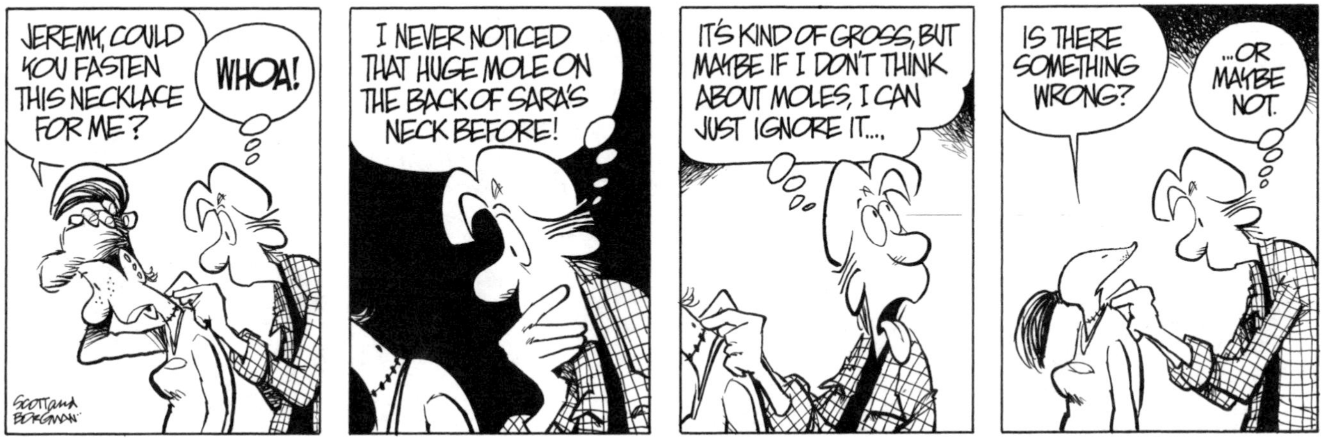
JEREMY, COULD YOU FASTEN THIS NECKLACE FOR ME?
WHOA!
SCOTT and BORGMAN
I NEVER NOTICED THAT HUGE MOLE ON THE BACK OF SARA'S NECK BEFORE!
IT'S KIND OF GROSS, BUT MAYBE IF I DON'T THINK ABOUT MOLES, I CAN JUST IGNORE IT....
IS THERE SOMETHING WRONG?
...OR MAYBE NOT.

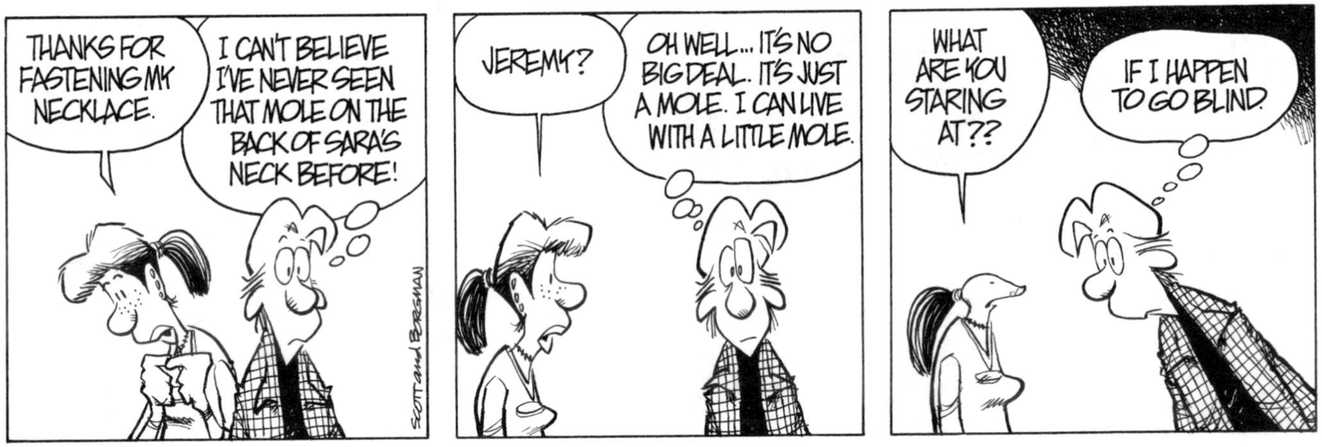
THANKS FOR FASTENING MY NECKLACE.
I CAN'T BELIEVE I'VE NEVER SEEN THAT MOLE ON THE BACK OF SARA'S NECK BEFORE!
SCOTT and BORGMAN
JEREMY?
OH WELL... IT'S NO BIG DEAL. IT'S JUST A MOLE. I CAN LIVE WITH A LITTLE MOLE.
WHAT ARE YOU STARING AT??
IF I HAPPEN TO GO BLIND.

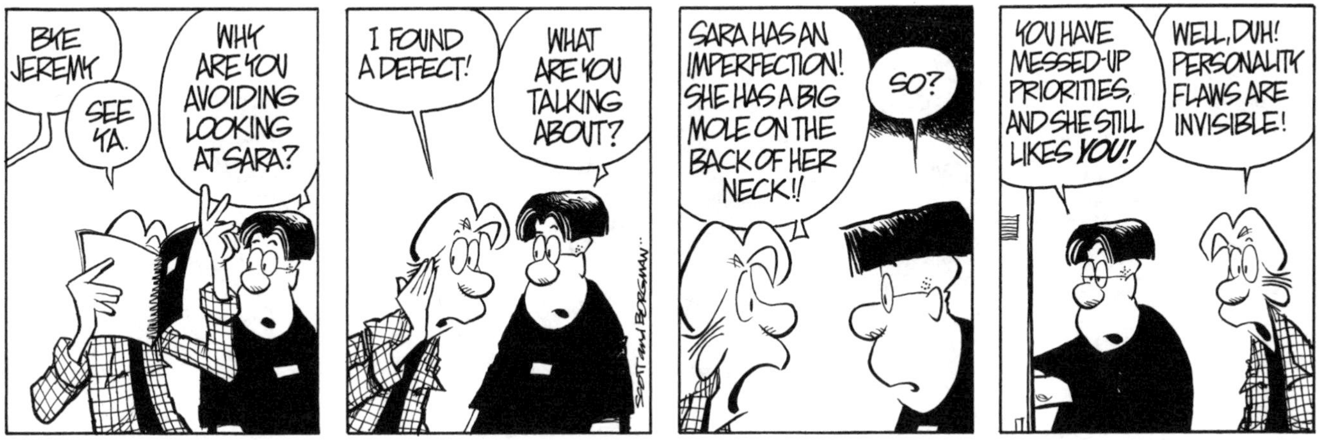
BYE JEREMY
SEE YA.
WHY ARE YOU AVOIDING LOOKING AT SARA?
I FOUND A DEFECT!
WHAT ARE YOU TALKING ABOUT?
SCOTT and BORGMAN
SARA HAS AN IMPERFECTION! SHE HAS A BIG MOLE ON THE BACK OF HER NECK!!
SO?
YOU HAVE MESSED-UP PRIORITIES, AND SHE STILL LIKES YOU!
WELL, DUH! PERSONALITY FLAWS ARE INVISIBLE!

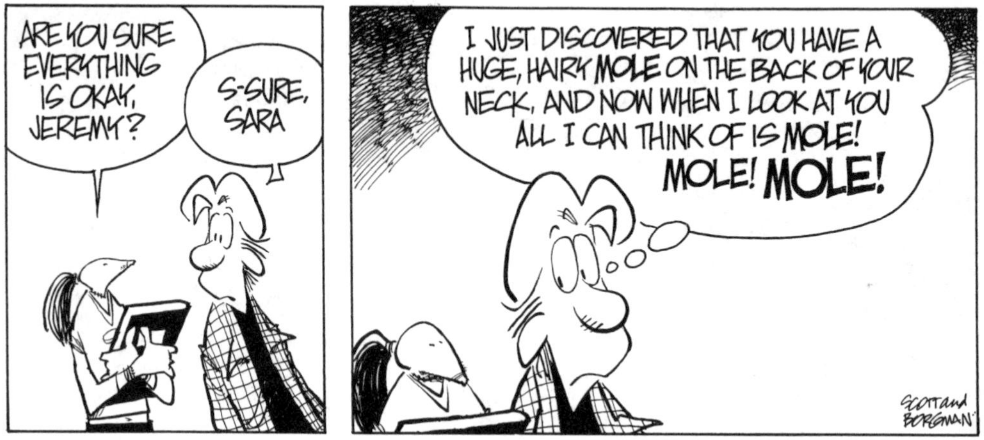
ARE YOU SURE EVERYTHING IS OKAY, JEREMY?
S-SURE, SARA
I JUST DISCOVERED THAT YOU HAVE A HUGE, HAIRY MOLE ON THE BACK OF YOUR NECK, AND NOW WHEN I LOOK AT YOU ALL I CAN THINK OF IS MOLE! MOLE! MOLE!
SCOTT and BORGMAN
BECAUSE YOU'RE ACTING KIND OF--
EVERYTHING IS FINE, OKAY?? FINE!!

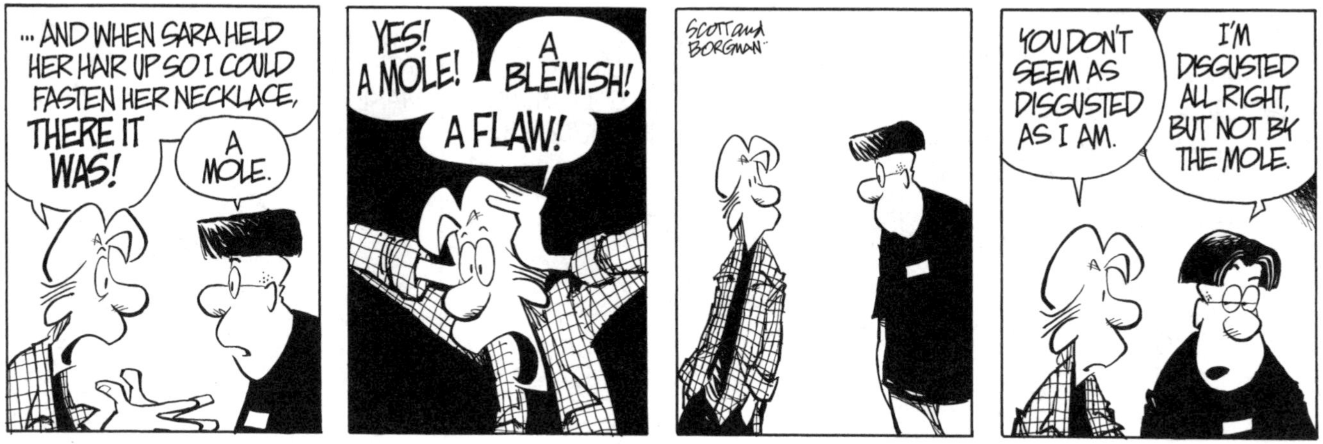
...AND WHEN SARA HELD HER HAIR UP SO I COULD FASTEN HER NECKLACE, THERE IT WAS!
A MOLE.
YES! A MOLE!
A BLEMISH!
A FLAW!
SCOTT and BORGMAN
YOU DON'T SEEM AS DISGUSTED AS I AM.
I'M DISGUSTED ALL RIGHT, BUT NOT BY THE MOLE.

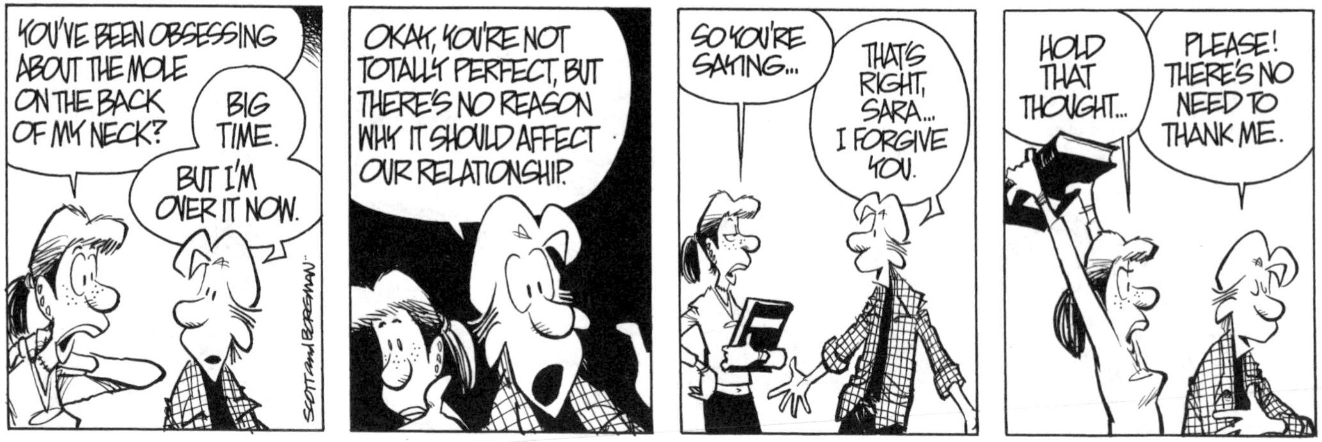
YOU'VE BEEN OBSESSING ABOUT THE MOLE ON THE BACK OF MY NECK?
BIG TIME.
BUT I'M OVER IT NOW.
SCOTT and BORGMAN
OKAY, YOU'RE NOT TOTALLY PERFECT, BUT THERE'S NO REASON WHY IT SHOULD AFFECT OUR RELATIONSHIP.
SO YOU'RE SAYING...
THAT'S RIGHT, SARA... I FORGIVE YOU.
HOLD THAT THOUGHT...
PLEASE! THERE'S NO NEED TO THANK ME.

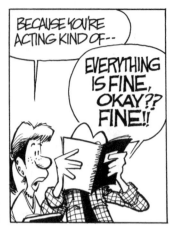

Zits®

by JERRY SCOTT and JIM BORGMAN

I'M NOT SLEEPY. LET'S WATCH THE NEWS.
OKAY.
CLICK!
DRUGS
TEENAGE ALCOHOLISM
AIDS
DRUGS
GUNS
RAPE
MURDER
SUICIDE
TRAFFIC FATALITIES
AIDS
DEPRESSION
DRUGS
GANGS
THIS BETTER HAVE A REALLY GOOD EXPLANATION, OR BE A RE-E-E-ALLY BAD DREAM.
SCOTT and BORGMAN

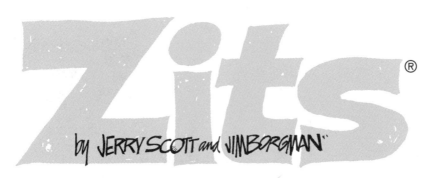

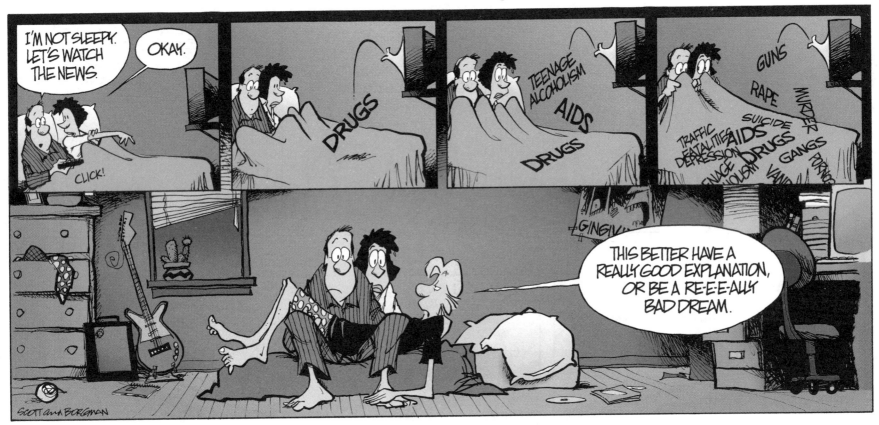

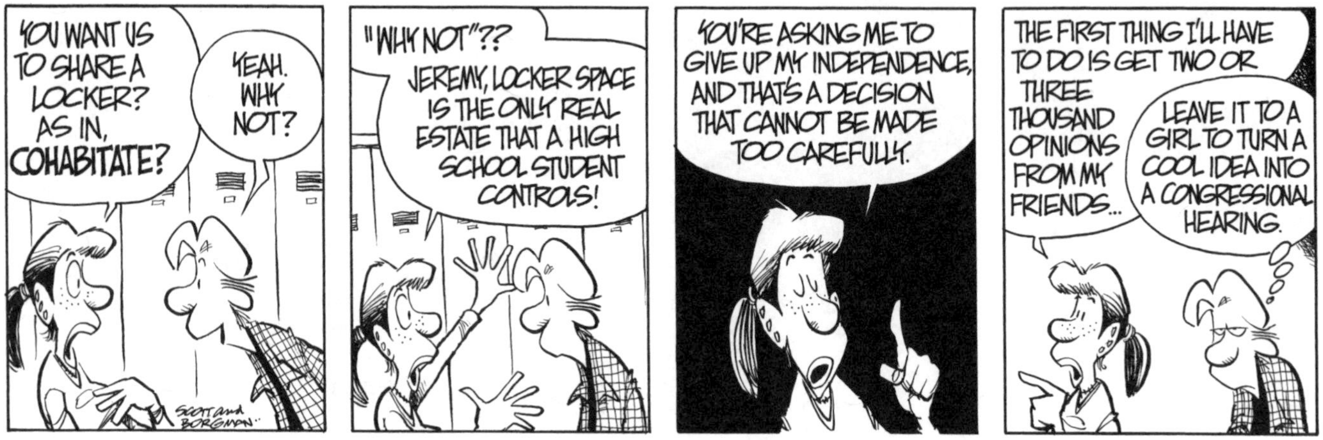
YOU WANT US TO SHARE A LOCKER? AS IN, COHABITATE?
YEAH. WHY NOT?
SCOTT and BORGMAN
"WHY NOT"??
JEREMY, LOCKER SPACE IS THE ONLY REAL ESTATE THAT A HIGH SCHOOL STUDENT CONTROLS!
YOU'RE ASKING ME TO GIVE UP MY INDEPENDENCE, AND THAT'S A DECISION THAT CANNOT BE MADE TOO CAREFULLY.
THE FIRST THING I'LL HAVE TO DO IS GET TWO OR THREE THOUSAND OPINIONS FROM MY FRIENDS...
LEAVE IT TO A GIRL TO TURN A COOL IDEA INTO A CONGRESSIONAL HEARING.

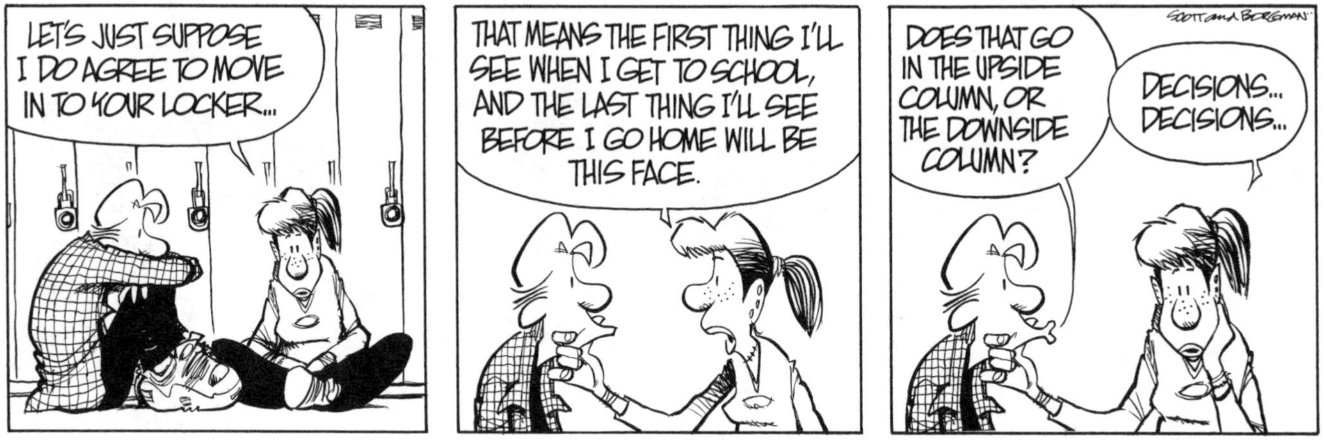
LET'S JUST SUPPOSE I DO AGREE TO MOVE IN TO YOUR LOCKER...
THAT MEANS THE FIRST THING I'LL SEE WHEN I GET TO SCHOOL, AND THE LAST THING I'LL SEE BEFORE I GO HOME WILL BE THIS FACE.
SCOTT and BORGMAN
DOES THAT GO IN THE UPSIDE COLUMN, OR THE DOWNSIDE COLUMN?
DECISIONS... DECISIONS...

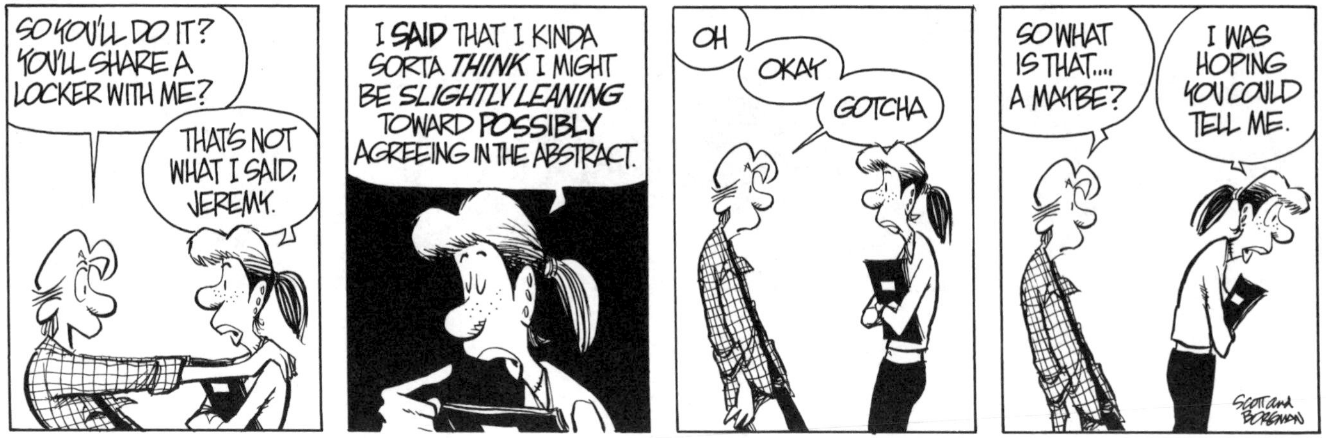
SO YOU'LL DO IT? YOU'LL SHARE A LOCKER WITH ME?
THAT'S NOT WHAT I SAID, JEREMY.
I SAID THAT I KINDA SORTA THINK I MIGHT BE SLIGHTLY LEANING TOWARD POSSIBLY AGREEING IN THE ABSTRACT.
OH
OKAY
GOTCHA
SO WHAT IS THAT.... A MAYBE?
I WAS HOPING YOU COULD TELL ME.
SCOTT and BORGMAN

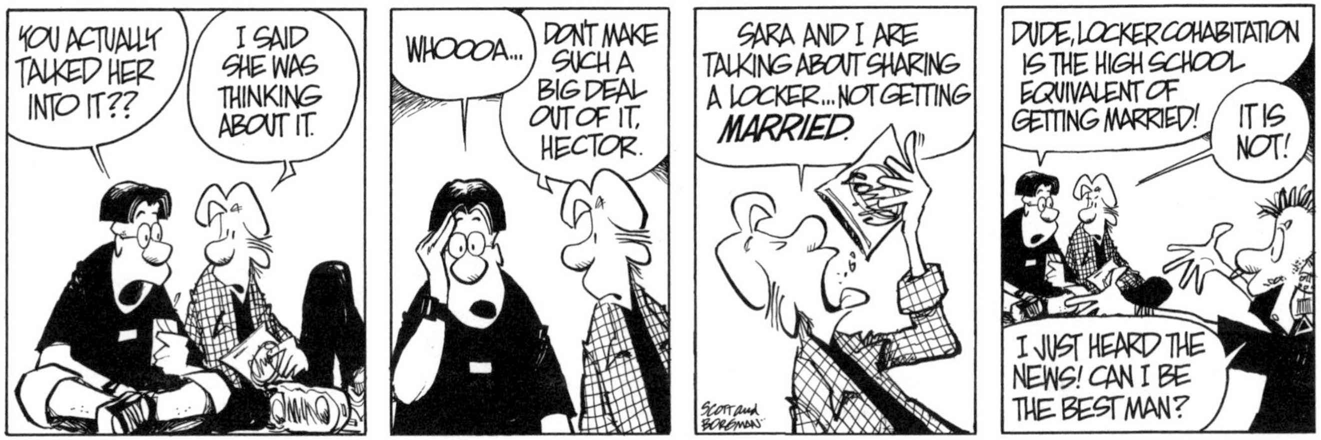
YOU ACTUALLY TALKED HER INTO IT??
I SAID SHE WAS THINKING ABOUT IT.
WHOOOA...
DON'T MAKE SUCH A BIG DEAL OUT OF IT, HECTOR.
SARA AND I ARE TALKING ABOUT SHARING A LOCKER... NOT GETTING MARRIED.
SCOTT and BORGMAN
DUDE, LOCKER COHABITATION IS THE HIGH SCHOOL EQUIVALENT OF GETTING MARRIED!
IT IS NOT!
I JUST HEARD THE NEWS! CAN I BE THE BEST MAN?

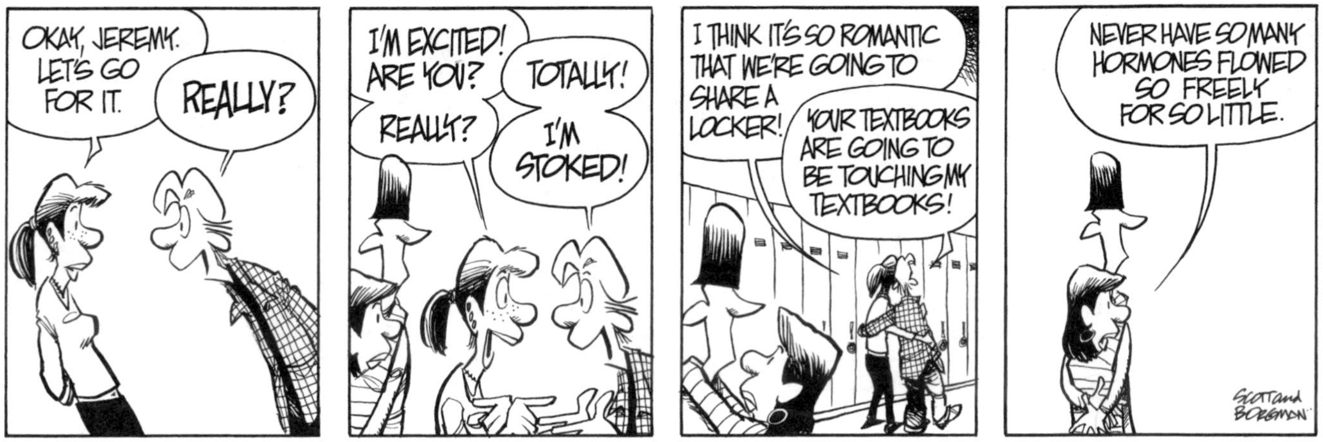
OKAY, JEREMY. LET'S GO FOR IT.
REALLY?
I'M EXCITED! ARE YOU?
TOTALLY!
REALLY?
I'M STOKED!
I THINK IT'S SO ROMANTIC THAT WE'RE GOING TO SHARE A LOCKER!
YOUR TEXTBOOKS ARE GOING TO BE TOUCHING MY TEXTBOOKS!
NEVER HAVE SO MANY HORMONES FLOWED SO FREELY FOR SO LITTLE.
SCOTT and BORGMAN

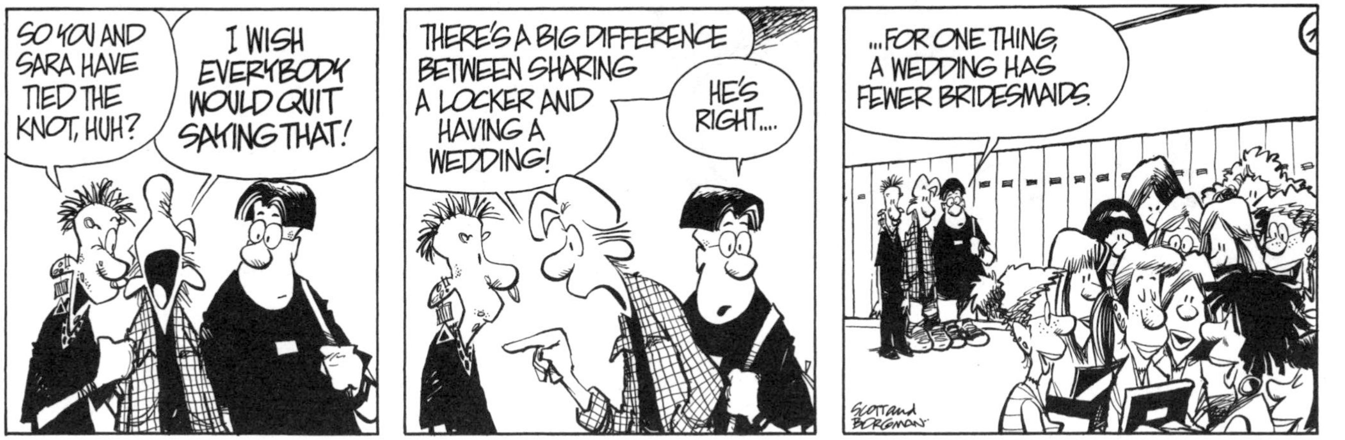
SO YOU AND SARA HAVE TIED THE KNOT, HUH?
I WISH EVERYBODY WOULD QUIT SAYING THAT!
THERE'S A BIG DIFFERENCE BETWEEN SHARING A LOCKER AND HAVING A WEDDING!
HE'S RIGHT....
...FOR ONE THING, A WEDDING HAS FEWER BRIDESMAIDS.
SCOTT and BORGMAN

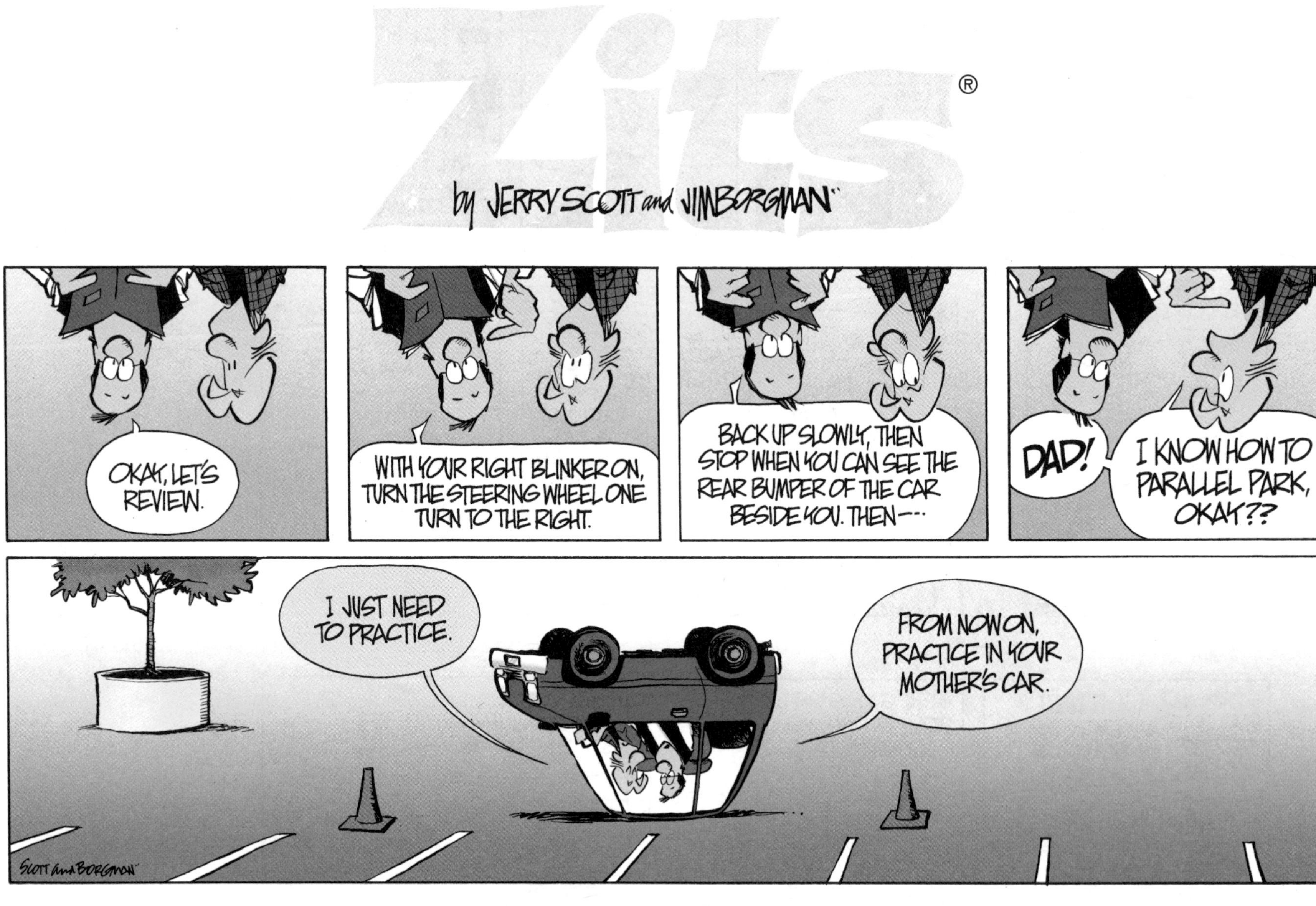
Zits®
by JERRY SCOTT and JIM BORGMAN
OKAY, LET'S REVIEW.
WITH YOUR RIGHT BLINKER ON, TURN THE STEERING WHEEL ONE TURN TO THE RIGHT.
BACK UP SLOWLY, THEN STOP WHEN YOU CAN SEE THE REAR BUMPER OF THE CAR BESIDE YOU. THEN---
DAD!
I KNOW HOW TO PARALLEL PARK, OKAY??
I JUST NEED TO PRACTICE.
FROM NOW ON, PRACTICE IN YOUR MOTHER'S CAR.
SCOTT AND BORGMAN

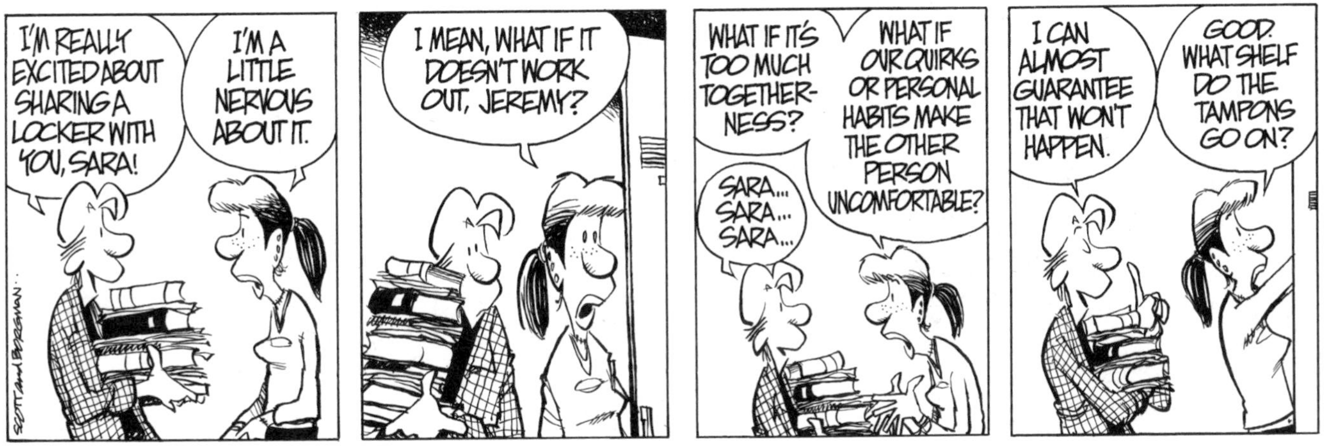
I'M REALLY EXCITED ABOUT SHARING A LOCKER WITH YOU, SARA!
I'M A LITTLE NERVOUS ABOUT IT.
I MEAN, WHAT IF IT DOESN'T WORK OUT, JEREMY?
WHAT IF IT'S TOO MUCH TOGETHER-NESS?
WHAT IF OUR QUIRKS OR PERSONAL HABITS MAKE THE OTHER PERSON UNCOMFORTABLE?
SARA... SARA... SARA...
I CAN ALMOST GUARANTEE THAT WON'T HAPPEN.
GOOD. WHAT SHELF DO THE TAMPONS GO ON?

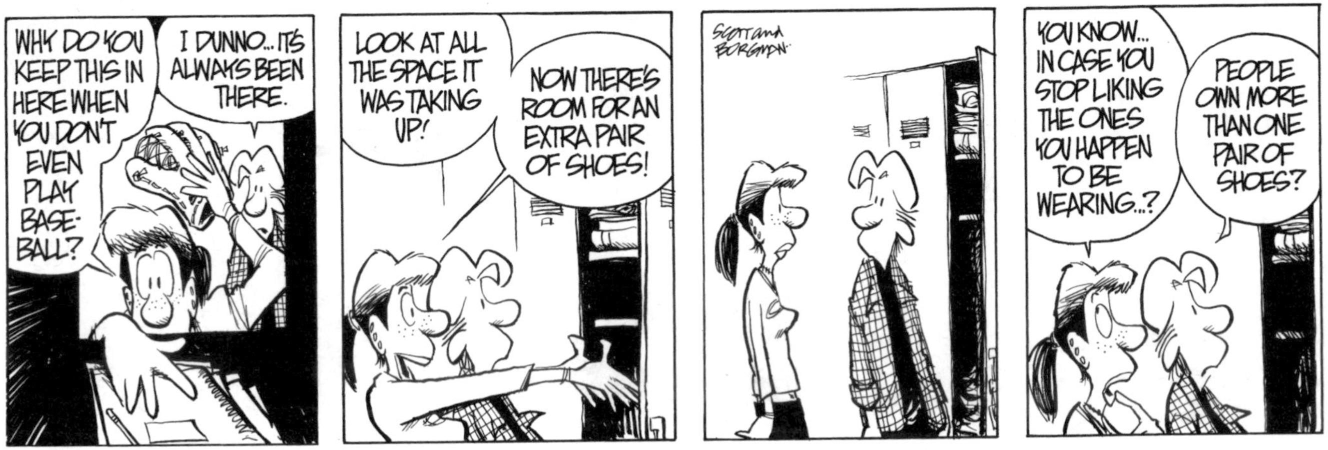
WHY DO YOU KEEP THIS IN HERE WHEN YOU DON'T EVEN PLAY BASE-BALL?
I DUNNO... IT'S ALWAYS BEEN THERE.
LOOK AT ALL THE SPACE IT WAS TAKING UP!
NOW THERE'S ROOM FOR AN EXTRA PAIR OF SHOES!
YOU KNOW... IN CASE YOU STOP LIKING THE ONES YOU HAPPEN TO BE WEARING..?
PEOPLE OWN MORE THAN ONE PAIR OF SHOES?

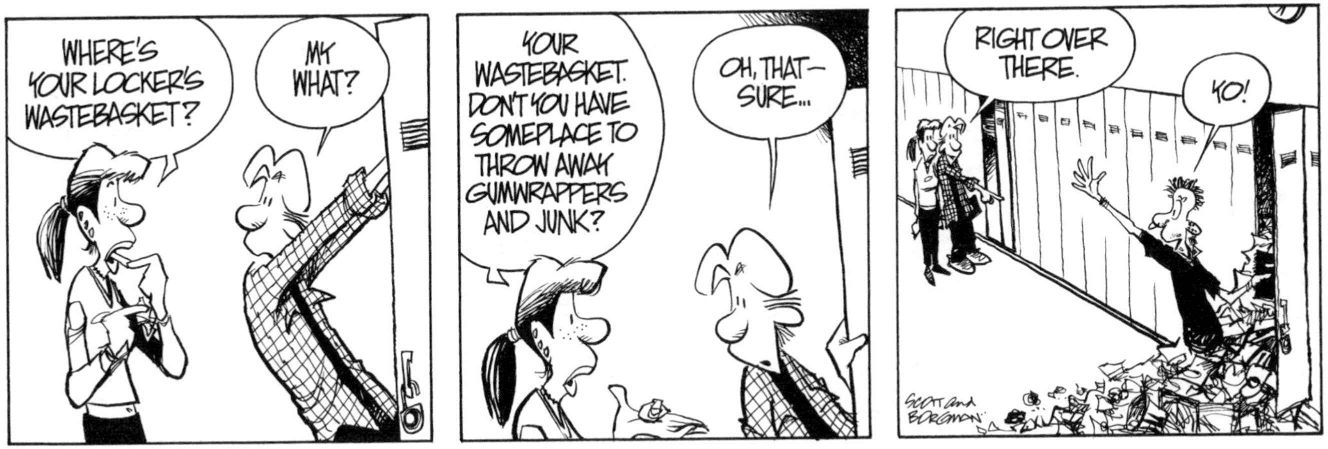
WHERE'S YOUR LOCKER'S WASTEBASKET?
MY WHAT?
YOUR WASTEBASKET. DON'T YOU HAVE SOMEPLACE TO THROW AWAY GUMWRAPPERS AND JUNK?
OH, THAT-SURE...
RIGHT OVER THERE.
YO!

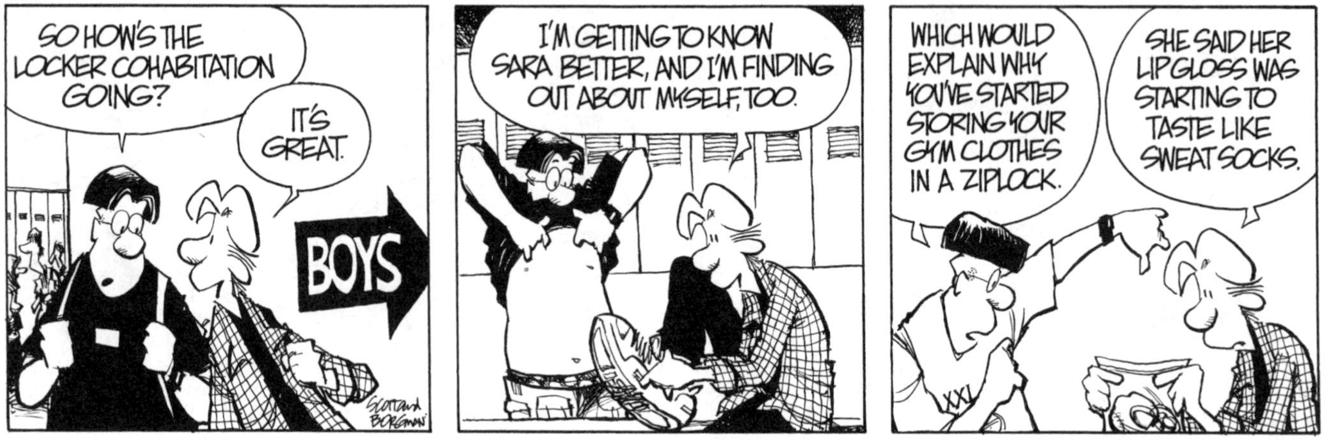
SO HOW'S THE LOCKER COHABITATION GOING?
IT'S GREAT.
BOYS
I'M GETTING TO KNOW SARA BETTER, AND I'M FINDING OUT ABOUT MYSELF, TOO.
WHICH WOULD EXPLAIN WHY YOU'VE STARTED STORING YOUR GYM CLOTHES IN A ZIPLOCK.
SHE SAID HER LIP GLOSS WAS STARTING TO TASTE LIKE SWEAT SOCKS.
XXL
SCOTT AND BORGMAN

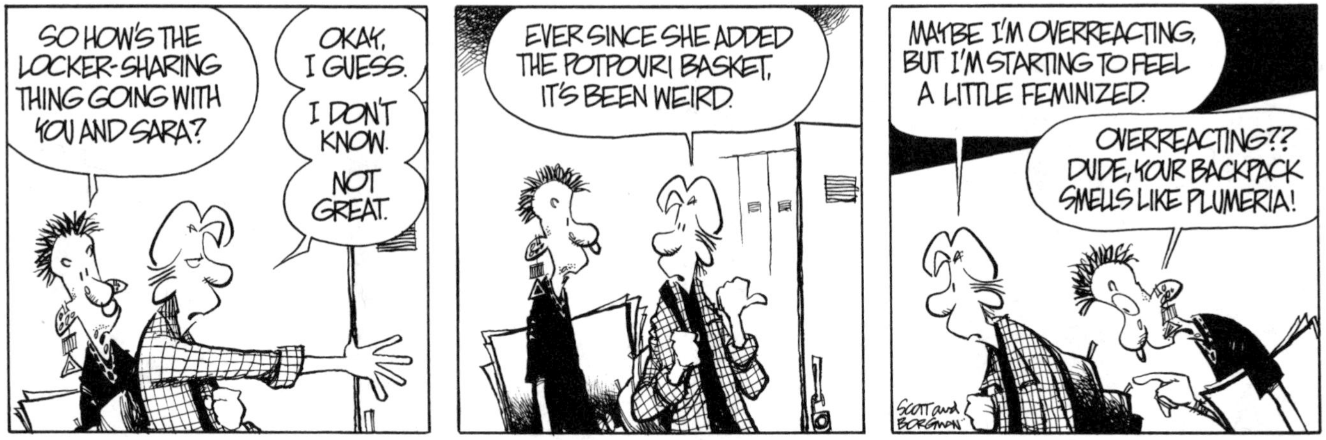
SO HOW'S THE LOCKER-SHARING THING GOING WITH YOU AND SARA?
OKAY, I GUESS.
I DON'T KNOW.
NOT GREAT.
EVER SINCE SHE ADDED THE POTPOURRI BASKET, IT'S BEEN WEIRD.
MAYBE I'M OVERREACTING, BUT I'M STARTING TO FEEL A LITTLE FEMINIZED.
OVERREACTING?? DUDE, YOUR BACKPACK SMELLS LIKE PLUMERIA!
SCOTT AND BORGMAN

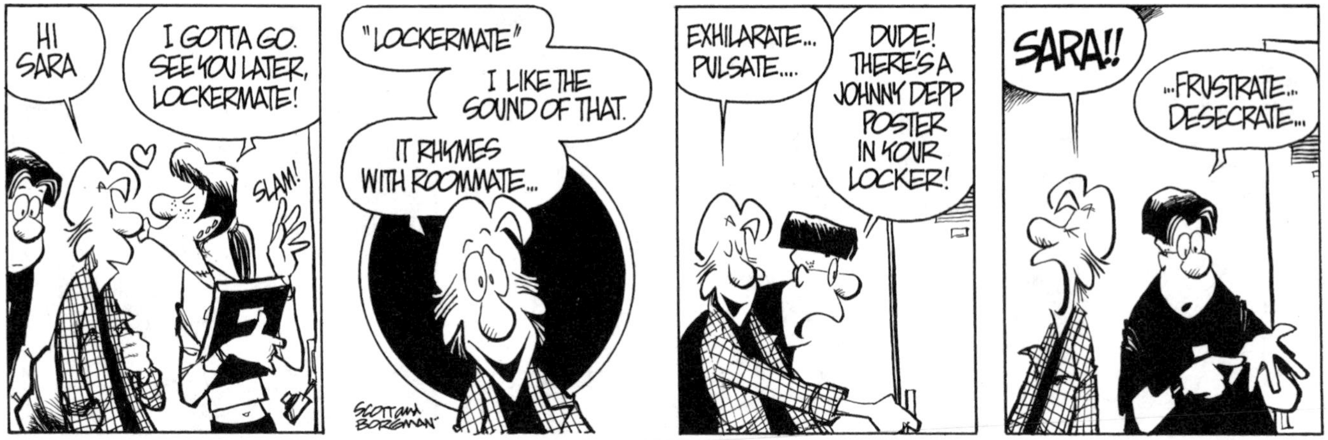
HI SARA
I GOTTA GO. SEE YOU LATER, LOCKERMATE!
SLAM!
"LOCKERMATE"
I LIKE THE SOUND OF THAT.
IT RHYMES WITH ROOMMATE...
SCOTT AND BORGMAN
EXHILARATE... PULSATE....
DUDE! THERE'S A JOHNNY DEPP POSTER IN YOUR LOCKER!
SARA!!
...FRUSTRATE... DESECRATE...

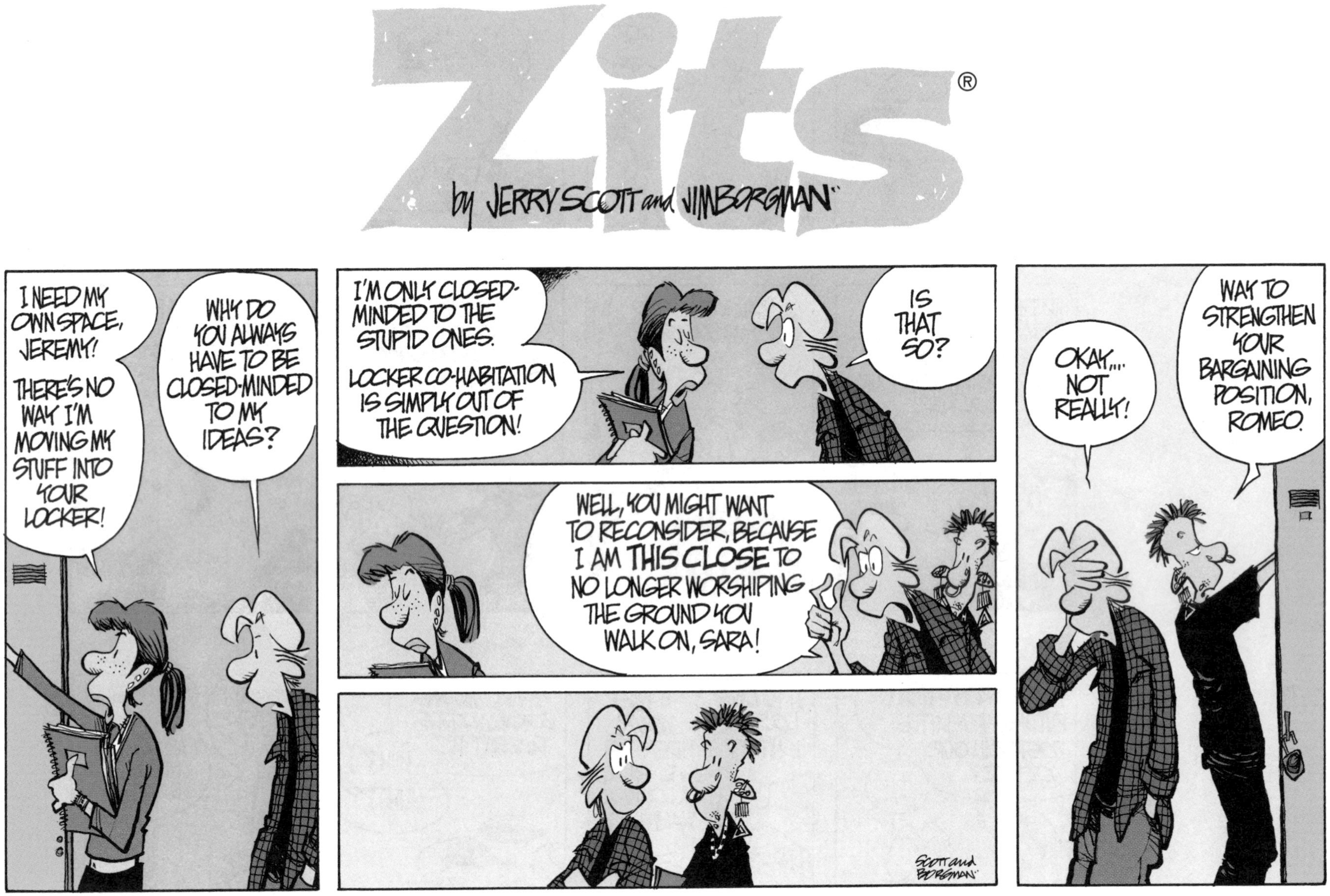

Zits®
by JERRY SCOTT and JIM BORGMAN
I NEED MY OWN SPACE, JEREMY!
THERE'S NO WAY I'M MOVING MY STUFF INTO YOUR LOCKER!
WHY DO YOU ALWAYS HAVE TO BE CLOSED-MINDED TO MY IDEAS?
I'M ONLY CLOSED-MINDED TO THE STUPID ONES.
LOCKER CO-HABITATION IS SIMPLY OUT OF THE QUESTION!
IS THAT SO?
WELL, YOU MIGHT WANT TO RECONSIDER, BECAUSE I AM THIS CLOSE TO NO LONGER WORSHIPING THE GROUND YOU WALK ON, SARA!
OKAY,... NOT REALLY!
WAY TO STRENGTHEN YOUR BARGAINING POSITION, ROMEO.
SCOTT and BORGMAN

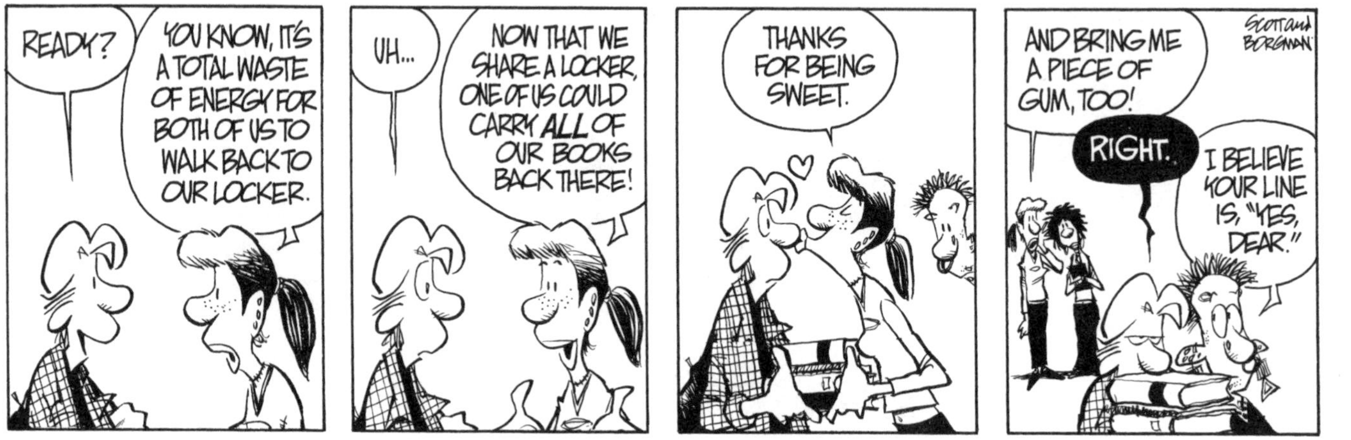
READY?
YOU KNOW, IT'S A TOTAL WASTE OF ENERGY FOR BOTH OF US TO WALK BACK TO OUR LOCKER.
UH...
NOW THAT WE SHARE A LOCKER, ONE OF US COULD CARRY ALL OF OUR BOOKS BACK THERE!
THANKS FOR BEING SWEET.
AND BRING ME A PIECE OF GUM, TOO!
RIGHT.
I BELIEVE YOUR LINE IS, "YES, DEAR."

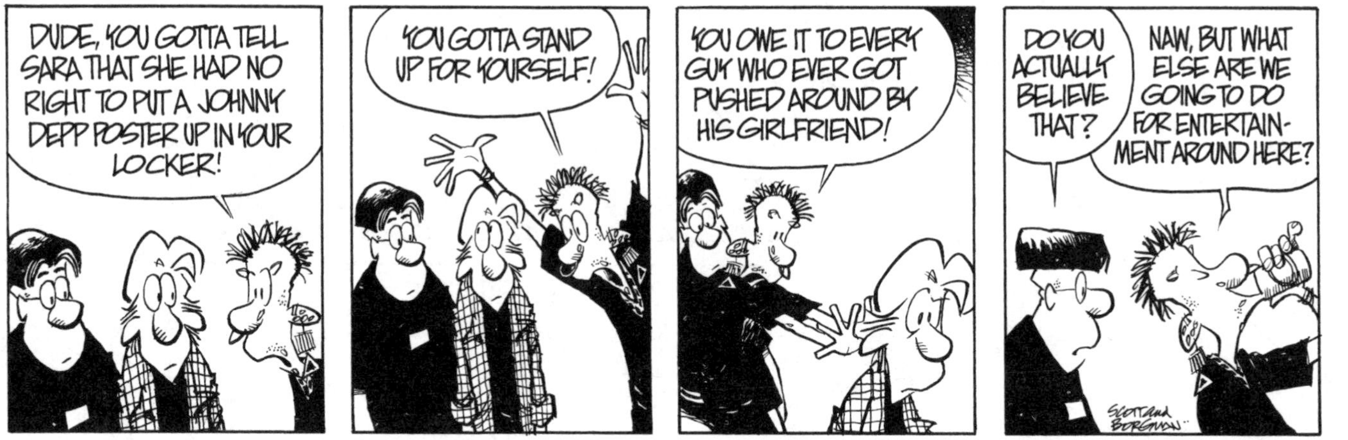
DUDE, YOU GOTTA TELL SARA THAT SHE HAD NO RIGHT TO PUT A JOHNNY DEPP POSTER UP IN YOUR LOCKER!
YOU GOTTA STAND UP FOR YOURSELF!
YOU OWE IT TO EVERY GUY WHO EVER GOT PUSHED AROUND BY HIS GIRLFRIEND!
DO YOU ACTUALLY BELIEVE THAT?
NAW, BUT WHAT ELSE ARE WE GOING TO DO FOR ENTERTAINMENT AROUND HERE?

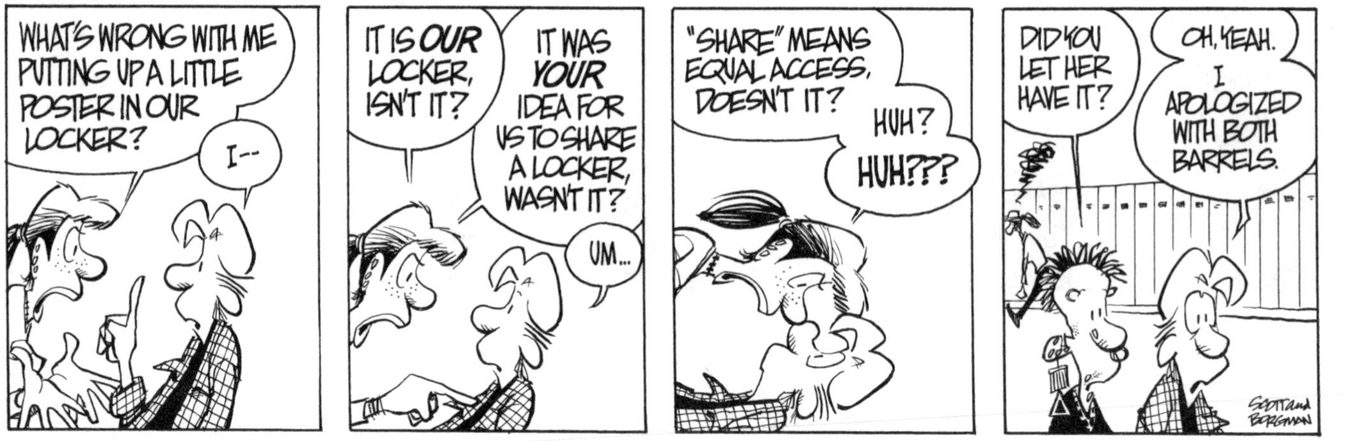
WHAT'S WRONG WITH ME PUTTING UP A LITTLE POSTER IN OUR LOCKER?
I--
IT IS OUR LOCKER, ISN'T IT?
IT WAS YOUR IDEA FOR US TO SHARE A LOCKER, WASN'T IT?
UM...
"SHARE" MEANS EQUAL ACCESS, DOESN'T IT?
HUH?
HUH???
DID YOU LET HER HAVE IT?
OH, YEAH.
I APOLOGIZED WITH BOTH BARRELS.

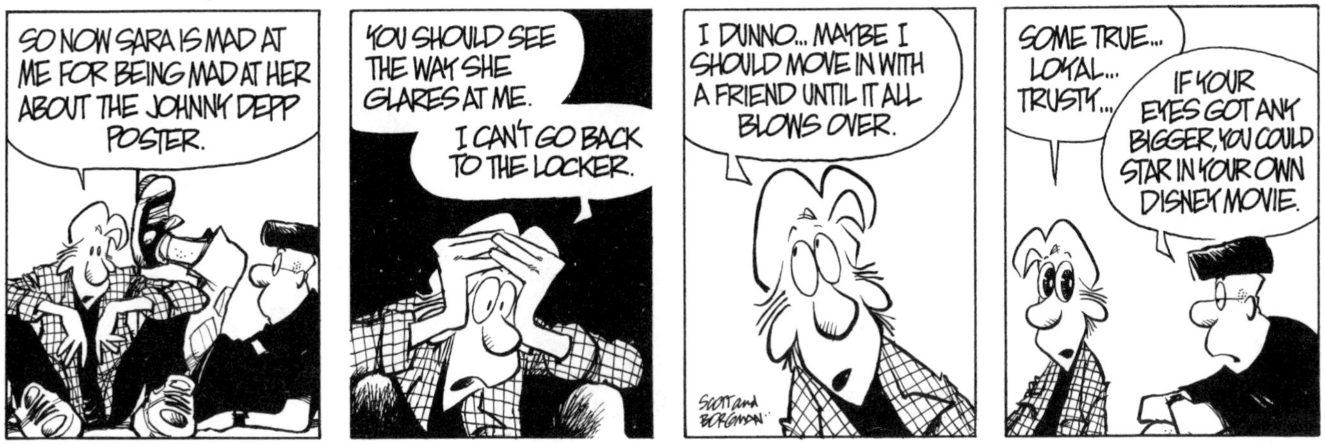
SO NOW SARA IS MAD AT ME FOR BEING MAD AT HER ABOUT THE JOHNNY DEPP POSTER.
YOU SHOULD SEE THE WAY SHE GLARES AT ME.
I CAN'T GO BACK TO THE LOCKER.
I DUNNO... MAYBE I SHOULD MOVE IN WITH A FRIEND UNTIL IT ALL BLOWS OVER.
SCOTT and BORGMAN
SOME TRUE... LOYAL... TRUSTY...
IF YOUR EYES GOT ANY BIGGER, YOU COULD STAR IN YOUR OWN DISNEY MOVIE.

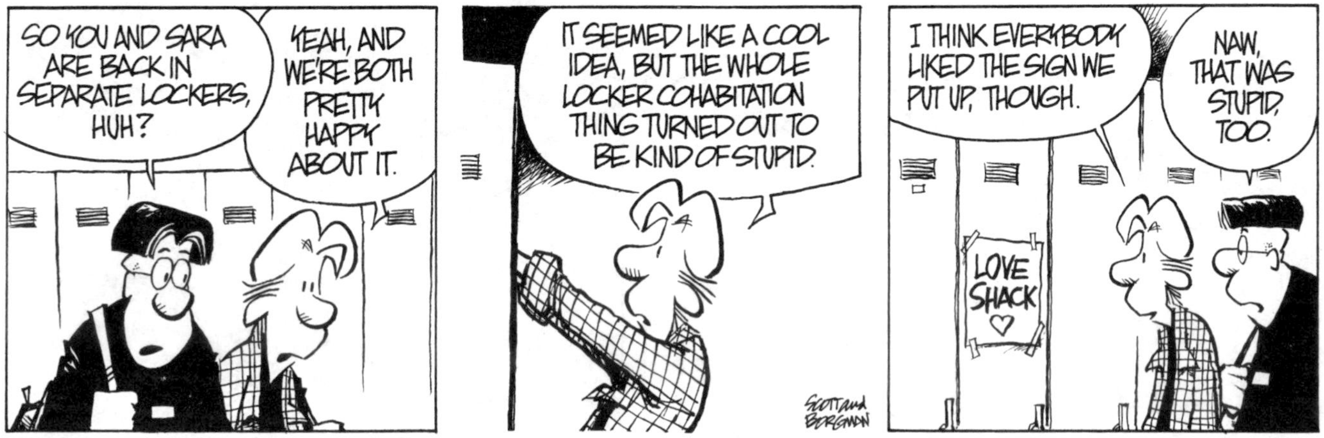
SO YOU AND SARA ARE BACK IN SEPARATE LOCKERS, HUH?
YEAH, AND WE'RE BOTH PRETTY HAPPY ABOUT IT.
IT SEEMED LIKE A COOL IDEA, BUT THE WHOLE LOCKER COHABITATION THING TURNED OUT TO BE KIND OF STUPID.
SCOTT and BORGMAN
I THINK EVERYBODY LIKED THE SIGN WE PUT UP, THOUGH.
NAW, THAT WAS STUPID, TOO.
LOVE SHACK

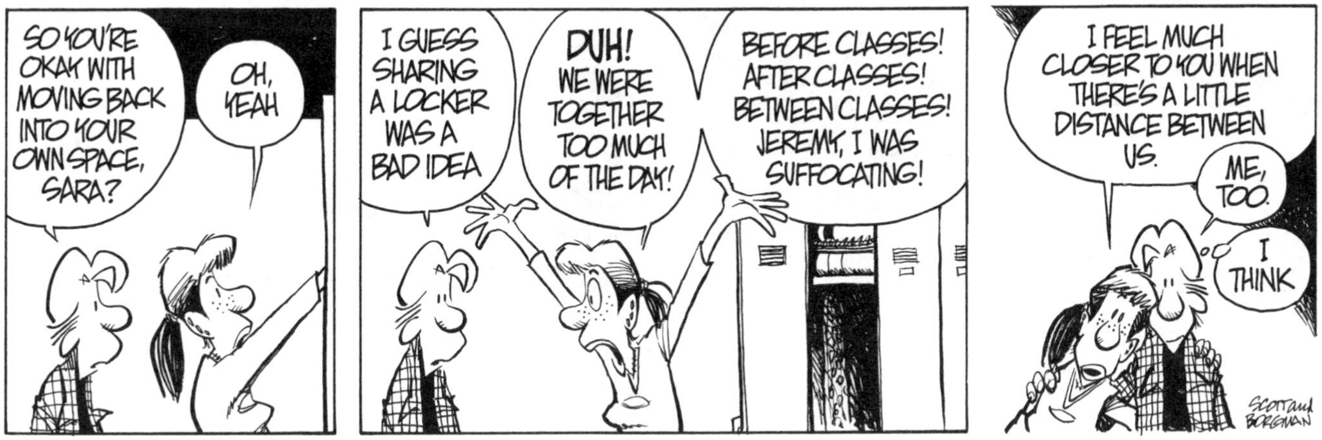
SO YOU'RE OKAY WITH MOVING BACK INTO YOUR OWN SPACE, SARA?
OH, YEAH
I GUESS SHARING A LOCKER WAS A BAD IDEA
DUH! WE WERE TOGETHER TOO MUCH OF THE DAY!
BEFORE CLASSES! AFTER CLASSES! BETWEEN CLASSES! JEREMY, I WAS SUFFOCATING!
I FEEL MUCH CLOSER TO YOU WHEN THERE'S A LITTLE DISTANCE BETWEEN US.
ME, TOO.
I THINK
SCOTT and BORGMAN

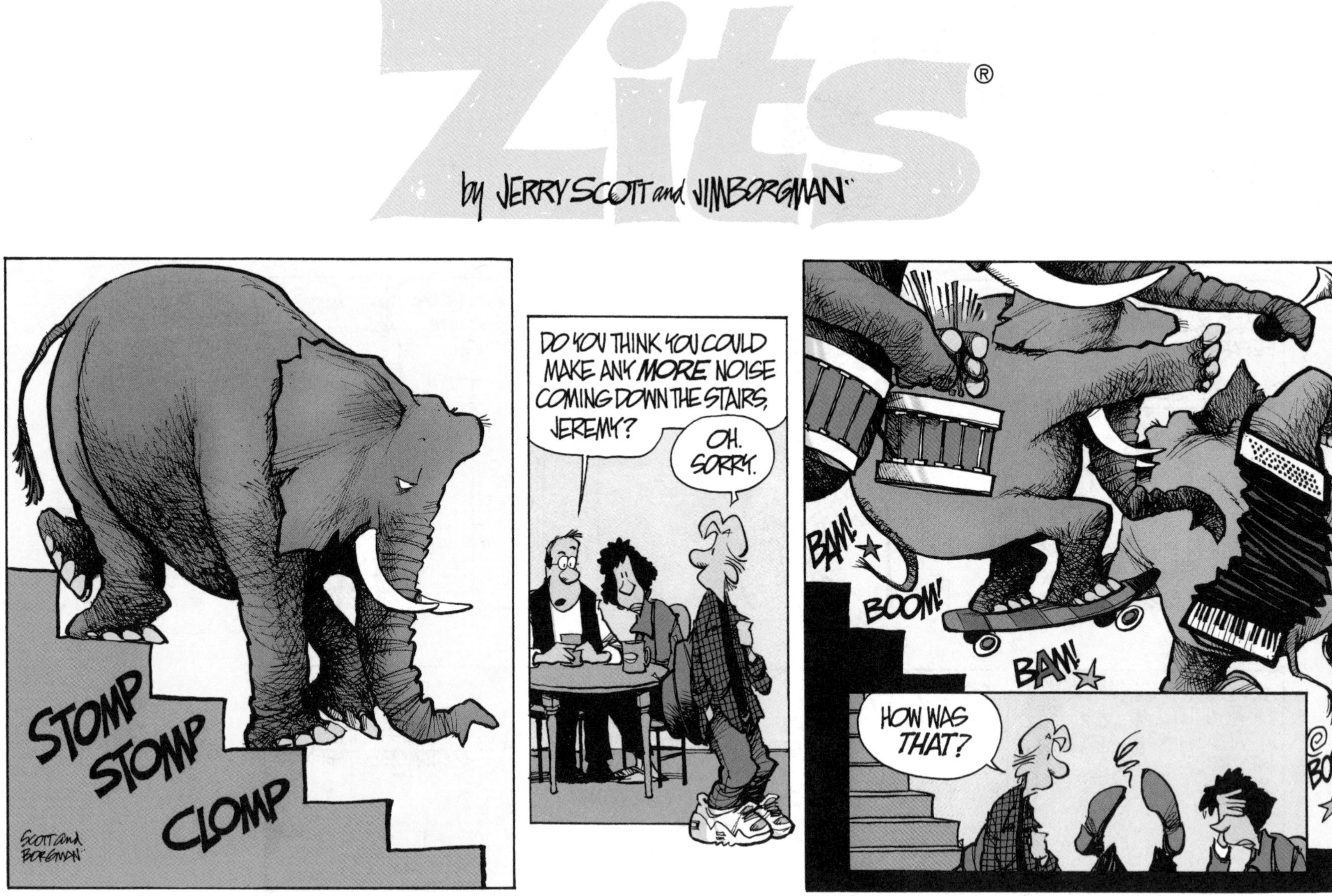
Zits®
by JERRY SCOTT and JIM BORGMAN
STOMP
STOMP
CLOMP
SCOTT and BORGMAN
DO YOU THINK YOU COULD MAKE ANY MORE NOISE COMING DOWN THE STAIRS, JEREMY?
OH. SORRY.
BAM!
BOOM!
BAM!
HOW WAS THAT?

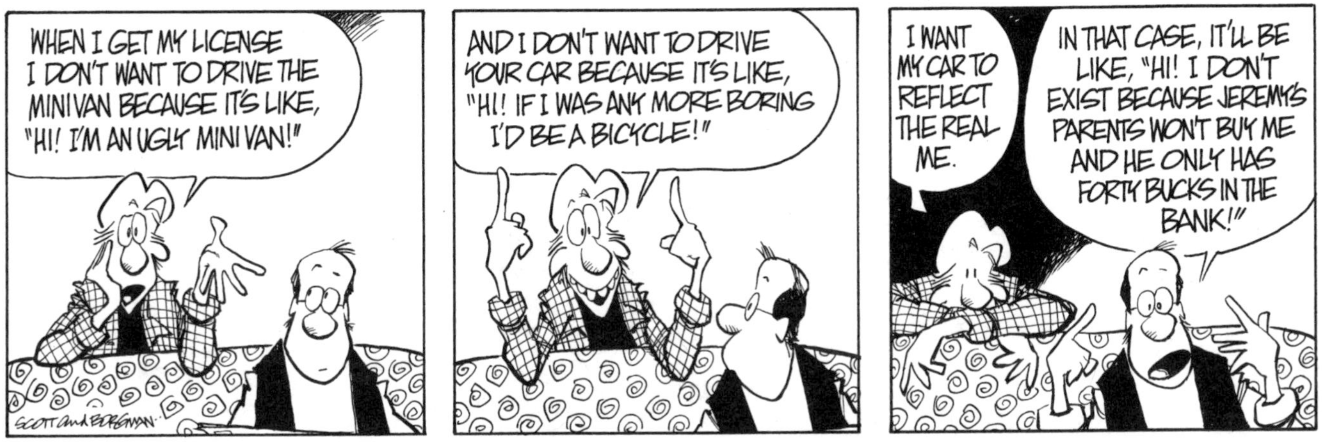
WHEN I GET MY LICENSE I DON'T WANT TO DRIVE THE MINIVAN BECAUSE IT'S LIKE, "HI! I'M AN UGLY MINIVAN!"
SCOTT and BORGMAN
AND I DON'T WANT TO DRIVE YOUR CAR BECAUSE IT'S LIKE, "HI! IF I WAS ANY MORE BORING I'D BE A BICYCLE!"
I WANT MY CAR TO REFLECT THE REAL ME.
IN THAT CASE, IT'LL BE LIKE, "HI! I DON'T EXIST BECAUSE JEREMY'S PARENTS WON'T BUY ME AND HE ONLY HAS FORTY BUCKS IN THE BANK!"

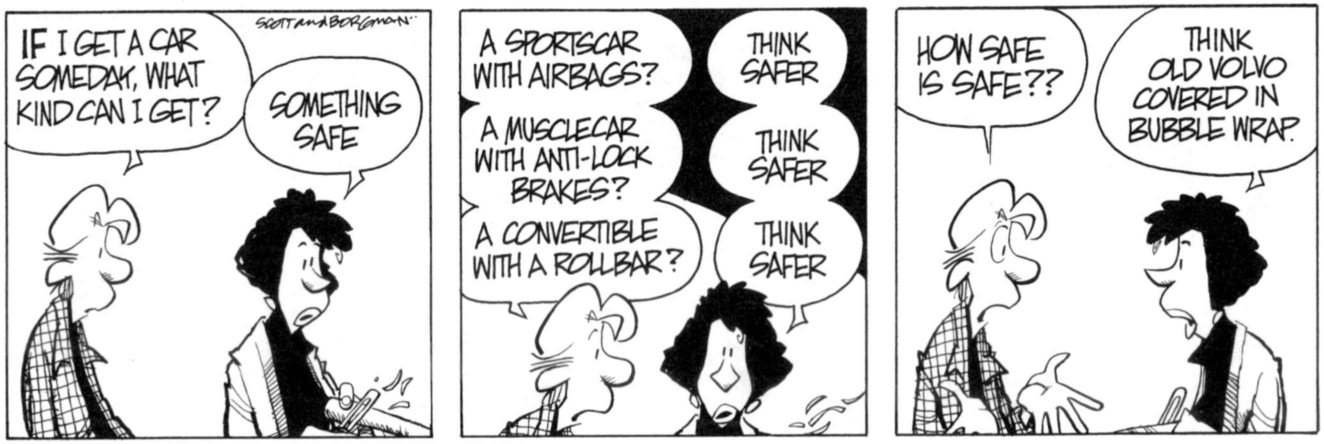
SCOTT and BORGMAN
IF I GET A CAR SOMEDAY, WHAT KIND CAN I GET?
SOMETHING SAFE
A SPORTSCAR WITH AIRBAGS?
THINK SAFER
A MUSCLECAR WITH ANTI-LOCK BRAKES?
THINK SAFER
A CONVERTIBLE WITH A ROLLBAR?
THINK SAFER
HOW SAFE IS SAFE??
THINK OLD VOLVO COVERED IN BUBBLE WRAP.

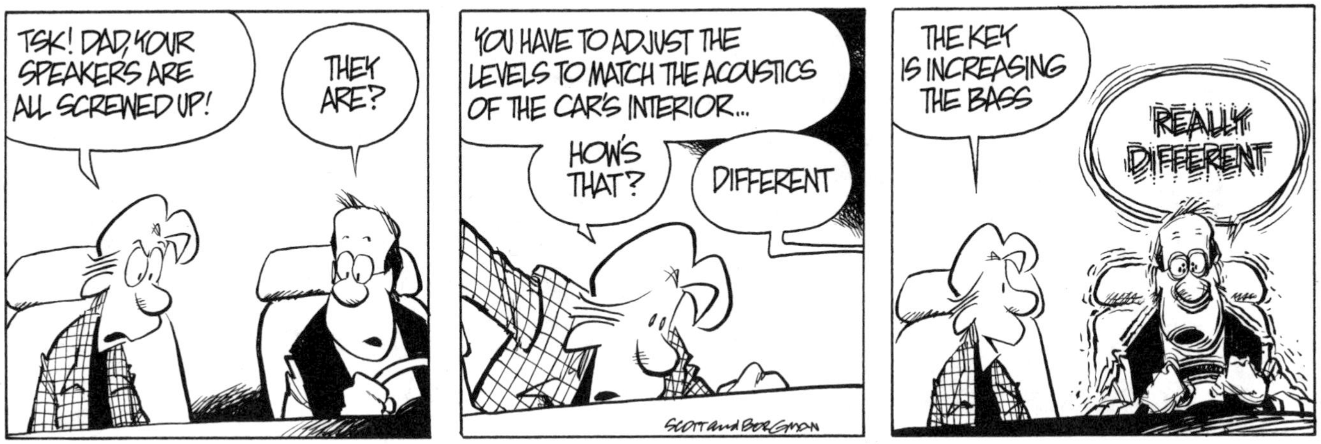
TSK! DAD, YOUR SPEAKERS ARE ALL SCREWED UP!
THEY ARE?
YOU HAVE TO ADJUST THE LEVELS TO MATCH THE ACOUSTICS OF THE CAR'S INTERIOR...
HOW'S THAT?
DIFFERENT
SCOTT and BORGMAN
THE KEY IS INCREASING THE BASS
REALLY DIFFERENT

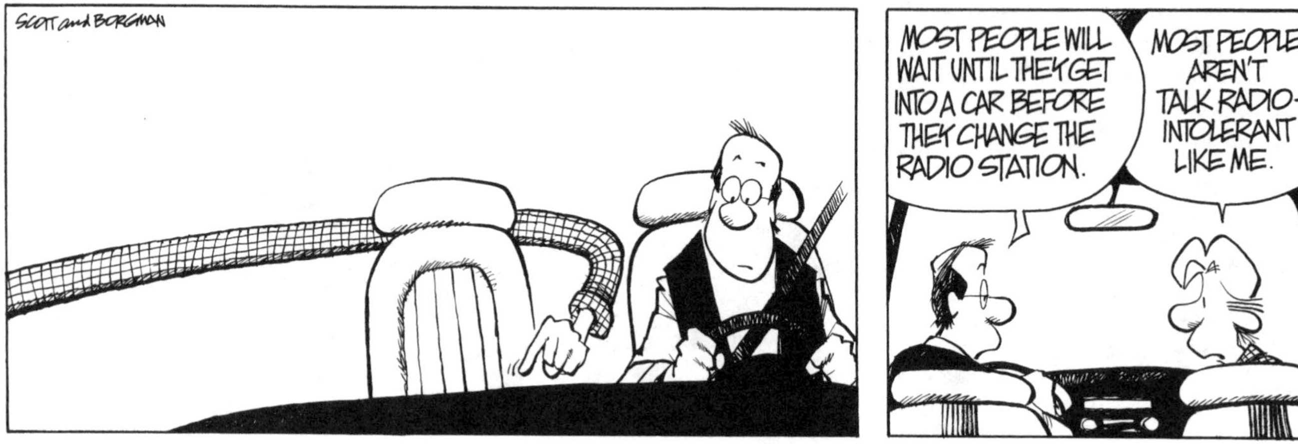
SCOTT and BORGMAN
MOST PEOPLE WILL WAIT UNTIL THEY GET INTO A CAR BEFORE THEY CHANGE THE RADIO STATION.
MOST PEOPLE AREN'T TALK RADIO-INTOLERANT LIKE ME.

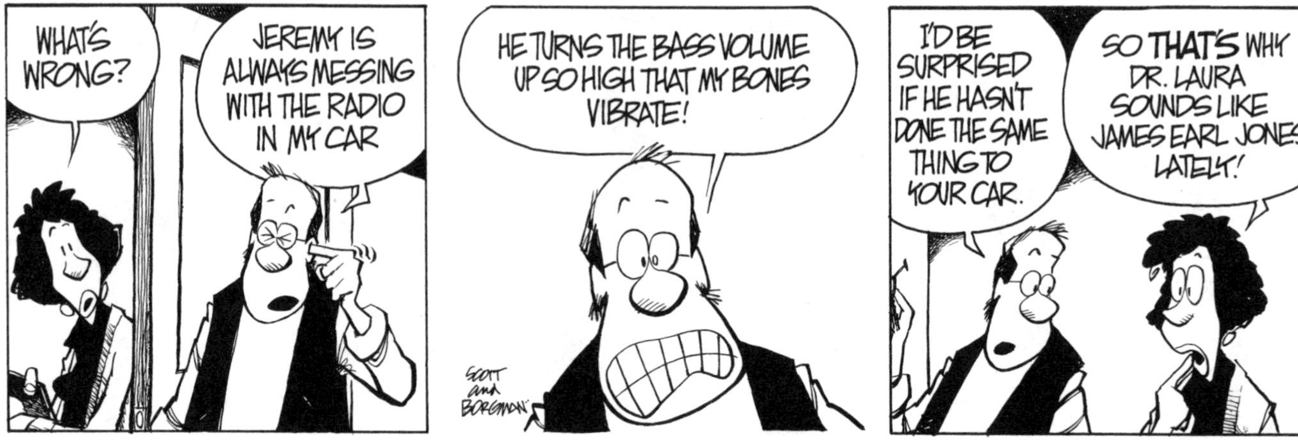
WHAT'S WRONG?
JEREMY IS ALWAYS MESSING WITH THE RADIO IN MY CAR
HE TURNS THE BASS VOLUME UP SO HIGH THAT MY BONES VIBRATE!
SCOTT and BORGMAN
I'D BE SURPRISED IF HE HASN'T DONE THE SAME THING TO YOUR CAR.
SO **THAT'S** WHY DR. LAURA SOUNDS LIKE JAMES EARL JONES LATELY!

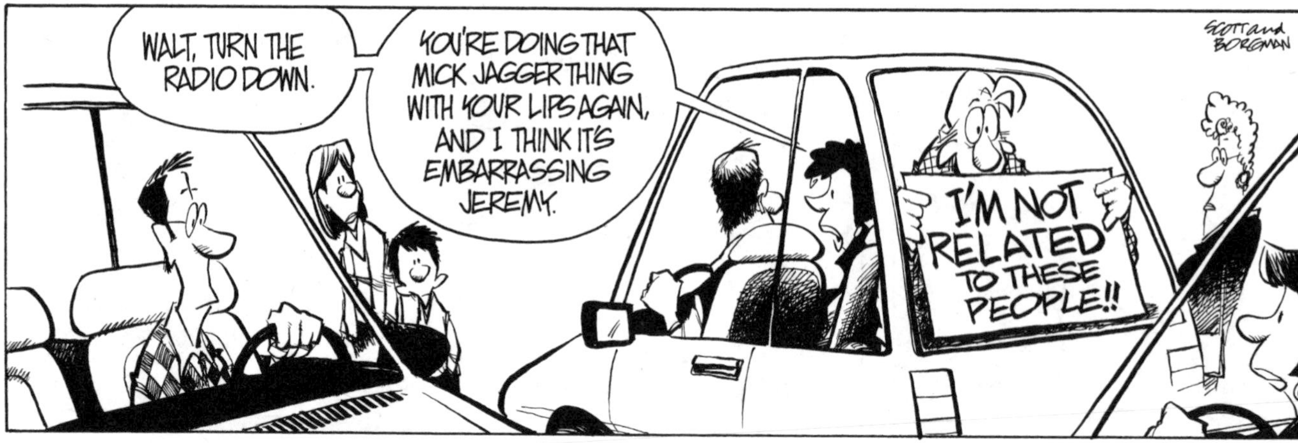
SCOTT and BORGMAN
WALT, TURN THE RADIO DOWN.
YOU'RE DOING THAT MICK JAGGER THING WITH YOUR LIPS AGAIN, AND I THINK IT'S EMBARRASSING JEREMY.
I'M NOT RELATED TO THESE PEOPLE!!

Zits®

by JERRY SCOTT and JIM BORGMAN

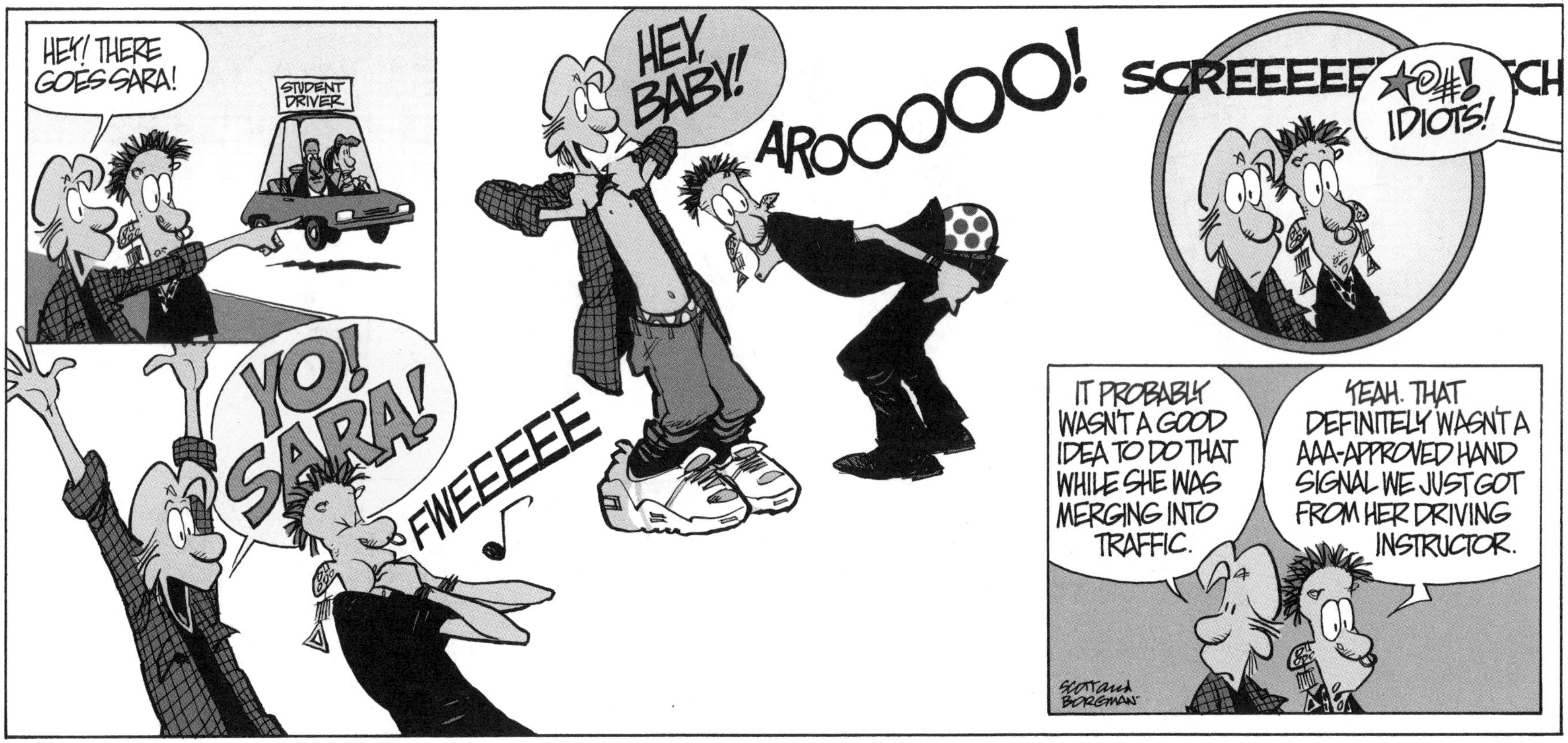

HEY! THERE GOES SARA!
STUDENT DRIVER
YO! SARA!
FWEEEEEE
HEY, BABY!
AROOOOOO!
SCREEEEEE
ECH
★@#! IDIOTS!
IT PROBABLY WASN'T A GOOD IDEA TO DO THAT WHILE SHE WAS MERGING INTO TRAFFIC.
YEAH. THAT DEFINITELY WASN'T A AAA-APPROVED HAND SIGNAL WE JUST GOT FROM HER DRIVING INSTRUCTOR.
SCOTT and BORGMAN

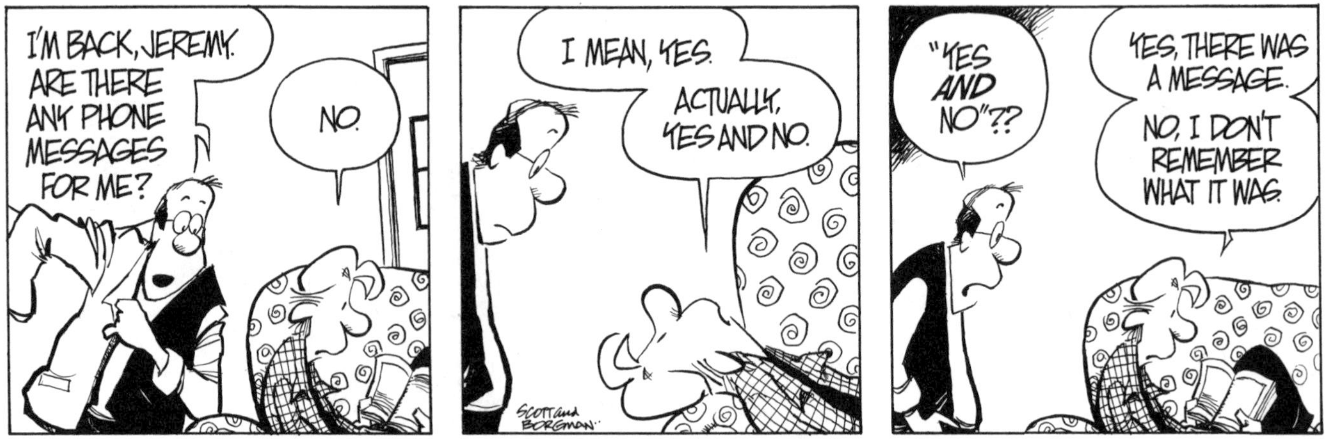
I'M BACK, JEREMY. ARE THERE ANY PHONE MESSAGES FOR ME?
NO.
I MEAN, YES.
ACTUALLY, YES AND NO.
"YES AND NO"??
YES, THERE WAS A MESSAGE.
NO, I DON'T REMEMBER WHAT IT WAS.

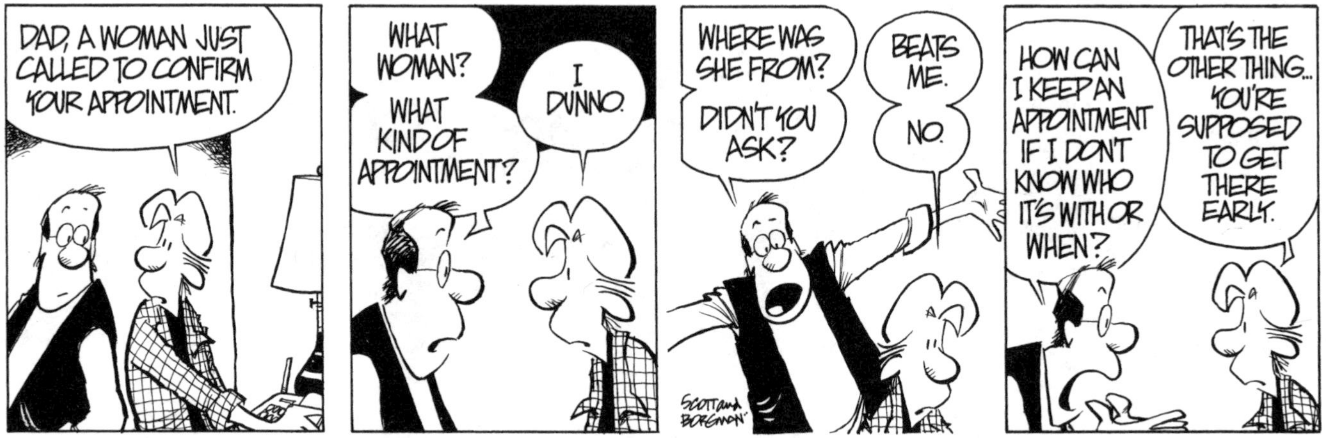
DAD, A WOMAN JUST CALLED TO CONFIRM YOUR APPOINTMENT.
WHAT WOMAN?
WHAT KIND OF APPOINTMENT?
I DUNNO.
WHERE WAS SHE FROM?
DIDN'T YOU ASK?
BEATS ME.
NO.
HOW CAN I KEEP AN APPOINTMENT IF I DON'T KNOW WHO IT'S WITH OR WHEN?
THAT'S THE OTHER THING... YOU'RE SUPPOSED TO GET THERE EARLY.

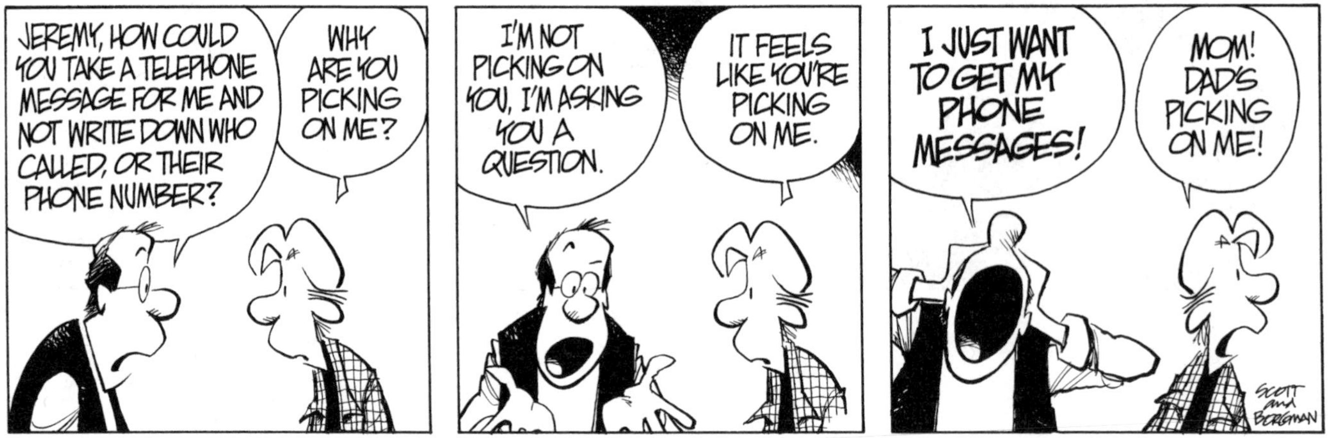
JEREMY, HOW COULD YOU TAKE A TELEPHONE MESSAGE FOR ME AND NOT WRITE DOWN WHO CALLED, OR THEIR PHONE NUMBER?
WHY ARE YOU PICKING ON ME?
I'M NOT PICKING ON YOU, I'M ASKING YOU A QUESTION.
IT FEELS LIKE YOU'RE PICKING ON ME.
I JUST WANT TO GET MY PHONE MESSAGES!
MOM! DAD'S PICKING ON ME!

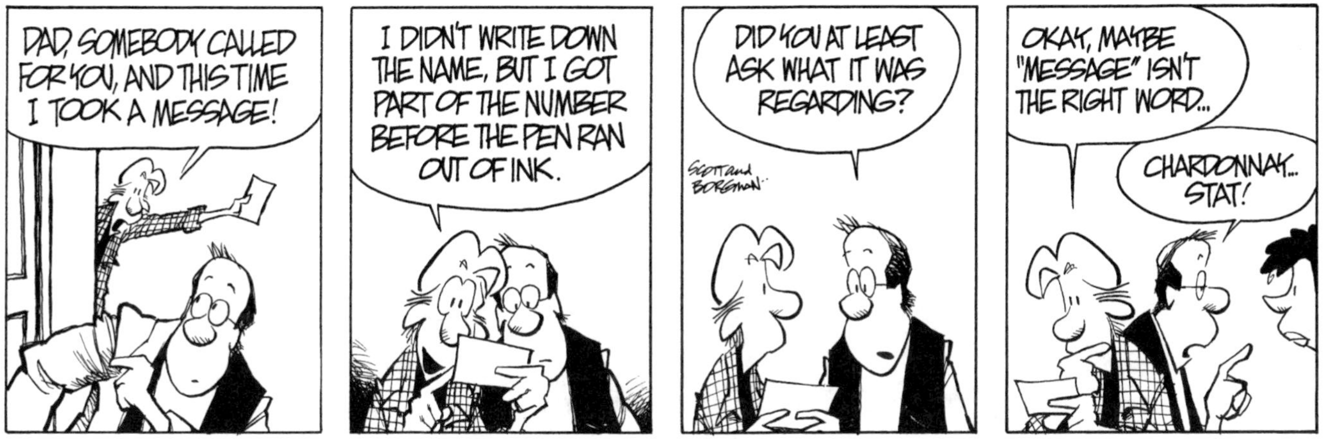
DAD, SOMEBODY CALLED FOR YOU, AND THIS TIME I TOOK A MESSAGE!
I DIDN'T WRITE DOWN THE NAME, BUT I GOT PART OF THE NUMBER BEFORE THE PEN RAN OUT OF INK.
DID YOU AT LEAST ASK WHAT IT WAS REGARDING?
OKAY, MAYBE "MESSAGE" ISN'T THE RIGHT WORD...
CHARDONNAY... STAT!

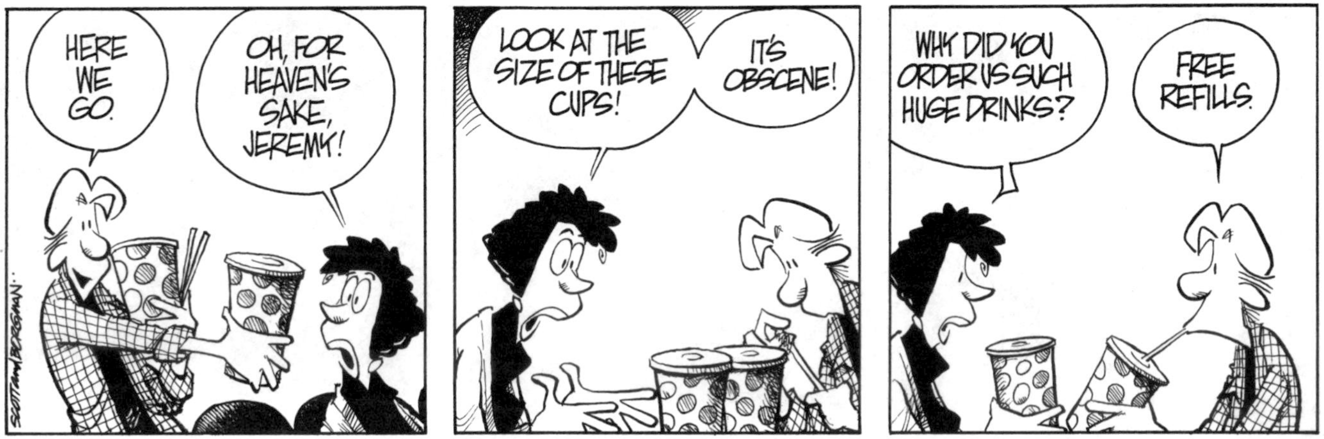
HERE WE GO.
OH, FOR HEAVEN'S SAKE, JEREMY!
LOOK AT THE SIZE OF THESE CUPS!
IT'S OBSCENE!
WHY DID YOU ORDER US SUCH HUGE DRINKS?
FREE REFILLS.

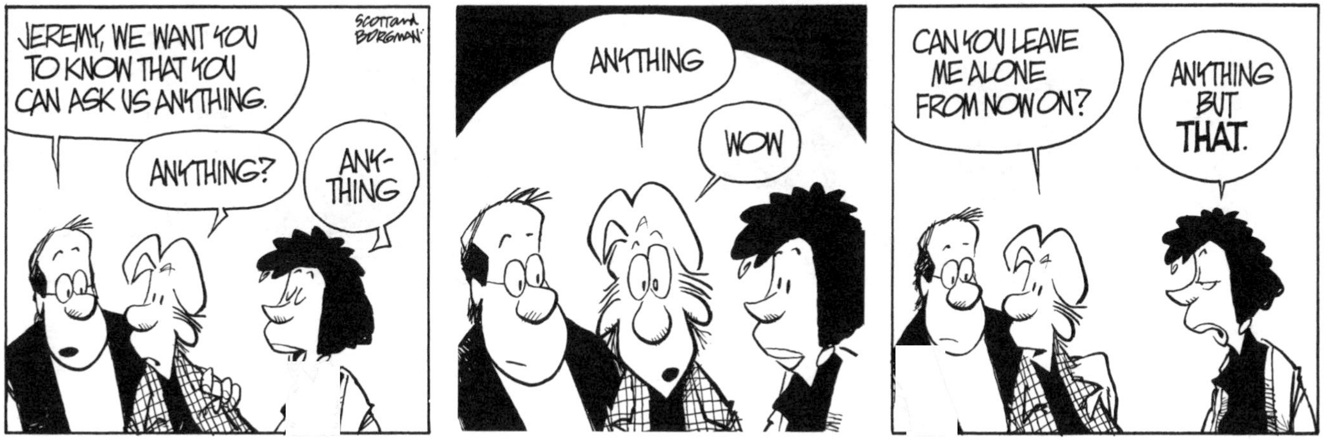
JEREMY, WE WANT YOU TO KNOW THAT YOU CAN ASK US ANYTHING.
ANYTHING?
ANY-THING
ANYTHING
WOW
CAN YOU LEAVE ME ALONE FROM NOW ON?
ANYTHING BUT THAT.

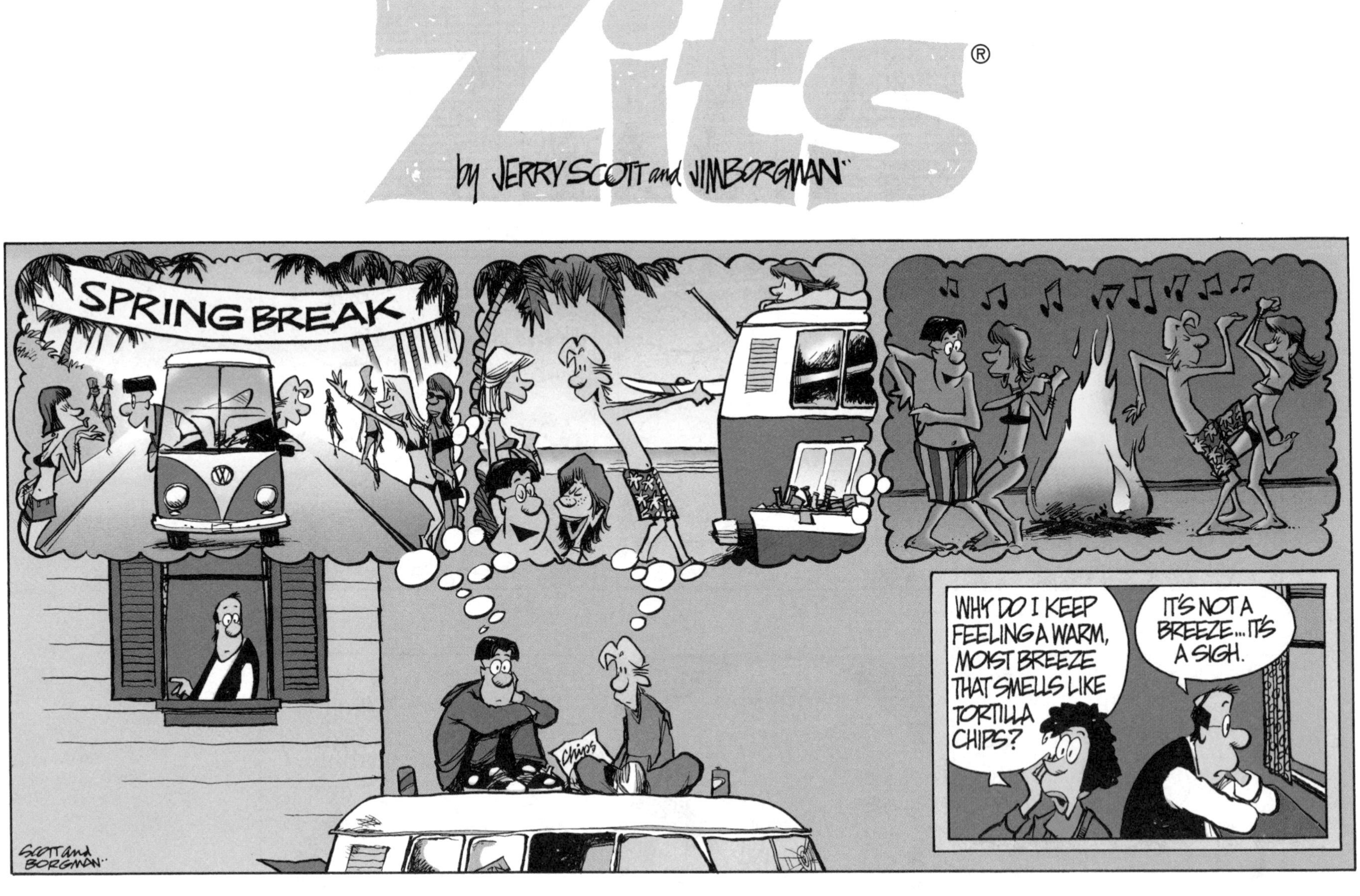
Zits®
by JERRY SCOTT and JIM BORGMAN
SPRING BREAK
WHY DO I KEEP FEELING A WARM, MOIST BREEZE THAT SMELLS LIKE TORTILLA CHIPS?
IT'S NOT A BREEZE... IT'S A SIGH.
CHIPS
SCOTT and BORGMAN

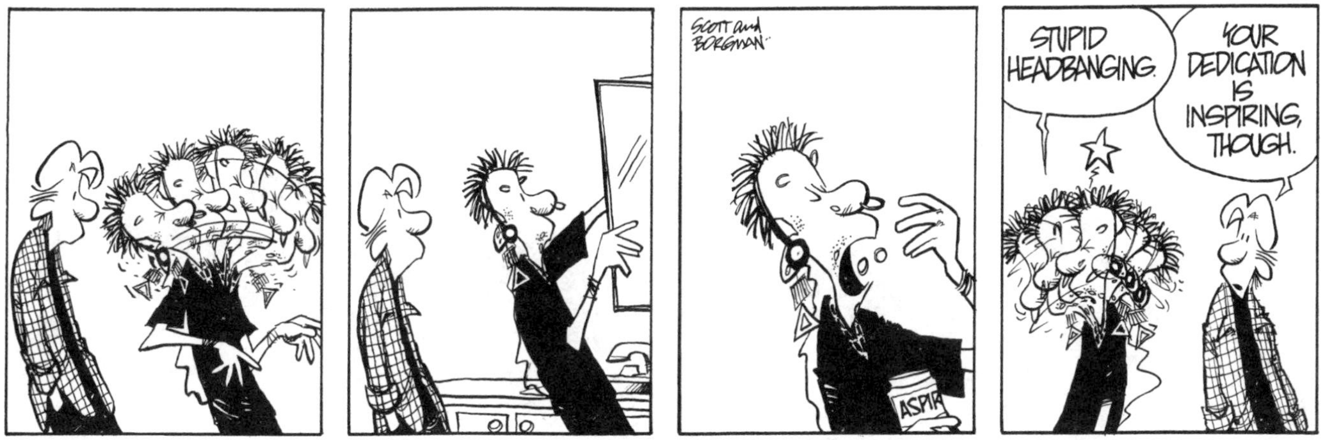
SCOTT and BORGMAN
ASPIR
STUPID HEADBANGING.
YOUR DEDICATION IS INSPIRING, THOUGH.

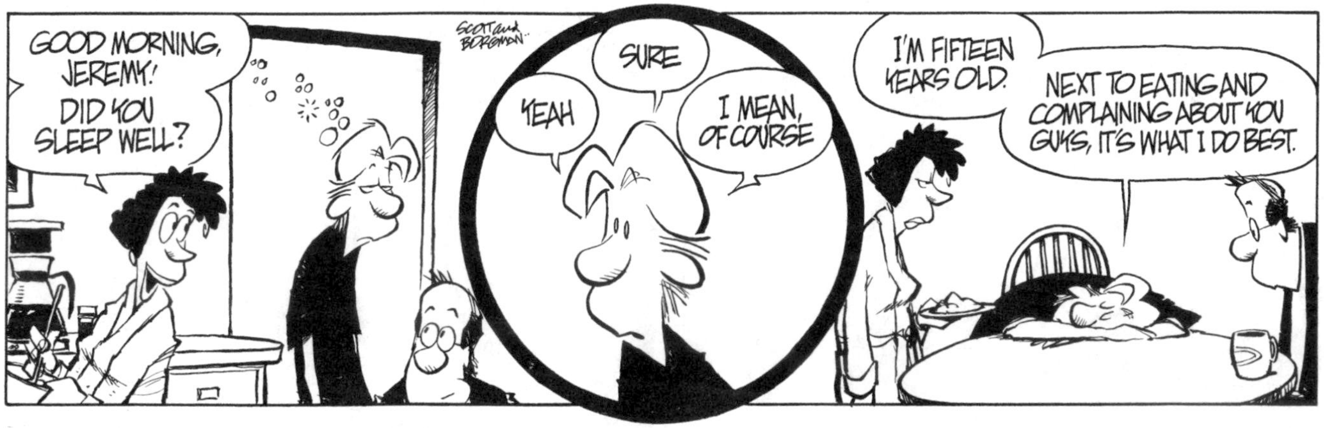
GOOD MORNING, JEREMY! DID YOU SLEEP WELL?
SCOTT and BORGMAN
YEAH
SURE
I MEAN, OF COURSE
I'M FIFTEEN YEARS OLD.
NEXT TO EATING AND COMPLAINING ABOUT YOU GUYS, IT'S WHAT I DO BEST.

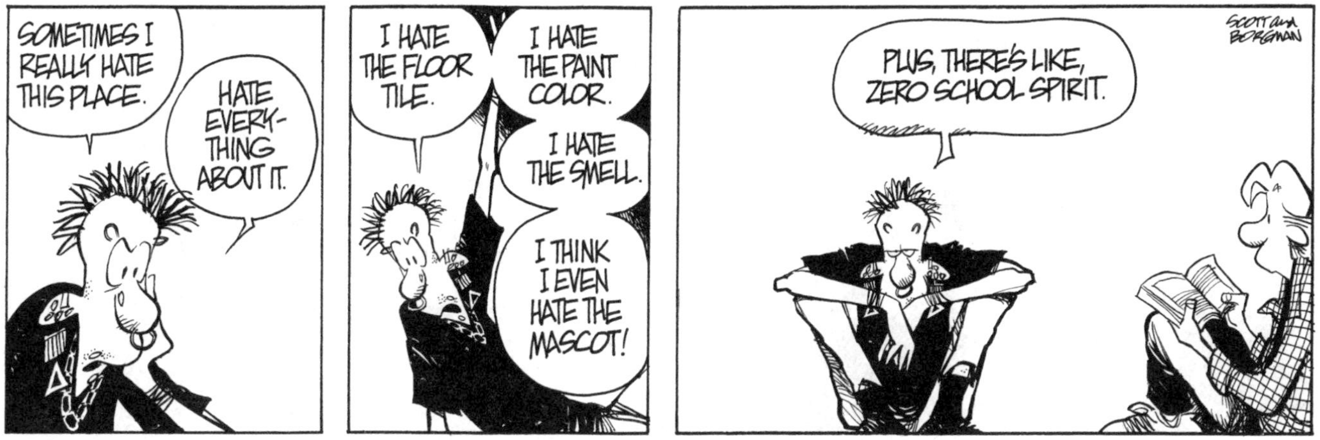
SOMETIMES I REALLY HATE THIS PLACE.
HATE EVERY-THING ABOUT IT.
I HATE THE FLOOR TILE.
I HATE THE PAINT COLOR.
I HATE THE SMELL.
I THINK I EVEN HATE THE MASCOT!
SCOTT and BORGMAN
PLUS, THERE'S LIKE, ZERO SCHOOL SPIRIT.

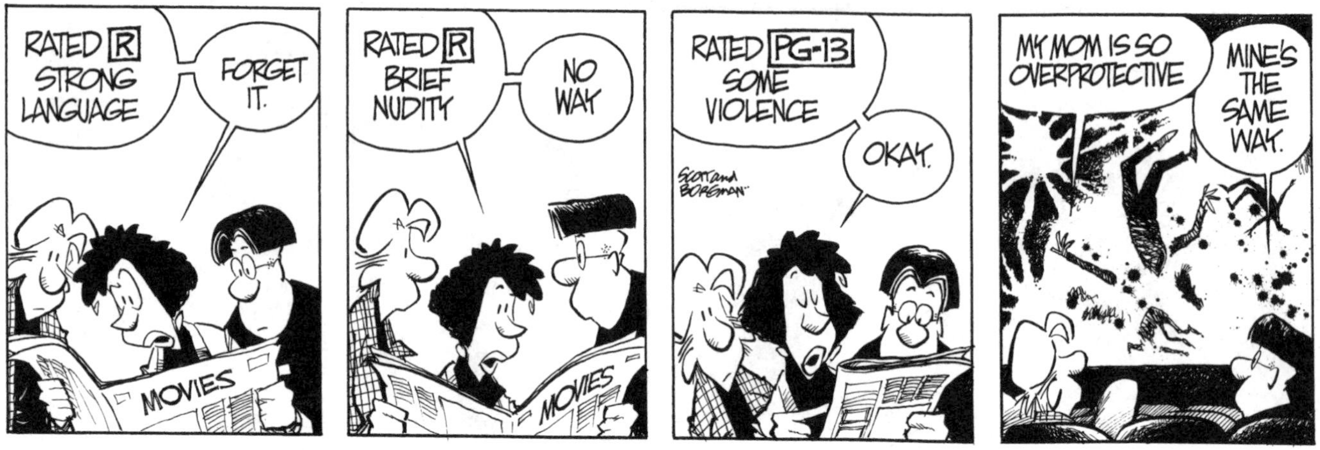
RATED R STRONG LANGUAGE
FORGET IT.
RATED R BRIEF NUDITY
NO WAY
RATED PG-13 SOME VIOLENCE
OKAY.
SCOTT and BORGMAN
MY MOM IS SO OVERPROTECTIVE
MINE'S THE SAME WAY.

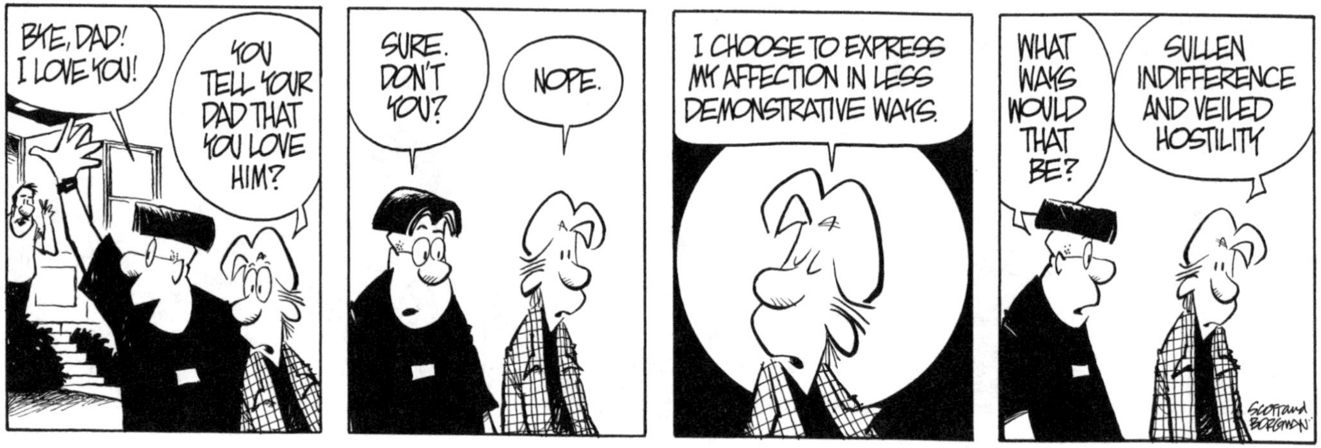
BYE, DAD! I LOVE YOU!
YOU TELL YOUR DAD THAT YOU LOVE HIM?
SURE. DON'T YOU?
NOPE.
I CHOOSE TO EXPRESS MY AFFECTION IN LESS DEMONSTRATIVE WAYS.
WHAT WAYS WOULD THAT BE?
SULLEN INDIFFERENCE AND VEILED HOSTILITY
SCOTT and BORGMAN

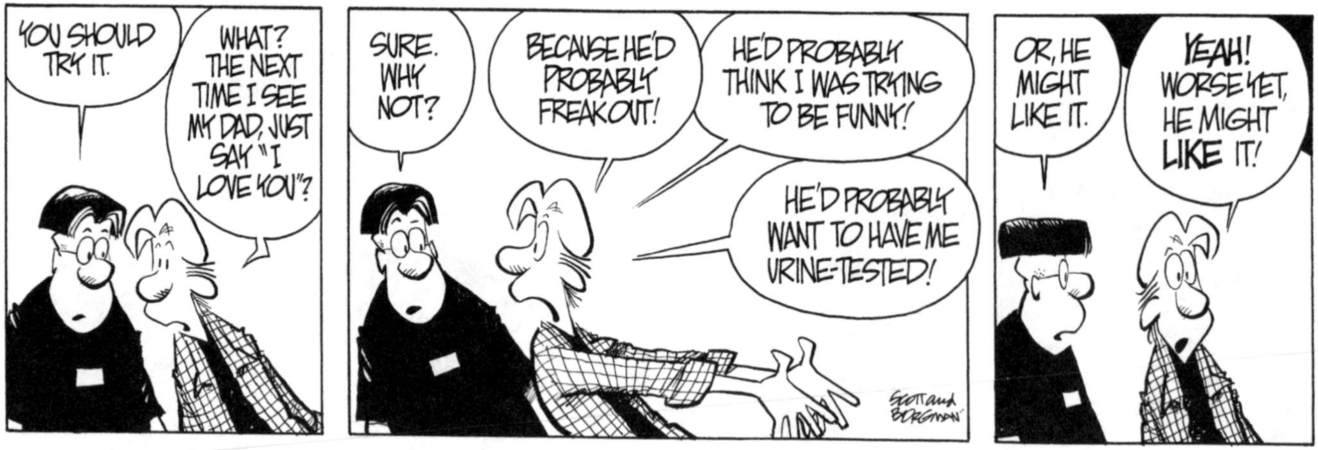
YOU SHOULD TRY IT.
WHAT? THE NEXT TIME I SEE MY DAD, JUST SAY "I LOVE YOU"?
SURE. WHY NOT?
BECAUSE HE'D PROBABLY FREAK OUT!
HE'D PROBABLY THINK I WAS TRYING TO BE FUNNY!
HE'D PROBABLY WANT TO HAVE ME URINE-TESTED!
SCOTT and BORGMAN
OR, HE MIGHT LIKE IT.
YEAH! WORSE YET, HE MIGHT LIKE IT!

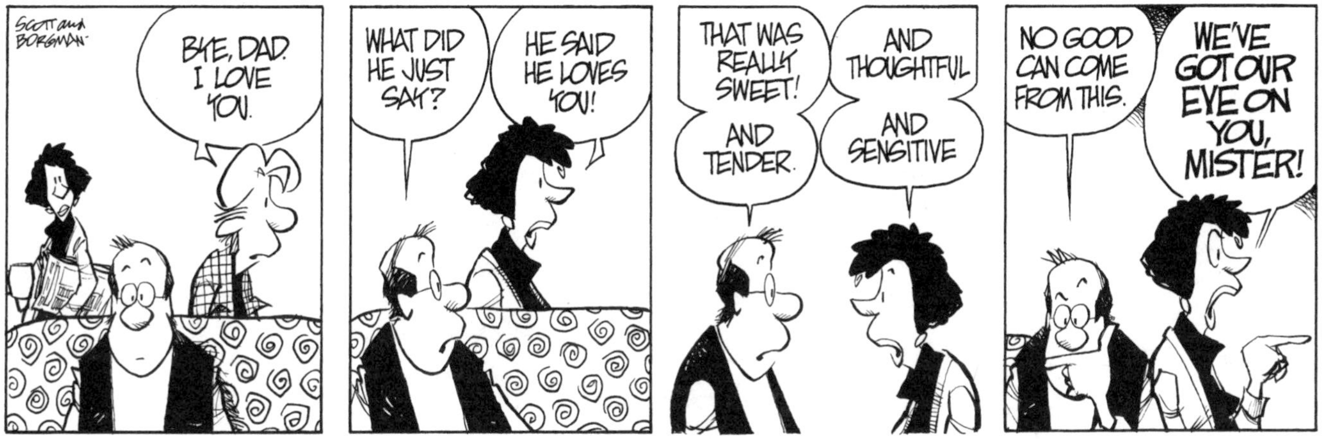
SCOTT and BORGMAN
BYE, DAD. I LOVE YOU.
WHAT DID HE JUST SAY?
HE SAID HE LOVES YOU!
THAT WAS REALLY SWEET!
AND THOUGHTFUL
AND TENDER.
AND SENSITIVE
NO GOOD CAN COME FROM THIS.
WE'VE GOT OUR EYE ON YOU, MISTER!

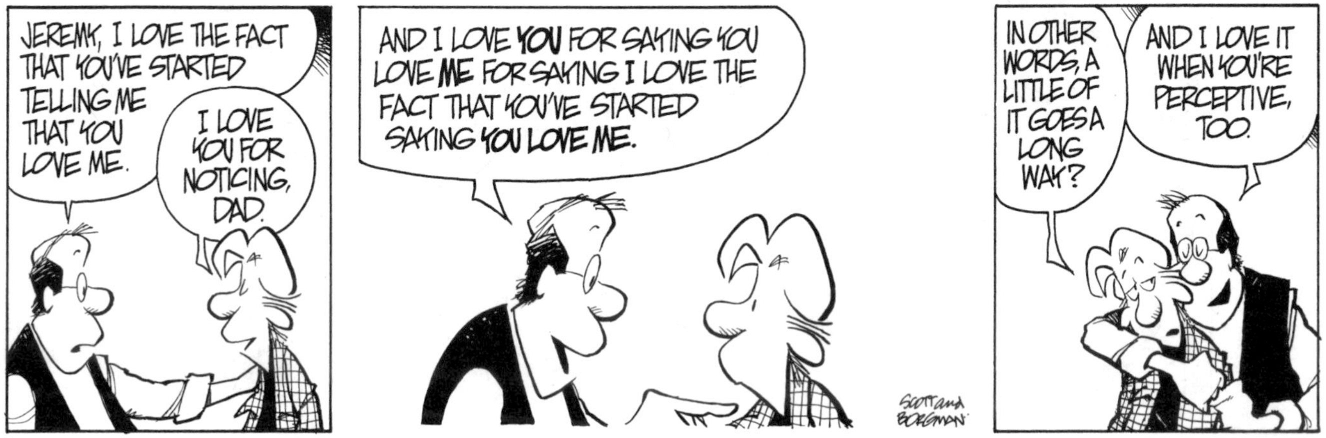
JEREMY, I LOVE THE FACT THAT YOU'VE STARTED TELLING ME THAT YOU LOVE ME.
I LOVE YOU FOR NOTICING, DAD.
AND I LOVE **YOU** FOR SAYING YOU LOVE **ME** FOR SAYING I LOVE THE FACT THAT YOU'VE STARTED SAYING **YOU LOVE ME.**
SCOTT and BORGMAN
IN OTHER WORDS, A LITTLE OF IT GOES A LONG WAY?
AND I LOVE IT WHEN YOU'RE PERCEPTIVE, TOO.

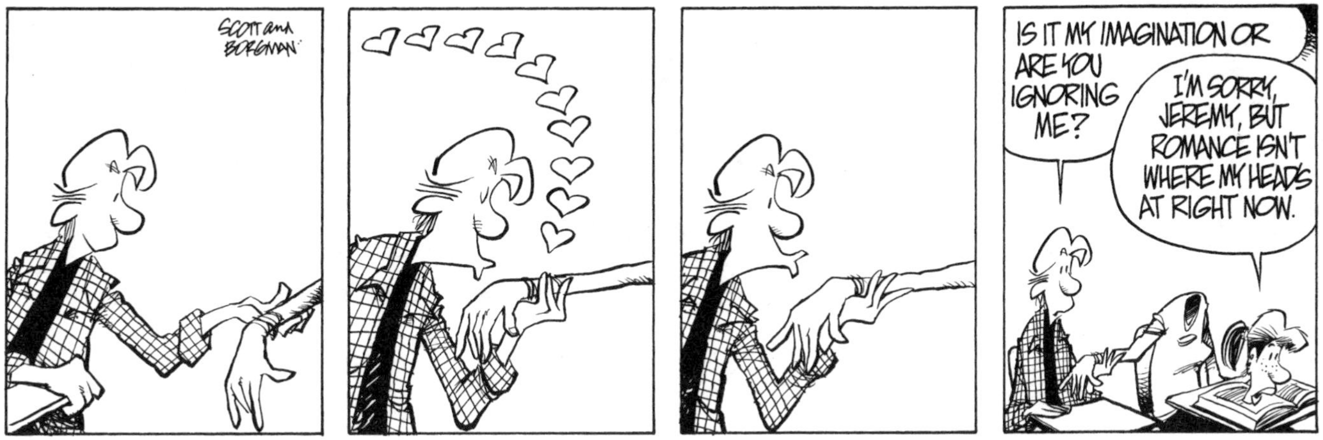
SCOTT and BORGMAN
IS IT MY IMAGINATION OR ARE YOU IGNORING ME?
I'M SORRY, JEREMY, BUT ROMANCE ISN'T WHERE MY HEAD'S AT RIGHT NOW.

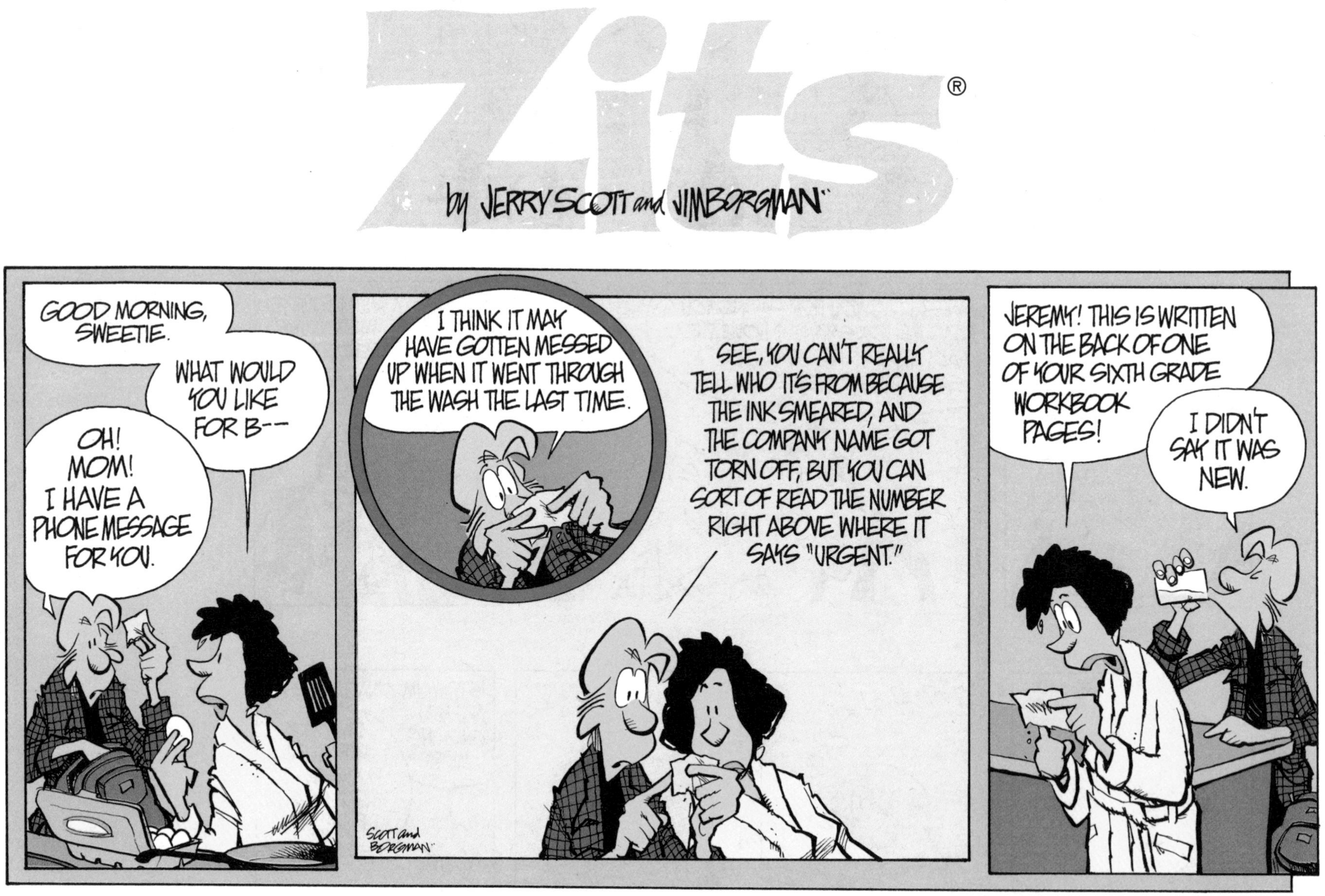
Zits®
by JERRY SCOTT and JIM BORGMAN
GOOD MORNING, SWEETIE.
WHAT WOULD YOU LIKE FOR B--
OH! MOM! I HAVE A PHONE MESSAGE FOR YOU.
I THINK IT MAY HAVE GOTTEN MESSED UP WHEN IT WENT THROUGH THE WASH THE LAST TIME.
SEE, YOU CAN'T REALLY TELL WHO IT'S FROM BECAUSE THE INK SMEARED, AND THE COMPANY NAME GOT TORN OFF, BUT YOU CAN SORT OF READ THE NUMBER RIGHT ABOVE WHERE IT SAYS "URGENT."
SCOTT and BORGMAN
JEREMY! THIS IS WRITTEN ON THE BACK OF ONE OF YOUR SIXTH GRADE WORKBOOK PAGES!
I DIDN'T SAY IT WAS NEW.

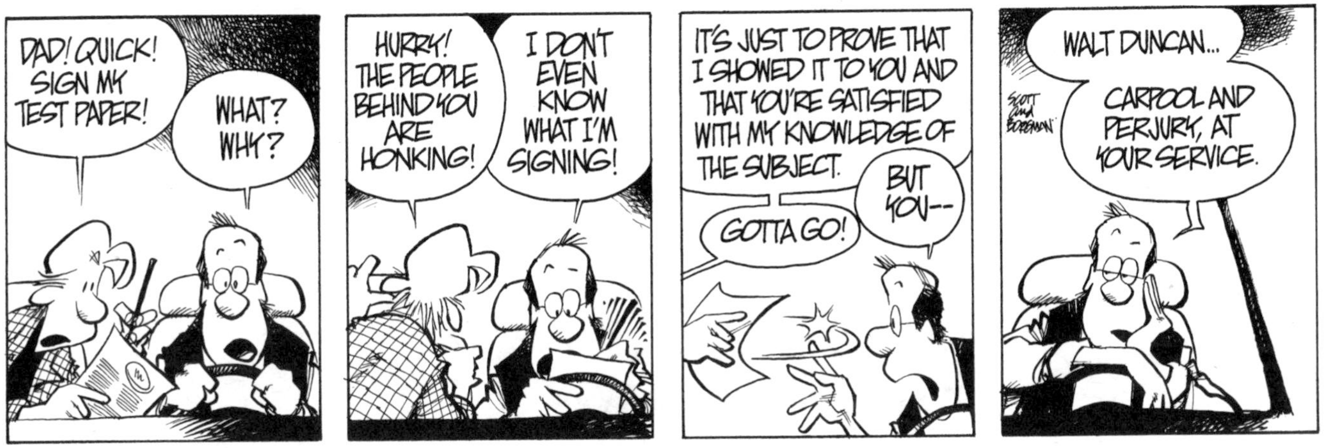
DAD! QUICK! SIGN MY TEST PAPER!
WHAT? WHY?
HURRY! THE PEOPLE BEHIND YOU ARE HONKING!
I DON'T EVEN KNOW WHAT I'M SIGNING!
IT'S JUST TO PROVE THAT I SHOWED IT TO YOU AND THAT YOU'RE SATISFIED WITH MY KNOWLEDGE OF THE SUBJECT.
GOTTA GO!
BUT YOU--
WALT DUNCAN...
CARPOOL AND PERJURY, AT YOUR SERVICE.

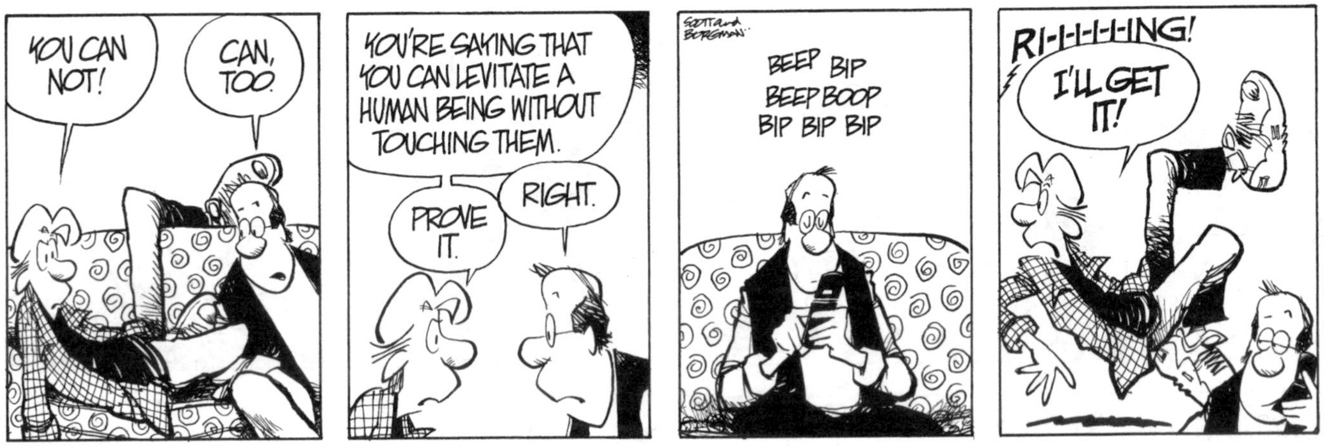
YOU CAN NOT!
CAN, TOO.
YOU'RE SAYING THAT YOU CAN LEVITATE A HUMAN BEING WITHOUT TOUCHING THEM.
PROVE IT.
RIGHT.
BEEP BIP BEEP BOOP BIP BIP BIP
RI-I-I-I-I-ING!
I'LL GET IT!

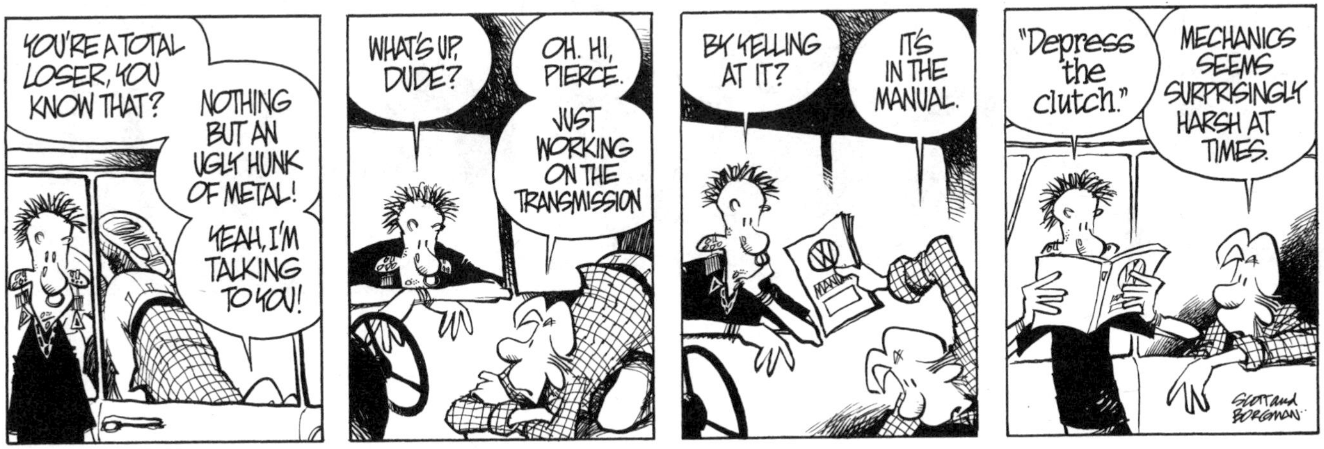
YOU'RE A TOTAL LOSER, YOU KNOW THAT?
NOTHING BUT AN UGLY HUNK OF METAL!
YEAH, I'M TALKING TO YOU!
WHAT'S UP, DUDE?
OH. HI, PIERCE.
JUST WORKING ON THE TRANSMISSION
BY YELLING AT IT?
IT'S IN THE MANUAL.
"Depress the clutch."
MECHANICS SEEMS SURPRISINGLY HARSH AT TIMES.

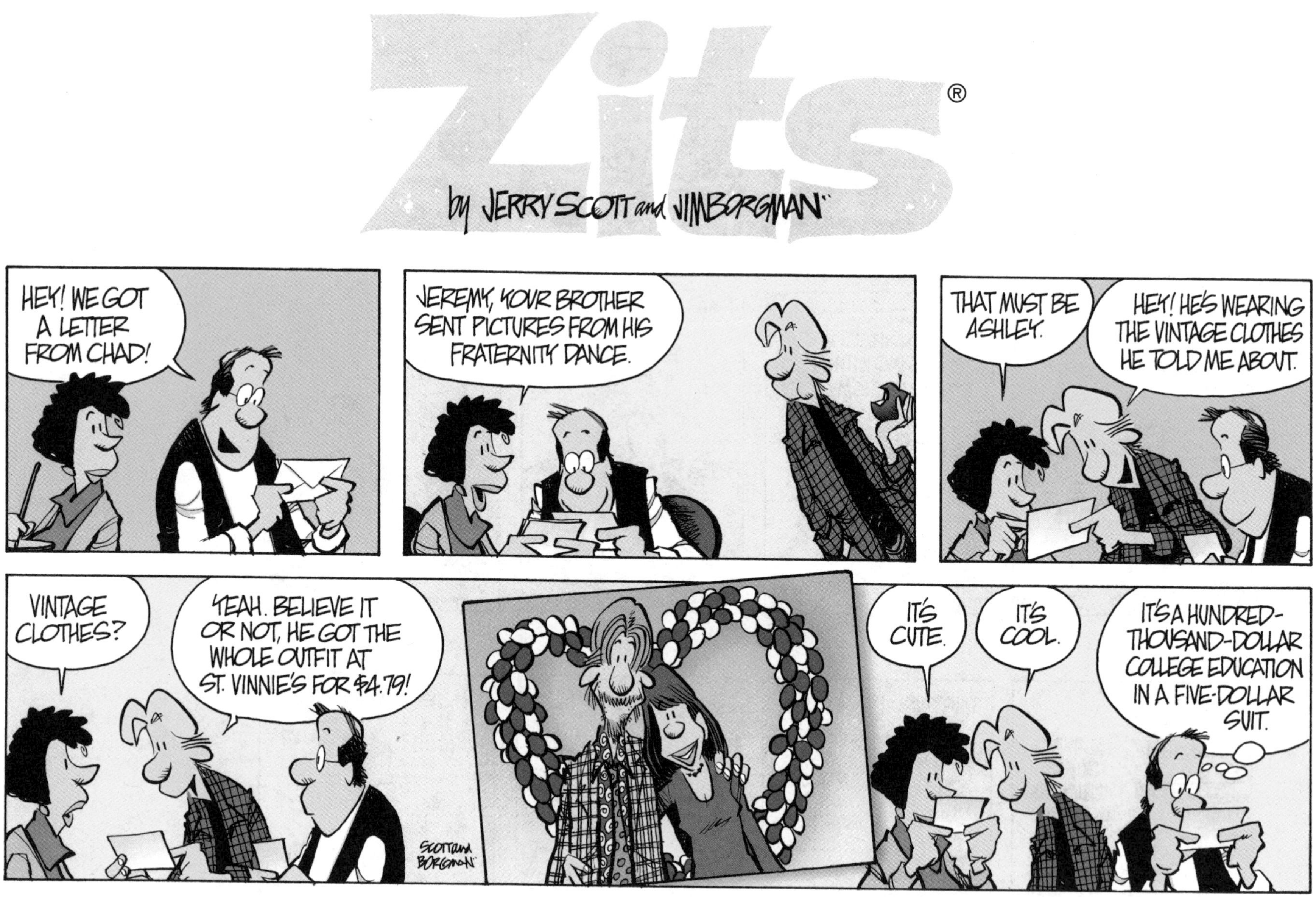
Zits®
by JERRY SCOTT and JIM BORGMAN
HEY! WE GOT A LETTER FROM CHAD!
JEREMY, YOUR BROTHER SENT PICTURES FROM HIS FRATERNITY DANCE.
THAT MUST BE ASHLEY.
HEY! HE'S WEARING THE VINTAGE CLOTHES HE TOLD ME ABOUT.
VINTAGE CLOTHES?
YEAH. BELIEVE IT OR NOT, HE GOT THE WHOLE OUTFIT AT ST. VINNIE'S FOR $4.79!
IT'S CUTE.
IT'S COOL.
IT'S A HUNDRED-THOUSAND-DOLLAR COLLEGE EDUCATION IN A FIVE-DOLLAR SUIT.

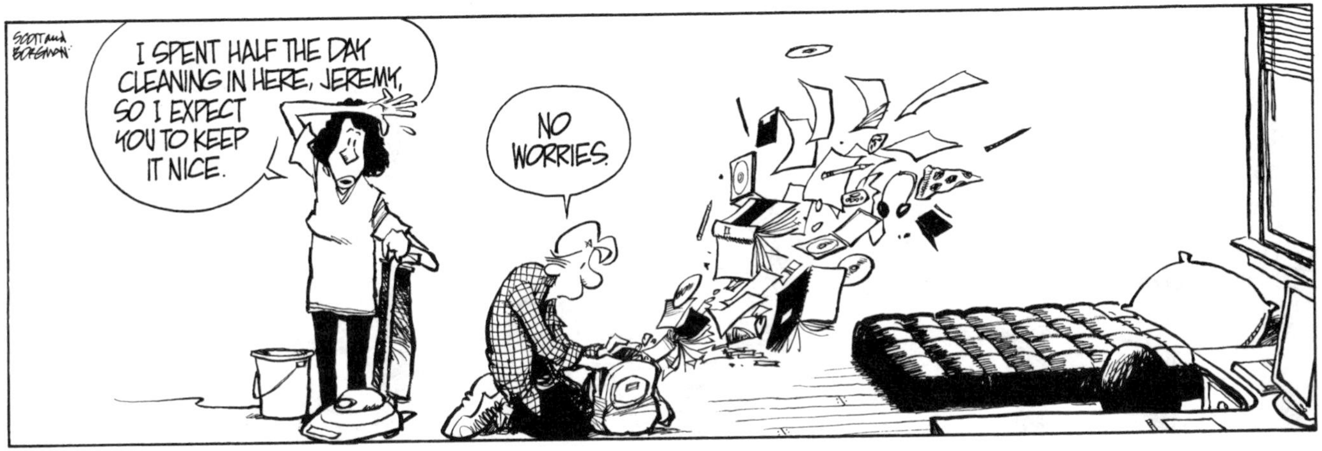
SCOTT and BORGMAN
I SPENT HALF THE DAY CLEANING IN HERE, JEREMY, SO I EXPECT YOU TO KEEP IT NICE.
NO WORRIES.

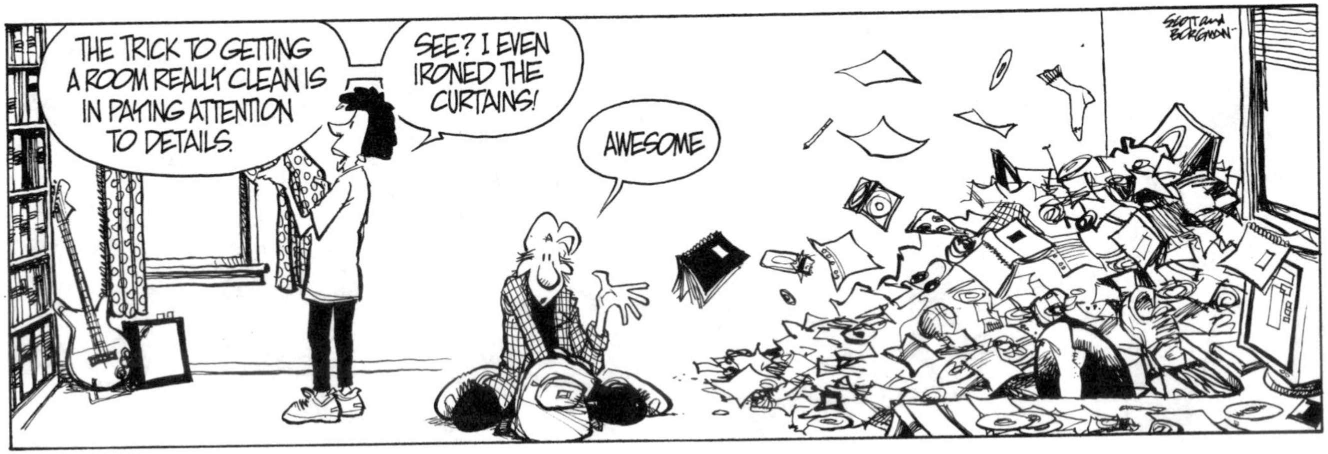
SCOTT and BORGMAN
THE TRICK TO GETTING A ROOM REALLY CLEAN IS IN PAYING ATTENTION TO DETAILS.
SEE? I EVEN IRONED THE CURTAINS!
AWESOME

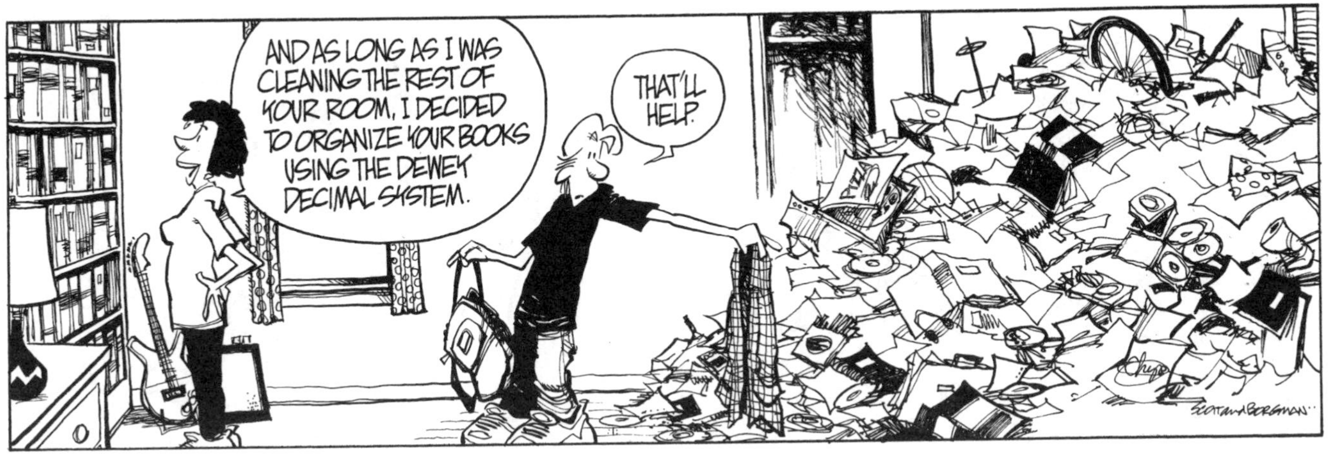
AND AS LONG AS I WAS CLEANING THE REST OF YOUR ROOM, I DECIDED TO ORGANIZE YOUR BOOKS USING THE DEWEY DECIMAL SYSTEM.
THAT'LL HELP.
SCOTT and BORGMAN

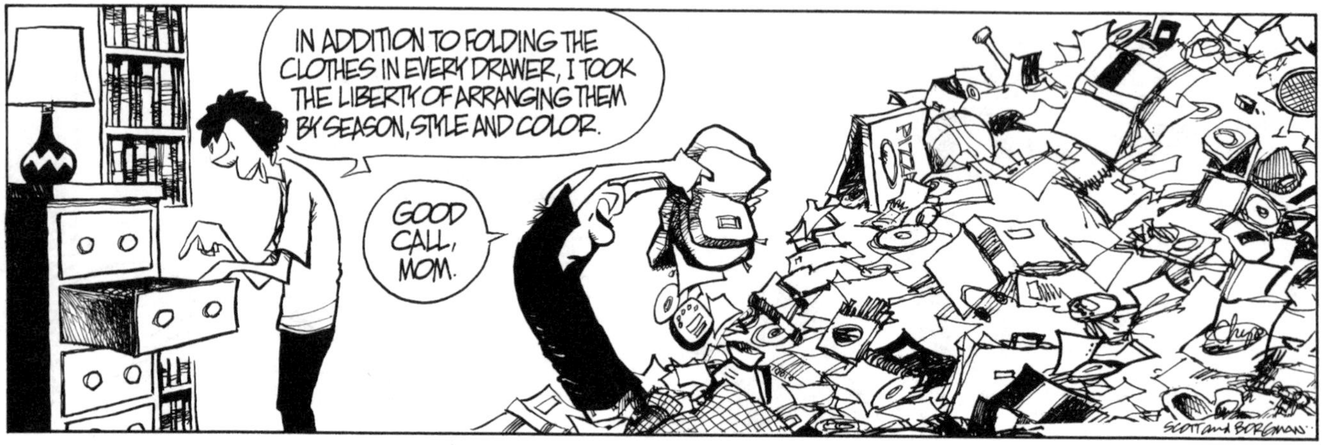
IN ADDITION TO FOLDING THE CLOTHES IN EVERY DRAWER, I TOOK THE LIBERTY OF ARRANGING THEM BY SEASON, STYLE AND COLOR.
GOOD CALL, MOM.
SCOTT AND BORGMAN

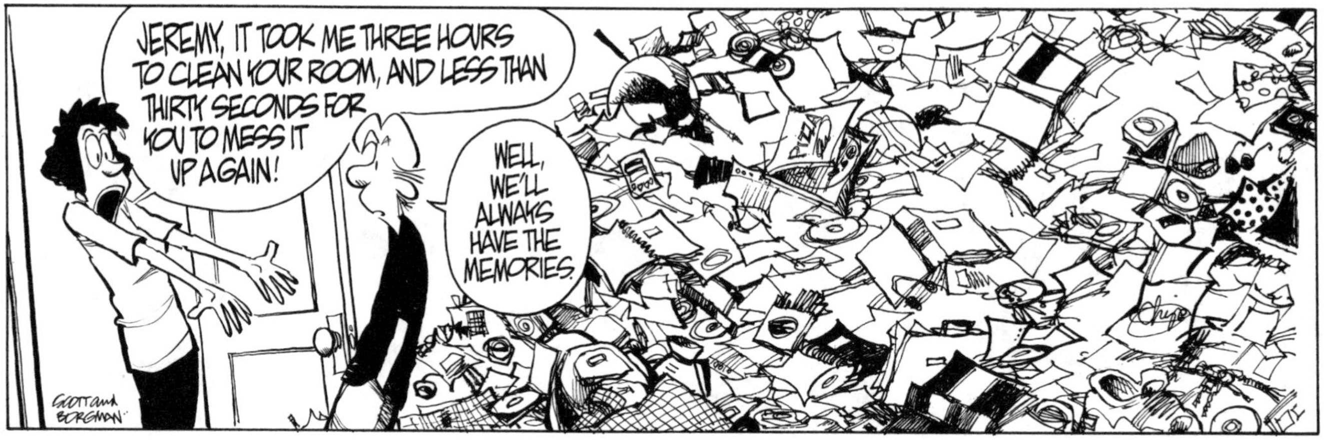
JEREMY, IT TOOK ME THREE HOURS TO CLEAN YOUR ROOM, AND LESS THAN THIRTY SECONDS FOR YOU TO MESS IT UP AGAIN!
WELL, WE'LL ALWAYS HAVE THE MEMORIES.
SCOTT AND BORGMAN

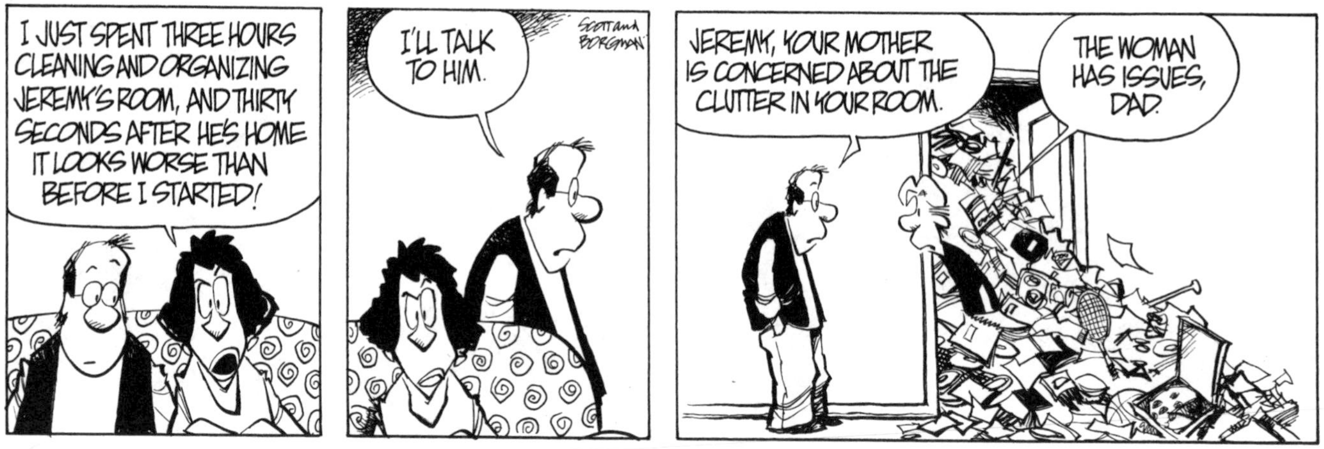
I JUST SPENT THREE HOURS CLEANING AND ORGANIZING JEREMY'S ROOM, AND THIRTY SECONDS AFTER HE'S HOME IT LOOKS WORSE THAN BEFORE I STARTED!
I'LL TALK TO HIM.
SCOTT AND BORGMAN
JEREMY, YOUR MOTHER IS CONCERNED ABOUT THE CLUTTER IN YOUR ROOM.
THE WOMAN HAS ISSUES, DAD.

Zits®

by JERRY SCOTT and JIM BORGMAN

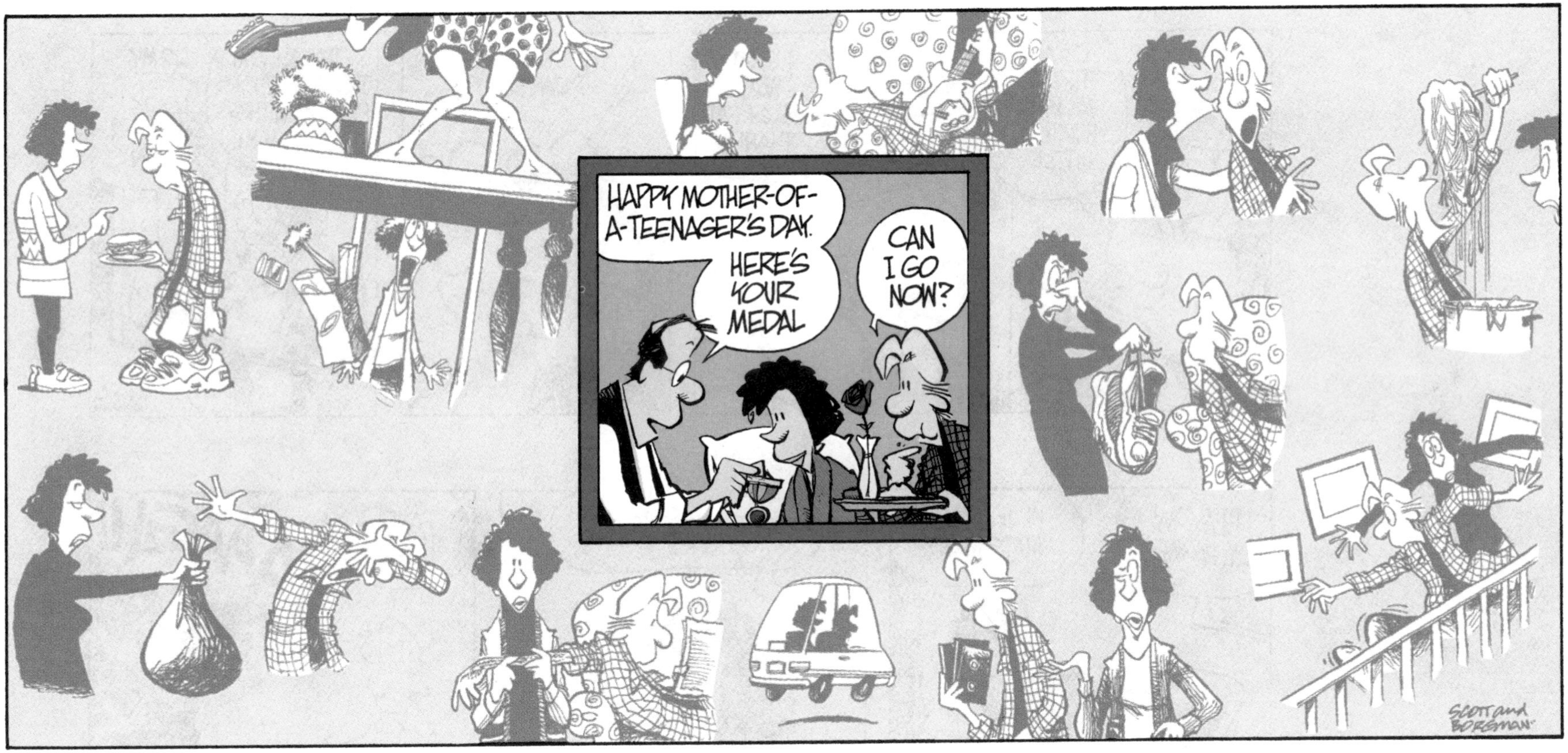
HAPPY MOTHER-OF-A-TEENAGER'S DAY.
HERE'S YOUR MEDAL
CAN I GO NOW?
SCOTT and BORGMAN

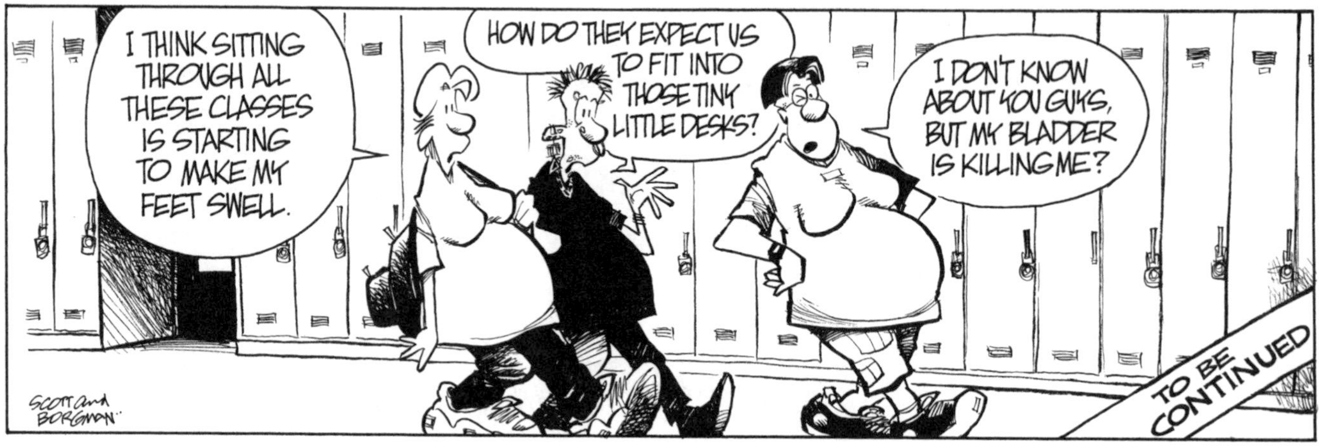
I THINK SITTING THROUGH ALL THESE CLASSES IS STARTING TO MAKE MY FEET SWELL.
HOW DO THEY EXPECT US TO FIT INTO THOSE TINY LITTLE DESKS?
I DON'T KNOW ABOUT YOU GUYS, BUT MY BLADDER IS KILLING ME?
TO BE CONTINUED

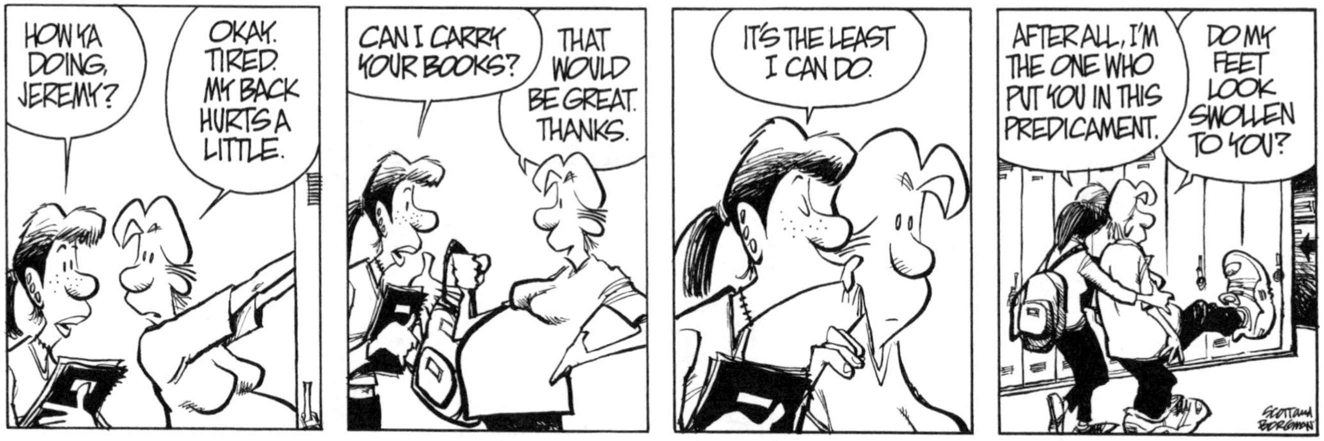
HOW YA DOING, JEREMY?
OKAY. TIRED. MY BACK HURTS A LITTLE.
CAN I CARRY YOUR BOOKS?
THAT WOULD BE GREAT. THANKS.
IT'S THE LEAST I CAN DO.
AFTER ALL, I'M THE ONE WHO PUT YOU IN THIS PREDICAMENT.
DO MY FEET LOOK SWOLLEN TO YOU?

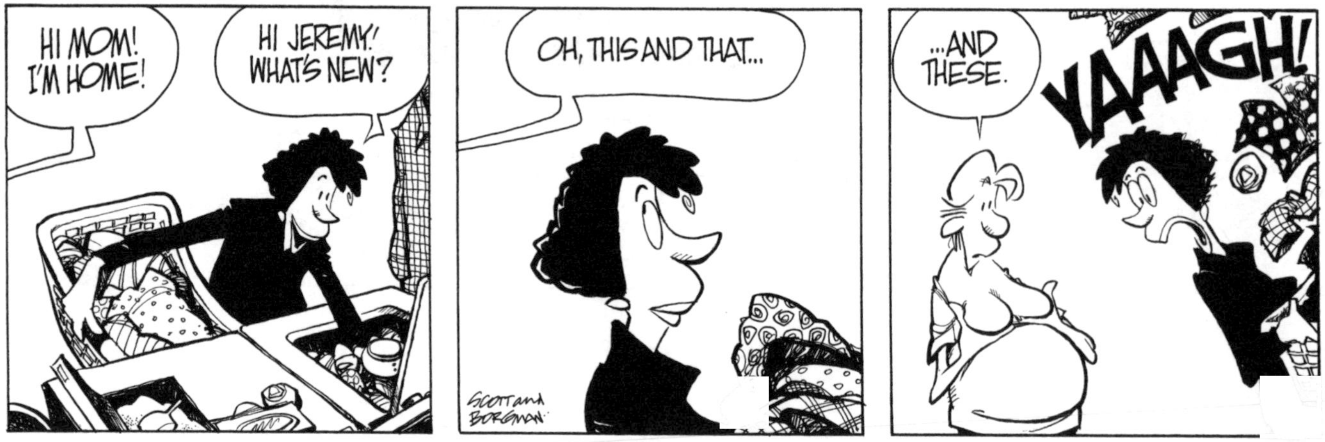
HI MOM! I'M HOME!
HI JEREMY! WHAT'S NEW?
OH, THIS AND THAT...
...AND THESE.
YAAAGH!

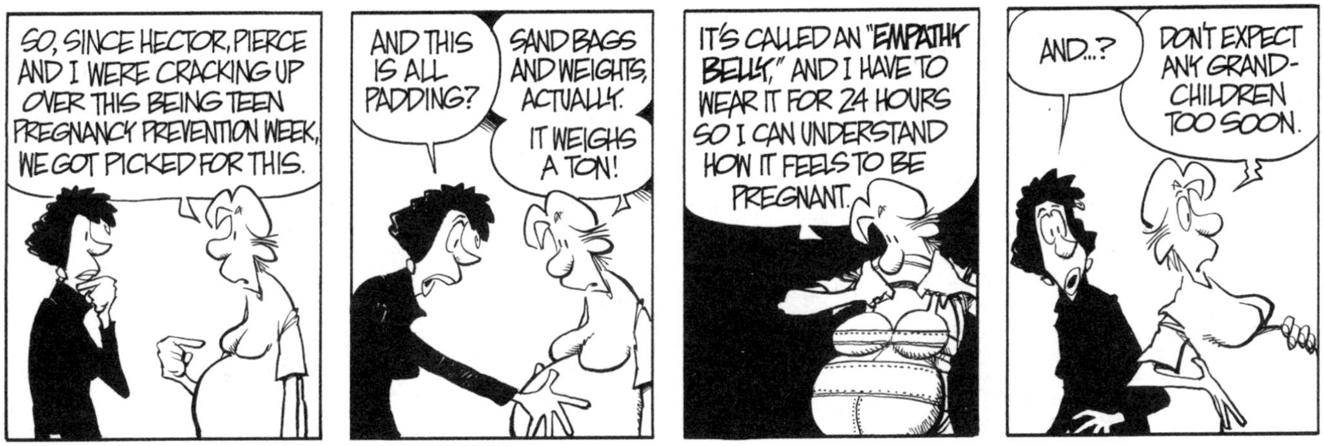
SO, SINCE HECTOR, PIERCE AND I WERE CRACKING UP OVER THIS BEING TEEN PREGNANCY PREVENTION WEEK, WE GOT PICKED FOR THIS.
AND THIS IS ALL PADDING?
SAND BAGS AND WEIGHTS, ACTUALLY.
IT WEIGHS A TON!
IT'S CALLED AN "EMPATHY BELLY," AND I HAVE TO WEAR IT FOR 24 HOURS SO I CAN UNDERSTAND HOW IT FEELS TO BE PREGNANT.
AND...?
DON'T EXPECT ANY GRAND-CHILDREN TOO SOON.

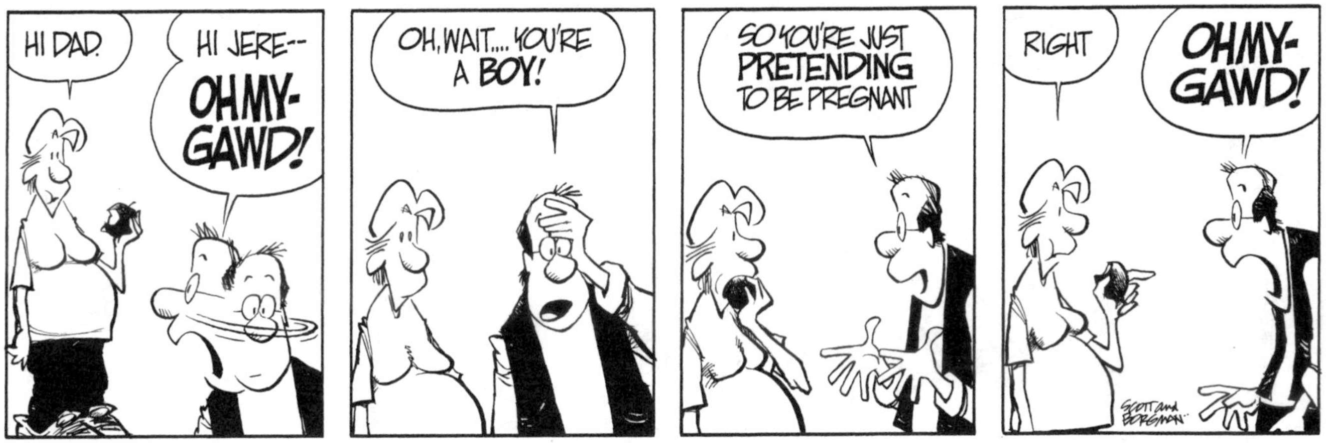
HI DAD.
HI JERE--
OHMY-GAWD!
OH, WAIT.... YOU'RE A BOY!
SO YOU'RE JUST PRETENDING TO BE PREGNANT
RIGHT
OHMY-GAWD!
SCOTT and BORGMAN

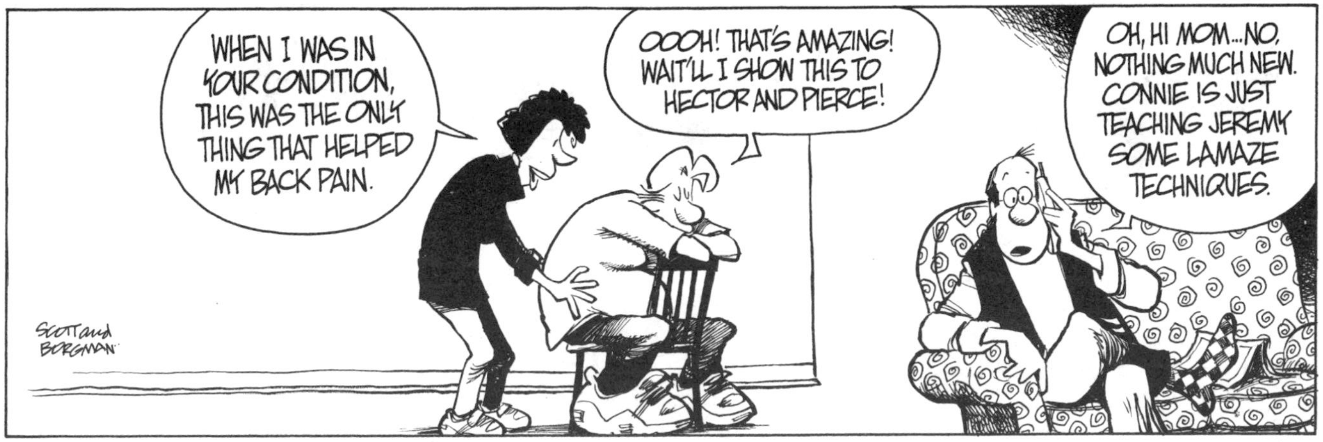
WHEN I WAS IN YOUR CONDITION, THIS WAS THE ONLY THING THAT HELPED MY BACK PAIN.
OOOH! THAT'S AMAZING! WAIT'LL I SHOW THIS TO HECTOR AND PIERCE!
OH, HI MOM...NO, NOTHING MUCH NEW. CONNIE IS JUST TEACHING JEREMY SOME LAMAZE TECHNIQUES.
SCOTT and BORGMAN

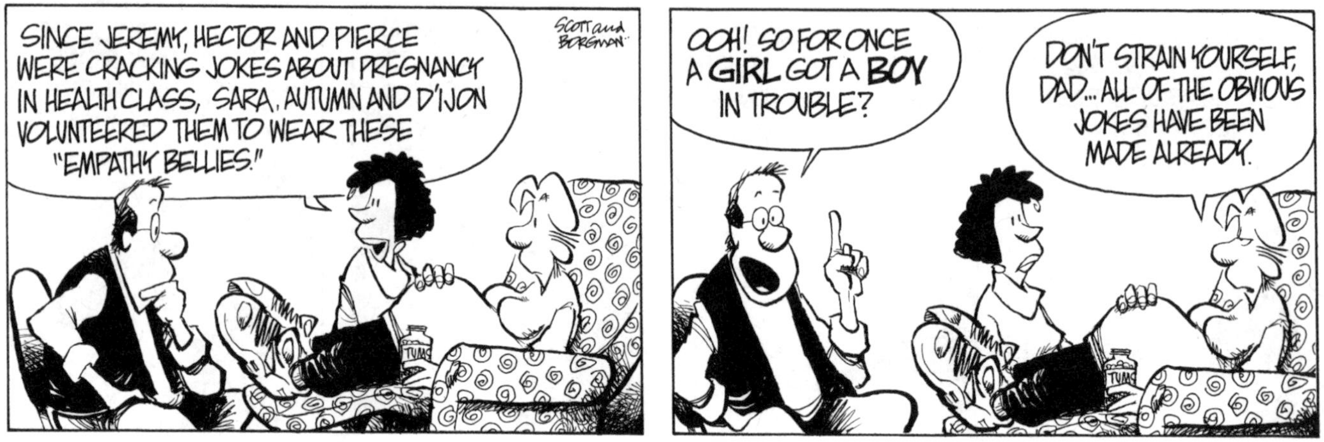
SINCE JEREMY, HECTOR AND PIERCE WERE CRACKING JOKES ABOUT PREGNANCY IN HEALTH CLASS, SARA, AUTUMN AND D'IJON VOLUNTEERED THEM TO WEAR THESE "EMPATHY BELLIES."
SCOTT and BORGMAN
TUMS
OOH! SO FOR ONCE A **GIRL** GOT A **BOY** IN TROUBLE?
DON'T STRAIN YOURSELF, DAD... ALL OF THE OBVIOUS JOKES HAVE BEEN MADE ALREADY.
TUMS

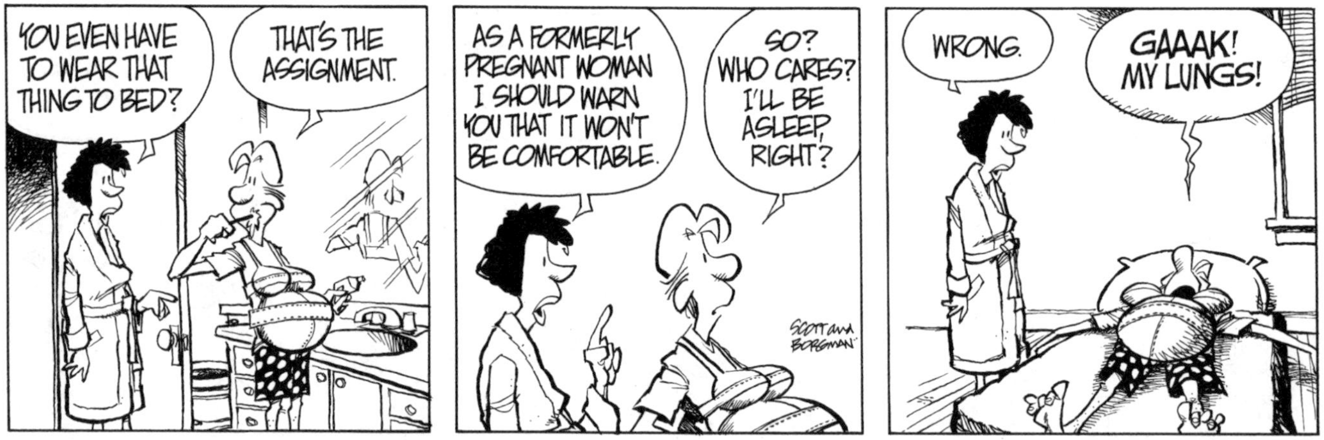
YOU EVEN HAVE TO WEAR THAT THING TO BED?
THAT'S THE ASSIGNMENT.
AS A FORMERLY PREGNANT WOMAN I SHOULD WARN YOU THAT IT WON'T BE COMFORTABLE.
SO? WHO CARES? I'LL BE ASLEEP, RIGHT?
SCOTT and BORGMAN
WRONG.
GAAAK! MY LUNGS!

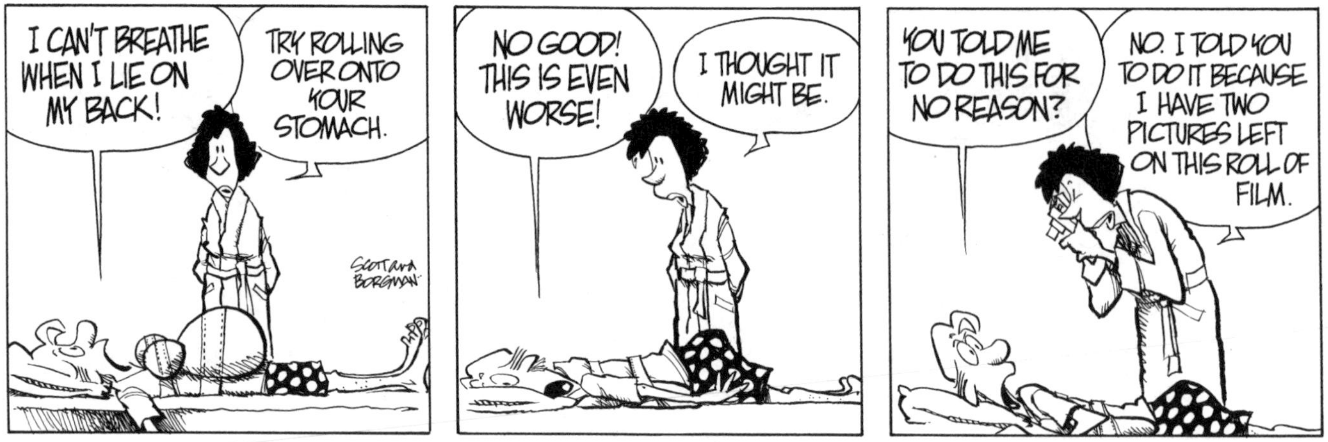
I CAN'T BREATHE WHEN I LIE ON MY BACK!
TRY ROLLING OVER ONTO YOUR STOMACH.
SCOTT and BORGMAN
NO GOOD! THIS IS EVEN WORSE!
I THOUGHT IT MIGHT BE.
YOU TOLD ME TO DO THIS FOR NO REASON?
NO. I TOLD YOU TO DO IT BECAUSE I HAVE TWO PICTURES LEFT ON THIS ROLL OF FILM.

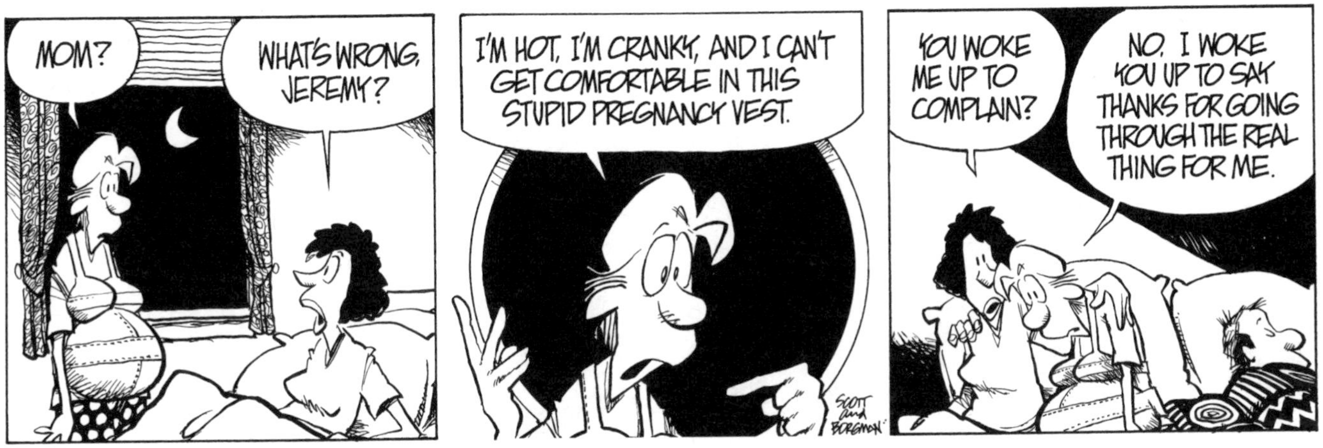
MOM?
WHAT'S WRONG, JEREMY?
I'M HOT, I'M CRANKY, AND I CAN'T GET COMFORTABLE IN THIS STUPID PREGNANCY VEST.
YOU WOKE ME UP TO COMPLAIN?
NO, I WOKE YOU UP TO SAY THANKS FOR GOING THROUGH THE REAL THING FOR ME.
SCOTT and BORGMAN

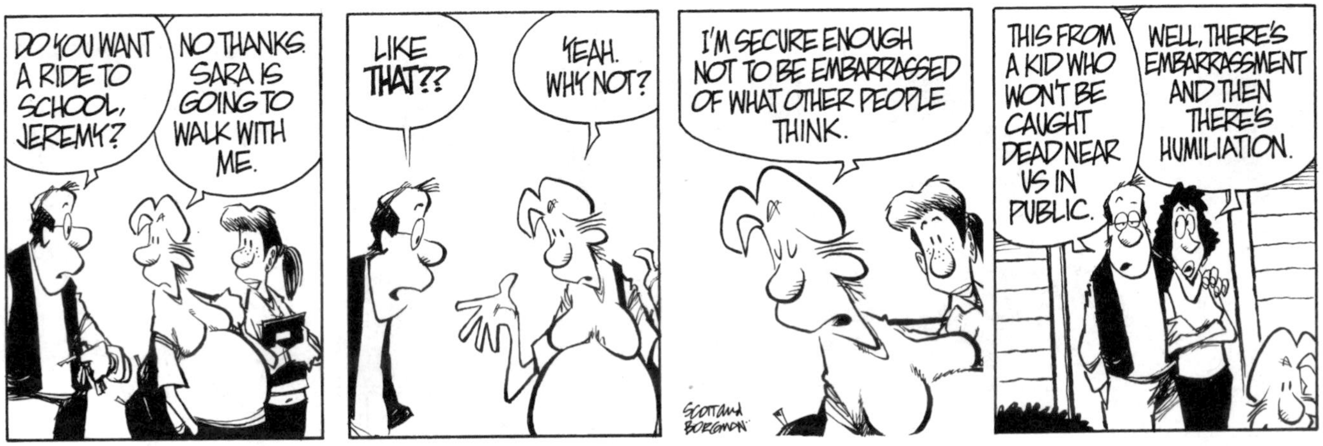
DO YOU WANT A RIDE TO SCHOOL, JEREMY?
NO THANKS. SARA IS GOING TO WALK WITH ME.
LIKE THAT??
YEAH. WHY NOT?
I'M SECURE ENOUGH NOT TO BE EMBARRASSED OF WHAT OTHER PEOPLE THINK.
SCOTT and BORGMAN
THIS FROM A KID WHO WON'T BE CAUGHT DEAD NEAR US IN PUBLIC.
WELL, THERE'S EMBARRASSMENT AND THEN THERE'S HUMILIATION.

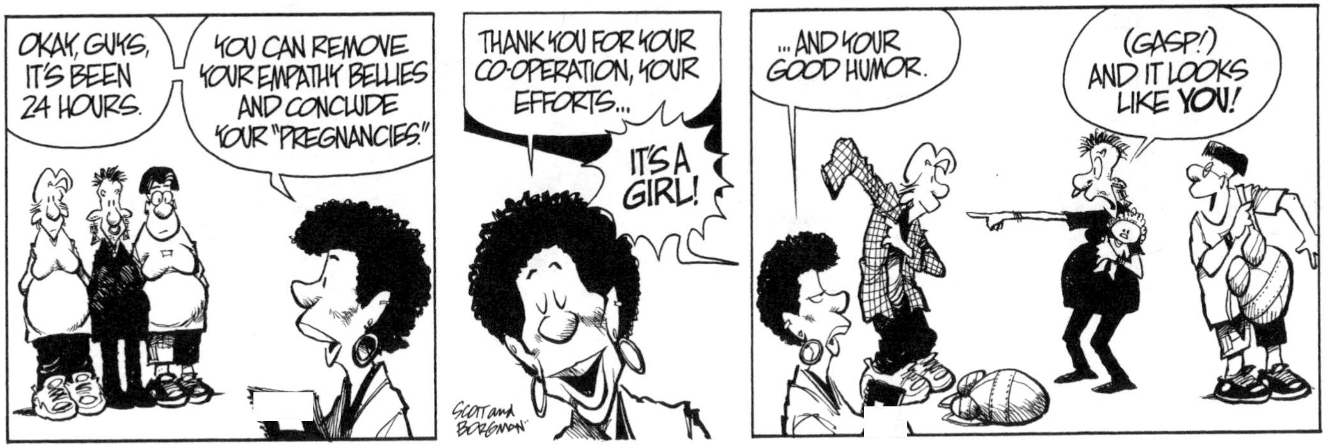
OKAY, GUYS, IT'S BEEN 24 HOURS.
YOU CAN REMOVE YOUR EMPATHY BELLIES AND CONCLUDE YOUR "PREGNANCIES."
THANK YOU FOR YOUR CO-OPERATION, YOUR EFFORTS...
IT'S A GIRL!
SCOTT and BORGMAN
...AND YOUR GOOD HUMOR.
(GASP!) AND IT LOOKS LIKE YOU!

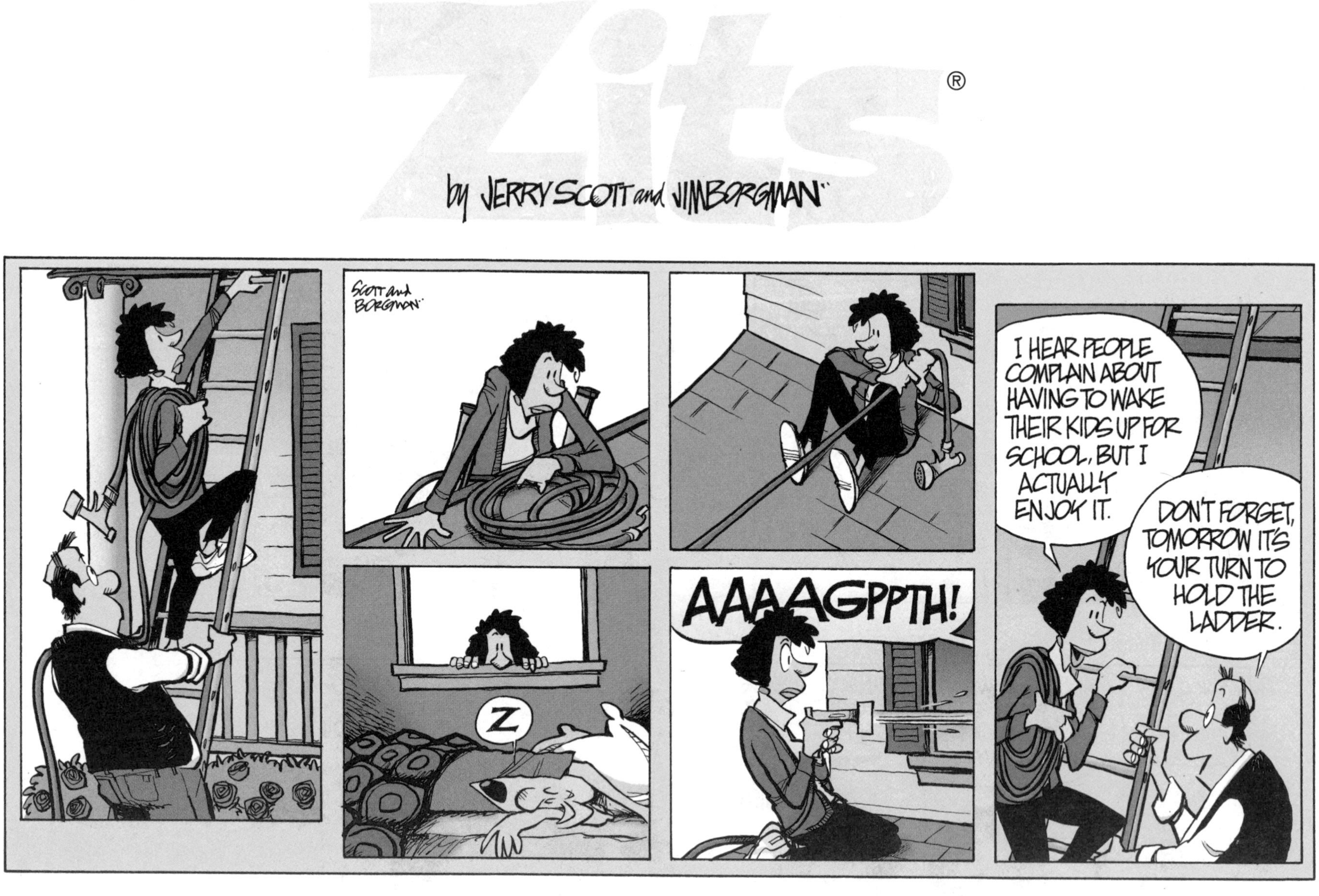
Zits®
by JERRY SCOTT and JIM BORGMAN
SCOTT and BORGMAN
Z
AAAAGPPTH!
I HEAR PEOPLE COMPLAIN ABOUT HAVING TO WAKE THEIR KIDS UP FOR SCHOOL, BUT I ACTUALLY ENJOY IT.
DON'T FORGET, TOMORROW IT'S YOUR TURN TO HOLD THE LADDER.

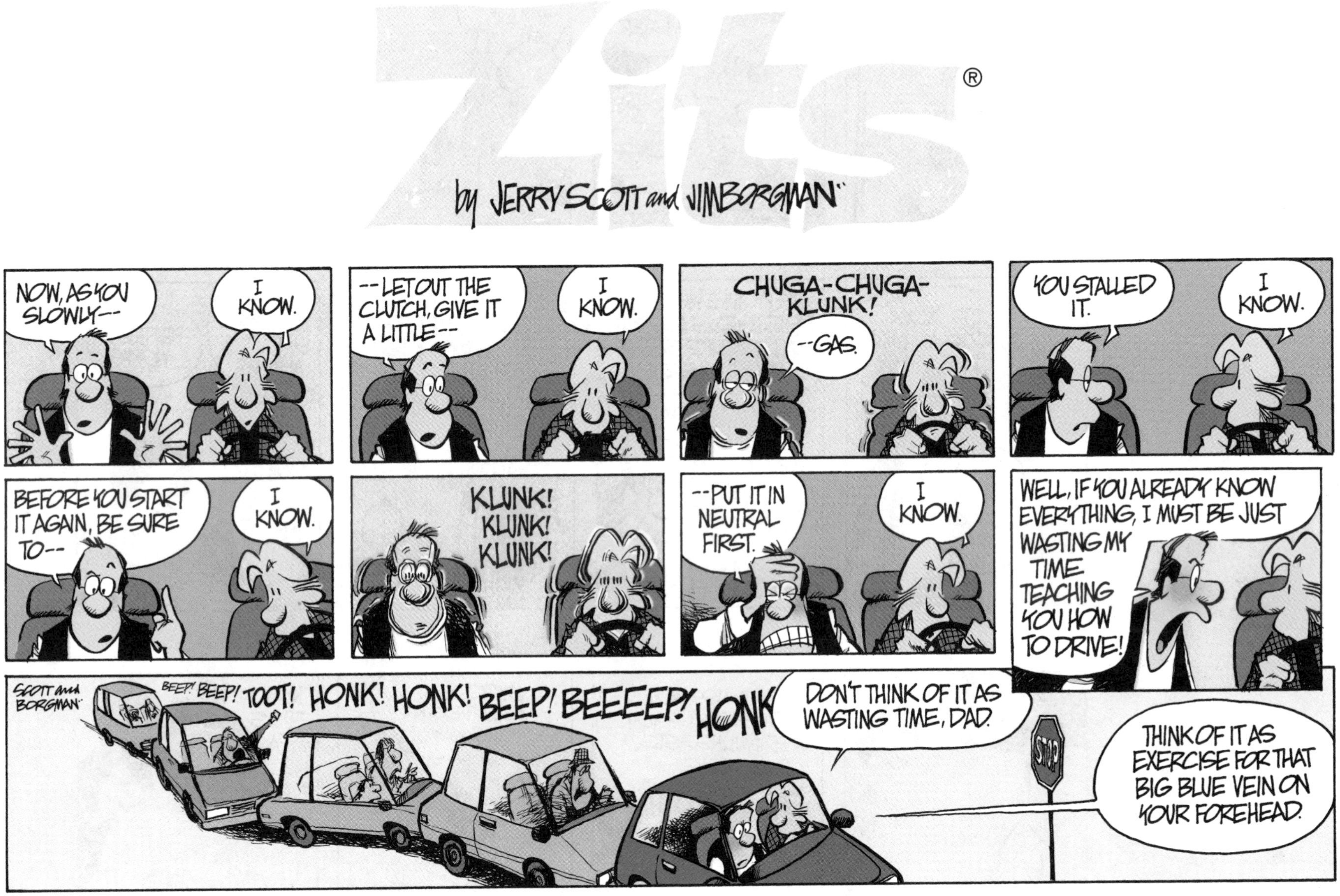
Zits®
by JERRY SCOTT and JIM BORGMAN
NOW, AS YOU SLOWLY--
I KNOW.
--LET OUT THE CLUTCH, GIVE IT A LITTLE--
I KNOW.
CHUGA-CHUGA-KLUNK!
--GAS.
YOU STALLED IT.
I KNOW.
BEFORE YOU START IT AGAIN, BE SURE TO--
I KNOW.
KLUNK! KLUNK! KLUNK!
--PUT IT IN NEUTRAL FIRST.
I KNOW.
WELL, IF YOU ALREADY KNOW EVERYTHING, I MUST BE JUST WASTING MY TIME TEACHING YOU HOW TO DRIVE!
SCOTT and BORGMAN
BEEP! BEEP! TOOT! HONK! HONK! BEEP! BEEEEP! HONK
DON'T THINK OF IT AS WASTING TIME, DAD.
STOP
THINK OF IT AS EXERCISE FOR THAT BIG BLUE VEIN ON YOUR FOREHEAD.

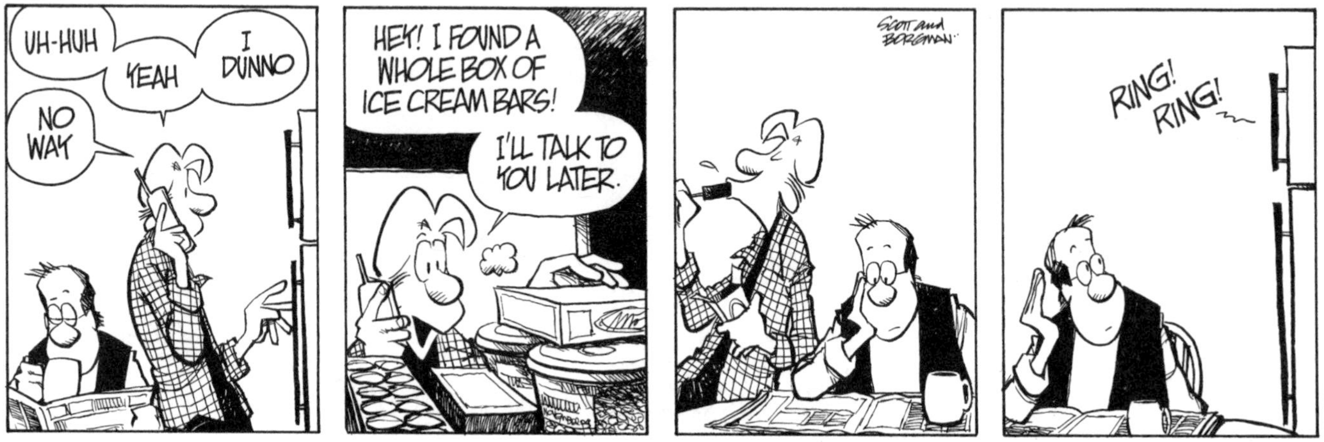
UH-HUH
NO WAY
YEAH
I DUNNO
HEY! I FOUND A WHOLE BOX OF ICE CREAM BARS!
I'LL TALK TO YOU LATER.
SCOTT AND BORGMAN
RING! RING!

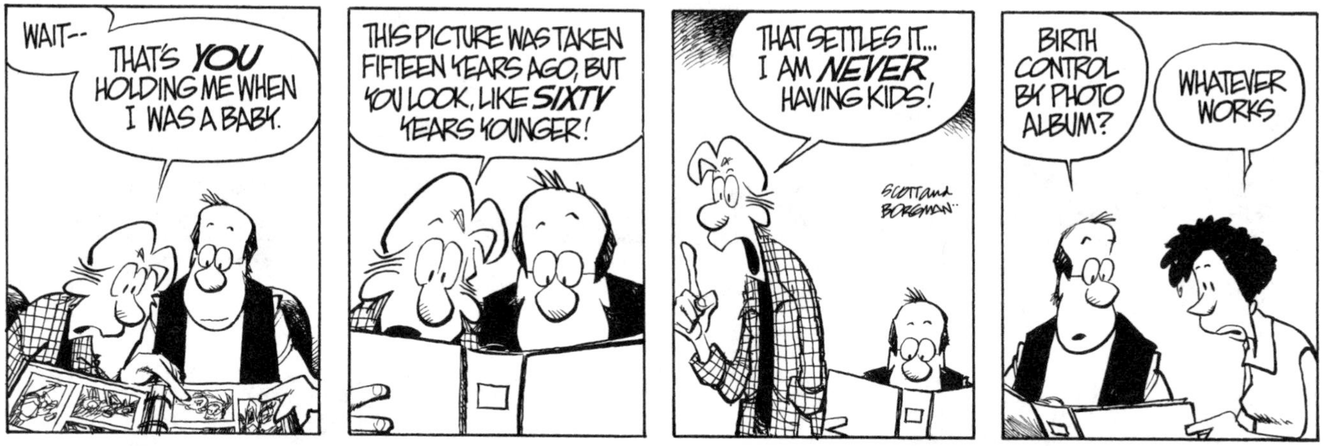
WAIT--
THAT'S **YOU** HOLDING ME WHEN I WAS A BABY.
THIS PICTURE WAS TAKEN FIFTEEN YEARS AGO, BUT YOU LOOK, LIKE **SIXTY** YEARS YOUNGER!
THAT SETTLES IT... I AM **NEVER** HAVING KIDS!
SCOTT AND BORGMAN
BIRTH CONTROL BY PHOTO ALBUM?
WHATEVER WORKS

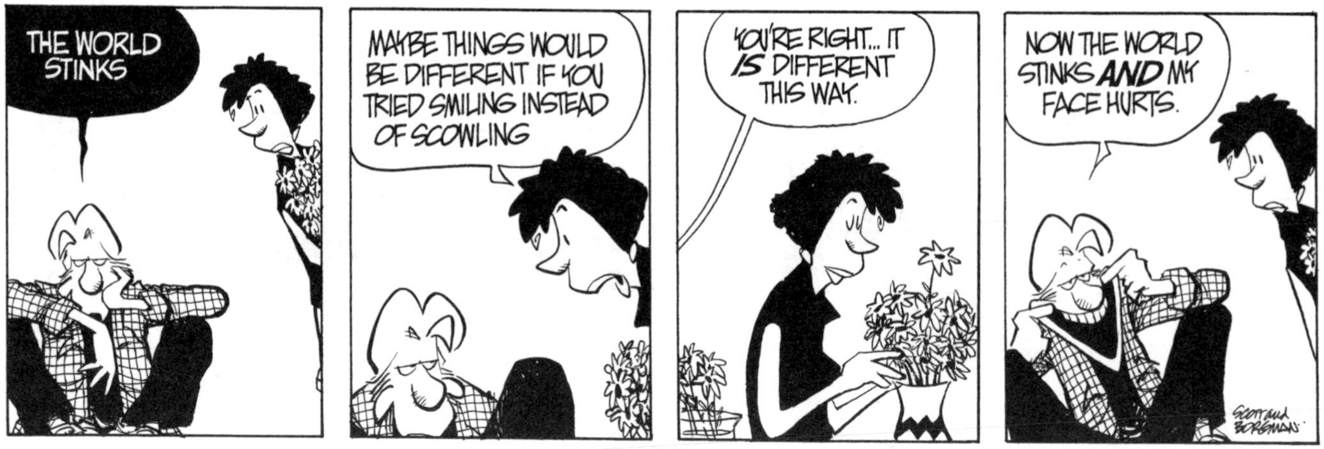
THE WORLD STINKS
MAYBE THINGS WOULD BE DIFFERENT IF YOU TRIED SMILING INSTEAD OF SCOWLING
YOU'RE RIGHT... IT **IS** DIFFERENT THIS WAY.
NOW THE WORLD STINKS **AND** MY FACE HURTS.
SCOTT AND BORGMAN

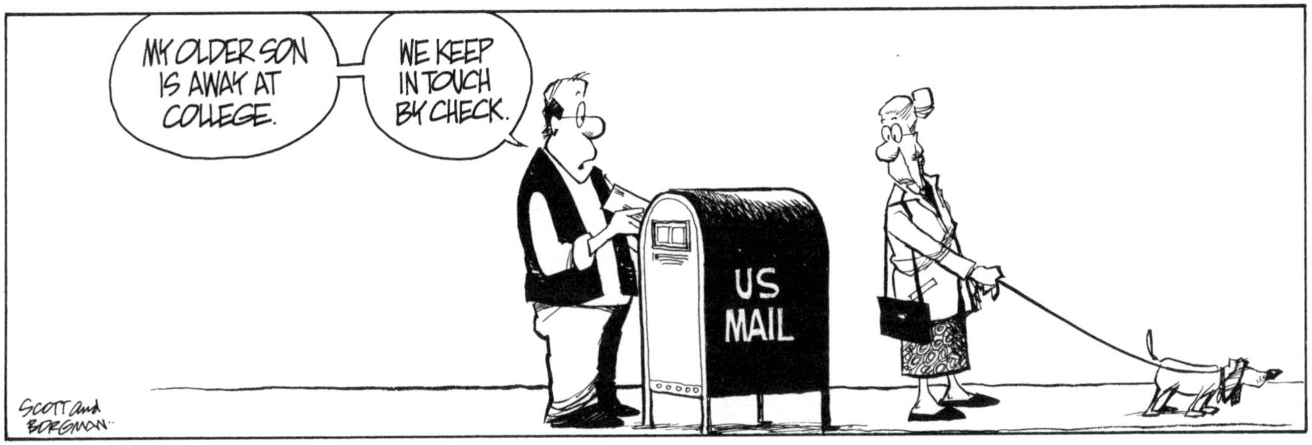
MY OLDER SON IS AWAY AT COLLEGE.
WE KEEP IN TOUCH BY CHECK.
US MAIL
SCOTT and BORGMAN

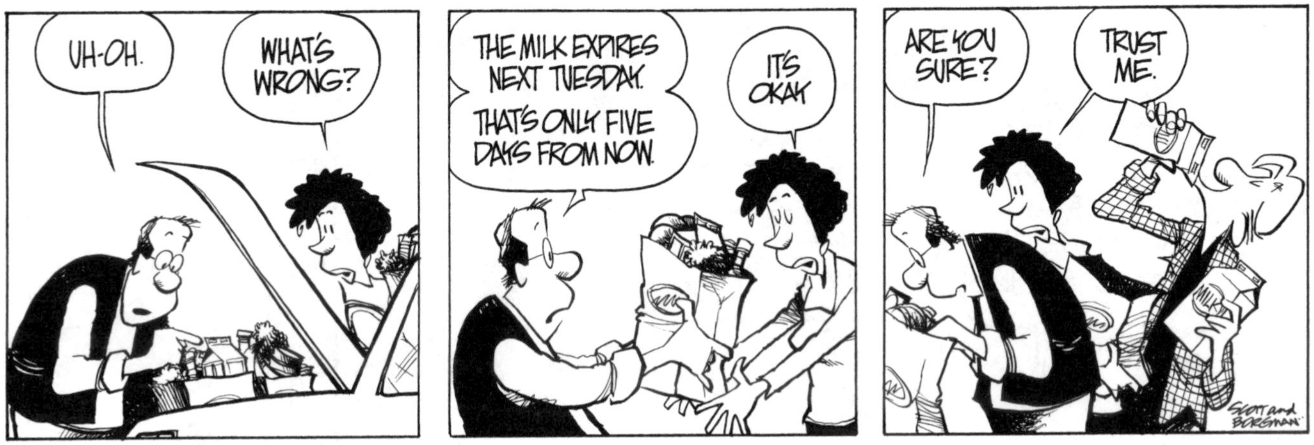
UH-OH.
WHAT'S WRONG?
THE MILK EXPIRES NEXT TUESDAY.
THAT'S ONLY FIVE DAYS FROM NOW.
IT'S OKAY
ARE YOU SURE?
TRUST ME.
SCOTT and BORGMAN

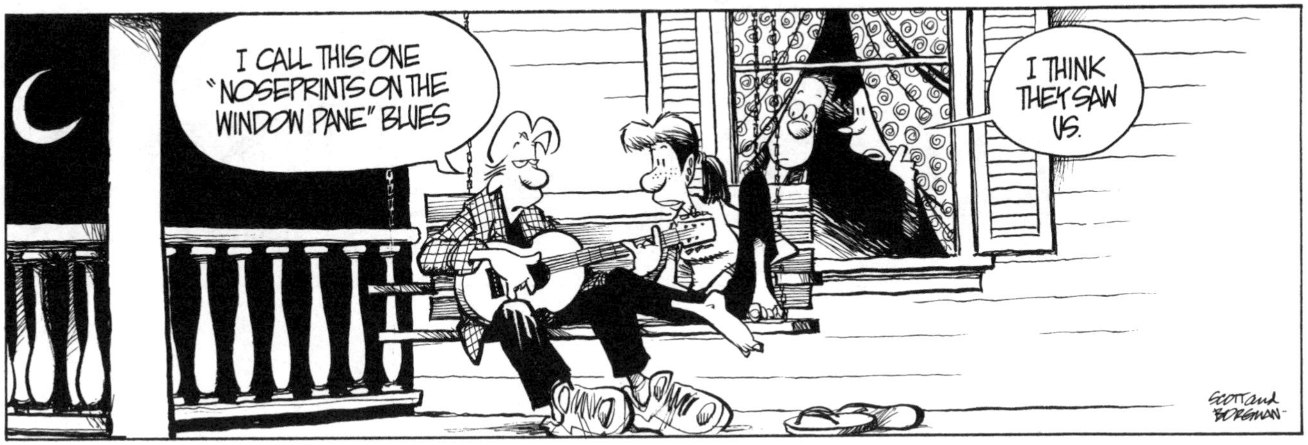
I CALL THIS ONE "NOSEPRINTS ON THE WINDOW PANE" BLUES
I THINK THEY SAW US.
SCOTT and BORGMAN

Zits®

by JERRY SCOTT and JIM BORGMAN

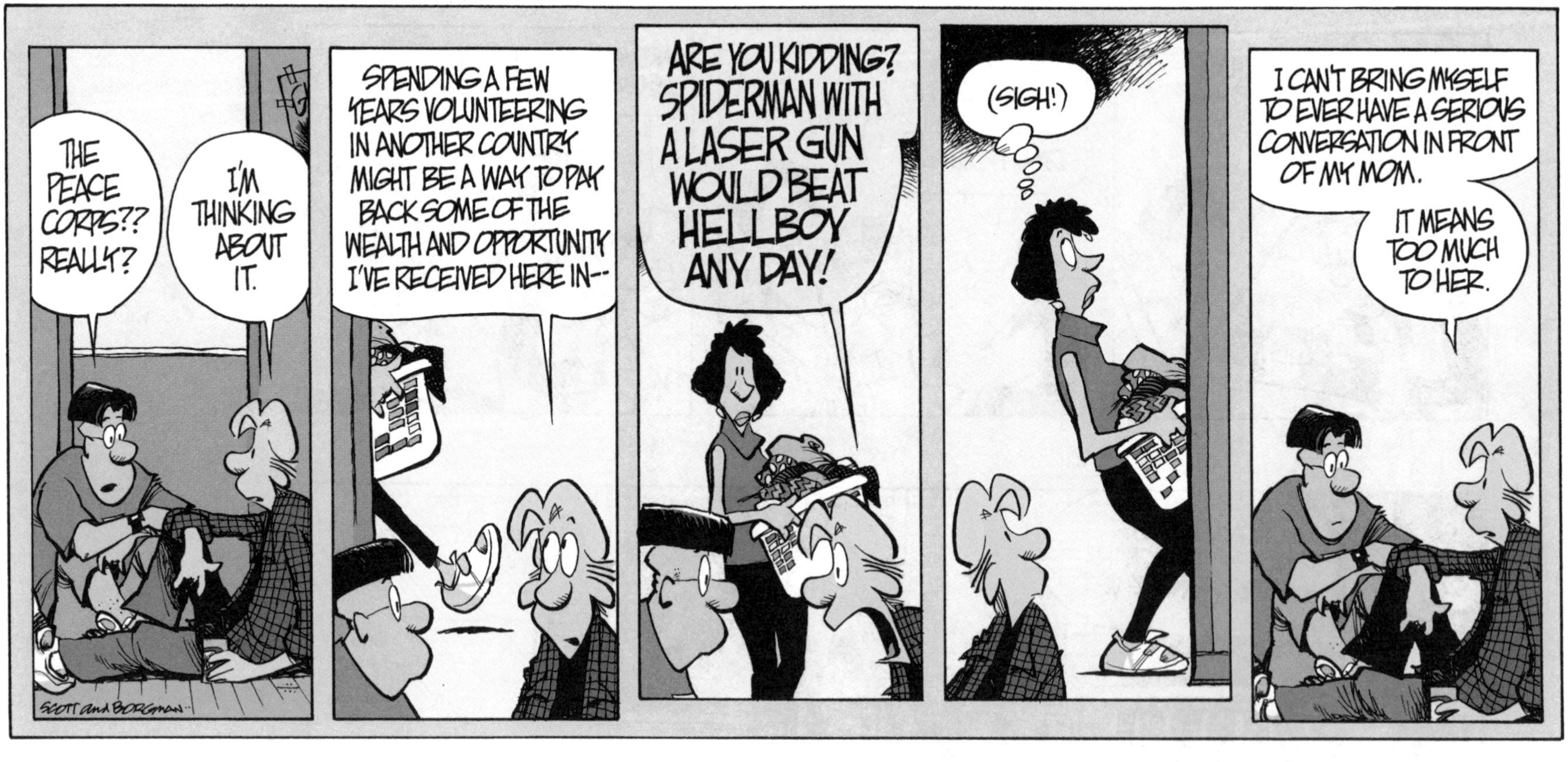
THE PEACE CORPS?? REALLY?
I'M THINKING ABOUT IT.
SPENDING A FEW YEARS VOLUNTEERING IN ANOTHER COUNTRY MIGHT BE A WAY TO PAY BACK SOME OF THE WEALTH AND OPPORTUNITY I'VE RECEIVED HERE IN--
ARE YOU KIDDING? SPIDERMAN WITH A LASER GUN WOULD BEAT HELLBOY ANY DAY!
(SIGH!)
I CAN'T BRING MYSELF TO EVER HAVE A SERIOUS CONVERSATION IN FRONT OF MY MOM.
IT MEANS TOO MUCH TO HER.
SCOTT and BORGMAN

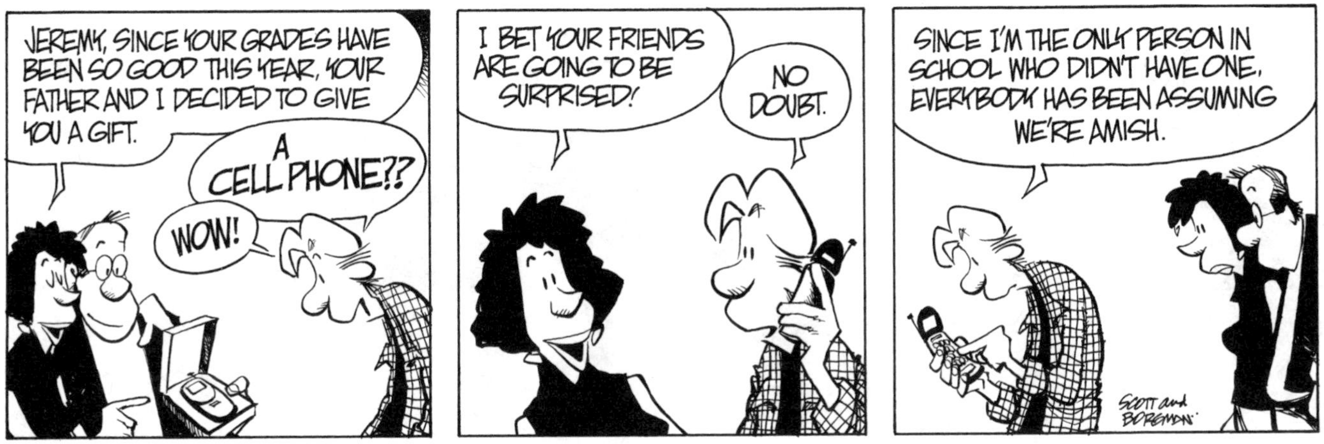
JEREMY, SINCE YOUR GRADES HAVE BEEN SO GOOD THIS YEAR, YOUR FATHER AND I DECIDED TO GIVE YOU A GIFT.
A CELL PHONE??
WOW!
I BET YOUR FRIENDS ARE GOING TO BE SURPRISED!
NO DOUBT.
SINCE I'M THE ONLY PERSON IN SCHOOL WHO DIDN'T HAVE ONE, EVERYBODY HAS BEEN ASSUMING WE'RE AMISH.
SCOTT and BORGMAN

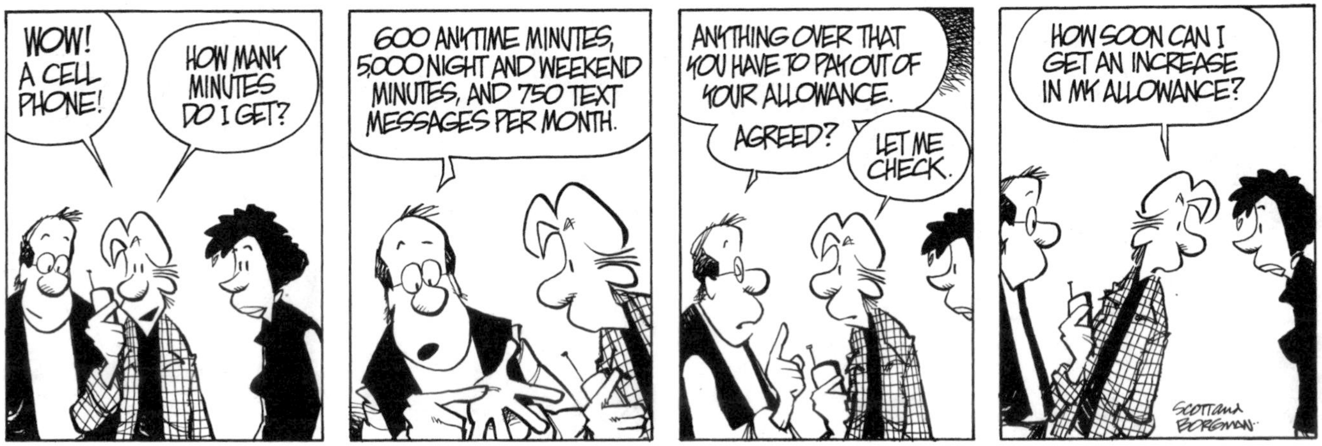
WOW! A CELL PHONE!
HOW MANY MINUTES DO I GET?
600 ANYTIME MINUTES, 5,000 NIGHT AND WEEKEND MINUTES, AND 750 TEXT MESSAGES PER MONTH.
ANYTHING OVER THAT YOU HAVE TO PAY OUT OF YOUR ALLOWANCE.
AGREED?
LET ME CHECK.
HOW SOON CAN I GET AN INCREASE IN MY ALLOWANCE?
SCOTT and BORGMAN

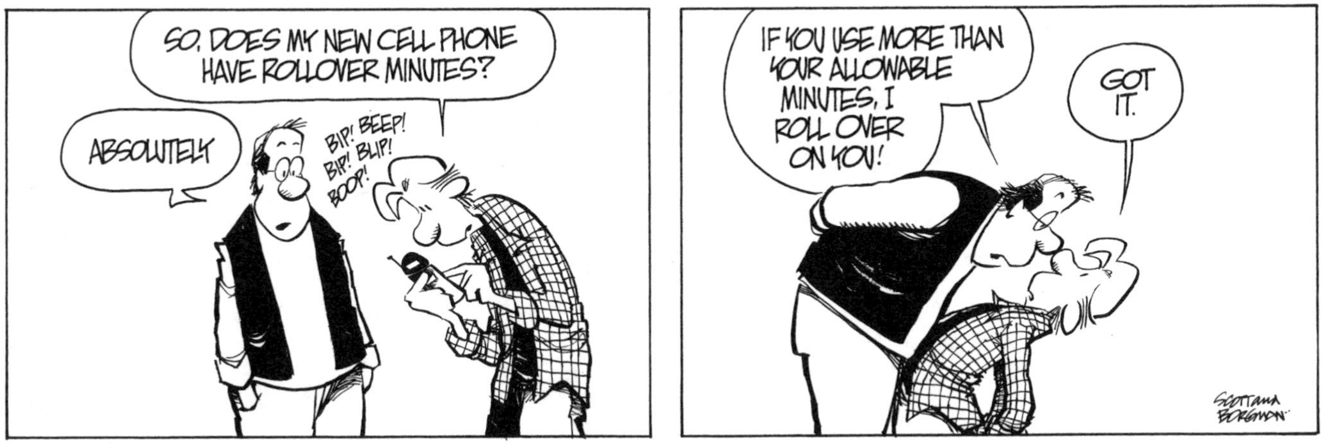
SO, DOES MY NEW CELL PHONE HAVE ROLLOVER MINUTES?
ABSOLUTELY.
BIP! BEEP! BIP! BLIP! BOOP!
IF YOU USE MORE THAN YOUR ALLOWABLE MINUTES, I ROLL OVER ON YOU!
GOT IT.
SCOTT and BORGMAN

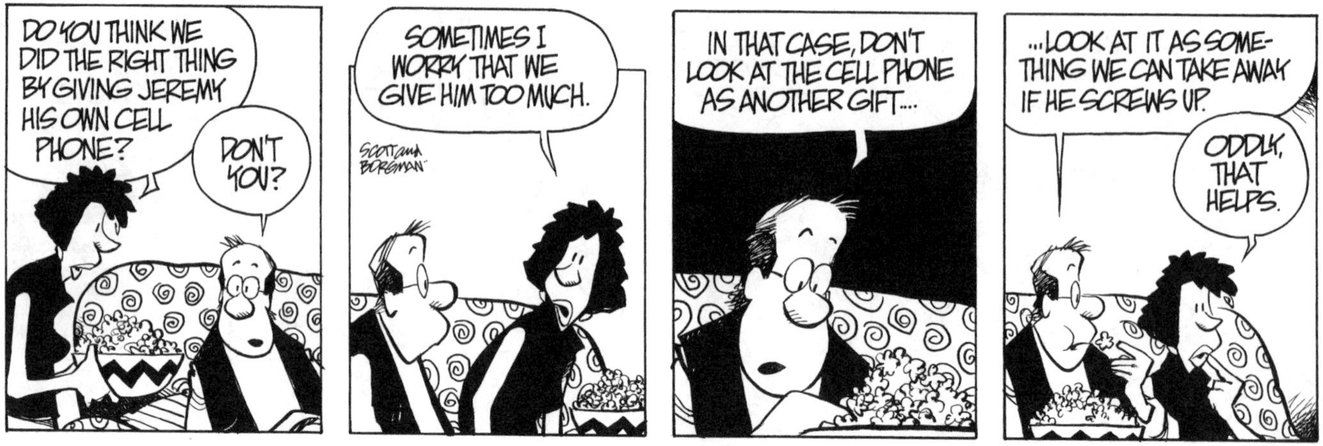
DO YOU THINK WE DID THE RIGHT THING BY GIVING JEREMY HIS OWN CELL PHONE?
DON'T YOU?
SOMETIMES I WORRY THAT WE GIVE HIM TOO MUCH.
IN THAT CASE, DON'T LOOK AT THE CELL PHONE AS ANOTHER GIFT....
...LOOK AT IT AS SOMETHING WE CAN TAKE AWAY IF HE SCREWS UP.
ODDLY, THAT HELPS.

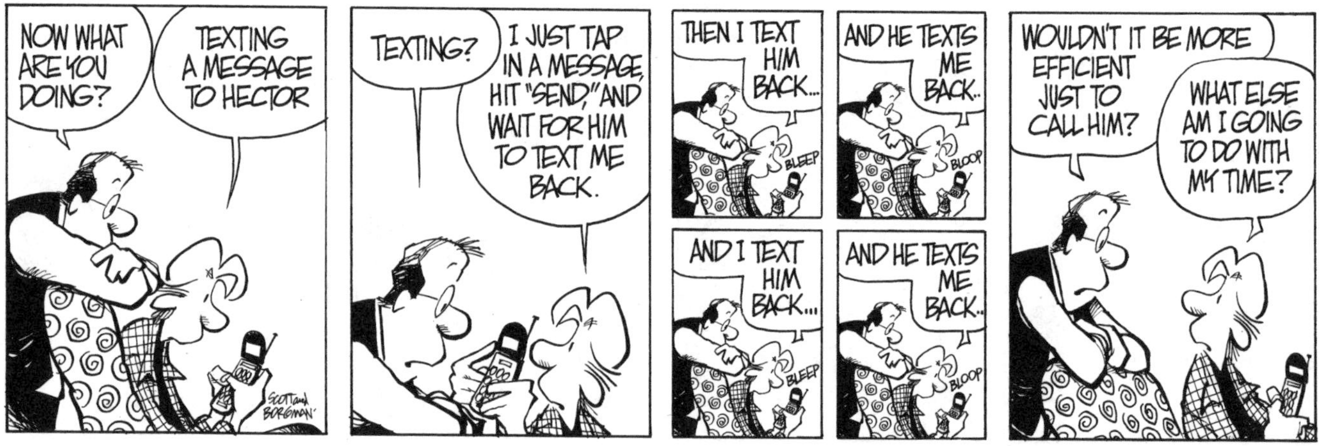
NOW WHAT ARE YOU DOING?
TEXTING A MESSAGE TO HECTOR
TEXTING?
I JUST TAP IN A MESSAGE, HIT "SEND," AND WAIT FOR HIM TO TEXT ME BACK.
THEN I TEXT HIM BACK...
BLEEP
AND HE TEXTS ME BACK..
BLOOP
AND I TEXT HIM BACK....
BLEEP
AND HE TEXTS ME BACK..
BLOOP
WOULDN'T IT BE MORE EFFICIENT JUST TO CALL HIM?
WHAT ELSE AM I GOING TO DO WITH MY TIME?

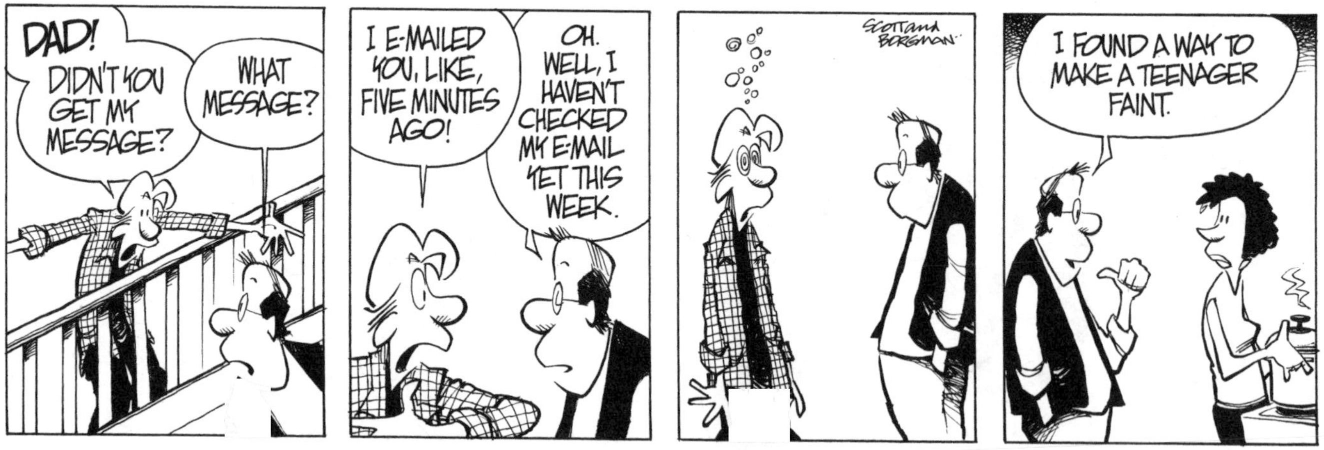
DAD!
DIDN'T YOU GET MY MESSAGE?
WHAT MESSAGE?
I E-MAILED YOU, LIKE, FIVE MINUTES AGO!
OH. WELL, I HAVEN'T CHECKED MY E-MAIL YET THIS WEEK.
I FOUND A WAY TO MAKE A TEENAGER FAINT.

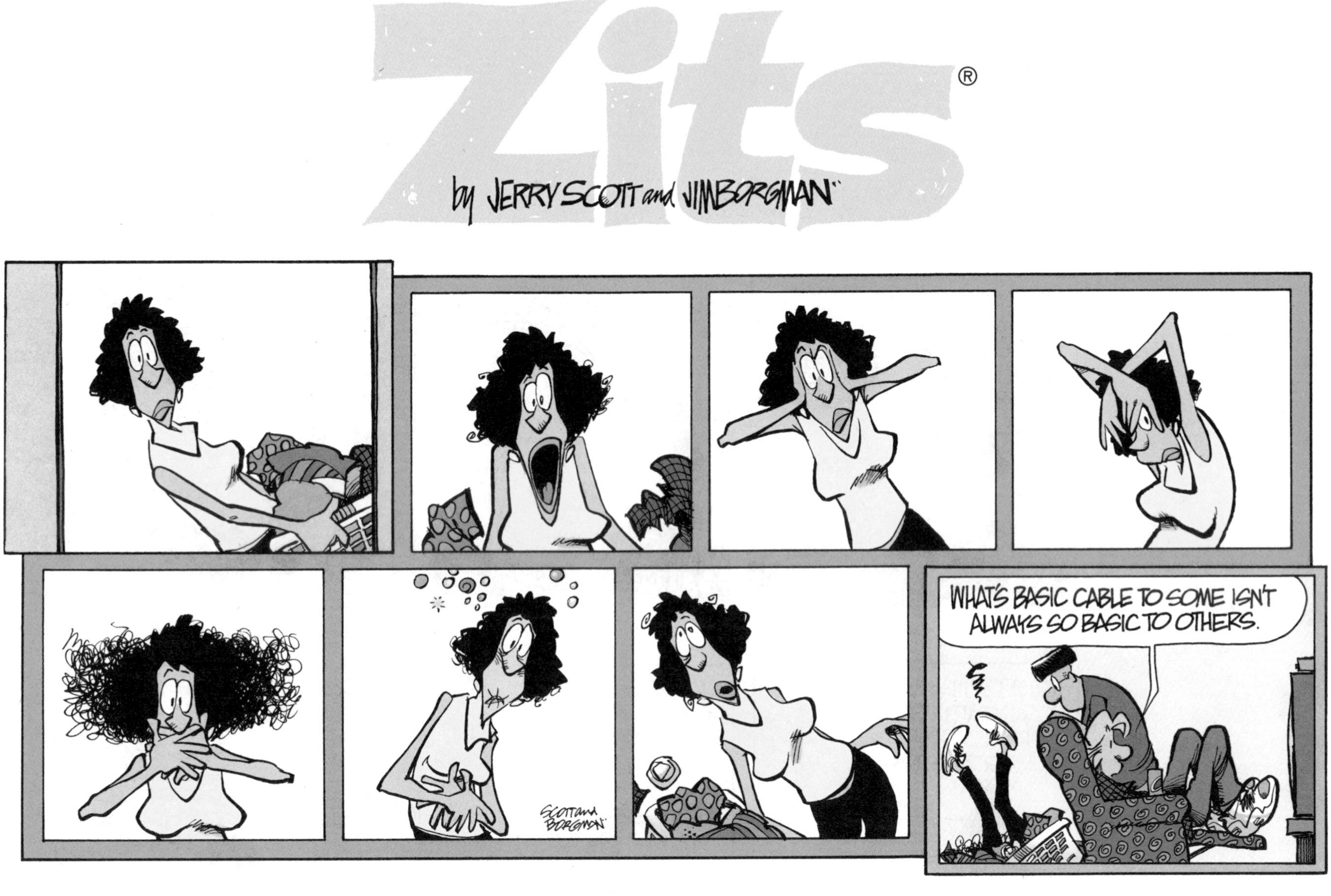
Zits®
by JERRY SCOTT and JIM BORGMAN
SCOTT and BORGMAN
WHAT'S BASIC CABLE TO SOME ISN'T ALWAYS SO BASIC TO OTHERS.

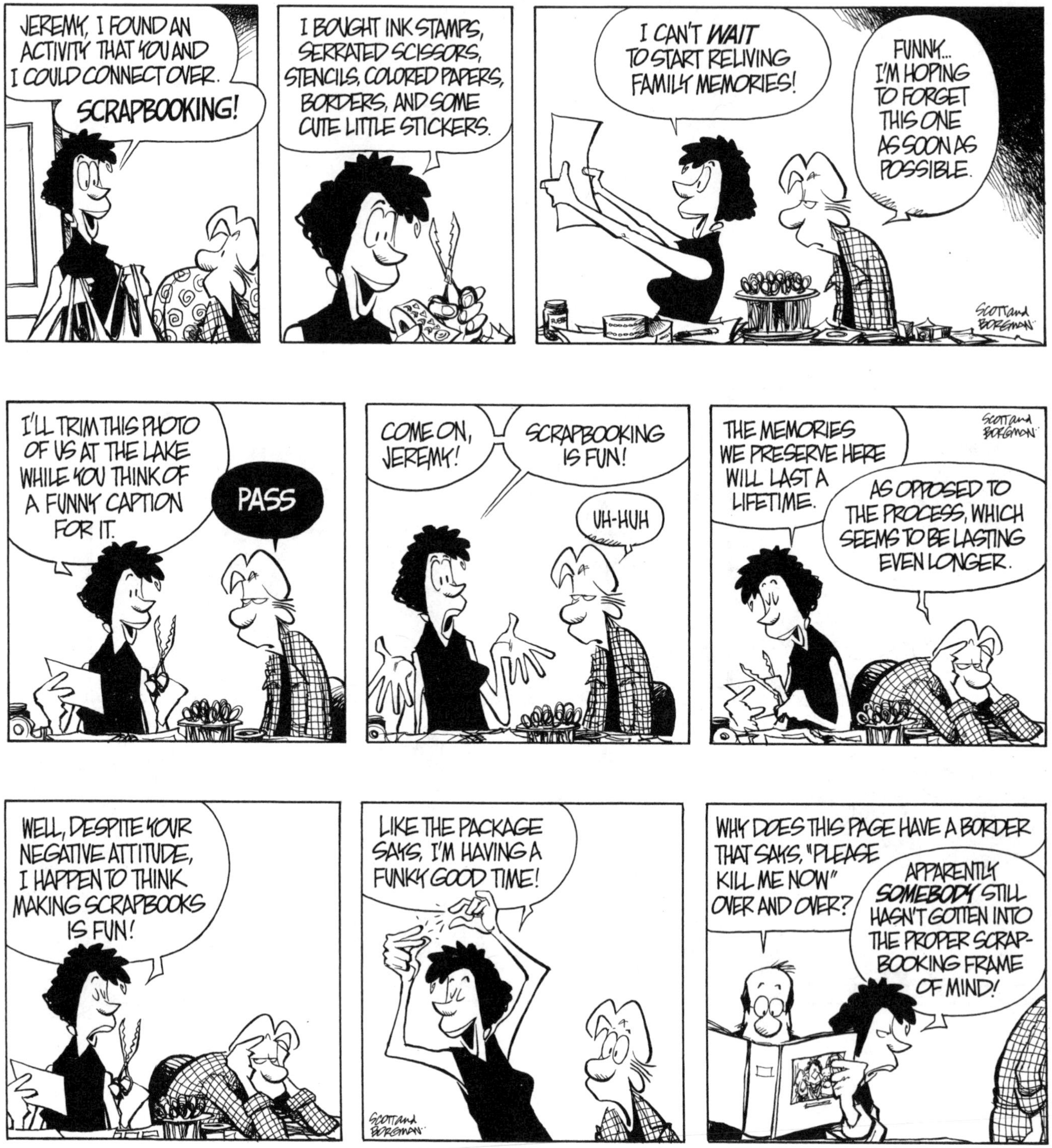
JEREMY, I FOUND AN ACTIVITY THAT YOU AND I COULD CONNECT OVER.
SCRAPBOOKING!
I BOUGHT INK STAMPS, SERRATED SCISSORS, STENCILS, COLORED PAPERS, BORDERS, AND SOME CUTE LITTLE STICKERS.
I CAN'T WAIT TO START RELIVING FAMILY MEMORIES!
FUNNY... I'M HOPING TO FORGET THIS ONE AS SOON AS POSSIBLE.
SCOTT and BORGMAN
I'LL TRIM THIS PHOTO OF US AT THE LAKE WHILE YOU THINK OF A FUNNY CAPTION FOR IT.
PASS
COME ON, JEREMY!
SCRAPBOOKING IS FUN!
UH-HUH
THE MEMORIES WE PRESERVE HERE WILL LAST A LIFETIME.
AS OPPOSED TO THE PROCESS, WHICH SEEMS TO BE LASTING EVEN LONGER.
SCOTT and BORGMAN
WELL, DESPITE YOUR NEGATIVE ATTITUDE, I HAPPEN TO THINK MAKING SCRAPBOOKS IS FUN!
LIKE THE PACKAGE SAYS, I'M HAVING A FUNKY GOOD TIME!
SCOTT and BORGMAN
WHY DOES THIS PAGE HAVE A BORDER THAT SAYS, "PLEASE KILL ME NOW" OVER AND OVER?
APPARENTLY SOMEBODY STILL HASN'T GOTTEN INTO THE PROPER SCRAP-BOOKING FRAME OF MIND!

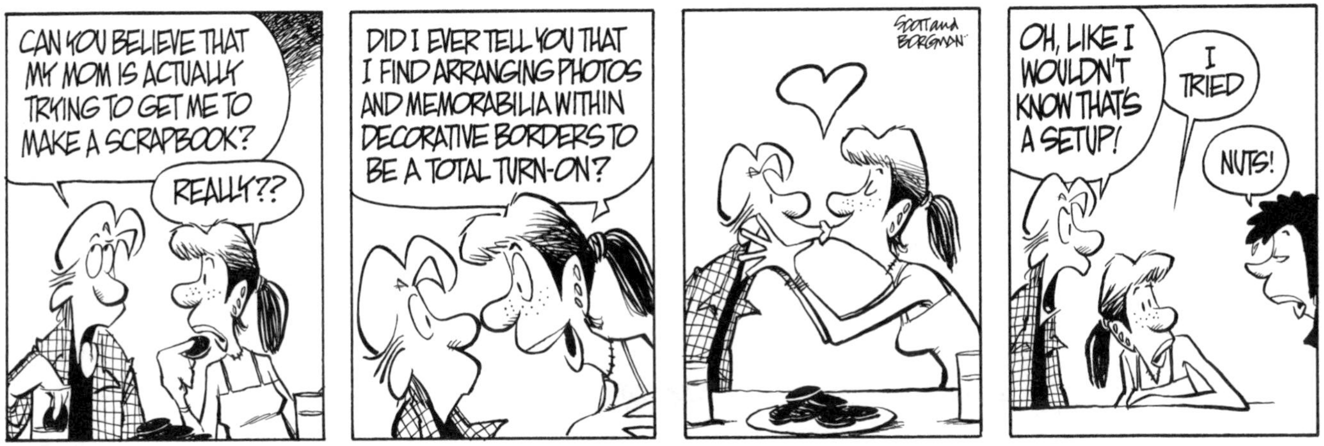
CAN YOU BELIEVE THAT MY MOM IS ACTUALLY TRYING TO GET ME TO MAKE A SCRAPBOOK?
REALLY??
DID I EVER TELL YOU THAT I FIND ARRANGING PHOTOS AND MEMORABILIA WITHIN DECORATIVE BORDERS TO BE A TOTAL TURN-ON?
SCOTT and BORGMAN
OH, LIKE I WOULDN'T KNOW THAT'S A SETUP!
I TRIED
NUTS!

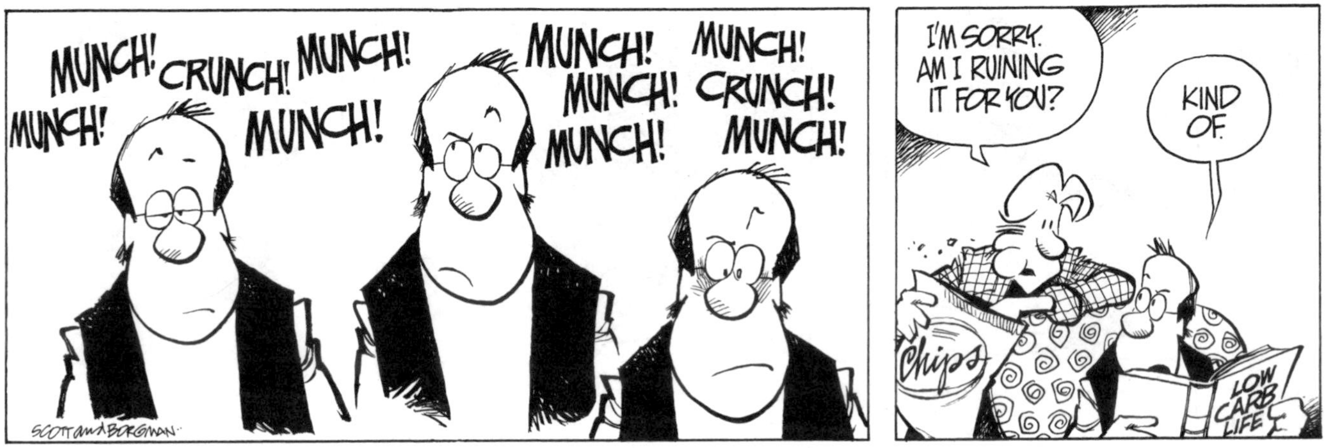
MUNCH! CRUNCH! MUNCH!
MUNCH!
MUNCH!
MUNCH! MUNCH! MUNCH!
MUNCH! CRUNCH! MUNCH!
SCOTT and BORGMAN
I'M SORRY. AM I RUINING IT FOR YOU?
KIND OF.
Chips
LOW CARB LIFE

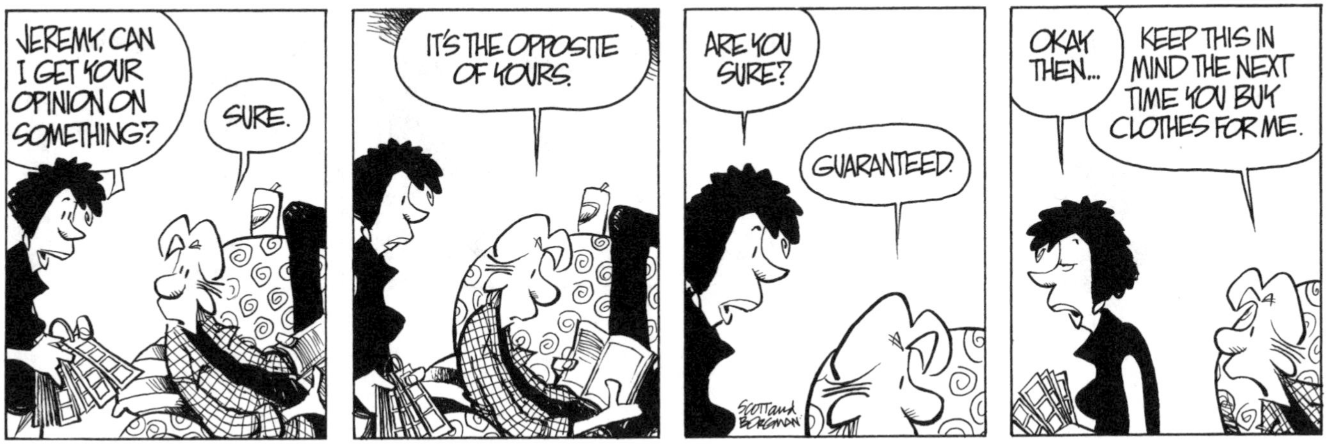
JEREMY, CAN I GET YOUR OPINION ON SOMETHING?
SURE.
IT'S THE OPPOSITE OF YOURS.
ARE YOU SURE?
GUARANTEED.
SCOTT and BORGMAN
OKAY THEN...
KEEP THIS IN MIND THE NEXT TIME YOU BUY CLOTHES FOR ME.

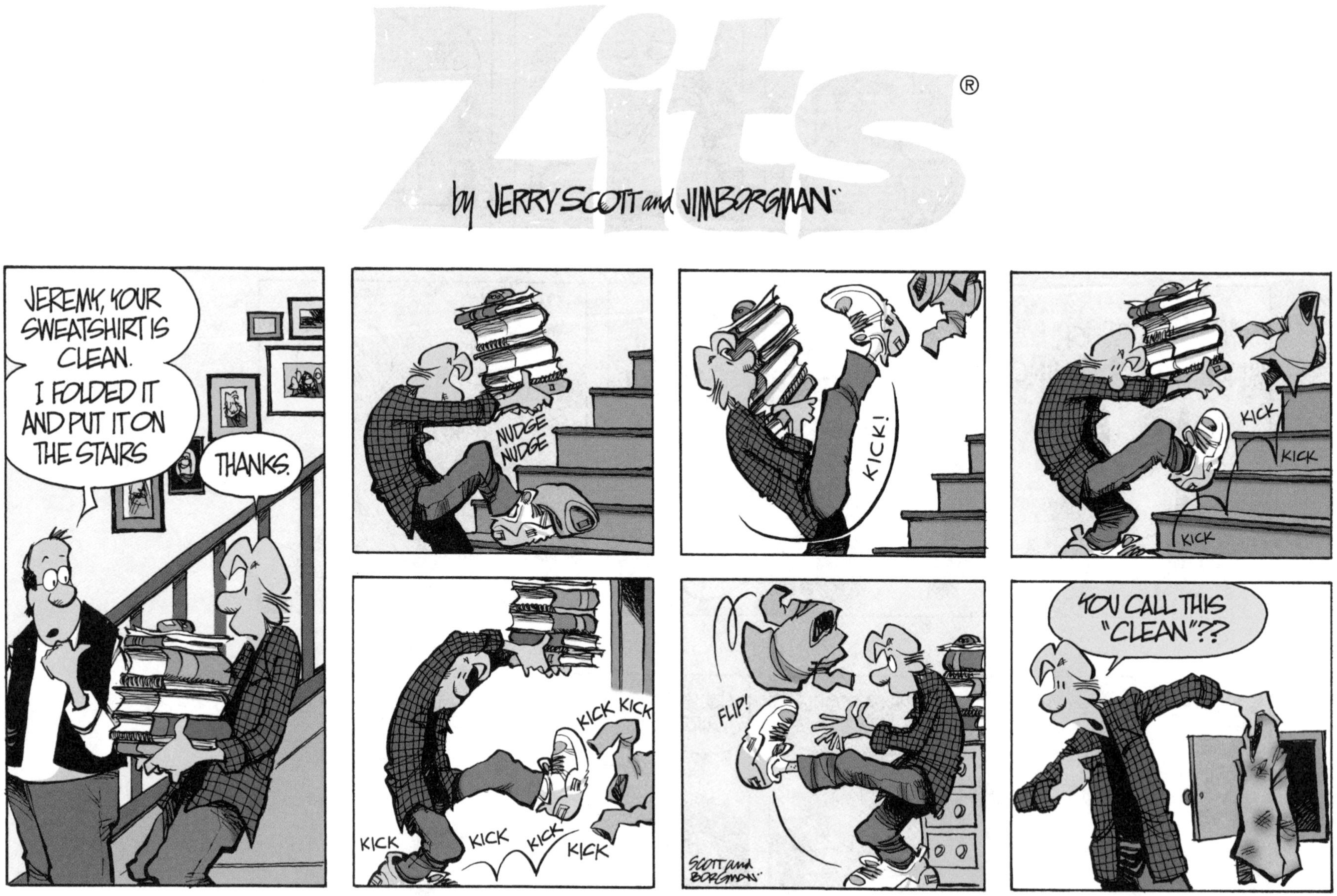
Zits®
by JERRY SCOTT and JIM BORGMAN
JEREMY, YOUR SWEATSHIRT IS CLEAN. I FOLDED IT AND PUT IT ON THE STAIRS
THANKS.
NUDGE NUDGE
KICK!
KICK
KICK
KICK
KICK KICK
KICK
KICK
KICK
KICK
FLIP!
SCOTT and BORGMAN
YOU CALL THIS "CLEAN"??

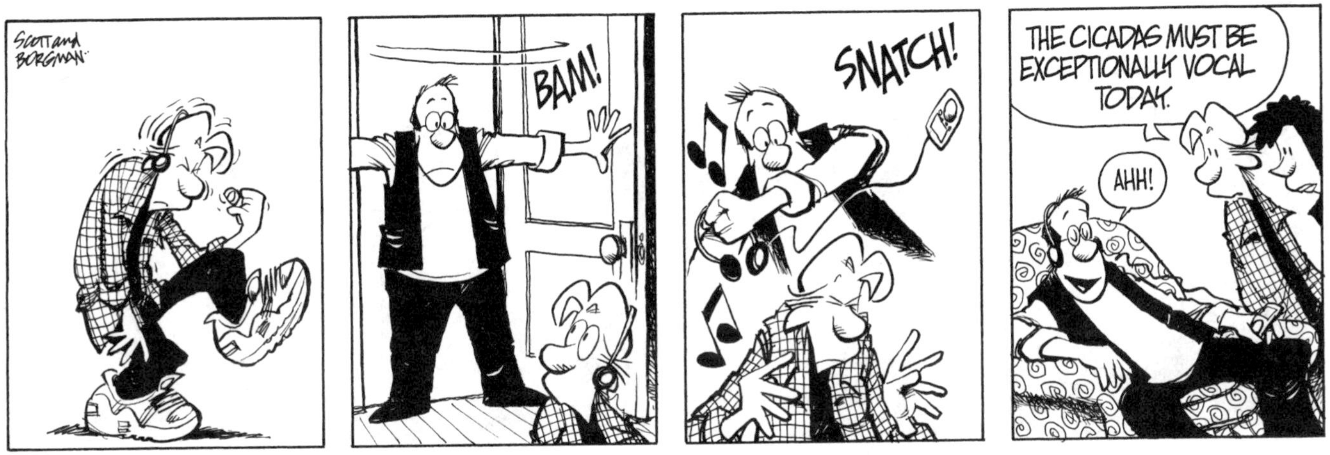
SCOTT and BORGMAN
BAM!
SNATCH!
THE CICADAS MUST BE EXCEPTIONALLY VOCAL TODAY.
AHH!

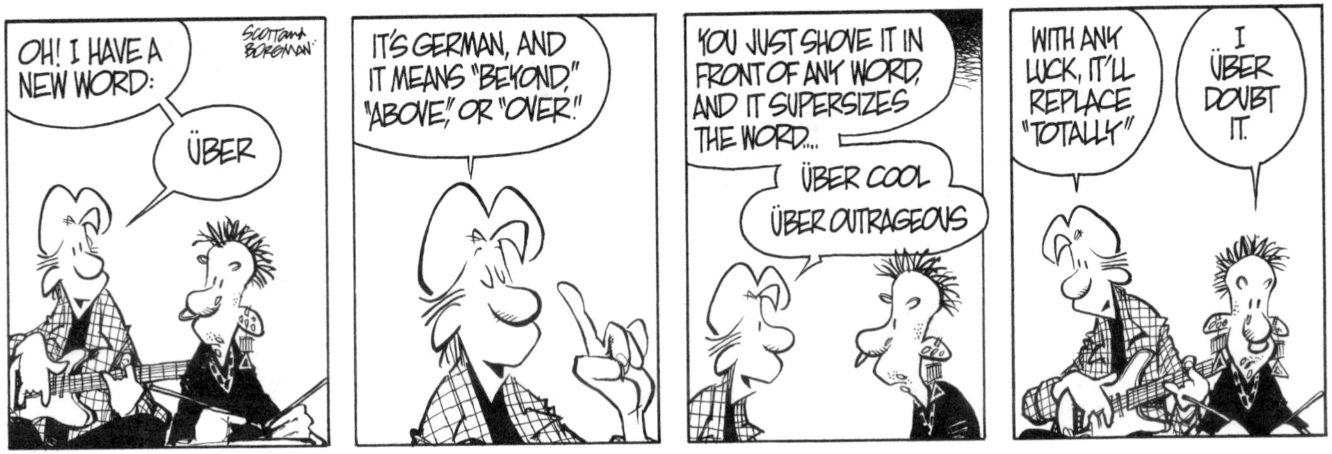
SCOTT and BORGMAN
OH! I HAVE A NEW WORD:
ÜBER
IT'S GERMAN, AND IT MEANS "BEYOND," "ABOVE," OR "OVER."
YOU JUST SHOVE IT IN FRONT OF ANY WORD, AND IT SUPERSIZES THE WORD...
ÜBER COOL
ÜBER OUTRAGEOUS
WITH ANY LUCK, IT'LL REPLACE "TOTALLY"
I ÜBER DOUBT IT.

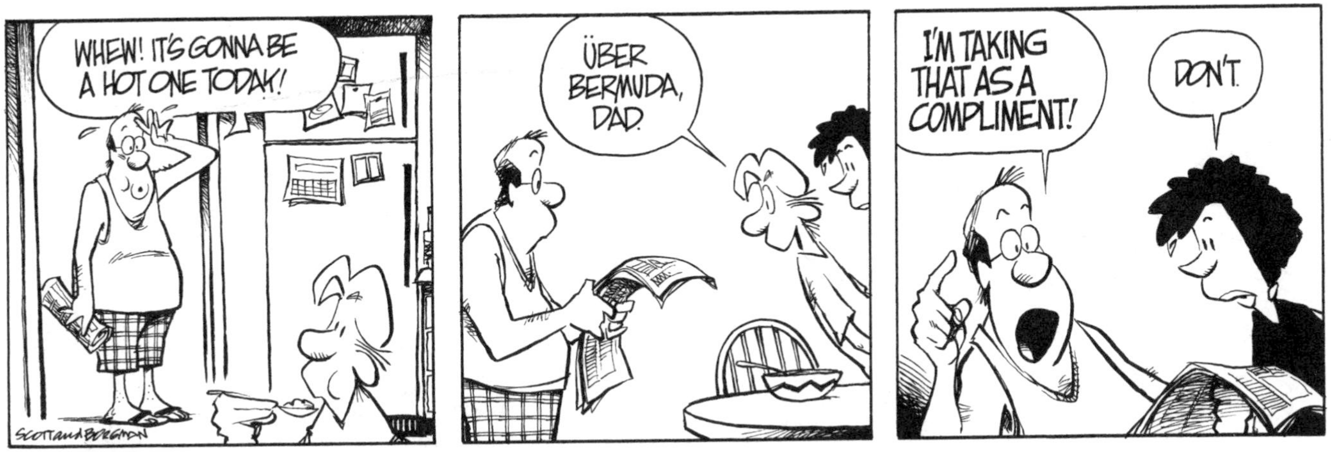
WHEW! IT'S GONNA BE A HOT ONE TODAY!
SCOTT and BORGMAN
ÜBER BERMUDA, DAD.
I'M TAKING THAT AS A COMPLIMENT!
DON'T.

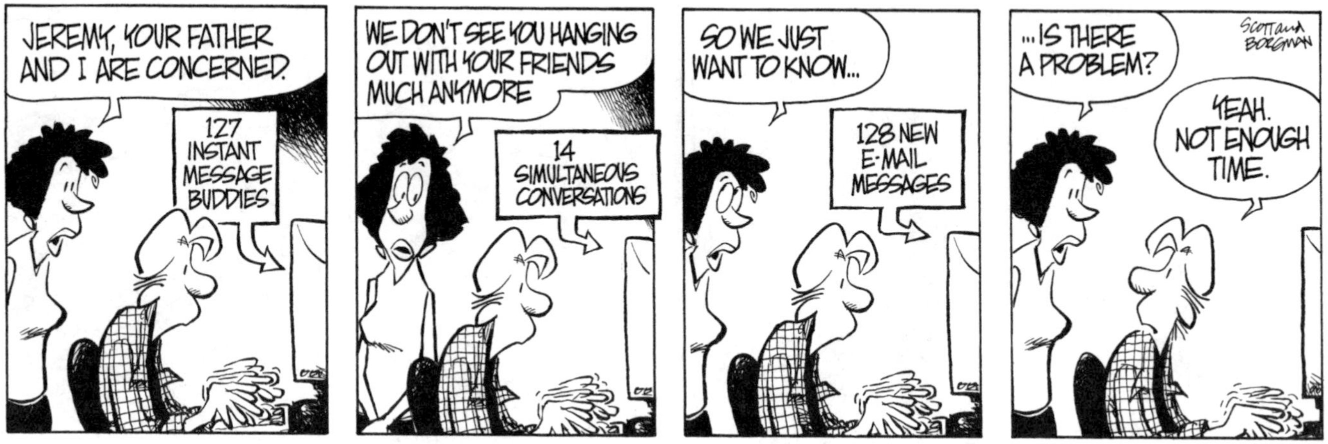
JEREMY, YOUR FATHER AND I ARE CONCERNED.
127 INSTANT MESSAGE BUDDIES
WE DON'T SEE YOU HANGING OUT WITH YOUR FRIENDS MUCH ANYMORE
14 SIMULTANEOUS CONVERSATIONS
SO WE JUST WANT TO KNOW...
128 NEW E-MAIL MESSAGES
...IS THERE A PROBLEM?
YEAH. NOT ENOUGH TIME.

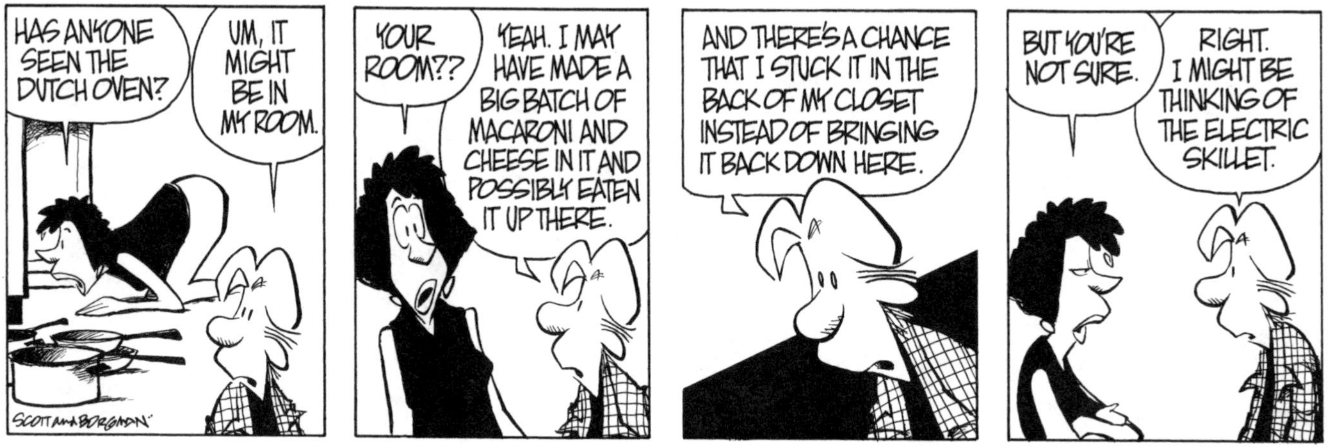
HAS ANYONE SEEN THE DUTCH OVEN?
UM, IT MIGHT BE IN MY ROOM.
YOUR ROOM??
YEAH. I MAY HAVE MADE A BIG BATCH OF MACARONI AND CHEESE IN IT AND POSSIBLY EATEN IT UP THERE.
AND THERE'S A CHANCE THAT I STUCK IT IN THE BACK OF MY CLOSET INSTEAD OF BRINGING IT BACK DOWN HERE.
BUT YOU'RE NOT SURE.
RIGHT. I MIGHT BE THINKING OF THE ELECTRIC SKILLET.

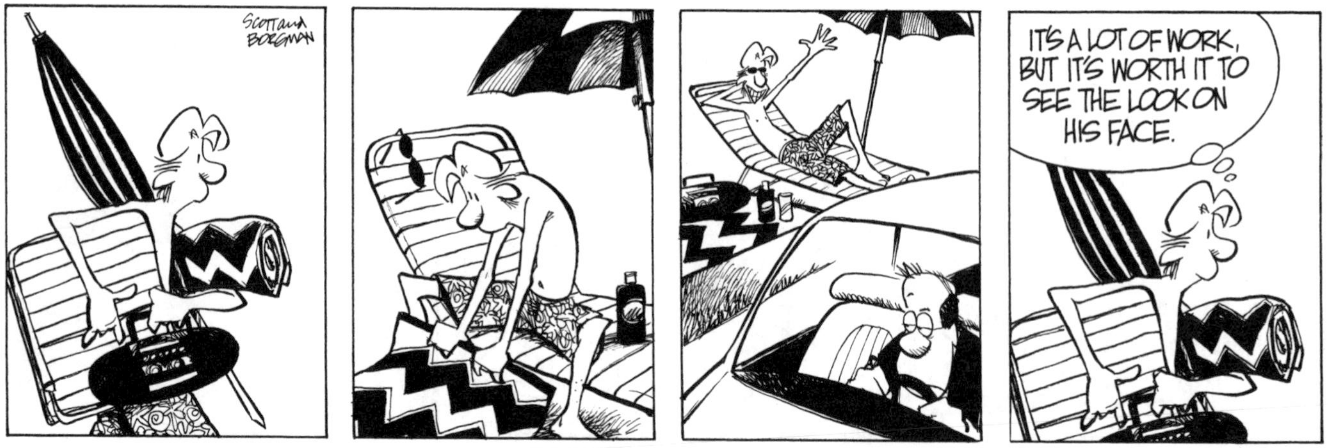
IT'S A LOT OF WORK, BUT IT'S WORTH IT TO SEE THE LOOK ON HIS FACE.

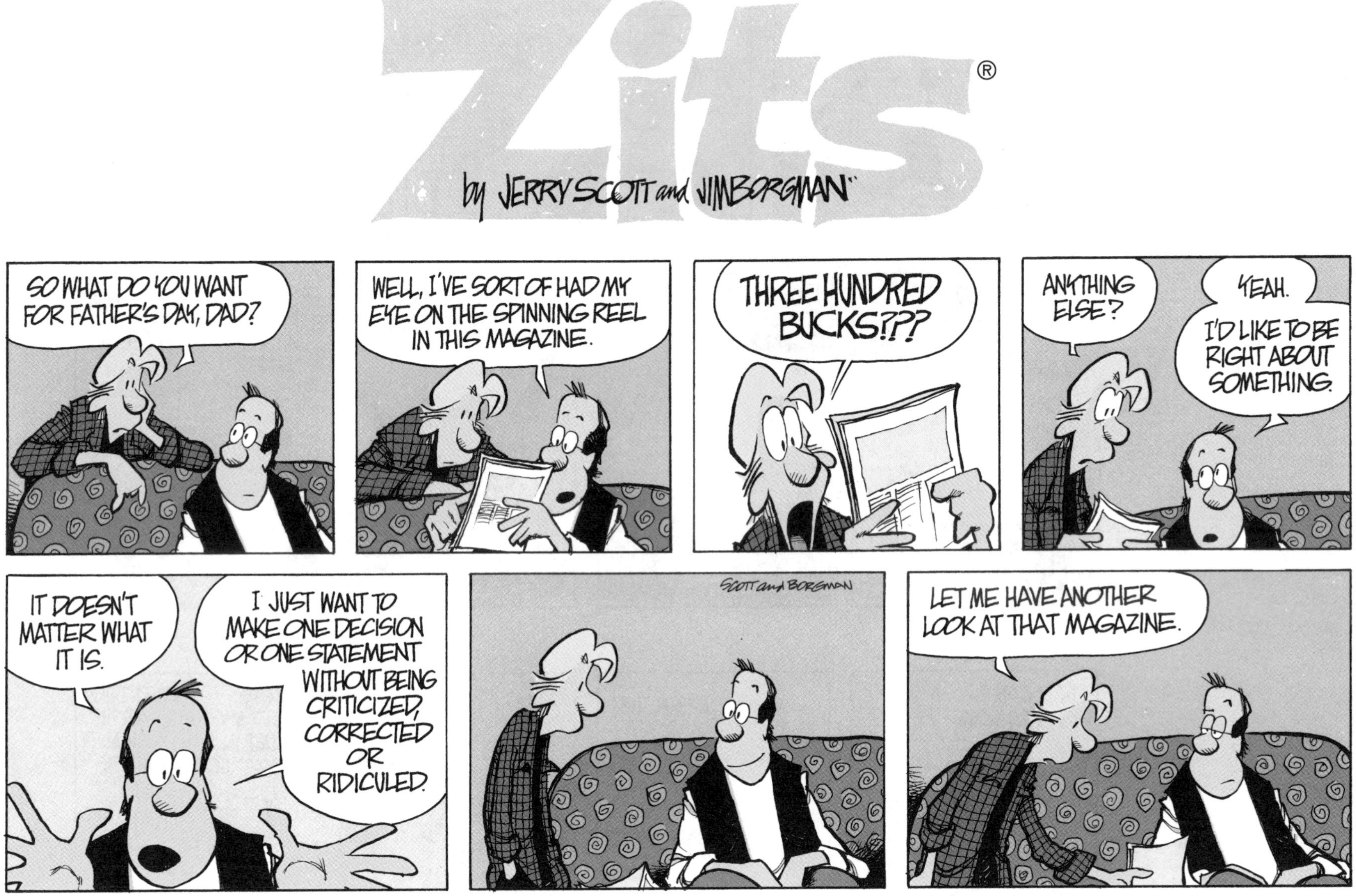

Zits®
by JERRY SCOTT and JIM BORGMAN
SO WHAT DO YOU WANT FOR FATHER'S DAY, DAD?
WELL, I'VE SORT OF HAD MY EYE ON THE SPINNING REEL IN THIS MAGAZINE.
THREE HUNDRED BUCKS???
ANYTHING ELSE?
YEAH.
I'D LIKE TO BE RIGHT ABOUT SOMETHING.
IT DOESN'T MATTER WHAT IT IS.
I JUST WANT TO MAKE ONE DECISION OR ONE STATEMENT WITHOUT BEING CRITICIZED, CORRECTED OR RIDICULED.
SCOTT and BORGMAN
LET ME HAVE ANOTHER LOOK AT THAT MAGAZINE.

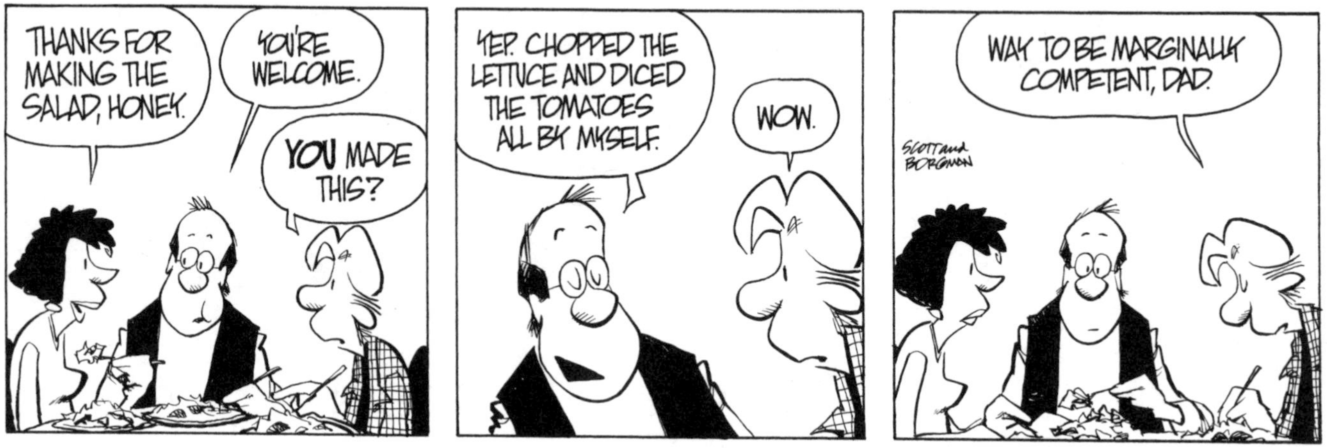
THANKS FOR MAKING THE SALAD, HONEY.
YOU'RE WELCOME.
YOU MADE THIS?
YEP. CHOPPED THE LETTUCE AND DICED THE TOMATOES ALL BY MYSELF.
WOW.
WAY TO BE MARGINALLY COMPETENT, DAD.

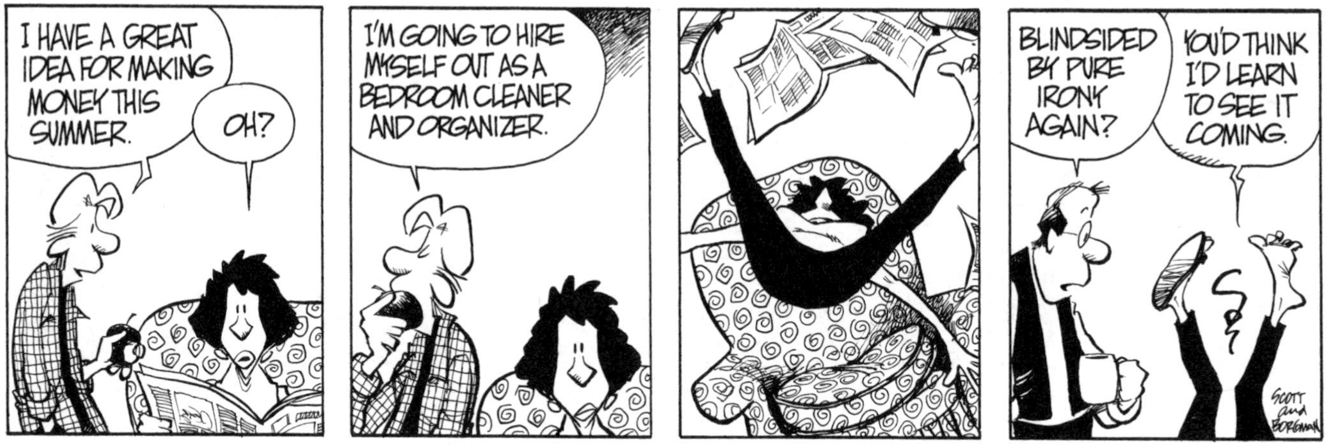
I HAVE A GREAT IDEA FOR MAKING MONEY THIS SUMMER.
OH?
I'M GOING TO HIRE MYSELF OUT AS A BEDROOM CLEANER AND ORGANIZER.
BLINDSIDED BY PURE IRONY AGAIN?
YOU'D THINK I'D LEARN TO SEE IT COMING.

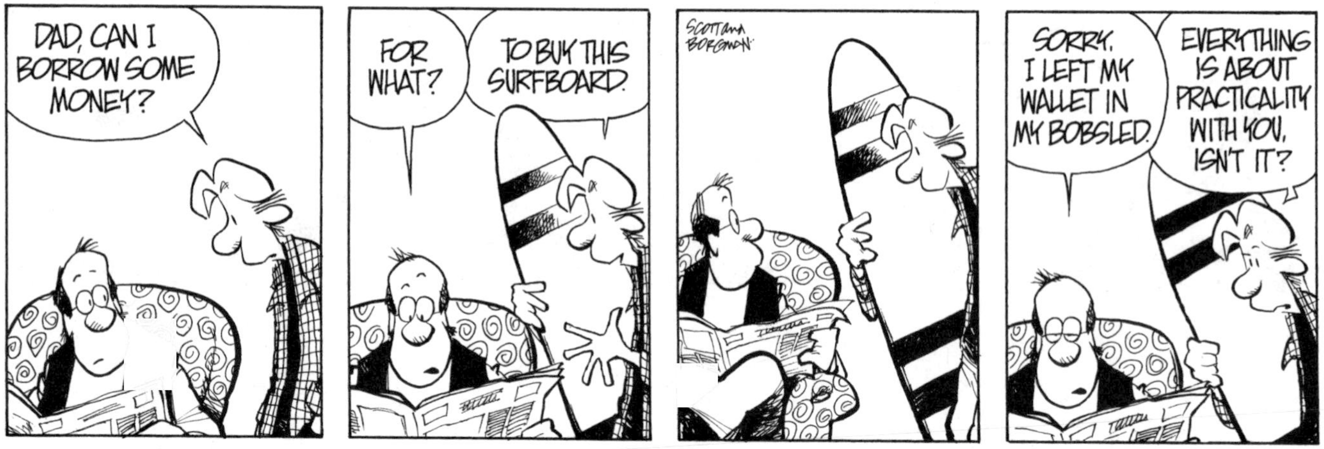
DAD, CAN I BORROW SOME MONEY?
FOR WHAT?
TO BUY THIS SURFBOARD.
SORRY. I LEFT MY WALLET IN MY BOBSLED.
EVERYTHING IS ABOUT PRACTICALITY WITH YOU, ISN'T IT?

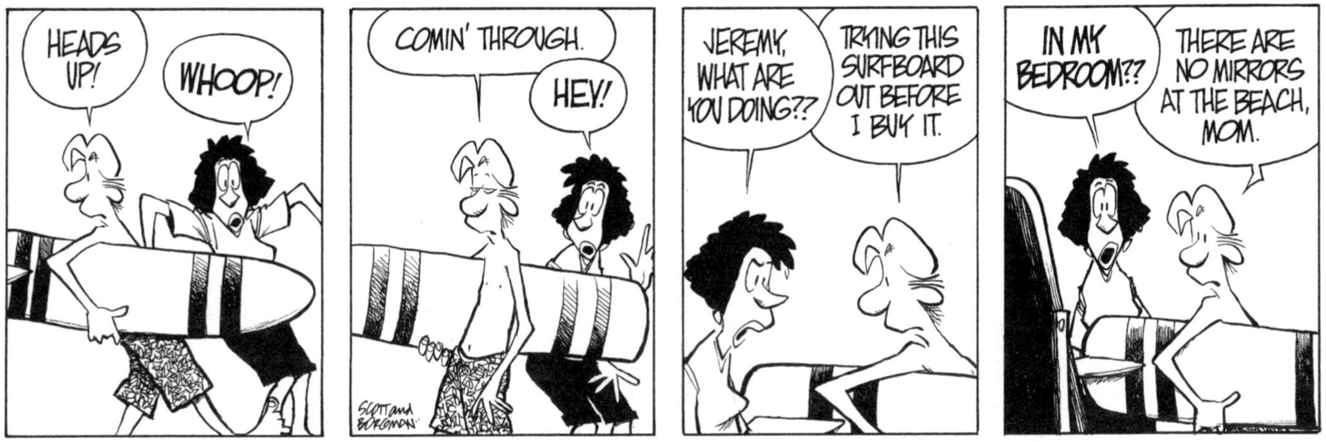
HEADS UP!
WHOOP!
COMIN' THROUGH.
HEY!
JEREMY, WHAT ARE YOU DOING??
TRYING THIS SURFBOARD OUT BEFORE I BUY IT.
IN MY BEDROOM??
THERE ARE NO MIRRORS AT THE BEACH, MOM.

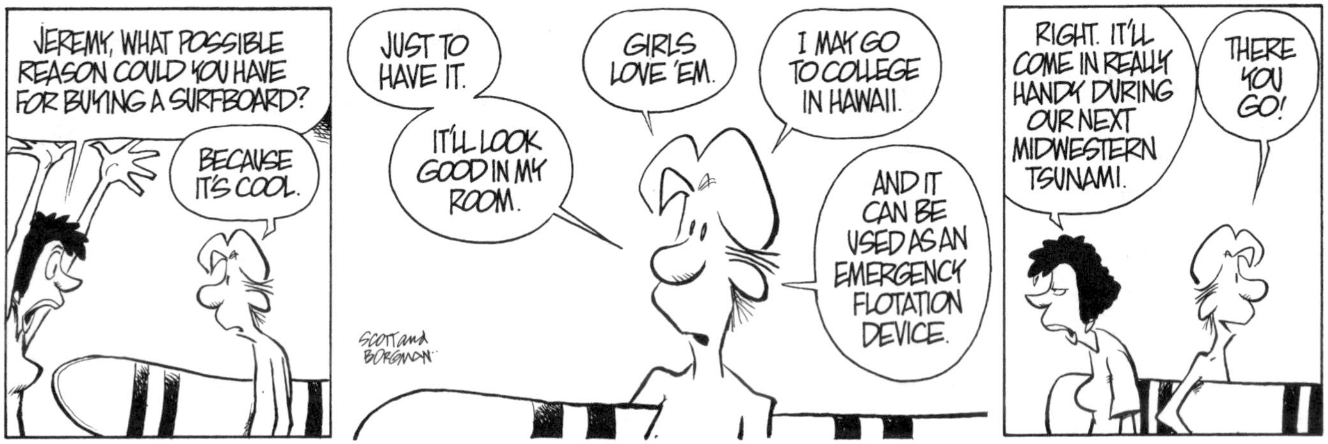
JEREMY, WHAT POSSIBLE REASON COULD YOU HAVE FOR BUYING A SURFBOARD?
BECAUSE IT'S COOL.
JUST TO HAVE IT.
IT'LL LOOK GOOD IN MY ROOM.
GIRLS LOVE 'EM.
I MAY GO TO COLLEGE IN HAWAII.
AND IT CAN BE USED AS AN EMERGENCY FLOTATION DEVICE.
RIGHT. IT'LL COME IN REALLY HANDY DURING OUR NEXT MIDWESTERN TSUNAMI.
THERE YOU GO!

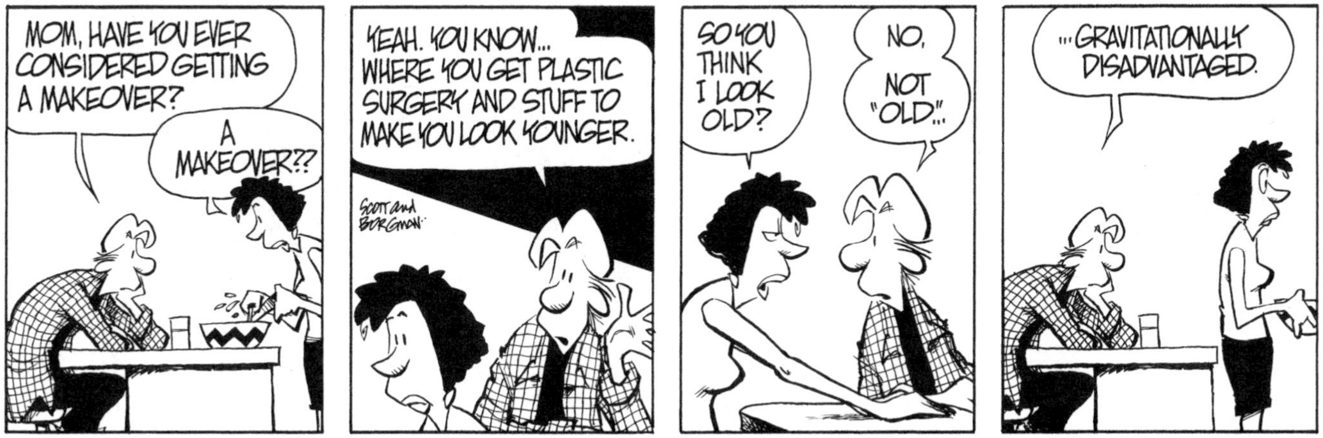
MOM, HAVE YOU EVER CONSIDERED GETTING A MAKEOVER?
A MAKEOVER??
YEAH. YOU KNOW... WHERE YOU GET PLASTIC SURGERY AND STUFF TO MAKE YOU LOOK YOUNGER.
SO YOU THINK I LOOK OLD?
NO,
NOT "OLD"...
...GRAVITATIONALLY DISADVANTAGED.

Zits®

by JERRY SCOTT and JIM BORGMAN

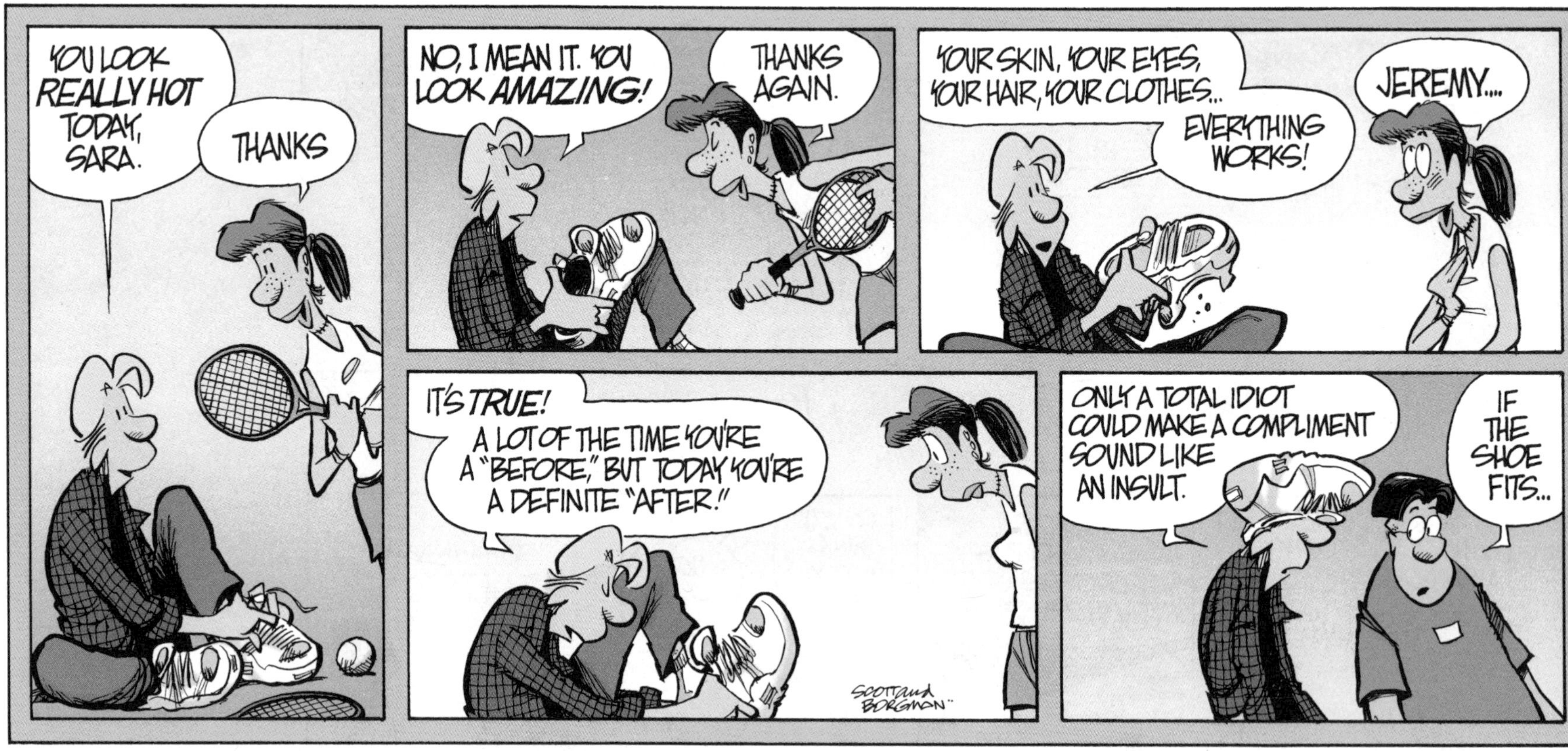
YOU LOOK REALLY HOT TODAY, SARA.
THANKS
NO, I MEAN IT. YOU LOOK AMAZING!
THANKS AGAIN.
YOUR SKIN, YOUR EYES, YOUR HAIR, YOUR CLOTHES...
EVERYTHING WORKS!
JEREMY....
IT'S TRUE!
A LOT OF THE TIME YOU'RE A "BEFORE," BUT TODAY YOU'RE A DEFINITE "AFTER."
SCOTT and BORGMAN
ONLY A TOTAL IDIOT COULD MAKE A COMPLIMENT SOUND LIKE AN INSULT.
IF THE SHOE FITS...

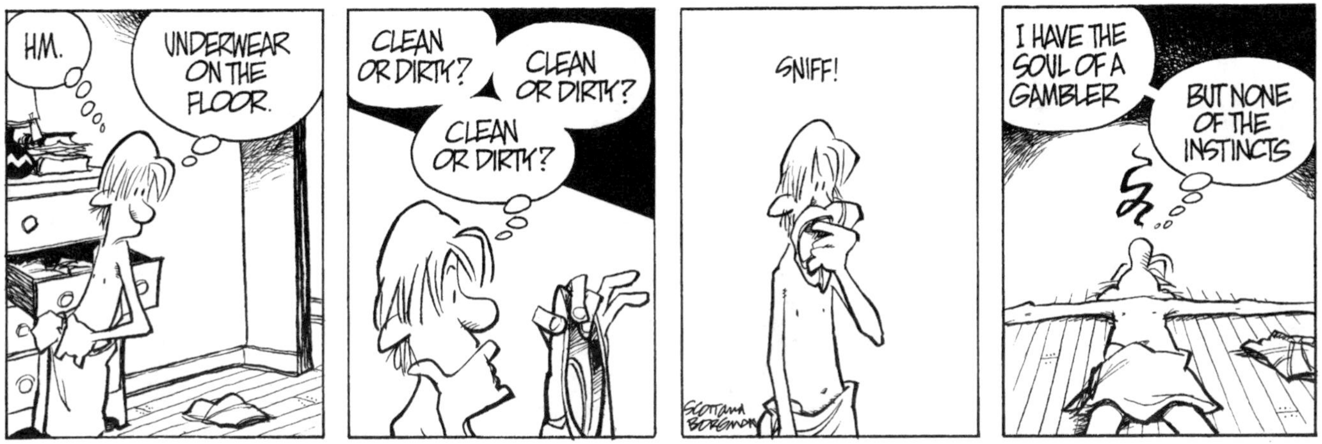
HM.
UNDERWEAR ON THE FLOOR.
CLEAN OR DIRTY?
CLEAN OR DIRTY?
CLEAN OR DIRTY?
SNIFF!
I HAVE THE SOUL OF A GAMBLER
BUT NONE OF THE INSTINCTS
SCOTT AND BORGMAN

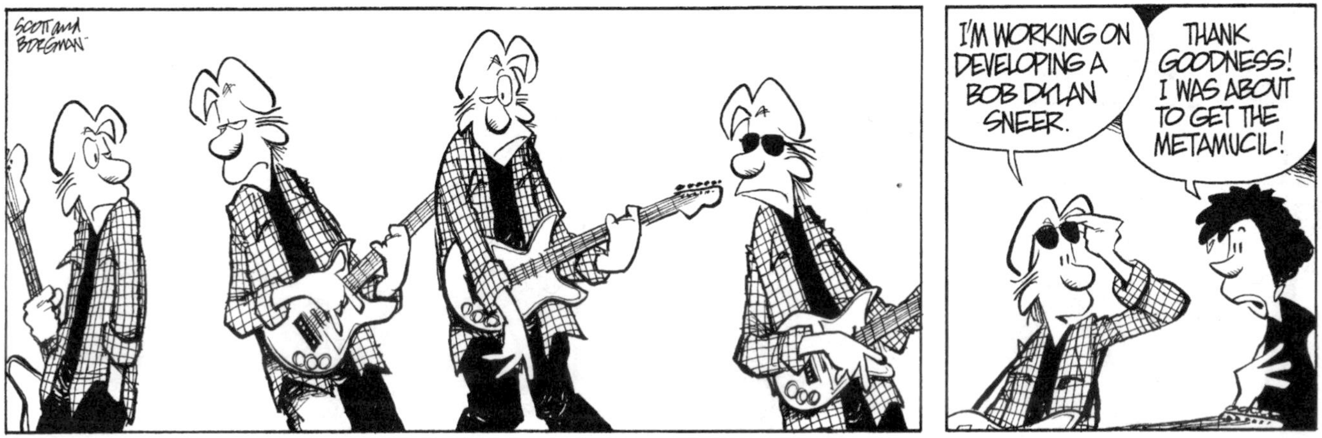
SCOTT AND BORGMAN
I'M WORKING ON DEVELOPING A BOB DYLAN SNEER.
THANK GOODNESS! I WAS ABOUT TO GET THE METAMUCIL!

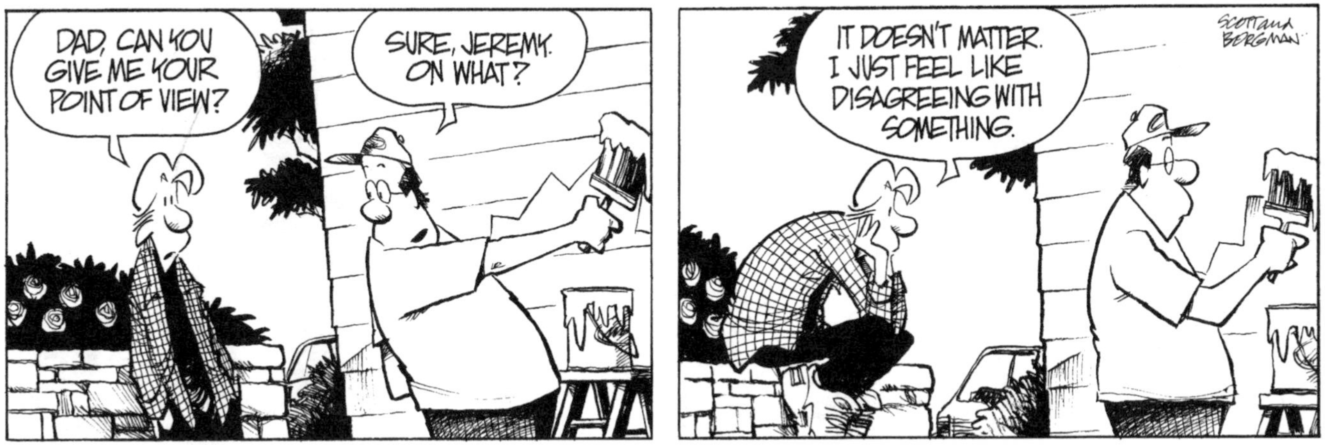
DAD, CAN YOU GIVE ME YOUR POINT OF VIEW?
SURE, JEREMY. ON WHAT?
IT DOESN'T MATTER. I JUST FEEL LIKE DISAGREEING WITH SOMETHING.
SCOTT AND BORGMAN

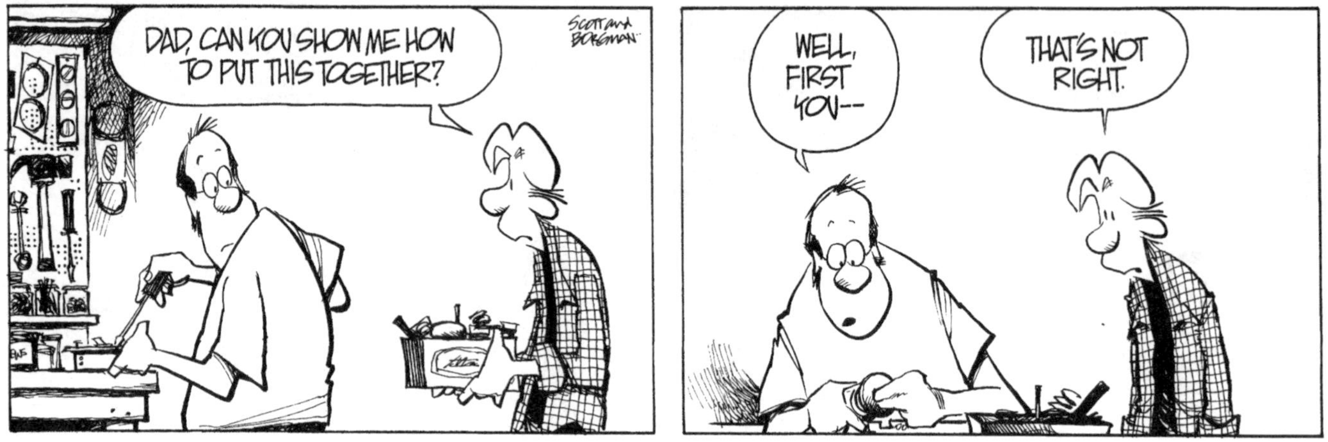
SCOTT and BORGMAN
DAD, CAN YOU SHOW ME HOW TO PUT THIS TOGETHER?
WELL, FIRST YOU--
THAT'S NOT RIGHT.

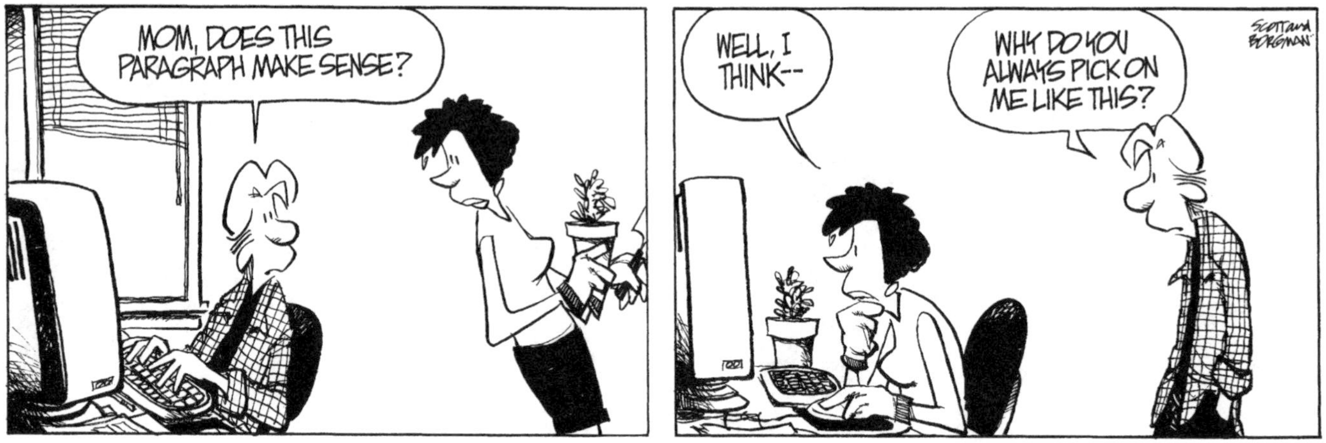
MOM, DOES THIS PARAGRAPH MAKE SENSE?
WELL, I THINK--
WHY DO YOU ALWAYS PICK ON ME LIKE THIS?
SCOTT and BORGMAN

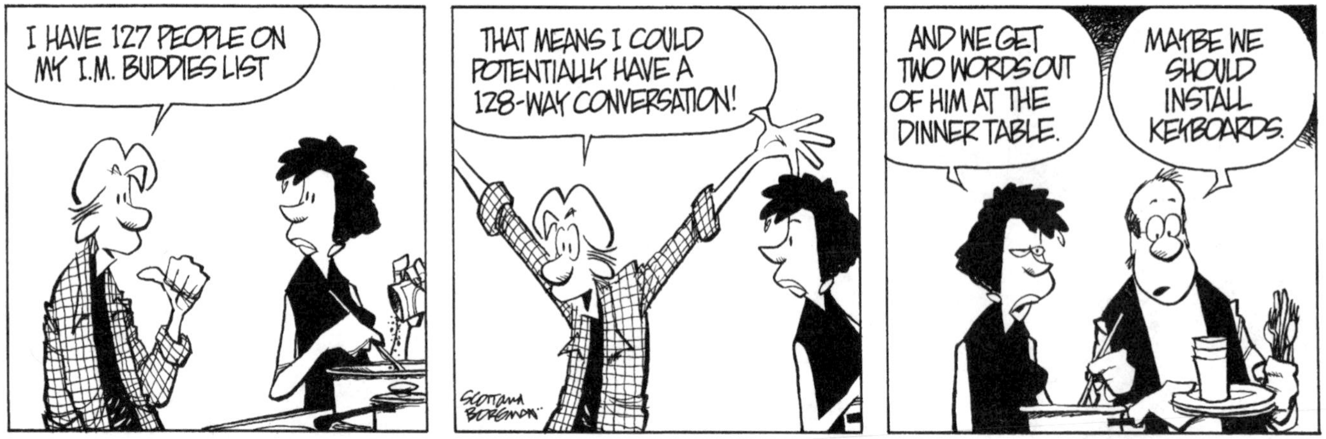
I HAVE 127 PEOPLE ON MY I.M. BUDDIES LIST
THAT MEANS I COULD POTENTIALLY HAVE A 128-WAY CONVERSATION!
SCOTT and BORGMAN
AND WE GET TWO WORDS OUT OF HIM AT THE DINNER TABLE.
MAYBE WE SHOULD INSTALL KEYBOARDS.

Zits®

by JERRY SCOTT and JIM BORGMAN

SCOTT and BORGMAN
ARE YOU *SURE* YOU DON'T HAVE ANYWHERE TO GO TODAY?
WHAT IS IT ABOUT SEEING A PERSON RELAX THAT BOTHERS YOU, MOM?

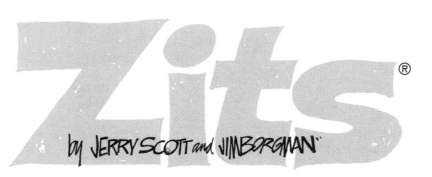

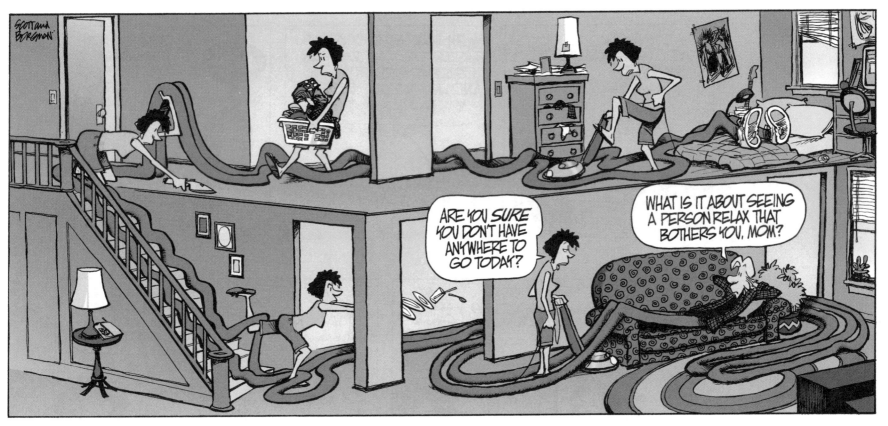

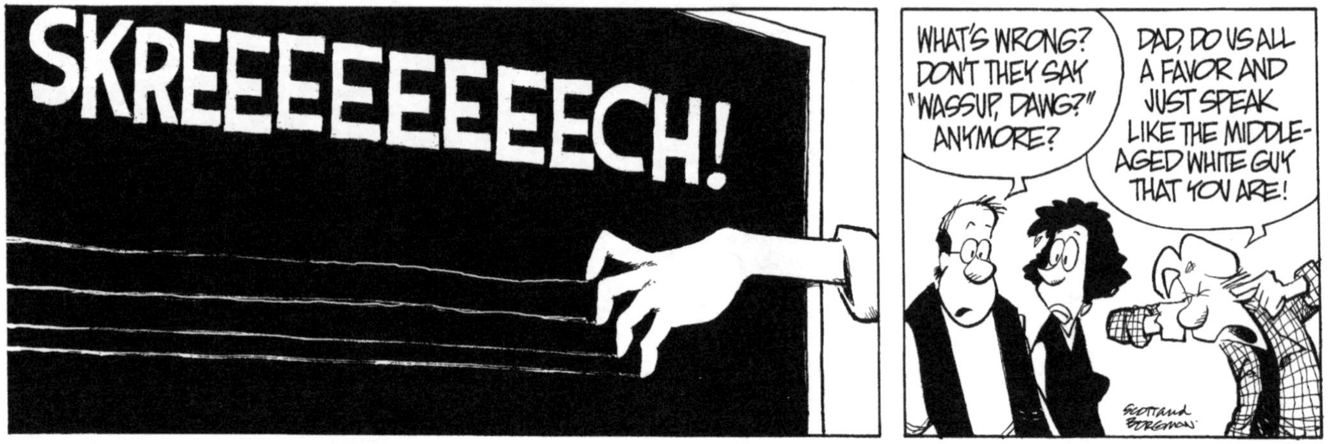
SKREEEEEEEEECH!
WHAT'S WRONG? DON'T THEY SAY "WASSUP, DAWG?" ANYMORE?
DAD, DO US ALL A FAVOR AND JUST SPEAK LIKE THE MIDDLE-AGED WHITE GUY THAT YOU ARE!
SCOTT AND BORGMAN

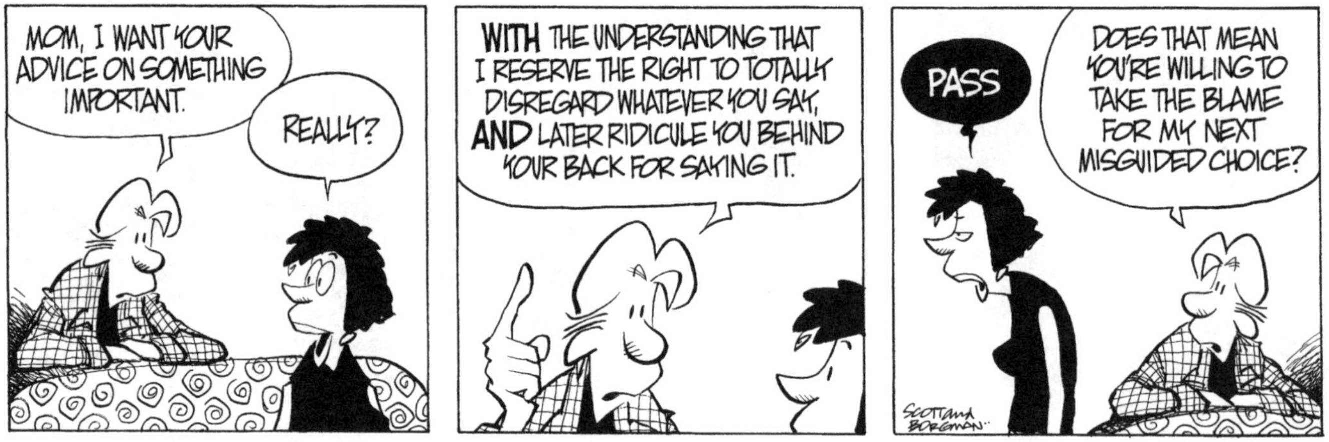
MOM, I WANT YOUR ADVICE ON SOMETHING IMPORTANT.
REALLY?
WITH THE UNDERSTANDING THAT I RESERVE THE RIGHT TO TOTALLY DISREGARD WHATEVER YOU SAY, AND LATER RIDICULE YOU BEHIND YOUR BACK FOR SAYING IT.
DOES THAT MEAN YOU'RE WILLING TO TAKE THE BLAME FOR MY NEXT MISGUIDED CHOICE?
PASS
SCOTT AND BORGMAN

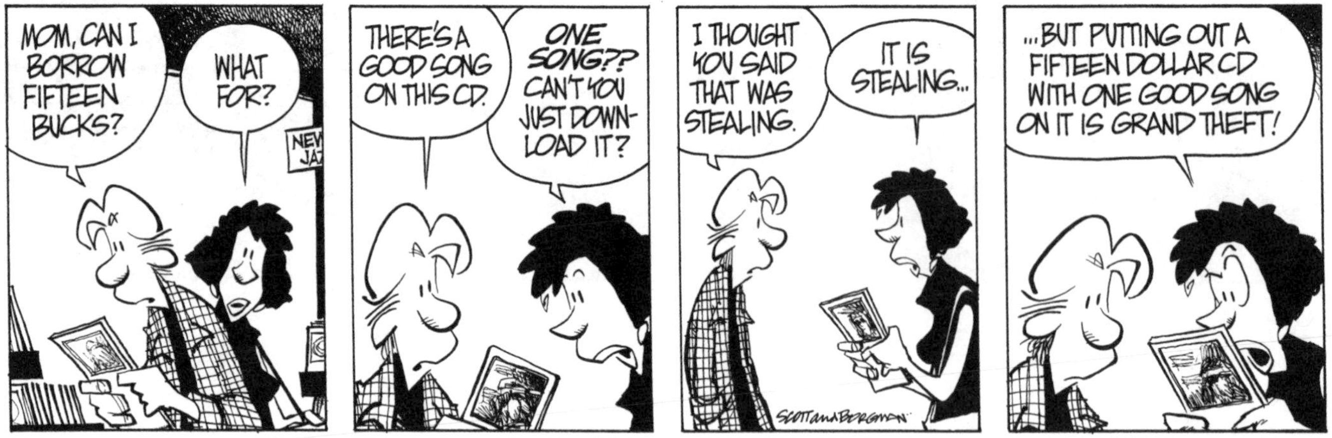
MOM, CAN I BORROW FIFTEEN BUCKS?
WHAT FOR?
THERE'S A GOOD SONG ON THIS CD.
ONE SONG?? CAN'T YOU JUST DOWN-LOAD IT?
I THOUGHT YOU SAID THAT WAS STEALING.
IT IS STEALING...
...BUT PUTTING OUT A FIFTEEN DOLLAR CD WITH ONE GOOD SONG ON IT IS GRAND THEFT!
SCOTT AND BORGMAN

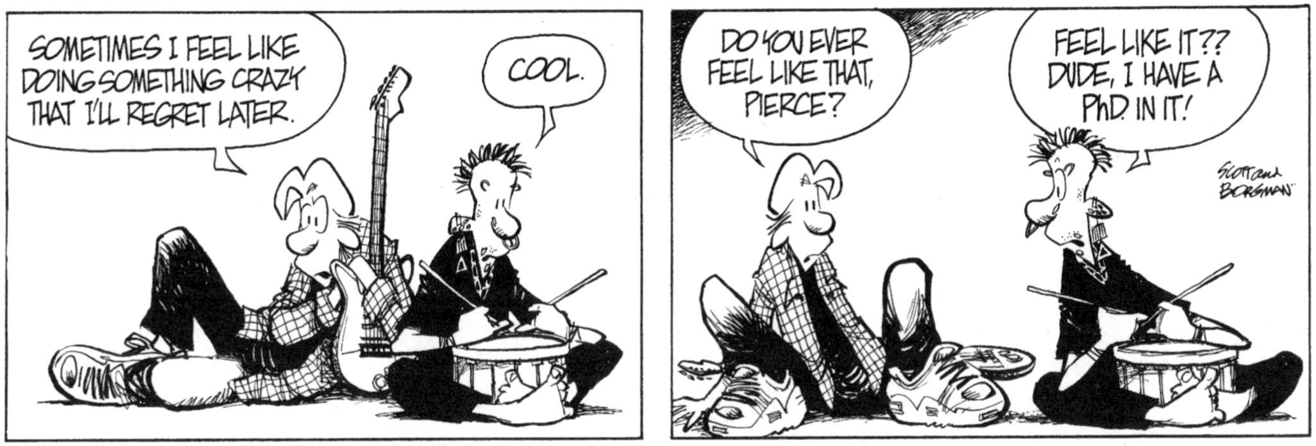
SOMETIMES I FEEL LIKE DOING SOMETHING CRAZY THAT I'LL REGRET LATER.
COOL.
DO YOU EVER FEEL LIKE THAT, PIERCE?
FEEL LIKE IT?? DUDE, I HAVE A PhD. IN IT!
SCOTT and BORGMAN

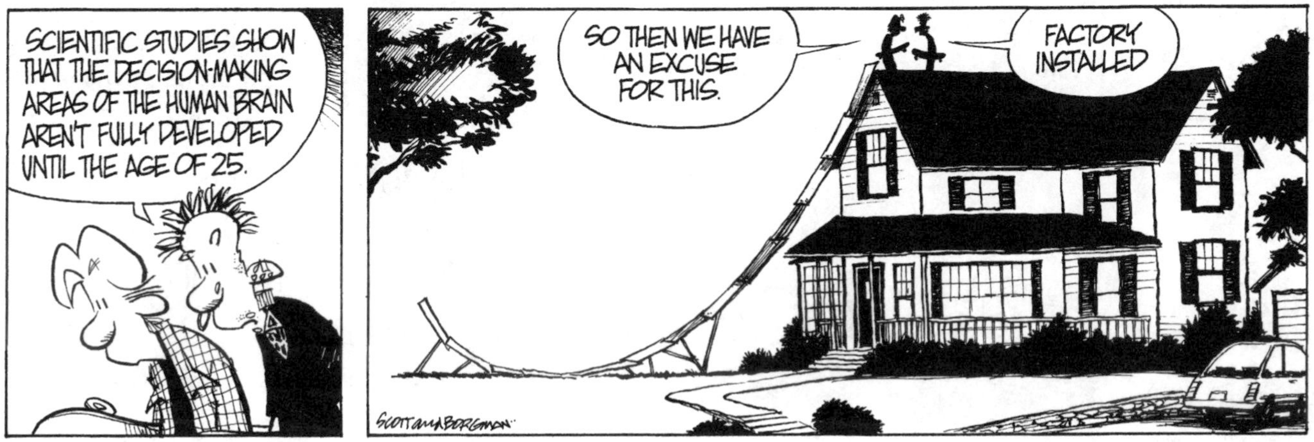
SCIENTIFIC STUDIES SHOW THAT THE DECISION-MAKING AREAS OF THE HUMAN BRAIN AREN'T FULLY DEVELOPED UNTIL THE AGE OF 25.
SO THEN WE HAVE AN EXCUSE FOR THIS.
FACTORY INSTALLED
SCOTT and BORGMAN

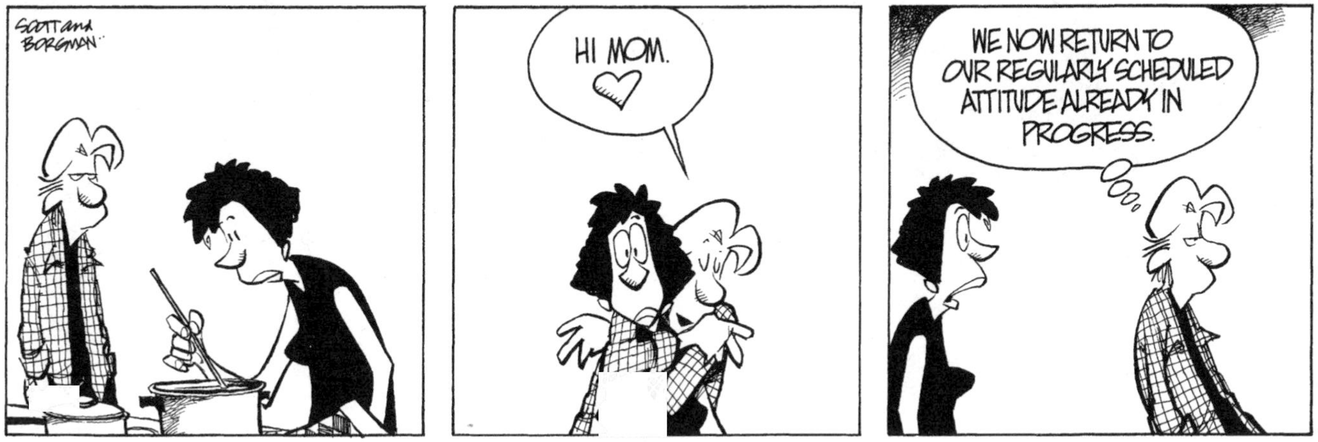
SCOTT and BORGMAN
HI MOM.
WE NOW RETURN TO OUR REGULARLY SCHEDULED ATTITUDE ALREADY IN PROGRESS.

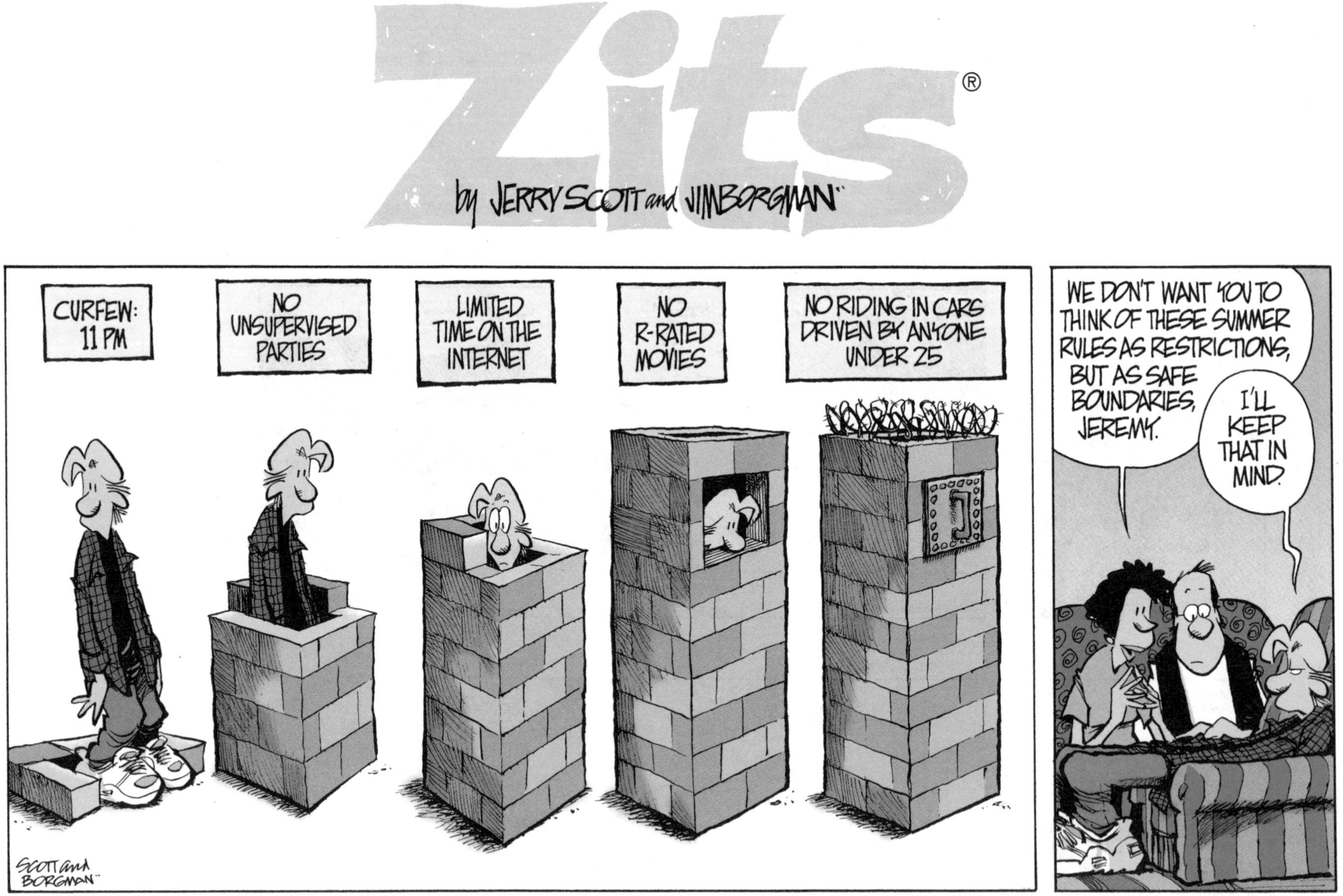
Zits®
by JERRY SCOTT and JIM BORGMAN
CURFEW: 11 PM
NO UNSUPERVISED PARTIES
LIMITED TIME ON THE INTERNET
NO R-RATED MOVIES
NO RIDING IN CARS DRIVEN BY ANYONE UNDER 25
SCOTT and BORGMAN
WE DON'T WANT YOU TO THINK OF THESE SUMMER RULES AS RESTRICTIONS, BUT AS SAFE BOUNDARIES, JEREMY.
I'LL KEEP THAT IN MIND.

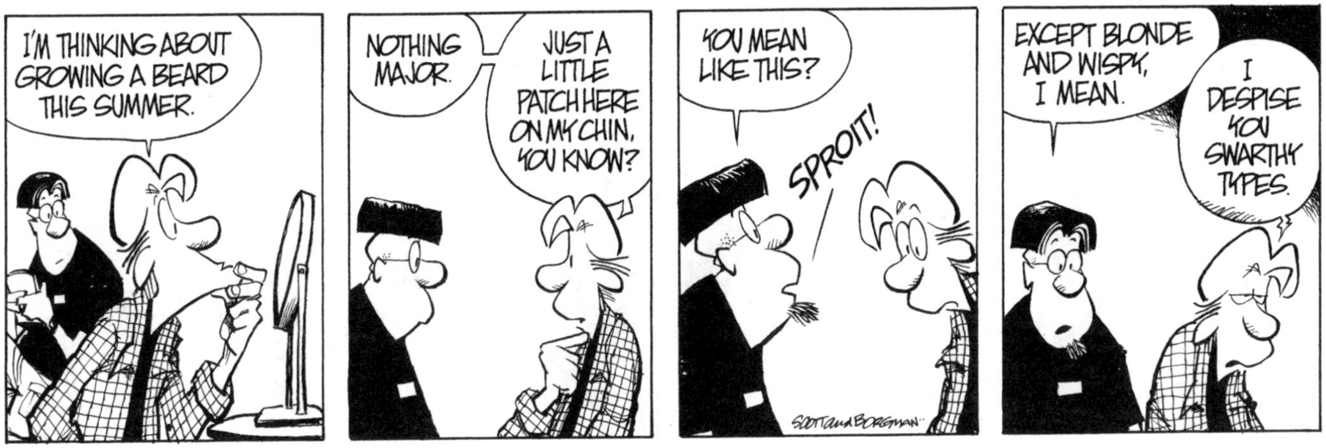
I'M THINKING ABOUT GROWING A BEARD THIS SUMMER.
NOTHING MAJOR.
JUST A LITTLE PATCH HERE ON MY CHIN, YOU KNOW?
YOU MEAN LIKE THIS?
SPROIT!
SCOTT and BORGMAN
EXCEPT BLONDE AND WISPY, I MEAN.
I DESPISE YOU SWARTHY TYPES.

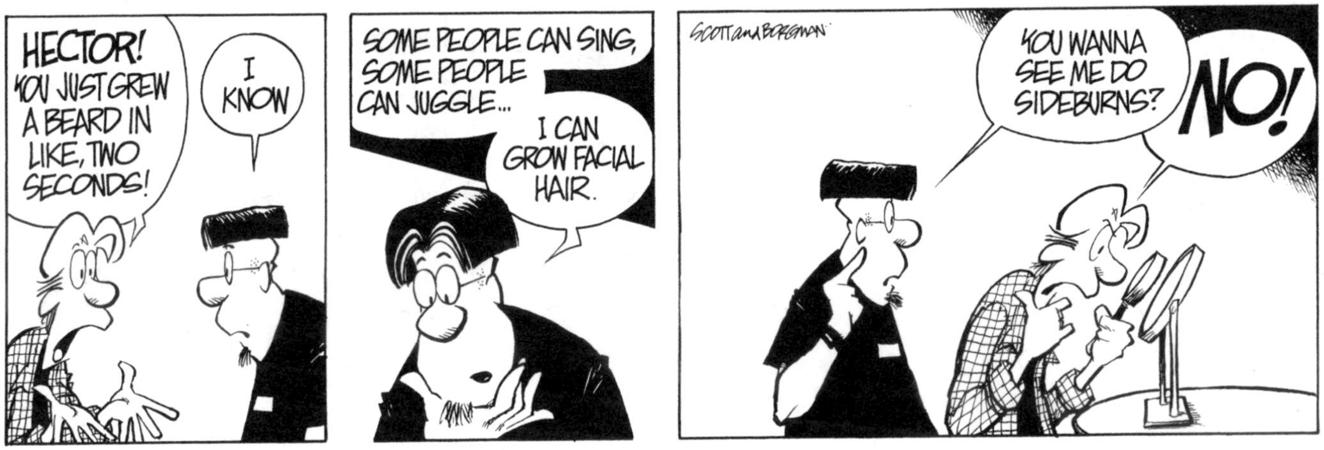
HECTOR! YOU JUST GREW A BEARD IN LIKE, TWO SECONDS!
I KNOW
SOME PEOPLE CAN SING, SOME PEOPLE CAN JUGGLE...
I CAN GROW FACIAL HAIR.
SCOTT and BORGMAN
YOU WANNA SEE ME DO SIDEBURNS?
NO!

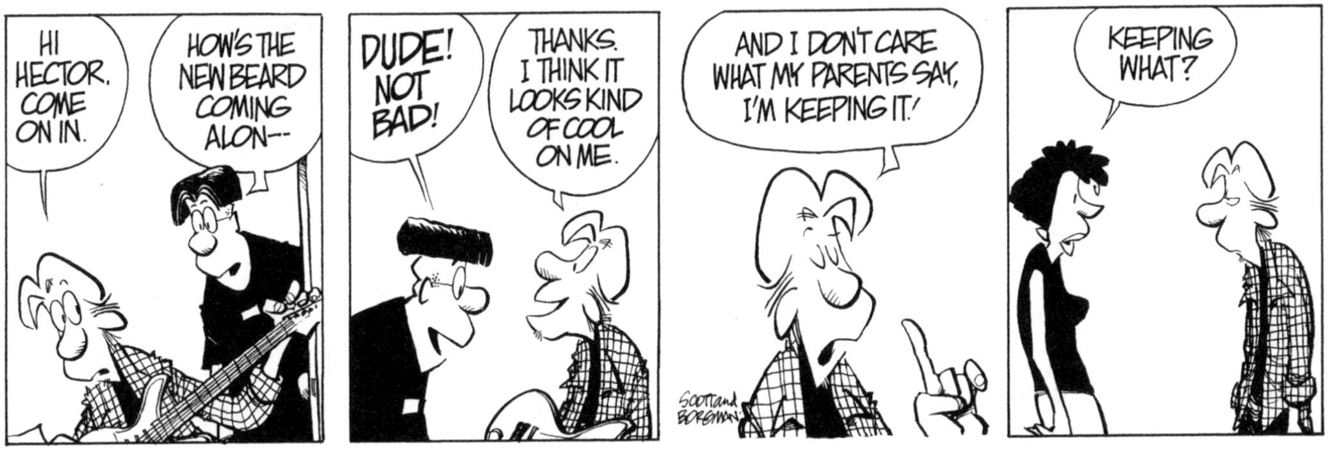
HI HECTOR. COME ON IN.
HOW'S THE NEW BEARD COMING ALON--
DUDE! NOT BAD!
THANKS. I THINK IT LOOKS KIND OF COOL ON ME.
AND I DON'T CARE WHAT MY PARENTS SAY, I'M KEEPING IT!
SCOTT and BORGMAN
KEEPING WHAT?

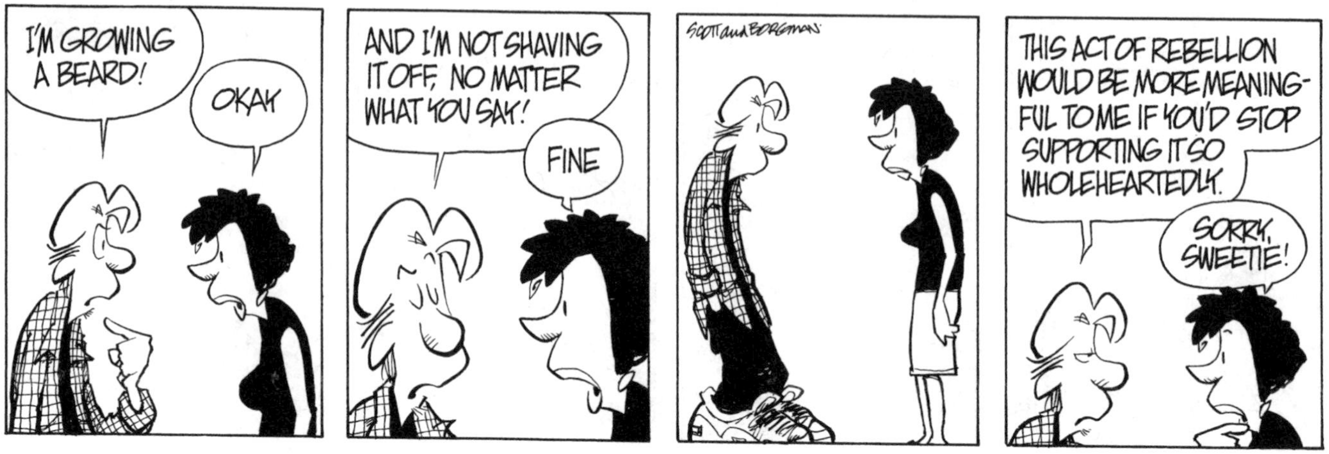
I'M GROWING A BEARD!
OKAY
AND I'M NOT SHAVING IT OFF, NO MATTER WHAT YOU SAY!
FINE
SCOTT and BORGMAN
THIS ACT OF REBELLION WOULD BE MORE MEANINGFUL TO ME IF YOU'D STOP SUPPORTING IT SO WHOLEHEARTEDLY.
SORRY, SWEETIE!

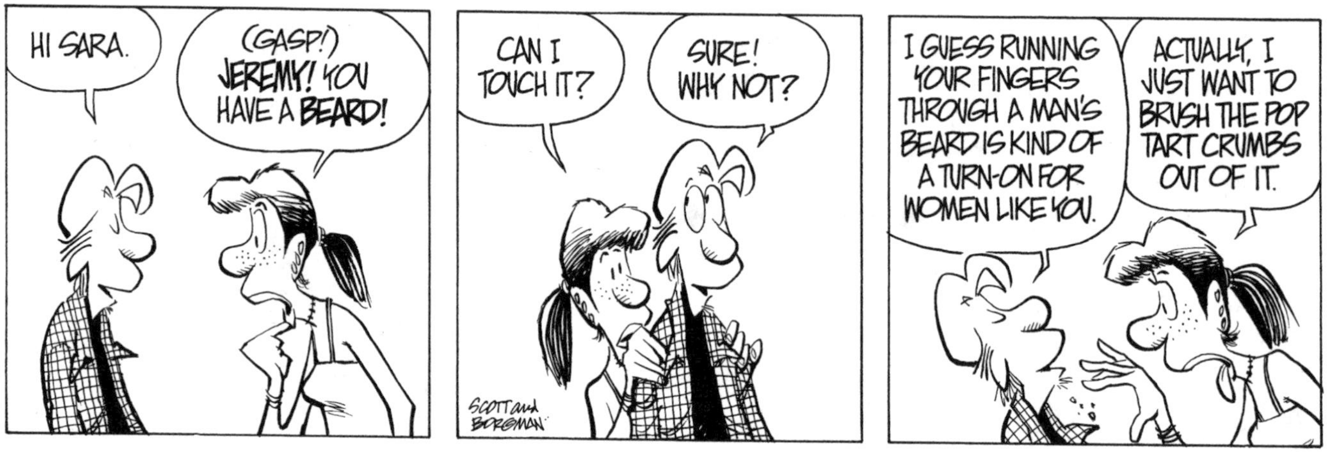
HI SARA.
(GASP!) JEREMY! YOU HAVE A BEARD!
CAN I TOUCH IT?
SURE! WHY NOT?
SCOTT and BORGMAN
I GUESS RUNNING YOUR FINGERS THROUGH A MAN'S BEARD IS KIND OF A TURN-ON FOR WOMEN LIKE YOU.
ACTUALLY, I JUST WANT TO BRUSH THE POP TART CRUMBS OUT OF IT.

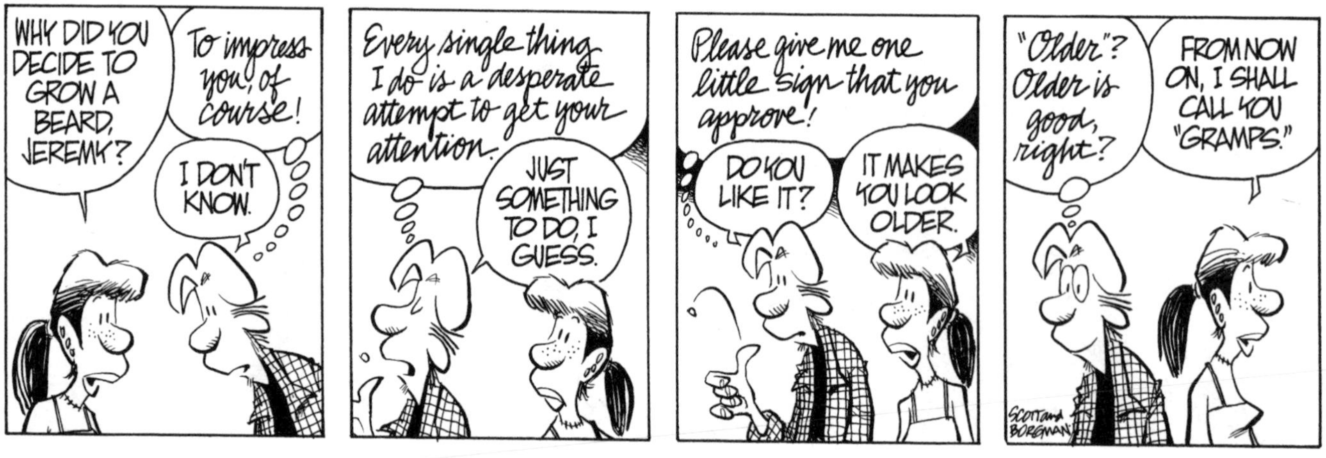
WHY DID YOU DECIDE TO GROW A BEARD, JEREMY?
To impress you, of course!
I DON'T KNOW.
Every single thing I do is a desperate attempt to get your attention.
JUST SOMETHING TO DO, I GUESS.
Please give me one little sign that you approve!
DO YOU LIKE IT?
IT MAKES YOU LOOK OLDER.
"Older"? Older is good, right?
FROM NOW ON, I SHALL CALL YOU "GRAMPS."
SCOTT and BORGMAN

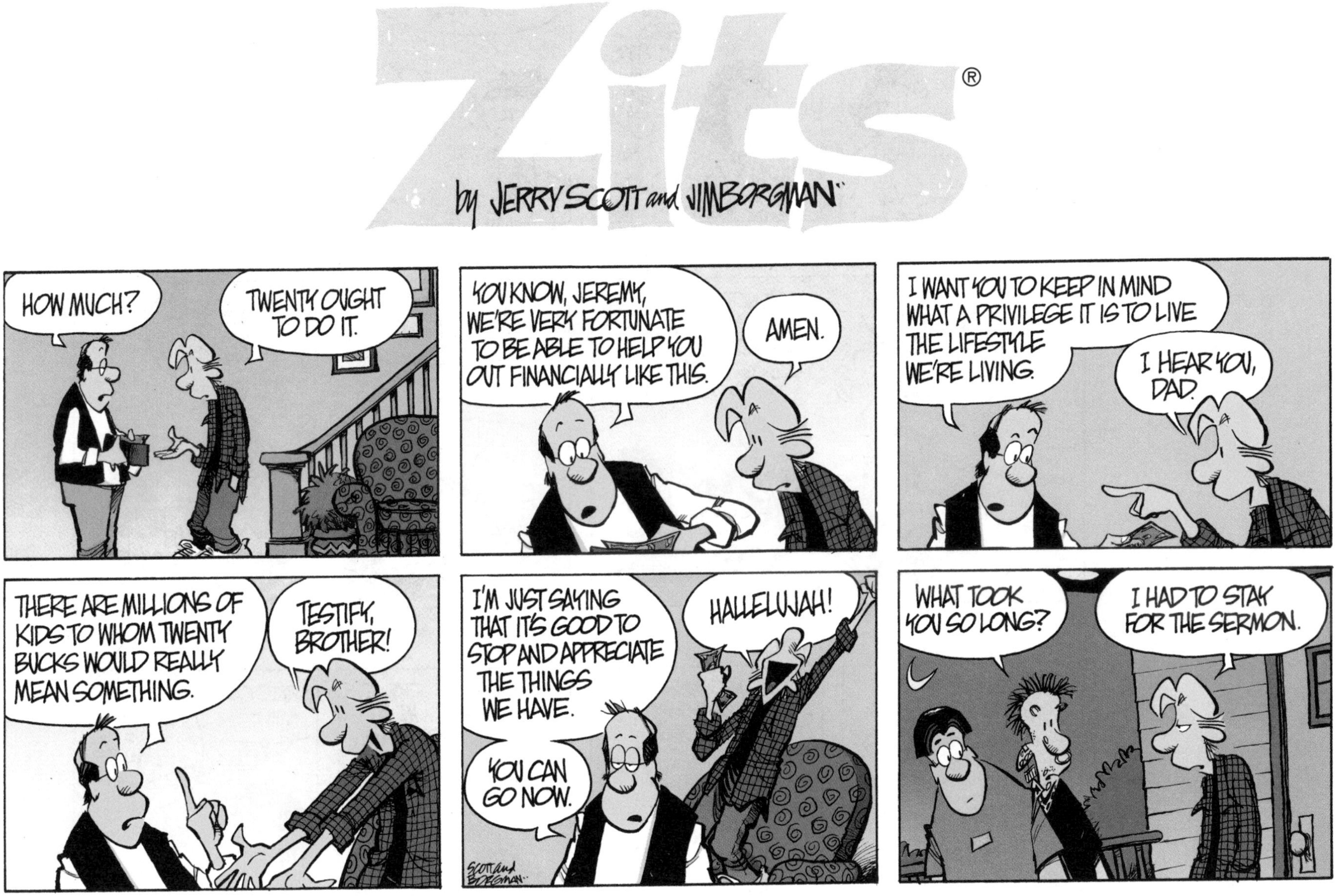
Zits®
by JERRY SCOTT and JIM BORGMAN
HOW MUCH?
TWENTY OUGHT TO DO IT.
YOU KNOW, JEREMY, WE'RE VERY FORTUNATE TO BE ABLE TO HELP YOU OUT FINANCIALLY LIKE THIS.
AMEN.
I WANT YOU TO KEEP IN MIND WHAT A PRIVILEGE IT IS TO LIVE THE LIFESTYLE WE'RE LIVING.
I HEAR YOU, DAD.
THERE ARE MILLIONS OF KIDS TO WHOM TWENTY BUCKS WOULD REALLY MEAN SOMETHING.
TESTIFY, BROTHER!
I'M JUST SAYING THAT IT'S GOOD TO STOP AND APPRECIATE THE THINGS WE HAVE.
HALLELUJAH!
YOU CAN GO NOW.
WHAT TOOK YOU SO LONG?
I HAD TO STAY FOR THE SERMON.

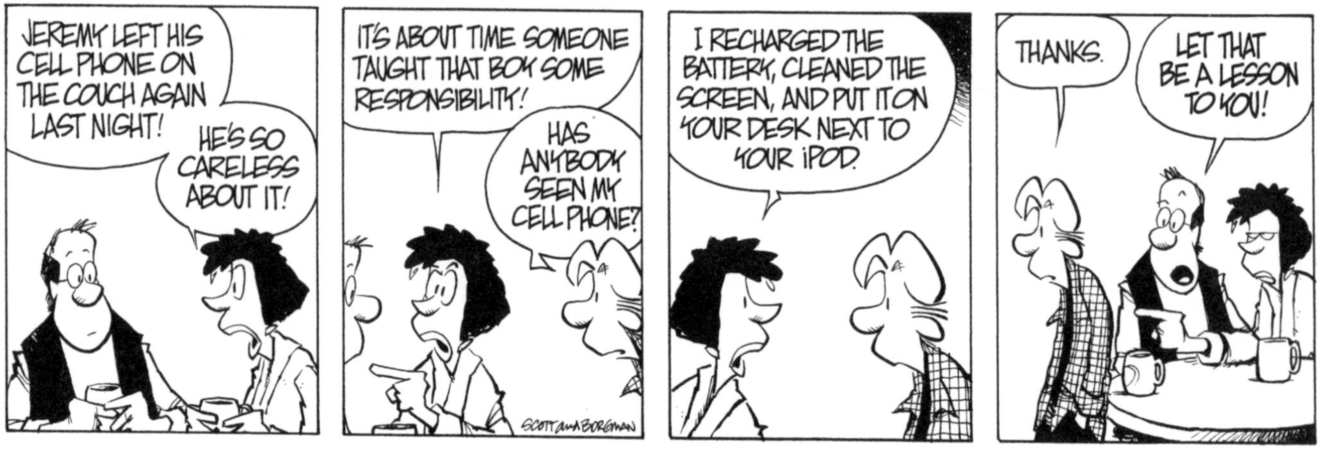
JEREMY LEFT HIS CELL PHONE ON THE COUCH AGAIN LAST NIGHT!
HE'S SO CARELESS ABOUT IT!
IT'S ABOUT TIME SOMEONE TAUGHT THAT BOY SOME RESPONSIBILITY!
HAS ANYBODY SEEN MY CELL PHONE?
I RECHARGED THE BATTERY, CLEANED THE SCREEN, AND PUT IT ON YOUR DESK NEXT TO YOUR iPOD.
THANKS.
LET THAT BE A LESSON TO YOU!

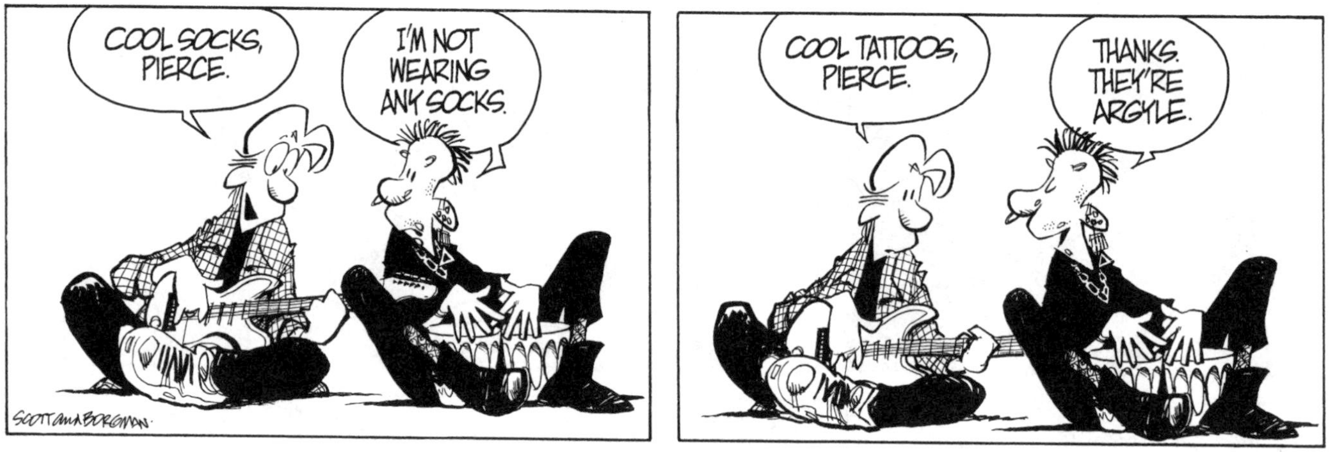
COOL SOCKS, PIERCE.
I'M NOT WEARING ANY SOCKS.
COOL TATTOOS, PIERCE.
THANKS. THEY'RE ARGYLE.

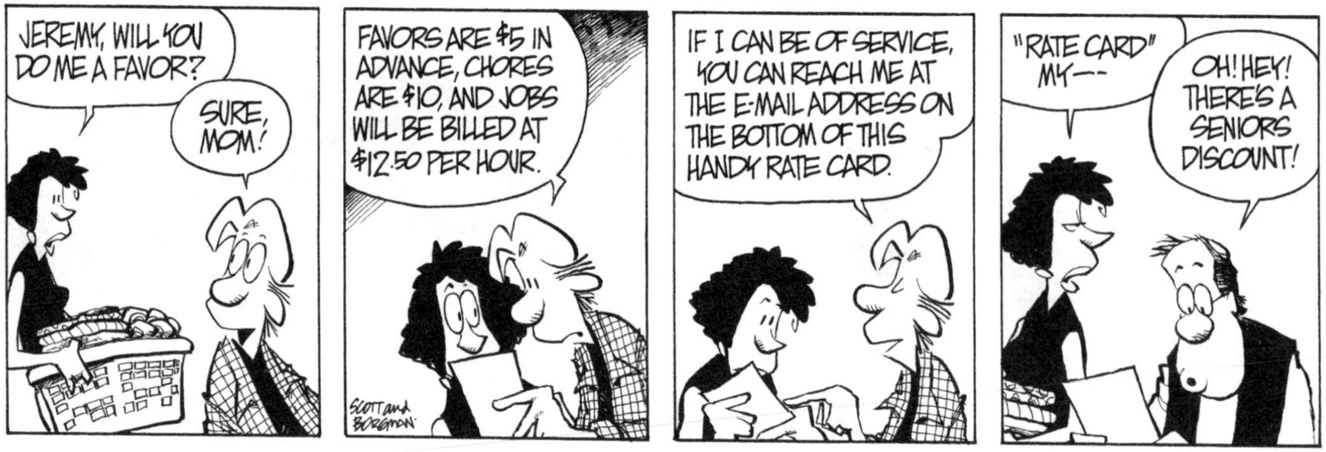
JEREMY, WILL YOU DO ME A FAVOR?
SURE, MOM!
FAVORS ARE $5 IN ADVANCE, CHORES ARE $10, AND JOBS WILL BE BILLED AT $12.50 PER HOUR.
IF I CAN BE OF SERVICE, YOU CAN REACH ME AT THE E-MAIL ADDRESS ON THE BOTTOM OF THIS HANDY RATE CARD.
"RATE CARD" MY--
OH! HEY! THERE'S A SENIORS DISCOUNT!

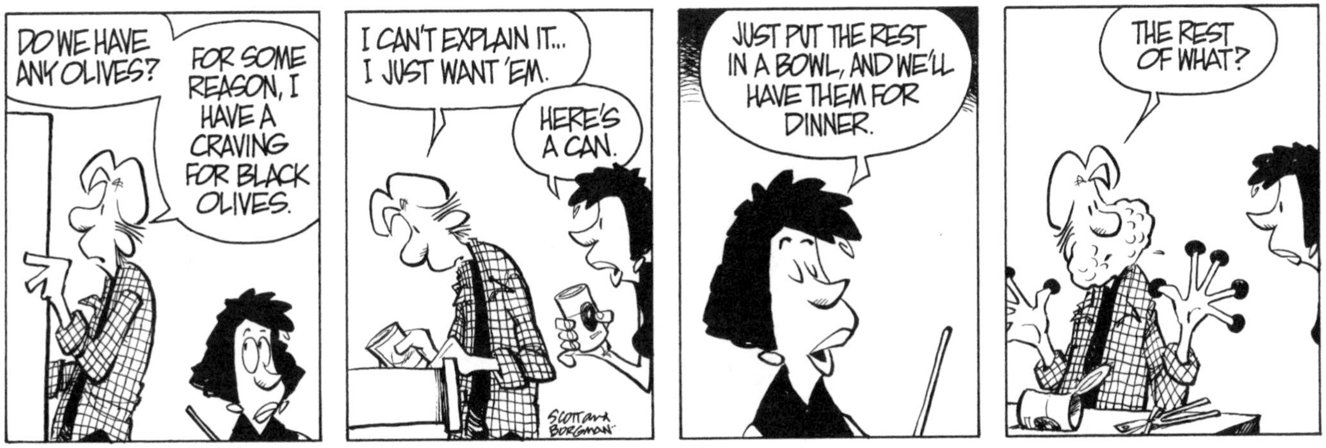
DO WE HAVE ANY OLIVES?
FOR SOME REASON, I HAVE A CRAVING FOR BLACK OLIVES.
I CAN'T EXPLAIN IT... I JUST WANT 'EM.
HERE'S A CAN.
JUST PUT THE REST IN A BOWL, AND WE'LL HAVE THEM FOR DINNER.
THE REST OF WHAT?

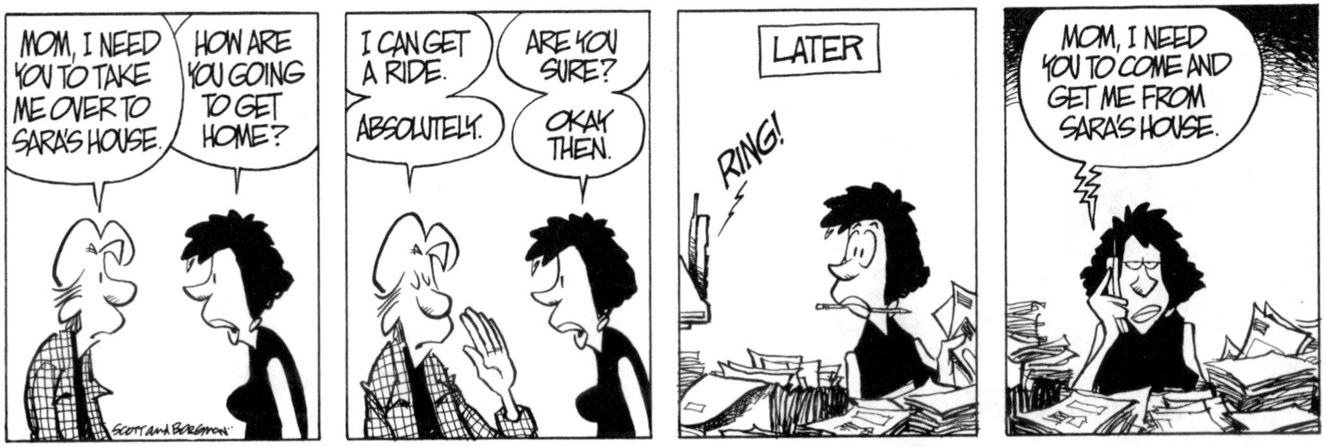
MOM, I NEED YOU TO TAKE ME OVER TO SARA'S HOUSE.
HOW ARE YOU GOING TO GET HOME?
I CAN GET A RIDE.
ARE YOU SURE?
ABSOLUTELY.
OKAY THEN.
LATER
RING!
MOM, I NEED YOU TO COME AND GET ME FROM SARA'S HOUSE.

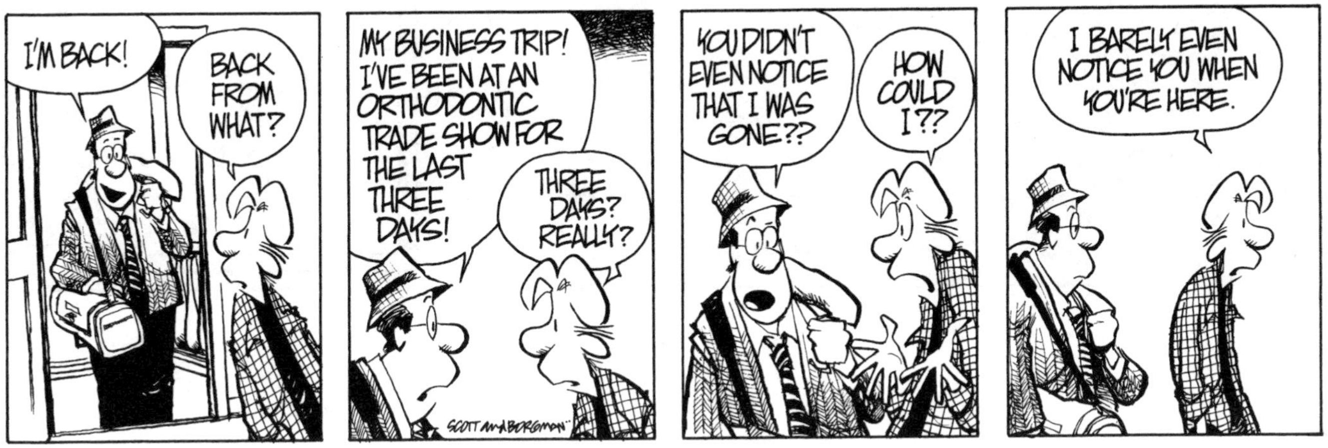
I'M BACK!
BACK FROM WHAT?
MY BUSINESS TRIP! I'VE BEEN AT AN ORTHODONTIC TRADE SHOW FOR THE LAST THREE DAYS!
THREE DAYS? REALLY?
YOU DIDN'T EVEN NOTICE THAT I WAS GONE??
HOW COULD I??
I BARELY EVEN NOTICE YOU WHEN YOU'RE HERE.

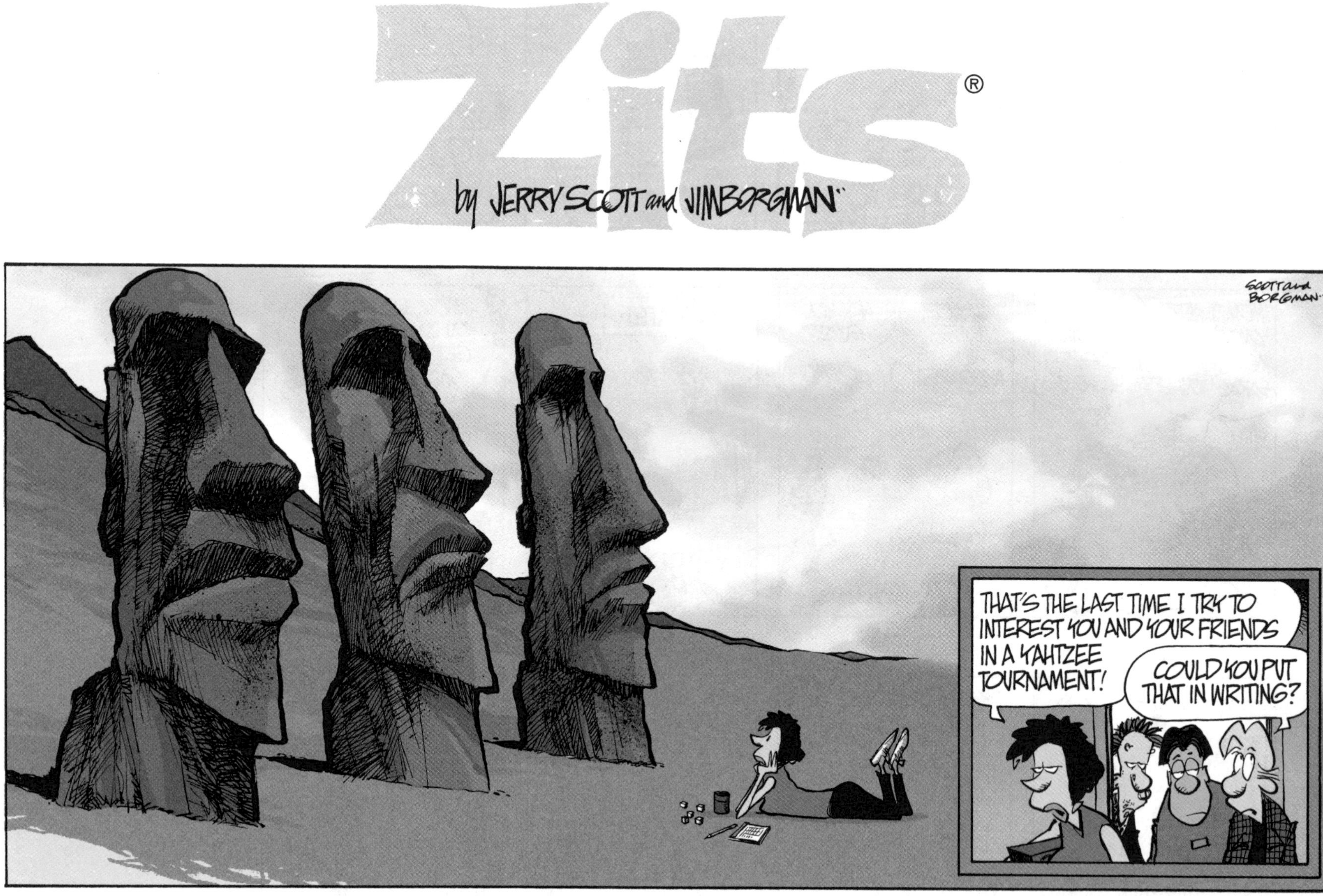
Zits®
by JERRY SCOTT and JIM BORGMAN
SCOTT and BORGMAN
THAT'S THE LAST TIME I TRY TO INTEREST YOU AND YOUR FRIENDS IN A YAHTZEE TOURNAMENT!
COULD YOU PUT THAT IN WRITING?

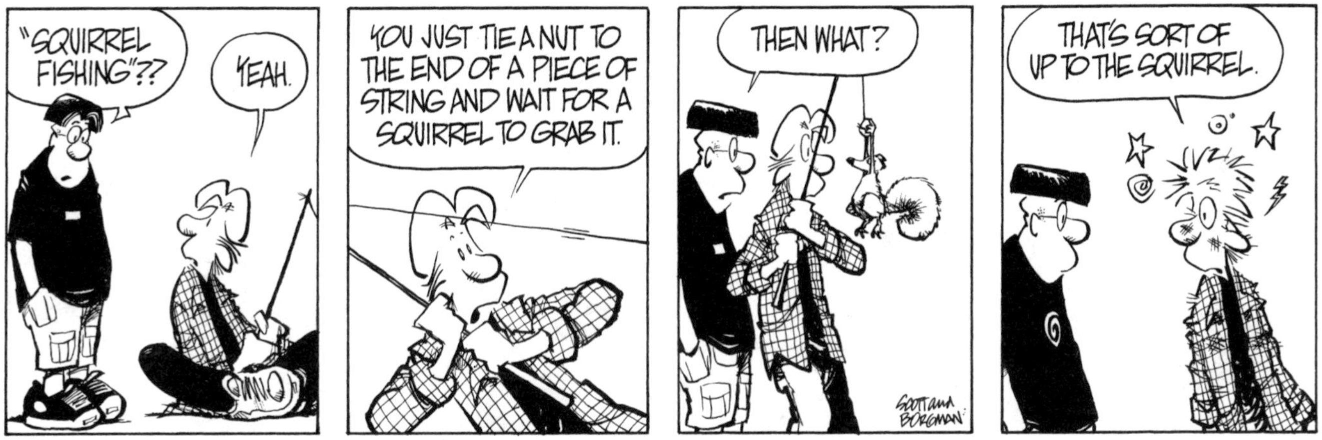
"SQUIRREL FISHING"??
YEAH.
YOU JUST TIE A NUT TO THE END OF A PIECE OF STRING AND WAIT FOR A SQUIRREL TO GRAB IT.
THEN WHAT?
THAT'S SORT OF UP TO THE SQUIRREL.

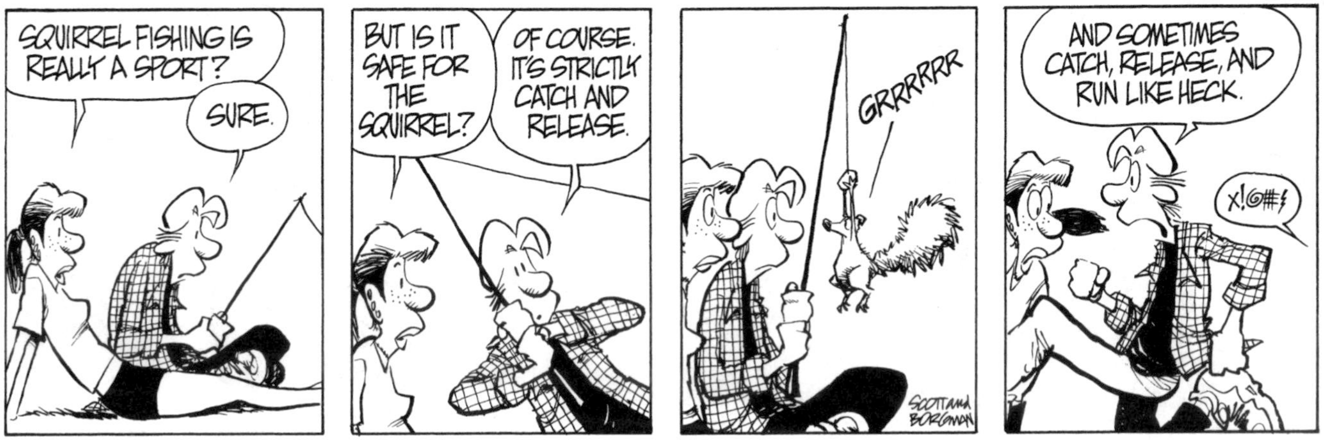
SQUIRREL FISHING IS REALLY A SPORT?
SURE.
BUT IS IT SAFE FOR THE SQUIRREL?
OF COURSE. IT'S STRICTLY CATCH AND RELEASE.
GRRRRRR
AND SOMETIMES CATCH, RELEASE, AND RUN LIKE HECK.

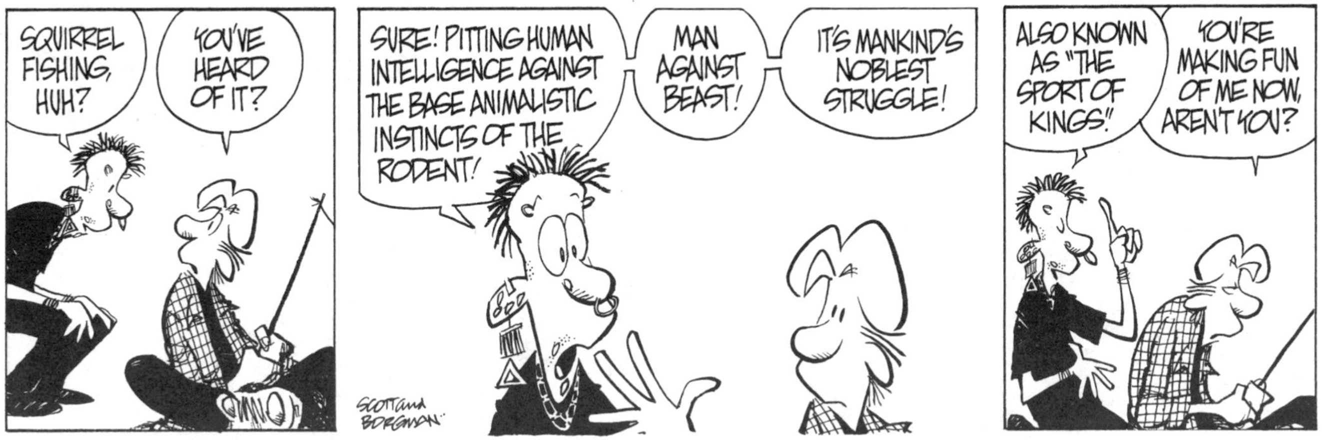
SQUIRREL FISHING, HUH?
YOU'VE HEARD OF IT?
SURE! PITTING HUMAN INTELLIGENCE AGAINST THE BASE ANIMALISTIC INSTINCTS OF THE RODENT!
MAN AGAINST BEAST!
IT'S MANKIND'S NOBLEST STRUGGLE!
ALSO KNOWN AS "THE SPORT OF KINGS."
YOU'RE MAKING FUN OF ME NOW, AREN'T YOU?

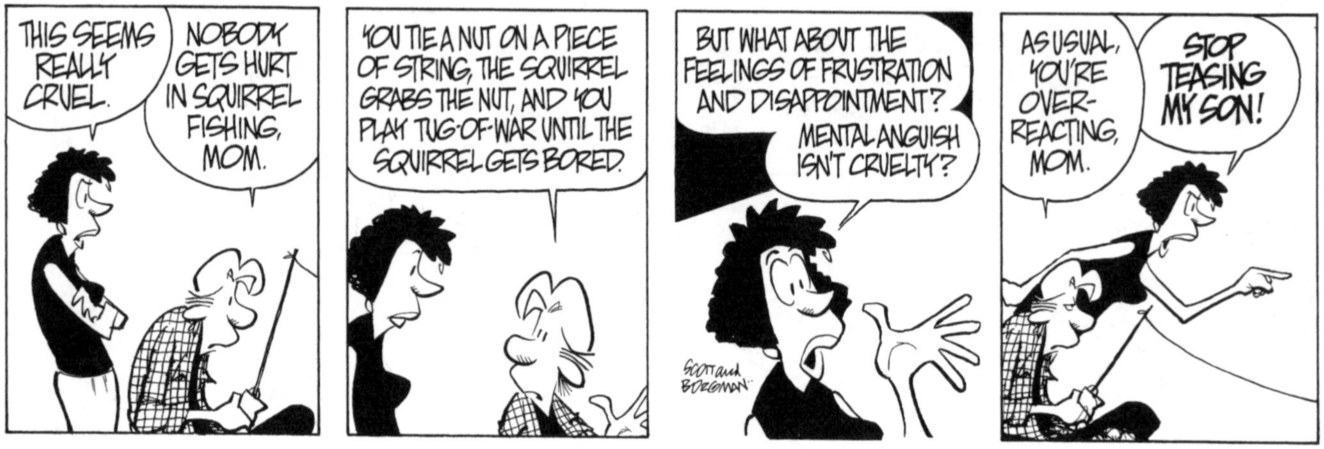
THIS SEEMS REALLY CRUEL.
NOBODY GETS HURT IN SQUIRREL FISHING, MOM.
YOU TIE A NUT ON A PIECE OF STRING, THE SQUIRREL GRABS THE NUT, AND YOU PLAY TUG-OF-WAR UNTIL THE SQUIRREL GETS BORED.
BUT WHAT ABOUT THE FEELINGS OF FRUSTRATION AND DISAPPOINTMENT?
MENTAL ANGUISH ISN'T CRUELTY?
SCOTT and BORGMAN
AS USUAL, YOU'RE OVER-REACTING, MOM.
STOP TEASING MY SON!

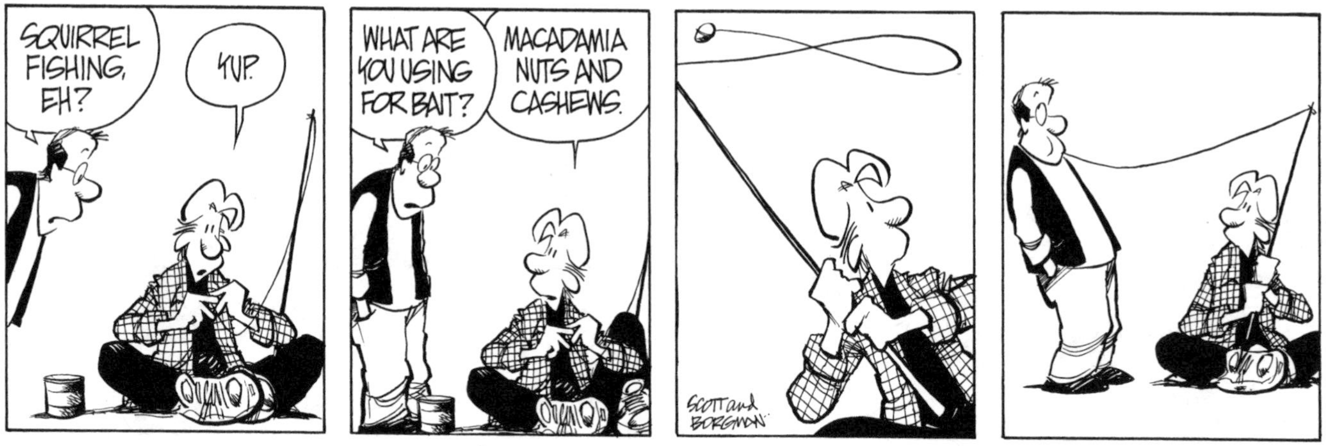
SQUIRREL FISHING, EH?
YUP.
WHAT ARE YOU USING FOR BAIT?
MACADAMIA NUTS AND CASHEWS.
SCOTT and BORGMAN

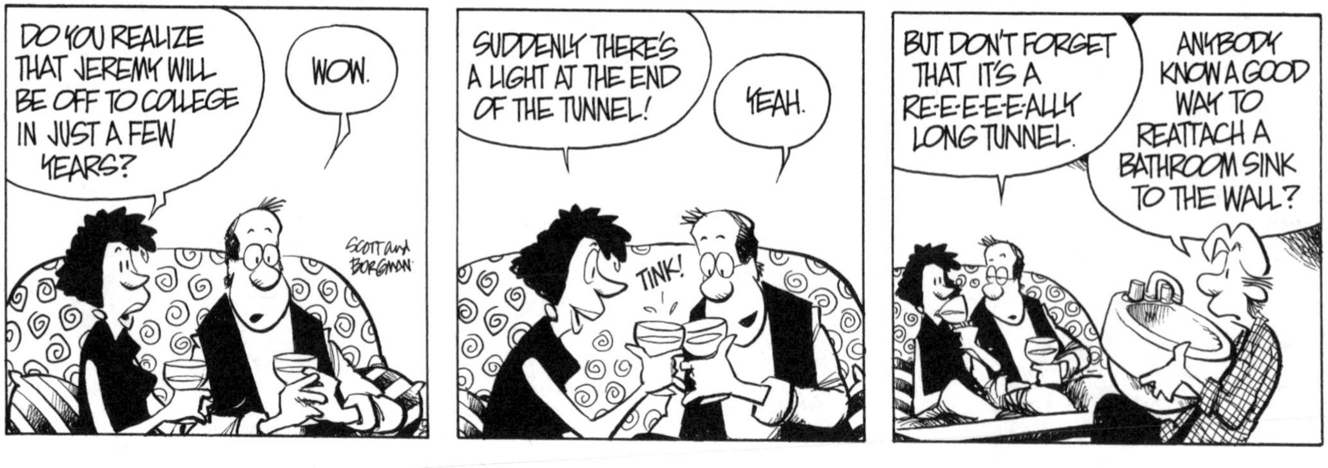
DO YOU REALIZE THAT JEREMY WILL BE OFF TO COLLEGE IN JUST A FEW YEARS?
WOW.
SCOTT and BORGMAN
SUDDENLY THERE'S A LIGHT AT THE END OF THE TUNNEL!
YEAH.
TINK!
BUT DON'T FORGET THAT IT'S A RE-E-E-E-E-ALLY LONG TUNNEL.
ANYBODY KNOW A GOOD WAY TO REATTACH A BATHROOM SINK TO THE WALL?

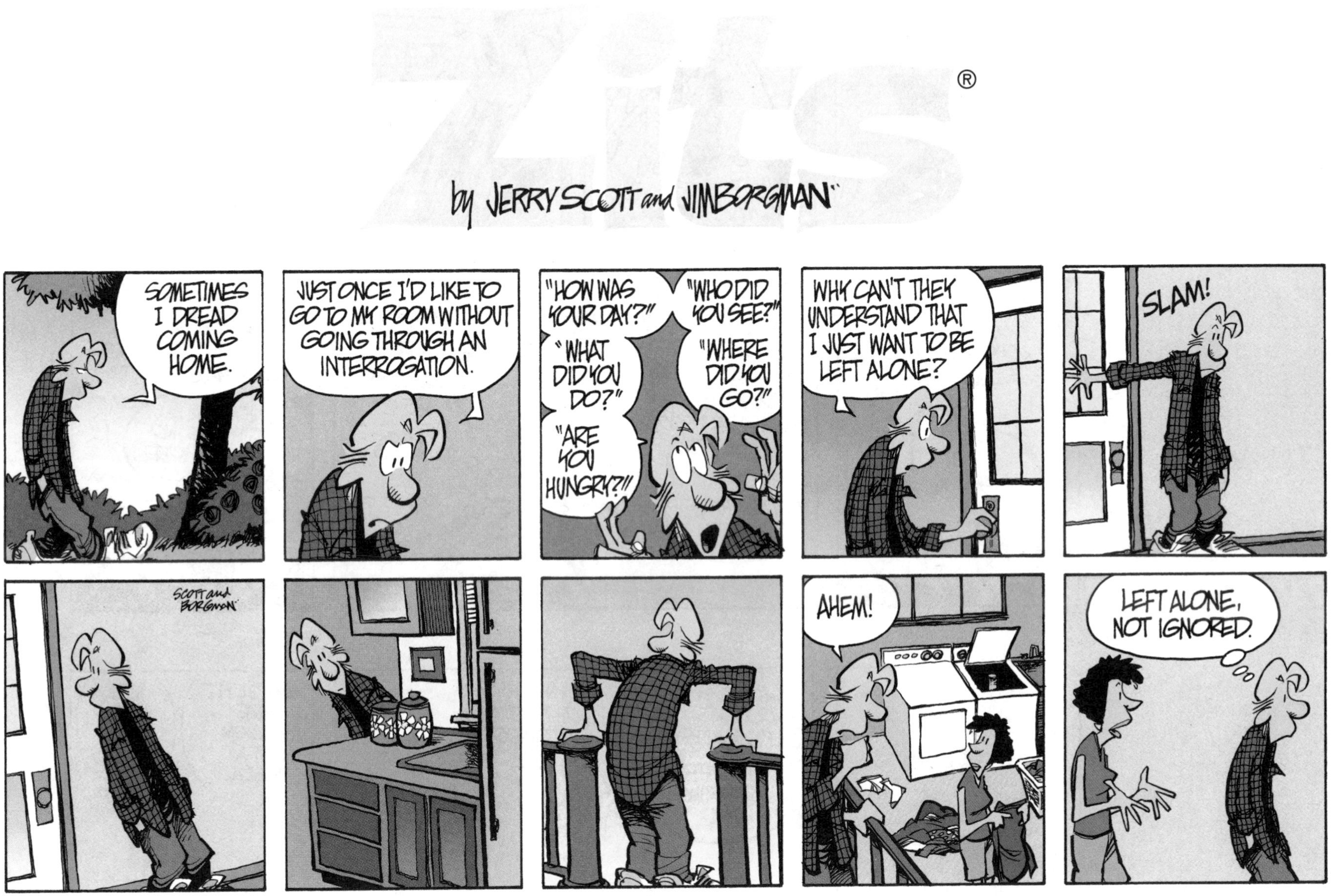
Zits®
by JERRY SCOTT and JIM BORGMAN
SOMETIMES I DREAD COMING HOME.
JUST ONCE I'D LIKE TO GO TO MY ROOM WITHOUT GOING THROUGH AN INTERROGATION.
"HOW WAS YOUR DAY?"
"WHAT DID YOU DO?"
"ARE YOU HUNGRY?!!"
"WHO DID YOU SEE?"
"WHERE DID YOU GO?"
WHY CAN'T THEY UNDERSTAND THAT I JUST WANT TO BE LEFT ALONE?
SLAM!
SCOTT and BORGMAN
AHEM!
LEFT ALONE, NOT IGNORED.

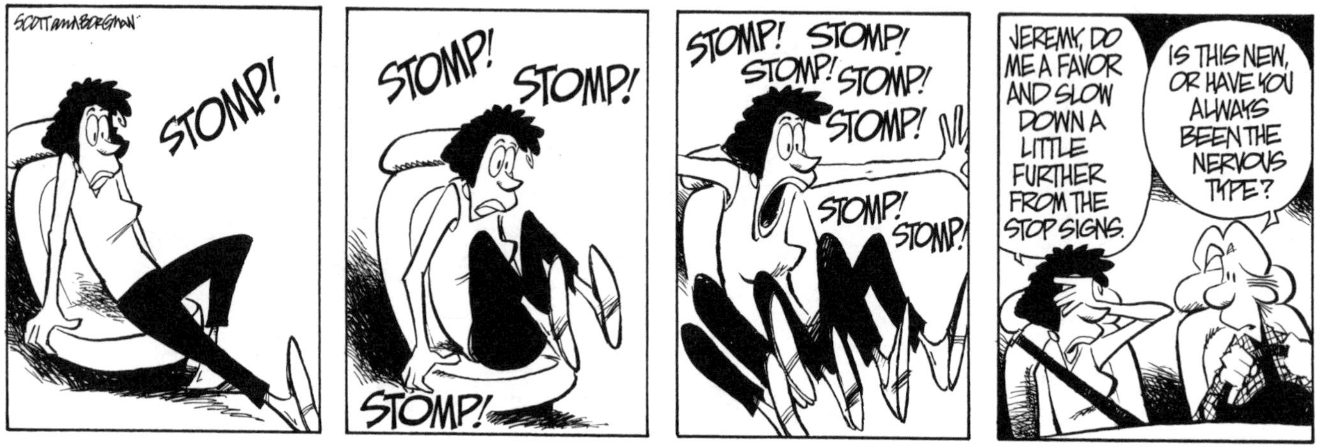
STOMP!
STOMP! STOMP!
STOMP!
STOMP! STOMP! STOMP! STOMP! STOMP!
STOMP! STOMP!
JEREMY, DO ME A FAVOR AND SLOW DOWN A LITTLE FURTHER FROM THE STOP SIGNS.
IS THIS NEW, OR HAVE YOU ALWAYS BEEN THE NERVOUS TYPE?

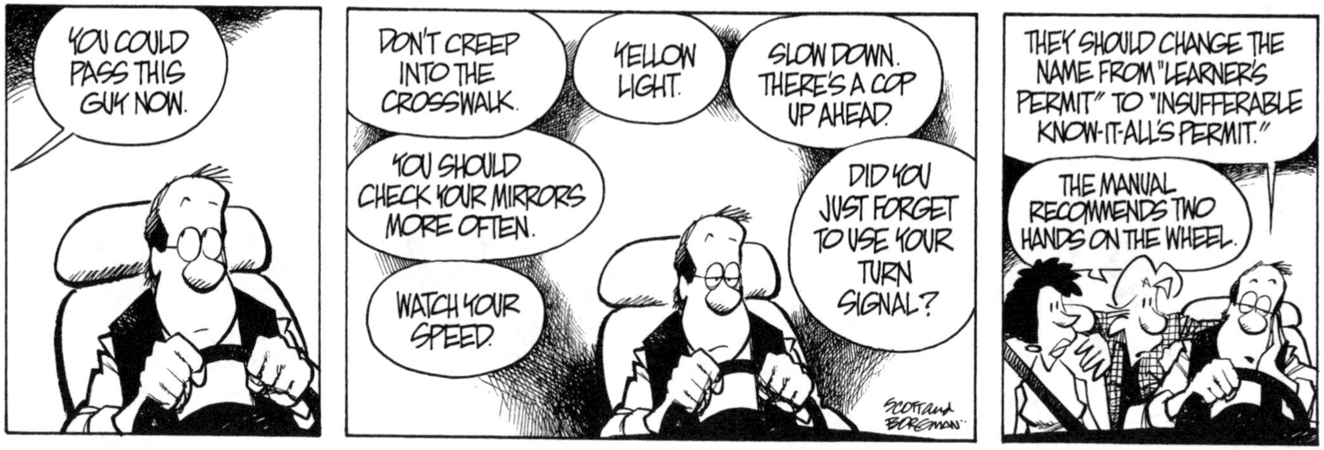
YOU COULD PASS THIS GUY NOW.
DON'T CREEP INTO THE CROSSWALK.
YELLOW LIGHT.
SLOW DOWN. THERE'S A COP UP AHEAD.
YOU SHOULD CHECK YOUR MIRRORS MORE OFTEN.
DID YOU JUST FORGET TO USE YOUR TURN SIGNAL?
WATCH YOUR SPEED.
THEY SHOULD CHANGE THE NAME FROM "LEARNER'S PERMIT" TO "INSUFFERABLE KNOW-IT-ALL'S PERMIT."
THE MANUAL RECOMMENDS TWO HANDS ON THE WHEEL.

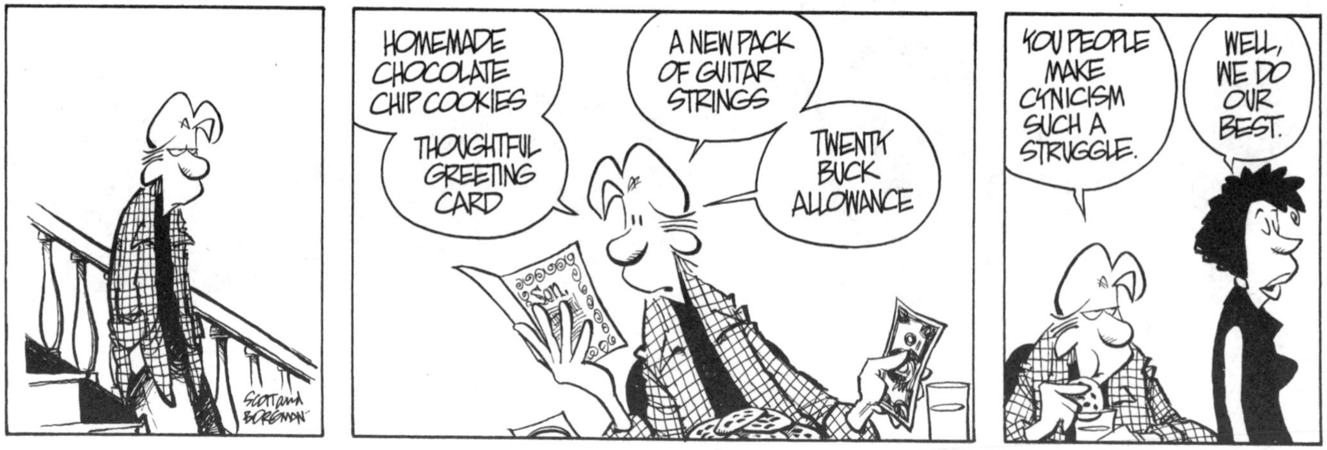
HOMEMADE CHOCOLATE CHIP COOKIES
A NEW PACK OF GUITAR STRINGS
THOUGHTFUL GREETING CARD
TWENTY BUCK ALLOWANCE
Son,
YOU PEOPLE MAKE CYNICISM SUCH A STRUGGLE.
WELL, WE DO OUR BEST.

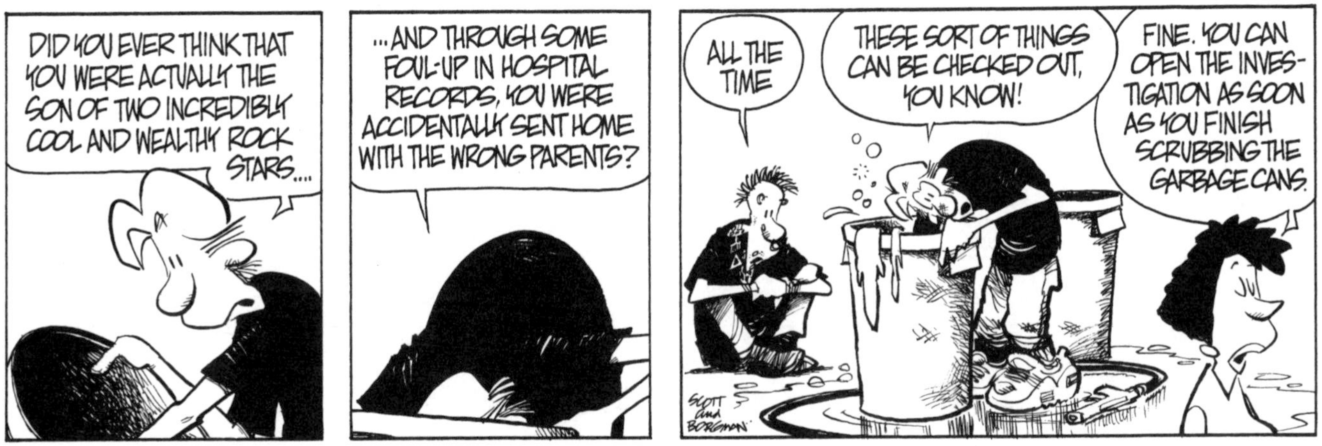

DID YOU EVER THINK THAT YOU WERE ACTUALLY THE SON OF TWO INCREDIBLY COOL AND WEALTHY ROCK STARS....
...AND THROUGH SOME FOUL-UP IN HOSPITAL RECORDS, YOU WERE ACCIDENTALLY SENT HOME WITH THE WRONG PARENTS?
ALL THE TIME
THESE SORT OF THINGS CAN BE CHECKED OUT, YOU KNOW!
FINE. YOU CAN OPEN THE INVESTIGATION AS SOON AS YOU FINISH SCRUBBING THE GARBAGE CANS.
SCOTT AND BORGMAN

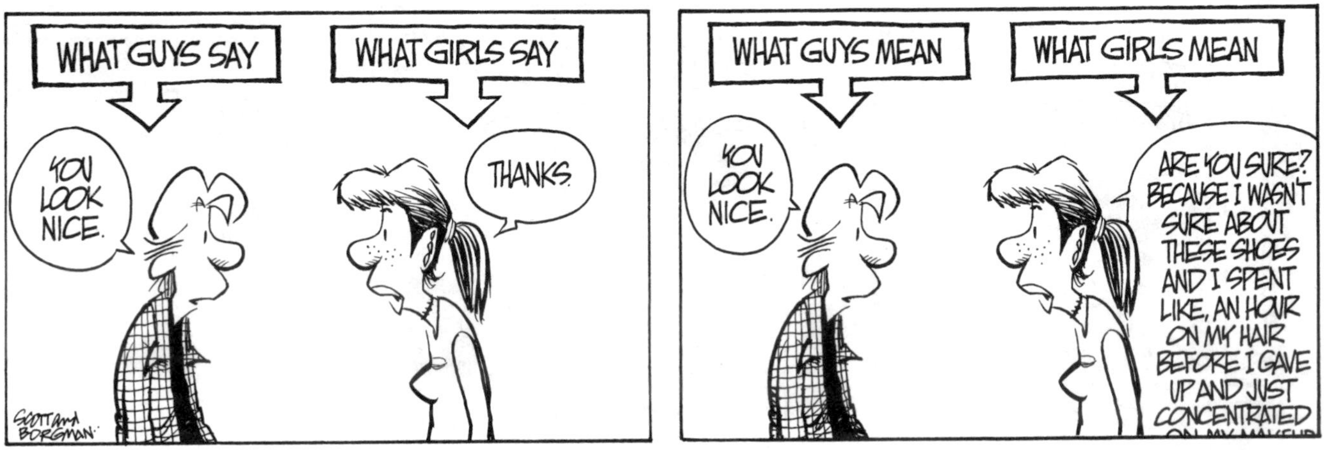

WHAT GUYS SAY
WHAT GIRLS SAY
YOU LOOK NICE.
THANKS.
SCOTT AND BORGMAN
WHAT GUYS MEAN
WHAT GIRLS MEAN
YOU LOOK NICE.
ARE YOU SURE? BECAUSE I WASN'T SURE ABOUT THESE SHOES AND I SPENT LIKE, AN HOUR ON MY HAIR BEFORE I GAVE UP AND JUST CONCENTRATED

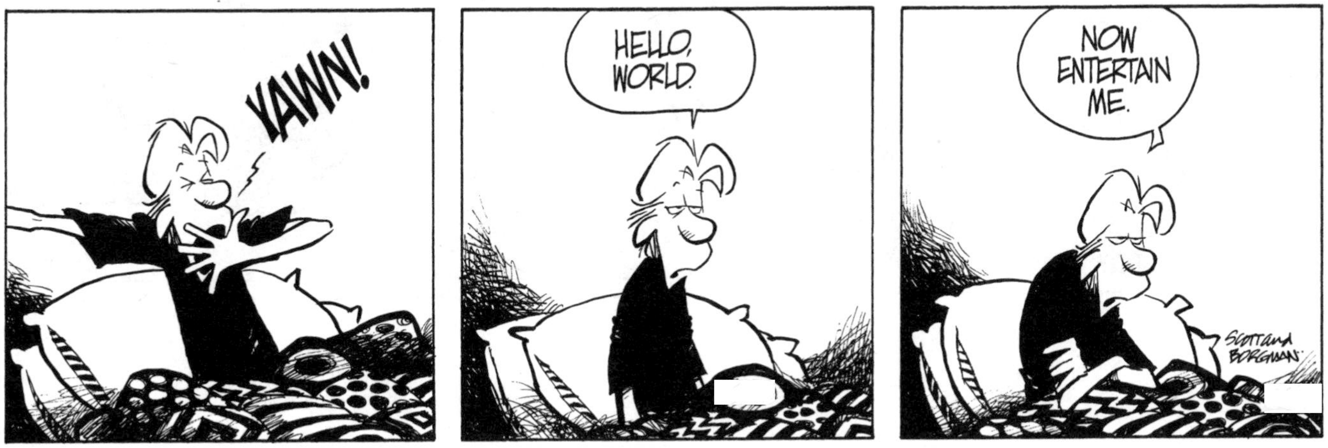

YAWN!
HELLO, WORLD.
NOW ENTERTAIN ME.
SCOTT AND BORGMAN

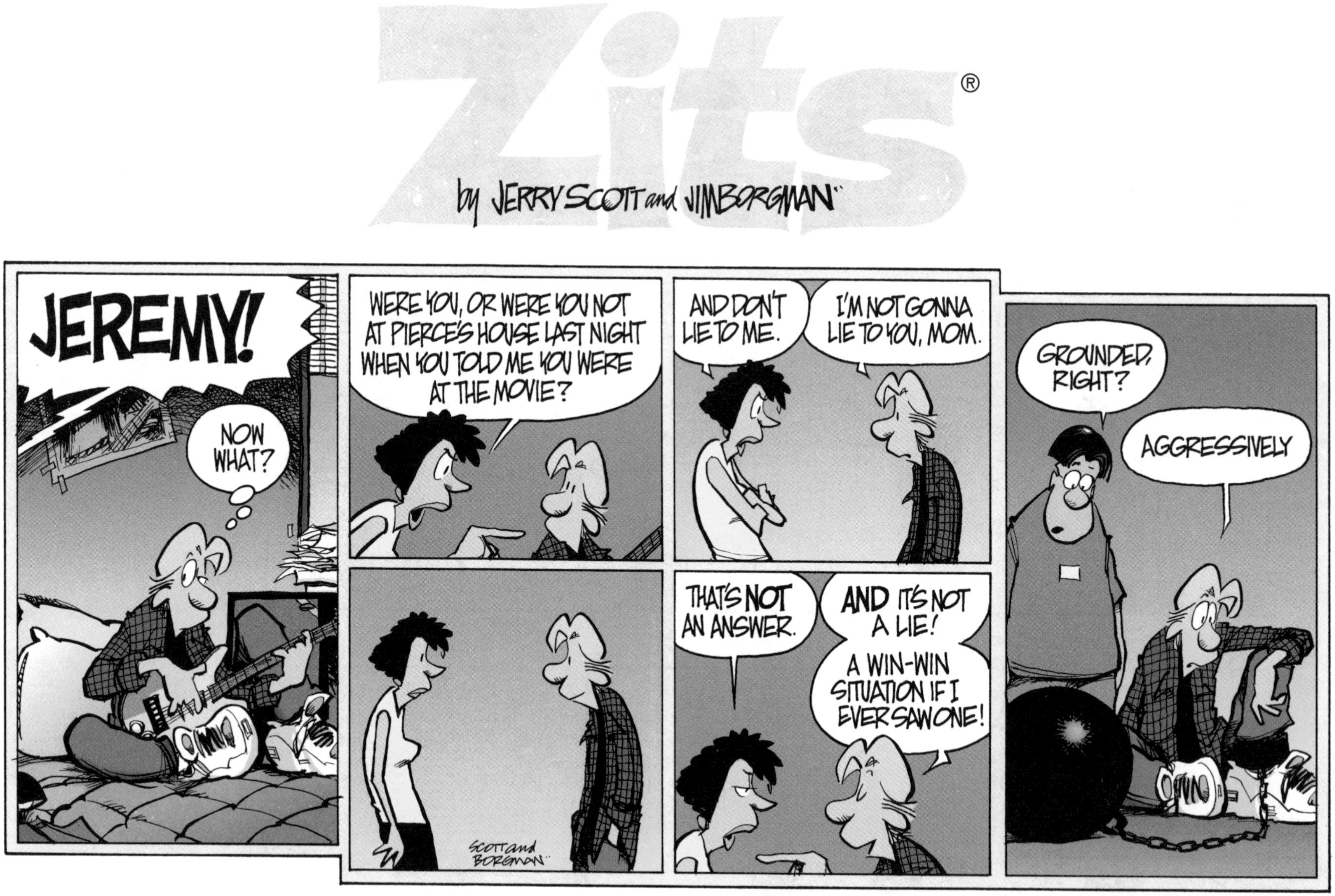
Zits®
by JERRY SCOTT and JIM BORGMAN
JEREMY!
NOW WHAT?
WERE YOU, OR WERE YOU NOT AT PIERCE'S HOUSE LAST NIGHT WHEN YOU TOLD ME YOU WERE AT THE MOVIE?
AND DON'T LIE TO ME.
I'M NOT GONNA LIE TO YOU, MOM.
SCOTT and BORGMAN
THAT'S NOT AN ANSWER.
AND IT'S NOT A LIE!
A WIN-WIN SITUATION IF I EVER SAW ONE!
GROUNDED, RIGHT?
AGGRESSIVELY

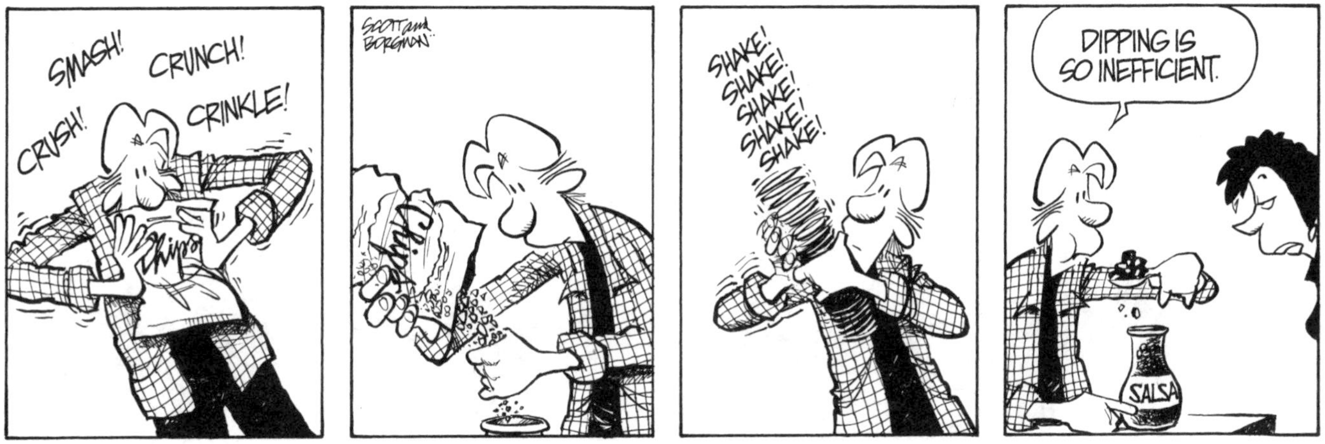
SMASH! CRUNCH!
CRUSH! CRINKLE!
Chips
SCOTT and BORGMAN
SHAKE! SHAKE! SHAKE! SHAKE! SHAKE!
DIPPING IS SO INEFFICIENT.
SALSA

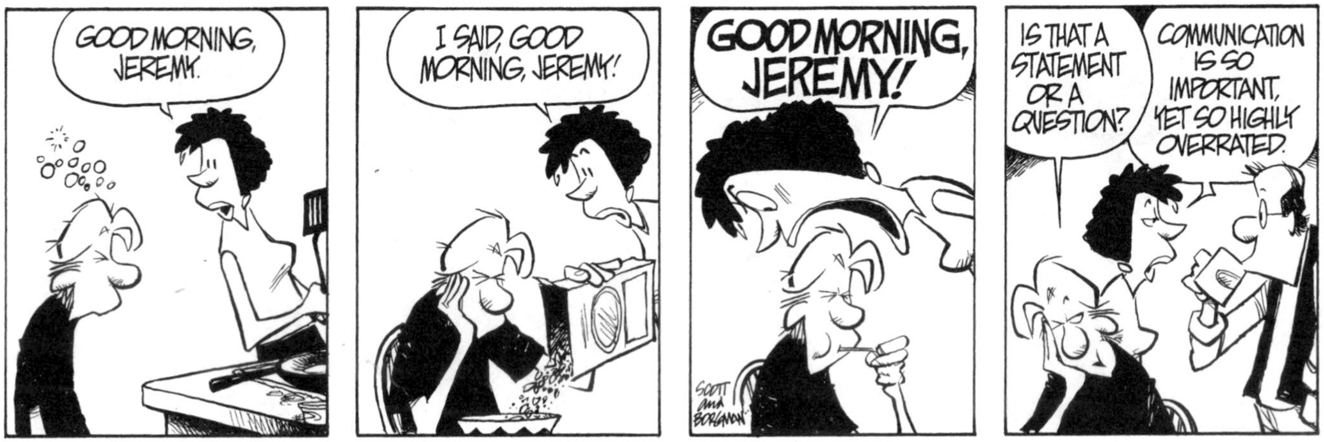
GOOD MORNING, JEREMY.
I SAID, GOOD MORNING, JEREMY!
GOOD MORNING, JEREMY!
SCOTT and BORGMAN
IS THAT A STATEMENT OR A QUESTION?
COMMUNICATION IS SO IMPORTANT, YET SO HIGHLY OVERRATED.

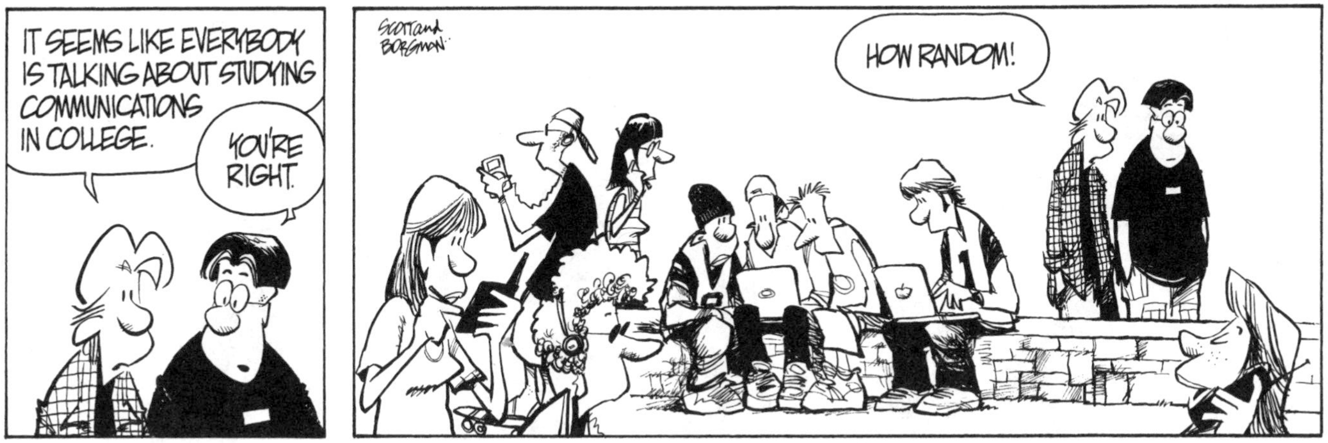
IT SEEMS LIKE EVERYBODY IS TALKING ABOUT STUDYING COMMUNICATIONS IN COLLEGE.
YOU'RE RIGHT.
SCOTT and BORGMAN
HOW RANDOM!

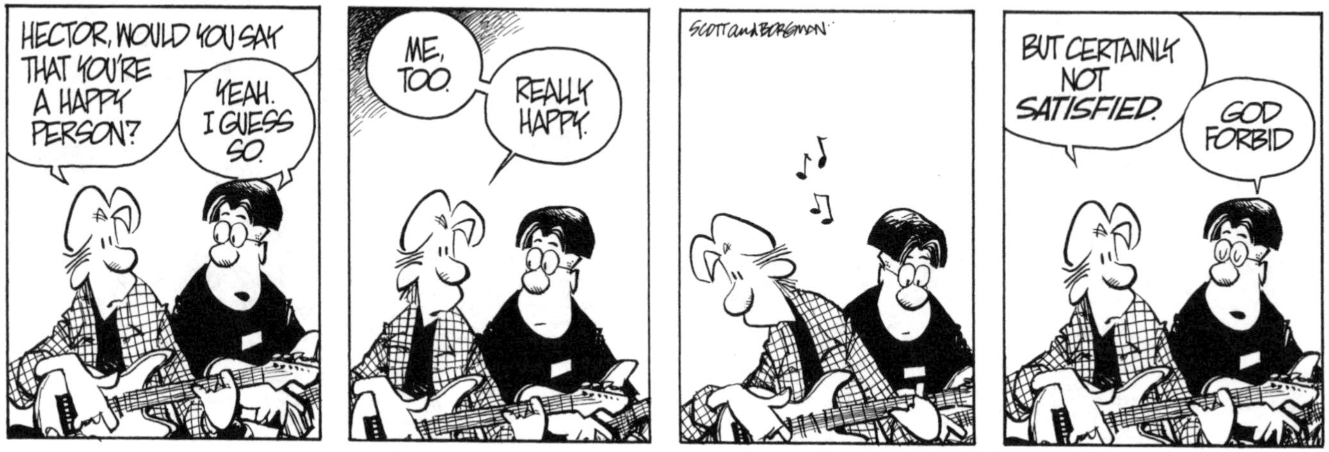
HECTOR, WOULD YOU SAY THAT YOU'RE A HAPPY PERSON?
YEAH. I GUESS SO.
ME, TOO.
REALLY HAPPY.
BUT CERTAINLY NOT SATISFIED.
GOD FORBID

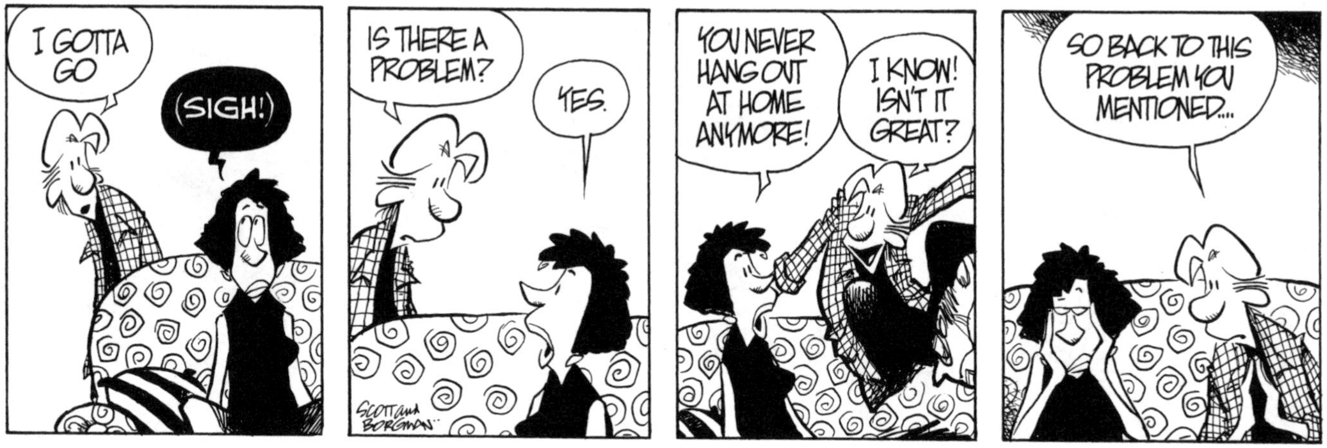
I GOTTA GO
(SIGH!)
IS THERE A PROBLEM?
YES.
YOU NEVER HANG OUT AT HOME ANYMORE!
I KNOW! ISN'T IT GREAT?
SO BACK TO THIS PROBLEM YOU MENTIONED....

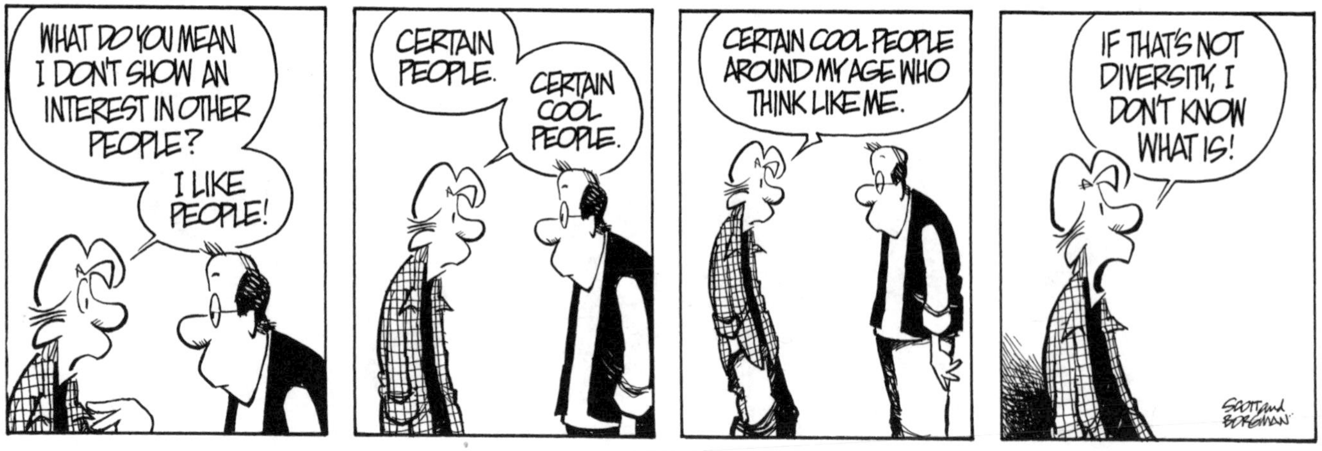
WHAT DO YOU MEAN I DON'T SHOW AN INTEREST IN OTHER PEOPLE?
I LIKE PEOPLE!
CERTAIN PEOPLE.
CERTAIN COOL PEOPLE.
CERTAIN COOL PEOPLE AROUND MY AGE WHO THINK LIKE ME.
IF THAT'S NOT DIVERSITY, I DON'T KNOW WHAT IS!

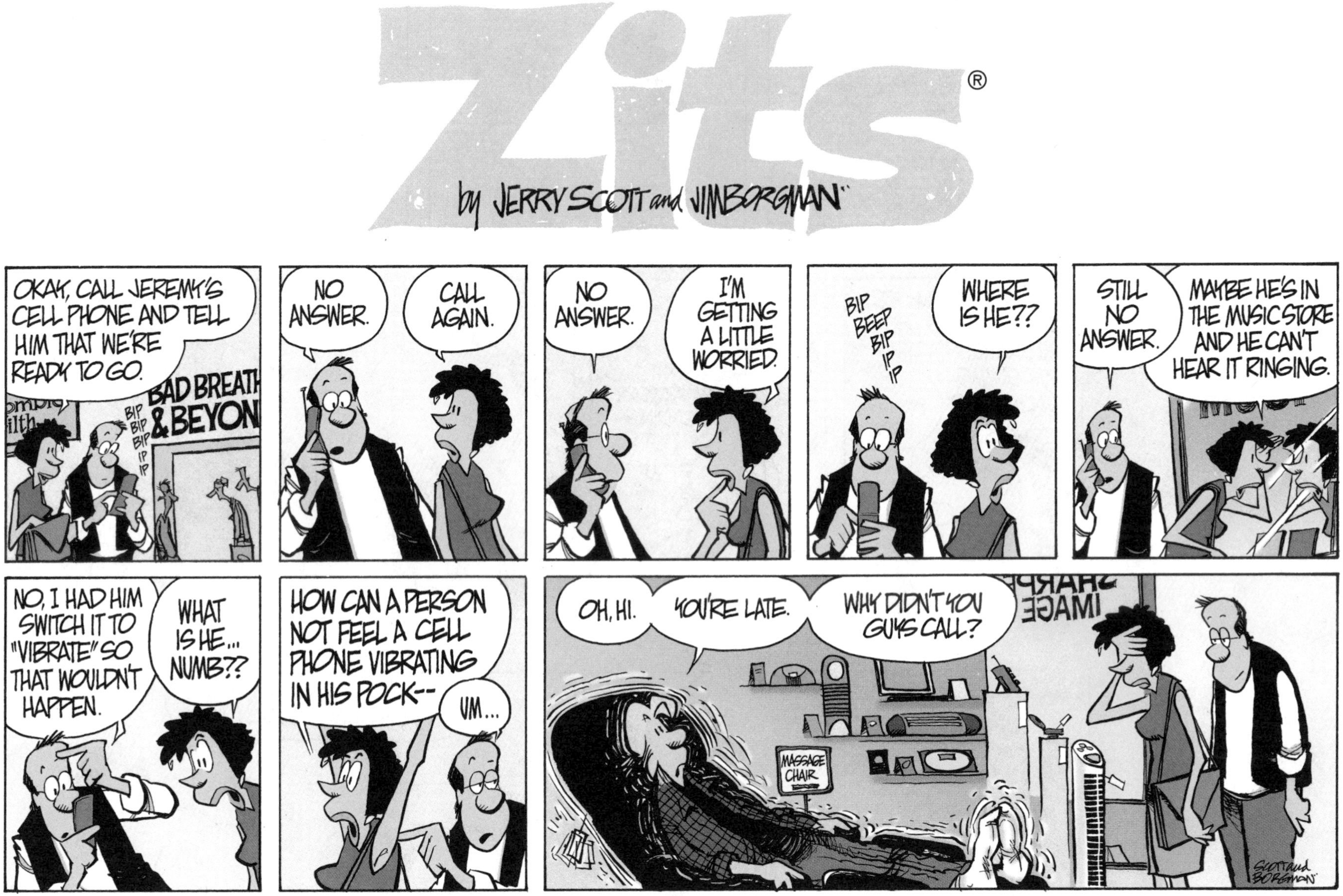
Zits®
by JERRY SCOTT and JIM BORGMAN
OKAY, CALL JEREMY'S CELL PHONE AND TELL HIM THAT WE'RE READY TO GO.
BAD BREATH & BEYOND
BIP BIP BIP IP IP
NO ANSWER.
CALL AGAIN.
NO ANSWER.
I'M GETTING A LITTLE WORRIED.
BIP BEEP BIP IP IP
WHERE IS HE??
STILL NO ANSWER.
MAYBE HE'S IN THE MUSIC STORE AND HE CAN'T HEAR IT RINGING.
NO, I HAD HIM SWITCH IT TO "VIBRATE" SO THAT WOULDN'T HAPPEN.
WHAT IS HE... NUMB??
HOW CAN A PERSON NOT FEEL A CELL PHONE VIBRATING IN HIS POCK--
UM...
OH, HI.
YOU'RE LATE.
WHY DIDN'T YOU GUYS CALL?
MASSAGE CHAIR
SCOTT and BORGMAN

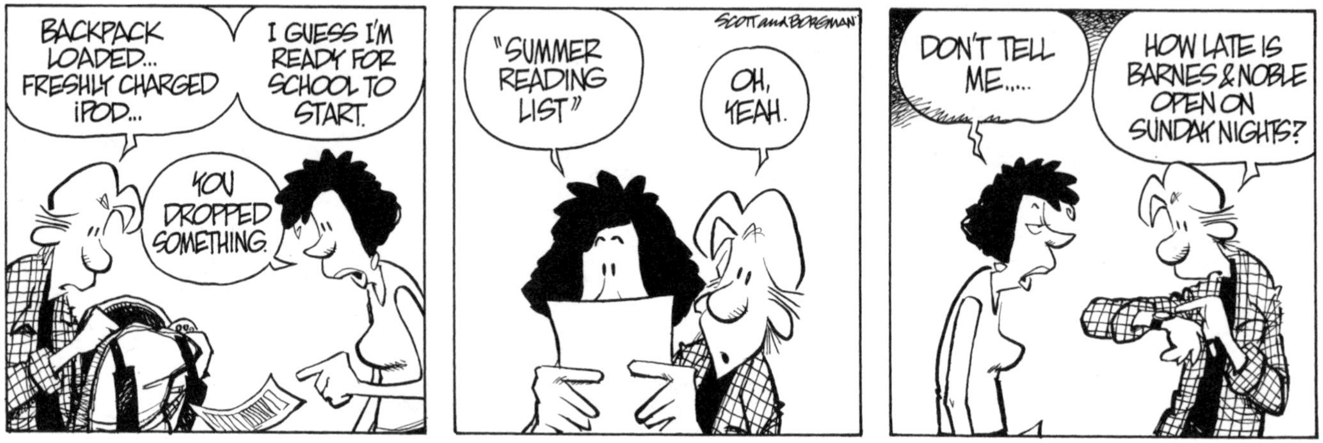
BACKPACK LOADED... FRESHLY CHARGED iPOD...
I GUESS I'M READY FOR SCHOOL TO START.
YOU DROPPED SOMETHING.
SCOTT and BORGMAN
"SUMMER READING LIST"
OH, YEAH.
DON'T TELL ME.....
HOW LATE IS BARNES & NOBLE OPEN ON SUNDAY NIGHTS?

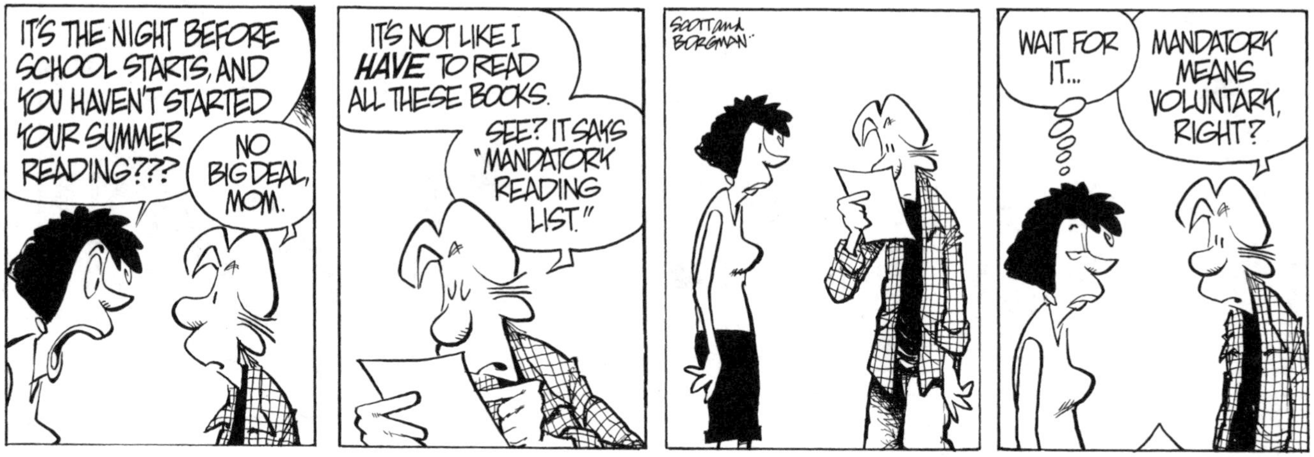
IT'S THE NIGHT BEFORE SCHOOL STARTS, AND YOU HAVEN'T STARTED YOUR SUMMER READING???
NO BIG DEAL, MOM.
IT'S NOT LIKE I HAVE TO READ ALL THESE BOOKS.
SEE? IT SAYS "MANDATORY READING LIST."
SCOTT and BORGMAN
WAIT FOR IT...
MANDATORY MEANS VOLUNTARY, RIGHT?

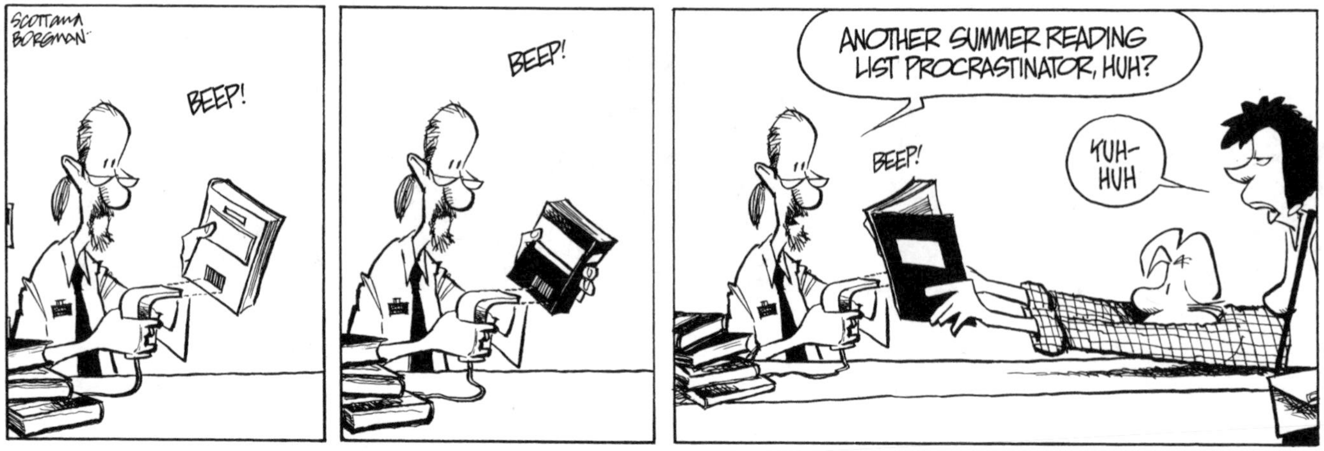
SCOTT and BORGMAN
BEEP!
BEEP!
ANOTHER SUMMER READING LIST PROCRASTINATOR, HUH?
BEEP!
YUH-HUH

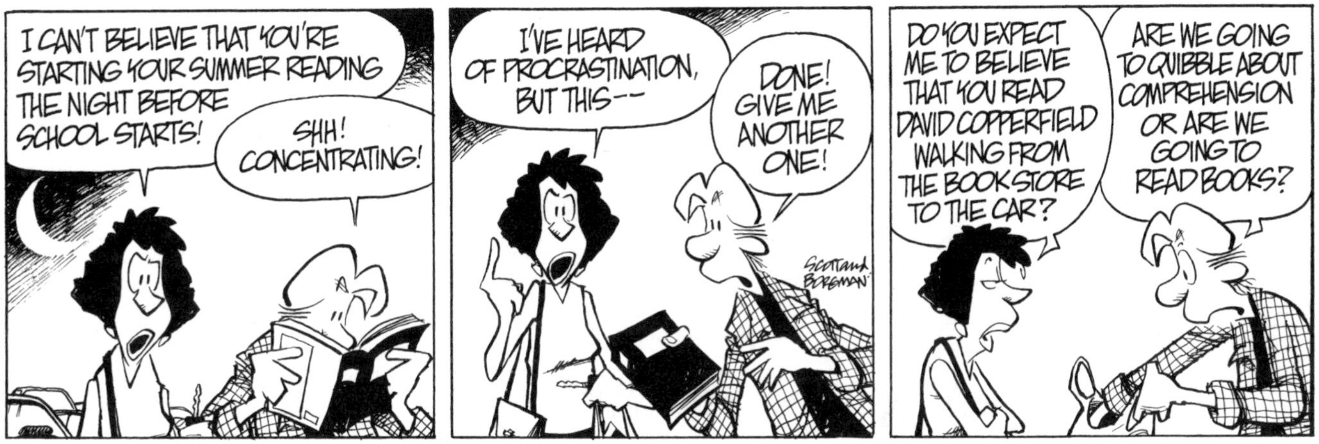
I CAN'T BELIEVE THAT YOU'RE STARTING YOUR SUMMER READING THE NIGHT BEFORE SCHOOL STARTS!
SHH! CONCENTRATING!
I'VE HEARD OF PROCRASTINATION, BUT THIS--
DONE! GIVE ME ANOTHER ONE!
SCOTT and BORGMAN
DO YOU EXPECT ME TO BELIEVE THAT YOU READ DAVID COPPERFIELD WALKING FROM THE BOOK STORE TO THE CAR?
ARE WE GOING TO QUIBBLE ABOUT COMPREHENSION OR ARE WE GOING TO READ BOOKS?

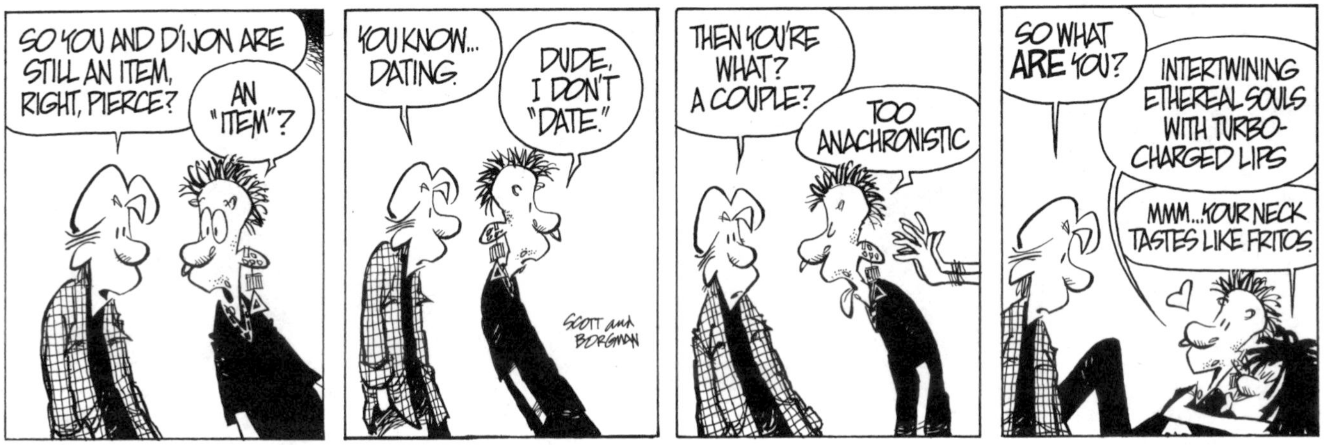
SO YOU AND D'IJON ARE STILL AN ITEM, RIGHT, PIERCE?
AN "ITEM"?
YOU KNOW... DATING.
DUDE, I DON'T "DATE."
SCOTT and BORGMAN
THEN YOU'RE WHAT? A COUPLE?
TOO ANACHRONISTIC
SO WHAT ARE YOU?
INTERTWINING ETHEREAL SOULS WITH TURBO-CHARGED LIPS
MMM...YOUR NECK TASTES LIKE FRITOS.

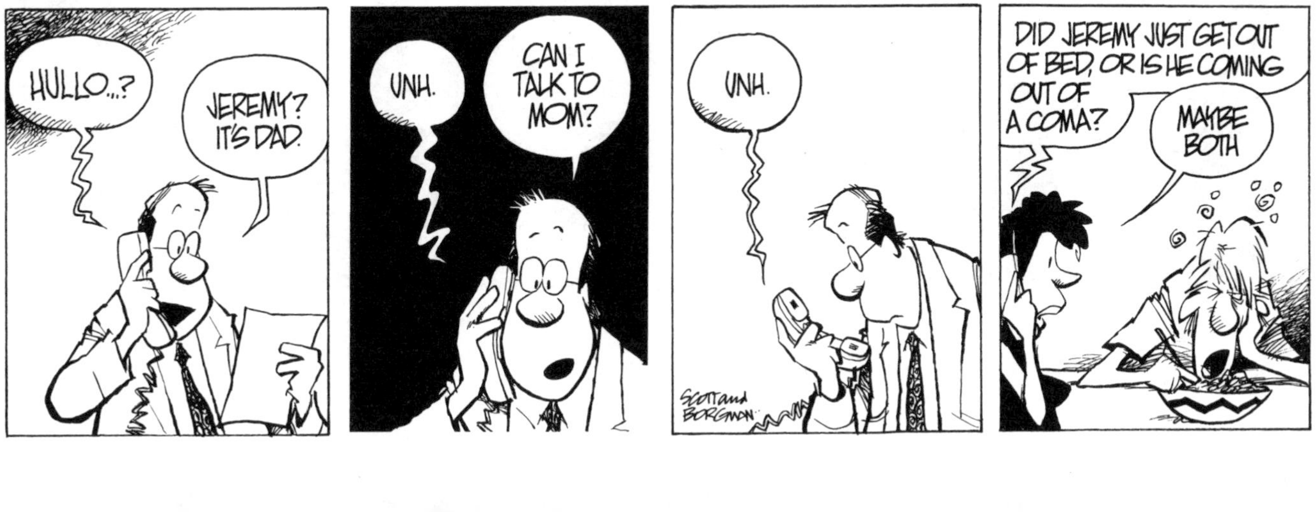
HULLO...?
JEREMY? IT'S DAD.
UNH.
CAN I TALK TO MOM?
UNH.
SCOTT and BORGMAN
DID JEREMY JUST GET OUT OF BED, OR IS HE COMING OUT OF A COMA?
MAYBE BOTH

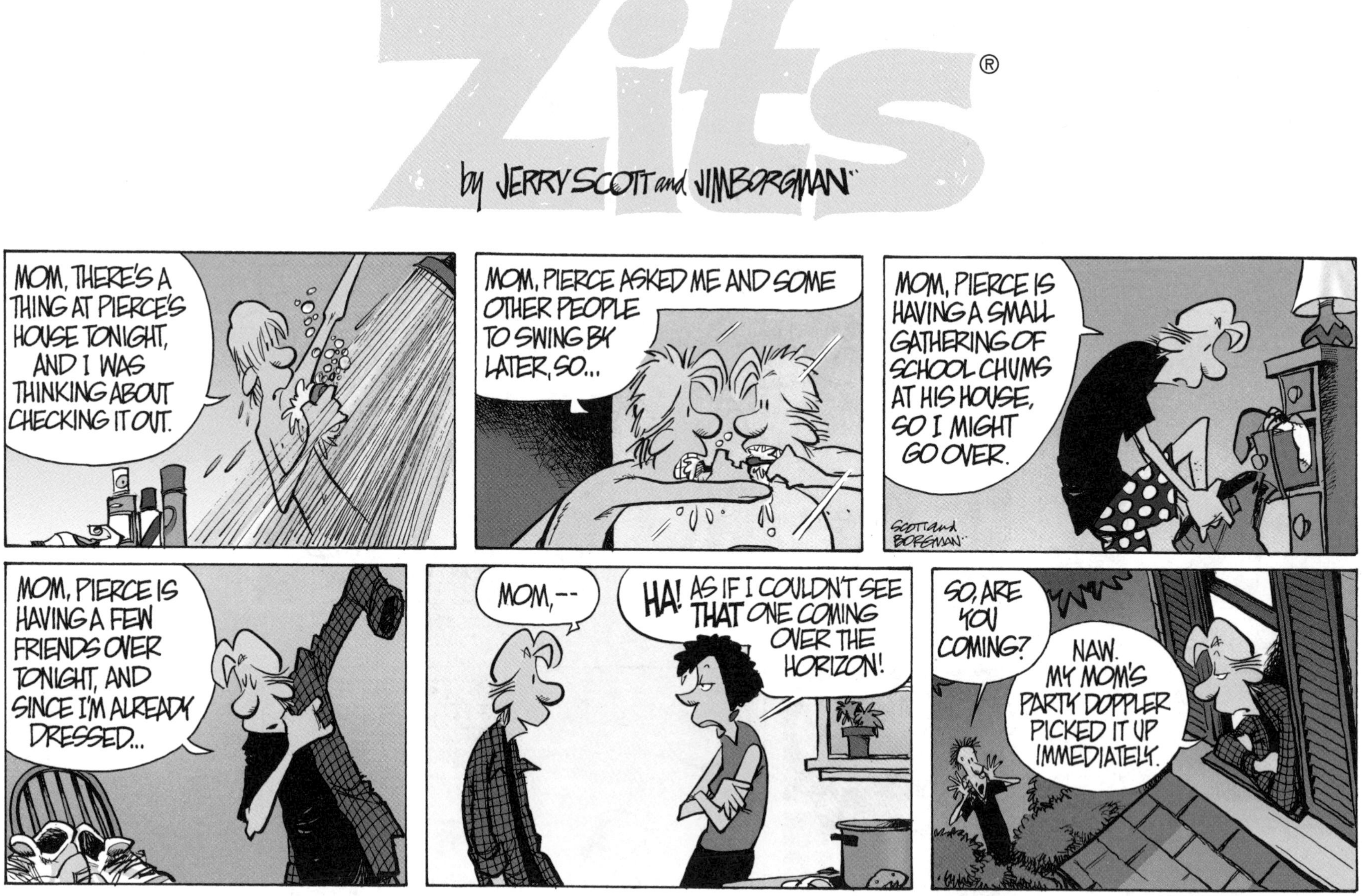
Zits®
by JERRY SCOTT and JIM BORGMAN
MOM, THERE'S A THING AT PIERCE'S HOUSE TONIGHT, AND I WAS THINKING ABOUT CHECKING IT OUT.
MOM, PIERCE ASKED ME AND SOME OTHER PEOPLE TO SWING BY LATER, SO...
MOM, PIERCE IS HAVING A SMALL GATHERING OF SCHOOL CHUMS AT HIS HOUSE, SO I MIGHT GO OVER.
SCOTT and BORGMAN
MOM, PIERCE IS HAVING A FEW FRIENDS OVER TONIGHT, AND SINCE I'M ALREADY DRESSED...
MOM, --
HA! AS IF I COULDN'T SEE THAT ONE COMING OVER THE HORIZON!
SO, ARE YOU COMING?
NAW. MY MOM'S PARTY DOPPLER PICKED IT UP IMMEDIATELY.

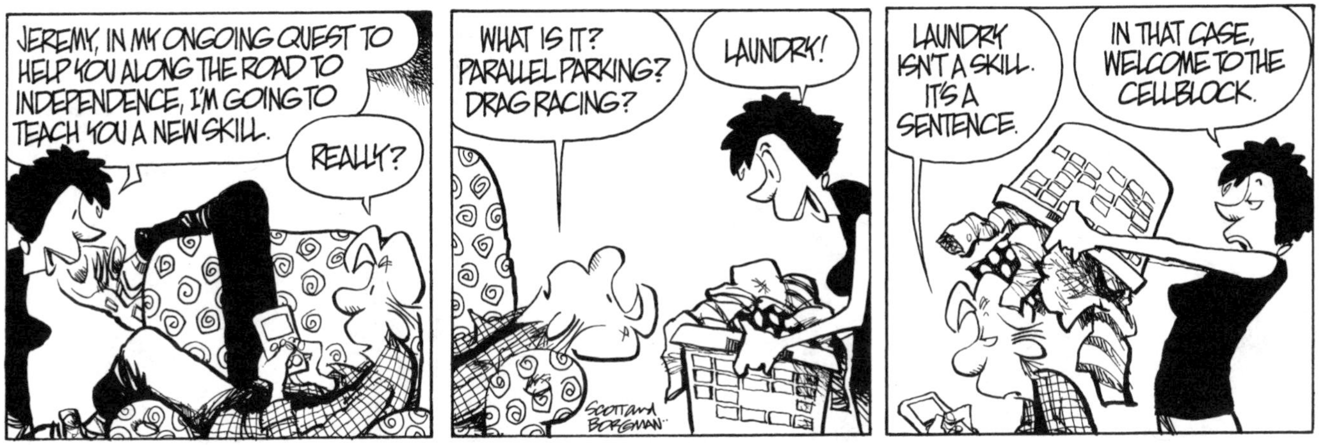
JEREMY, IN MY ONGOING QUEST TO HELP YOU ALONG THE ROAD TO INDEPENDENCE, I'M GOING TO TEACH YOU A NEW SKILL.
REALLY?
WHAT IS IT? PARALLEL PARKING? DRAG RACING?
LAUNDRY!
SCOTT and BORGMAN
LAUNDRY ISN'T A SKILL. IT'S A SENTENCE.
IN THAT CASE, WELCOME TO THE CELLBLOCK.

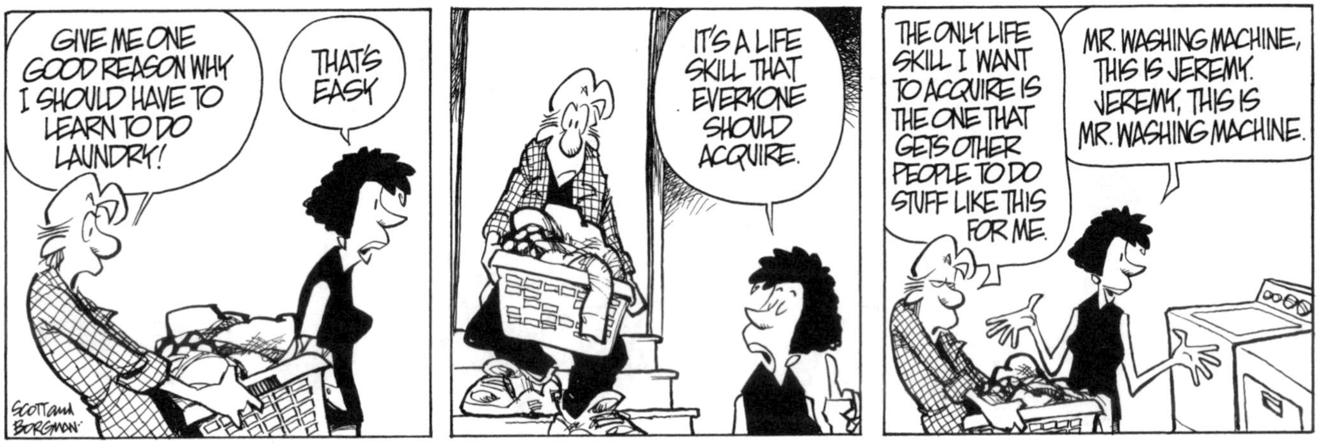
GIVE ME ONE GOOD REASON WHY I SHOULD HAVE TO LEARN TO DO LAUNDRY!
THAT'S EASY
SCOTT and BORGMAN
IT'S A LIFE SKILL THAT EVERYONE SHOULD ACQUIRE.
THE ONLY LIFE SKILL I WANT TO ACQUIRE IS THE ONE THAT GETS OTHER PEOPLE TO DO STUFF LIKE THIS FOR ME.
MR. WASHING MACHINE, THIS IS JEREMY. JEREMY, THIS IS MR. WASHING MACHINE.

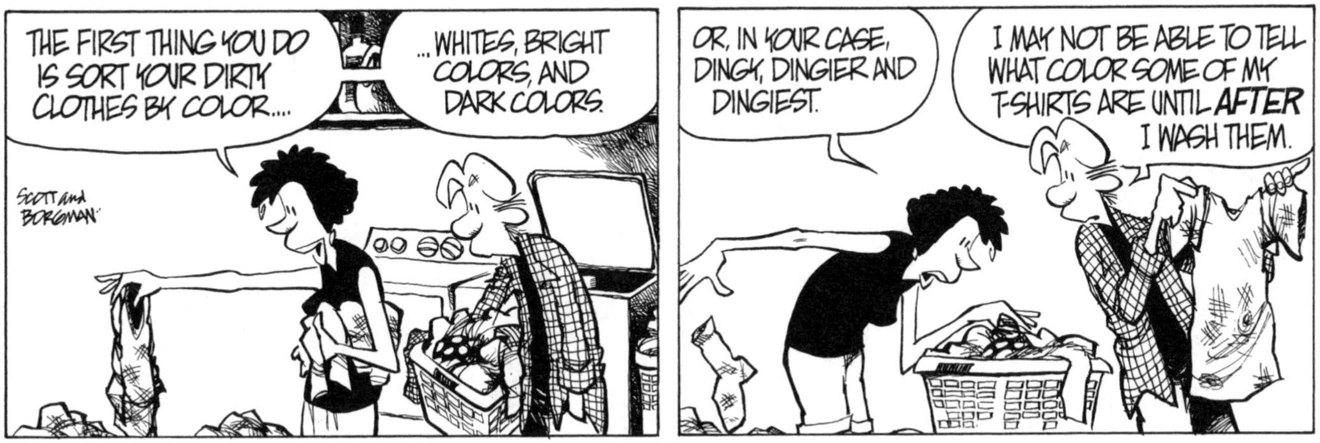
THE FIRST THING YOU DO IS SORT YOUR DIRTY CLOTHES BY COLOR....
...WHITES, BRIGHT COLORS, AND DARK COLORS.
SCOTT and BORGMAN
OR, IN YOUR CASE, DINGY, DINGIER AND DINGIEST.
I MAY NOT BE ABLE TO TELL WHAT COLOR SOME OF MY T-SHIRTS ARE UNTIL **AFTER** I WASH THEM.

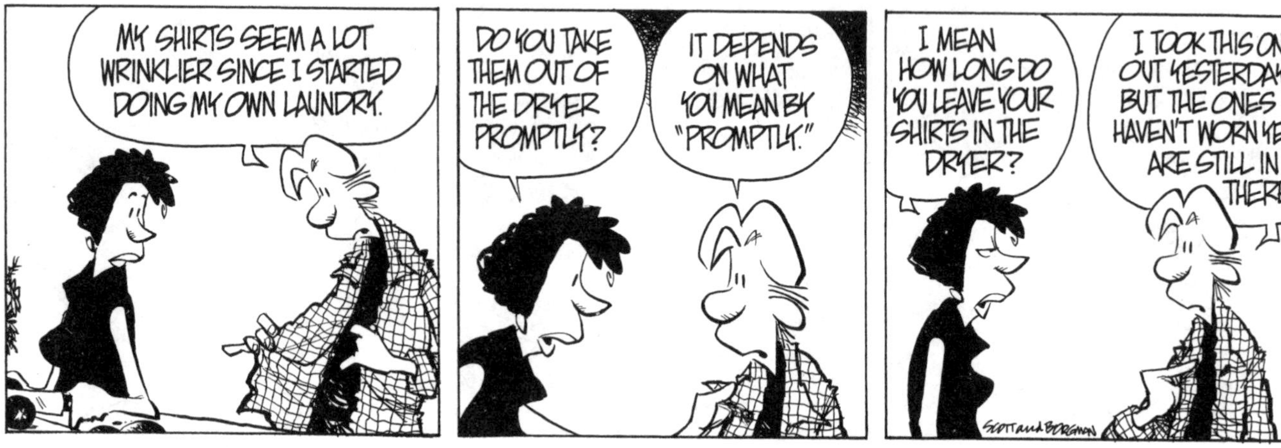
MY SHIRTS SEEM A LOT WRINKLIER SINCE I STARTED DOING MY OWN LAUNDRY.
DO YOU TAKE THEM OUT OF THE DRYER PROMPTLY?
IT DEPENDS ON WHAT YOU MEAN BY "PROMPTLY."
I MEAN HOW LONG DO YOU LEAVE YOUR SHIRTS IN THE DRYER?
I TOOK THIS ONE OUT YESTERDAY, BUT THE ONES I HAVEN'T WORN YET ARE STILL IN THERE.
SCOTT and BORGMAN

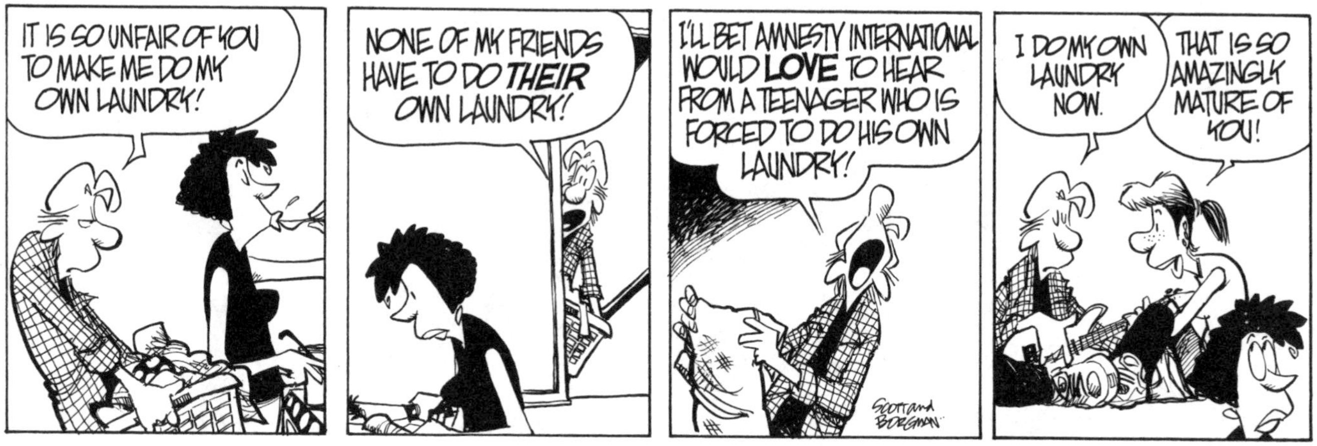
IT IS SO UNFAIR OF YOU TO MAKE ME DO MY OWN LAUNDRY!
NONE OF MY FRIENDS HAVE TO DO THEIR OWN LAUNDRY!
I'LL BET AMNESTY INTERNATIONAL WOULD LOVE TO HEAR FROM A TEENAGER WHO IS FORCED TO DO HIS OWN LAUNDRY!
SCOTT and BORGMAN
I DO MY OWN LAUNDRY NOW.
THAT IS SO AMAZINGLY MATURE OF YOU!

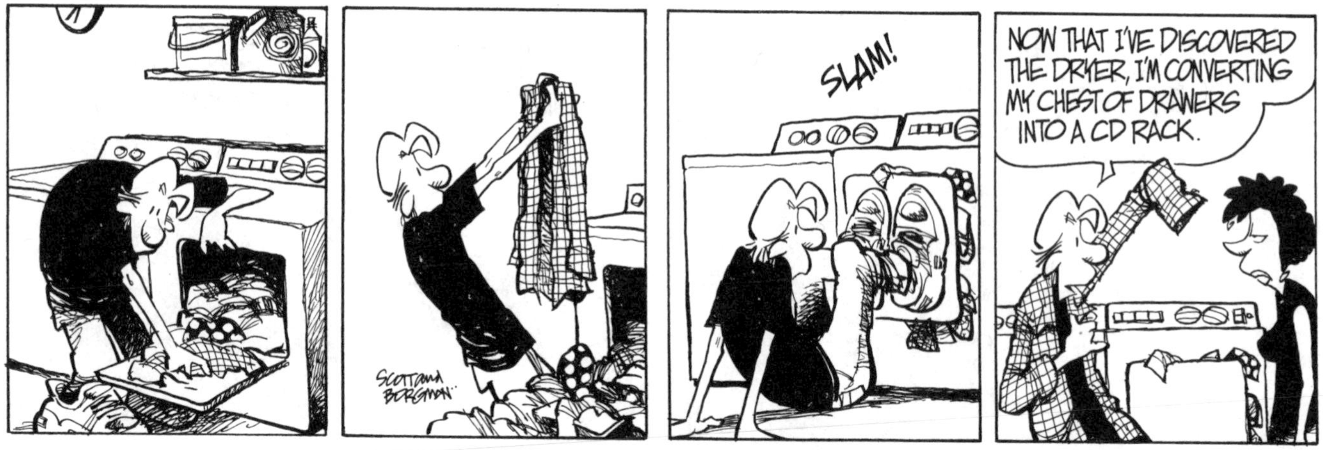
SCOTT and BORGMAN
SLAM!
NOW THAT I'VE DISCOVERED THE DRYER, I'M CONVERTING MY CHEST OF DRAWERS INTO A CD RACK.

Zits®

by JERRY SCOTT and JIM BORGMAN

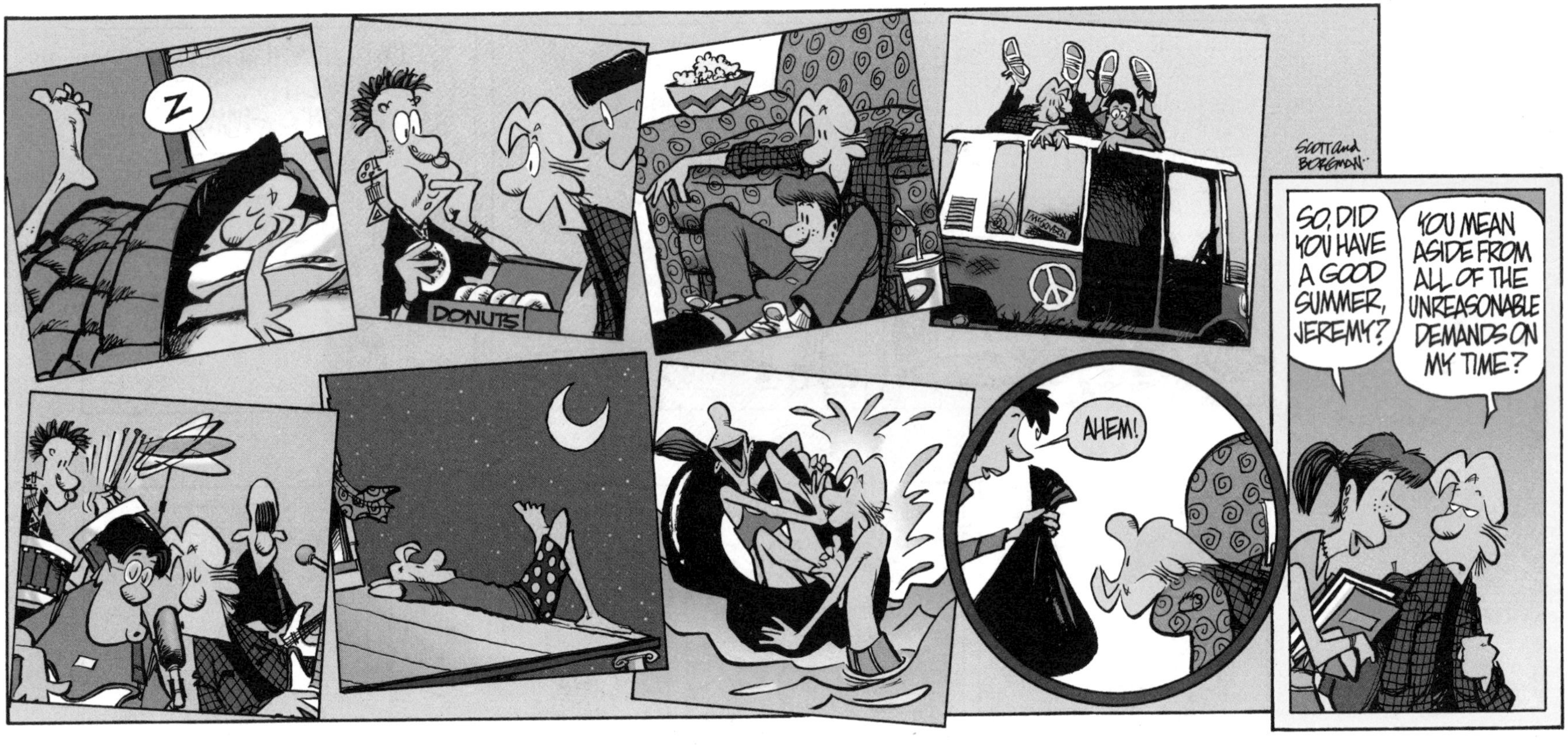
Z
DONUTS
SCOTT and BORGMAN
AHEM!
SO, DID YOU HAVE A GOOD SUMMER, JEREMY?
YOU MEAN ASIDE FROM ALL OF THE UNREASONABLE DEMANDS ON MY TIME?

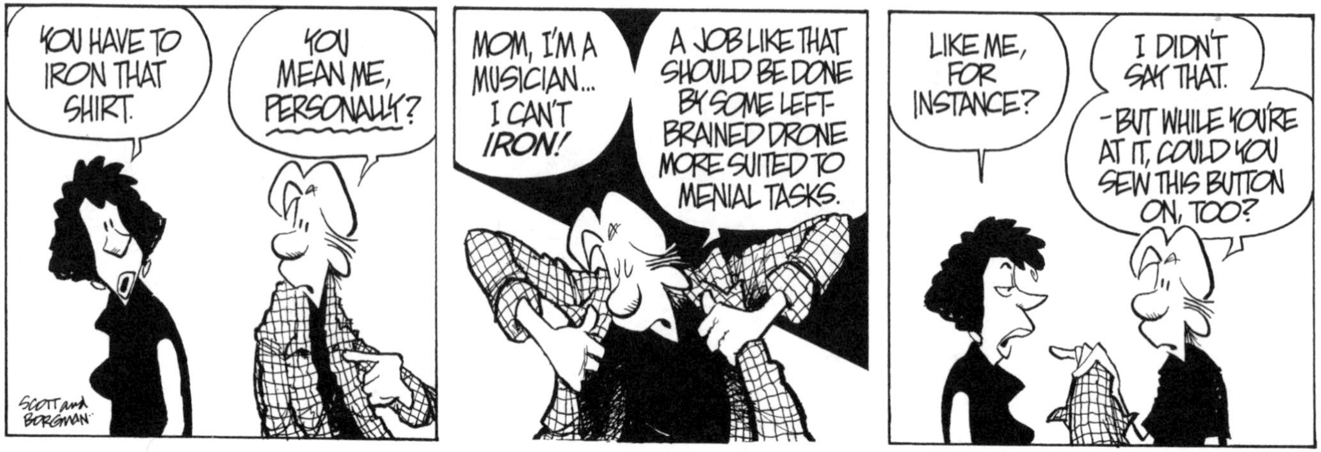
YOU HAVE TO IRON THAT SHIRT.
YOU MEAN ME, PERSONALLY?
MOM, I'M A MUSICIAN... I CAN'T IRON!
A JOB LIKE THAT SHOULD BE DONE BY SOME LEFT-BRAINED DRONE MORE SUITED TO MENIAL TASKS.
LIKE ME, FOR INSTANCE?
I DIDN'T SAY THAT.
-BUT WHILE YOU'RE AT IT, COULD YOU SEW THIS BUTTON ON, TOO?
SCOTT and BORGMAN

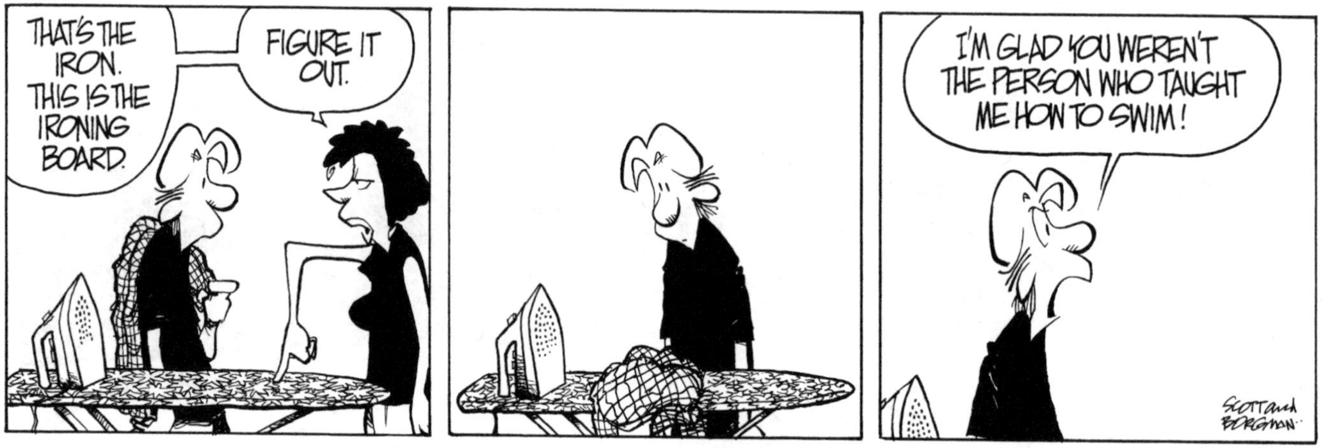
THAT'S THE IRON. THIS IS THE IRONING BOARD.
FIGURE IT OUT.
I'M GLAD YOU WEREN'T THE PERSON WHO TAUGHT ME HOW TO SWIM!
SCOTT and BORGMAN

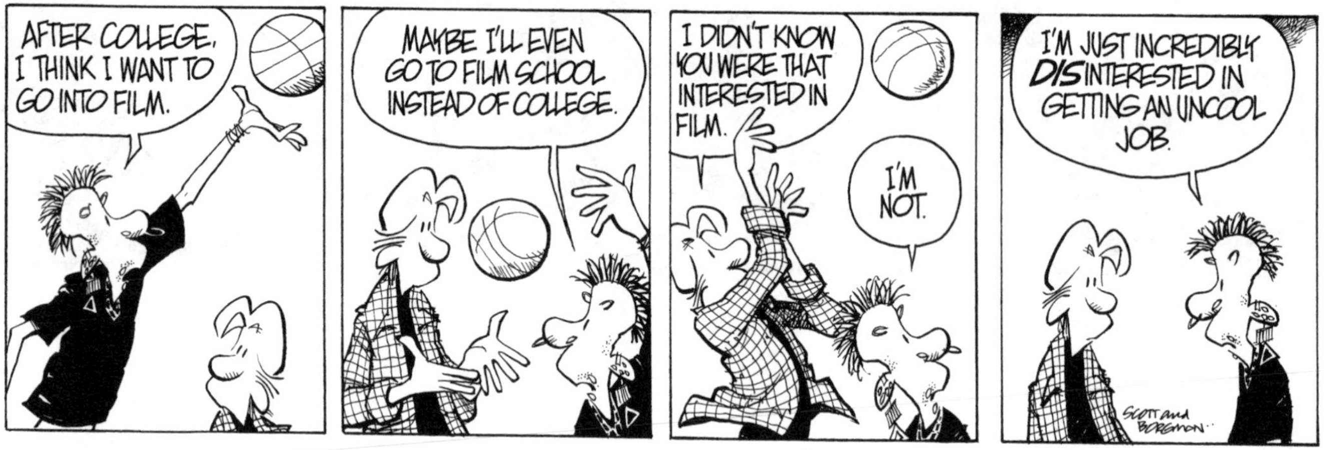
AFTER COLLEGE, I THINK I WANT TO GO INTO FILM.
MAYBE I'LL EVEN GO TO FILM SCHOOL INSTEAD OF COLLEGE.
I DIDN'T KNOW YOU WERE THAT INTERESTED IN FILM.
I'M NOT.
I'M JUST INCREDIBLY DISINTERESTED IN GETTING AN UNCOOL JOB.
SCOTT and BORGMAN

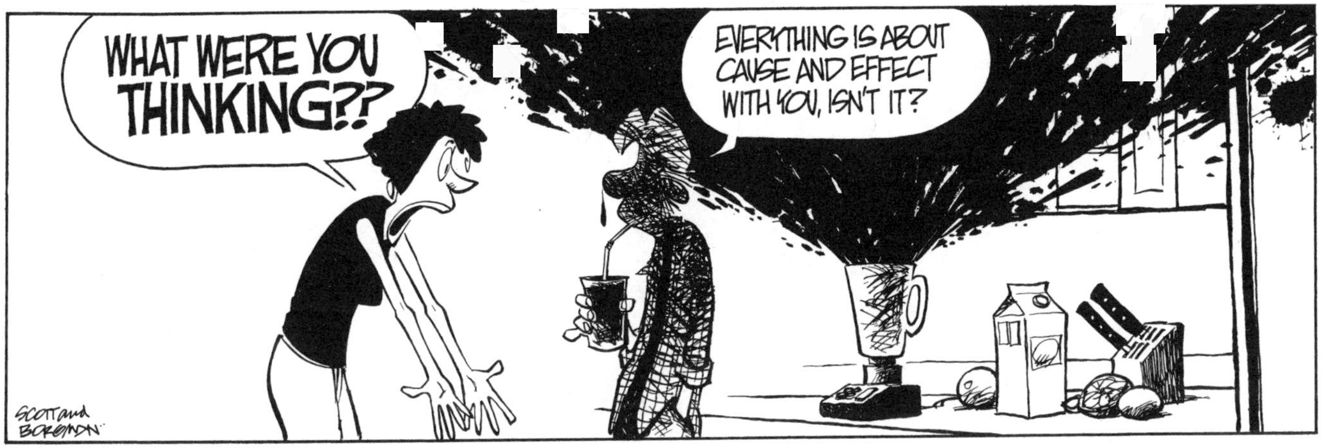
WHAT WERE YOU THINKING??
EVERYTHING IS ABOUT CAUSE AND EFFECT WITH YOU, ISN'T IT?

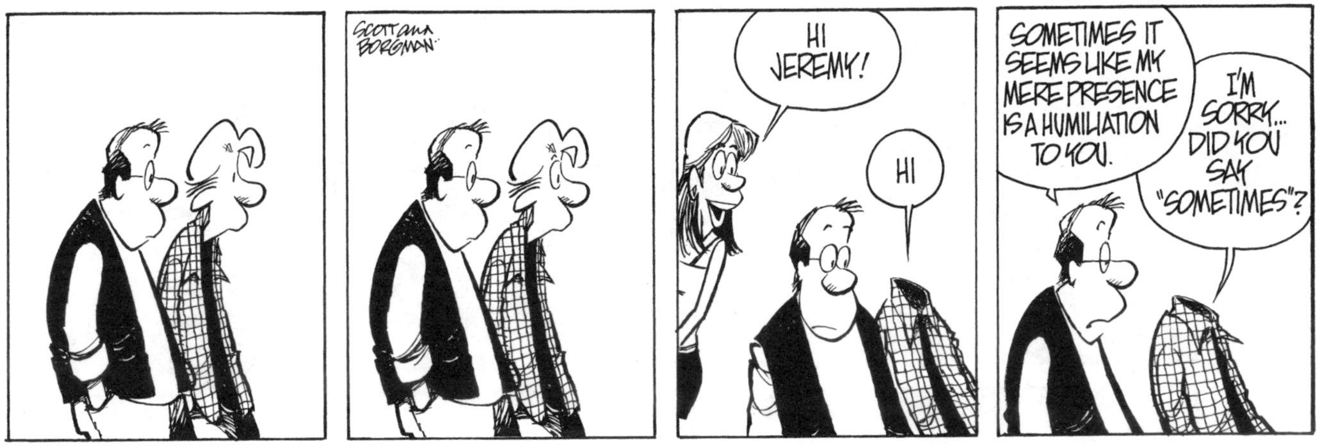
HI JEREMY!
HI
SOMETIMES IT SEEMS LIKE MY MERE PRESENCE IS A HUMILIATION TO YOU.
I'M SORRY... DID YOU SAY "SOMETIMES"?

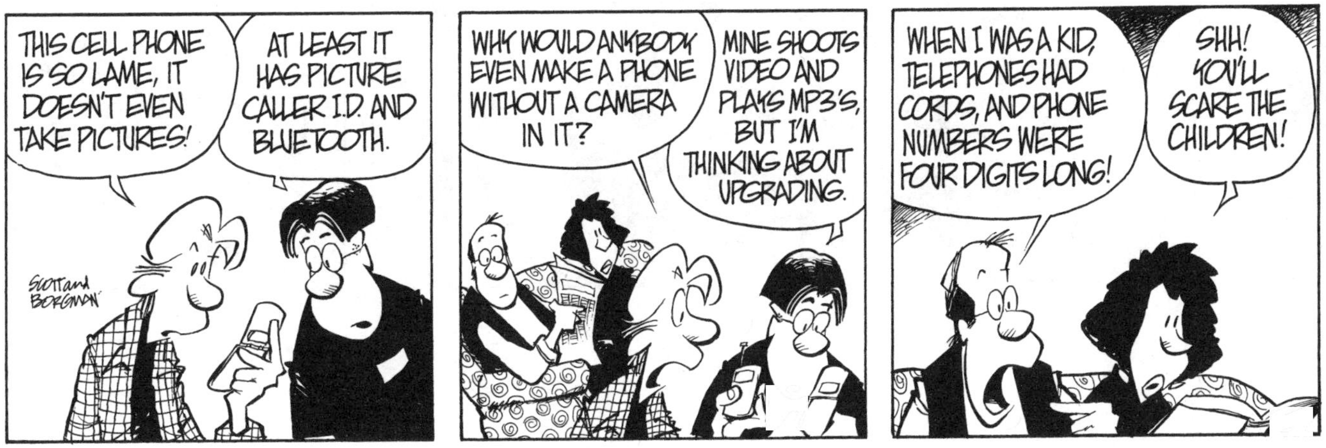
THIS CELL PHONE IS SO LAME, IT DOESN'T EVEN TAKE PICTURES!
AT LEAST IT HAS PICTURE CALLER I.D. AND BLUETOOTH.
WHY WOULD ANYBODY EVEN MAKE A PHONE WITHOUT A CAMERA IN IT?
MINE SHOOTS VIDEO AND PLAYS MP3'S, BUT I'M THINKING ABOUT UPGRADING.
WHEN I WAS A KID, TELEPHONES HAD CORDS, AND PHONE NUMBERS WERE FOUR DIGITS LONG!
SHH! YOU'LL SCARE THE CHILDREN!

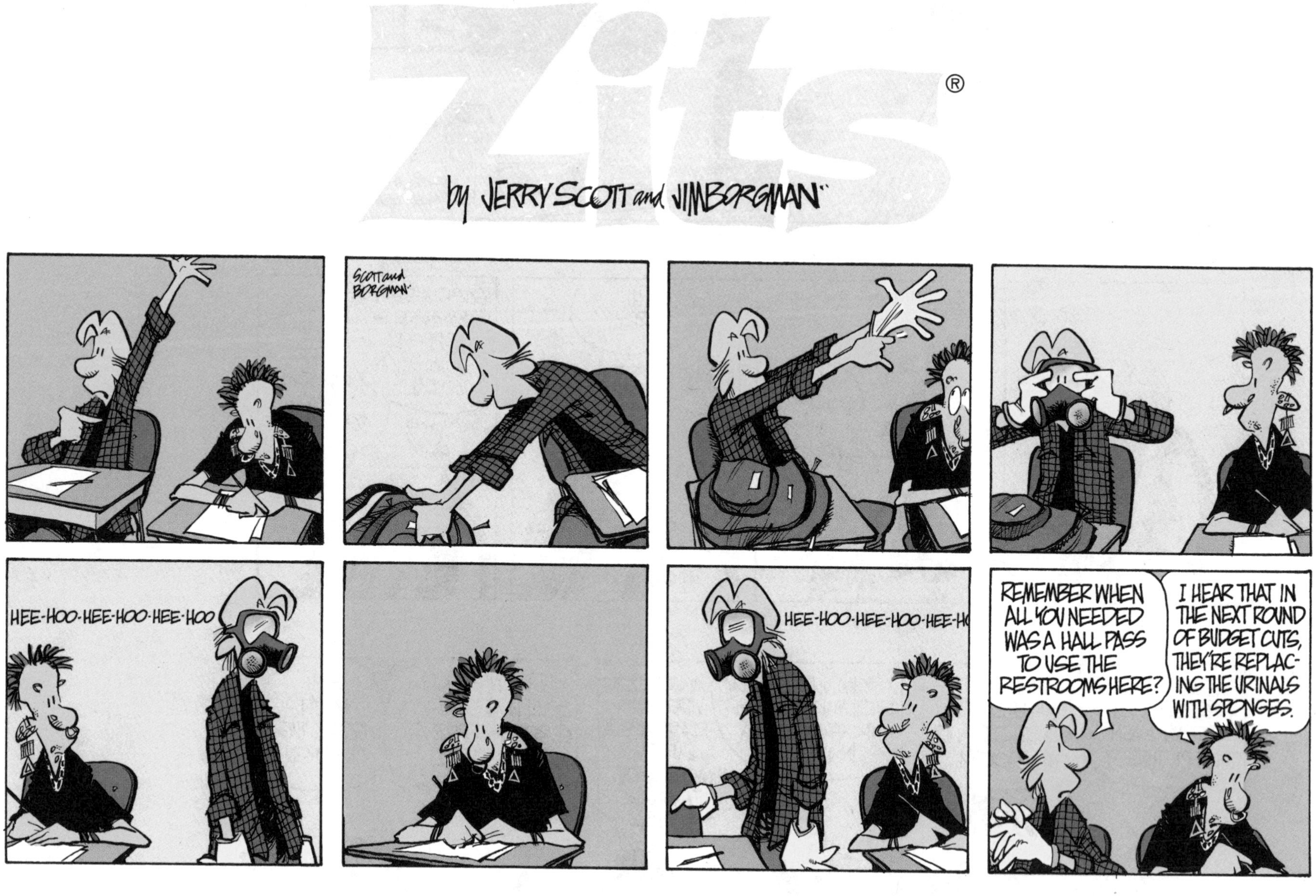
Zits®
by JERRY SCOTT and JIM BORGMAN
SCOTT and BORGMAN
HEE-HOO-HEE-HOO-HEE-HOO
HEE-HOO-HEE-HOO-HEE-HO
REMEMBER WHEN ALL YOU NEEDED WAS A HALL PASS TO USE THE RESTROOMS HERE?
I HEAR THAT IN THE NEXT ROUND OF BUDGET CUTS, THEY'RE REPLACING THE URINALS WITH SPONGES.

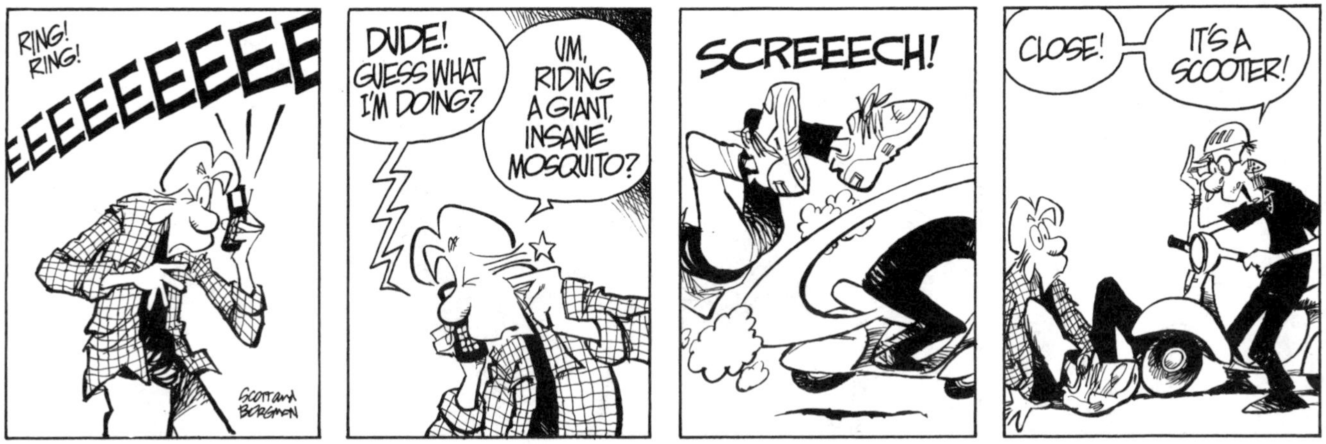
RING! RING!
EEEEEEEEEEEE
DUDE! GUESS WHAT I'M DOING?
UM, RIDING A GIANT, INSANE MOSQUITO?
SCREEECH!
CLOSE!
IT'S A SCOOTER!

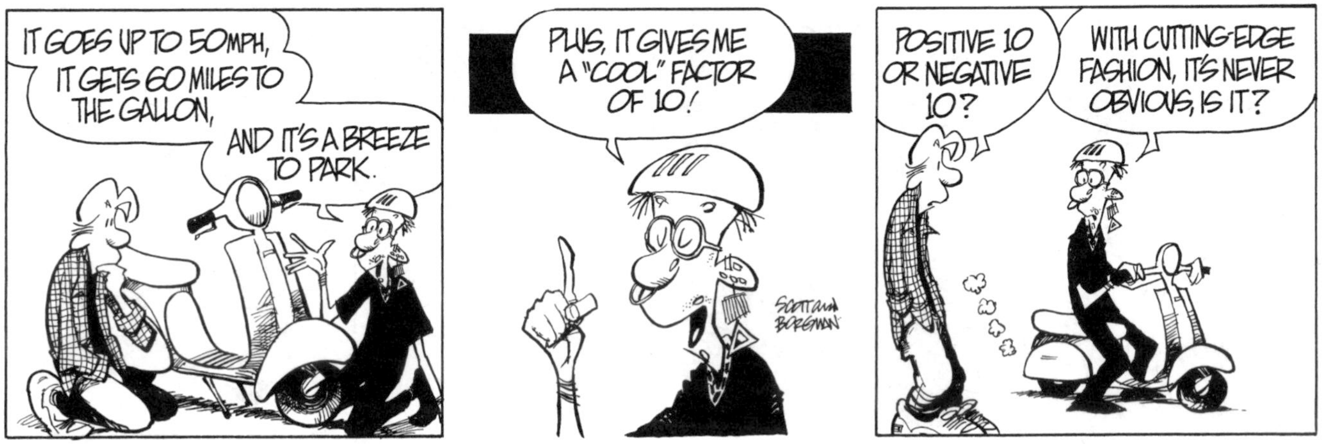
IT GOES UP TO 50MPH, IT GETS 60 MILES TO THE GALLON,
AND IT'S A BREEZE TO PARK.
PLUS, IT GIVES ME A "COOL" FACTOR OF 10!
POSITIVE 10 OR NEGATIVE 10?
WITH CUTTING-EDGE FASHION, IT'S NEVER OBVIOUS, IS IT?

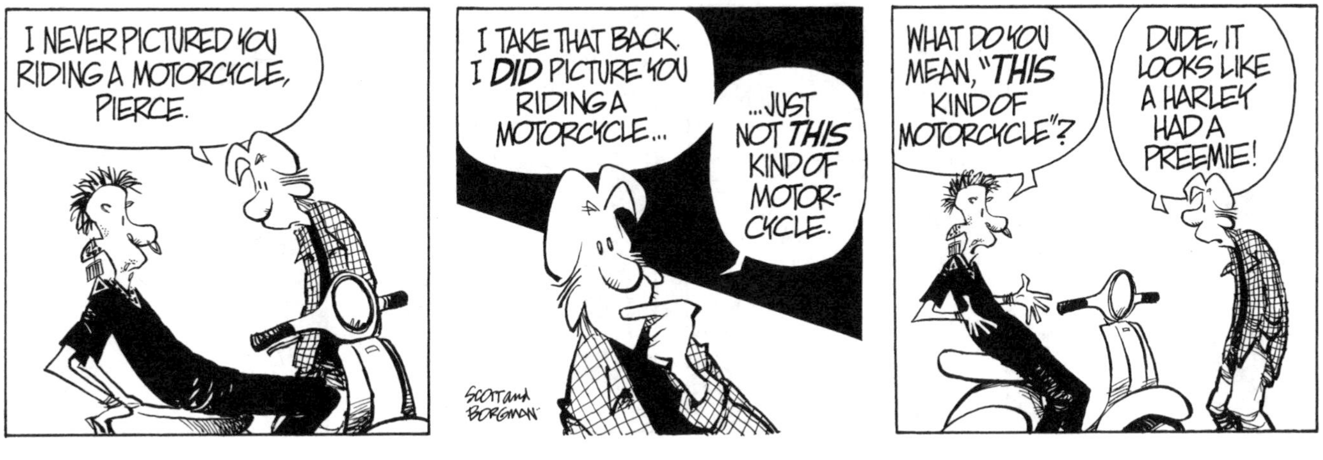
I NEVER PICTURED YOU RIDING A MOTORCYCLE, PIERCE.
I TAKE THAT BACK. I **DID** PICTURE YOU RIDING A MOTORCYCLE...
...JUST NOT **THIS** KIND OF MOTOR-CYCLE.
WHAT DO YOU MEAN, "**THIS** KIND OF MOTORCYCLE"?
DUDE, IT LOOKS LIKE A HARLEY HAD A PREEMIE!

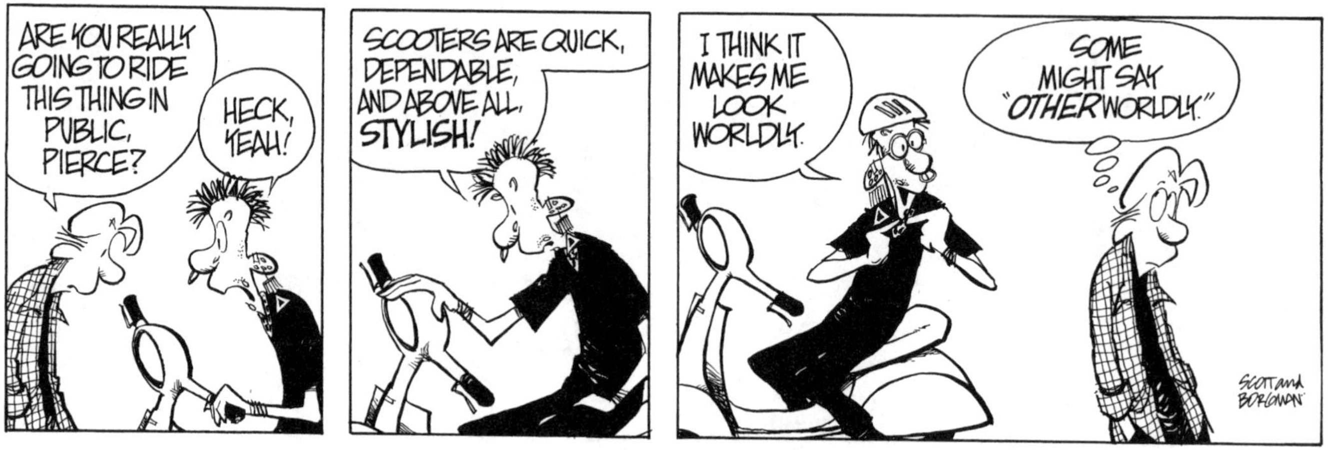
ARE YOU REALLY GOING TO RIDE THIS THING IN PUBLIC, PIERCE?
HECK, YEAH!
SCOOTERS ARE QUICK, DEPENDABLE, AND ABOVE ALL, STYLISH!
I THINK IT MAKES ME LOOK WORLDLY.
SOME MIGHT SAY "OTHER WORLDLY."
SCOTT and BORGMAN

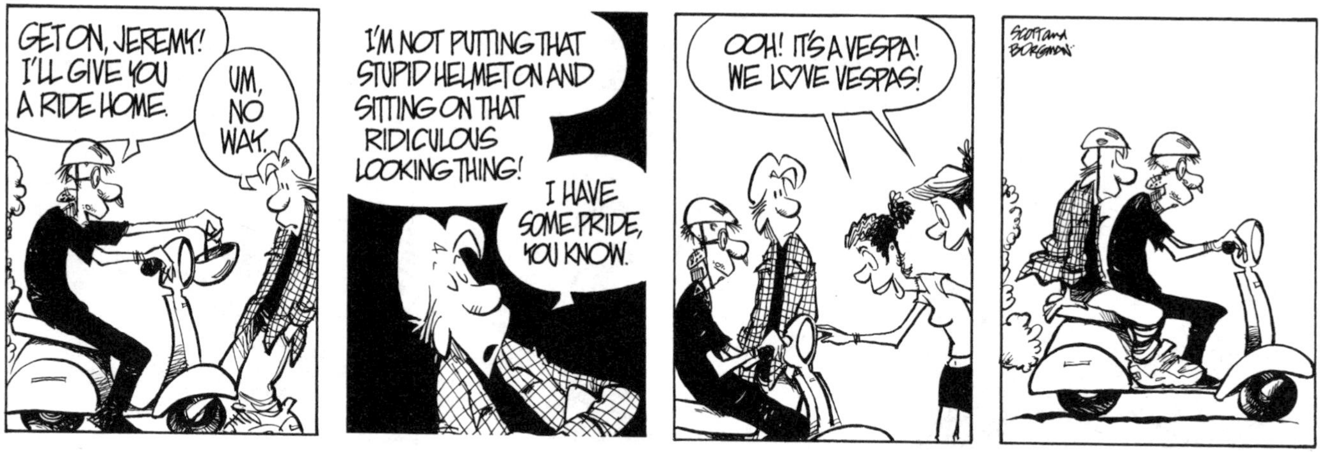
GET ON, JEREMY! I'LL GIVE YOU A RIDE HOME.
UM, NO WAY.
I'M NOT PUTTING THAT STUPID HELMET ON AND SITTING ON THAT RIDICULOUS LOOKING THING!
I HAVE SOME PRIDE, YOU KNOW.
OOH! IT'S A VESPA! WE LOVE VESPAS!
SCOTT and BORGMAN

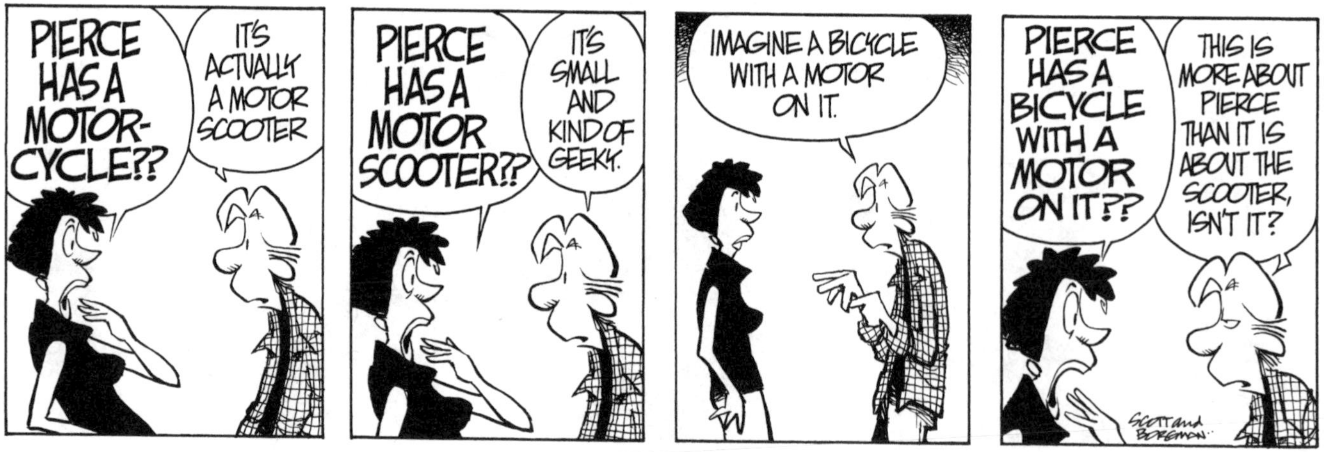
PIERCE HAS A MOTOR-CYCLE??
IT'S ACTUALLY A MOTOR SCOOTER
PIERCE HAS A MOTOR SCOOTER??
IT'S SMALL AND KIND OF GEEKY.
IMAGINE A BICYCLE WITH A MOTOR ON IT.
PIERCE HAS A BICYCLE WITH A MOTOR ON IT??
THIS IS MORE ABOUT PIERCE THAN IT IS ABOUT THE SCOOTER, ISN'T IT?
SCOTT and BORGMAN

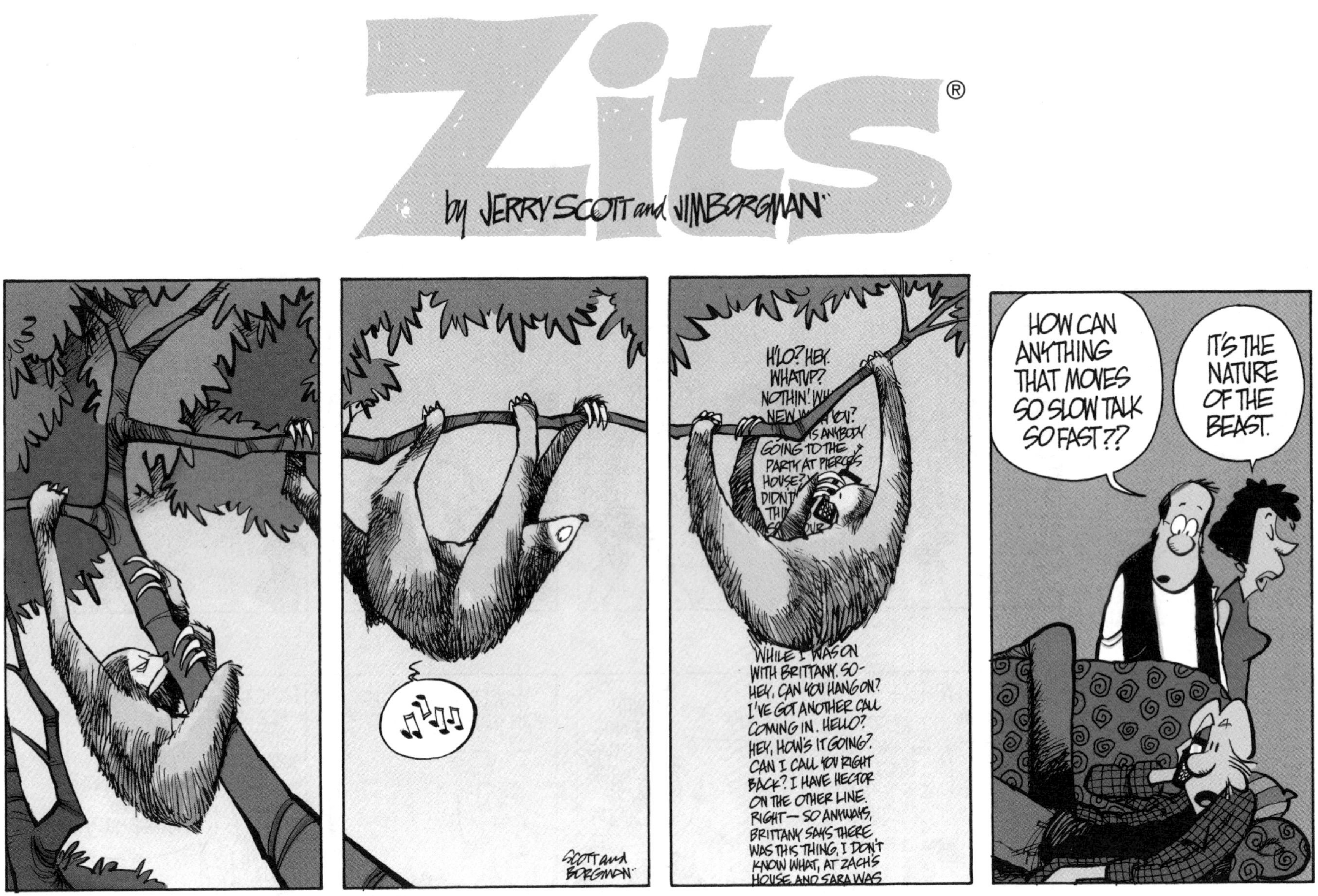
Zits®
by JERRY SCOTT and JIM BORGMAN
H'LO? HEY. WHATUP? NOTHIN'.
IS ANYBODY GOING TO THE PARTY AT
HOUSE?
WHILE I WAS ON WITH BRITTANY. SO- HEY, CAN YOU HANG ON? I'VE GOT ANOTHER CALL COMING IN. HELLO? HEY, HOW'S IT GOING? CAN I CALL YOU RIGHT BACK? I HAVE HECTOR ON THE OTHER LINE. RIGHT— SO ANYWAYS, BRITTANY SAYS THERE WAS THIS THING, I DON'T KNOW WHAT, AT ZACH'S HOUSE AND SARA WAS
SCOTT and BORGMAN
HOW CAN ANYTHING THAT MOVES SO SLOW TALK SO FAST??
IT'S THE NATURE OF THE BEAST.

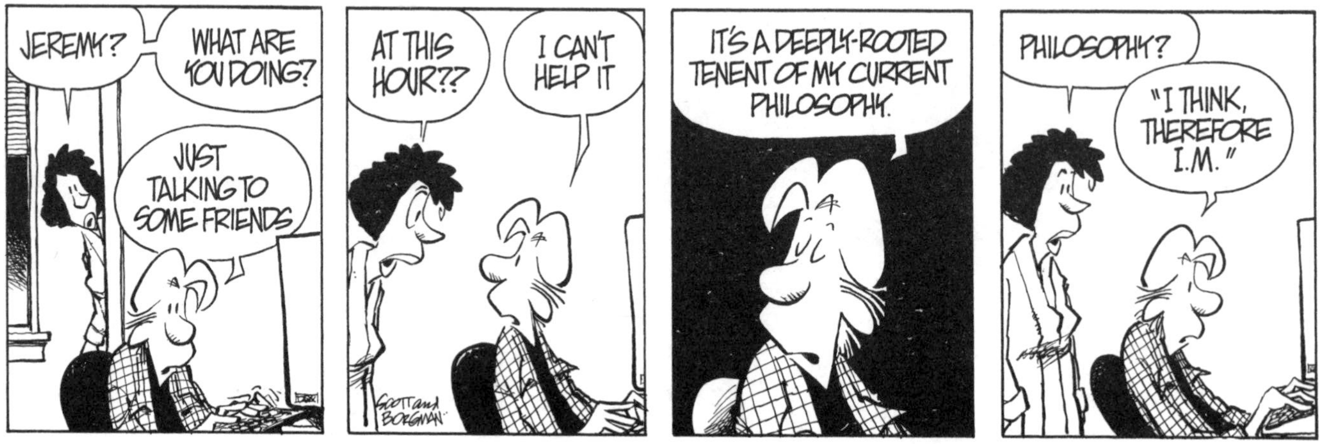
JEREMY?
WHAT ARE YOU DOING?
JUST TALKING TO SOME FRIENDS.
AT THIS HOUR??
I CAN'T HELP IT
SCOTT and BORGMAN
IT'S A DEEPLY-ROOTED TENENT OF MY CURRENT PHILOSOPHY.
PHILOSOPHY?
"I THINK, THEREFORE I.M."

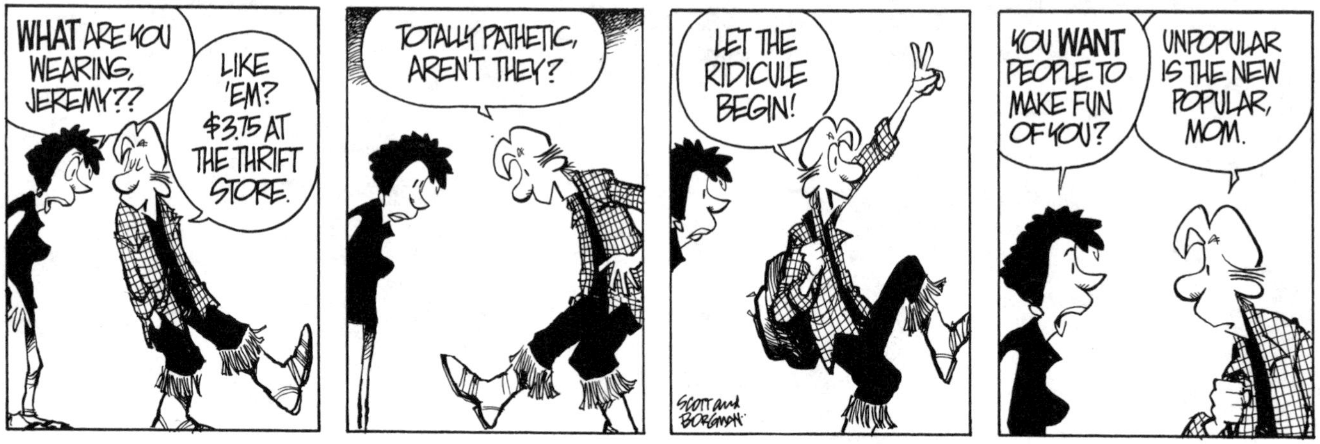
WHAT ARE YOU WEARING, JEREMY??
LIKE 'EM? $3.75 AT THE THRIFT STORE.
TOTALLY PATHETIC, AREN'T THEY?
LET THE RIDICULE BEGIN!
SCOTT and BORGMAN
YOU WANT PEOPLE TO MAKE FUN OF YOU?
UNPOPULAR IS THE NEW POPULAR, MOM.

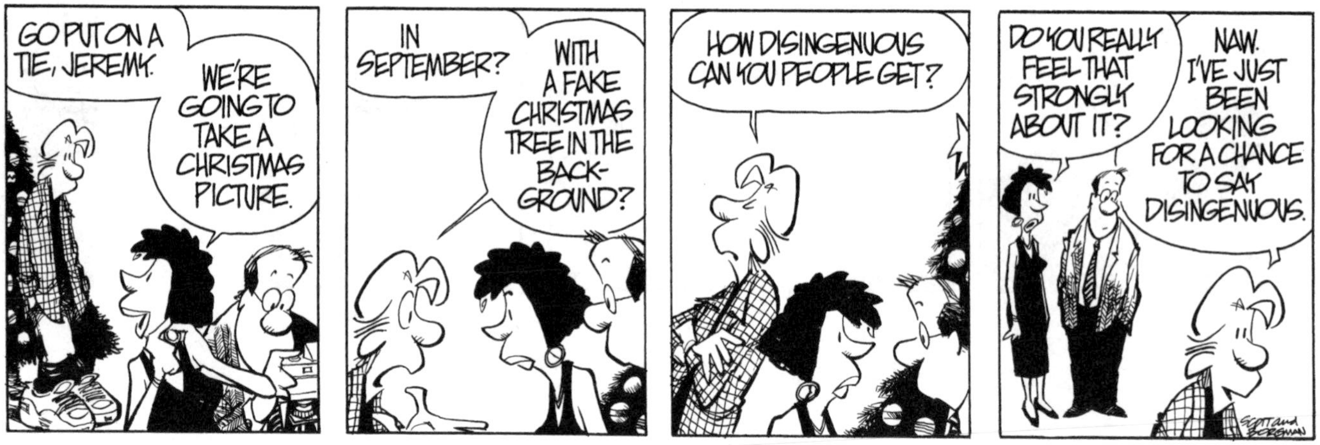
GO PUT ON A TIE, JEREMY.
WE'RE GOING TO TAKE A CHRISTMAS PICTURE.
IN SEPTEMBER?
WITH A FAKE CHRISTMAS TREE IN THE BACK-GROUND?
HOW DISINGENUOUS CAN YOU PEOPLE GET?
DO YOU REALLY FEEL THAT STRONGLY ABOUT IT?
NAW. I'VE JUST BEEN LOOKING FOR A CHANCE TO SAY DISINGENUOUS.
SCOTT and BORGMAN

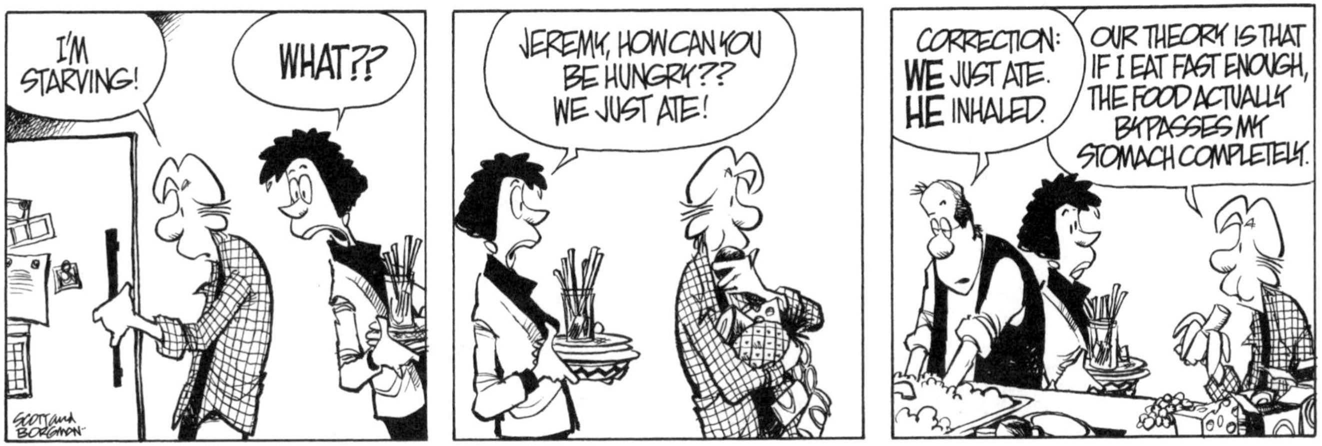
I'M STARVING!
WHAT??
JEREMY, HOW CAN YOU BE HUNGRY?? WE JUST ATE!
CORRECTION: WE JUST ATE. HE INHALED.
OUR THEORY IS THAT IF I EAT FAST ENOUGH, THE FOOD ACTUALLY BYPASSES MY STOMACH COMPLETELY.
SCOTT and BORGMAN

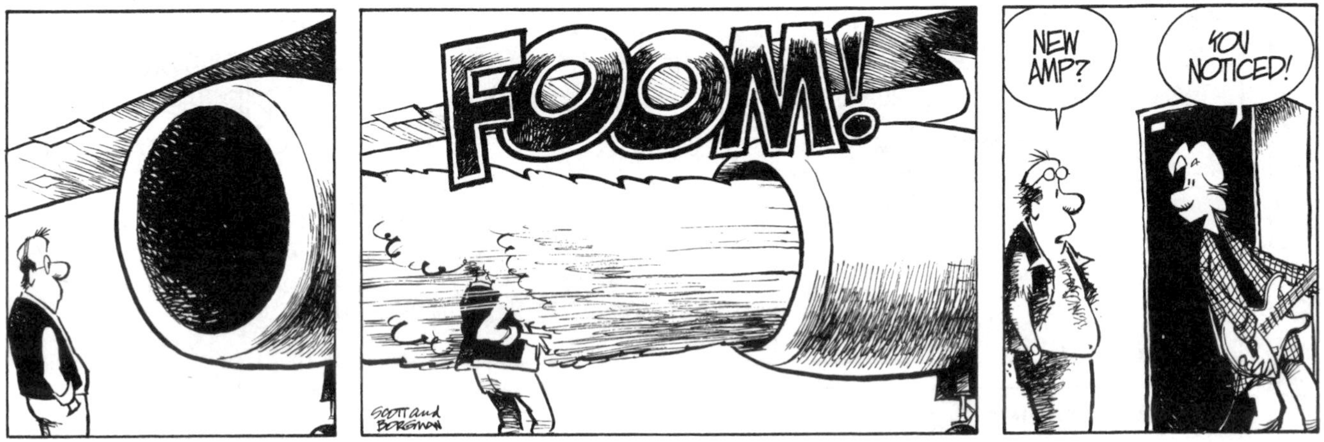
FOOM!
SCOTT and BORGMAN
NEW AMP?
YOU NOTICED!

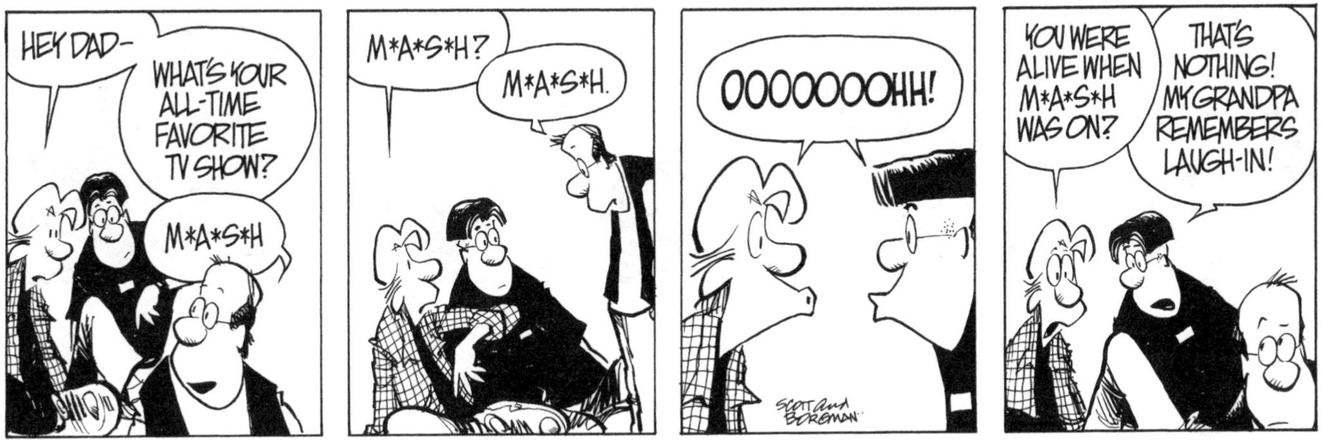
HEY DAD-
WHAT'S YOUR ALL-TIME FAVORITE TV SHOW?
M*A*S*H
M*A*S*H?
M*A*S*H.
OOOOOOOHH!
SCOTT and BORGMAN
YOU WERE ALIVE WHEN M*A*S*H WAS ON?
THAT'S NOTHING! MY GRANDPA REMEMBERS LAUGH-IN!

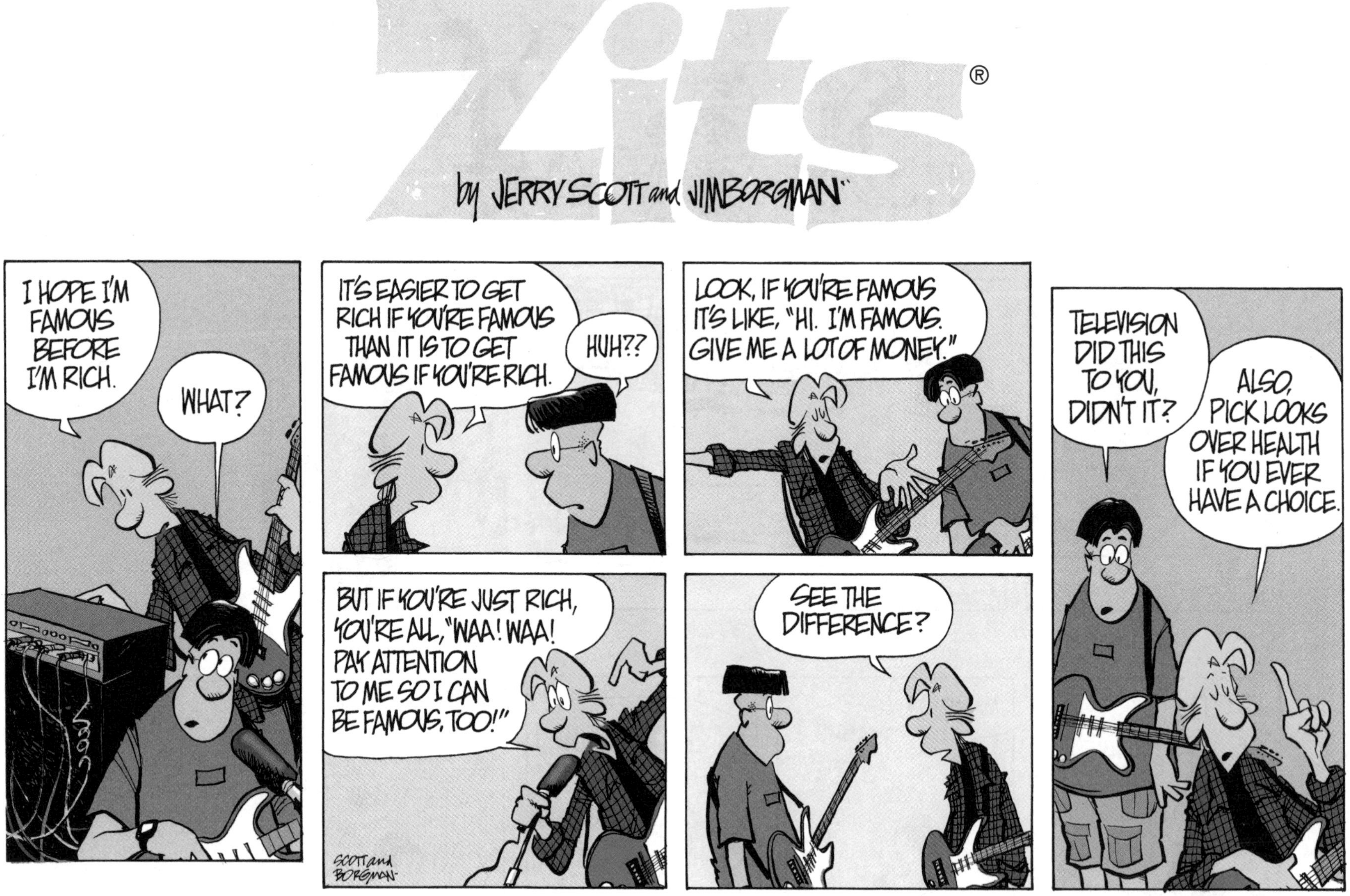
Zits®
by JERRY SCOTT and JIM BORGMAN
I HOPE I'M FAMOUS BEFORE I'M RICH.
WHAT?
IT'S EASIER TO GET RICH IF YOU'RE FAMOUS THAN IT IS TO GET FAMOUS IF YOU'RE RICH.
HUH??
LOOK, IF YOU'RE FAMOUS IT'S LIKE, "HI. I'M FAMOUS. GIVE ME A LOT OF MONEY."
BUT IF YOU'RE JUST RICH, YOU'RE ALL, "WAA! WAA! PAY ATTENTION TO ME SO I CAN BE FAMOUS, TOO!"
SCOTT and BORGMAN
SEE THE DIFFERENCE?
TELEVISION DID THIS TO YOU, DIDN'T IT?
ALSO, PICK LOOKS OVER HEALTH IF YOU EVER HAVE A CHOICE.

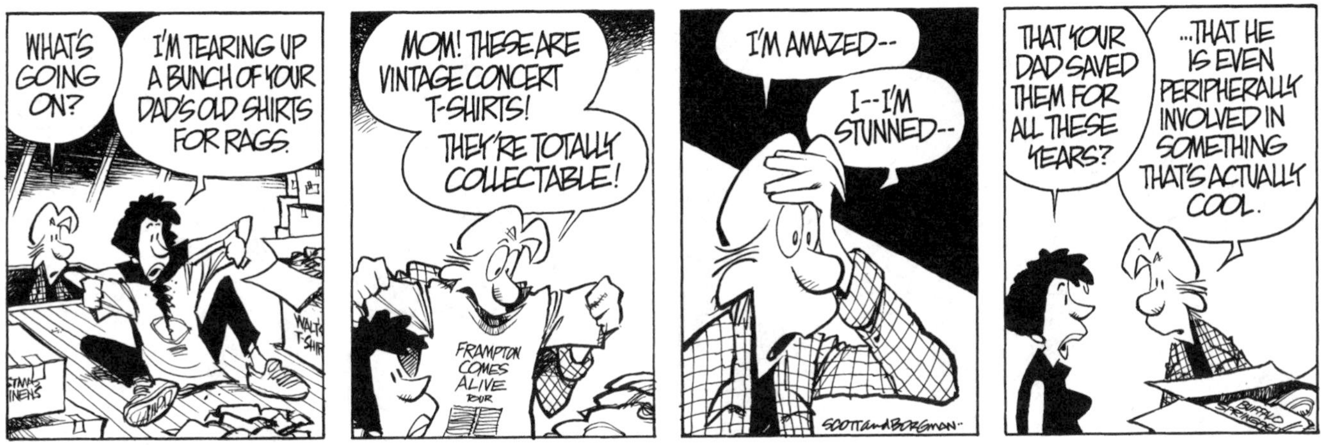
WHAT'S GOING ON?
I'M TEARING UP A BUNCH OF YOUR DAD'S OLD SHIRTS FOR RAGS.
MOM! THESE ARE VINTAGE CONCERT T-SHIRTS!
THEY'RE TOTALLY COLLECTABLE!
FRAMPTON COMES ALIVE TOUR
I'M AMAZED--
I--I'M STUNNED--
THAT YOUR DAD SAVED THEM FOR ALL THESE YEARS?
...THAT HE IS EVEN PERIPHERALLY INVOLVED IN SOMETHING THAT'S ACTUALLY COOL.

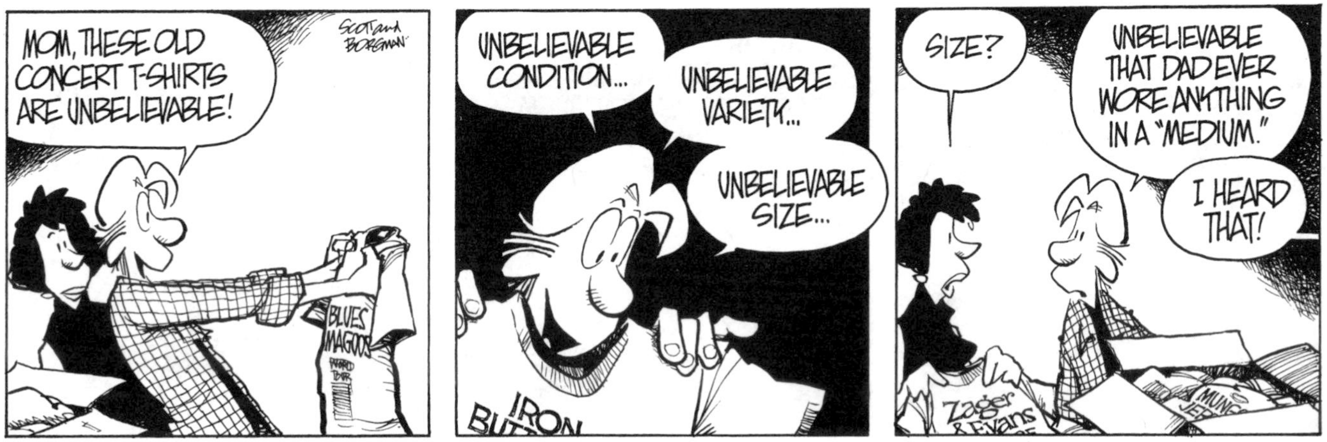
MOM, THESE OLD CONCERT T-SHIRTS ARE UNBELIEVABLE!
BLUES MAGOOS
UNBELIEVABLE CONDITION...
UNBELIEVABLE VARIETY...
UNBELIEVABLE SIZE...
SIZE?
UNBELIEVABLE THAT DAD EVER WORE ANYTHING IN A "MEDIUM."
I HEARD THAT!
Zager & Evans

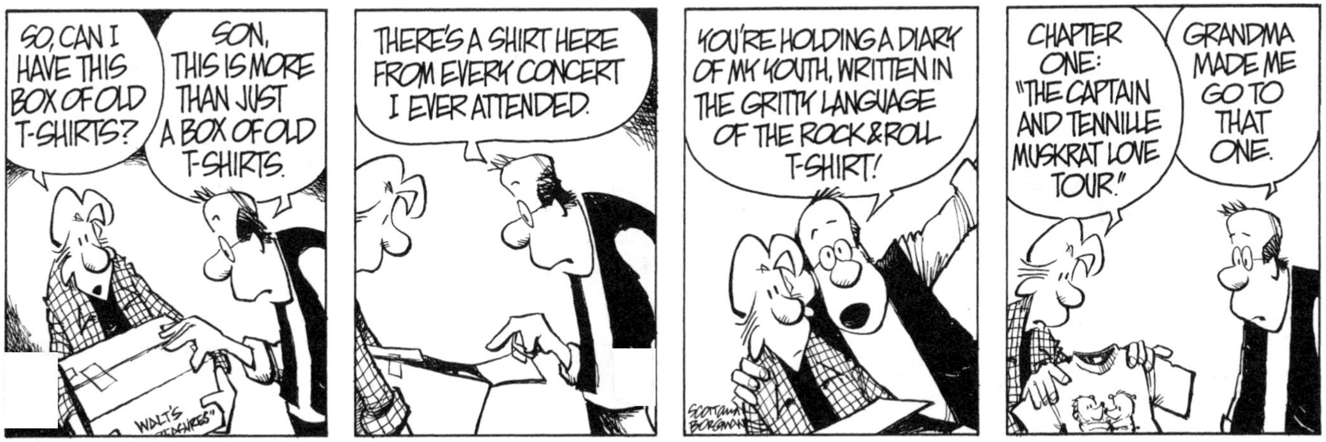
SO, CAN I HAVE THIS BOX OF OLD T-SHIRTS?
SON, THIS IS MORE THAN JUST A BOX OF OLD T-SHIRTS.
THERE'S A SHIRT HERE FROM EVERY CONCERT I EVER ATTENDED.
YOU'RE HOLDING A DIARY OF MY YOUTH, WRITTEN IN THE GRITTY LANGUAGE OF THE ROCK & ROLL T-SHIRT!
CHAPTER ONE: "THE CAPTAIN AND TENNILLE MUSKRAT LOVE TOUR."
GRANDMA MADE ME GO TO THAT ONE.

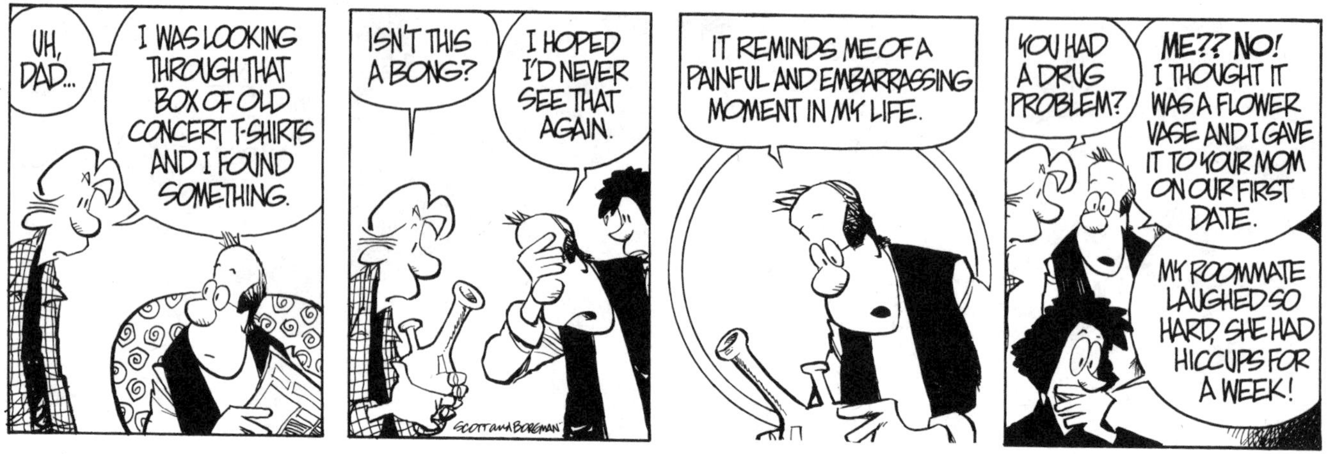
UH, DAD...
I WAS LOOKING THROUGH THAT BOX OF OLD CONCERT T-SHIRTS AND I FOUND SOMETHING.
ISN'T THIS A BONG?
I HOPED I'D NEVER SEE THAT AGAIN.
IT REMINDS ME OF A PAINFUL AND EMBARRASSING MOMENT IN MY LIFE.
YOU HAD A DRUG PROBLEM?
ME?? NO! I THOUGHT IT WAS A FLOWER VASE AND I GAVE IT TO YOUR MOM ON OUR FIRST DATE.
MY ROOMMATE LAUGHED SO HARD, SHE HAD HICCUPS FOR A WEEK!

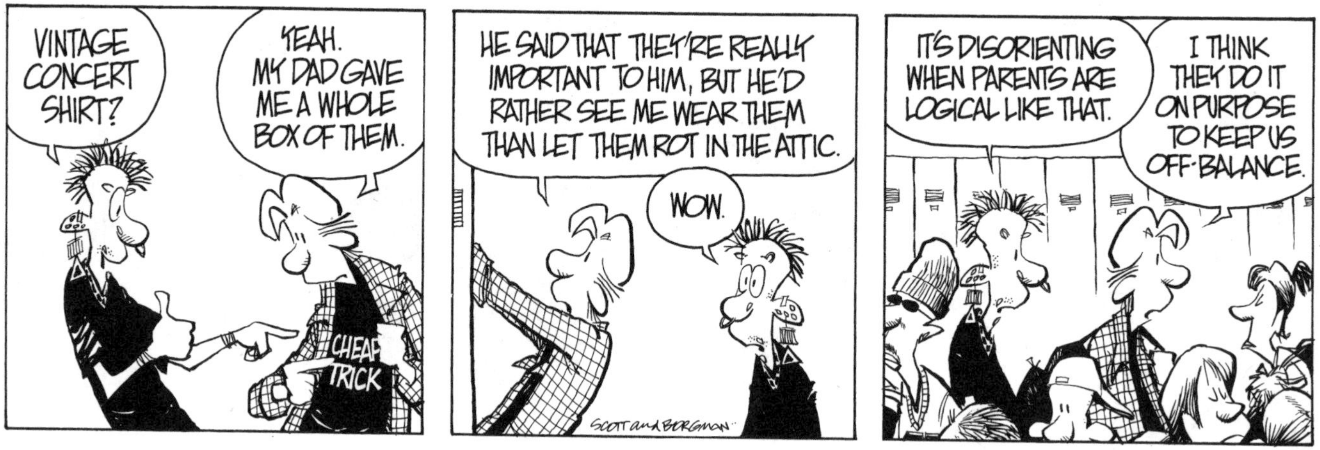
VINTAGE CONCERT SHIRT?
YEAH. MY DAD GAVE ME A WHOLE BOX OF THEM.
CHEAP TRICK
HE SAID THAT THEY'RE REALLY IMPORTANT TO HIM, BUT HE'D RATHER SEE ME WEAR THEM THAN LET THEM ROT IN THE ATTIC.
WOW.
IT'S DISORIENTING WHEN PARENTS ARE LOGICAL LIKE THAT.
I THINK THEY DO IT ON PURPOSE TO KEEP US OFF-BALANCE.

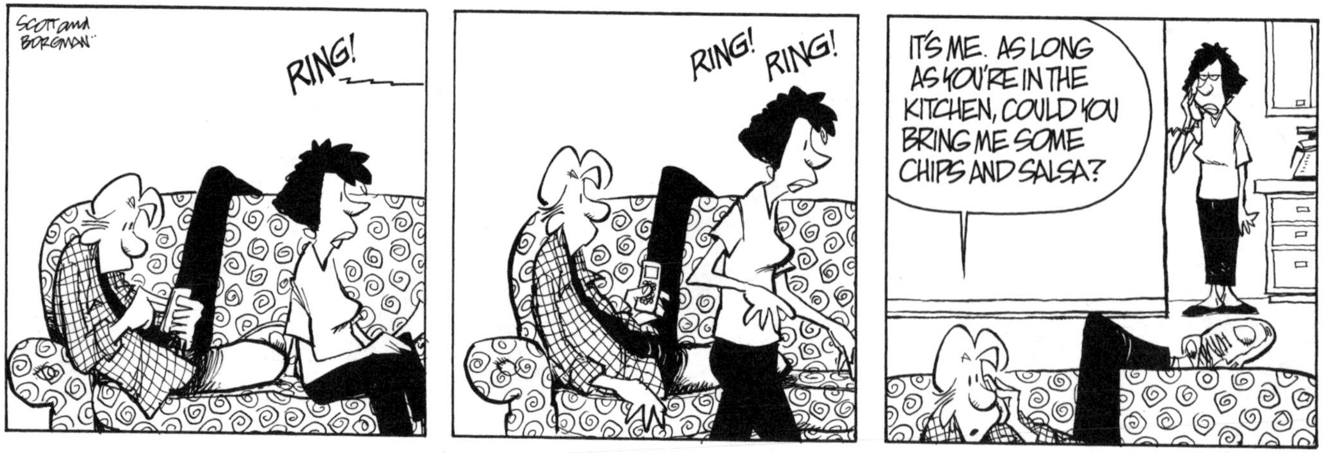
RING!
RING! RING!
IT'S ME. AS LONG AS YOU'RE IN THE KITCHEN, COULD YOU BRING ME SOME CHIPS AND SALSA?

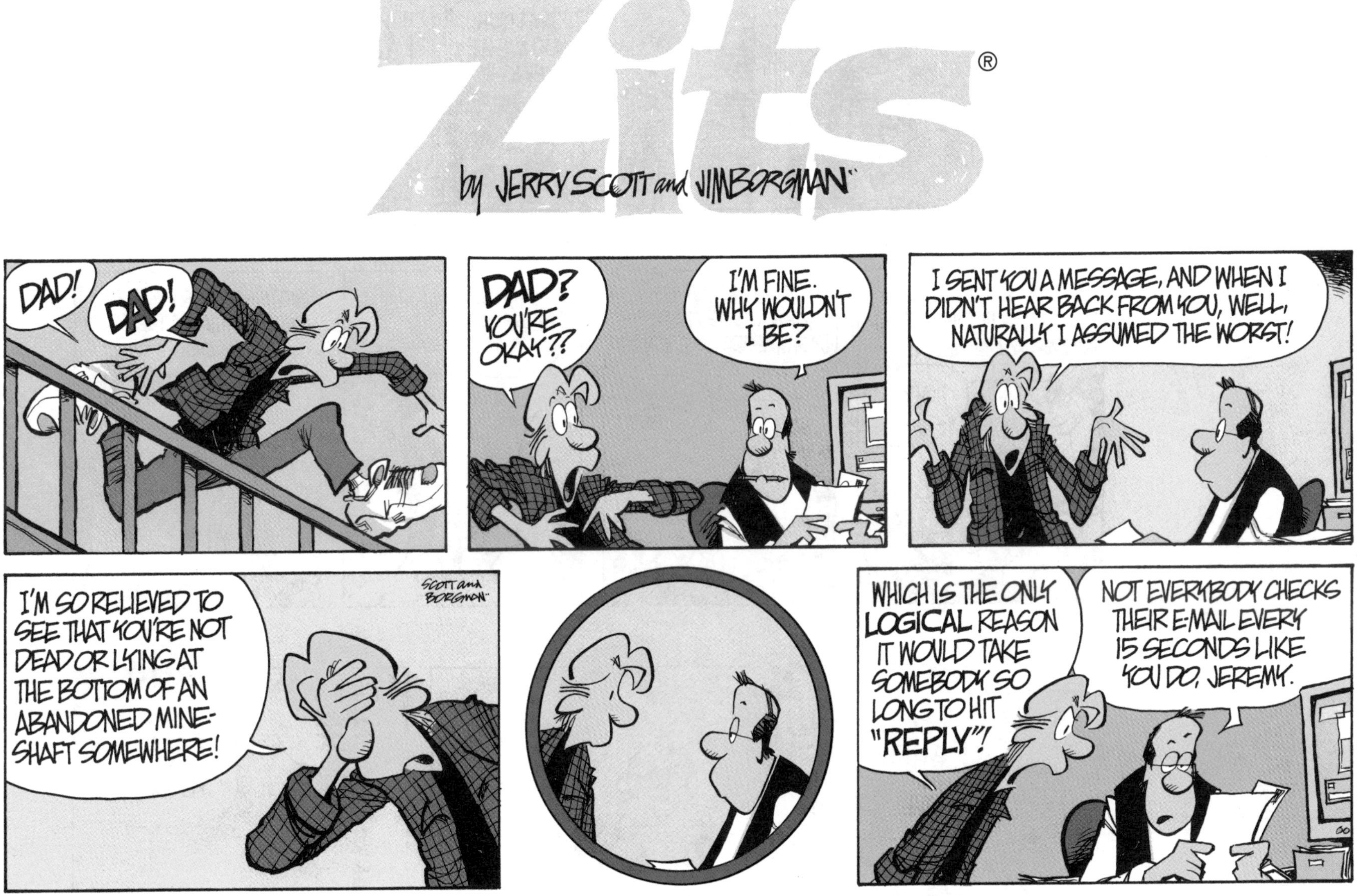
Zits®
by JERRY SCOTT and JIM BORGMAN
DAD!
DAD!
DAD? YOU'RE OKAY??
I'M FINE. WHY WOULDN'T I BE?
I SENT YOU A MESSAGE, AND WHEN I DIDN'T HEAR BACK FROM YOU, WELL, NATURALLY I ASSUMED THE WORST!
I'M SO RELIEVED TO SEE THAT YOU'RE NOT DEAD OR LYING AT THE BOTTOM OF AN ABANDONED MINE-SHAFT SOMEWHERE!
SCOTT and BORGMAN
WHICH IS THE ONLY LOGICAL REASON IT WOULD TAKE SOMEBODY SO LONG TO HIT "REPLY"!
NOT EVERYBODY CHECKS THEIR E-MAIL EVERY 15 SECONDS LIKE YOU DO, JEREMY.

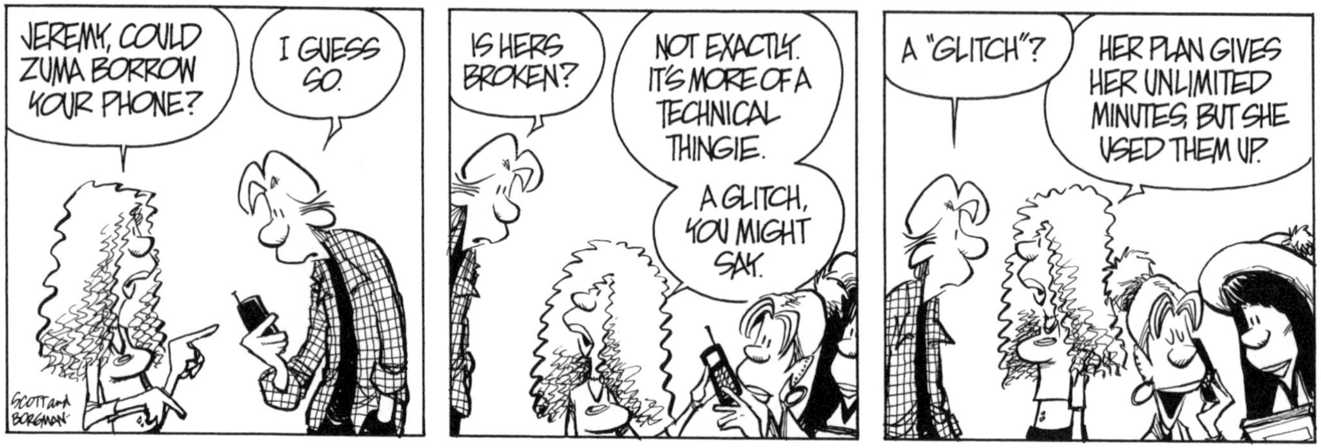
JEREMY, COULD ZUMA BORROW YOUR PHONE?
I GUESS SO.
IS HERS BROKEN?
NOT EXACTLY. IT'S MORE OF A TECHNICAL THINGIE.
A GLITCH, YOU MIGHT SAY.
A "GLITCH"?
HER PLAN GIVES HER UNLIMITED MINUTES, BUT SHE USED THEM UP.

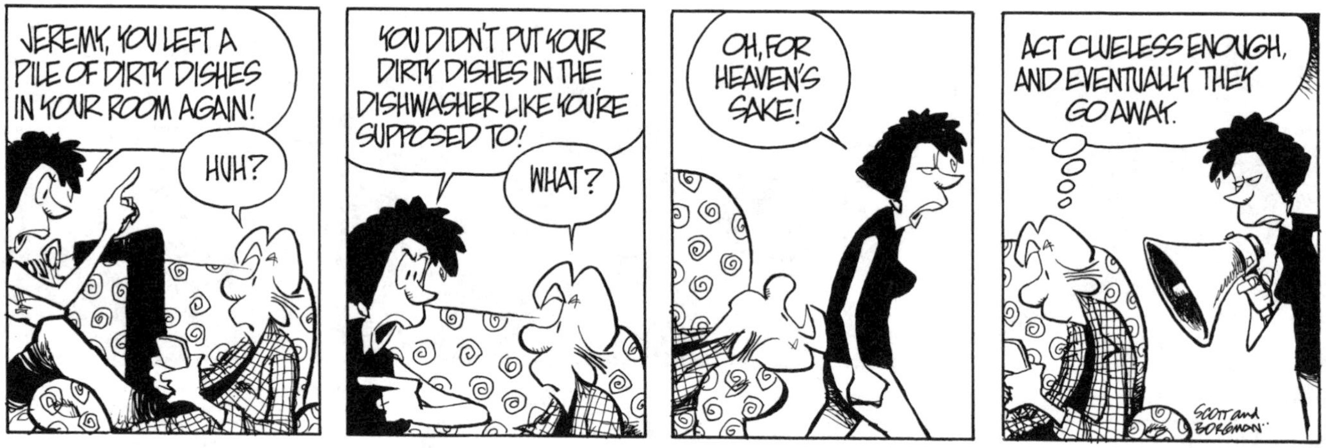
JEREMY, YOU LEFT A PILE OF DIRTY DISHES IN YOUR ROOM AGAIN!
HUH?
YOU DIDN'T PUT YOUR DIRTY DISHES IN THE DISHWASHER LIKE YOU'RE SUPPOSED TO!
WHAT?
OH, FOR HEAVEN'S SAKE!
ACT CLUELESS ENOUGH, AND EVENTUALLY THEY GO AWAY.

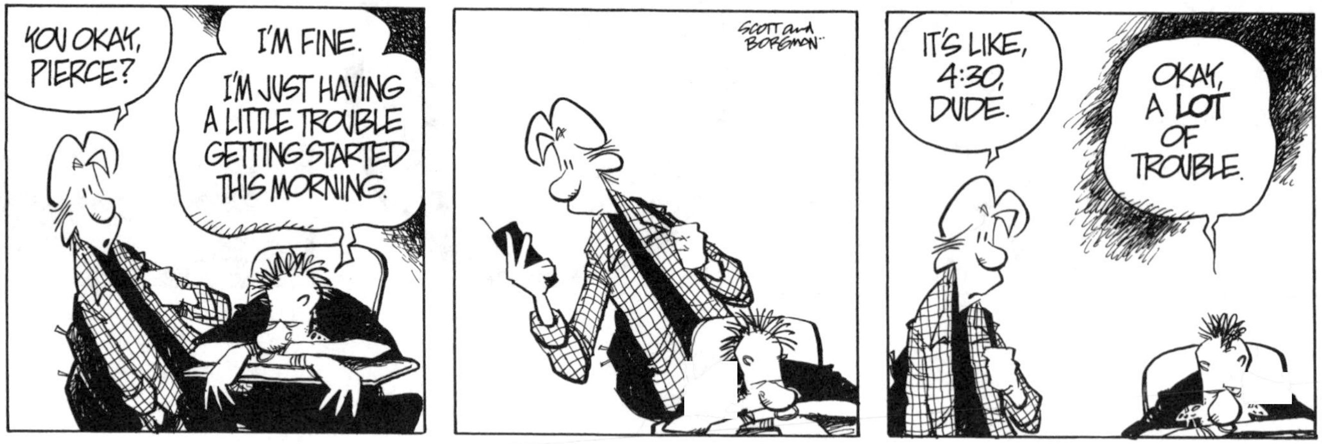
YOU OKAY, PIERCE?
I'M FINE.
I'M JUST HAVING A LITTLE TROUBLE GETTING STARTED THIS MORNING.
IT'S LIKE, 4:30, DUDE.
OKAY, A **LOT** OF TROUBLE.

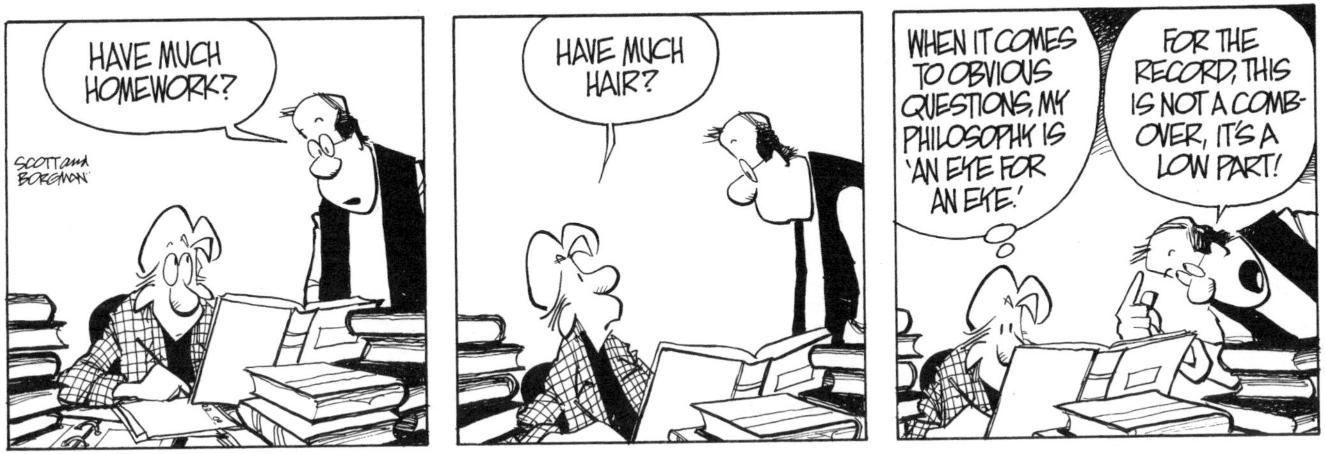
SCOTT and BORGMAN
HAVE MUCH HOMEWORK?
HAVE MUCH HAIR?
WHEN IT COMES TO OBVIOUS QUESTIONS, MY PHILOSOPHY IS 'AN EYE FOR AN EYE.'
FOR THE RECORD, THIS IS NOT A COMB-OVER, IT'S A LOW PART!

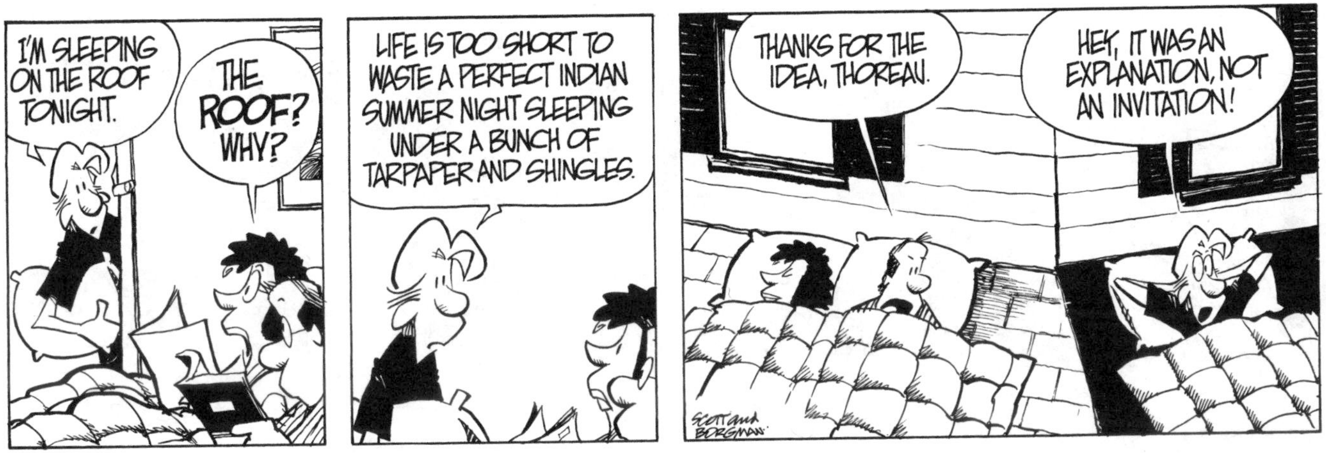
I'M SLEEPING ON THE ROOF TONIGHT.
THE ROOF? WHY?
LIFE IS TOO SHORT TO WASTE A PERFECT INDIAN SUMMER NIGHT SLEEPING UNDER A BUNCH OF TARPAPER AND SHINGLES.
THANKS FOR THE IDEA, THOREAU.
HEY, IT WAS AN EXPLANATION, NOT AN INVITATION!
SCOTT and BORGMAN

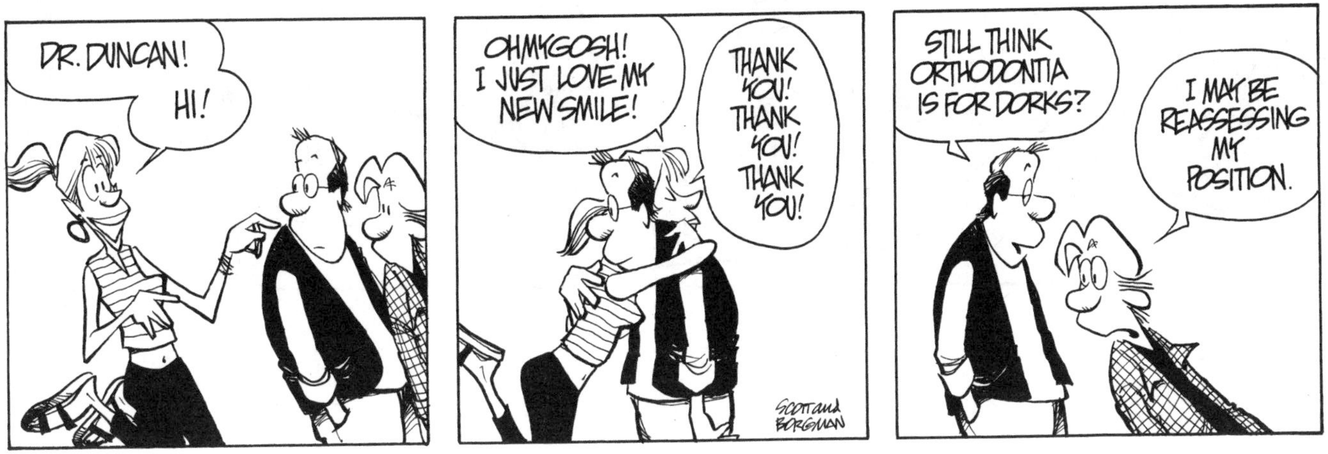
DR. DUNCAN!
HI!
OHMYGOSH! I JUST LOVE MY NEW SMILE!
THANK YOU! THANK YOU! THANK YOU!
SCOTT and BORGMAN
STILL THINK ORTHODONTIA IS FOR DORKS?
I MAY BE REASSESSING MY POSITION.

Zits®

by JERRY SCOTT and JIM BORGMAN

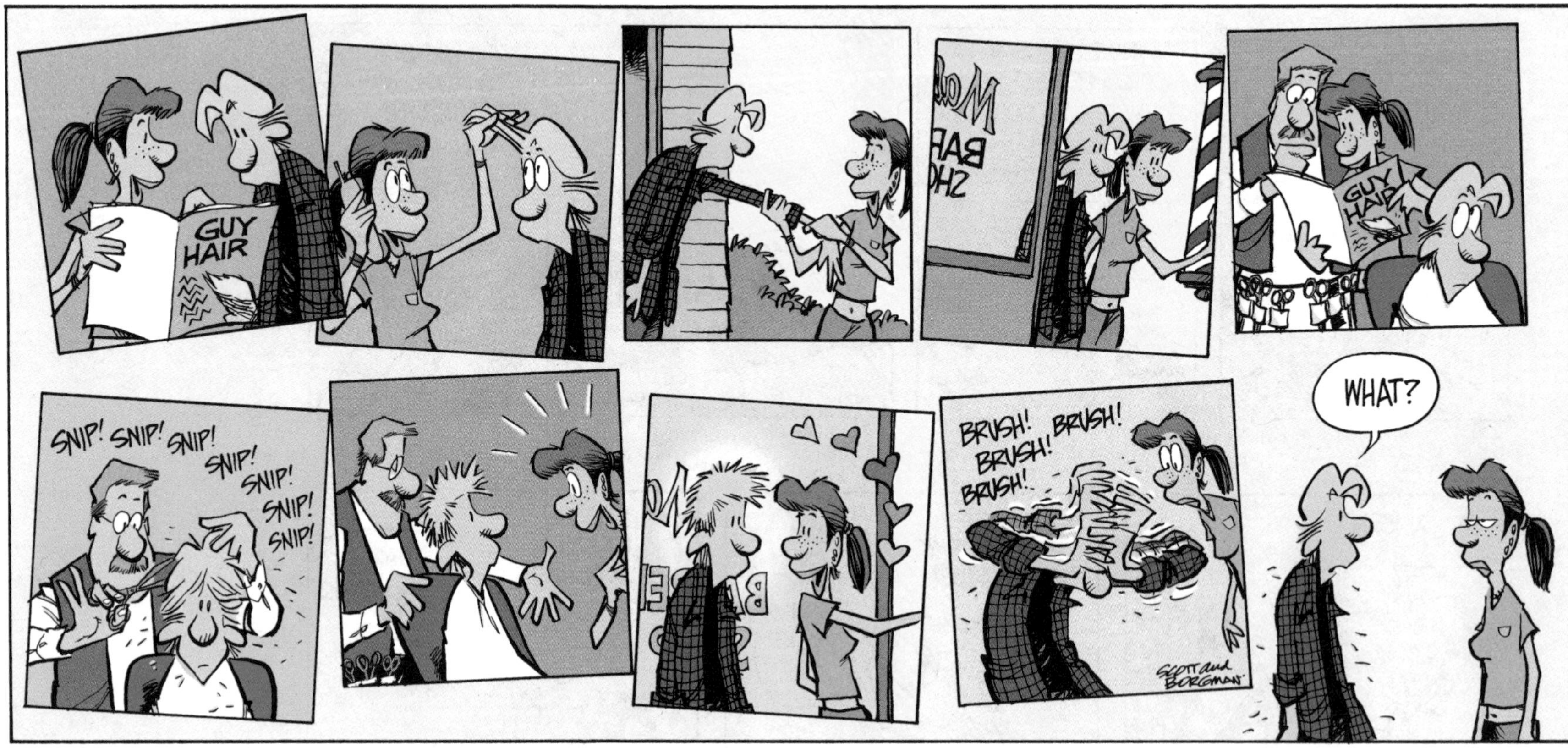
GUY HAIR
GUY HAIR
SNIP! SNIP! SNIP!
SNIP!
SNIP!
SNIP!
SNIP!
BRUSH! BRUSH!
BRUSH!
BRUSH!
SCOTT and BORGMAN
WHAT?

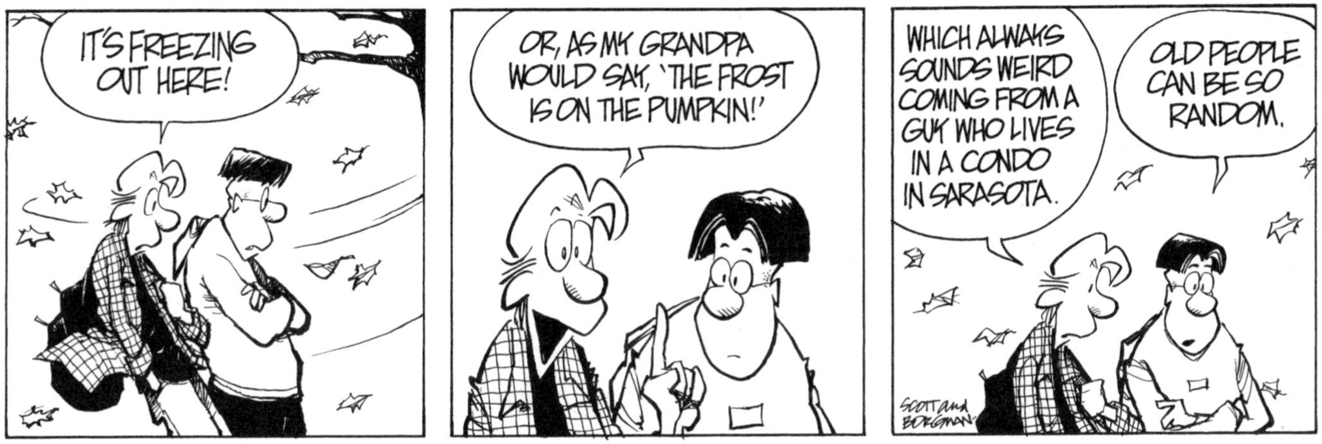
IT'S FREEZING OUT HERE!
OR, AS MY GRANDPA WOULD SAY, 'THE FROST IS ON THE PUMPKIN!'
WHICH ALWAYS SOUNDS WEIRD COMING FROM A GUY WHO LIVES IN A CONDO IN SARASOTA.
OLD PEOPLE CAN BE SO RANDOM.
SCOTT AND BORGMAN

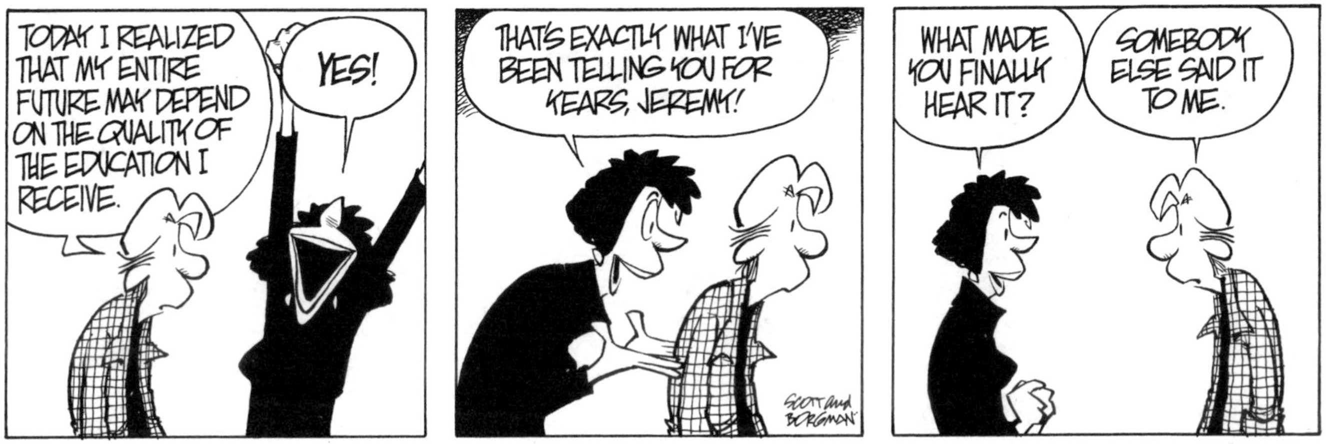
TODAY I REALIZED THAT MY ENTIRE FUTURE MAY DEPEND ON THE QUALITY OF THE EDUCATION I RECEIVE.
YES!
THAT'S EXACTLY WHAT I'VE BEEN TELLING YOU FOR YEARS, JEREMY!
SCOTT AND BORGMAN
WHAT MADE YOU FINALLY HEAR IT?
SOMEBODY ELSE SAID IT TO ME.

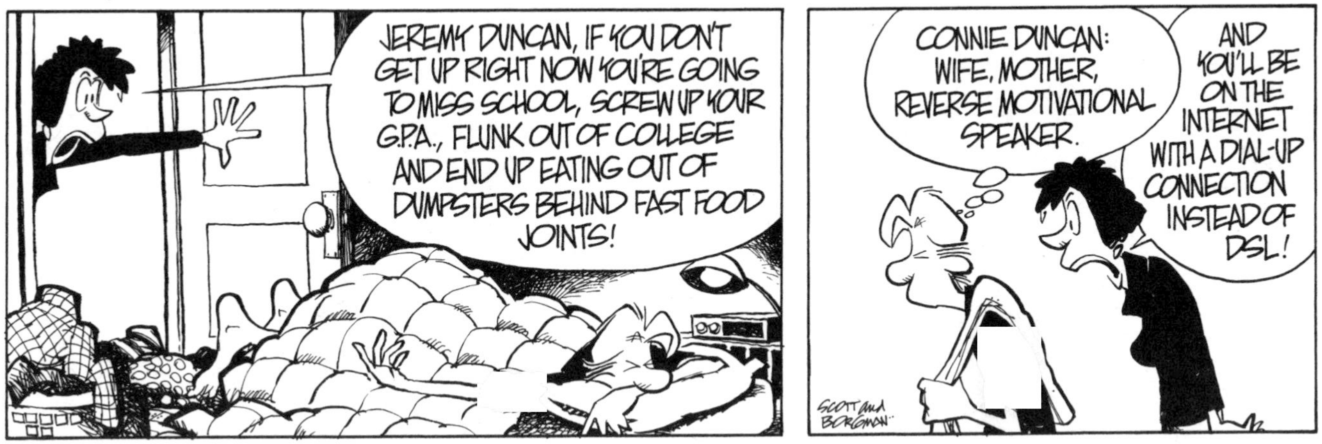
JEREMY DUNCAN, IF YOU DON'T GET UP RIGHT NOW YOU'RE GOING TO MISS SCHOOL, SCREW UP YOUR G.P.A., FLUNK OUT OF COLLEGE AND END UP EATING OUT OF DUMPSTERS BEHIND FAST FOOD JOINTS!
CONNIE DUNCAN: WIFE, MOTHER, REVERSE MOTIVATIONAL SPEAKER.
AND YOU'LL BE ON THE INTERNET WITH A DIAL-UP CONNECTION INSTEAD OF DSL!
SCOTT AND BORGMAN

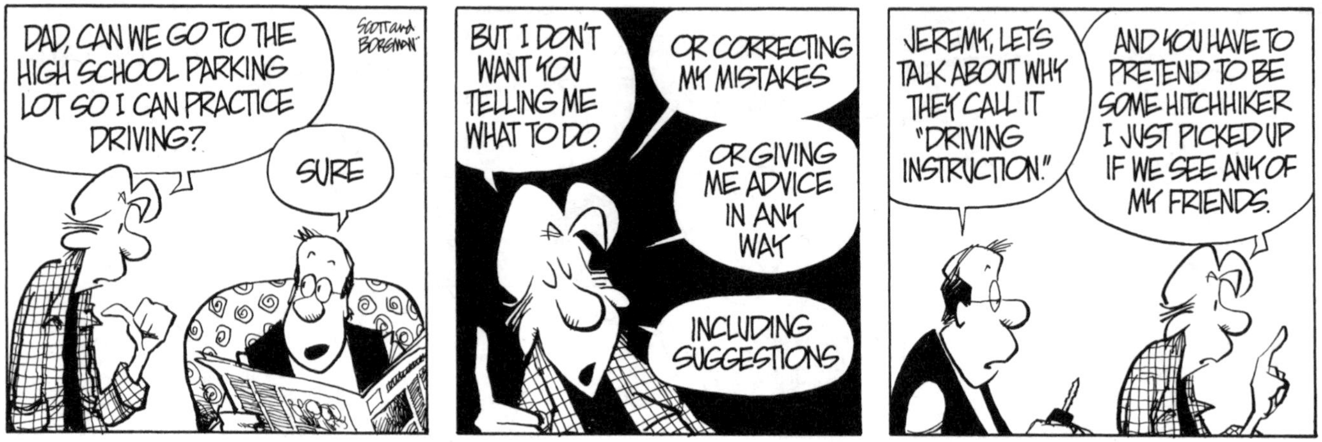
DAD, CAN WE GO TO THE HIGH SCHOOL PARKING LOT SO I CAN PRACTICE DRIVING?
SURE
BUT I DON'T WANT YOU TELLING ME WHAT TO DO.
OR CORRECTING MY MISTAKES
OR GIVING ME ADVICE IN ANY WAY
INCLUDING SUGGESTIONS
JEREMY, LET'S TALK ABOUT WHY THEY CALL IT "DRIVING INSTRUCTION."
AND YOU HAVE TO PRETEND TO BE SOME HITCHHIKER I JUST PICKED UP IF WE SEE ANY OF MY FRIENDS.

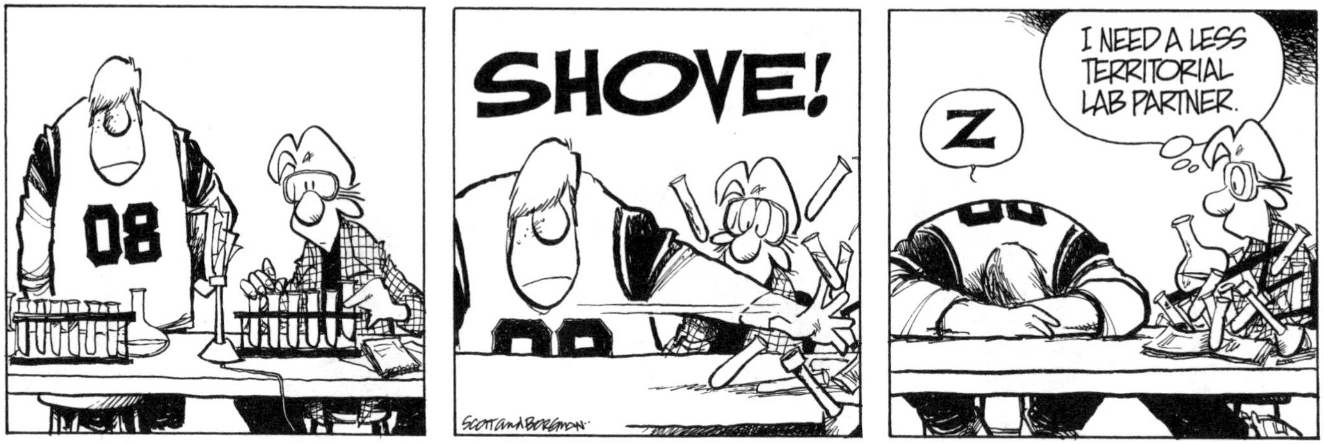
08
SHOVE!
Z
I NEED A LESS TERRITORIAL LAB PARTNER.

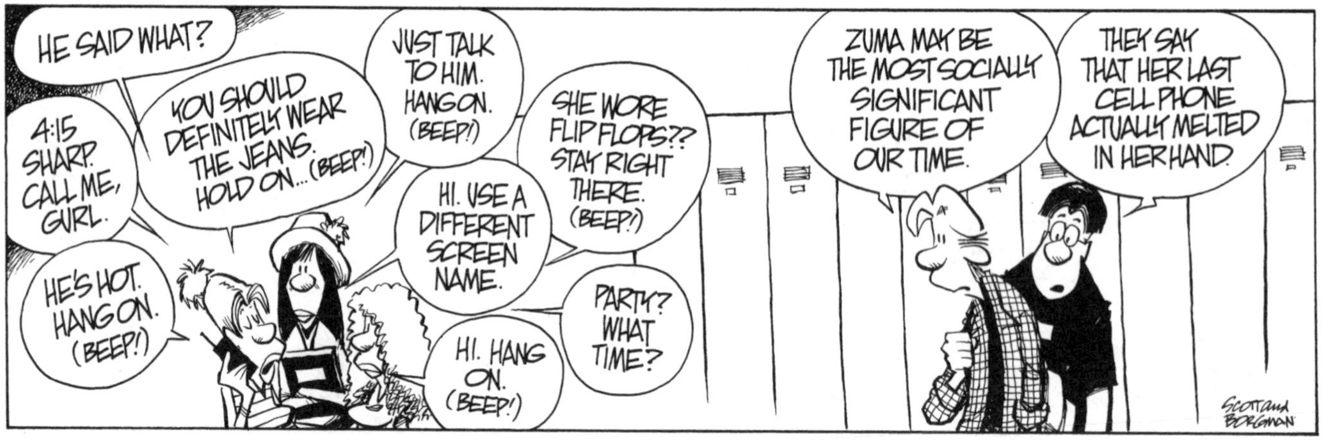
HE SAID WHAT?
4:15 SHARP. CALL ME, GURL.
YOU SHOULD DEFINITELY WEAR THE JEANS. HOLD ON... (BEEP!)
JUST TALK TO HIM. HANG ON. (BEEP!)
HE'S HOT. HANG ON. (BEEP!)
HI. USE A DIFFERENT SCREEN NAME.
SHE WORE FLIP FLOPS?? STAY RIGHT THERE. (BEEP!)
HI. HANG ON. (BEEP!)
PARTY? WHAT TIME?
ZUMA MAY BE THE MOST SOCIALLY SIGNIFICANT FIGURE OF OUR TIME.
THEY SAY THAT HER LAST CELL PHONE ACTUALLY MELTED IN HER HAND.

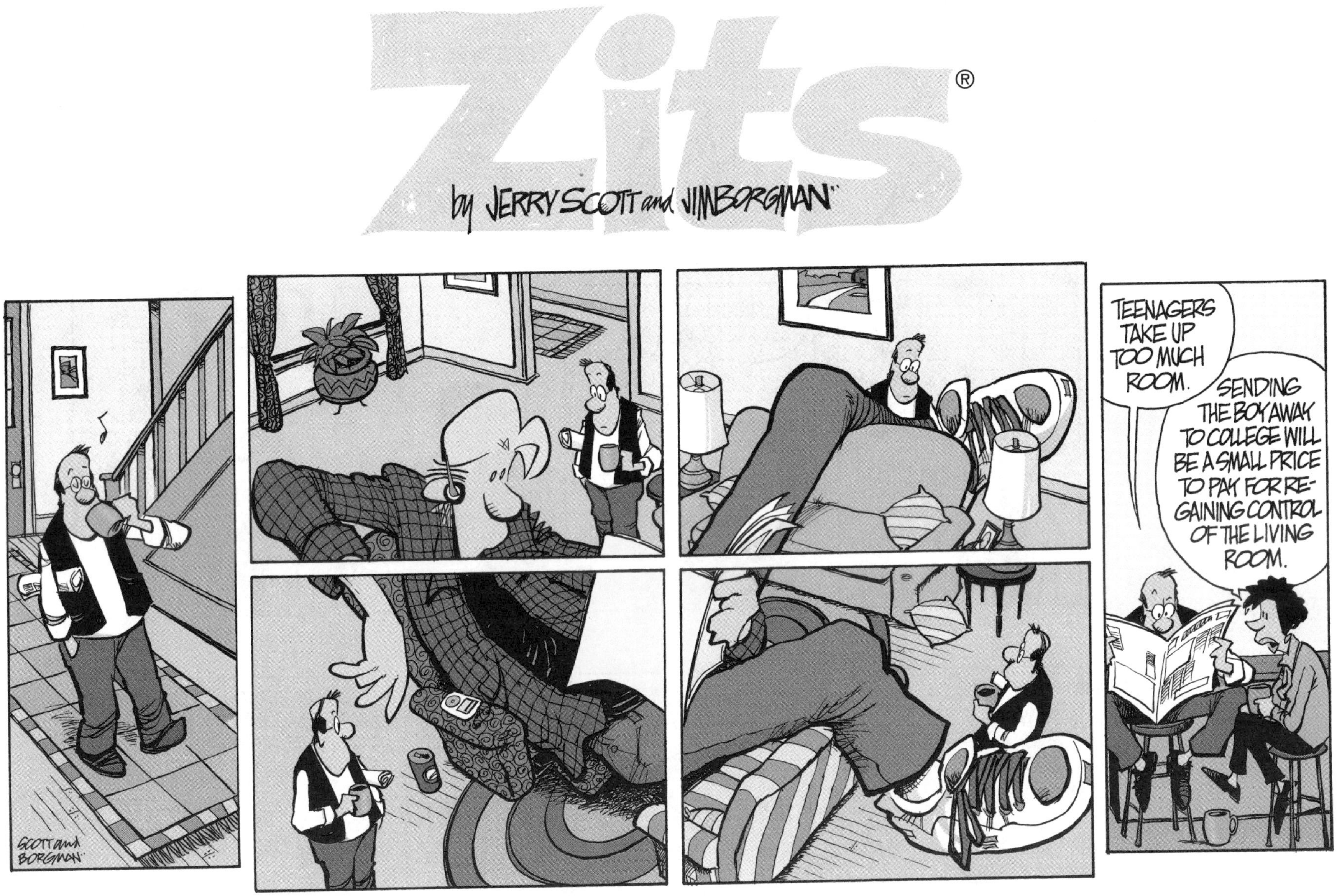
Zits®
by JERRY SCOTT and JIM BORGMAN
SCOTT and BORGMAN
TEENAGERS TAKE UP TOO MUCH ROOM.
SENDING THE BOY AWAY TO COLLEGE WILL BE A SMALL PRICE TO PAY FOR RE-GAINING CONTROL OF THE LIVING ROOM.

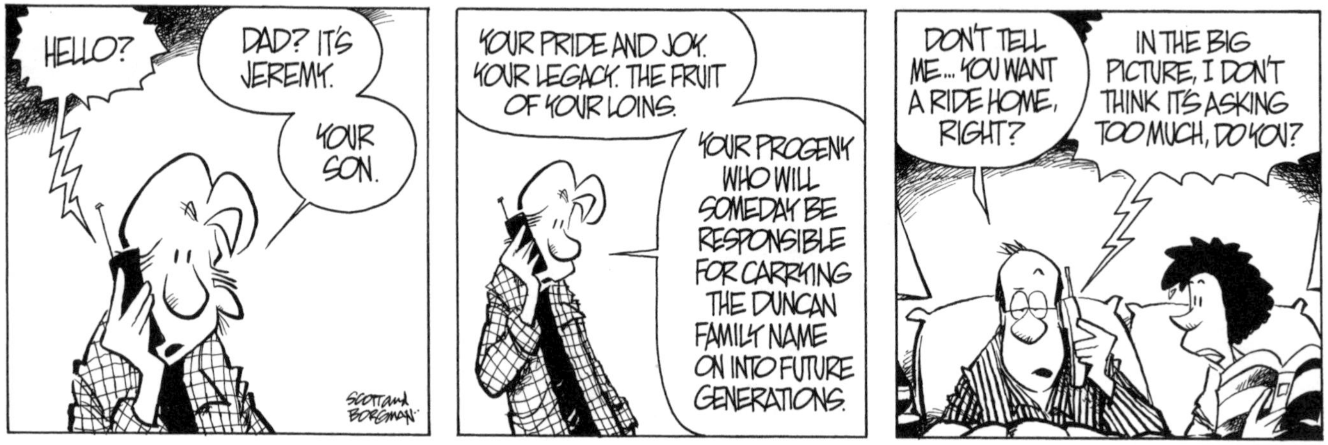
HELLO?
DAD? IT'S JEREMY.
YOUR SON.
SCOTT and BORGMAN
YOUR PRIDE AND JOY. YOUR LEGACY. THE FRUIT OF YOUR LOINS.
YOUR PROGENY WHO WILL SOMEDAY BE RESPONSIBLE FOR CARRYING THE DUNCAN FAMILY NAME ON INTO FUTURE GENERATIONS.
DON'T TELL ME... YOU WANT A RIDE HOME, RIGHT?
IN THE BIG PICTURE, I DON'T THINK IT'S ASKING TOO MUCH, DO YOU?

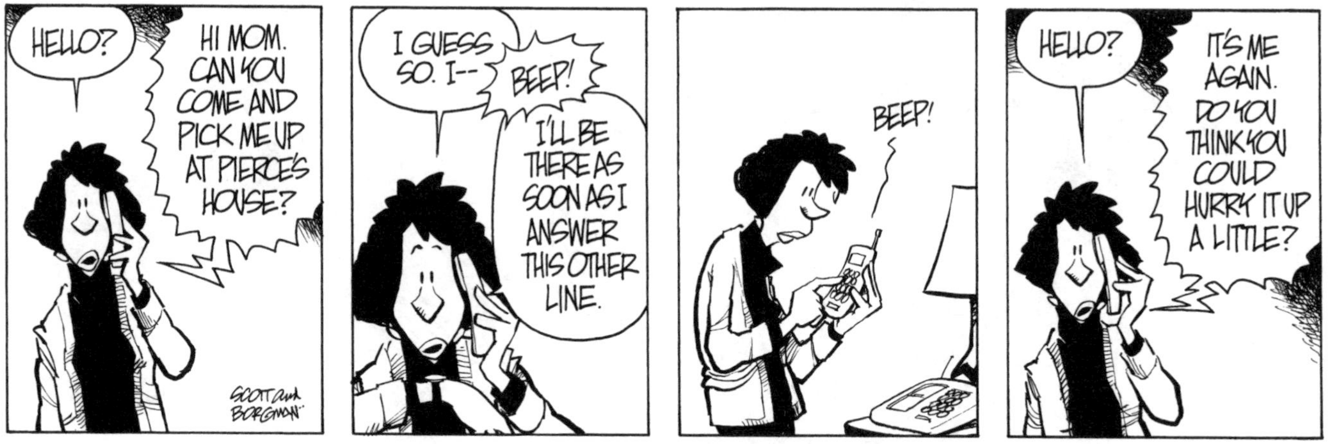
HELLO?
HI MOM. CAN YOU COME AND PICK ME UP AT PIERCE'S HOUSE?
SCOTT and BORGMAN
I GUESS SO. I--
BEEP!
I'LL BE THERE AS SOON AS I ANSWER THIS OTHER LINE.
BEEP!
HELLO?
IT'S ME AGAIN. DO YOU THINK YOU COULD HURRY IT UP A LITTLE?

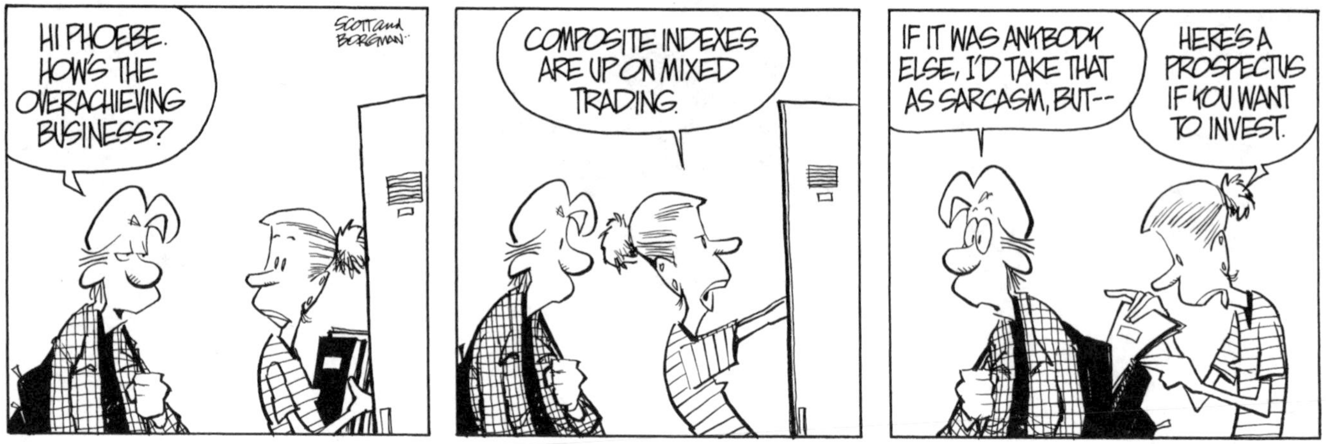
HI PHOEBE. HOW'S THE OVERACHIEVING BUSINESS?
SCOTT and BORGMAN
COMPOSITE INDEXES ARE UP ON MIXED TRADING.
IF IT WAS ANYBODY ELSE, I'D TAKE THAT AS SARCASM, BUT--
HERE'S A PROSPECTUS IF YOU WANT TO INVEST.

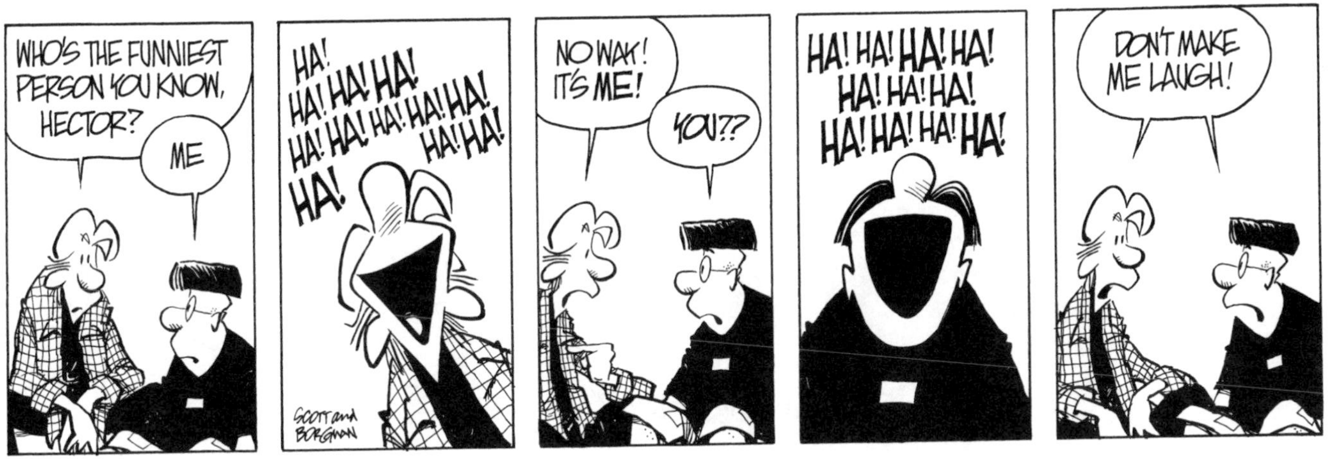

WHO'S THE FUNNIEST PERSON YOU KNOW, HECTOR?
ME
HA! HA! HA! HA! HA! HA! HA! HA! HA! HA! HA! HA!
NO WAY! IT'S ME!
YOU??
HA! HA! HA! HA! HA! HA! HA! HA! HA! HA! HA!
DON'T MAKE ME LAUGH!
SCOTT and BORGMAN

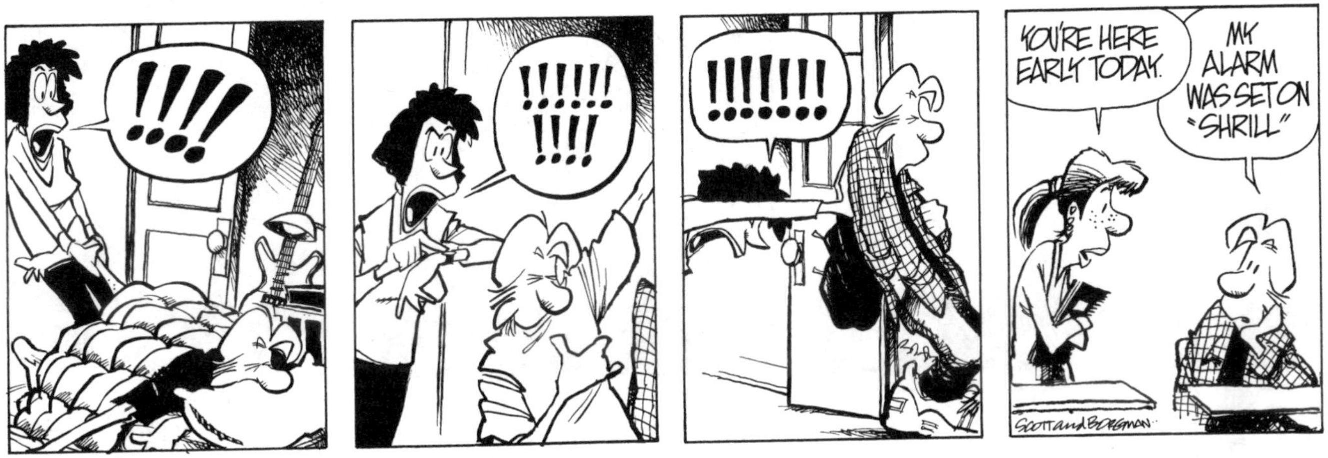

!!!!
!!!!!!! !!!!
!!!!!!!
YOU'RE HERE EARLY TODAY.
MY ALARM WAS SET ON "SHRILL"
SCOTT and BORGMAN

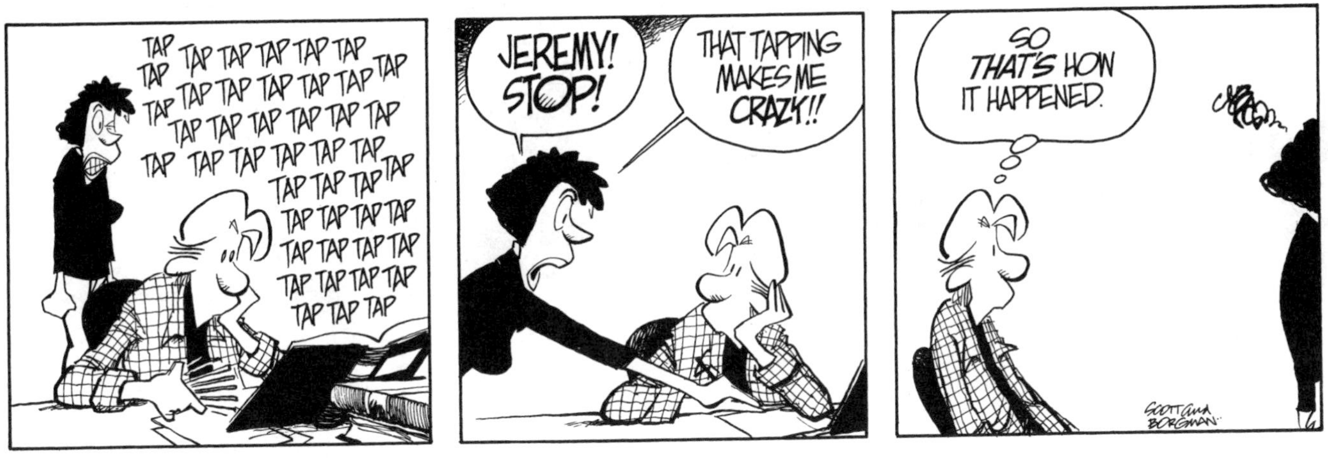

TAP TAP TAP TAP TAP TAP TAP
TAP TAP TAP TAP TAP TAP TAP TAP
TAP TAP TAP TAP TAP TAP TAP TAP
TAP TAP TAP TAP TAP TAP TAP
TAP TAP TAP TAP TAP TAP TAP TAP
TAP TAP TAP TAP
TAP TAP TAP TAP
TAP TAP TAP TAP
TAP TAP TAP TAP
TAP TAP TAP
JEREMY! STOP!
THAT TAPPING MAKES ME CRAZY!!
SO THAT'S HOW IT HAPPENED.
SCOTT and BORGMAN

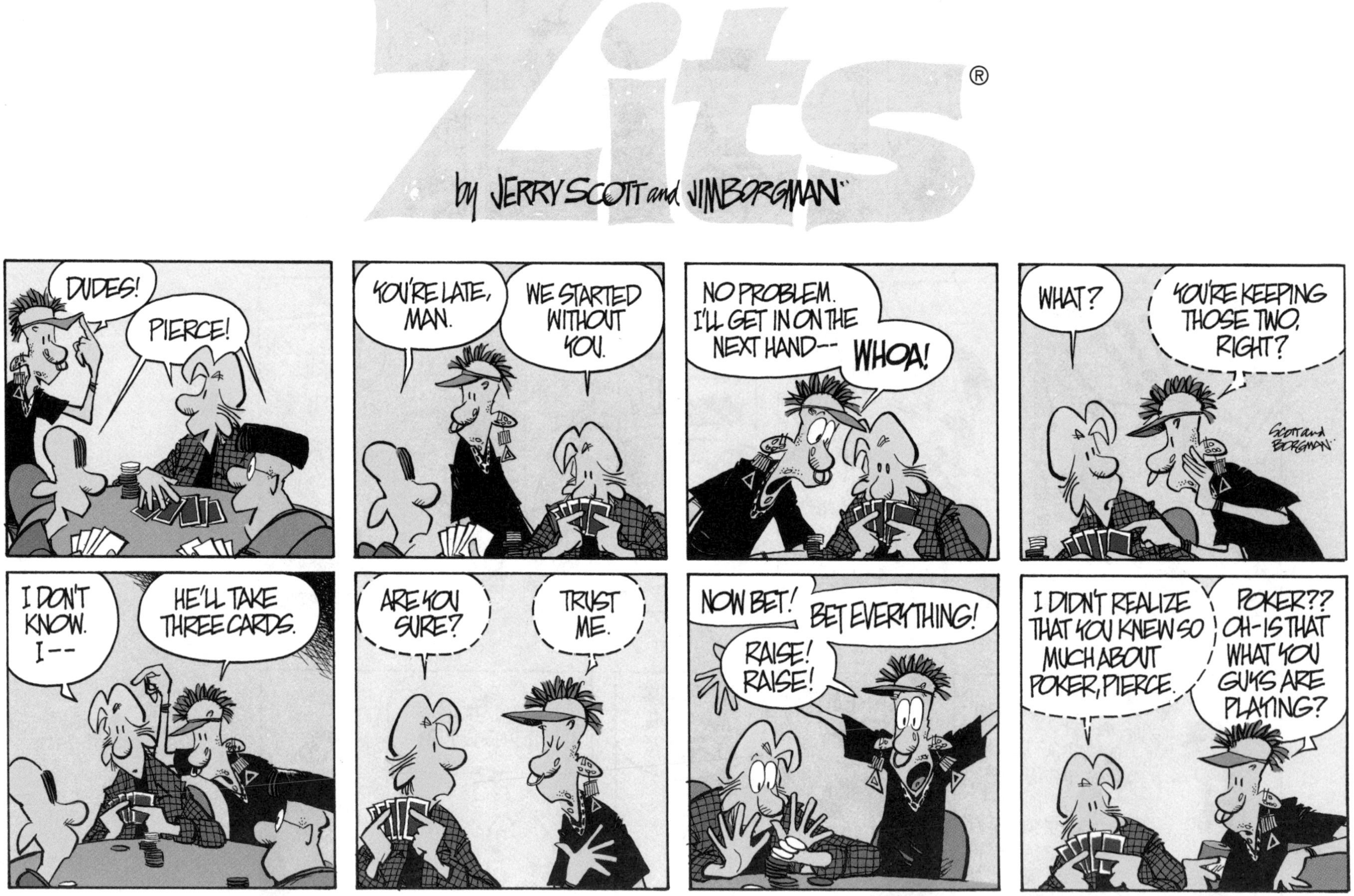
Zits®
by JERRY SCOTT and JIM BORGMAN
DUDES!
PIERCE!
YOU'RE LATE, MAN.
WE STARTED WITHOUT YOU.
NO PROBLEM. I'LL GET IN ON THE NEXT HAND--
WHOA!
WHAT?
YOU'RE KEEPING THOSE TWO, RIGHT?
SCOTT and BORGMAN
I DON'T KNOW. I --
HE'LL TAKE THREE CARDS.
ARE YOU SURE?
TRUST ME.
NOW BET!
BET EVERYTHING!
RAISE! RAISE!
I DIDN'T REALIZE THAT YOU KNEW SO MUCH ABOUT POKER, PIERCE.
POKER?? OH-IS THAT WHAT YOU GUYS ARE PLAYING?

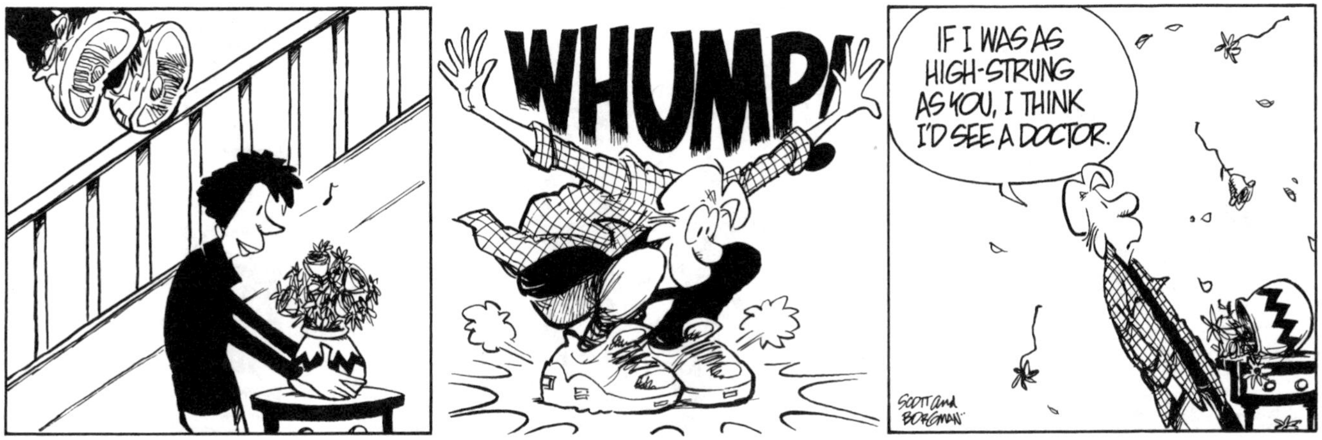
WHUMP!
IF I WAS AS HIGH-STRUNG AS YOU, I THINK I'D SEE A DOCTOR.

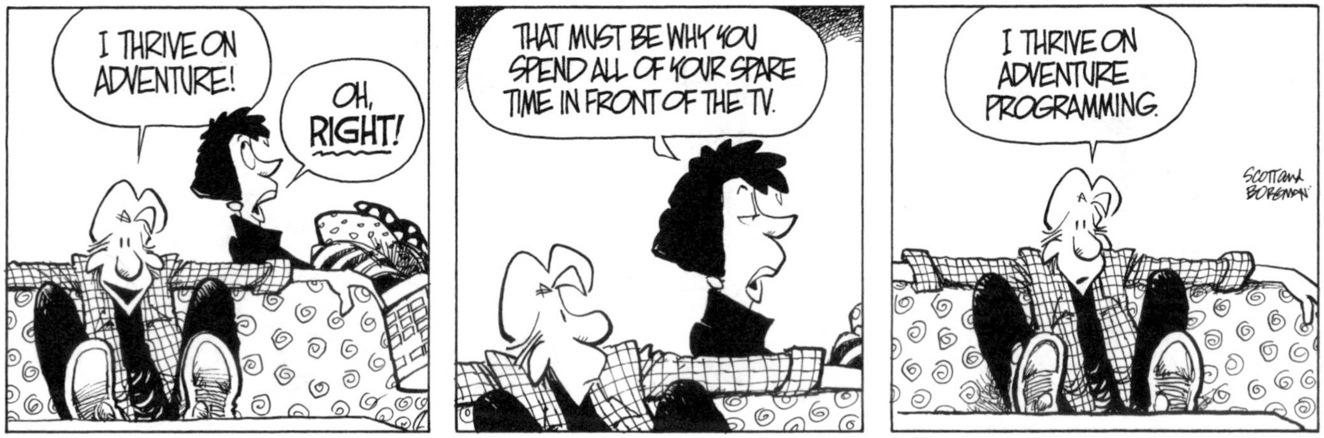
I THRIVE ON ADVENTURE!
OH, RIGHT!
THAT MUST BE WHY YOU SPEND ALL OF YOUR SPARE TIME IN FRONT OF THE TV.
I THRIVE ON ADVENTURE PROGRAMMING.

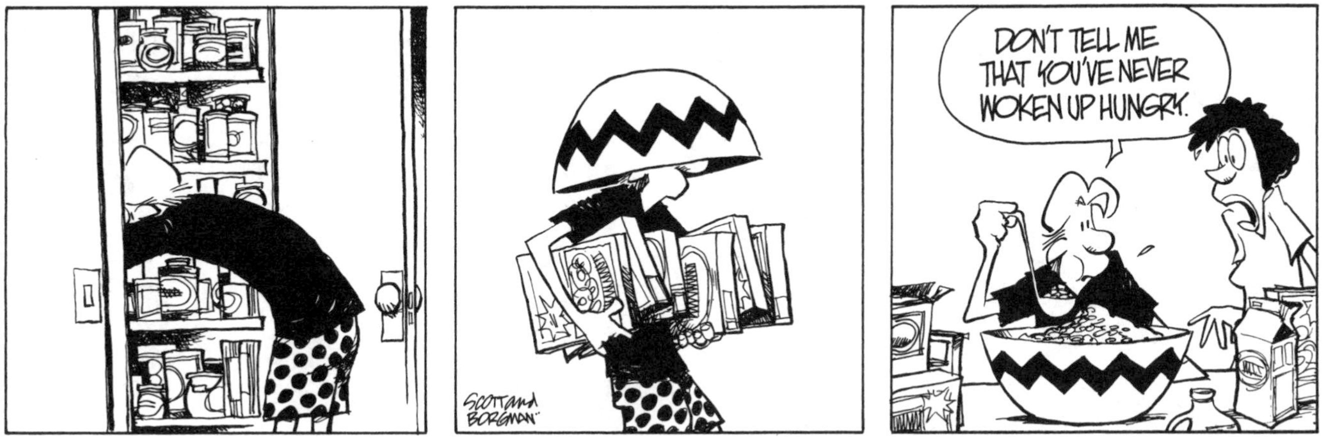
DON'T TELL ME THAT YOU'VE NEVER WOKEN UP HUNGRY.

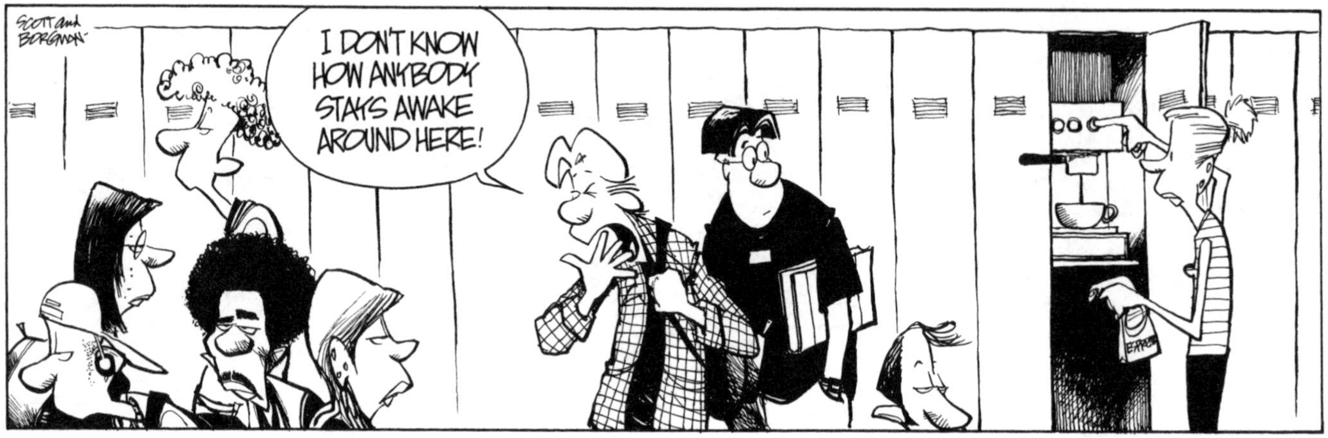
SCOTT and BORGMAN
I DON'T KNOW HOW ANYBODY STAYS AWAKE AROUND HERE!

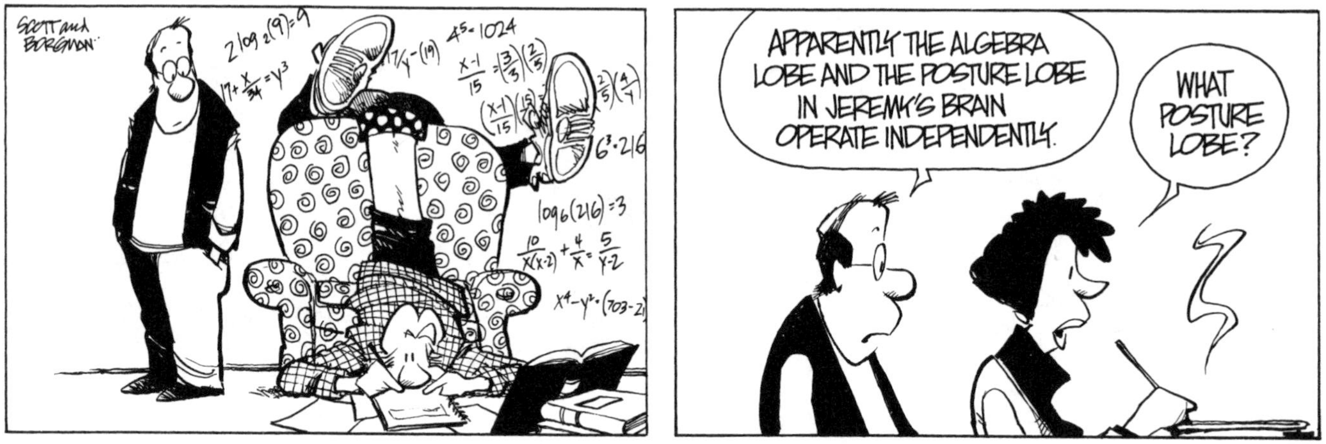
SCOTT and BORGMAN
APPARENTLY THE ALGEBRA LOBE AND THE POSTURE LOBE IN JEREMY'S BRAIN OPERATE INDEPENDENTLY.
WHAT POSTURE LOBE?

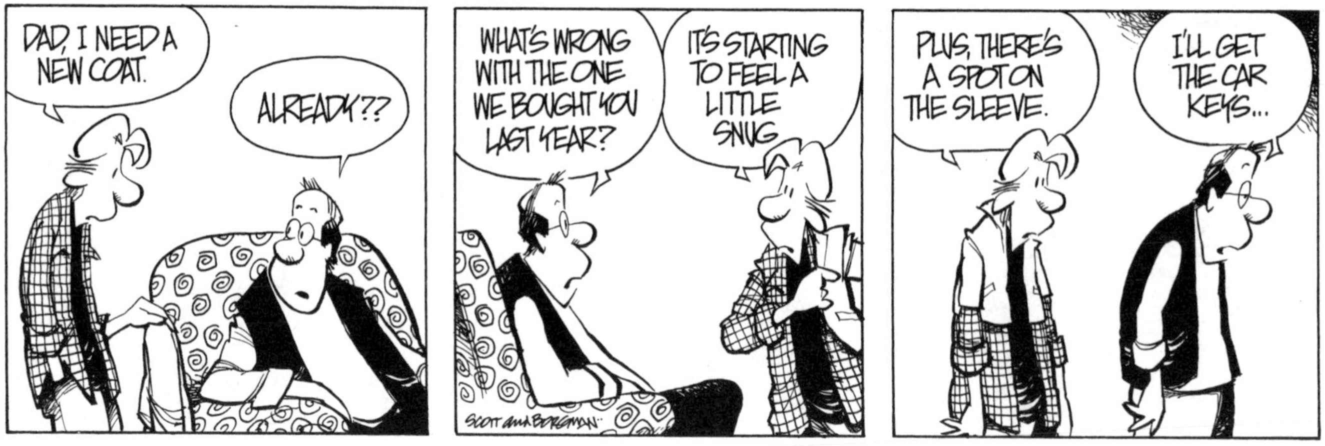
DAD, I NEED A NEW COAT.
ALREADY??
WHAT'S WRONG WITH THE ONE WE BOUGHT YOU LAST YEAR?
IT'S STARTING TO FEEL A LITTLE SNUG.
SCOTT and BORGMAN
PLUS, THERE'S A SPOT ON THE SLEEVE.
I'LL GET THE CAR KEYS...

Zits®

by JERRY SCOTT and JIM BORGMAN

UP! UP! UP!
EAT! EAT! EAT!
HURRY! HURRY! HURRY!
GO! GO! GO!
SCOTT and BORGMAN
I THINK WHAT I ENJOY MOST ABOUT HIGH SCHOOL IS THE INDEPENDENCE.
WHO DOESN'T?
LUNCH MONEY

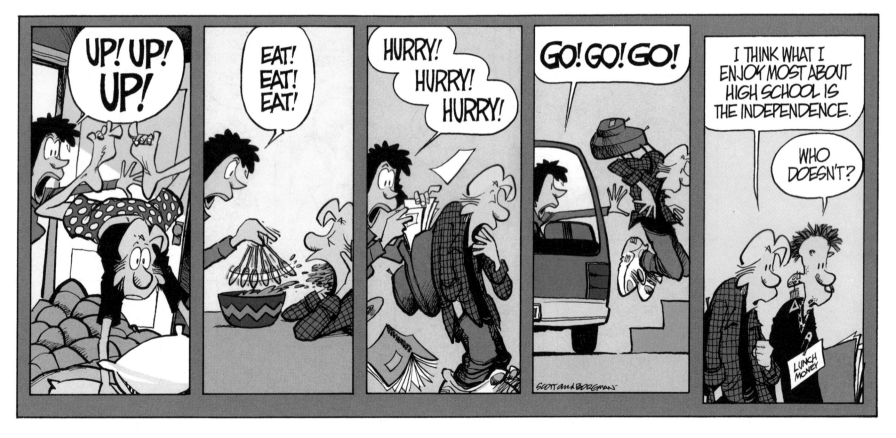

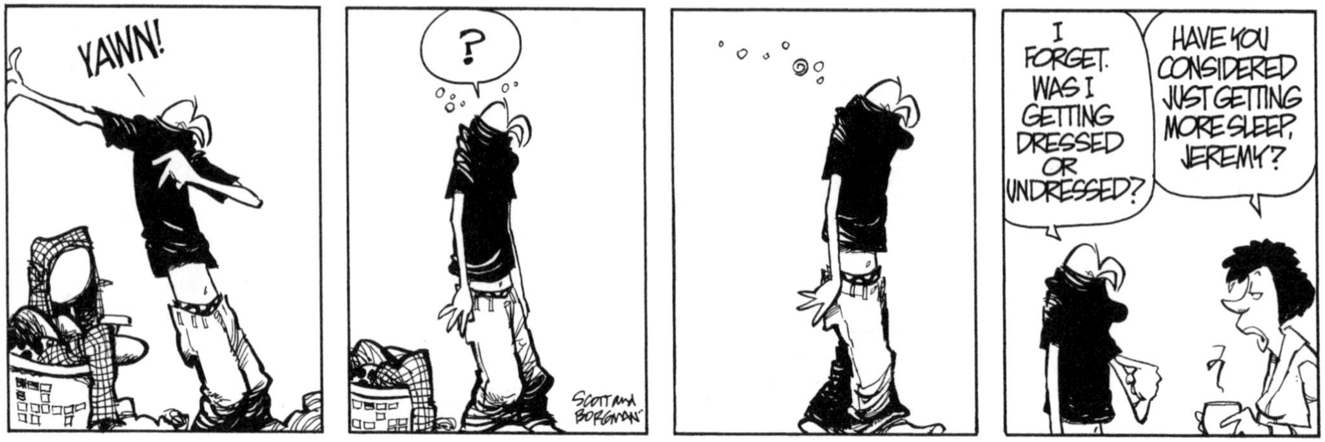
YAWN!
?
I FORGET. WAS I GETTING DRESSED OR UNDRESSED?
HAVE YOU CONSIDERED JUST GETTING MORE SLEEP, JEREMY?

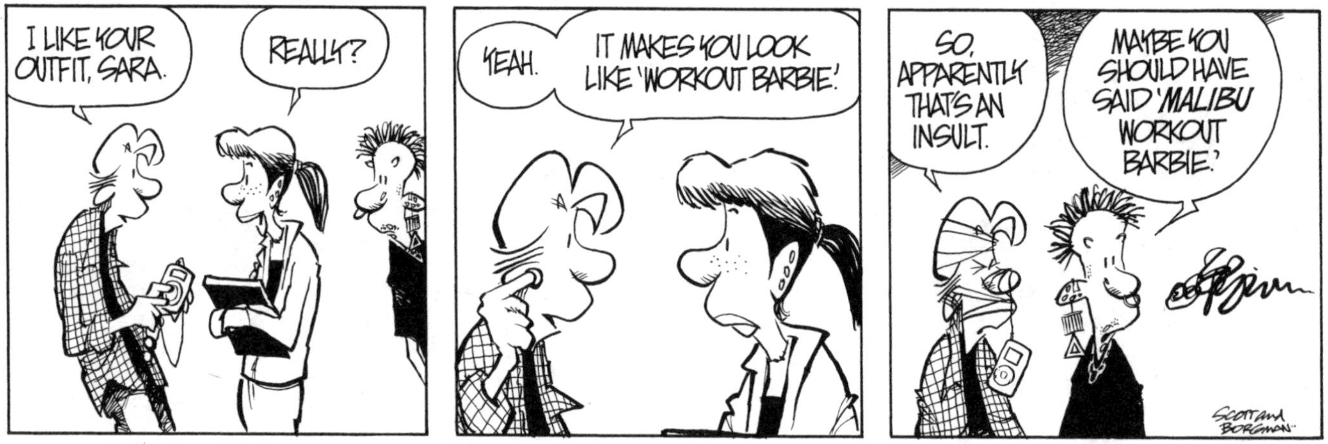
I LIKE YOUR OUTFIT, SARA.
REALLY?
YEAH.
IT MAKES YOU LOOK LIKE 'WORKOUT BARBIE.'
SO, APPARENTLY THAT'S AN INSULT.
MAYBE YOU SHOULD HAVE SAID '*MALIBU* WORKOUT BARBIE.'

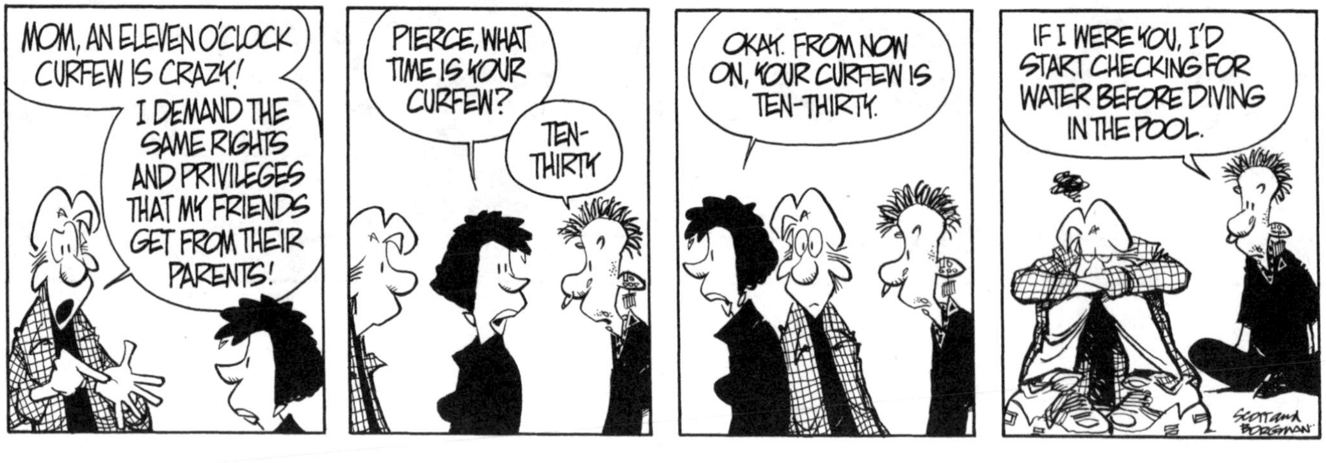
MOM, AN ELEVEN O'CLOCK CURFEW IS CRAZY!
I DEMAND THE SAME RIGHTS AND PRIVILEGES THAT MY FRIENDS GET FROM THEIR PARENTS!
PIERCE, WHAT TIME IS YOUR CURFEW?
TEN-THIRTY
OKAY. FROM NOW ON, YOUR CURFEW IS TEN-THIRTY.
IF I WERE YOU, I'D START CHECKING FOR WATER BEFORE DIVING IN THE POOL.

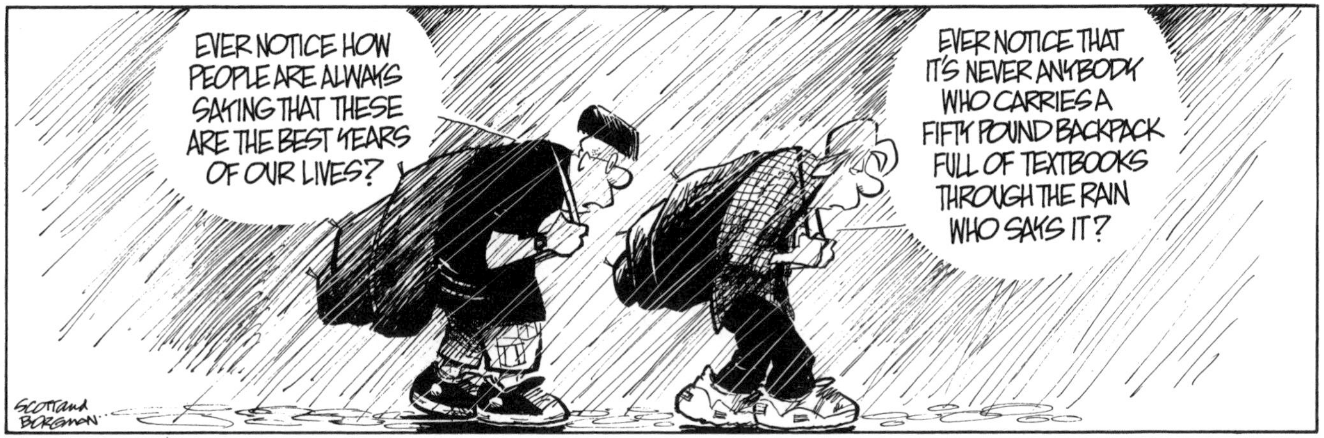
EVER NOTICE HOW PEOPLE ARE ALWAYS SAYING THAT THESE ARE THE BEST YEARS OF OUR LIVES?
EVER NOTICE THAT IT'S NEVER ANYBODY WHO CARRIES A FIFTY POUND BACKPACK FULL OF TEXTBOOKS THROUGH THE RAIN WHO SAYS IT?
SCOTT and BORGMAN

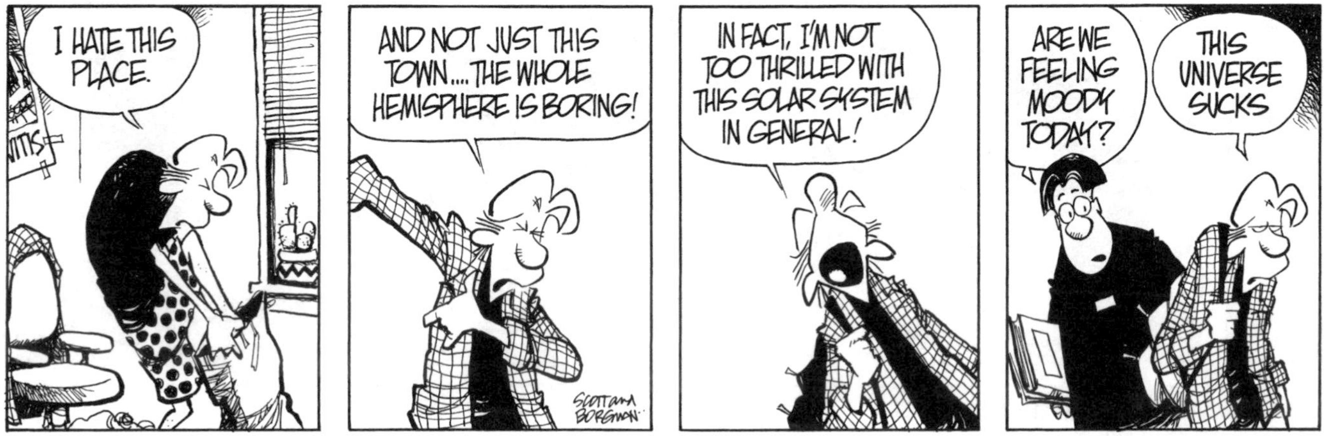
I HATE THIS PLACE.
AND NOT JUST THIS TOWN.... THE WHOLE HEMISPHERE IS BORING!
SCOTT and BORGMAN
IN FACT, I'M NOT TOO THRILLED WITH THIS SOLAR SYSTEM IN GENERAL!
ARE WE FEELING MOODY TODAY?
THIS UNIVERSE SUCKS

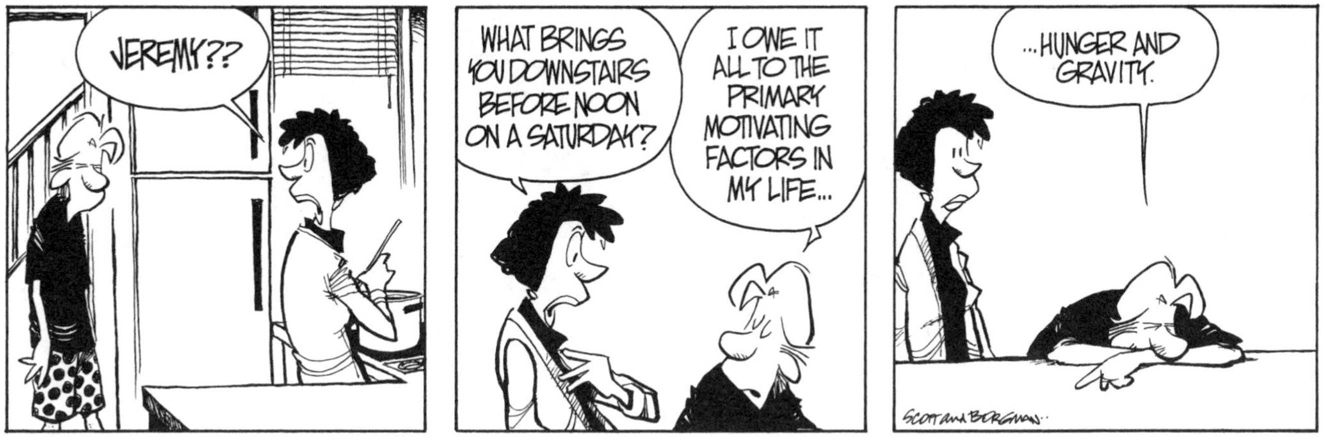
JEREMY??
WHAT BRINGS YOU DOWNSTAIRS BEFORE NOON ON A SATURDAY?
I OWE IT ALL TO THE PRIMARY MOTIVATING FACTORS IN MY LIFE...
...HUNGER AND GRAVITY.
SCOTT and BORGMAN

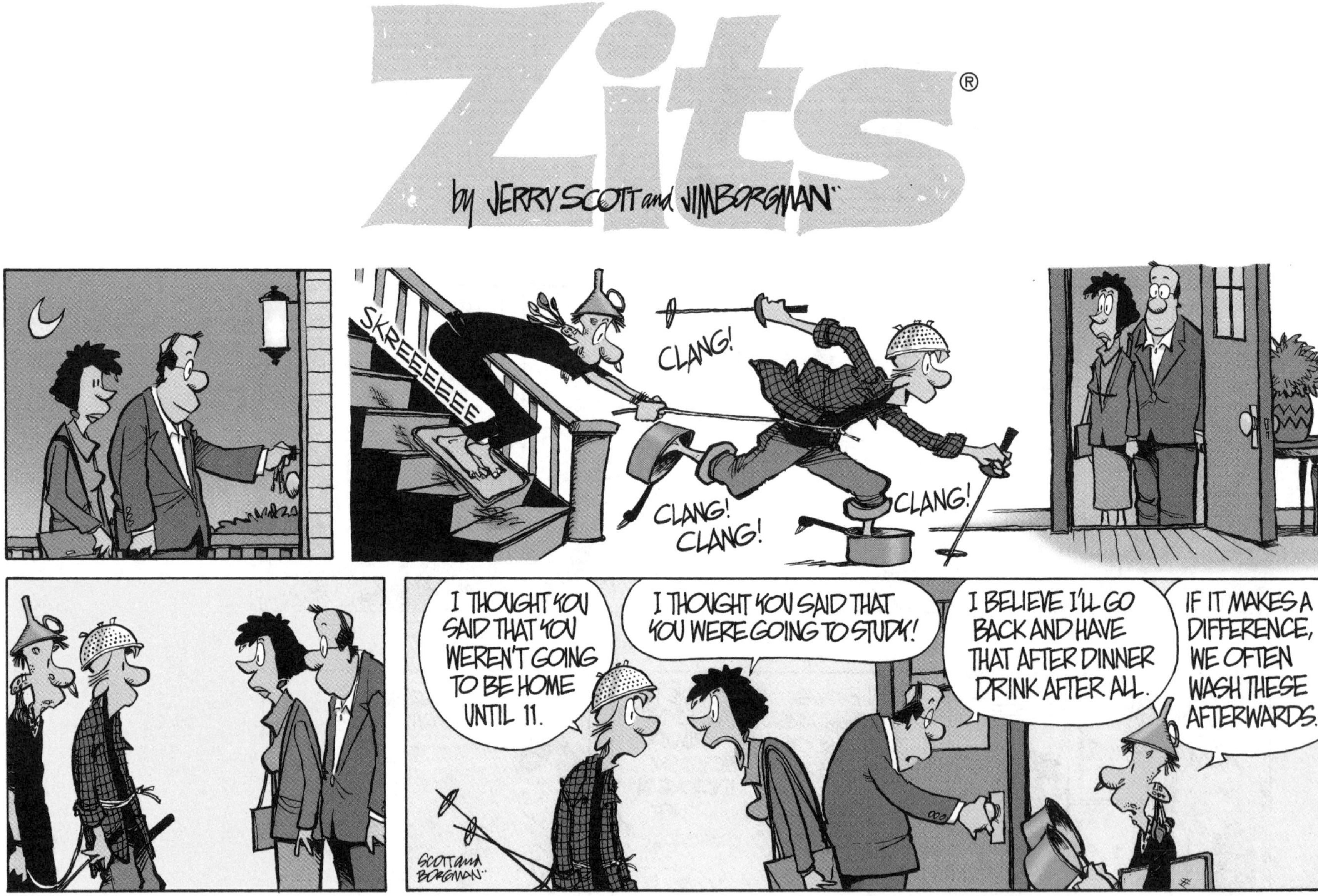
Zits®
by JERRY SCOTT and JIM BORGMAN
SKREEEEEEEE
CLANG!
CLANG!
CLANG!
CLANG!
I THOUGHT YOU SAID THAT YOU WEREN'T GOING TO BE HOME UNTIL 11.
I THOUGHT YOU SAID THAT YOU WERE GOING TO STUDY!
I BELIEVE I'LL GO BACK AND HAVE THAT AFTER DINNER DRINK AFTER ALL.
IF IT MAKES A DIFFERENCE, WE OFTEN WASH THESE AFTERWARDS.
SCOTT and BORGMAN

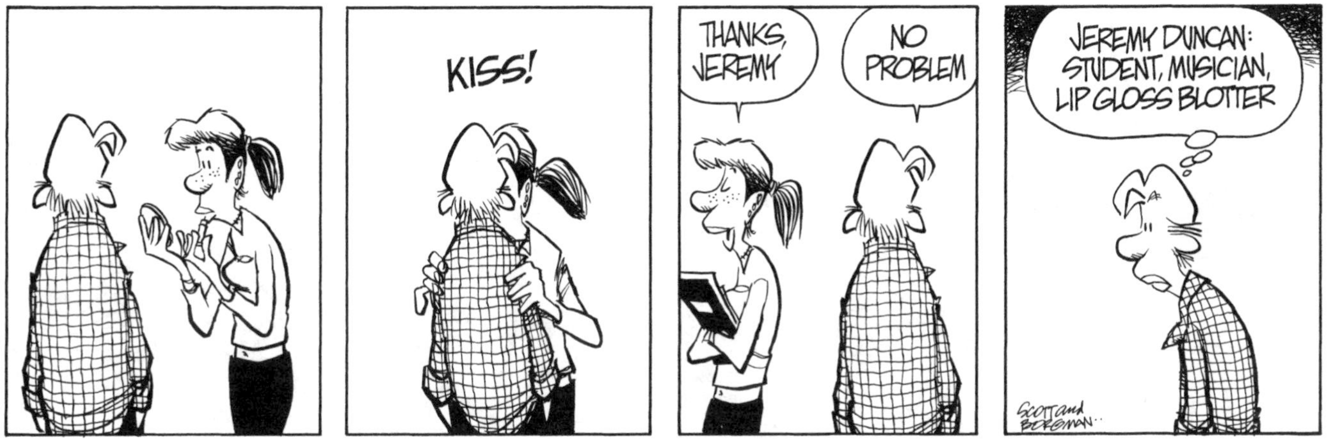
KISS!
THANKS, JEREMY
NO PROBLEM
JEREMY DUNCAN: STUDENT, MUSICIAN, LIP GLOSS BLOTTER
SCOTT and BORGMAN

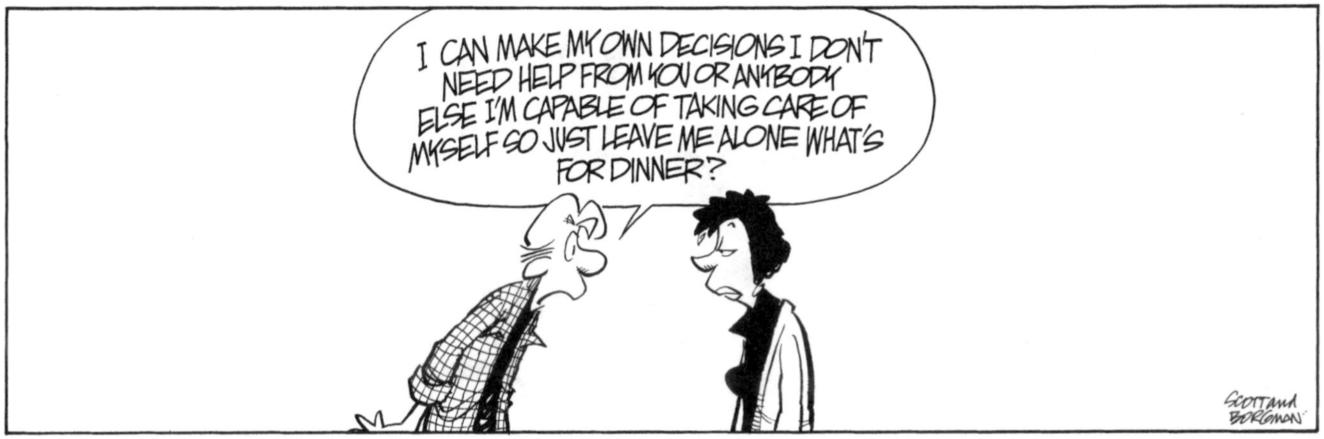
I CAN MAKE MY OWN DECISIONS I DON'T NEED HELP FROM YOU OR ANYBODY ELSE I'M CAPABLE OF TAKING CARE OF MYSELF SO JUST LEAVE ME ALONE WHAT'S FOR DINNER?
SCOTT and BORGMAN

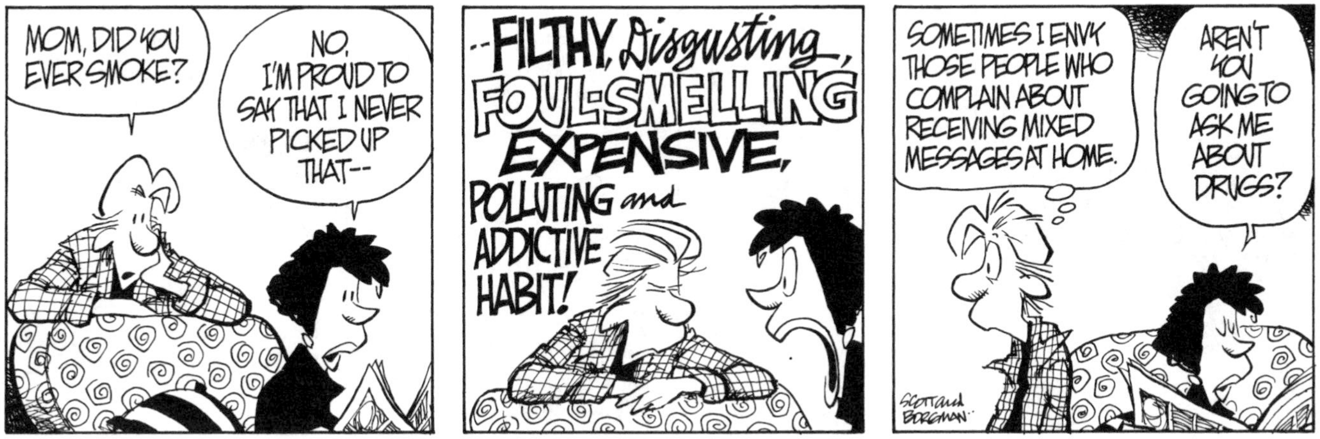
MOM, DID YOU EVER SMOKE?
NO. I'M PROUD TO SAY THAT I NEVER PICKED UP THAT--
--FILTHY, Disgusting, FOUL-SMELLING EXPENSIVE, POLLUTING and ADDICTIVE HABIT!
SOMETIMES I ENVY THOSE PEOPLE WHO COMPLAIN ABOUT RECEIVING MIXED MESSAGES AT HOME.
AREN'T YOU GOING TO ASK ME ABOUT DRUGS?
SCOTT and BORGMAN

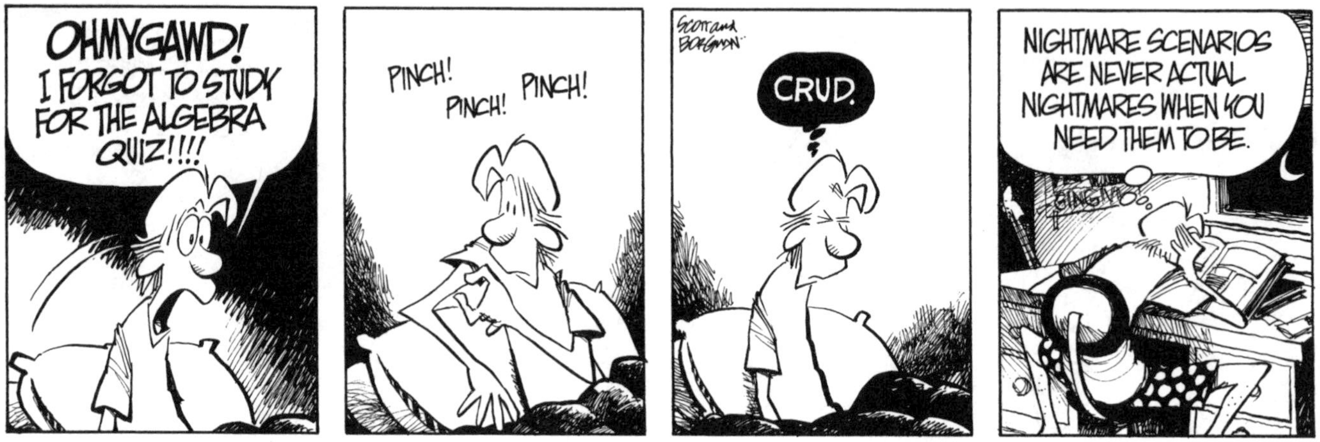
OHMYGAWD! I FORGOT TO STUDY FOR THE ALGEBRA QUIZ!!!!
PINCH! PINCH! PINCH!
CRUD.
NIGHTMARE SCENARIOS ARE NEVER ACTUAL NIGHTMARES WHEN YOU NEED THEM TO BE.

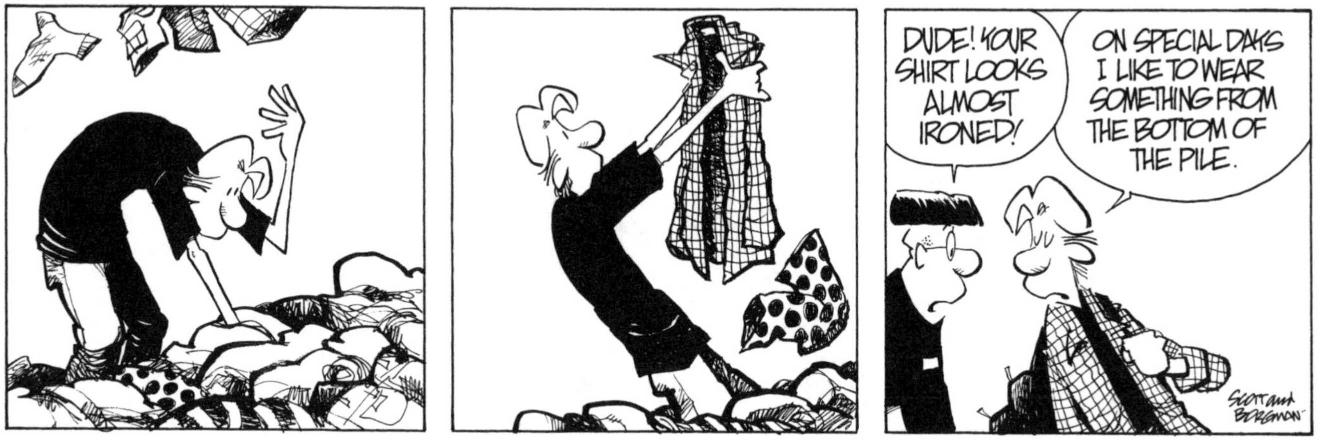
DUDE! YOUR SHIRT LOOKS ALMOST IRONED!
ON SPECIAL DAYS I LIKE TO WEAR SOMETHING FROM THE BOTTOM OF THE PILE.

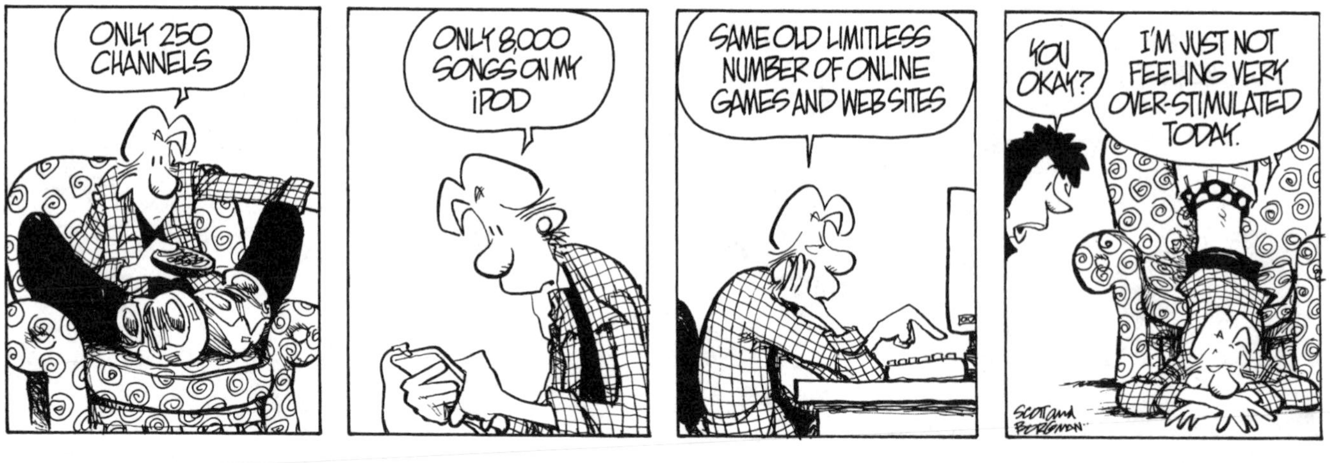
ONLY 250 CHANNELS
ONLY 8,000 SONGS ON MY iPOD
SAME OLD LIMITLESS NUMBER OF ONLINE GAMES AND WEB SITES
YOU OKAY?
I'M JUST NOT FEELING VERY OVER-STIMULATED TODAY.

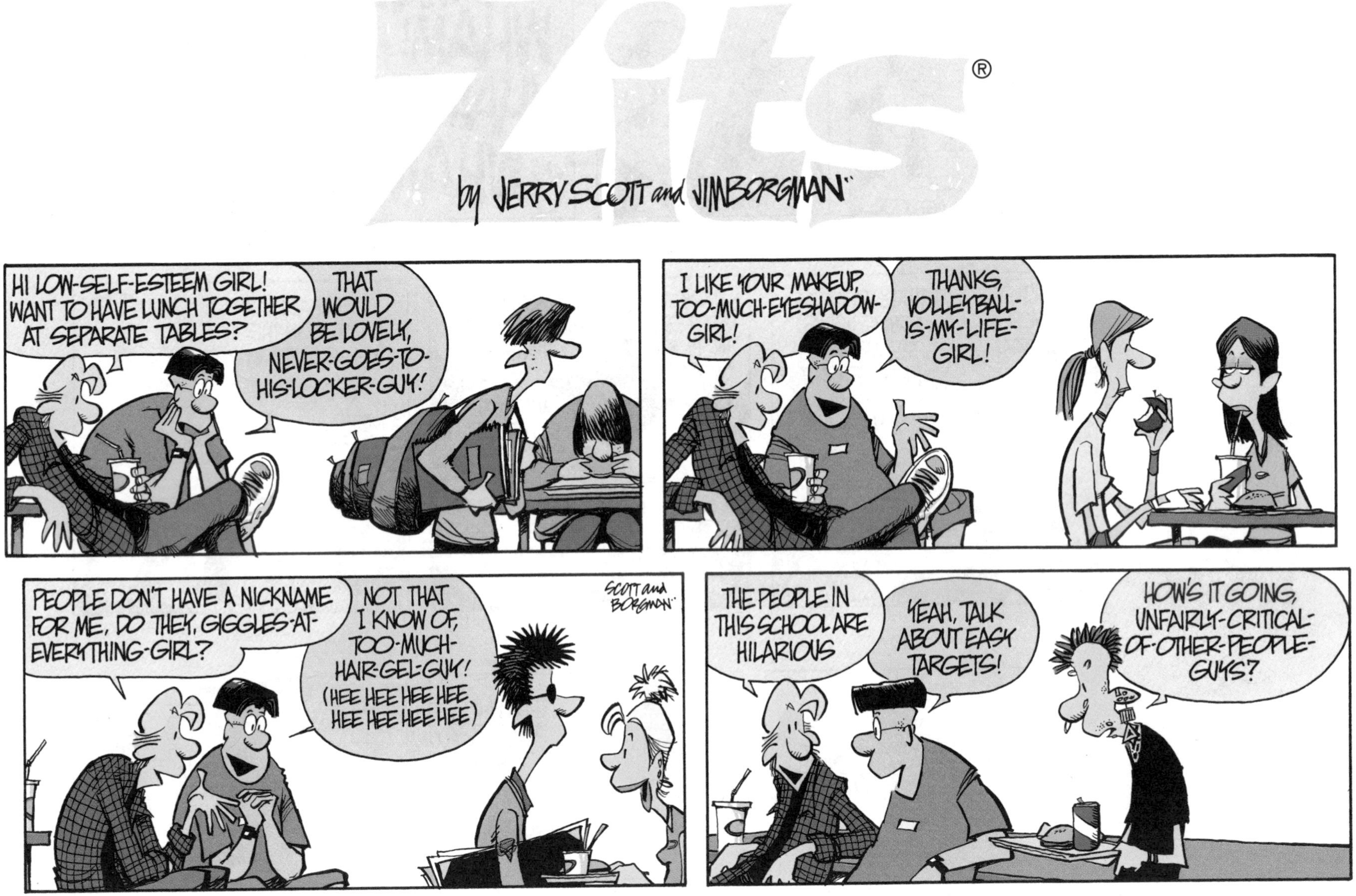
Zits®
by JERRY SCOTT and JIM BORGMAN
HI LOW-SELF-ESTEEM GIRL! WANT TO HAVE LUNCH TOGETHER AT SEPARATE TABLES?
THAT WOULD BE LOVELY, NEVER-GOES-TO-HIS-LOCKER-GUY!
I LIKE YOUR MAKEUP, TOO-MUCH-EYESHADOW-GIRL!
THANKS, VOLLEYBALL-IS-MY-LIFE-GIRL!
PEOPLE DON'T HAVE A NICKNAME FOR ME, DO THEY, GIGGLES-AT-EVERYTHING-GIRL?
NOT THAT I KNOW OF, TOO-MUCH-HAIR-GEL-GUY! (HEE HEE HEE HEE HEE HEE HEE HEE)
SCOTT and BORGMAN
THE PEOPLE IN THIS SCHOOL ARE HILARIOUS
YEAH, TALK ABOUT EASY TARGETS!
HOW'S IT GOING, UNFAIRLY-CRITICAL-OF-OTHER-PEOPLE-GUYS?

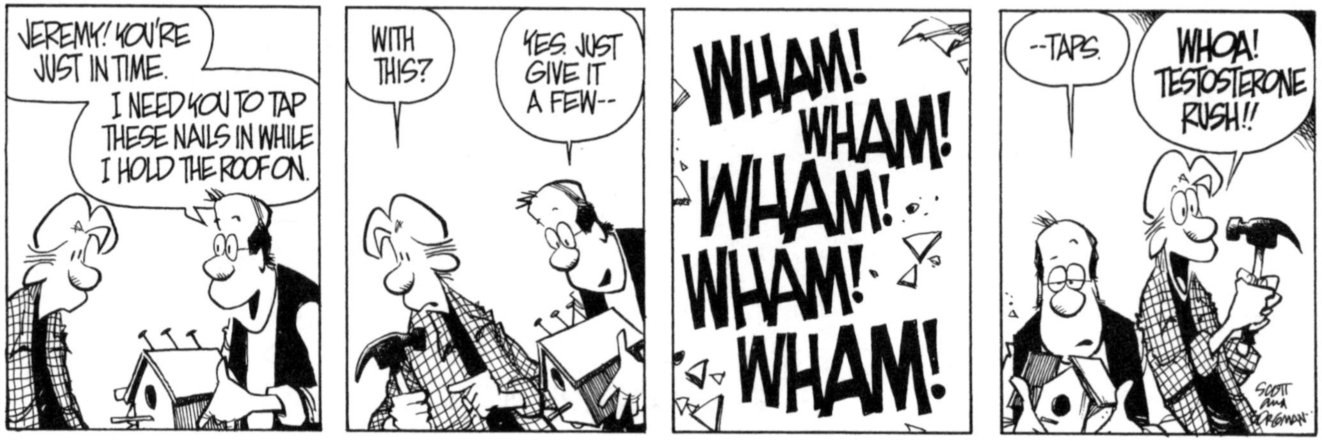
JEREMY! YOU'RE JUST IN TIME.
I NEED YOU TO TAP THESE NAILS IN WHILE I HOLD THE ROOF ON.
WITH THIS?
YES. JUST GIVE IT A FEW--
WHAM! WHAM! WHAM! WHAM! WHAM!
--TAPS.
WHOA! TESTOSTERONE RUSH!!
SCOTT AND BORGMAN

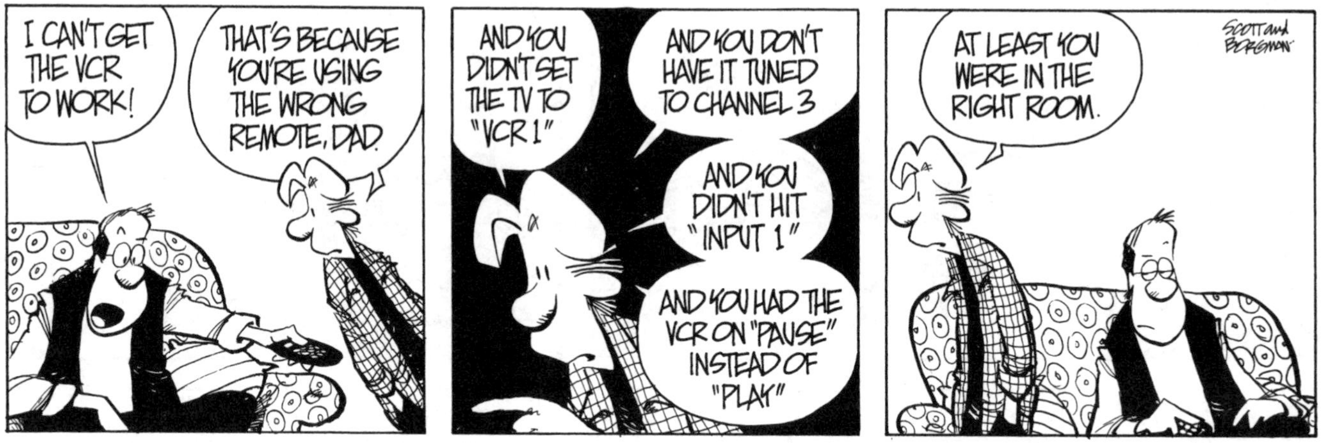
I CAN'T GET THE VCR TO WORK!
THAT'S BECAUSE YOU'RE USING THE WRONG REMOTE, DAD.
AND YOU DIDN'T SET THE TV TO "VCR 1"
AND YOU DON'T HAVE IT TUNED TO CHANNEL 3
AND YOU DIDN'T HIT "INPUT 1"
AND YOU HAD THE VCR ON "PAUSE" INSTEAD OF "PLAY"
AT LEAST YOU WERE IN THE RIGHT ROOM.
SCOTT AND BORGMAN

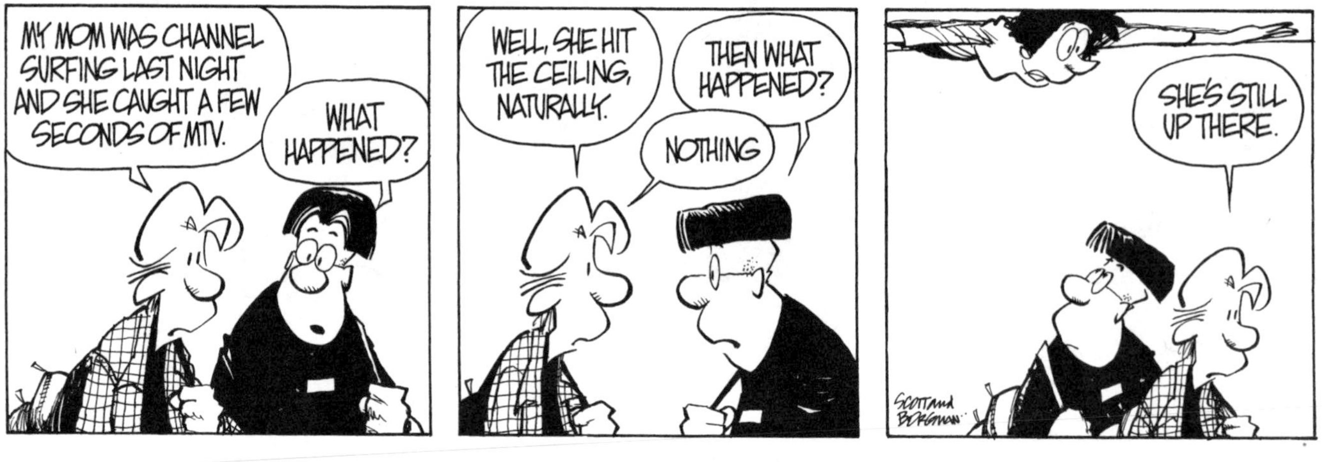
MY MOM WAS CHANNEL SURFING LAST NIGHT AND SHE CAUGHT A FEW SECONDS OF MTV.
WHAT HAPPENED?
WELL, SHE HIT THE CEILING, NATURALLY.
THEN WHAT HAPPENED?
NOTHING
SHE'S STILL UP THERE.
SCOTT AND BORGMAN

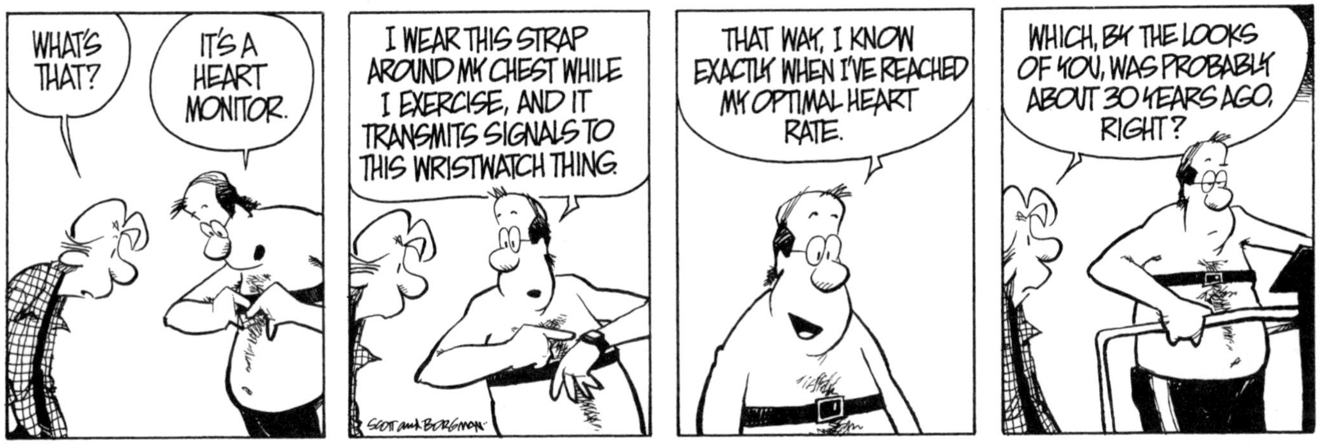
WHAT'S THAT?
IT'S A HEART MONITOR.
I WEAR THIS STRAP AROUND MY CHEST WHILE I EXERCISE, AND IT TRANSMITS SIGNALS TO THIS WRISTWATCH THING.
THAT WAY, I KNOW EXACTLY WHEN I'VE REACHED MY OPTIMAL HEART RATE.
WHICH, BY THE LOOKS OF YOU, WAS PROBABLY ABOUT 30 YEARS AGO, RIGHT?
SCOTT and BORGMAN

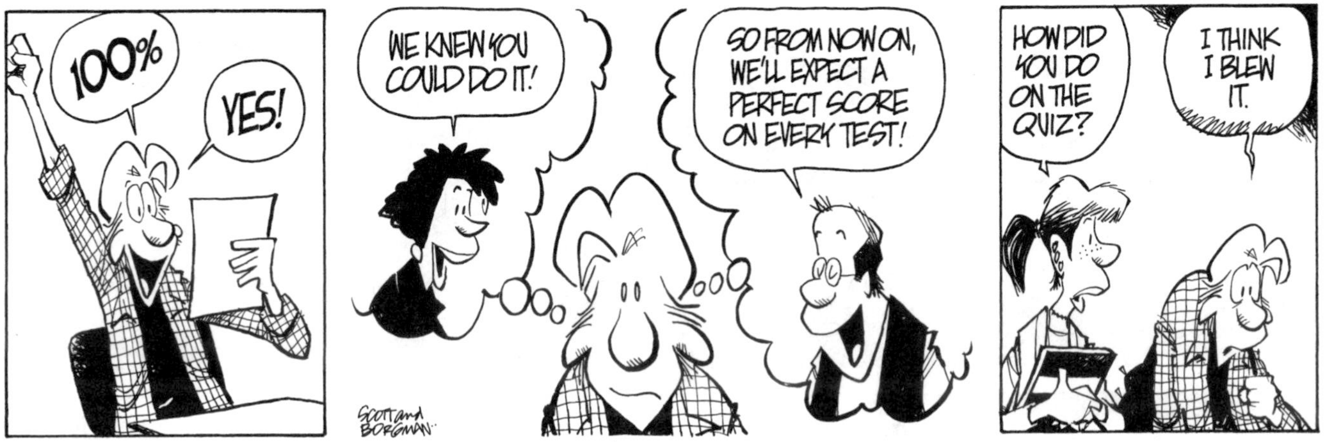
100%
YES!
WE KNEW YOU COULD DO IT!
SO FROM NOW ON, WE'LL EXPECT A PERFECT SCORE ON EVERY TEST!
HOW DID YOU DO ON THE QUIZ?
I THINK I BLEW IT.
SCOTT and BORGMAN

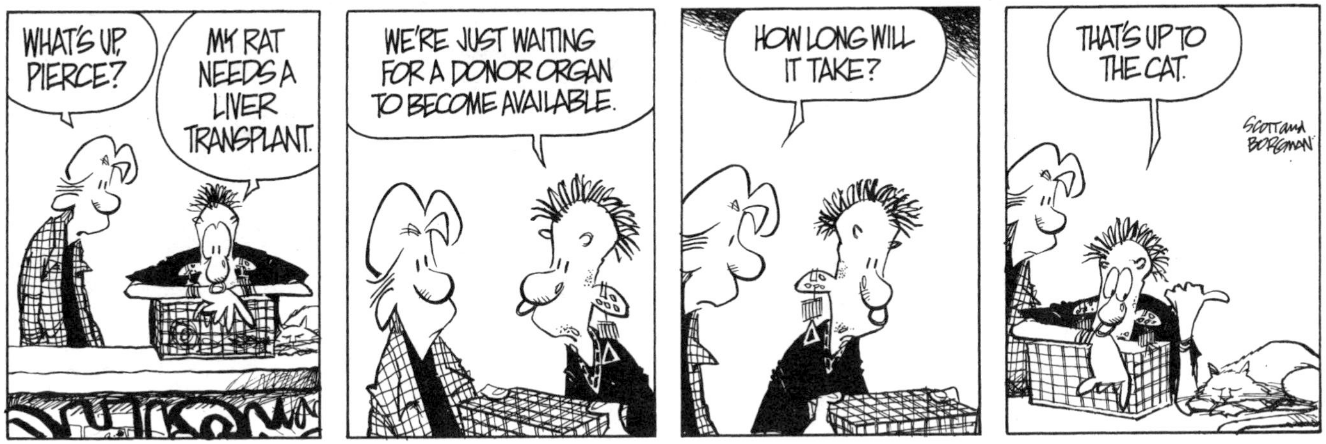
WHAT'S UP, PIERCE?
MY RAT NEEDS A LIVER TRANSPLANT.
WE'RE JUST WAITING FOR A DONOR ORGAN TO BECOME AVAILABLE.
HOW LONG WILL IT TAKE?
THAT'S UP TO THE CAT.
SCOTT and BORGMAN

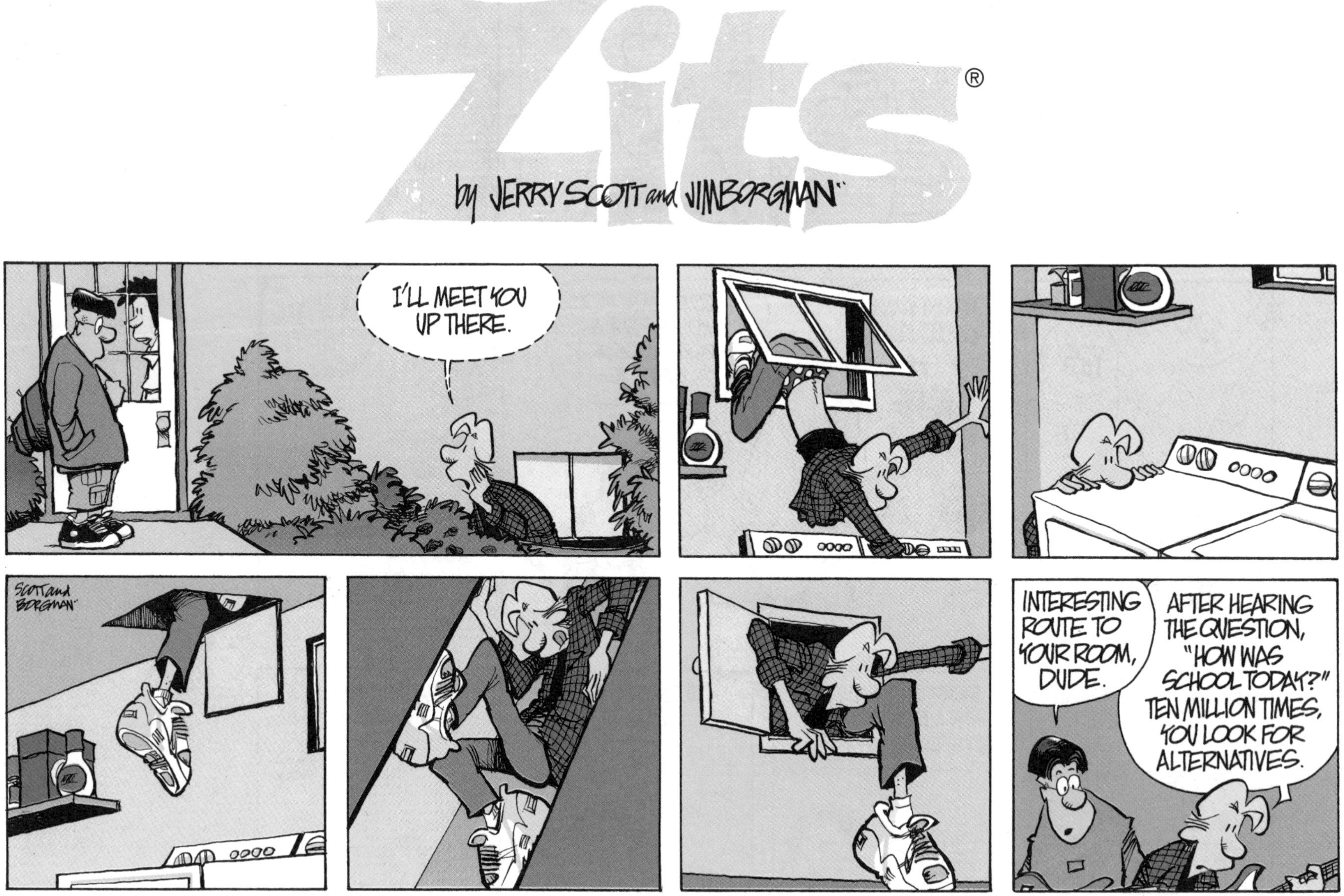
Zits®
by JERRY SCOTT and JIM BORGMAN
I'LL MEET YOU UP THERE.
SCOTT and BORGMAN
INTERESTING ROUTE TO YOUR ROOM, DUDE.
AFTER HEARING THE QUESTION, "HOW WAS SCHOOL TODAY?" TEN MILLION TIMES, YOU LOOK FOR ALTERNATIVES.

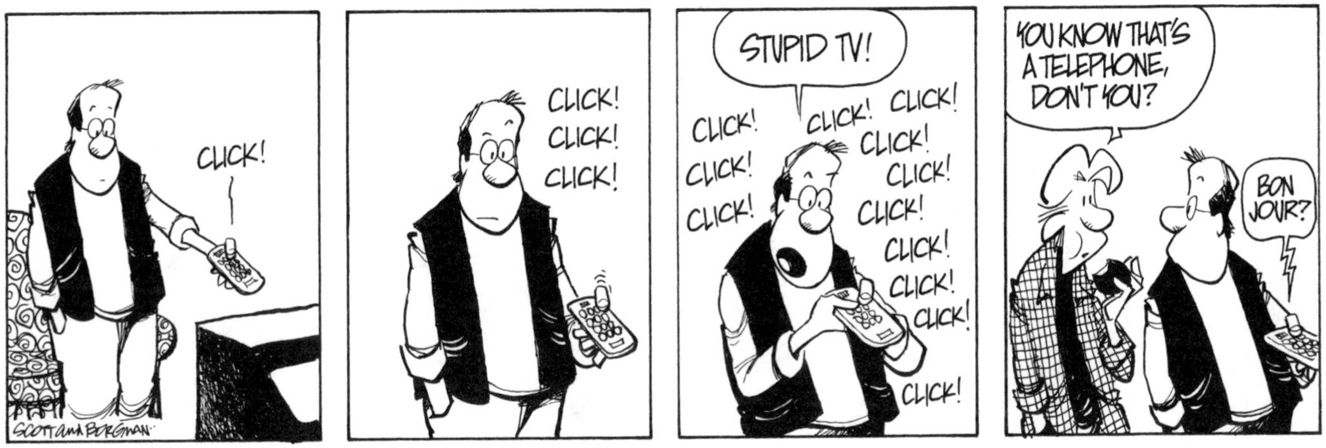
SCOTT AND BORGMAN
CLICK!
CLICK! CLICK! CLICK!
STUPID TV!
CLICK! CLICK! CLICK! CLICK! CLICK! CLICK! CLICK! CLICK! CLICK! CLICK! CLICK!
CLICK!
YOU KNOW THAT'S A TELEPHONE, DON'T YOU?
BON JOUR?

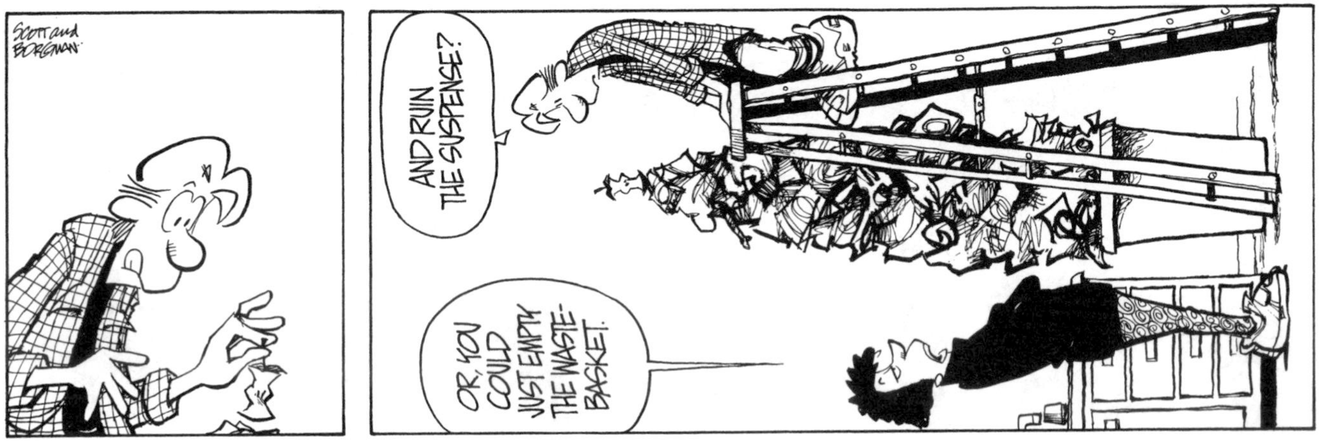
SCOTT AND BORGMAN
OR, YOU COULD JUST EMPTY THE WASTE-BASKET.
AND RUIN THE SUSPENSE?

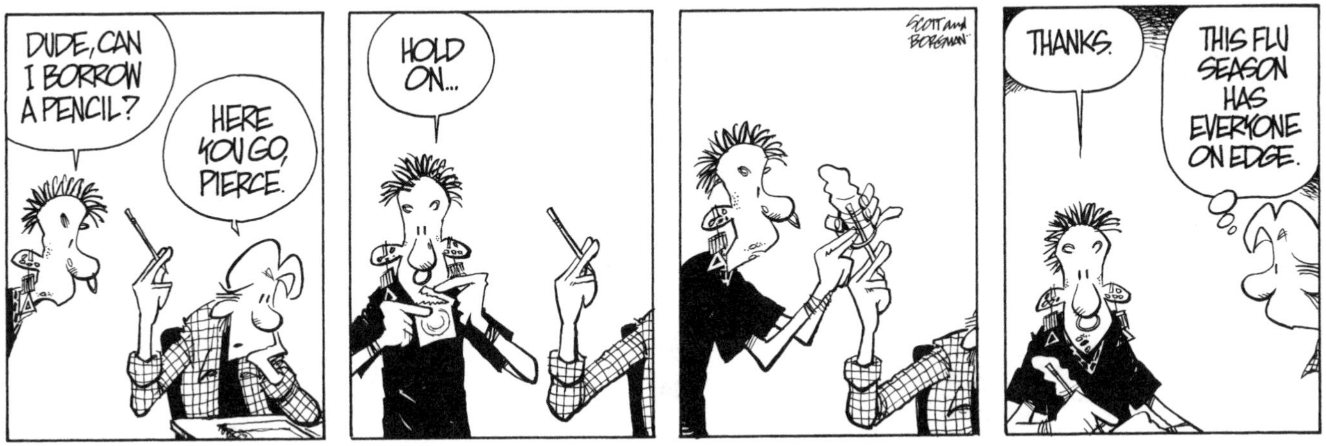
DUDE, CAN I BORROW A PENCIL?
HERE YOU GO, PIERCE.
HOLD ON...
SCOTT AND BORGMAN
THANKS.
THIS FLU SEASON HAS EVERYONE ON EDGE.

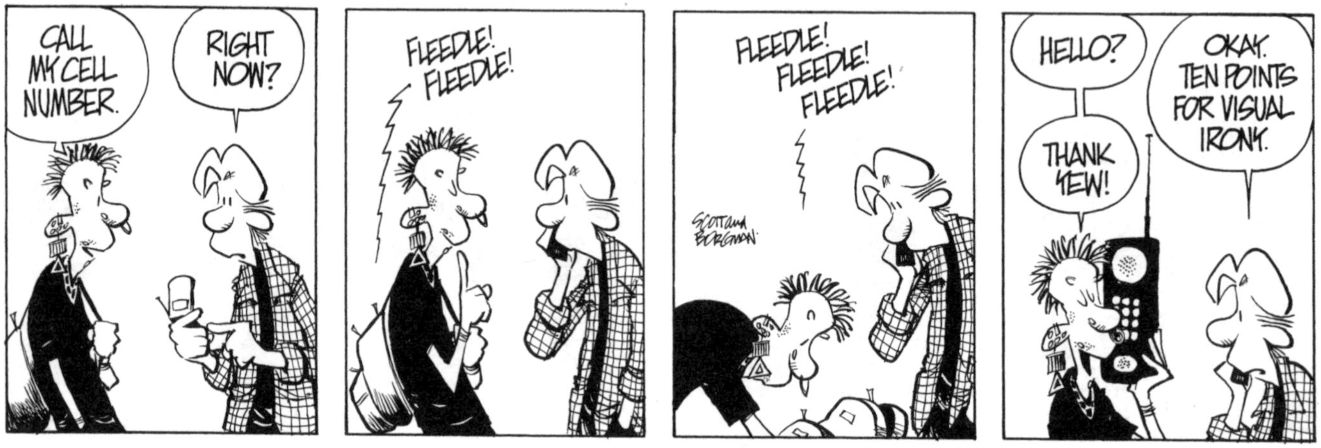
CALL MY CELL NUMBER.
RIGHT NOW?
FLEEDLE! FLEEDLE!
FLEEDLE! FLEEDLE! FLEEDLE!
SCOTT AND BORGMAN
HELLO?
THANK YEW!
OKAY. TEN POINTS FOR VISUAL IRONY.

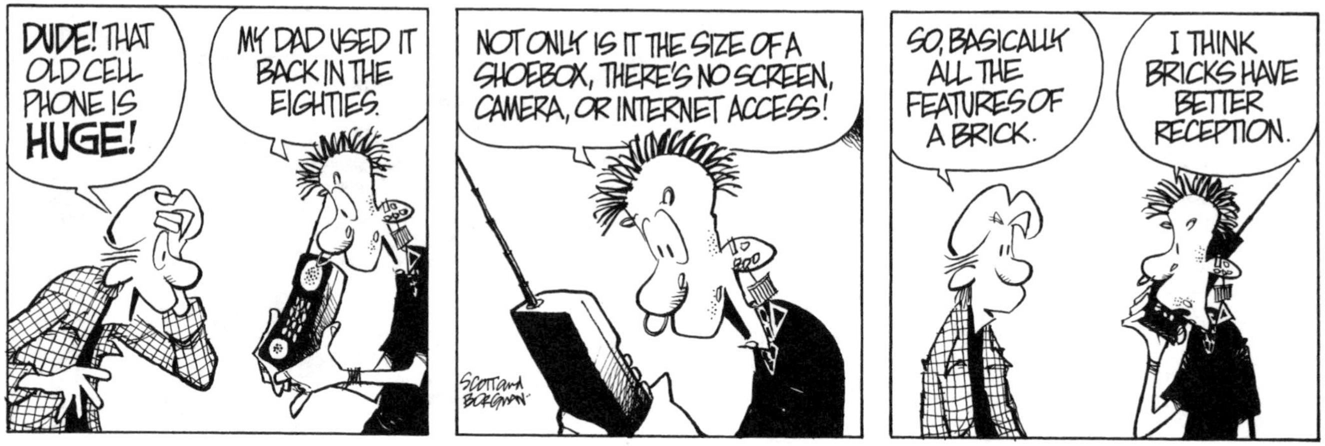
DUDE! THAT OLD CELL PHONE IS HUGE!
MY DAD USED IT BACK IN THE EIGHTIES.
NOT ONLY IS IT THE SIZE OF A SHOEBOX, THERE'S NO SCREEN, CAMERA, OR INTERNET ACCESS!
SCOTT AND BORGMAN
SO, BASICALLY ALL THE FEATURES OF A BRICK.
I THINK BRICKS HAVE BETTER RECEPTION.

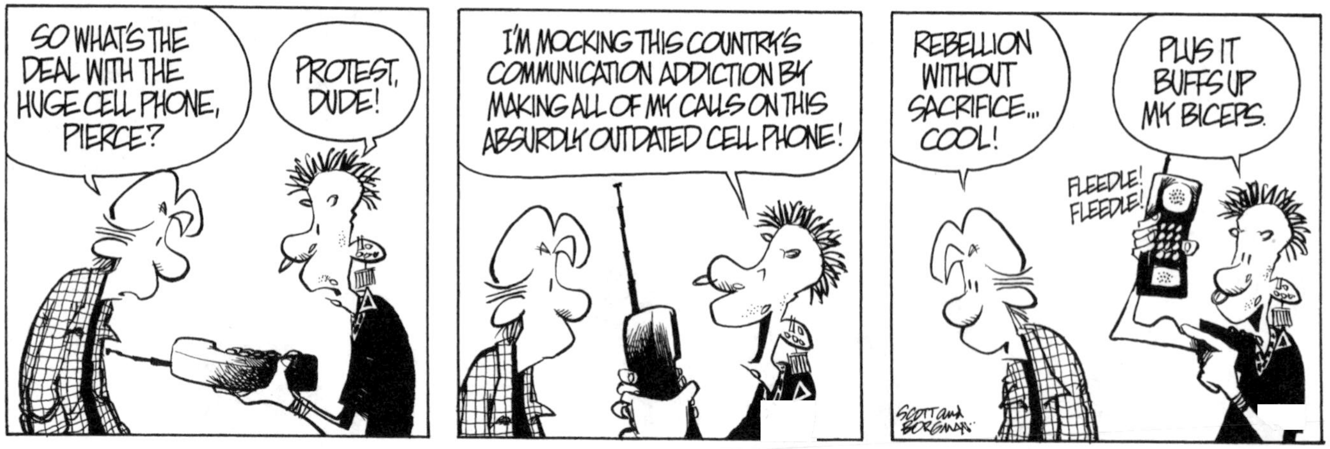
SO WHAT'S THE DEAL WITH THE HUGE CELL PHONE, PIERCE?
PROTEST, DUDE!
I'M MOCKING THIS COUNTRY'S COMMUNICATION ADDICTION BY MAKING ALL OF MY CALLS ON THIS ABSURDLY OUTDATED CELL PHONE!
REBELLION WITHOUT SACRIFICE... COOL!
PLUS IT BUFFS UP MY BICEPS.
FLEEDLE! FLEEDLE!
SCOTT AND BORGMAN

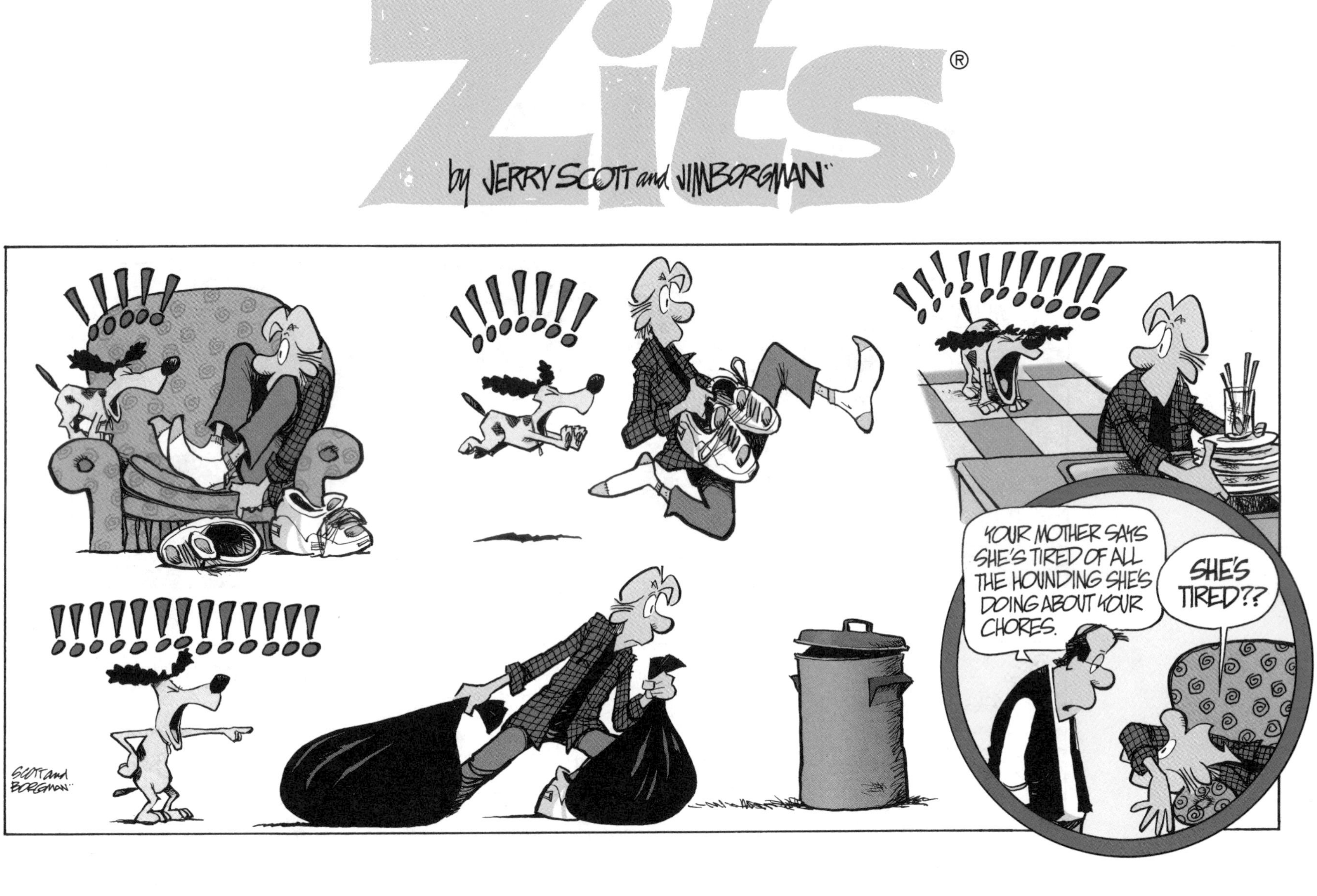
Zits®
by JERRY SCOTT and JIM BORGMAN
!!!!!
!!!!!!!
!!!!!!!!!!!
!!!!!!!!!!!!!!!
SCOTT and BORGMAN
YOUR MOTHER SAYS SHE'S TIRED OF ALL THE HOUNDING SHE'S DOING ABOUT YOUR CHORES.
SHE'S TIRED??

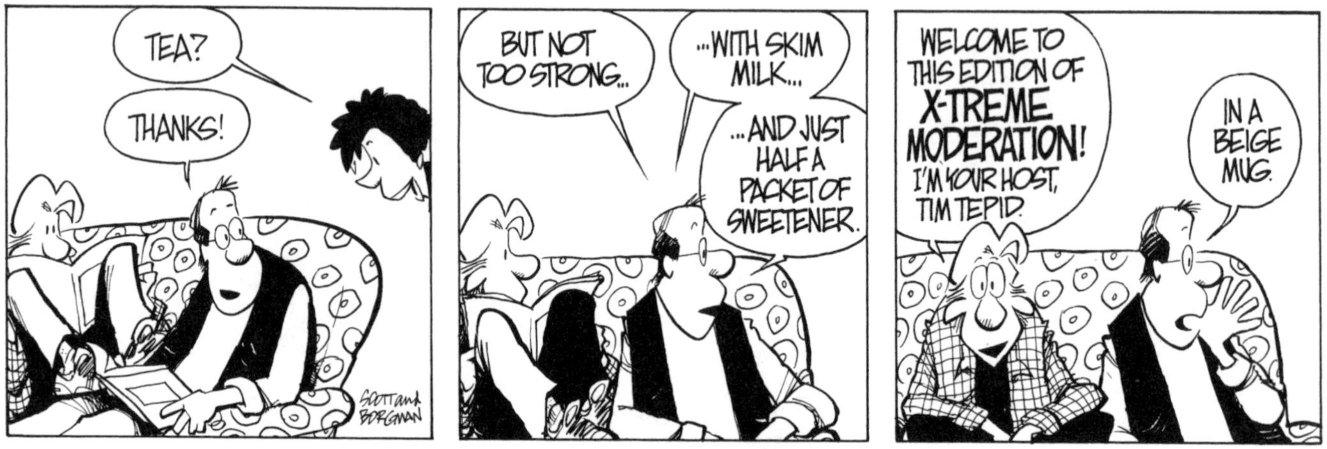
TEA?
THANKS!
BUT NOT TOO STRONG...
...WITH SKIM MILK...
...AND JUST HALF A PACKET OF SWEETENER.
WELCOME TO THIS EDITION OF X-TREME MODERATION! I'M YOUR HOST, TIM TEPID.
IN A BEIGE MUG.
SCOTT AND BORGMAN

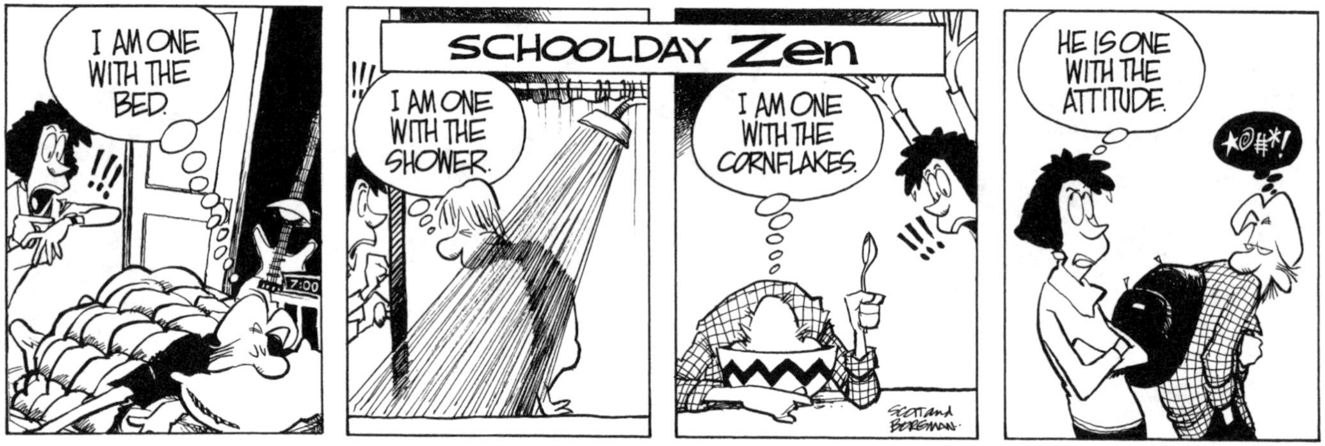
SCHOOLDAY Zen
I AM ONE WITH THE BED.
!!!
7:00
I AM ONE WITH THE SHOWER.
!!!
I AM ONE WITH THE CORNFLAKES.
!!!
HE IS ONE WITH THE ATTITUDE.
SCOTT AND BORGMAN

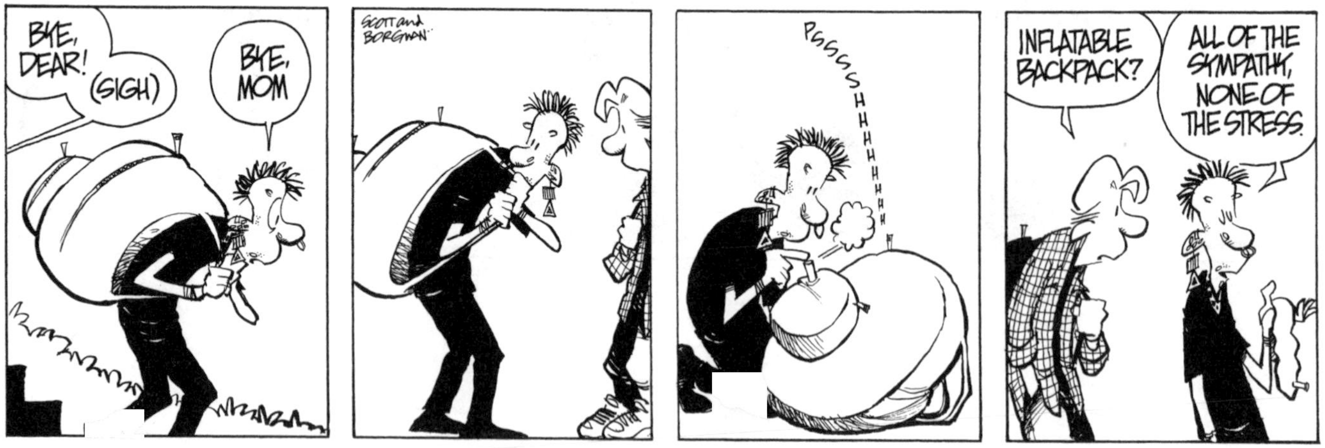
BYE, DEAR!
(SIGH)
BYE, MOM
SCOTT AND BORGMAN
PSSSSSHHHHHHHH
INFLATABLE BACKPACK?
ALL OF THE SYMPATHY, NONE OF THE STRESS.

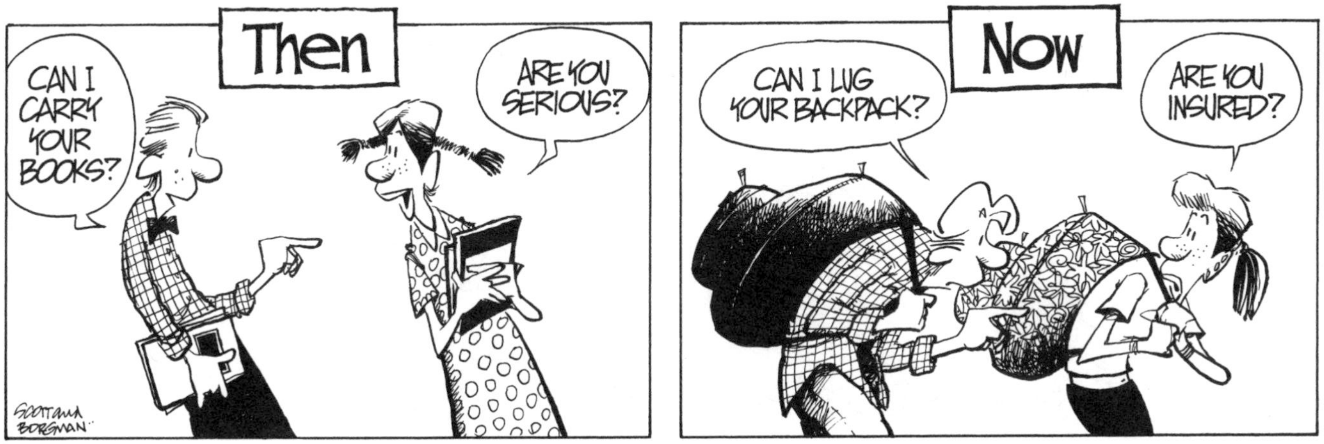
Then
CAN I CARRY YOUR BOOKS?
ARE YOU SERIOUS?
Now
CAN I LUG YOUR BACKPACK?
ARE YOU INSURED?
SCOTT AND BORGMAN

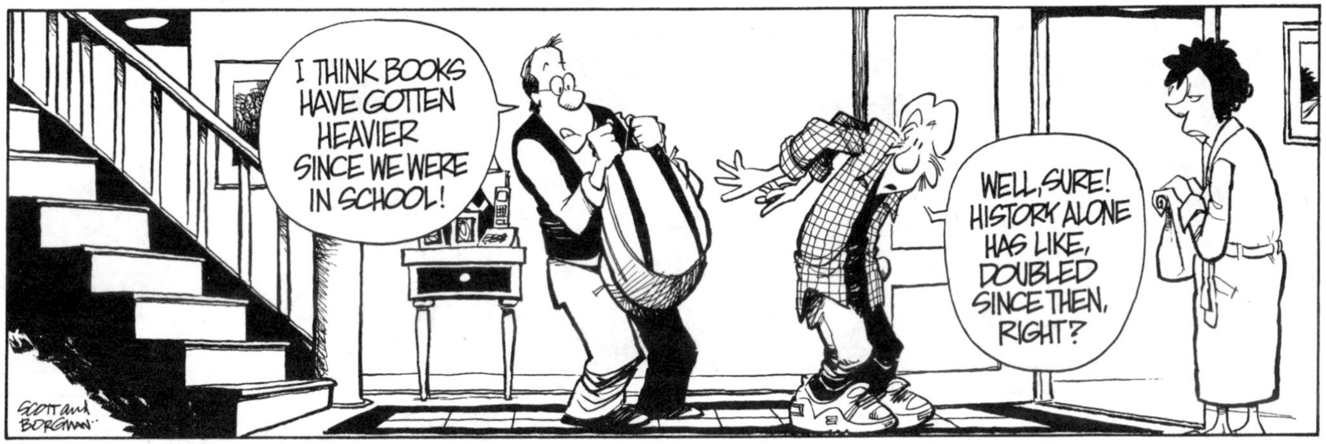
I THINK BOOKS HAVE GOTTEN HEAVIER SINCE WE WERE IN SCHOOL!
WELL, SURE! HISTORY ALONE HAS LIKE, DOUBLED SINCE THEN, RIGHT?
SCOTT AND BORGMAN

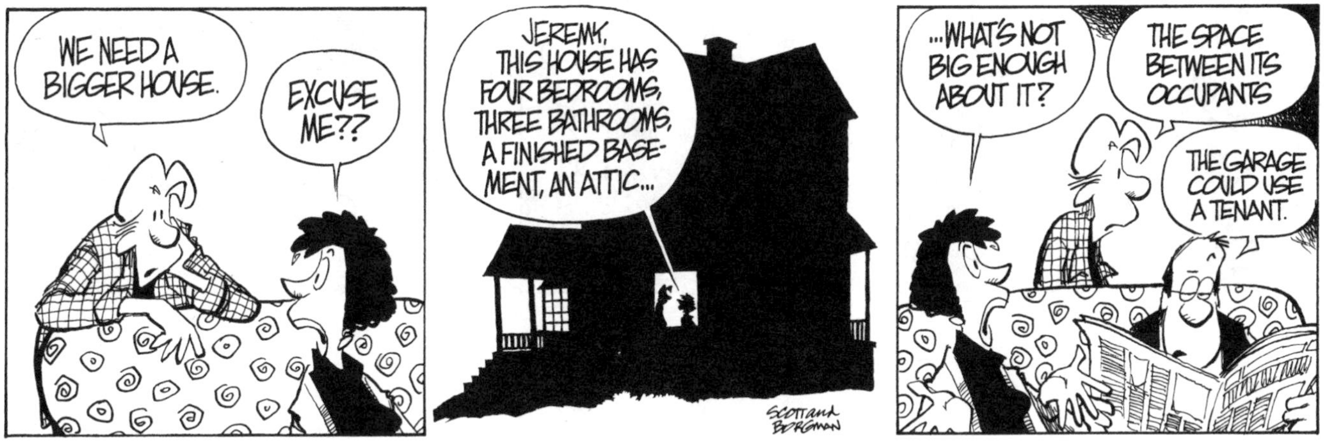
WE NEED A BIGGER HOUSE.
EXCUSE ME??
JEREMY, THIS HOUSE HAS FOUR BEDROOMS, THREE BATHROOMS, A FINISHED BASEMENT, AN ATTIC...
SCOTT AND BORGMAN
...WHAT'S NOT BIG ENOUGH ABOUT IT?
THE SPACE BETWEEN ITS OCCUPANTS
THE GARAGE COULD USE A TENANT.

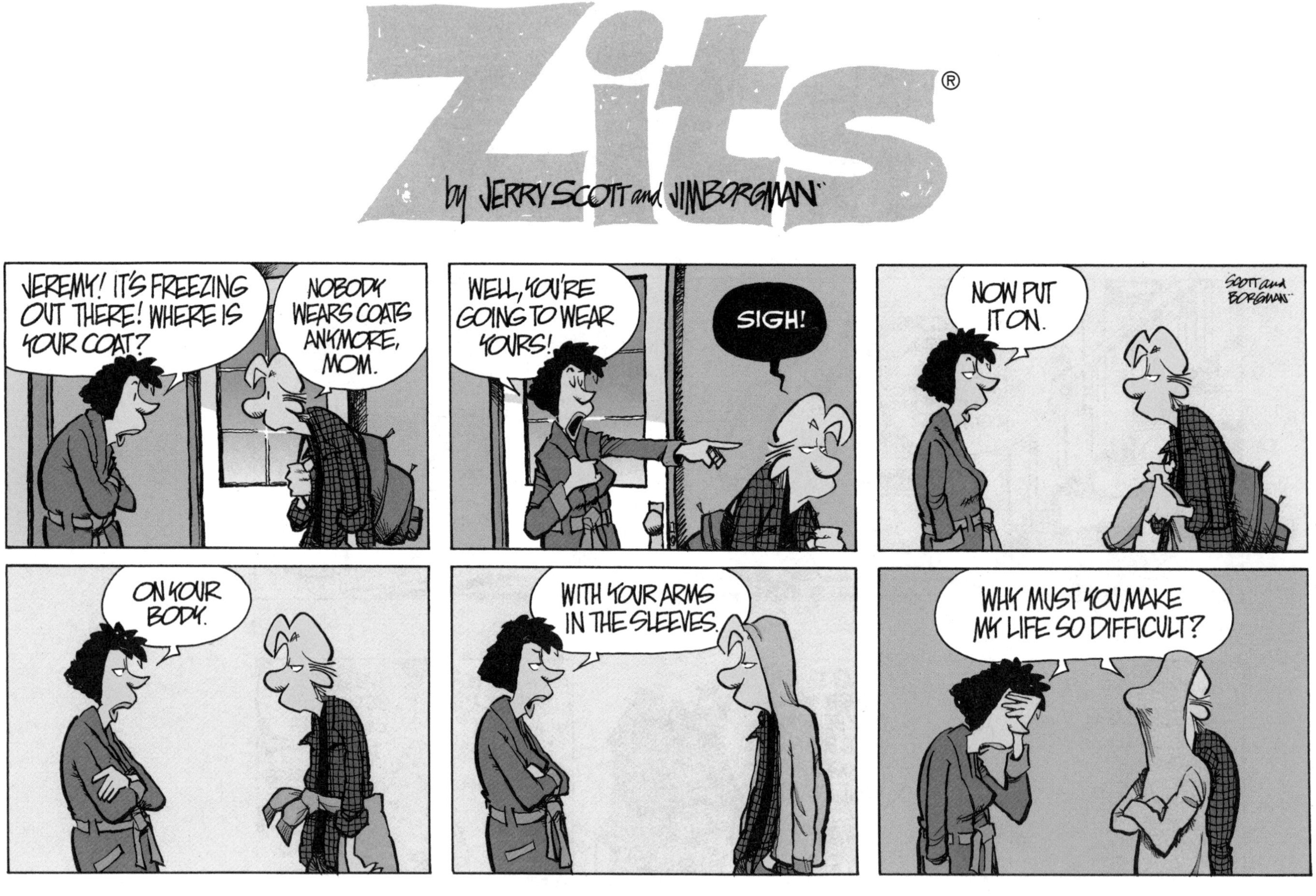
Zits®
by JERRY SCOTT and JIM BORGMAN
JEREMY! IT'S FREEZING OUT THERE! WHERE IS YOUR COAT?
NOBODY WEARS COATS ANYMORE, MOM.
WELL, YOU'RE GOING TO WEAR YOURS!
SIGH!
NOW PUT IT ON.
SCOTT and BORGMAN
ON YOUR BODY.
WITH YOUR ARMS IN THE SLEEVES.
WHY MUST YOU MAKE MY LIFE SO DIFFICULT?

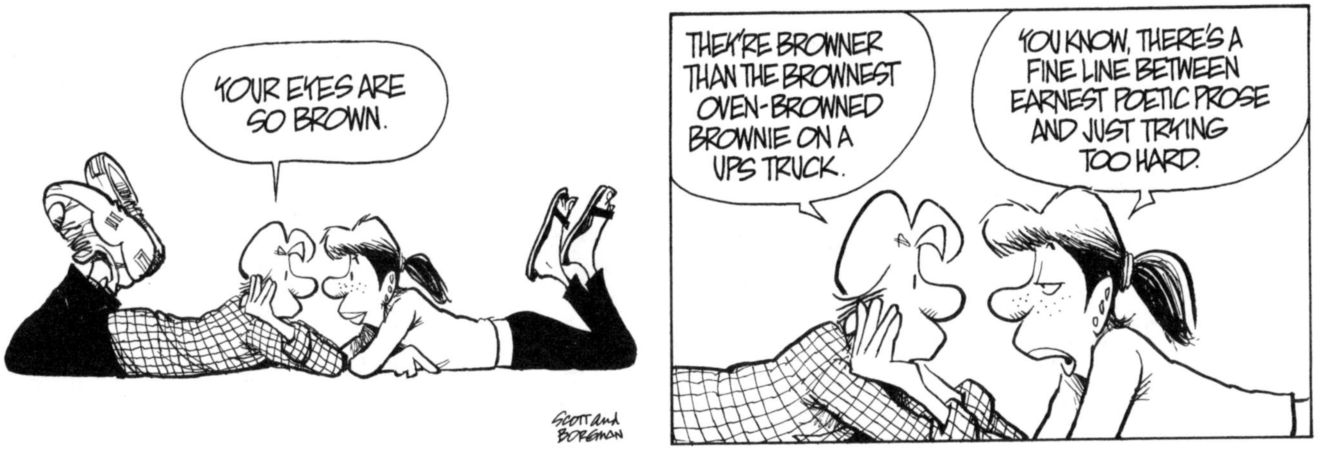
YOUR EYES ARE SO BROWN.
THEY'RE BROWNER THAN THE BROWNEST OVEN-BROWNED BROWNIE ON A UPS TRUCK.
YOU KNOW, THERE'S A FINE LINE BETWEEN EARNEST POETIC PROSE AND JUST TRYING TOO HARD.

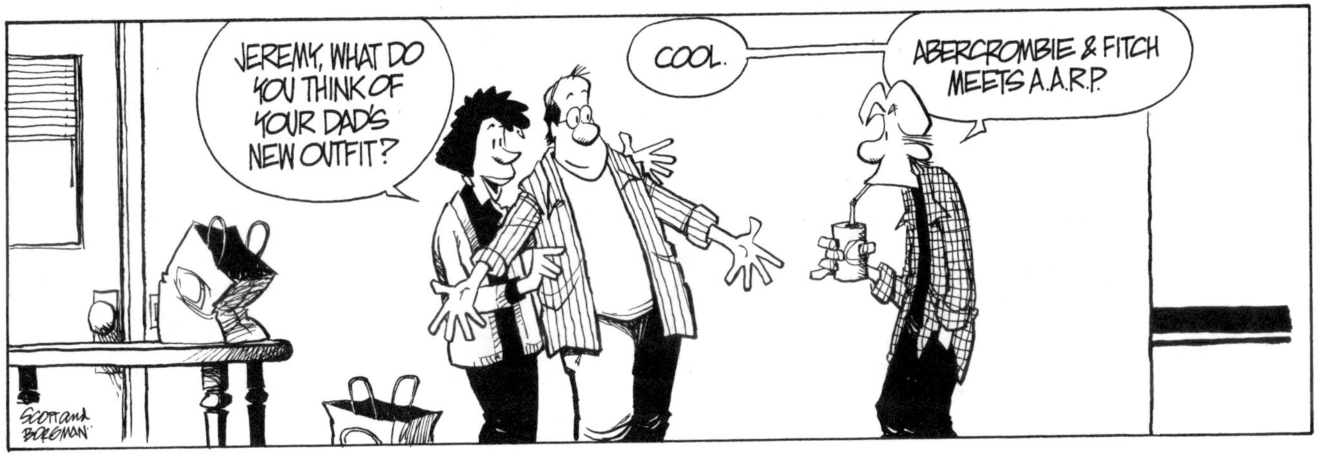
JEREMY, WHAT DO YOU THINK OF YOUR DAD'S NEW OUTFIT?
COOL.
ABERCROMBIE & FITCH MEETS A.A.R.P.

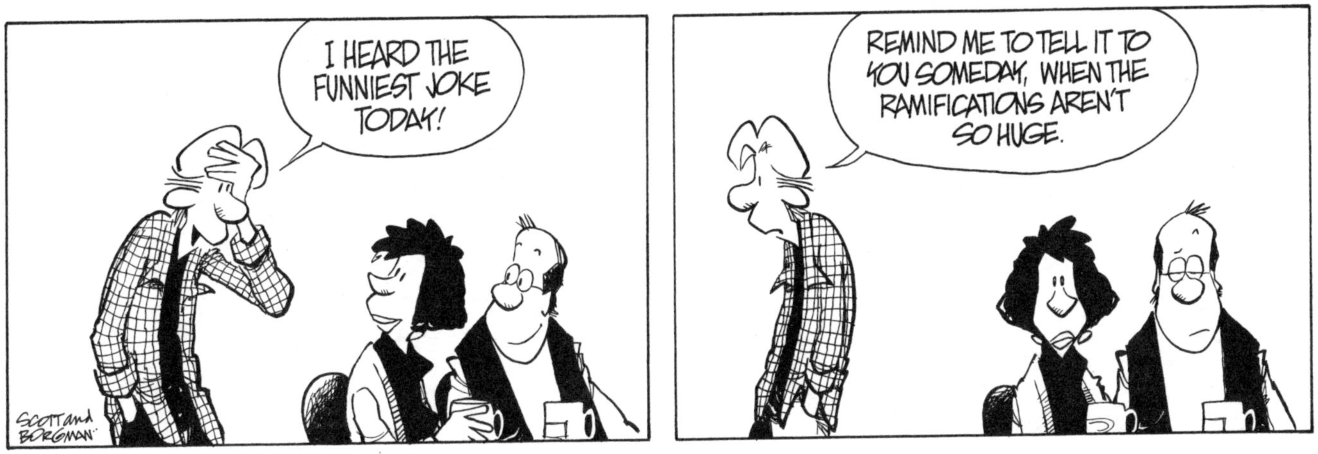
I HEARD THE FUNNIEST JOKE TODAY!
REMIND ME TO TELL IT TO YOU SOMEDAY, WHEN THE RAMIFICATIONS AREN'T SO HUGE.

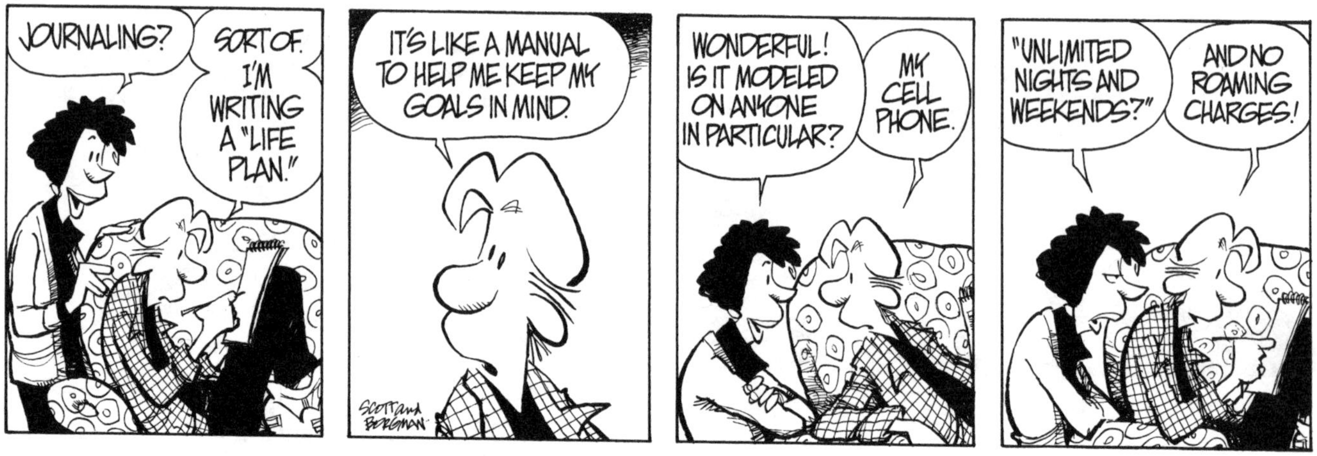
JOURNALING?
SORT OF. I'M WRITING A "LIFE PLAN."
IT'S LIKE A MANUAL TO HELP ME KEEP MY GOALS IN MIND.
WONDERFUL! IS IT MODELED ON ANYONE IN PARTICULAR?
MY CELL PHONE.
"UNLIMITED NIGHTS AND WEEKENDS?"
AND NO ROAMING CHARGES!

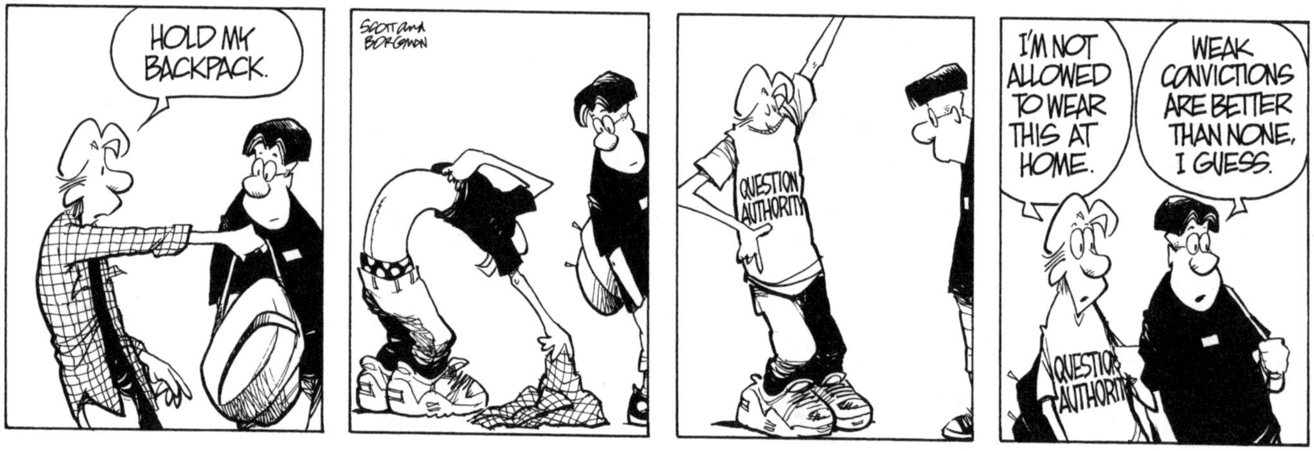
HOLD MY BACKPACK.
QUESTION AUTHORITY
I'M NOT ALLOWED TO WEAR THIS AT HOME.
WEAK CONVICTIONS ARE BETTER THAN NONE, I GUESS.
QUESTION AUTHORITY

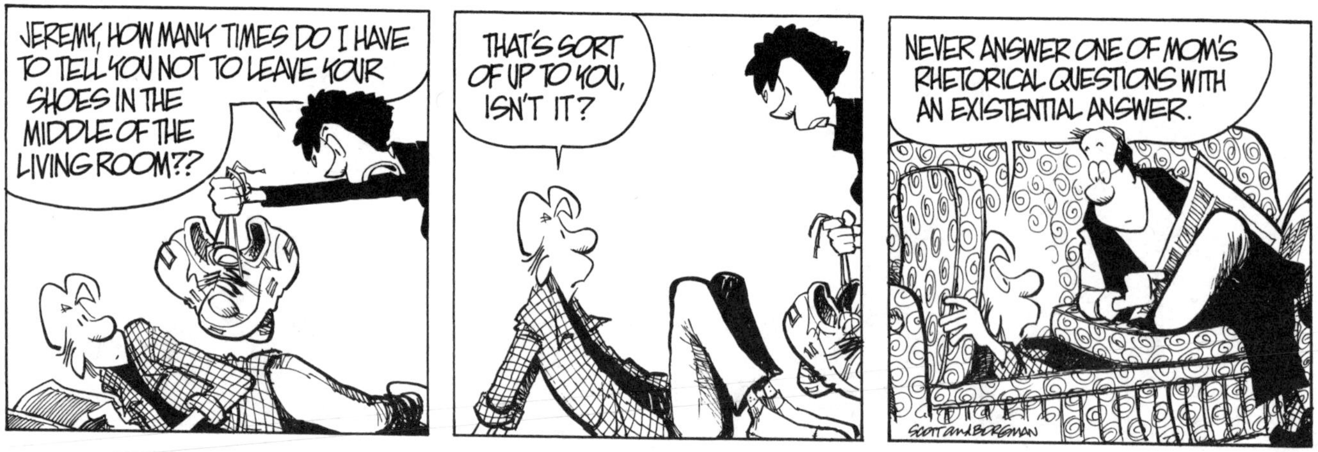
JEREMY, HOW MANY TIMES DO I HAVE TO TELL YOU NOT TO LEAVE YOUR SHOES IN THE MIDDLE OF THE LIVING ROOM??
THAT'S SORT OF UP TO YOU, ISN'T IT?
NEVER ANSWER ONE OF MOM'S RHETORICAL QUESTIONS WITH AN EXISTENTIAL ANSWER.

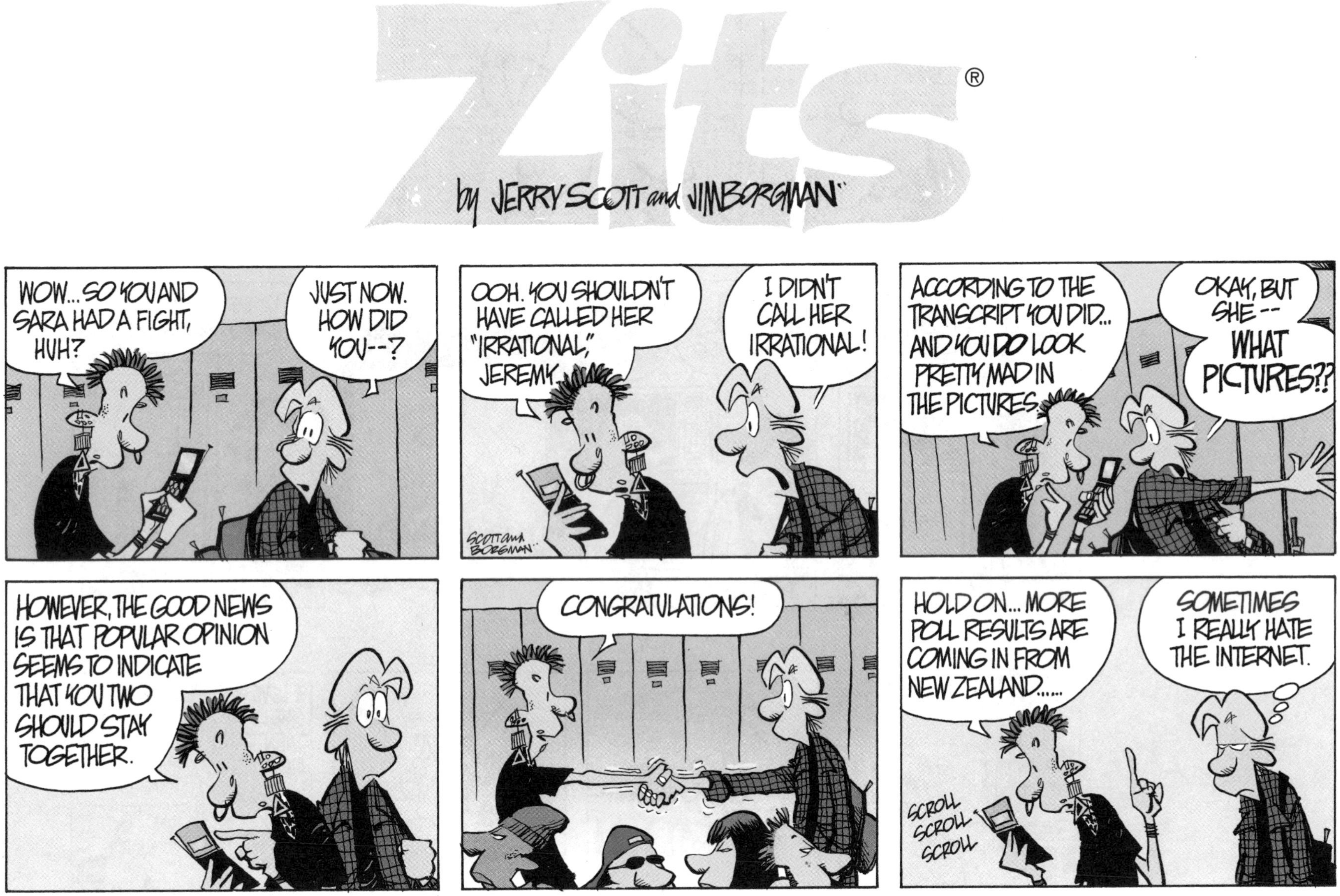
Zits®
by JERRY SCOTT and JIM BORGMAN
WOW... SO YOU AND SARA HAD A FIGHT, HUH?
JUST NOW. HOW DID YOU--?
OOH. YOU SHOULDN'T HAVE CALLED HER "IRRATIONAL," JEREMY.
I DIDN'T CALL HER IRRATIONAL!
ACCORDING TO THE TRANSCRIPT YOU DID... AND YOU DO LOOK PRETTY MAD IN THE PICTURES.
OKAY, BUT SHE -- WHAT PICTURES??
HOWEVER, THE GOOD NEWS IS THAT POPULAR OPINION SEEMS TO INDICATE THAT YOU TWO SHOULD STAY TOGETHER.
CONGRATULATIONS!
HOLD ON... MORE POLL RESULTS ARE COMING IN FROM NEW ZEALAND......
SCROLL SCROLL SCROLL
SOMETIMES I REALLY HATE THE INTERNET.

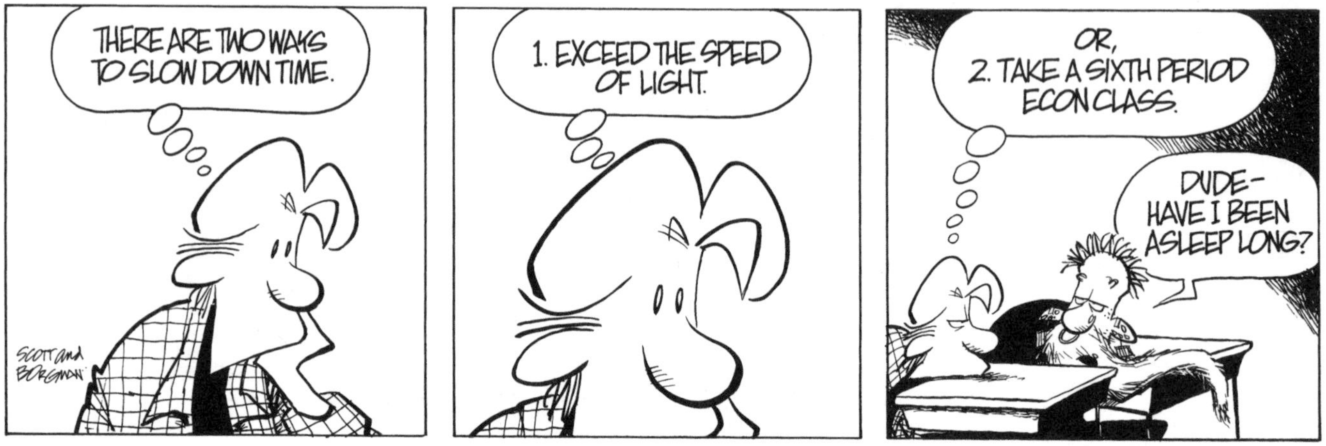
THERE ARE TWO WAYS TO SLOW DOWN TIME.
SCOTT and BORGMAN
1. EXCEED THE SPEED OF LIGHT.
OR, 2. TAKE A SIXTH PERIOD ECON CLASS.
DUDE- HAVE I BEEN ASLEEP LONG?

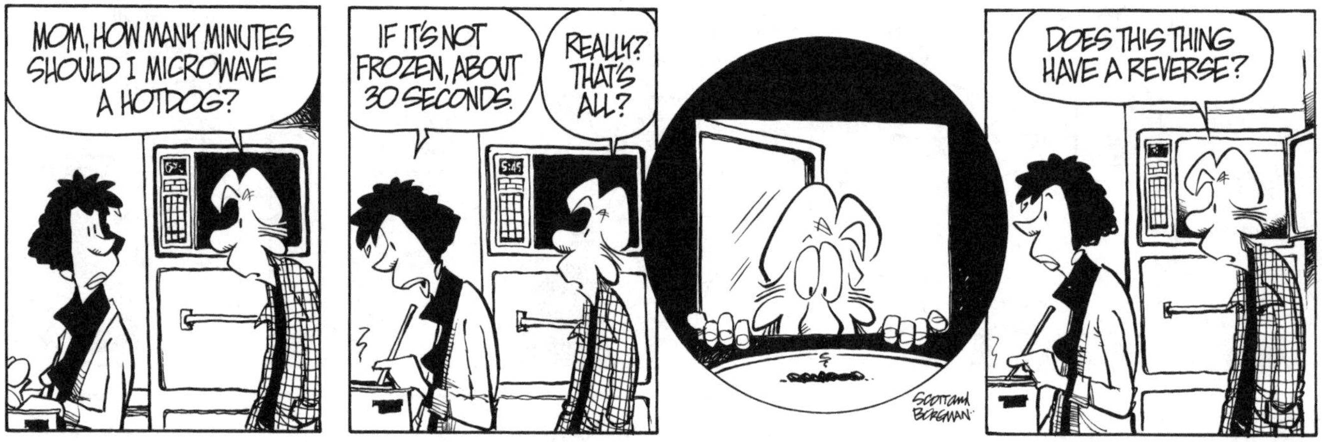
MOM, HOW MANY MINUTES SHOULD I MICROWAVE A HOTDOG?
IF IT'S NOT FROZEN, ABOUT 30 SECONDS.
REALLY? THAT'S ALL?
SCOTT and BORGMAN
DOES THIS THING HAVE A REVERSE?

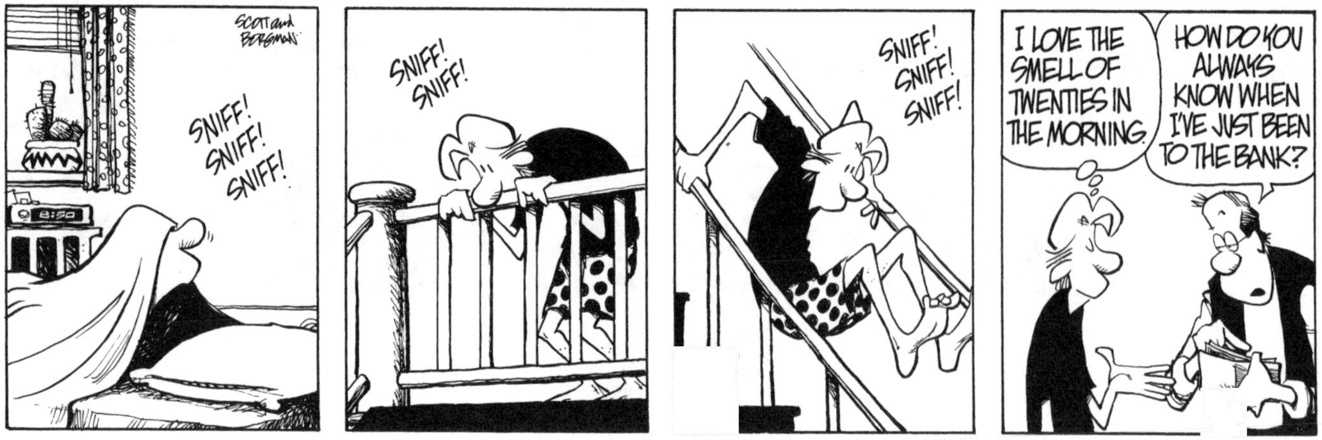
SCOTT and BORGMAN
SNIFF! SNIFF! SNIFF!
SNIFF! SNIFF!
SNIFF! SNIFF! SNIFF!
I LOVE THE SMELL OF TWENTIES IN THE MORNING.
HOW DO YOU ALWAYS KNOW WHEN I'VE JUST BEEN TO THE BANK?

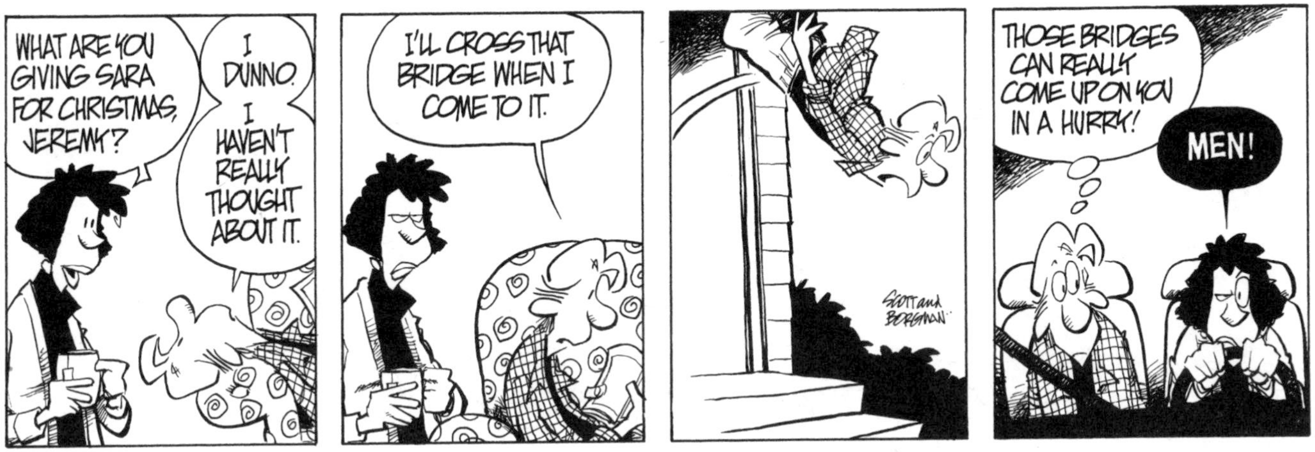
WHAT ARE YOU GIVING SARA FOR CHRISTMAS, JEREMY?
I DUNNO.
I HAVEN'T REALLY THOUGHT ABOUT IT.
I'LL CROSS THAT BRIDGE WHEN I COME TO IT.
SCOTT and BORGMAN
THOSE BRIDGES CAN REALLY COME UP ON YOU IN A HURRY!
MEN!

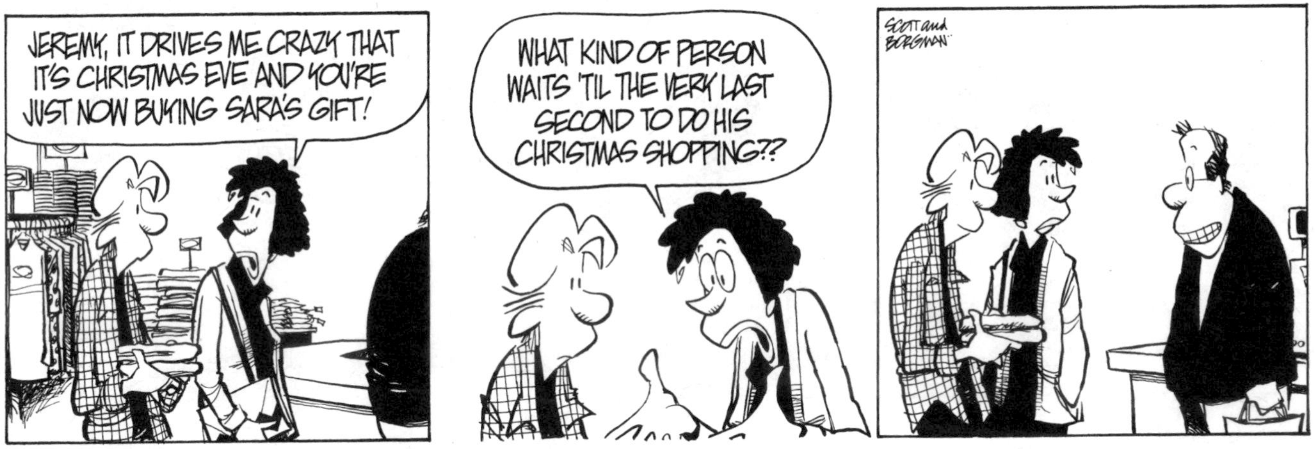
JEREMY, IT DRIVES ME CRAZY THAT IT'S CHRISTMAS EVE AND YOU'RE JUST NOW BUYING SARA'S GIFT!
WHAT KIND OF PERSON WAITS 'TIL THE VERY LAST SECOND TO DO HIS CHRISTMAS SHOPPING??
SCOTT and BORGMAN

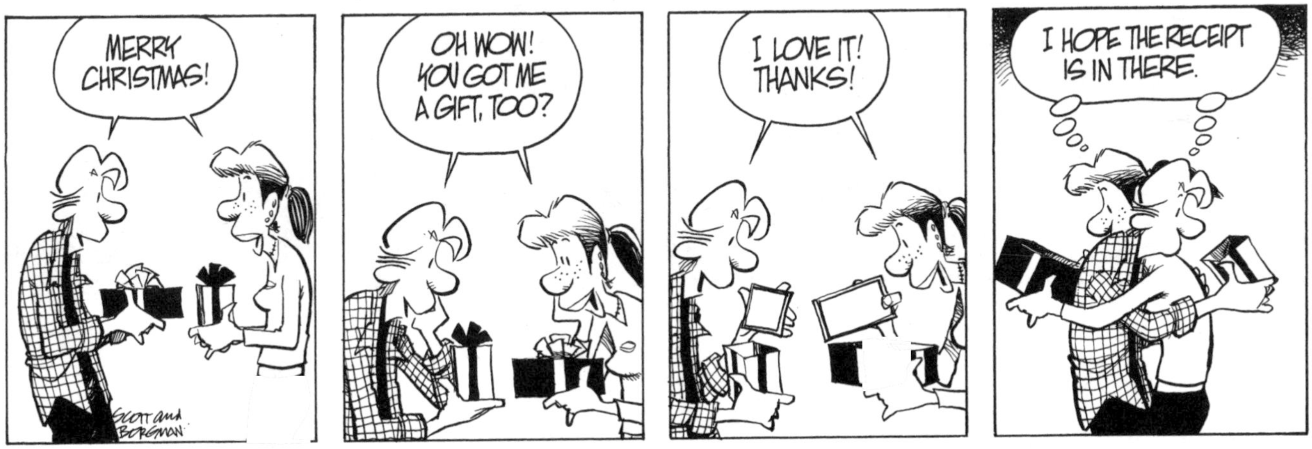
MERRY CHRISTMAS!
SCOTT and BORGMAN
OH WOW! YOU GOT ME A GIFT, TOO?
I LOVE IT! THANKS!
I HOPE THE RECEIPT IS IN THERE.

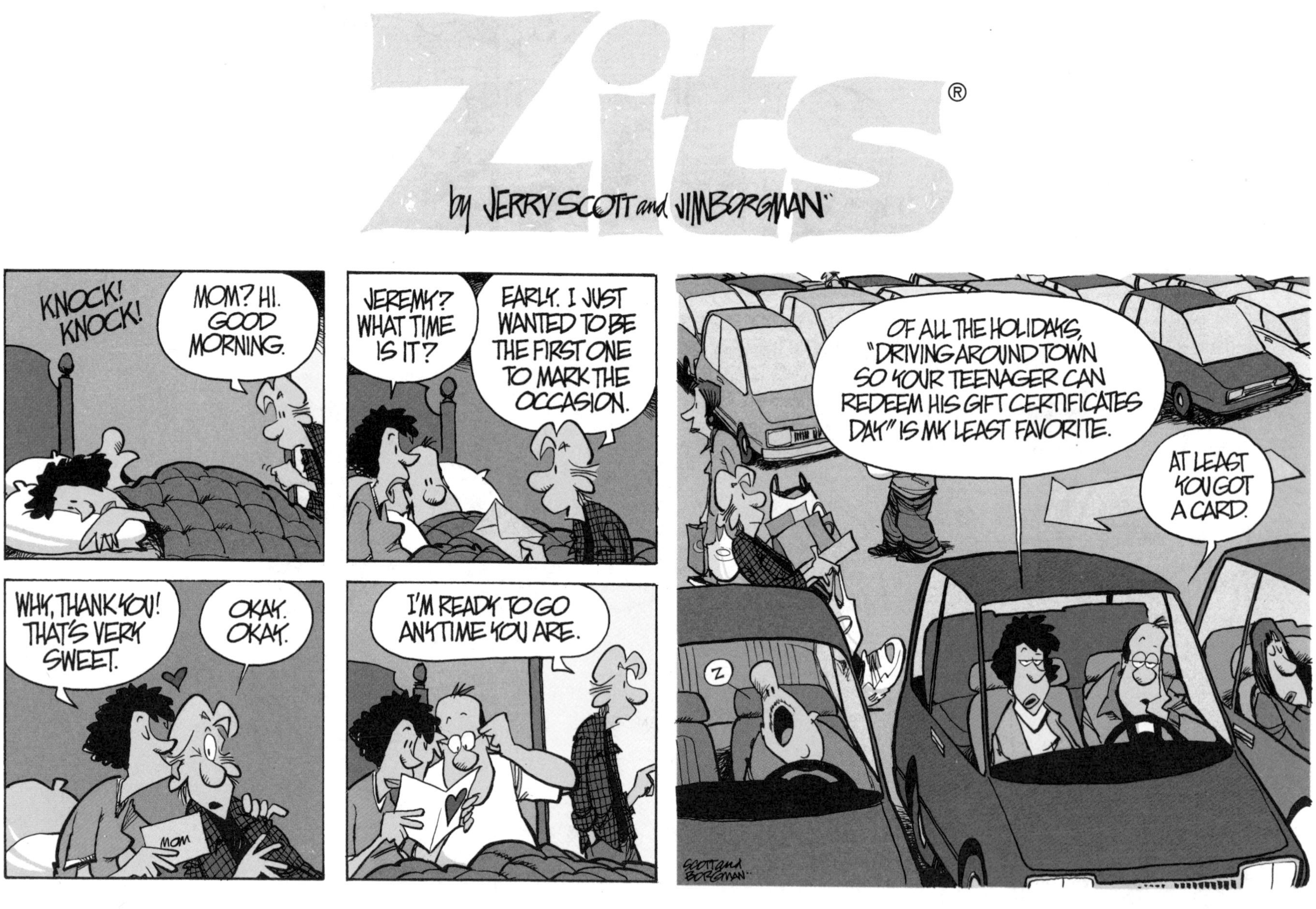
Zits®
by JERRY SCOTT and JIM BORGMAN
KNOCK! KNOCK!
MOM? HI. GOOD MORNING.
JEREMY? WHAT TIME IS IT?
EARLY. I JUST WANTED TO BE THE FIRST ONE TO MARK THE OCCASION.
WHY, THANK YOU! THAT'S VERY SWEET.
OKAY. OKAY.
MOM
I'M READY TO GO ANYTIME YOU ARE.
OF ALL THE HOLIDAYS, "DRIVING AROUND TOWN SO YOUR TEENAGER CAN REDEEM HIS GIFT CERTIFICATES DAY" IS MY LEAST FAVORITE.
AT LEAST YOU GOT A CARD.
Z
SCOTT and BORGMAN

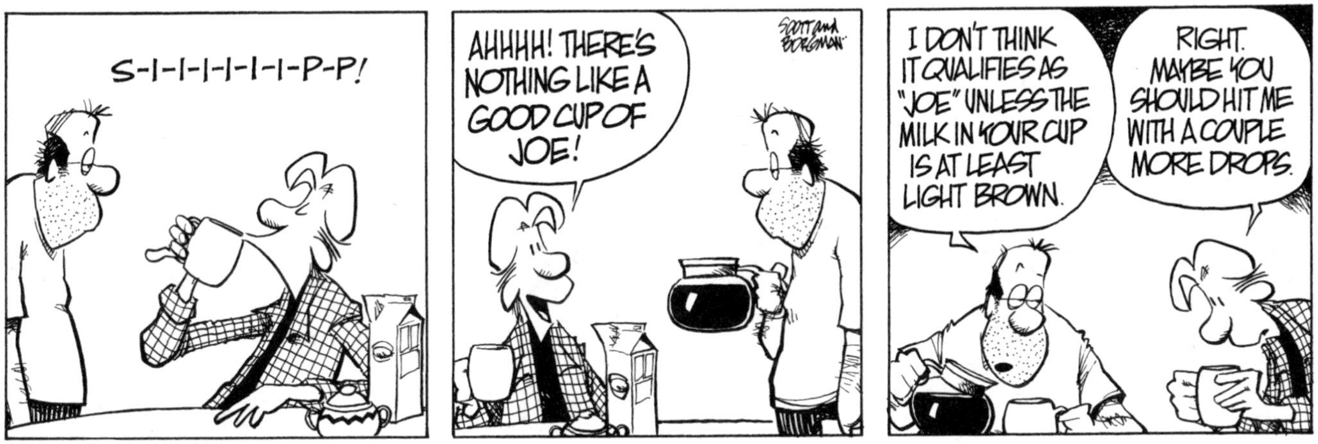
S-I-I-I-I-I-I-I-P-P!
AHHHH! THERE'S NOTHING LIKE A GOOD CUP OF JOE!
SCOTT AND BORGMAN
I DON'T THINK IT QUALIFIES AS "JOE" UNLESS THE MILK IN YOUR CUP IS AT LEAST LIGHT BROWN.
RIGHT. MAYBE YOU SHOULD HIT ME WITH A COUPLE MORE DROPS.

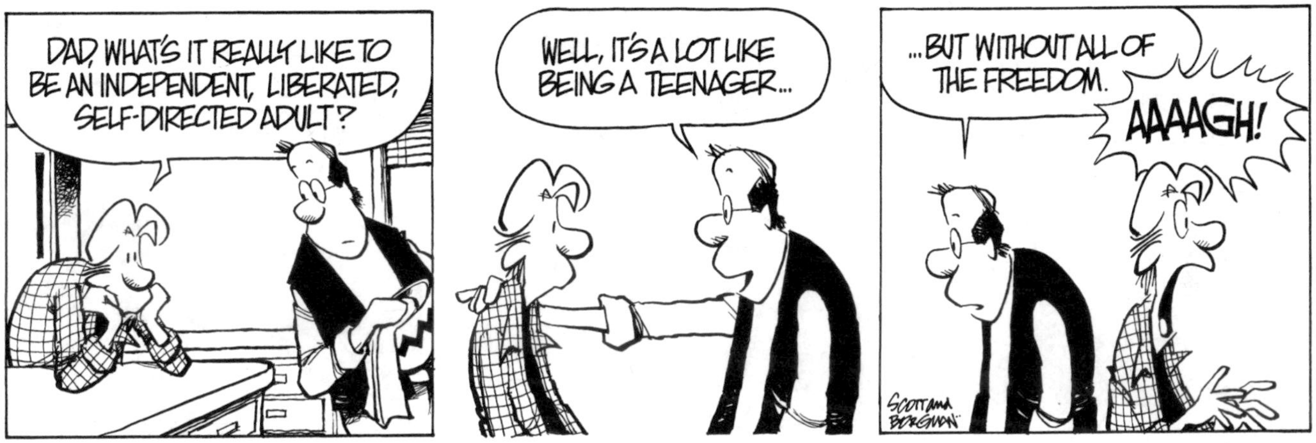
DAD, WHAT'S IT REALLY LIKE TO BE AN INDEPENDENT, LIBERATED, SELF-DIRECTED ADULT?
WELL, IT'S A LOT LIKE BEING A TEENAGER...
...BUT WITHOUT ALL OF THE FREEDOM.
AAAAGH!
SCOTT AND BORGMAN

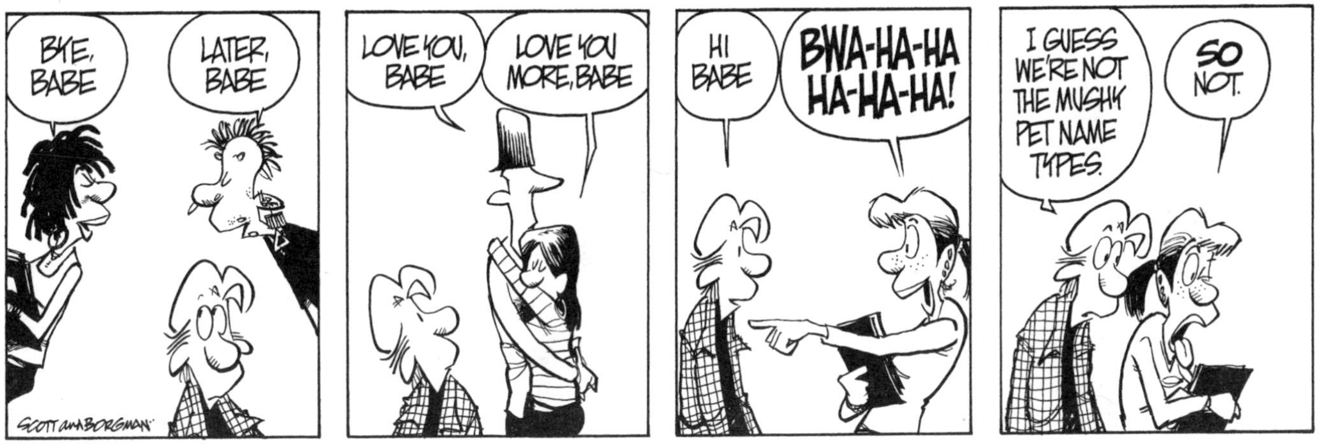
BYE, BABE
LATER, BABE
SCOTT AND BORGMAN
LOVE YOU, BABE
LOVE YOU MORE, BABE
HI BABE
BWA-HA-HA HA-HA-HA!
I GUESS WE'RE NOT THE MUSHY PET NAME TYPES.
SO NOT.

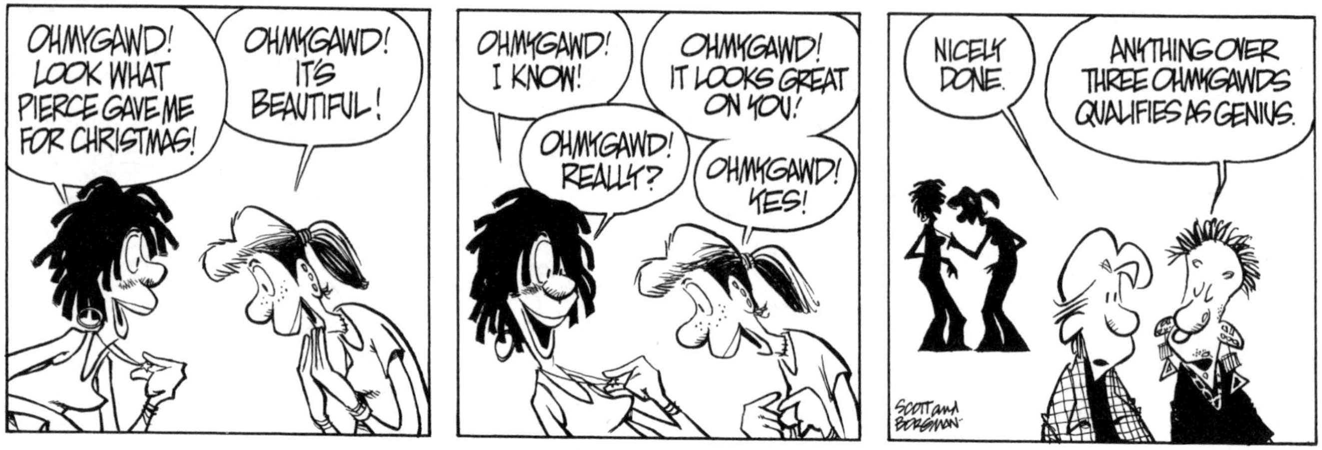

OHMYGAWD! LOOK WHAT PIERCE GAVE ME FOR CHRISTMAS!
OHMYGAWD! IT'S BEAUTIFUL!
OHMYGAWD! I KNOW!
OHMYGAWD! IT LOOKS GREAT ON YOU!
OHMYGAWD! REALLY?
OHMYGAWD! YES!
NICELY DONE.
ANYTHING OVER THREE OHMYGAWDS QUALIFIES AS GENIUS.
SCOTT and BORGMAN

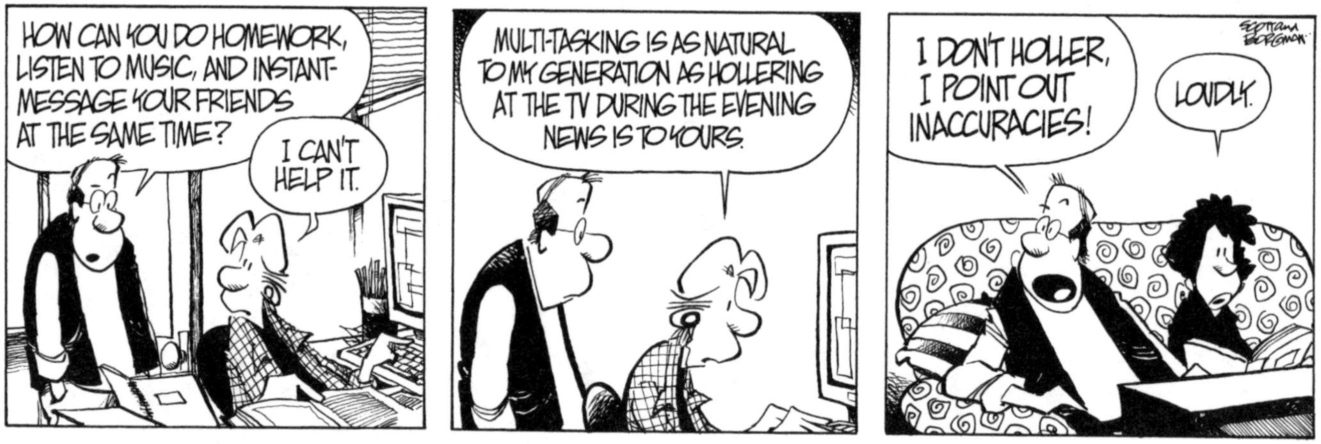

HOW CAN YOU DO HOMEWORK, LISTEN TO MUSIC, AND INSTANT-MESSAGE YOUR FRIENDS AT THE SAME TIME?
I CAN'T HELP IT.
MULTI-TASKING IS AS NATURAL TO MY GENERATION AS HOLLERING AT THE TV DURING THE EVENING NEWS IS TO YOURS.
I DON'T HOLLER, I POINT OUT INACCURACIES!
LOUDLY.
SCOTT and BORGMAN

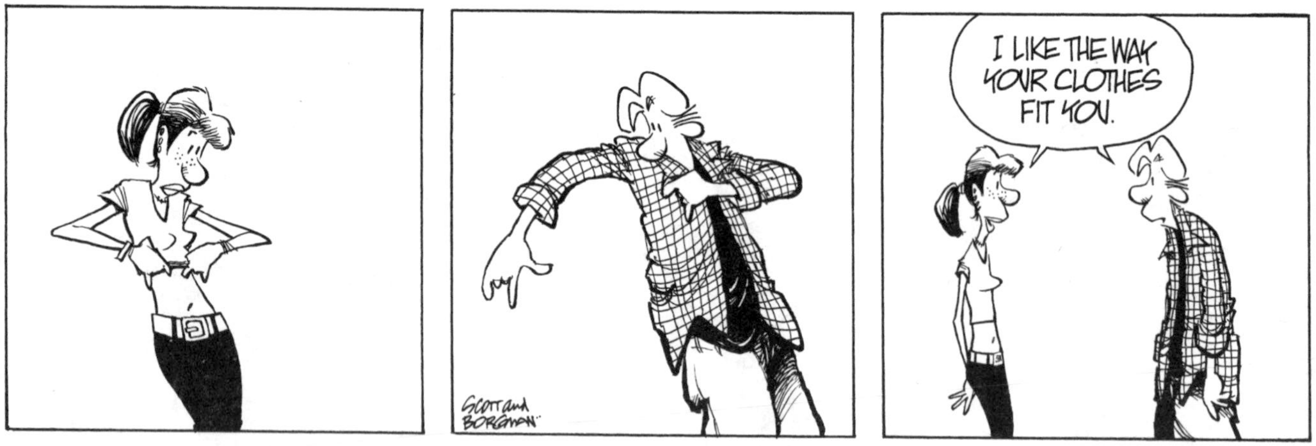

SCOTT and BORGMAN
I LIKE THE WAY YOUR CLOTHES FIT YOU.

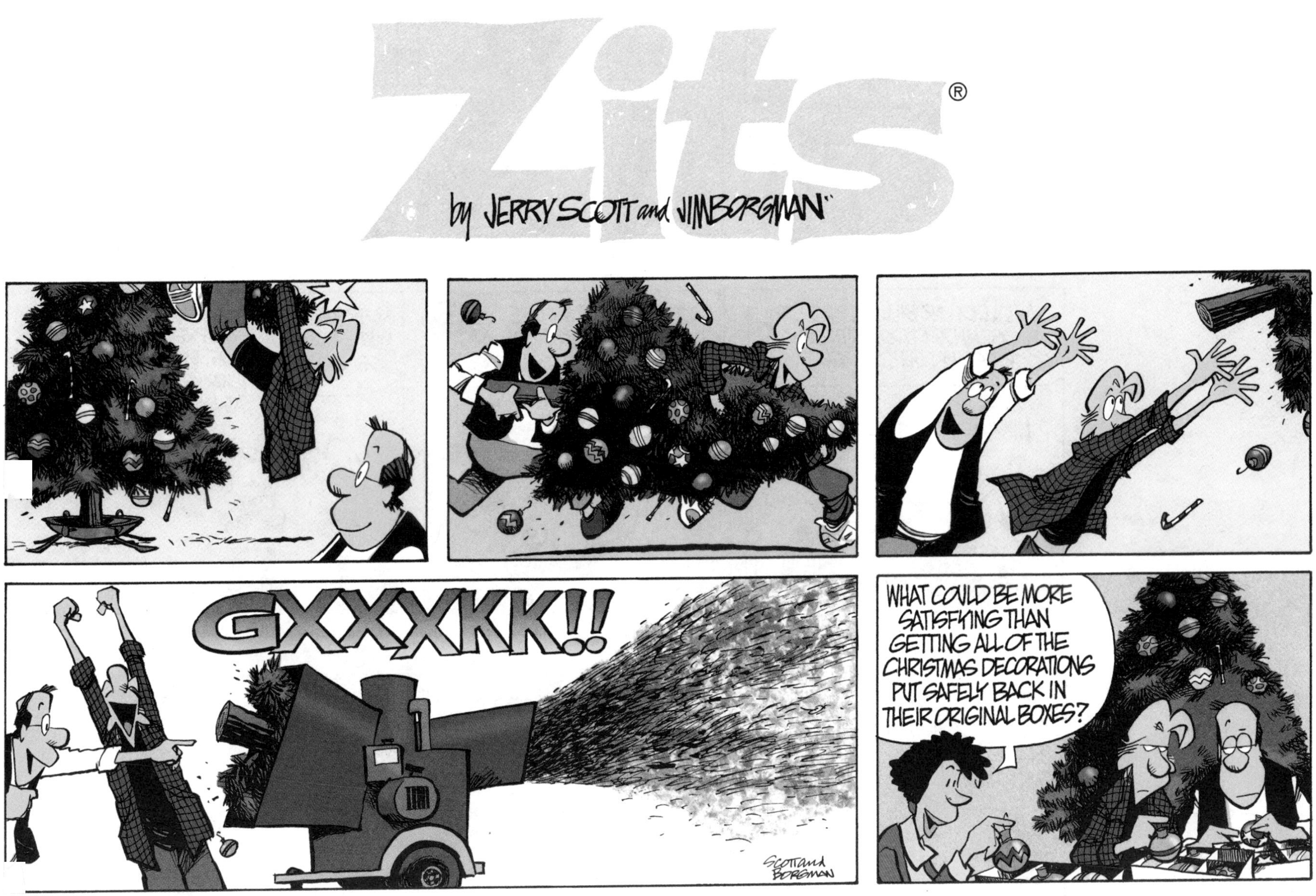
Zits®
by JERRY SCOTT and JIM BORGMAN
GXXXKK!!
SCOTT and BORGMAN
WHAT COULD BE MORE SATISFYING THAN GETTING ALL OF THE CHRISTMAS DECORATIONS PUT SAFELY BACK IN THEIR ORIGINAL BOXES?

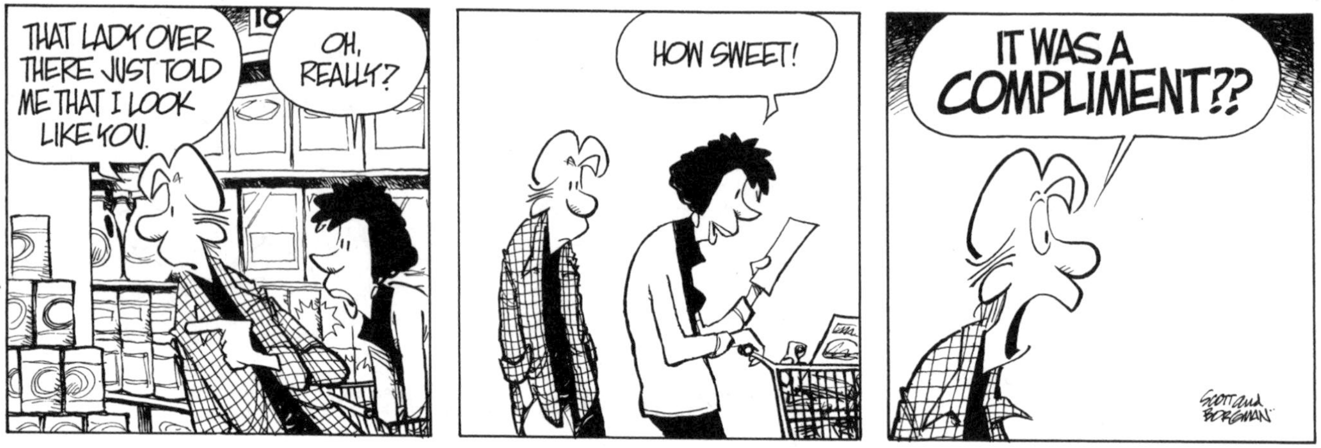
THAT LADY OVER THERE JUST TOLD ME THAT I LOOK LIKE YOU.
OH, REALLY?
HOW SWEET!
IT WAS A COMPLIMENT??

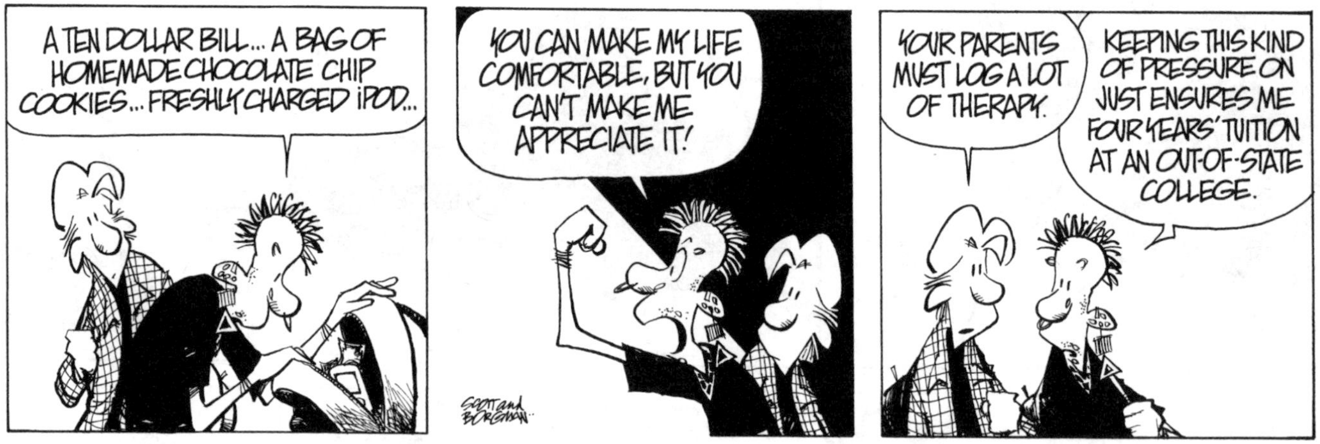
A TEN DOLLAR BILL... A BAG OF HOMEMADE CHOCOLATE CHIP COOKIES... FRESHLY CHARGED iPOD...
YOU CAN MAKE MY LIFE COMFORTABLE, BUT YOU CAN'T MAKE ME APPRECIATE IT!
YOUR PARENTS MUST LOG A LOT OF THERAPY.
KEEPING THIS KIND OF PRESSURE ON JUST ENSURES ME FOUR YEARS' TUITION AT AN OUT-OF-STATE COLLEGE.

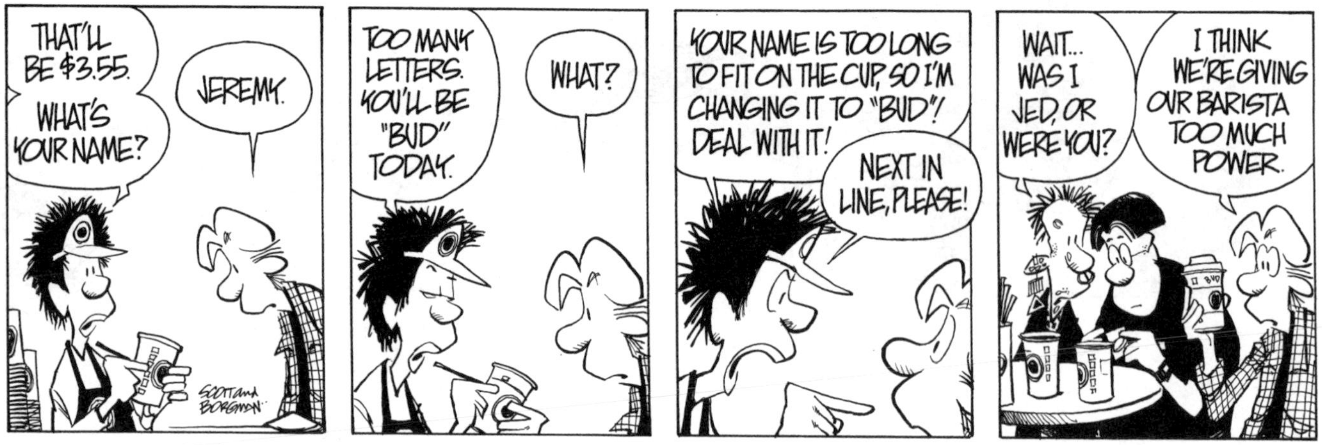
THAT'LL BE $3.55.
WHAT'S YOUR NAME?
JEREMY.
TOO MANY LETTERS. YOU'LL BE "BUD" TODAY.
WHAT?
YOUR NAME IS TOO LONG TO FIT ON THE CUP, SO I'M CHANGING IT TO "BUD"! DEAL WITH IT!
NEXT IN LINE, PLEASE!
WAIT... WAS I JED, OR WERE YOU?
I THINK WE'RE GIVING OUR BARISTA TOO MUCH POWER.

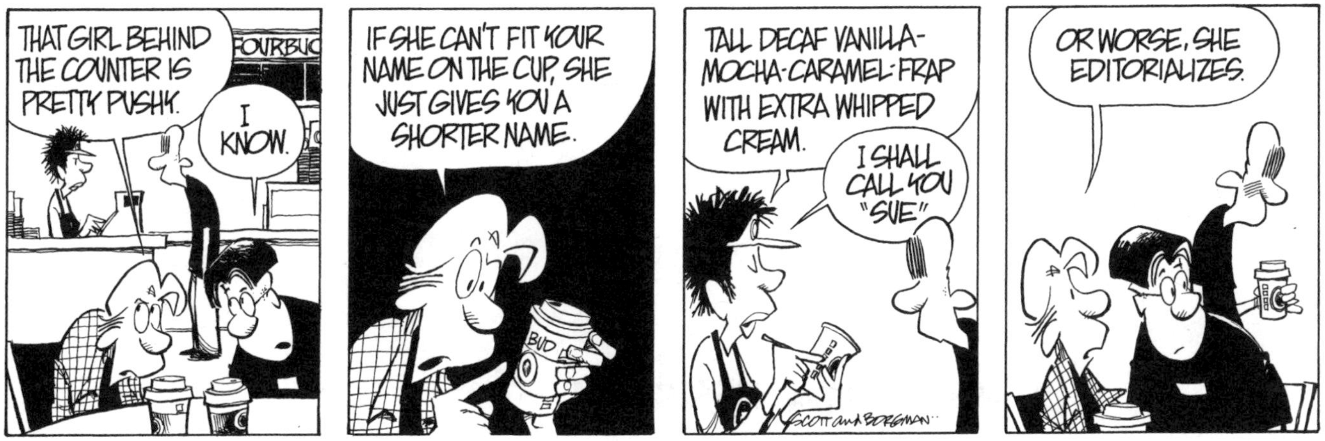
THAT GIRL BEHIND THE COUNTER IS PRETTY PUSHY.
I KNOW.
IF SHE CAN'T FIT YOUR NAME ON THE CUP, SHE JUST GIVES YOU A SHORTER NAME.
BUD
TALL DECAF VANILLA-MOCHA-CARAMEL-FRAP WITH EXTRA WHIPPED CREAM.
I SHALL CALL YOU "SUE"
OR WORSE, SHE EDITORIALIZES.
SCOTT AND BORGMAN

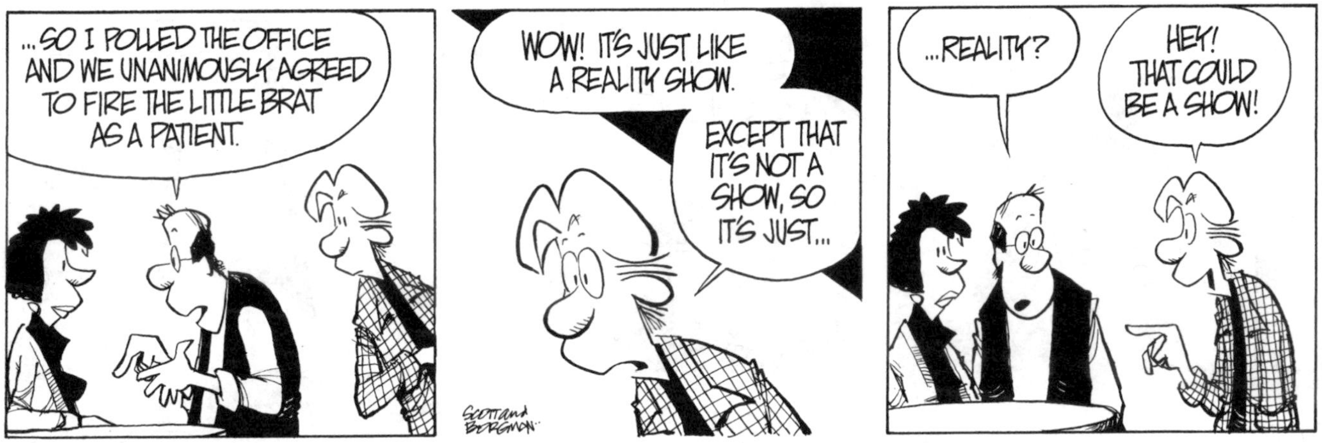
...SO I POLLED THE OFFICE AND WE UNANIMOUSLY AGREED TO FIRE THE LITTLE BRAT AS A PATIENT.
WOW! IT'S JUST LIKE A REALITY SHOW.
EXCEPT THAT IT'S NOT A SHOW, SO IT'S JUST...
...REALITY?
HEY! THAT COULD BE A SHOW!
SCOTT AND BORGMAN

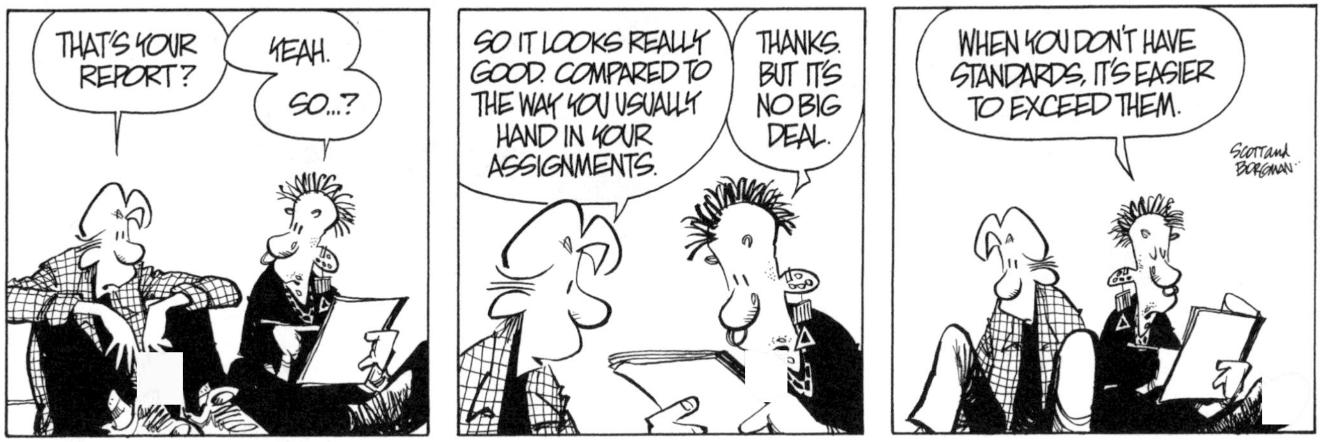
THAT'S YOUR REPORT?
YEAH.
SO...?
SO IT LOOKS REALLY GOOD. COMPARED TO THE WAY YOU USUALLY HAND IN YOUR ASSIGNMENTS.
THANKS. BUT IT'S NO BIG DEAL.
WHEN YOU DON'T HAVE STANDARDS, IT'S EASIER TO EXCEED THEM.
SCOTT AND BORGMAN

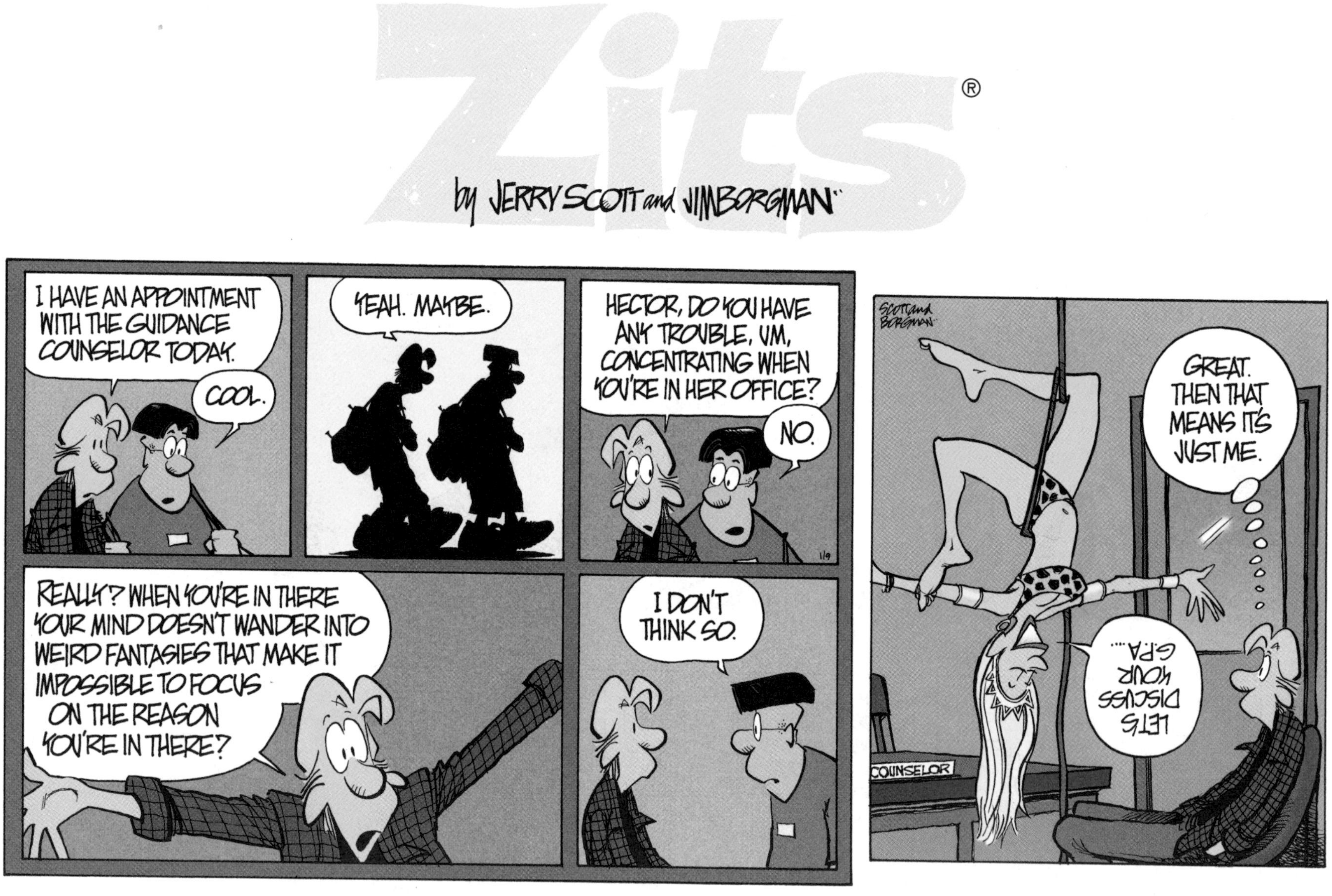
Zits®
by JERRY SCOTT and JIM BORGMAN
I HAVE AN APPOINTMENT WITH THE GUIDANCE COUNSELOR TODAY.
COOL.
YEAH. MAYBE.
HECTOR, DO YOU HAVE ANY TROUBLE, UM, CONCENTRATING WHEN YOU'RE IN HER OFFICE?
NO.
REALLY? WHEN YOU'RE IN THERE YOUR MIND DOESN'T WANDER INTO WEIRD FANTASIES THAT MAKE IT IMPOSSIBLE TO FOCUS ON THE REASON YOU'RE IN THERE?
I DON'T THINK SO.
SCOTT and BORGMAN
LET'S DISCUSS YOUR G.P.A....
GREAT. THEN THAT MEANS IT'S JUST ME.
COUNSELOR

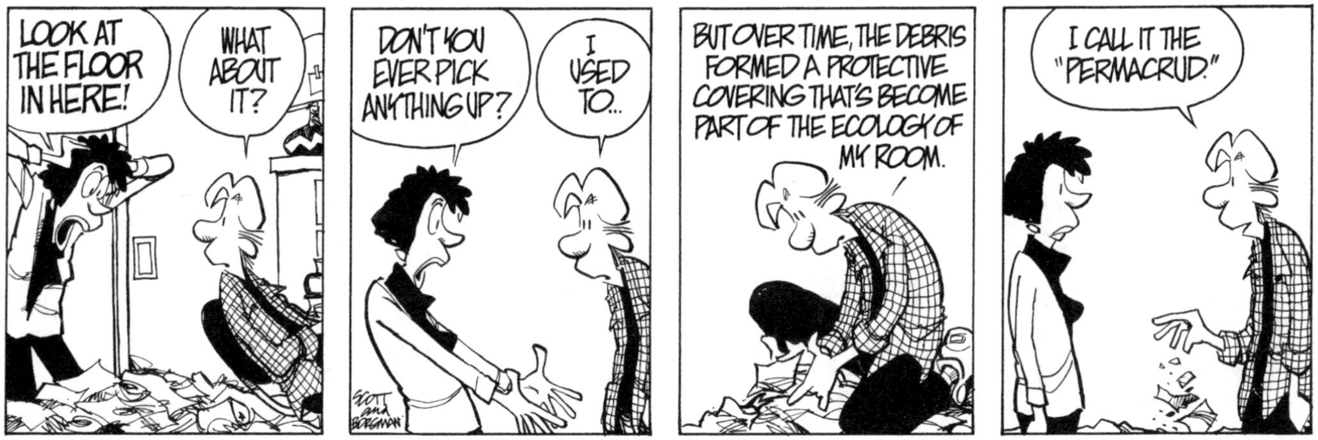
LOOK AT THE FLOOR IN HERE!
WHAT ABOUT IT?
DON'T YOU EVER PICK ANYTHING UP?
I USED TO...
BUT OVER TIME, THE DEBRIS FORMED A PROTECTIVE COVERING THAT'S BECOME PART OF THE ECOLOGY OF MY ROOM.
I CALL IT THE "PERMACRUD."

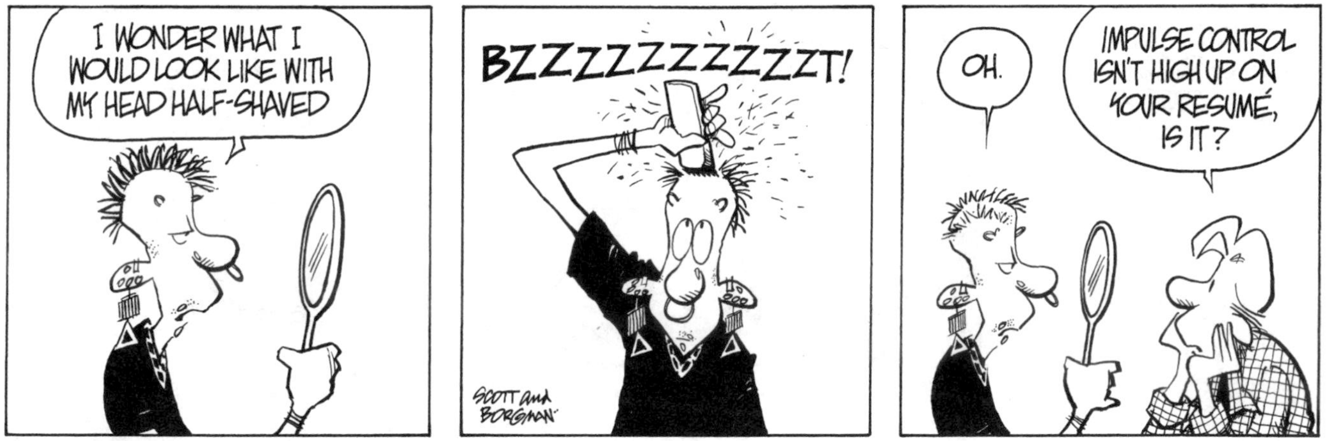
I WONDER WHAT I WOULD LOOK LIKE WITH MY HEAD HALF-SHAVED
BZZZZZZZZZZT!
OH.
IMPULSE CONTROL ISN'T HIGH UP ON YOUR RESUMÉ, IS IT?

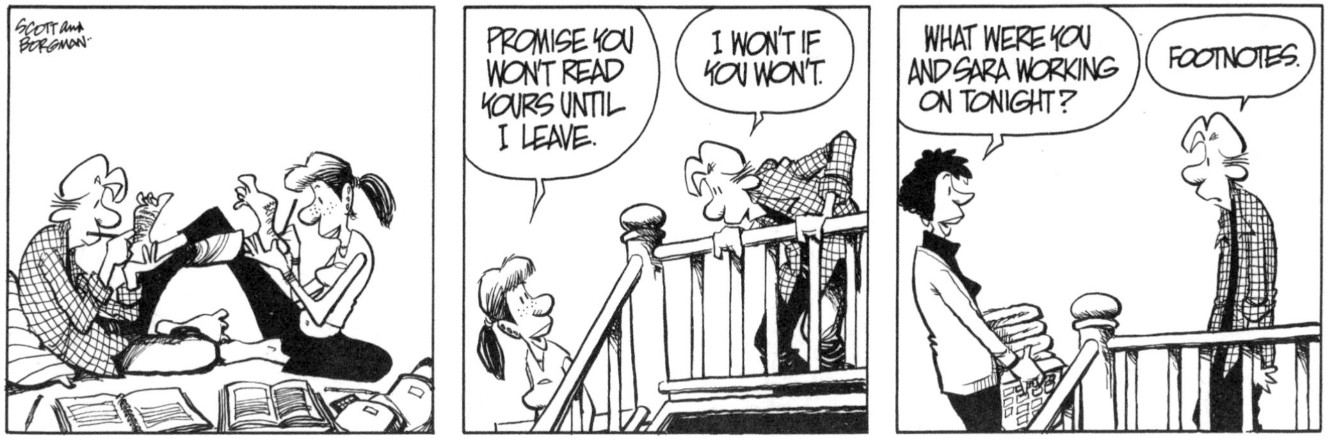
PROMISE YOU WON'T READ YOURS UNTIL I LEAVE.
I WON'T IF YOU WON'T.
WHAT WERE YOU AND SARA WORKING ON TONIGHT?
FOOTNOTES.

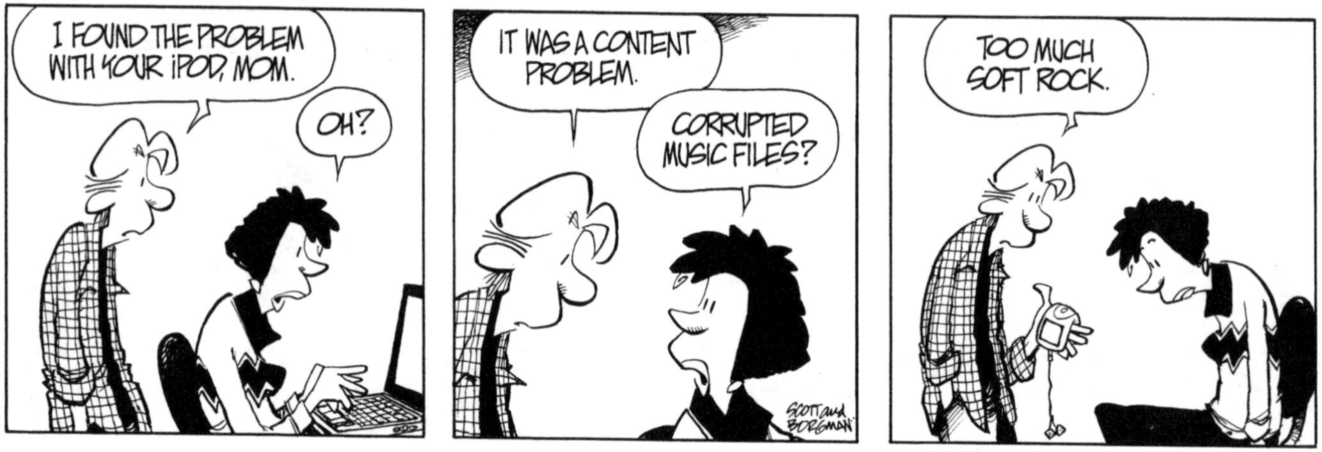
I FOUND THE PROBLEM WITH YOUR iPOD, MOM.
OH?
IT WAS A CONTENT PROBLEM.
CORRUPTED MUSIC FILES?
SCOTT and BORGMAN
TOO MUCH SOFT ROCK.

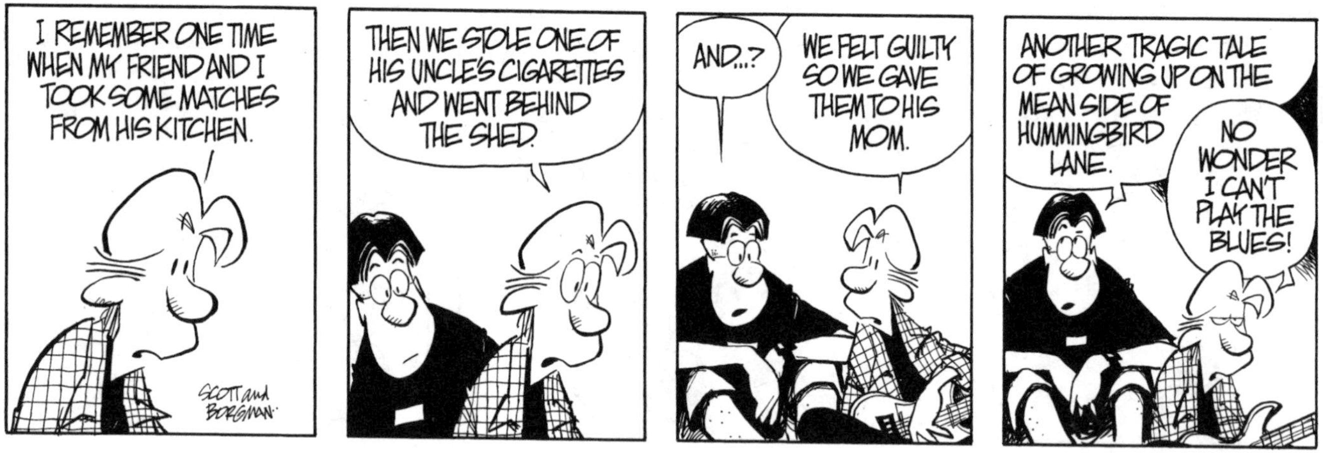
I REMEMBER ONE TIME WHEN MY FRIEND AND I TOOK SOME MATCHES FROM HIS KITCHEN.
SCOTT and BORGMAN
THEN WE STOLE ONE OF HIS UNCLE'S CIGARETTES AND WENT BEHIND THE SHED.
AND...?
WE FELT GUILTY SO WE GAVE THEM TO HIS MOM.
ANOTHER TRAGIC TALE OF GROWING UP ON THE MEAN SIDE OF HUMMINGBIRD LANE.
NO WONDER I CAN'T PLAY THE BLUES!

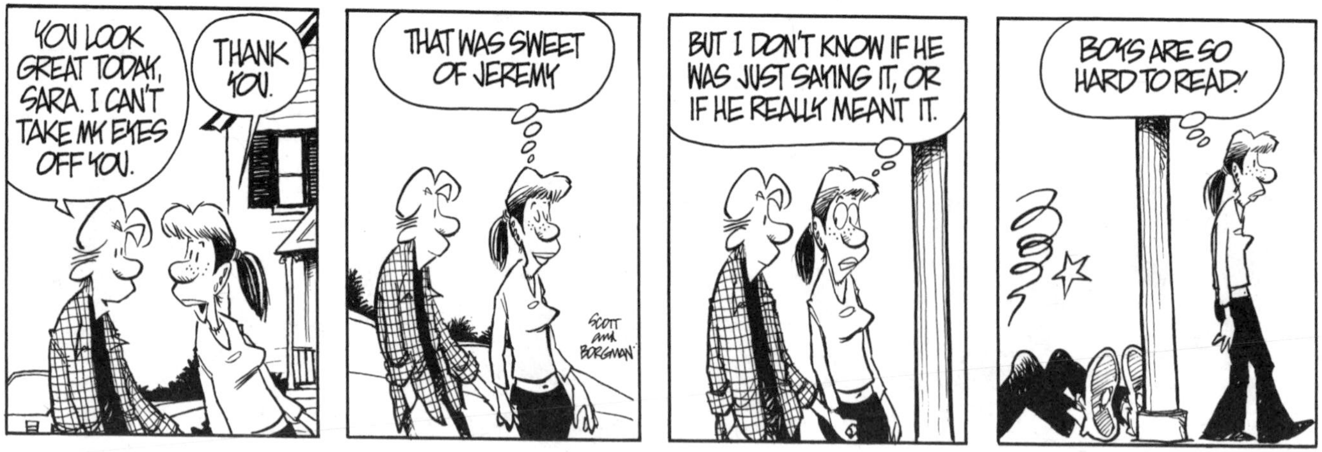
YOU LOOK GREAT TODAY, SARA. I CAN'T TAKE MY EYES OFF YOU.
THANK YOU.
THAT WAS SWEET OF JEREMY
SCOTT and BORGMAN
BUT I DON'T KNOW IF HE WAS JUST SAYING IT, OR IF HE REALLY MEANT IT.
BOYS ARE SO HARD TO READ!

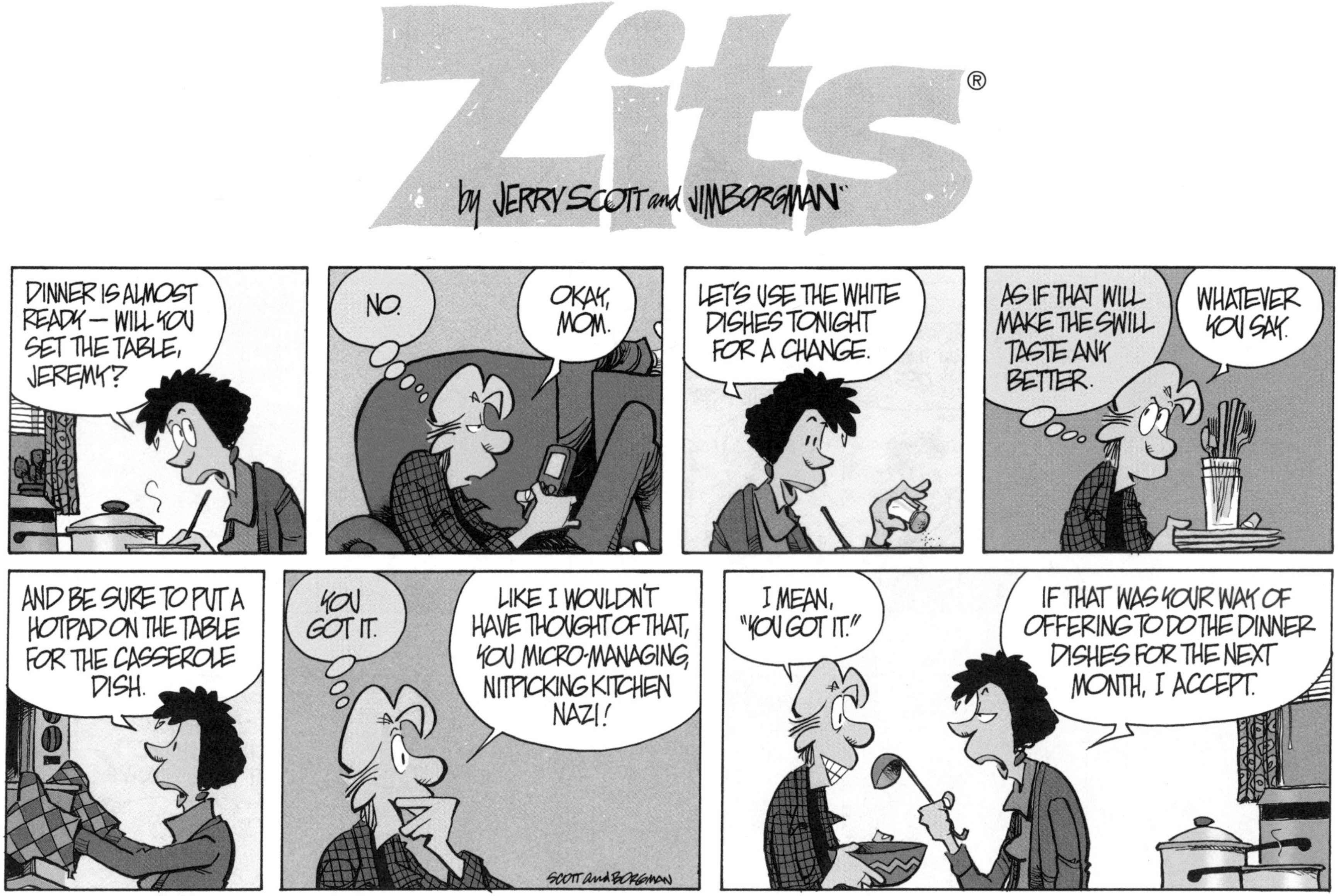
Zits®
by JERRY SCOTT and JIM BORGMAN
DINNER IS ALMOST READY — WILL YOU SET THE TABLE, JEREMY?
NO.
OKAY, MOM.
LET'S USE THE WHITE DISHES TONIGHT FOR A CHANGE.
AS IF THAT WILL MAKE THE SWILL TASTE ANY BETTER.
WHATEVER YOU SAY.
AND BE SURE TO PUT A HOTPAD ON THE TABLE FOR THE CASSEROLE DISH.
YOU GOT IT.
LIKE I WOULDN'T HAVE THOUGHT OF THAT, YOU MICRO-MANAGING, NITPICKING KITCHEN NAZI!
SCOTT and BORGMAN
I MEAN, "YOU GOT IT."
IF THAT WAS YOUR WAY OF OFFERING TO DO THE DINNER DISHES FOR THE NEXT MONTH, I ACCEPT.

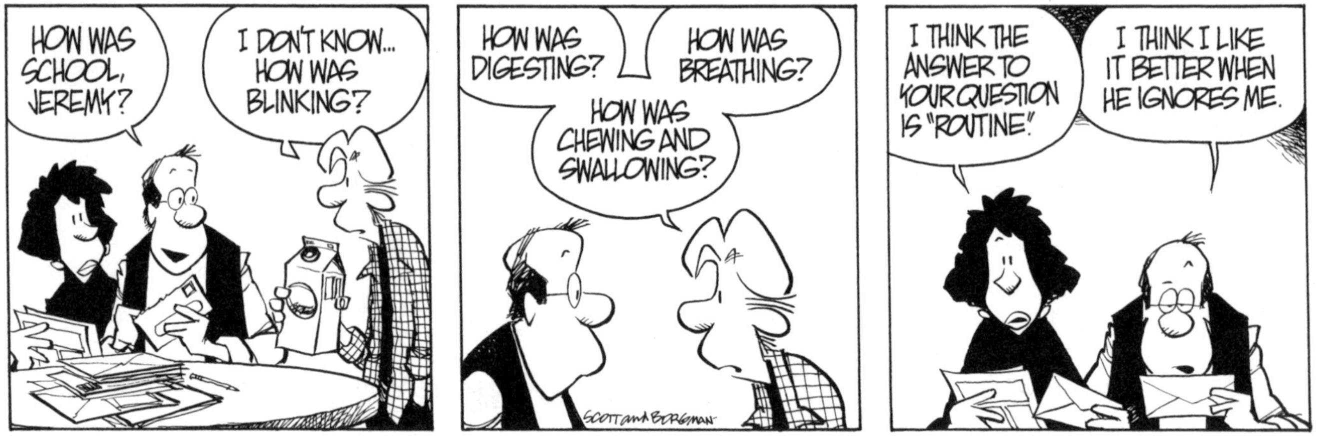
HOW WAS SCHOOL, JEREMY?
I DON'T KNOW... HOW WAS BLINKING?
HOW WAS DIGESTING?
HOW WAS BREATHING?
HOW WAS CHEWING AND SWALLOWING?
I THINK THE ANSWER TO YOUR QUESTION IS "ROUTINE."
I THINK I LIKE IT BETTER WHEN HE IGNORES ME.
SCOTT and BORGMAN

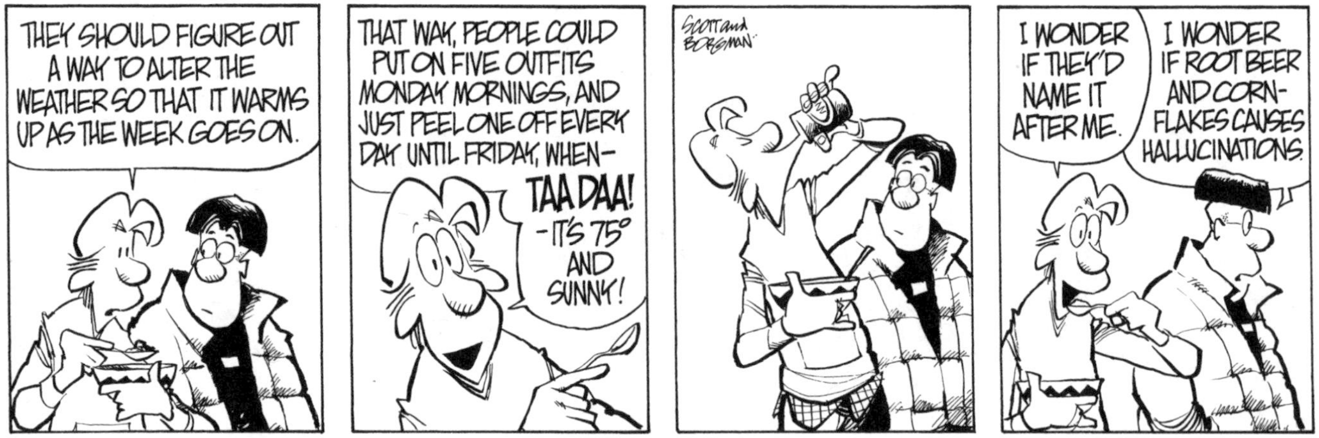
THEY SHOULD FIGURE OUT A WAY TO ALTER THE WEATHER SO THAT IT WARMS UP AS THE WEEK GOES ON.
THAT WAY, PEOPLE COULD PUT ON FIVE OUTFITS MONDAY MORNINGS, AND JUST PEEL ONE OFF EVERY DAY UNTIL FRIDAY, WHEN-
TAA DAA! -IT'S 75° AND SUNNY!
SCOTT and BORGMAN
I WONDER IF THEY'D NAME IT AFTER ME.
I WONDER IF ROOT BEER AND CORN-FLAKES CAUSES HALLUCINATIONS.

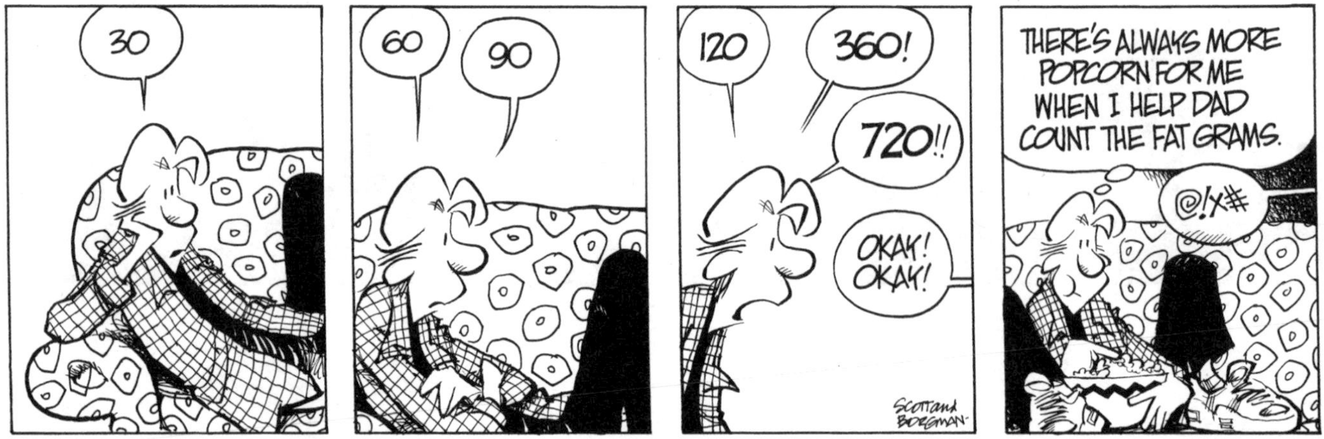
30
60
90
120
360!
720!!
OKAY! OKAY!
SCOTT and BORGMAN
THERE'S ALWAYS MORE POPCORN FOR ME WHEN I HELP DAD COUNT THE FAT GRAMS.
@!x#

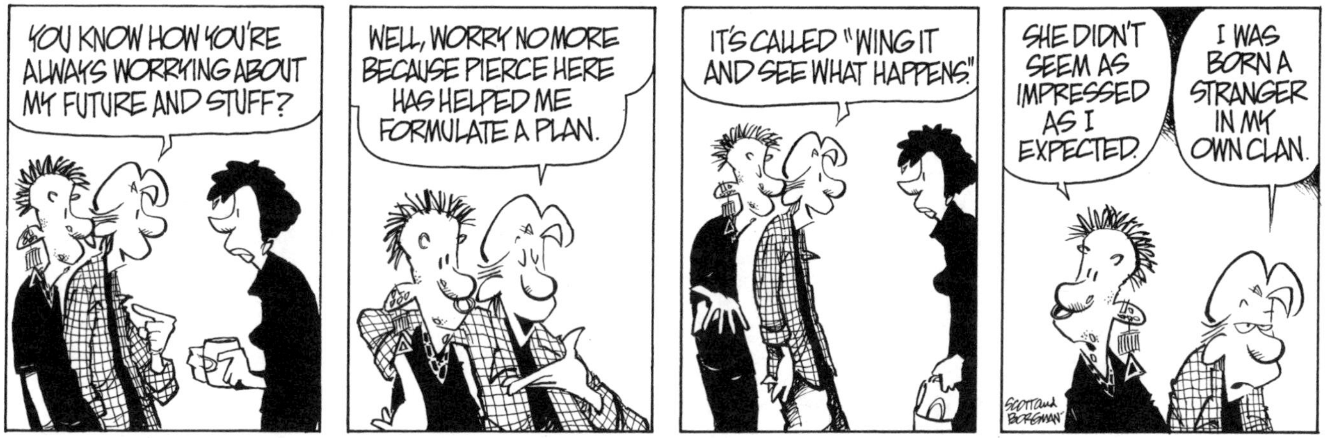
YOU KNOW HOW YOU'RE ALWAYS WORRYING ABOUT MY FUTURE AND STUFF?
WELL, WORRY NO MORE BECAUSE PIERCE HERE HAS HELPED ME FORMULATE A PLAN.
IT'S CALLED "WING IT AND SEE WHAT HAPPENS."
SHE DIDN'T SEEM AS IMPRESSED AS I EXPECTED.
I WAS BORN A STRANGER IN MY OWN CLAN.
SCOTT and BORGMAN

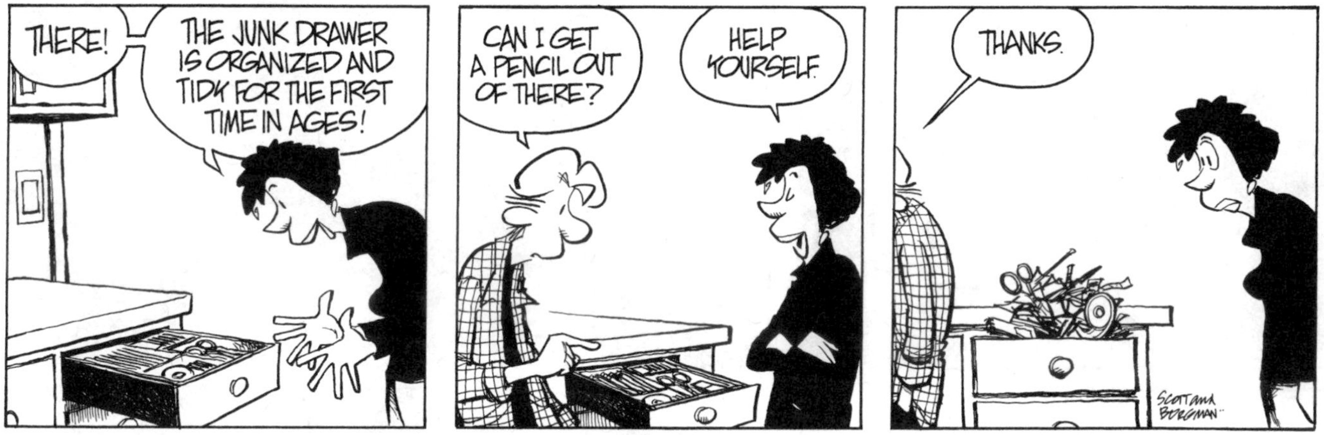
THERE!
THE JUNK DRAWER IS ORGANIZED AND TIDY FOR THE FIRST TIME IN AGES!
CAN I GET A PENCIL OUT OF THERE?
HELP YOURSELF.
THANKS.
SCOTT and BORGMAN

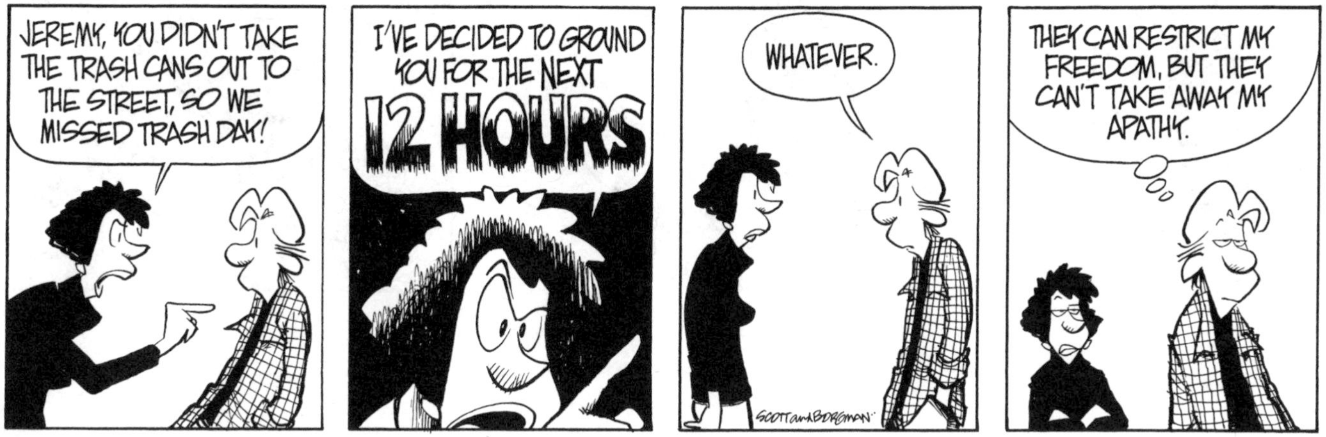
JEREMY, YOU DIDN'T TAKE THE TRASH CANS OUT TO THE STREET, SO WE MISSED TRASH DAY!
I'VE DECIDED TO GROUND YOU FOR THE NEXT
12 HOURS
WHATEVER.
SCOTT and BORGMAN
THEY CAN RESTRICT MY FREEDOM, BUT THEY CAN'T TAKE AWAY MY APATHY.

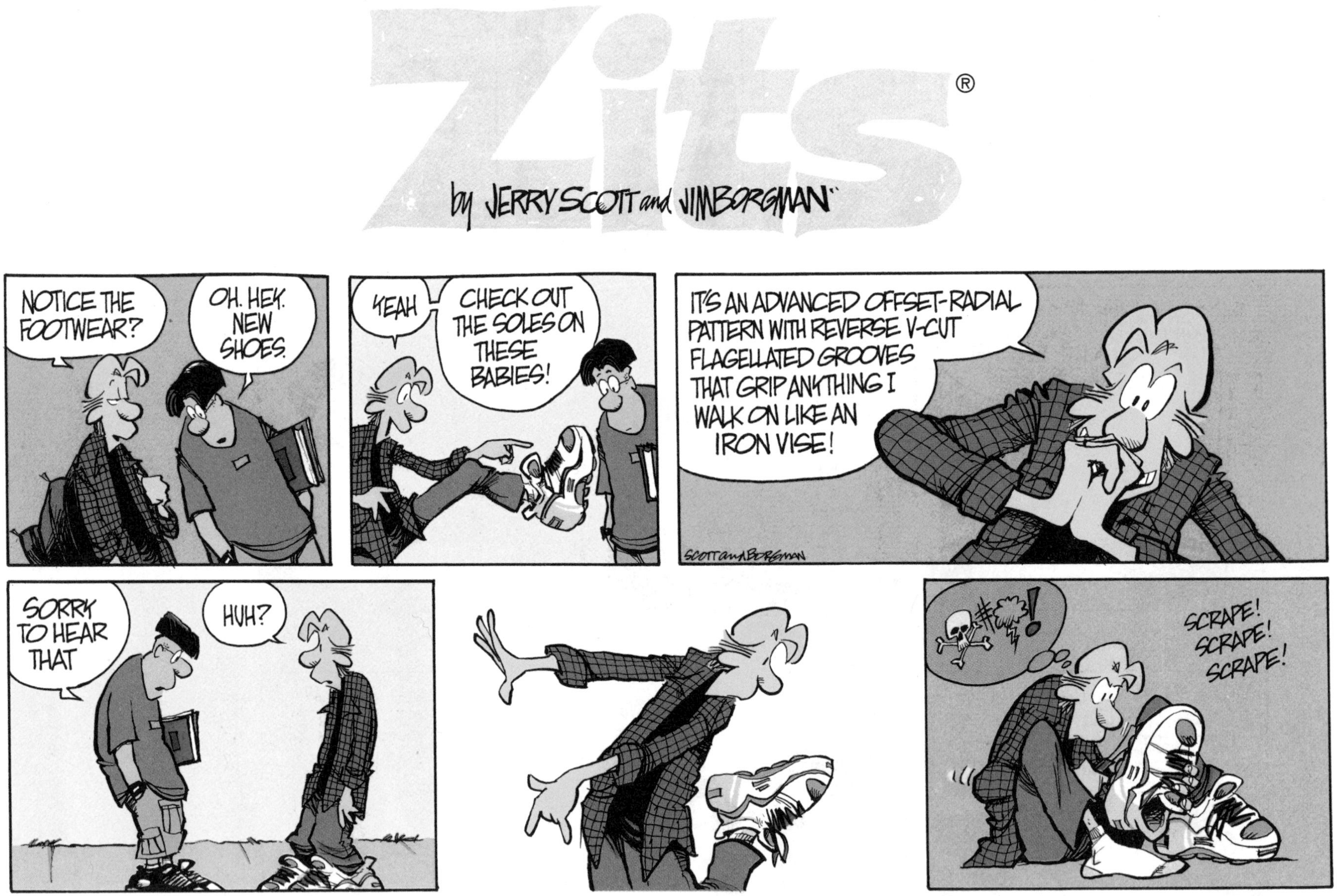
Zits®
by JERRY SCOTT and JIM BORGMAN
NOTICE THE FOOTWEAR?
OH. HEY. NEW SHOES.
YEAH
CHECK OUT THE SOLES ON THESE BABIES!
IT'S AN ADVANCED OFFSET-RADIAL PATTERN WITH REVERSE V-CUT FLAGELLATED GROOVES THAT GRIP ANYTHING I WALK ON LIKE AN IRON VISE!
SCOTT and BORGMAN
SORRY TO HEAR THAT
HUH?
SCRAPE! SCRAPE! SCRAPE!

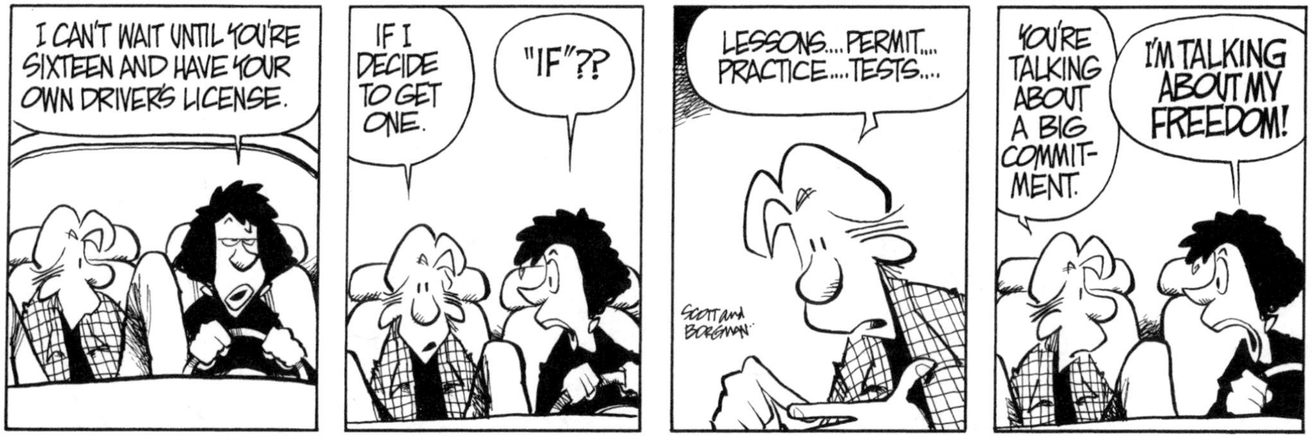
I CAN'T WAIT UNTIL YOU'RE SIXTEEN AND HAVE YOUR OWN DRIVER'S LICENSE.
IF I DECIDE TO GET ONE.
"IF"??
LESSONS.... PERMIT.... PRACTICE.... TESTS....
YOU'RE TALKING ABOUT A BIG COMMIT-MENT.
I'M TALKING ABOUT MY FREEDOM!

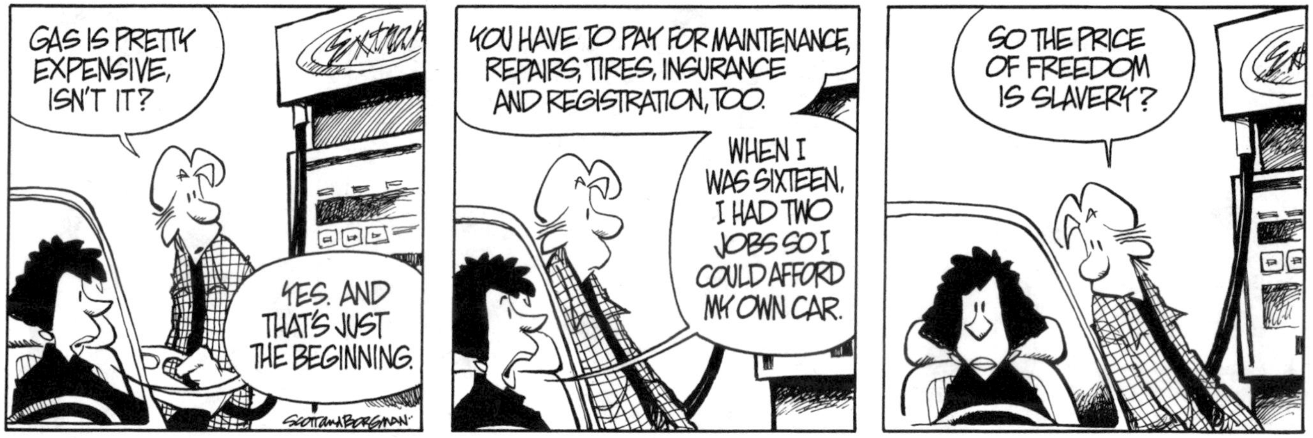
GAS IS PRETTY EXPENSIVE, ISN'T IT?
YES. AND THAT'S JUST THE BEGINNING.
YOU HAVE TO PAY FOR MAINTENANCE, REPAIRS, TIRES, INSURANCE AND REGISTRATION, TOO.
WHEN I WAS SIXTEEN, I HAD TWO JOBS SO I COULD AFFORD MY OWN CAR.
SO THE PRICE OF FREEDOM IS SLAVERY?

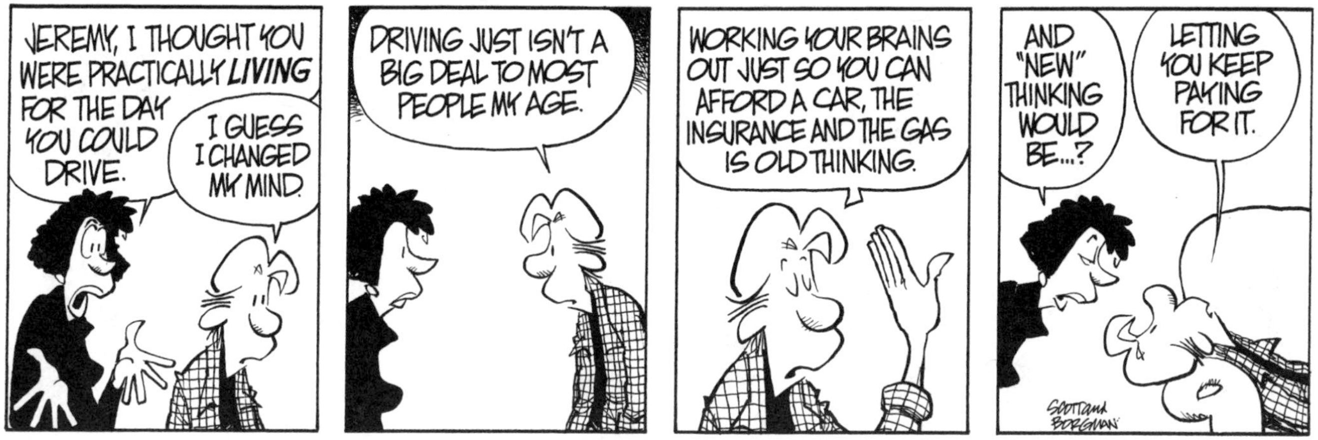
JEREMY, I THOUGHT YOU WERE PRACTICALLY *LIVING* FOR THE DAY YOU COULD DRIVE.
I GUESS I CHANGED MY MIND.
DRIVING JUST ISN'T A BIG DEAL TO MOST PEOPLE MY AGE.
WORKING YOUR BRAINS OUT JUST SO YOU CAN AFFORD A CAR, THE INSURANCE AND THE GAS IS OLD THINKING.
AND "NEW" THINKING WOULD BE...?
LETTING YOU KEEP PAYING FOR IT.

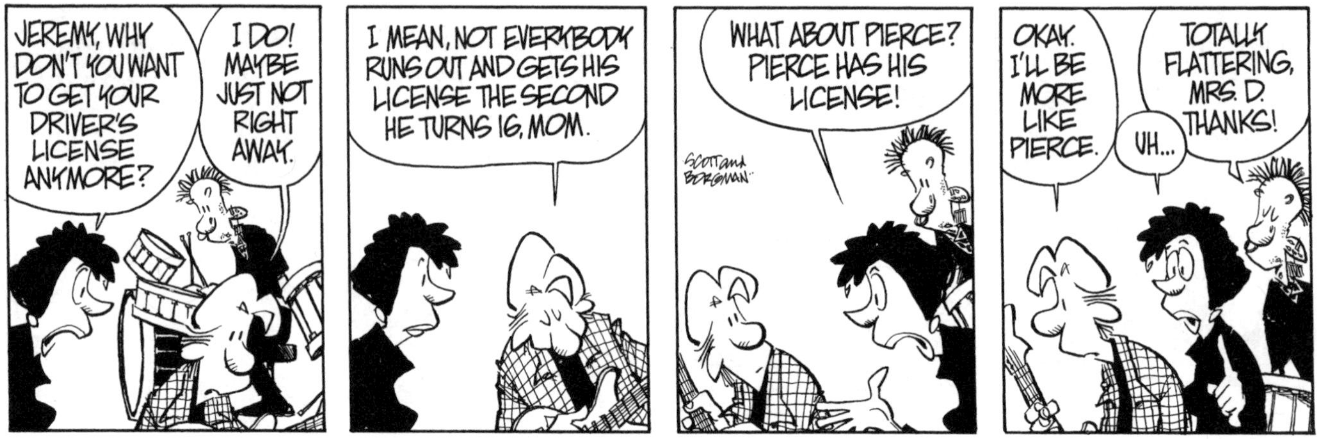
JEREMY, WHY DON'T YOU WANT TO GET YOUR DRIVER'S LICENSE ANYMORE?
I DO! MAYBE JUST NOT RIGHT AWAY.
I MEAN, NOT EVERYBODY RUNS OUT AND GETS HIS LICENSE THE SECOND HE TURNS 16, MOM.
WHAT ABOUT PIERCE? PIERCE HAS HIS LICENSE!
SCOTT and BORGMAN
OKAY. I'LL BE MORE LIKE PIERCE.
UH...
TOTALLY FLATTERING, MRS. D. THANKS!

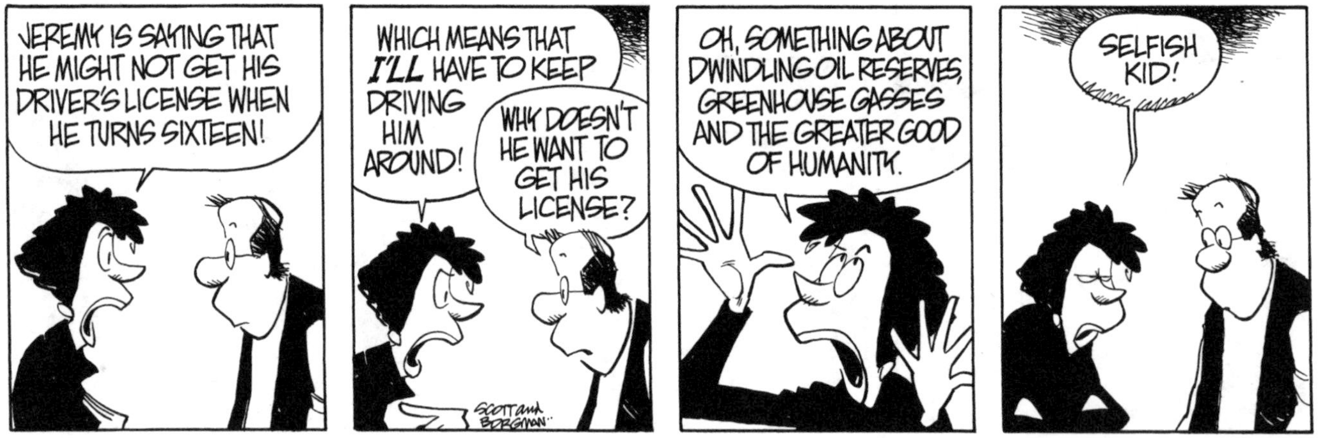
JEREMY IS SAYING THAT HE MIGHT NOT GET HIS DRIVER'S LICENSE WHEN HE TURNS SIXTEEN!
WHICH MEANS THAT I'LL HAVE TO KEEP DRIVING HIM AROUND!
WHY DOESN'T HE WANT TO GET HIS LICENSE?
SCOTT and BORGMAN
OH, SOMETHING ABOUT DWINDLING OIL RESERVES, GREENHOUSE GASSES AND THE GREATER GOOD OF HUMANITY.
SELFISH KID!

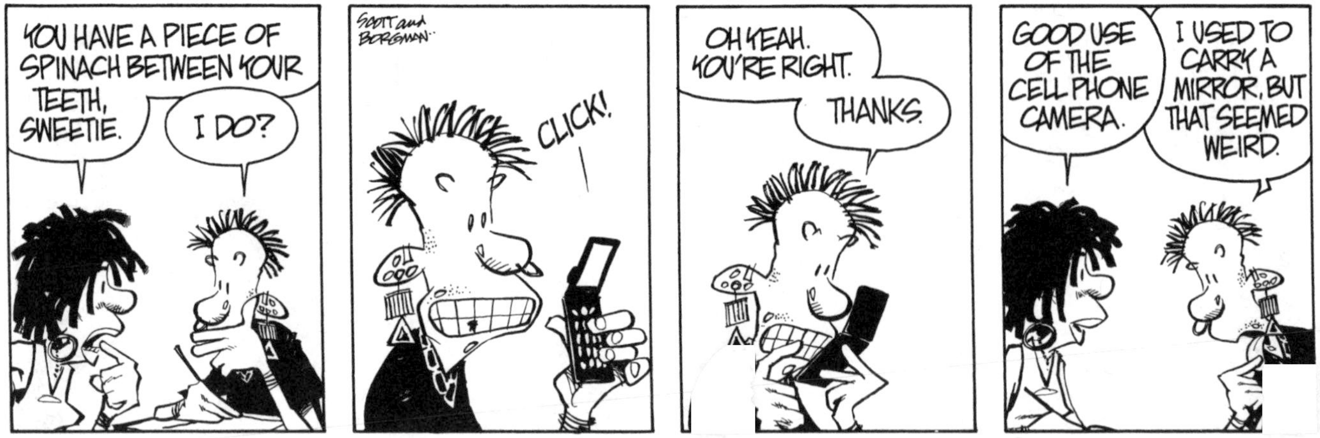
YOU HAVE A PIECE OF SPINACH BETWEEN YOUR TEETH, SWEETIE.
I DO?
SCOTT and BORGMAN
CLICK!
OH YEAH. YOU'RE RIGHT.
THANKS.
GOOD USE OF THE CELL PHONE CAMERA.
I USED TO CARRY A MIRROR, BUT THAT SEEMED WEIRD.

Zits®

by JERRY SCOTT and JIM BORGMAN

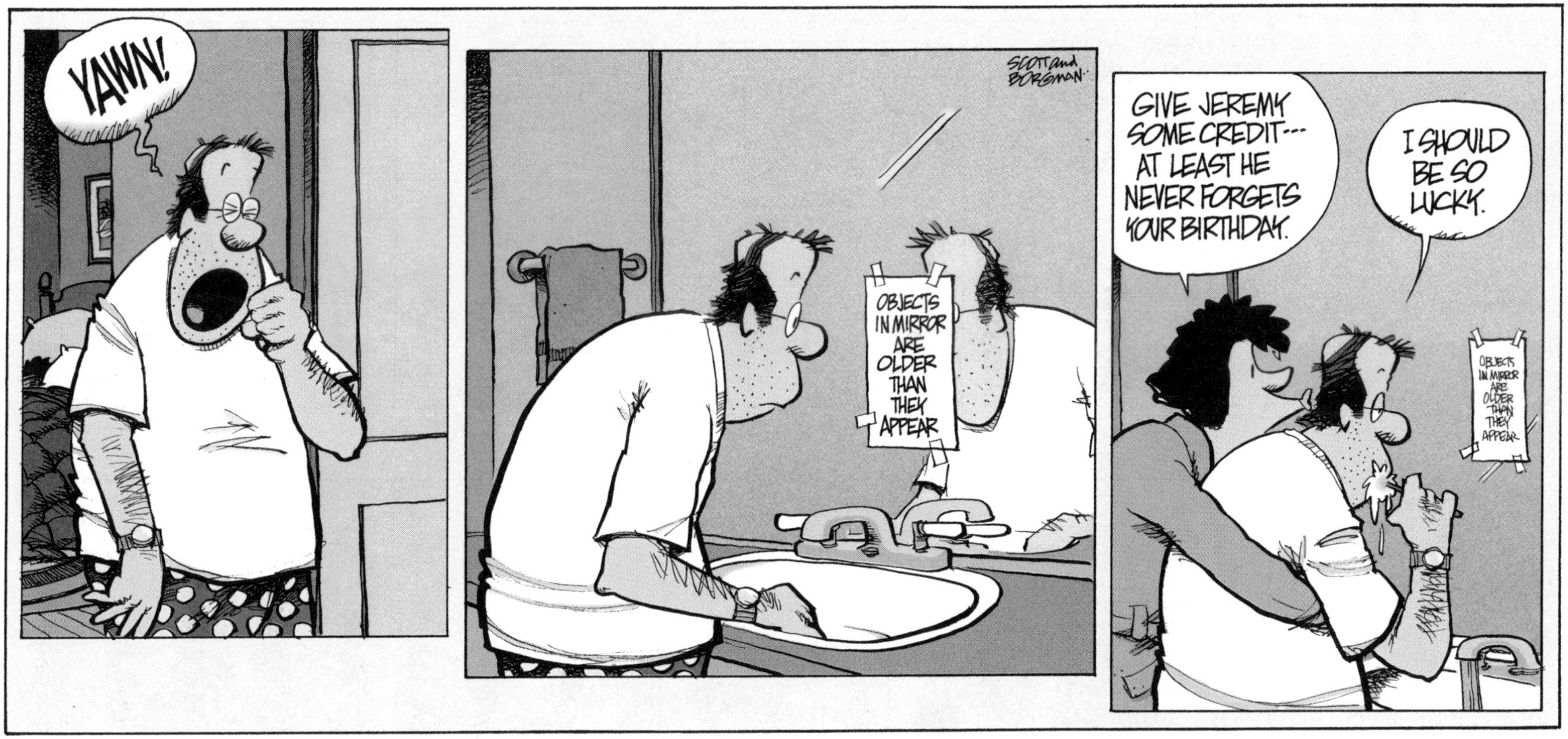
YAWN!
SCOTT and BORGMAN
OBJECTS IN MIRROR ARE OLDER THAN THEY APPEAR
GIVE JEREMY SOME CREDIT--- AT LEAST HE NEVER FORGETS YOUR BIRTHDAY.
I SHOULD BE SO LUCKY.

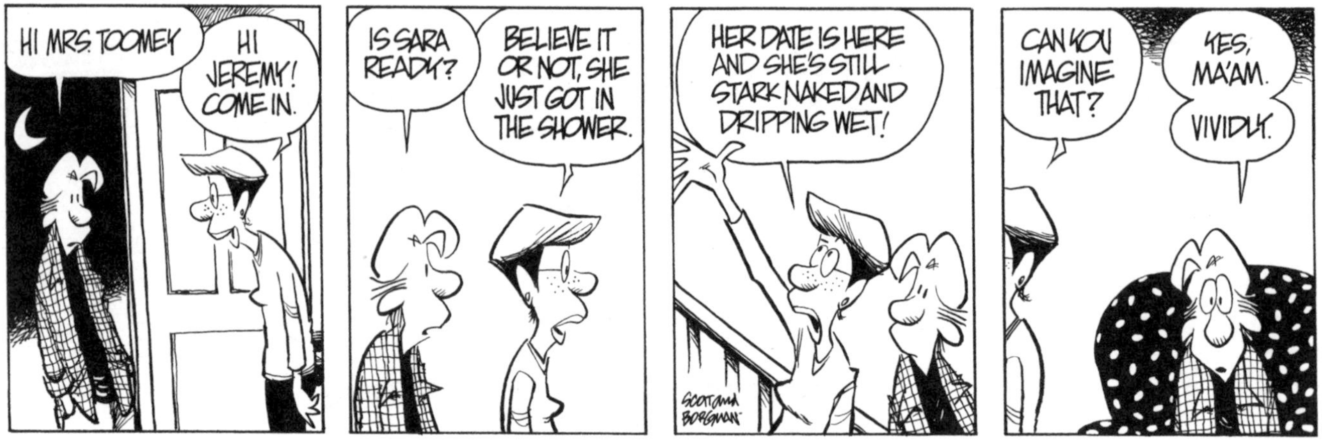
HI MRS. TOOMEY
HI JEREMY! COME IN.
IS SARA READY?
BELIEVE IT OR NOT, SHE JUST GOT IN THE SHOWER.
HER DATE IS HERE AND SHE'S STILL STARK NAKED AND DRIPPING WET!
SCOTT AND BORGMAN
CAN YOU IMAGINE THAT?
YES, MA'AM.
VIVIDLY.

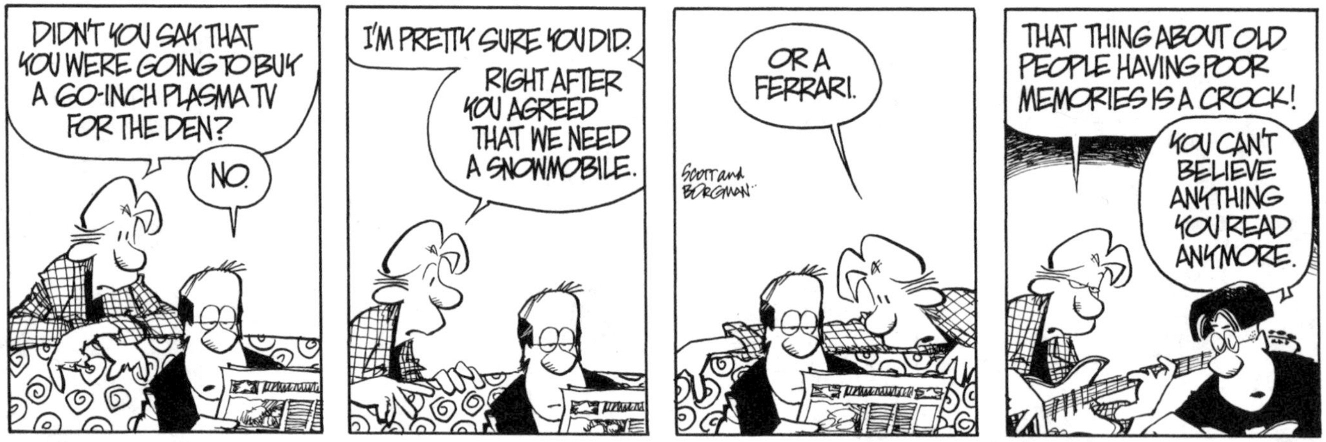
DIDN'T YOU SAY THAT YOU WERE GOING TO BUY A 60-INCH PLASMA TV FOR THE DEN?
NO.
I'M PRETTY SURE YOU DID.
RIGHT AFTER YOU AGREED THAT WE NEED A SNOWMOBILE.
SCOTT AND BORGMAN
OR A FERRARI.
THAT THING ABOUT OLD PEOPLE HAVING POOR MEMORIES IS A CROCK!
YOU CAN'T BELIEVE ANYTHING YOU READ ANYMORE.

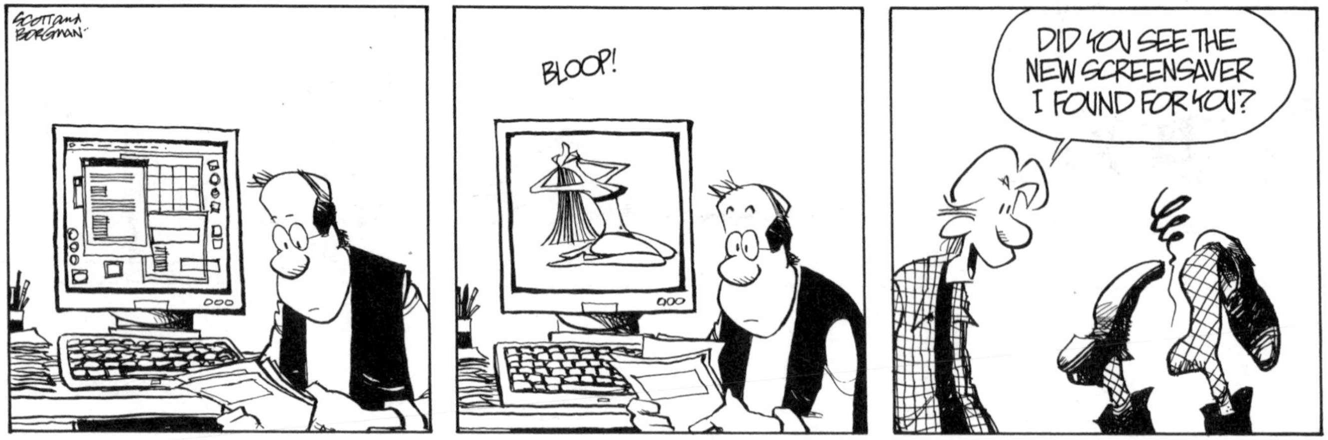
SCOTT AND BORGMAN
BLOOP!
DID YOU SEE THE NEW SCREENSAVER I FOUND FOR YOU?

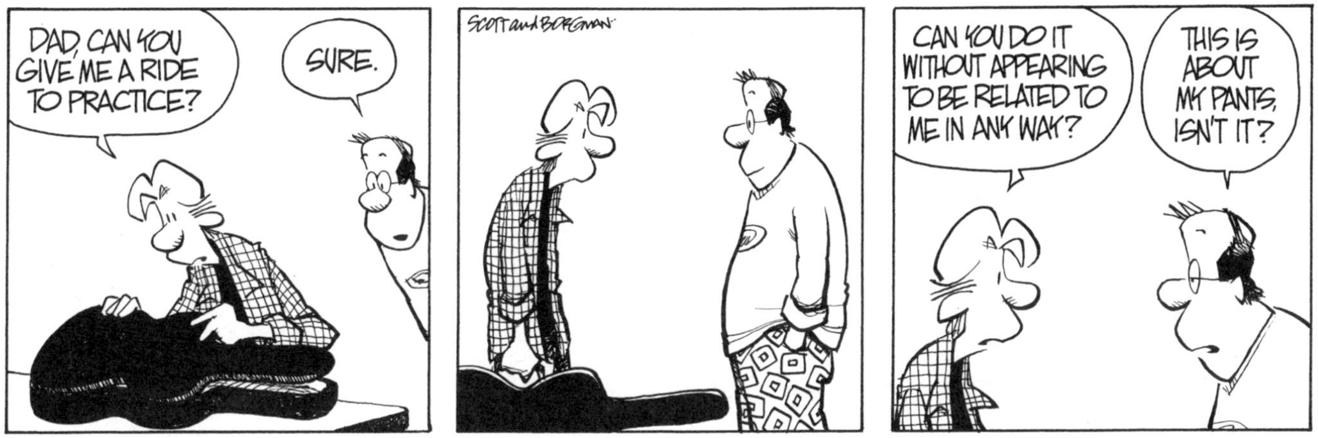
DAD, CAN YOU GIVE ME A RIDE TO PRACTICE?
SURE.
SCOTT and BORGMAN
CAN YOU DO IT WITHOUT APPEARING TO BE RELATED TO ME IN ANY WAY?
THIS IS ABOUT MY PANTS, ISN'T IT?

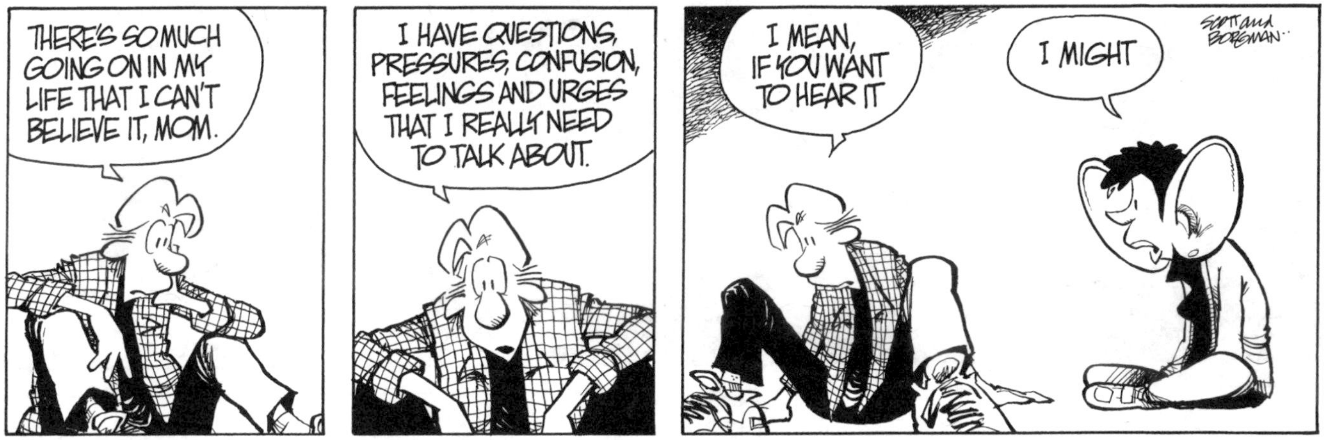
THERE'S SO MUCH GOING ON IN MY LIFE THAT I CAN'T BELIEVE IT, MOM.
I HAVE QUESTIONS, PRESSURES, CONFUSION, FEELINGS AND URGES THAT I REALLY NEED TO TALK ABOUT.
I MEAN, IF YOU WANT TO HEAR IT
I MIGHT
SCOTT and BORGMAN

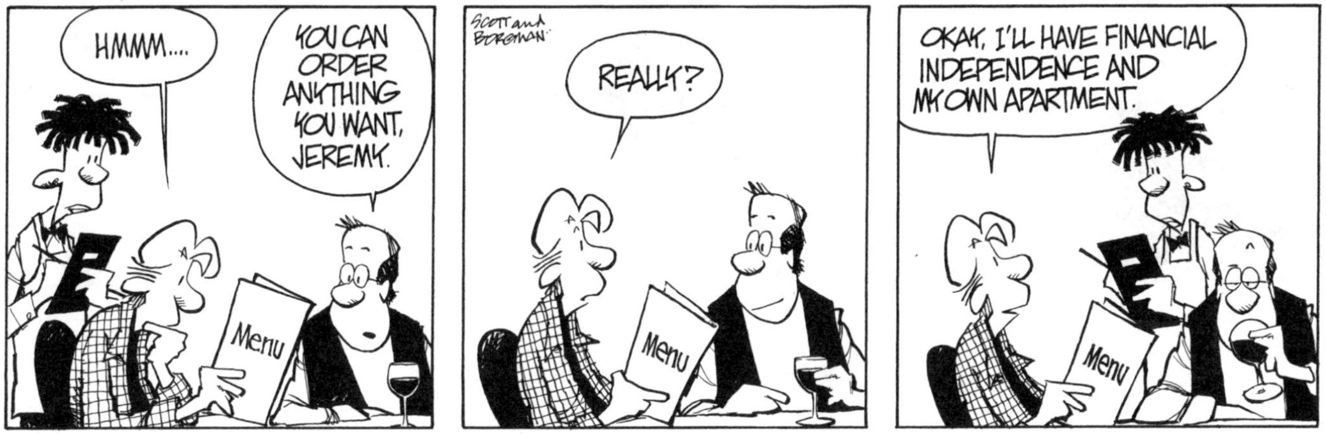
HMMM....
YOU CAN ORDER ANYTHING YOU WANT, JEREMY.
Menu
SCOTT and BORGMAN
REALLY?
Menu
OKAY, I'LL HAVE FINANCIAL INDEPENDENCE AND MY OWN APARTMENT.
Menu

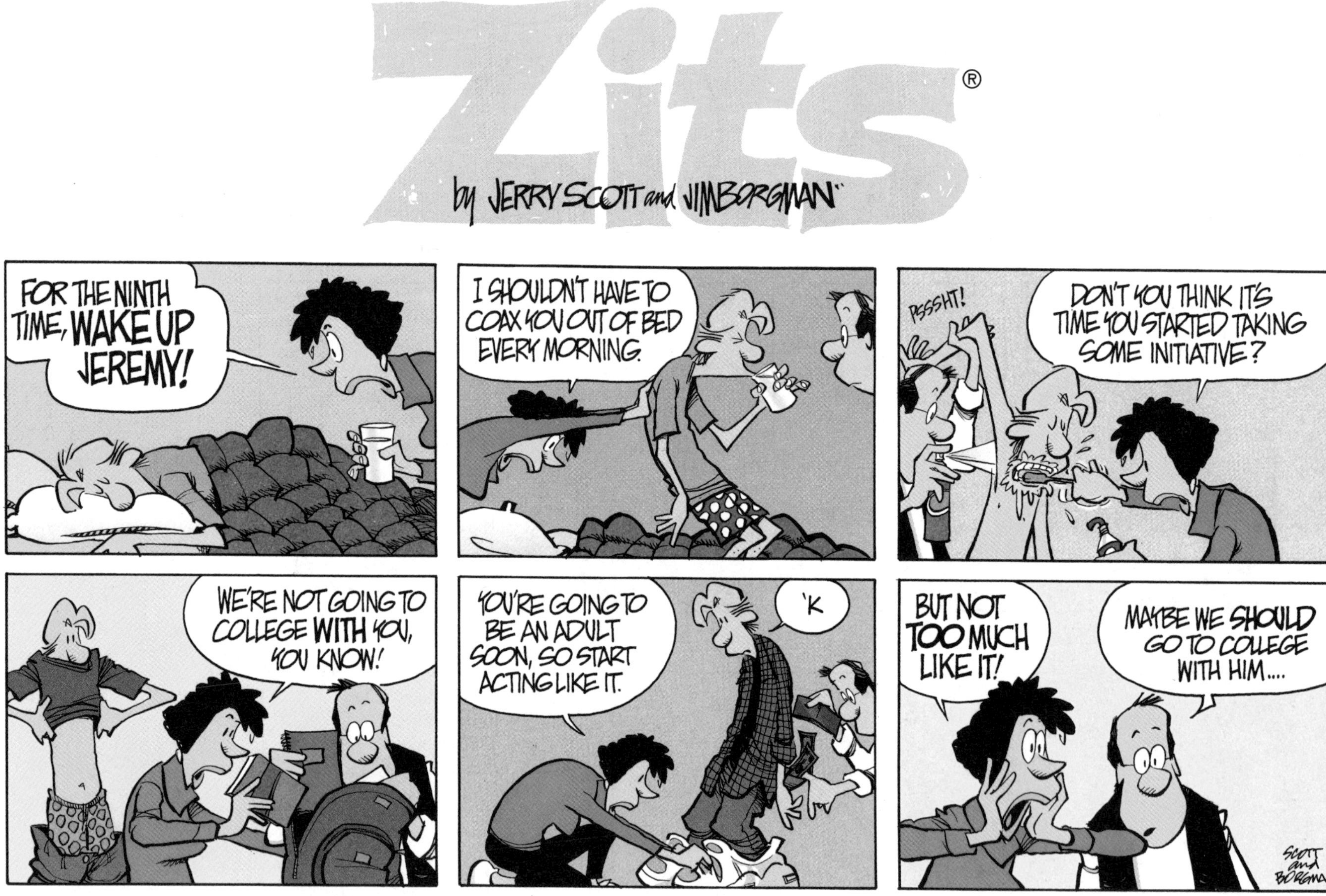
Zits®
by JERRY SCOTT and JIM BORGMAN
FOR THE NINTH TIME, WAKE UP JEREMY!
I SHOULDN'T HAVE TO COAX YOU OUT OF BED EVERY MORNING.
PSSSHT!
DON'T YOU THINK IT'S TIME YOU STARTED TAKING SOME INITIATIVE?
WE'RE NOT GOING TO COLLEGE WITH YOU, YOU KNOW!
YOU'RE GOING TO BE AN ADULT SOON, SO START ACTING LIKE IT.
'K
BUT NOT TOO MUCH LIKE IT!
MAYBE WE SHOULD GO TO COLLEGE WITH HIM....
SCOTT and BORGMAN

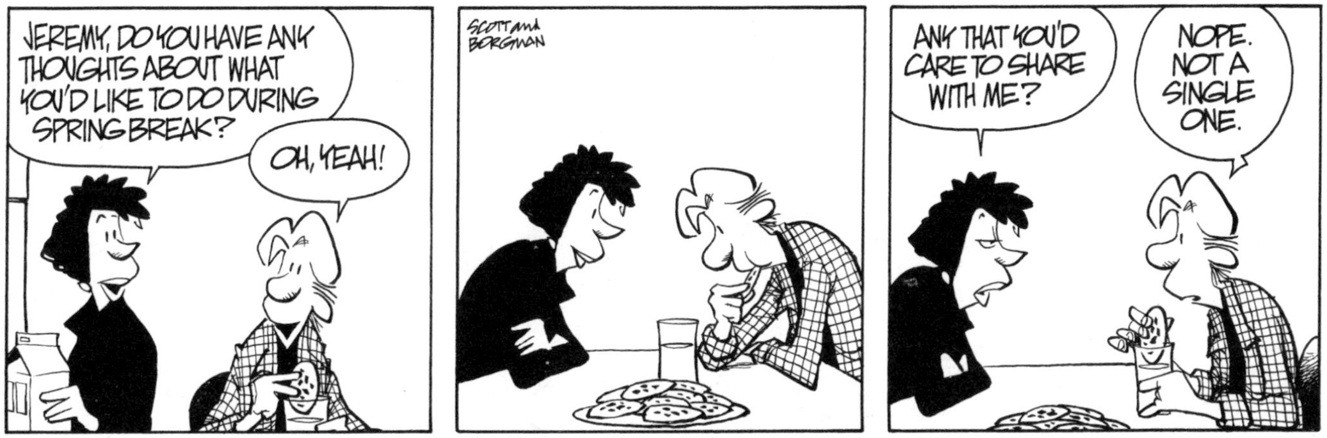
JEREMY, DO YOU HAVE ANY THOUGHTS ABOUT WHAT YOU'D LIKE TO DO DURING SPRING BREAK?
OH, YEAH!
SCOTT AND BORGMAN
ANY THAT YOU'D CARE TO SHARE WITH ME?
NOPE. NOT A SINGLE ONE.

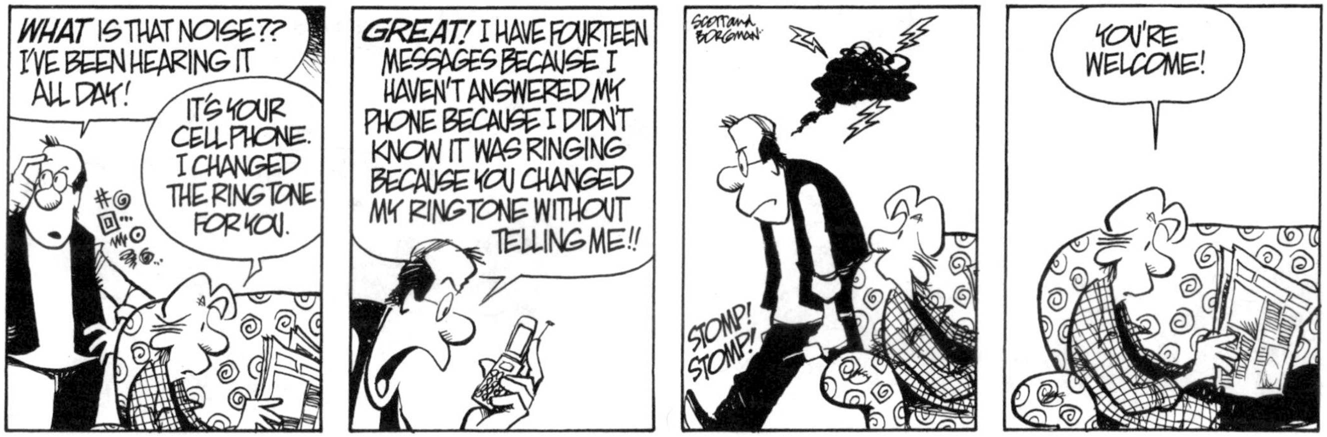
WHAT IS THAT NOISE?? I'VE BEEN HEARING IT ALL DAY!
IT'S YOUR CELL PHONE. I CHANGED THE RING TONE FOR YOU.
GREAT! I HAVE FOURTEEN MESSAGES BECAUSE I HAVEN'T ANSWERED MY PHONE BECAUSE I DIDN'T KNOW IT WAS RINGING BECAUSE YOU CHANGED MY RINGTONE WITHOUT TELLING ME!!
SCOTT AND BORGMAN
STOMP! STOMP!
YOU'RE WELCOME!

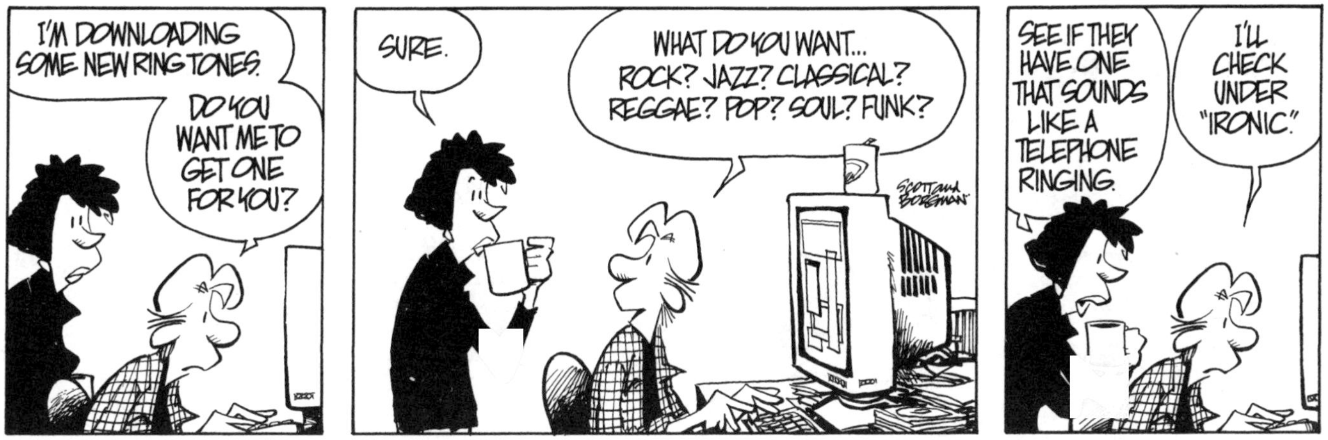
I'M DOWNLOADING SOME NEW RING TONES.
DO YOU WANT ME TO GET ONE FOR YOU?
SURE.
WHAT DO YOU WANT... ROCK? JAZZ? CLASSICAL? REGGAE? POP? SOUL? FUNK?
SCOTT AND BORGMAN
SEE IF THEY HAVE ONE THAT SOUNDS LIKE A TELEPHONE RINGING.
I'LL CHECK UNDER "IRONIC."

JEREMY, YOU SHOULD GET THE TRASH CANS OUT TO THE CURB BEFORE IT GETS DARK.
I KNOW. I'LL DO IT SOON.
SCOTT AND BORGMAN
AND BY "SOON" YOU MEAN...?
"NOT SOON"

WHAT A DAY!
I FEEL LIKE I'VE BEEN RUN OVER BY A BUS!
THERE YOU ARE!
SCOTT AND BORGMAN
!!!!!!!!
OKAY, A BUS FULL OF DRILL SERGEANTS

RRRRRRRRRRRRRR
RRRRRRRRRPTH.
SCOTT AND BORGMAN
WE'RE HERE. YOU CAN GET OFF NOW.
I'M WAITING FOR MY PANTS TO THAW.

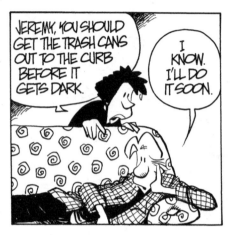

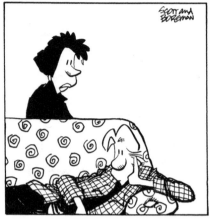

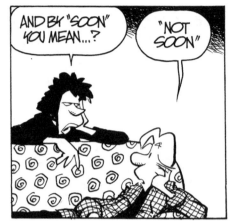

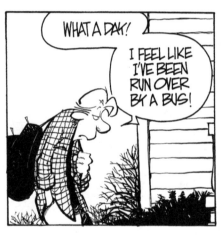

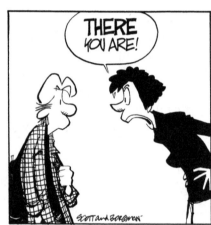

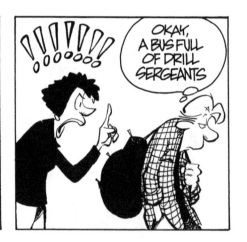

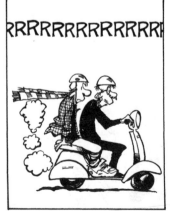

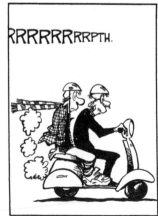

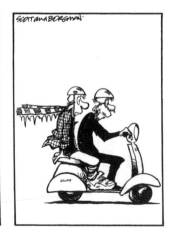

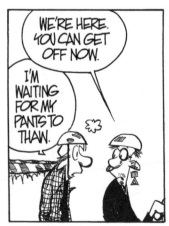

Zits®

by JERRY SCOTT and JIM BORGMAN

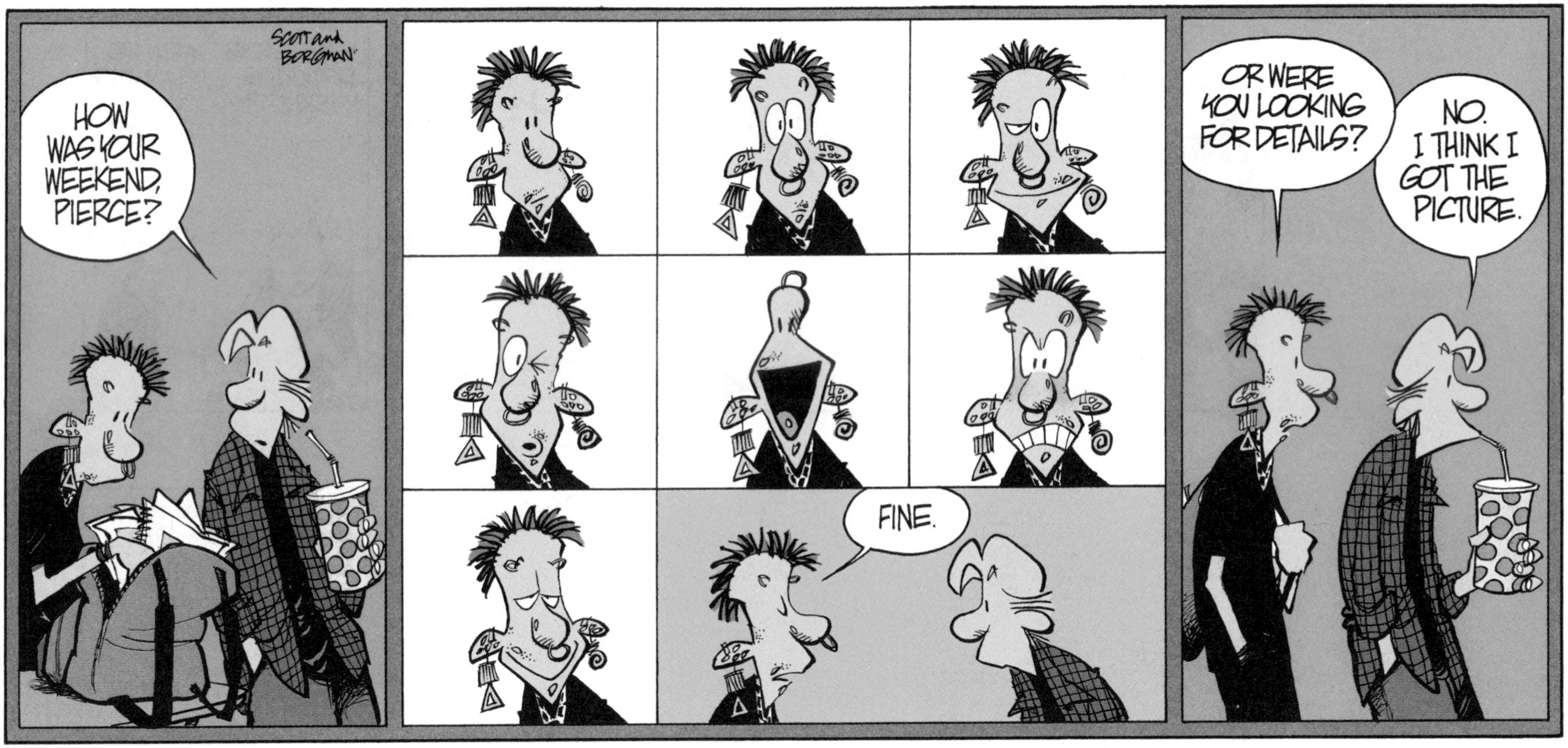
SCOTT and BORGMAN
HOW WAS YOUR WEEKEND, PIERCE?
FINE.
OR WERE YOU LOOKING FOR DETAILS?
NO. I THINK I GOT THE PICTURE.

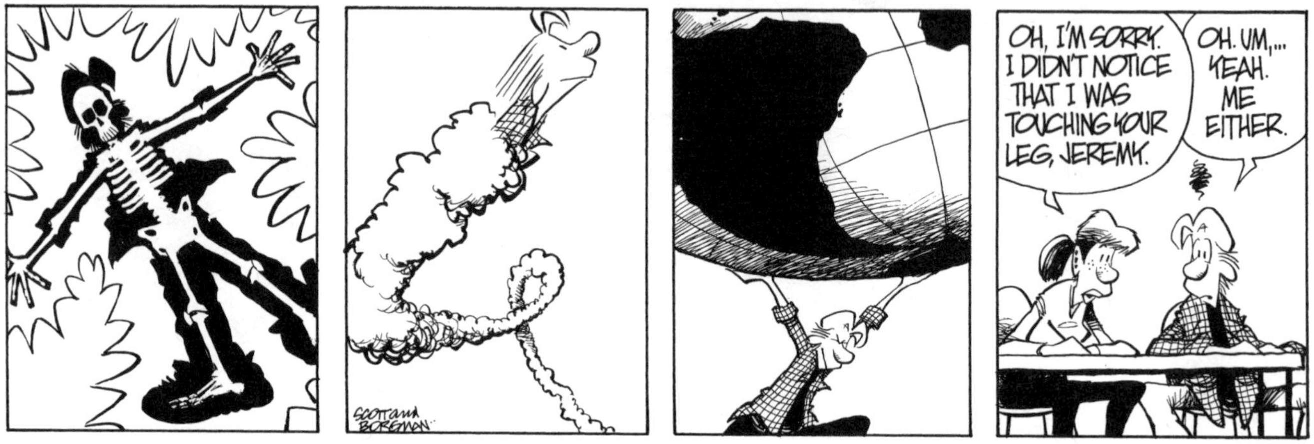
OH, I'M SORRY. I DIDN'T NOTICE THAT I WAS TOUCHING YOUR LEG, JEREMY.
OH. UM,... YEAH. ME EITHER.

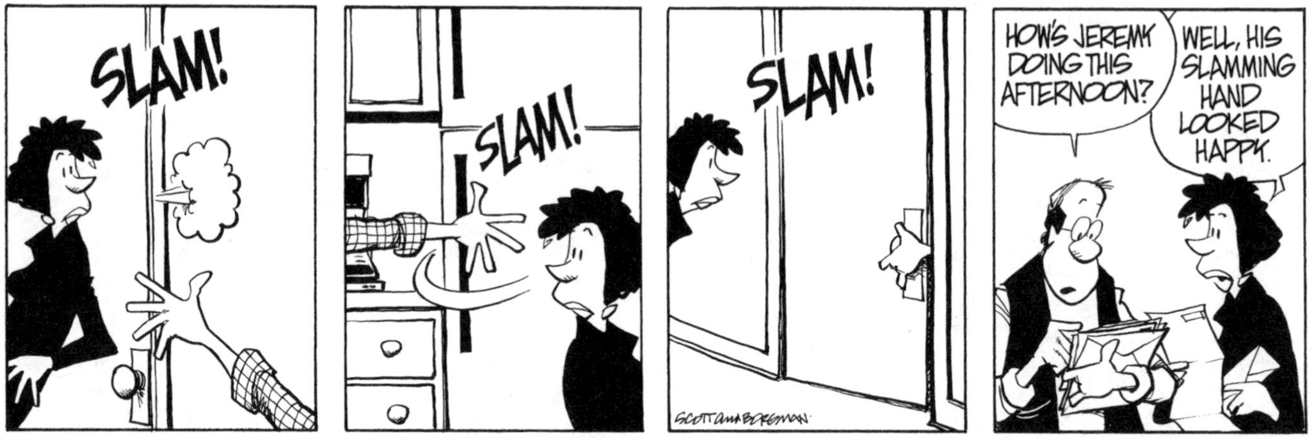
SLAM!
SLAM!
SLAM!
HOW'S JEREMY DOING THIS AFTERNOON?
WELL, HIS SLAMMING HAND LOOKED HAPPY.

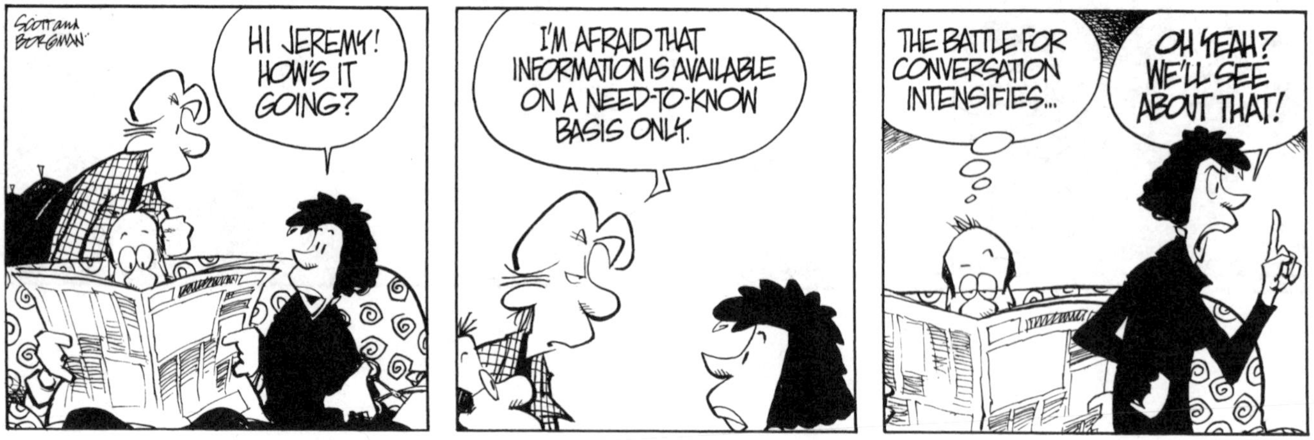
HI JEREMY! HOW'S IT GOING?
I'M AFRAID THAT INFORMATION IS AVAILABLE ON A NEED-TO-KNOW BASIS ONLY.
THE BATTLE FOR CONVERSATION INTENSIFIES...
OH YEAH? WE'LL SEE ABOUT THAT!

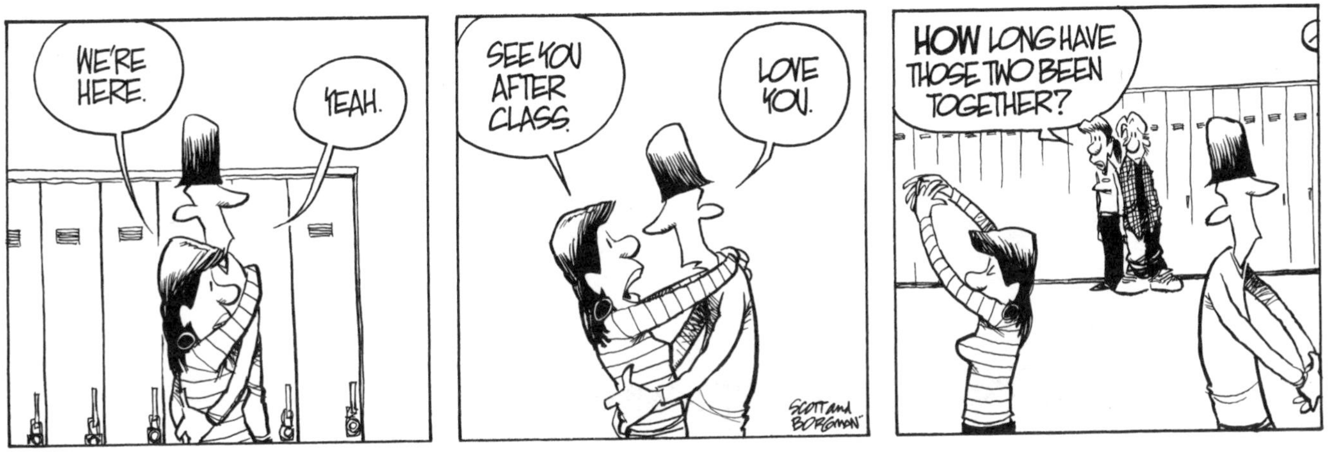
WE'RE HERE.
YEAH.
SEE YOU AFTER CLASS.
LOVE YOU.
SCOTT AND BORGMAN
HOW LONG HAVE THOSE TWO BEEN TOGETHER?

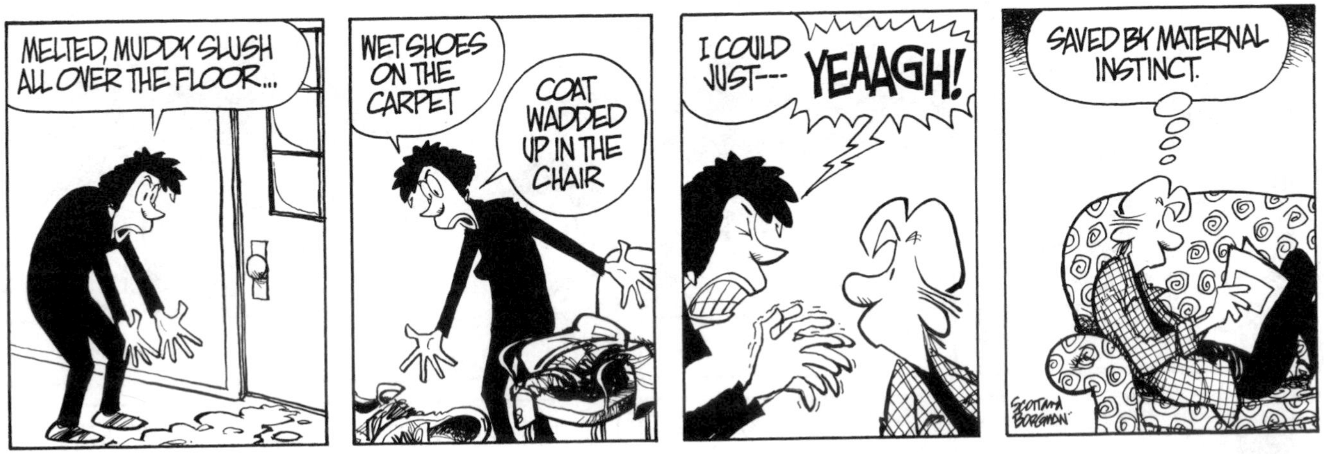
MELTED, MUDDY SLUSH ALL OVER THE FLOOR...
WET SHOES ON THE CARPET
COAT WADDED UP IN THE CHAIR
I COULD JUST---
YEAAGH!
SAVED BY MATERNAL INSTINCT.
SCOTT AND BORGMAN

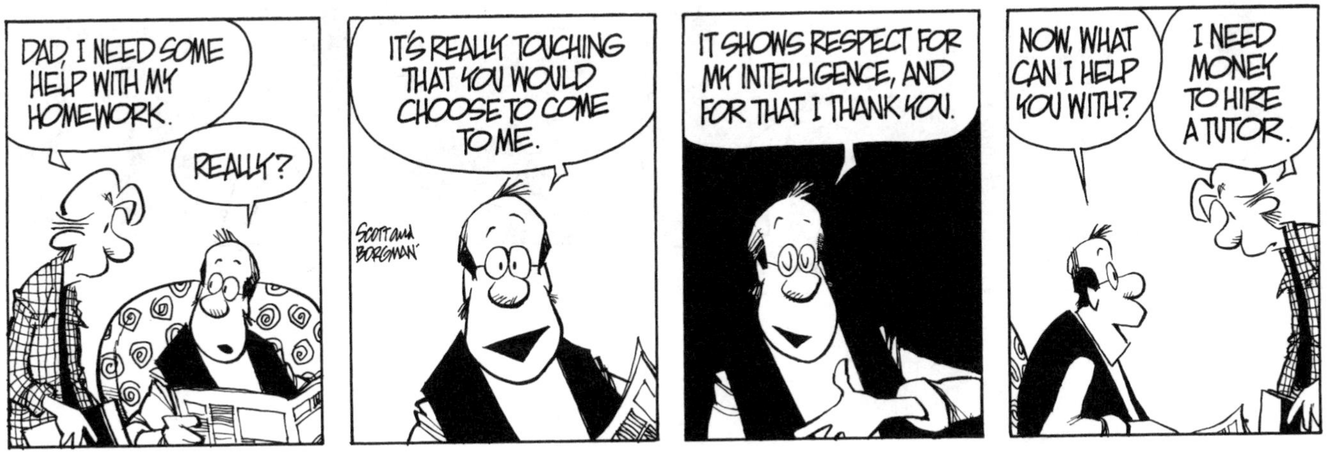
DAD, I NEED SOME HELP WITH MY HOMEWORK.
REALLY?
IT'S REALLY TOUCHING THAT YOU WOULD CHOOSE TO COME TO ME.
SCOTT AND BORGMAN
IT SHOWS RESPECT FOR MY INTELLIGENCE, AND FOR THAT I THANK YOU.
NOW, WHAT CAN I HELP YOU WITH?
I NEED MONEY TO HIRE A TUTOR.

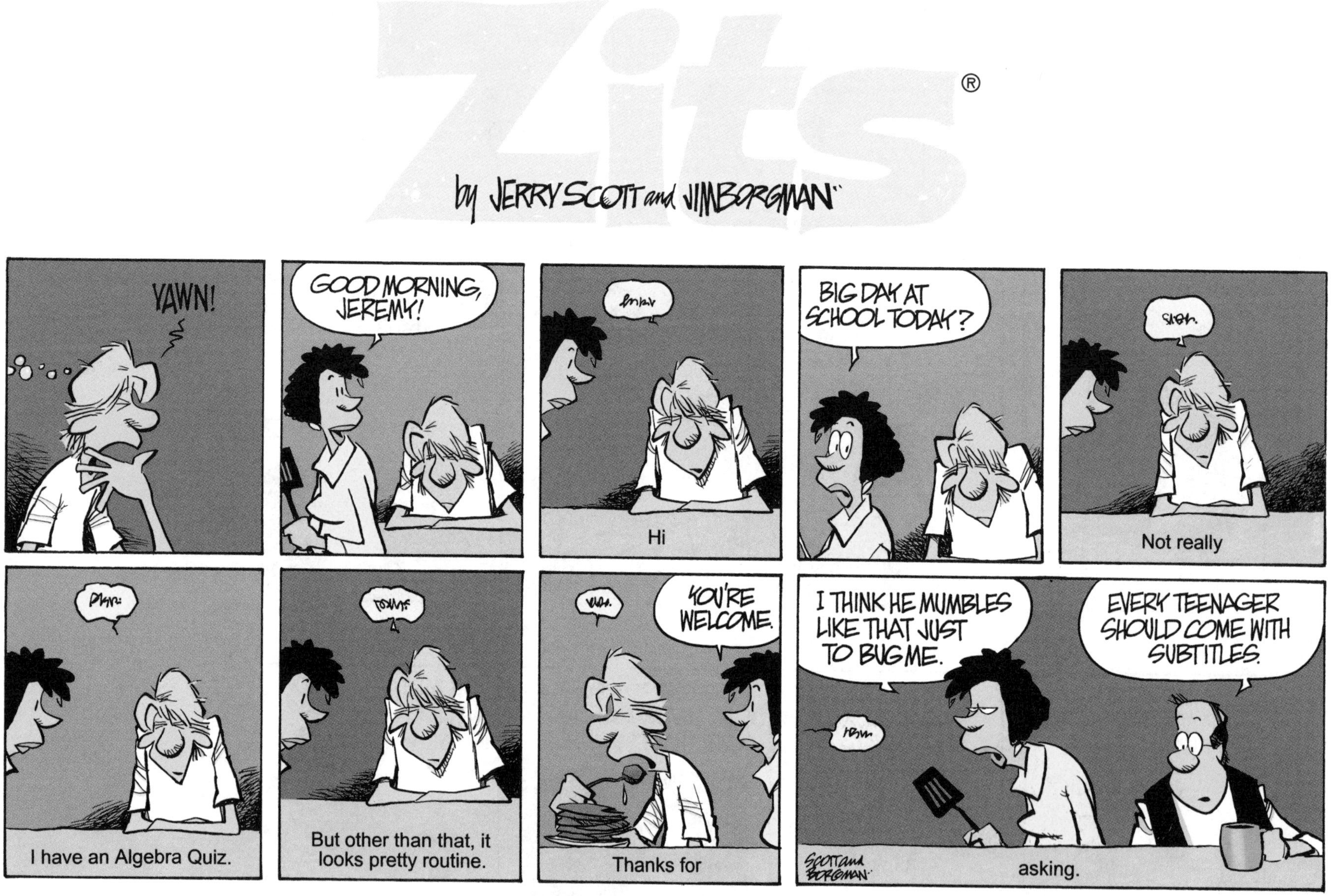
Zits®
by JERRY SCOTT and JIM BORGMAN
YAWN!
GOOD MORNING, JEREMY!
Hi
BIG DAY AT SCHOOL TODAY?
Not really
I have an Algebra Quiz.
But other than that, it looks pretty routine.
YOU'RE WELCOME.
Thanks for
I THINK HE MUMBLES LIKE THAT JUST TO BUG ME.
EVERY TEENAGER SHOULD COME WITH SUBTITLES.
asking.
SCOTT and BORGMAN

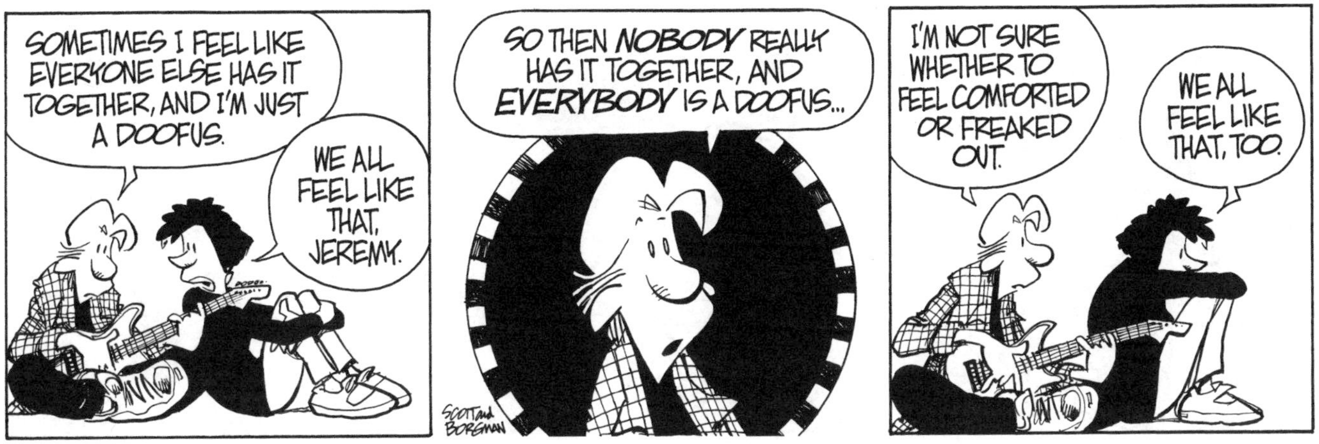

SOMETIMES I FEEL LIKE EVERYONE ELSE HAS IT TOGETHER, AND I'M JUST A DOOFUS.
WE ALL FEEL LIKE THAT, JEREMY.
SO THEN **NOBODY** REALLY HAS IT TOGETHER, AND **EVERYBODY** IS A DOOFUS...
SCOTT and BORGMAN
I'M NOT SURE WHETHER TO FEEL COMFORTED OR FREAKED OUT.
WE ALL FEEL LIKE THAT, TOO.

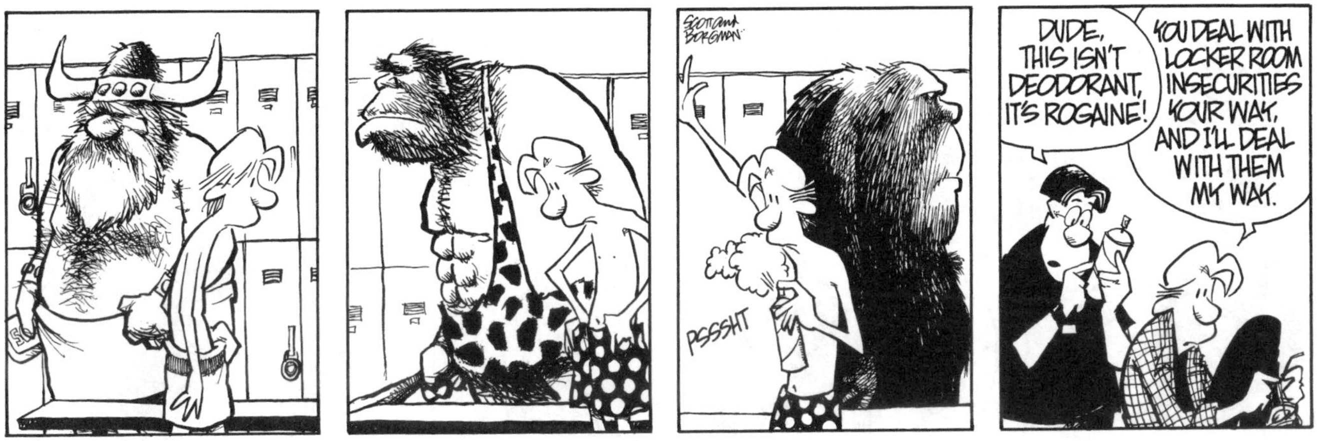

SCOTT and BORGMAN
PSSSHT
DUDE, THIS ISN'T DEODORANT, IT'S ROGAINE!
YOU DEAL WITH LOCKER ROOM INSECURITIES YOUR WAY, AND I'LL DEAL WITH THEM MY WAY.

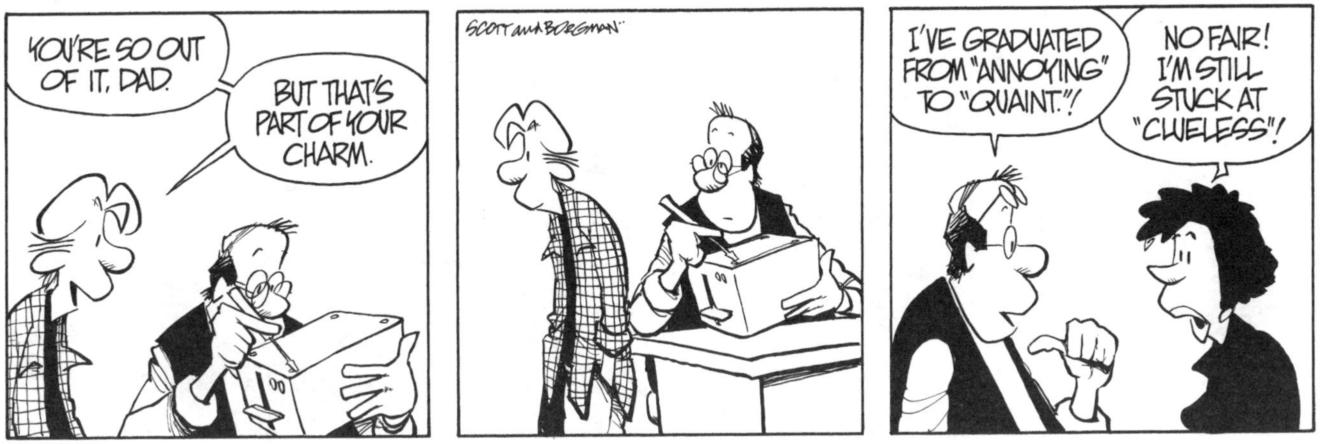

YOU'RE SO OUT OF IT, DAD.
BUT THAT'S PART OF YOUR CHARM.
SCOTT and BORGMAN
I'VE GRADUATED FROM "ANNOYING" TO "QUAINT."!
NO FAIR! I'M STILL STUCK AT "CLUELESS"!

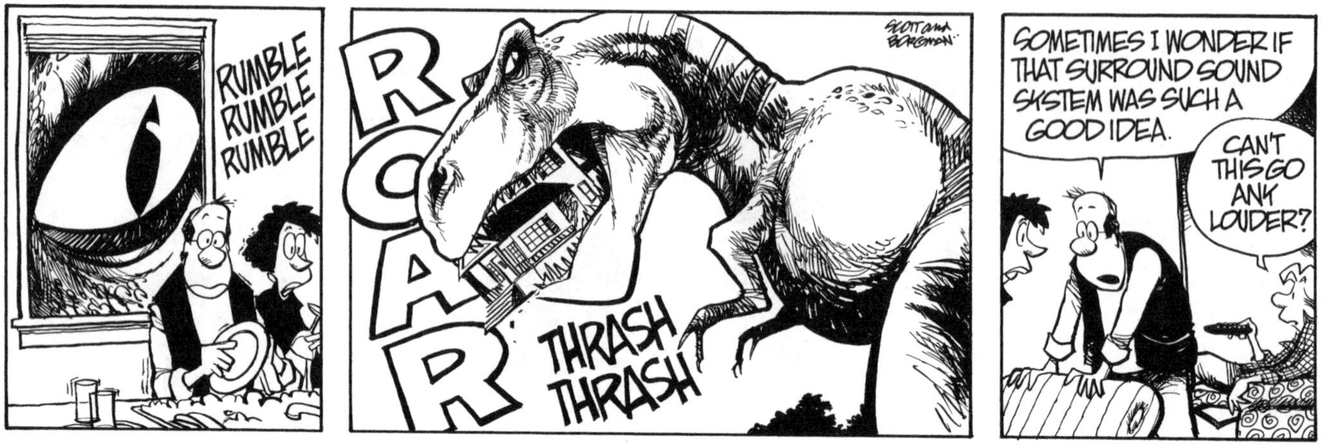
RUMBLE RUMBLE RUMBLE
ROAR
THRASH THRASH
SCOTT AND BORGMAN
SOMETIMES I WONDER IF THAT SURROUND SOUND SYSTEM WAS SUCH A GOOD IDEA.
CAN'T THIS GO ANY LOUDER?

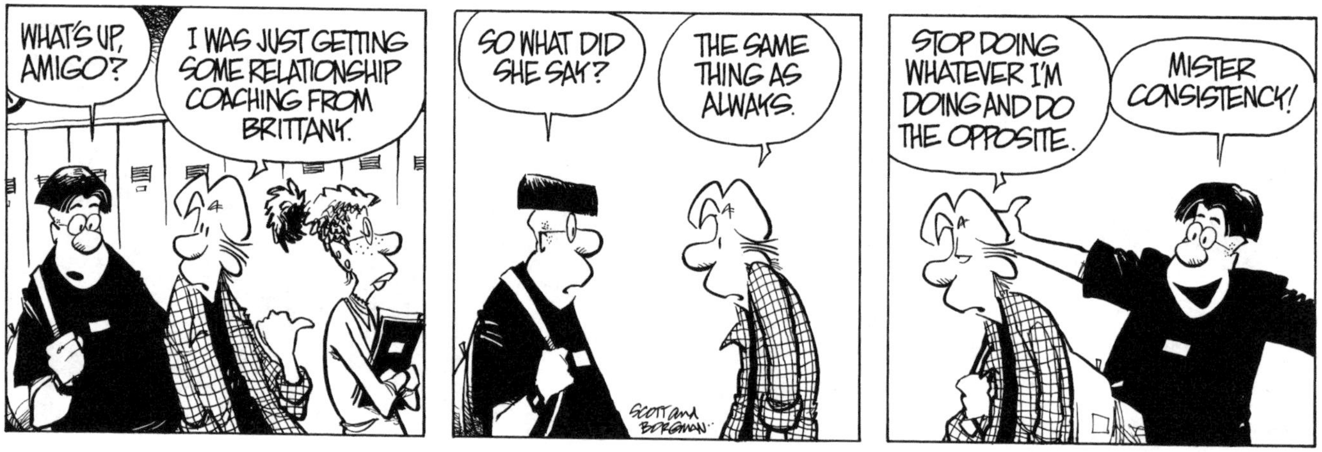
WHAT'S UP, AMIGO?
I WAS JUST GETTING SOME RELATIONSHIP COACHING FROM BRITTANY.
SO WHAT DID SHE SAY?
THE SAME THING AS ALWAYS.
SCOTT AND BORGMAN
STOP DOING WHATEVER I'M DOING AND DO THE OPPOSITE.
MISTER CONSISTENCY!

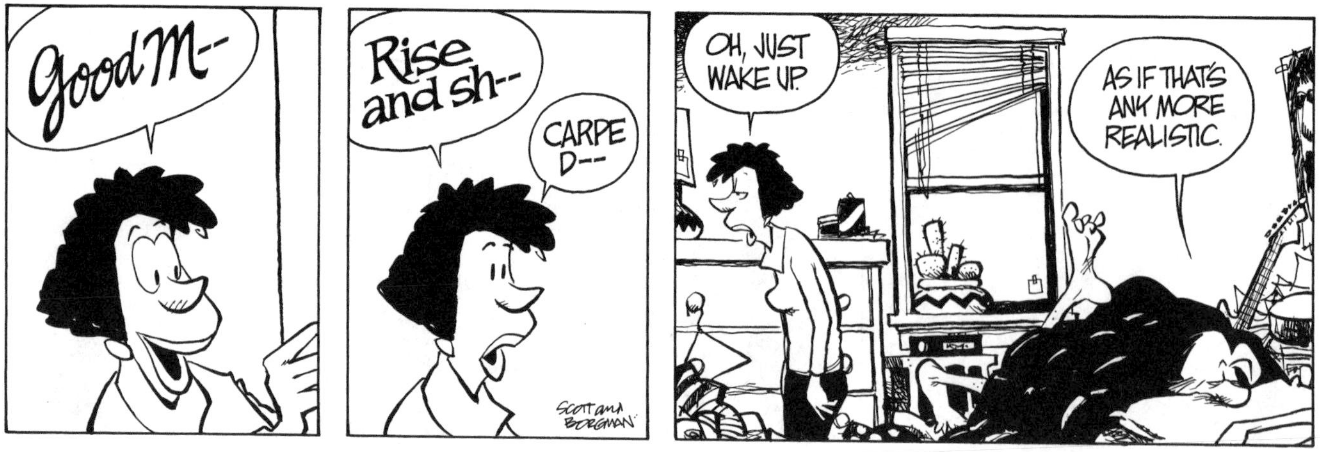
Good M--
Rise and sh--
CARPE D--
SCOTT AND BORGMAN
OH, JUST WAKE UP.
AS IF THAT'S ANY MORE REALISTIC.

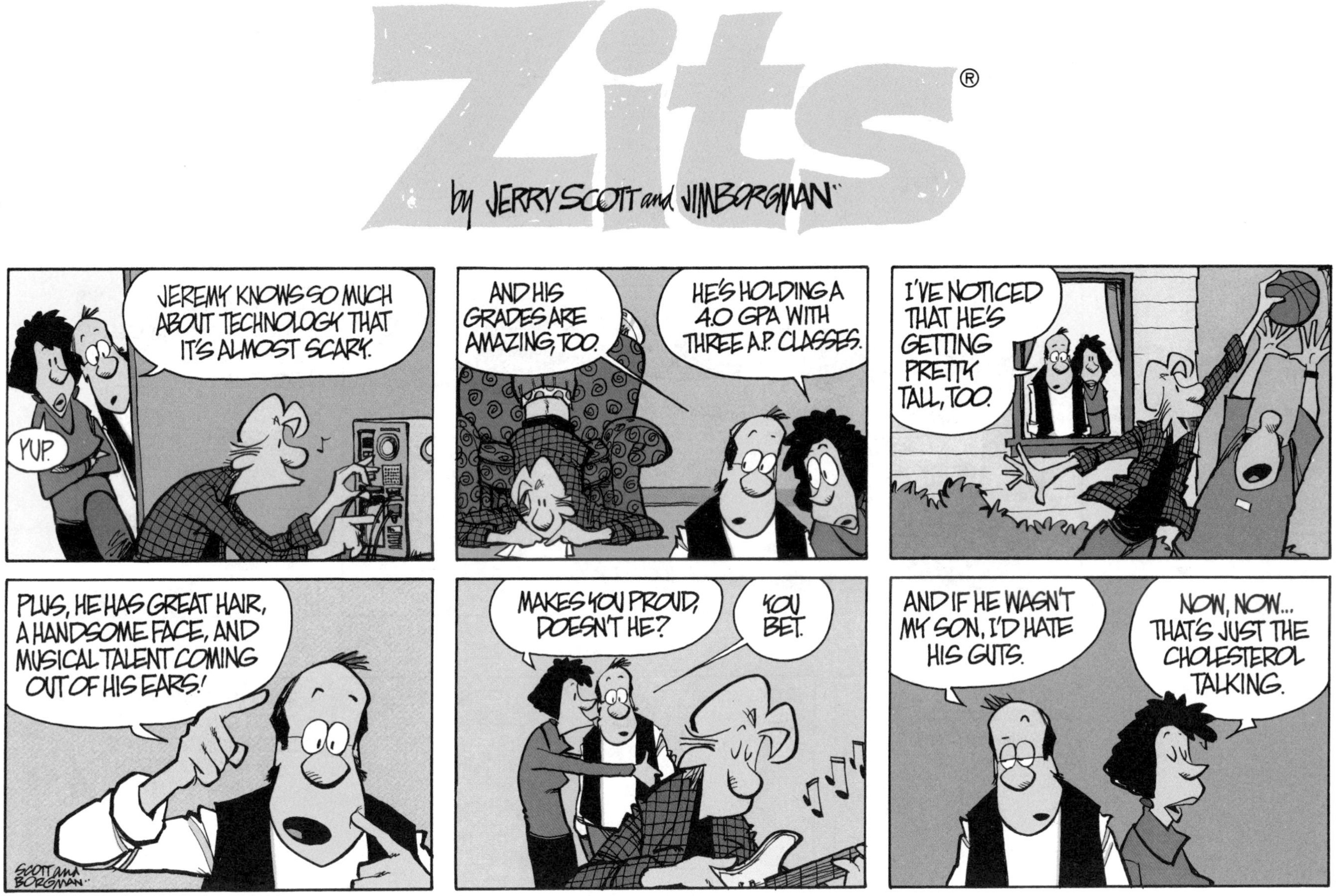
Zits®
by JERRY SCOTT and JIM BORGMAN
JEREMY KNOWS SO MUCH ABOUT TECHNOLOGY THAT IT'S ALMOST SCARY.
YUP.
AND HIS GRADES ARE AMAZING, TOO.
HE'S HOLDING A 4.0 GPA WITH THREE A.P. CLASSES.
I'VE NOTICED THAT HE'S GETTING PRETTY TALL, TOO.
PLUS, HE HAS GREAT HAIR, A HANDSOME FACE, AND MUSICAL TALENT COMING OUT OF HIS EARS!
SCOTT and BORGMAN
MAKES YOU PROUD, DOESN'T HE?
YOU BET.
AND IF HE WASN'T MY SON, I'D HATE HIS GUTS.
NOW, NOW... THAT'S JUST THE CHOLESTEROL TALKING.

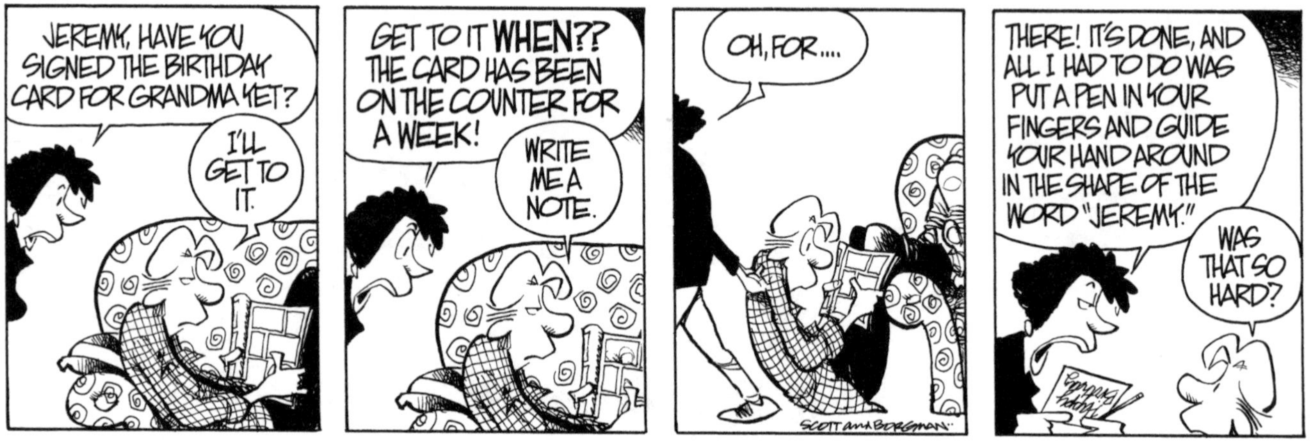
JEREMY, HAVE YOU SIGNED THE BIRTHDAY CARD FOR GRANDMA YET?
I'LL GET TO IT.
GET TO IT **WHEN??** THE CARD HAS BEEN ON THE COUNTER FOR A WEEK!
WRITE ME A NOTE.
OH, FOR....
THERE! IT'S DONE, AND ALL I HAD TO DO WAS PUT A PEN IN YOUR FINGERS AND GUIDE YOUR HAND AROUND IN THE SHAPE OF THE WORD "JEREMY."
WAS THAT SO HARD?

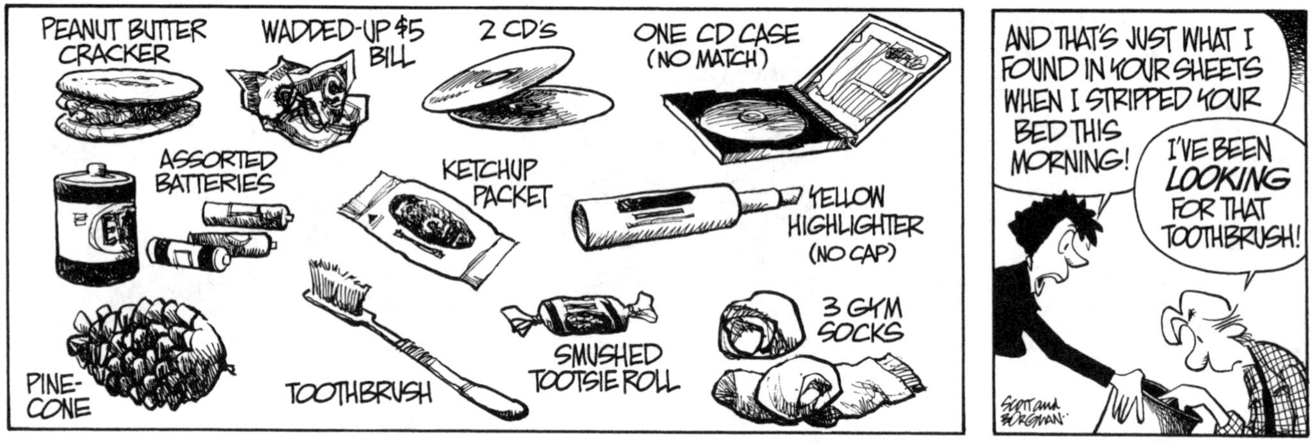
PEANUT BUTTER CRACKER
WADDED-UP $5 BILL
2 CD'S
ONE CD CASE (NO MATCH)
ASSORTED BATTERIES
KETCHUP PACKET
YELLOW HIGHLIGHTER (NO CAP)
PINE-CONE
TOOTHBRUSH
SMUSHED TOOTSIE ROLL
3 GYM SOCKS
AND THAT'S JUST WHAT I FOUND IN YOUR SHEETS WHEN I STRIPPED YOUR BED THIS MORNING!
I'VE BEEN *LOOKING* FOR THAT TOOTHBRUSH!

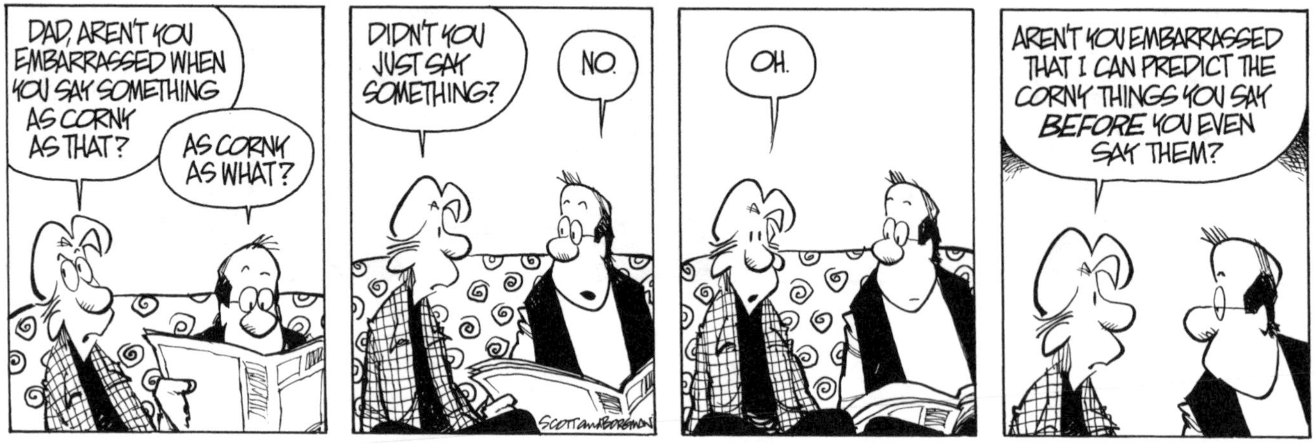
DAD, AREN'T YOU EMBARRASSED WHEN YOU SAY SOMETHING AS CORNY AS THAT?
AS CORNY AS WHAT?
DIDN'T YOU JUST SAY SOMETHING?
NO.
OH.
AREN'T YOU EMBARRASSED THAT I CAN PREDICT THE CORNY THINGS YOU SAY *BEFORE* YOU EVEN SAY THEM?

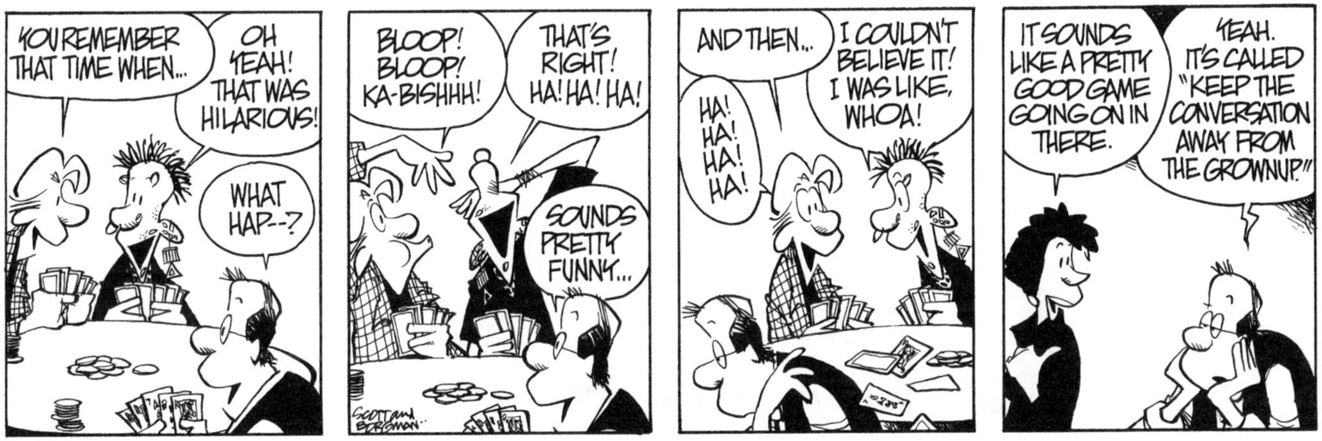
YOU REMEMBER THAT TIME WHEN...
OH YEAH! THAT WAS HILARIOUS!
WHAT HAP--?
BLOOP! BLOOP! KA-BISHHH!
THAT'S RIGHT! HA! HA! HA!
SOUNDS PRETTY FUNNY...
AND THEN...
I COULDN'T BELIEVE IT! I WAS LIKE, WHOA!
HA! HA! HA! HA!
IT SOUNDS LIKE A PRETTY GOOD GAME GOING ON IN THERE.
YEAH. IT'S CALLED "KEEP THE CONVERSATION AWAY FROM THE GROWNUP."

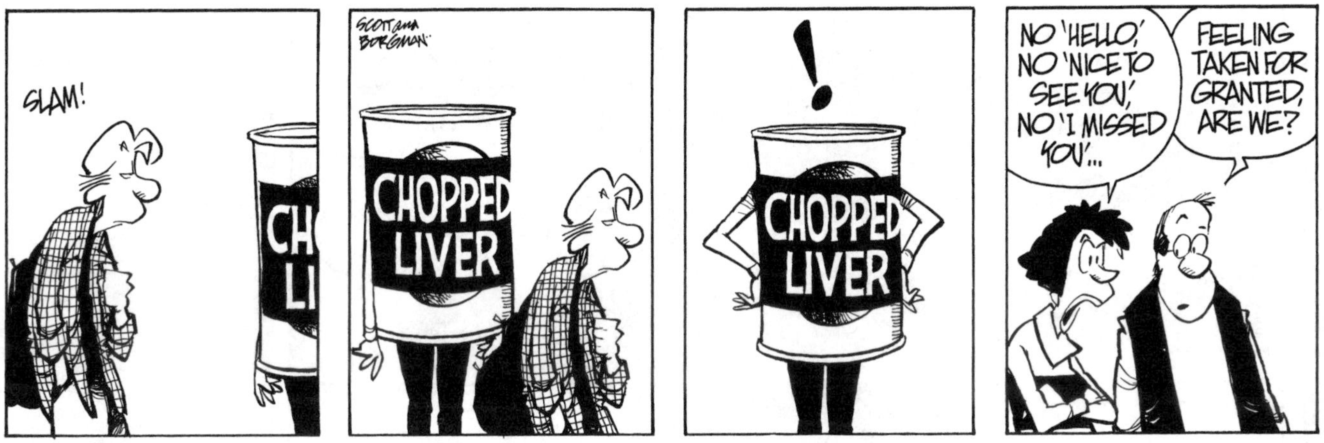
SLAM!
CHOPPED LIVER
CHOPPED LIVER
!
CHOPPED LIVER
NO 'HELLO,' NO 'NICE TO SEE YOU,' NO 'I MISSED YOU'...
FEELING TAKEN FOR GRANTED, ARE WE?

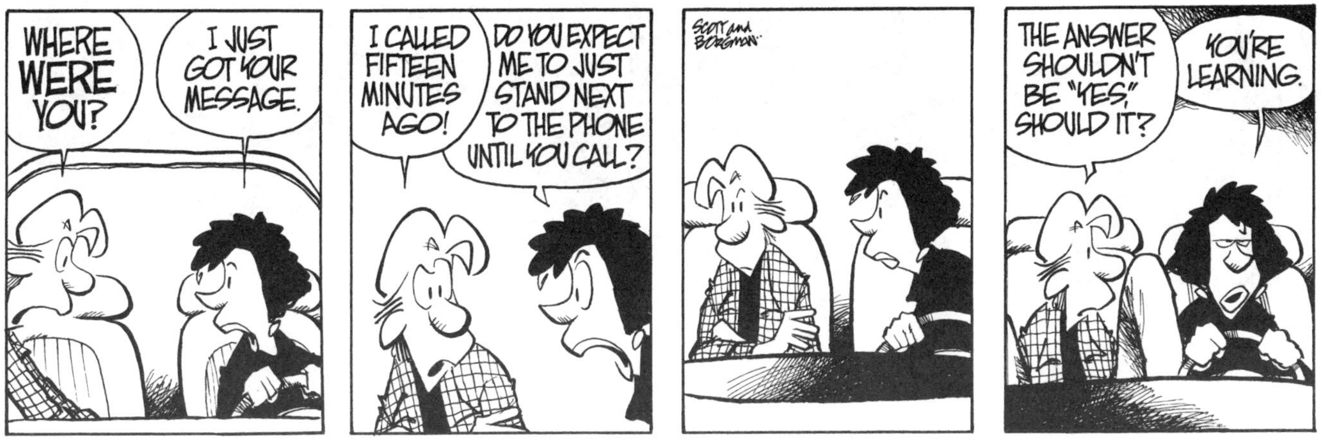
WHERE WERE YOU?
I JUST GOT YOUR MESSAGE.
I CALLED FIFTEEN MINUTES AGO!
DO YOU EXPECT ME TO JUST STAND NEXT TO THE PHONE UNTIL YOU CALL?
THE ANSWER SHOULDN'T BE "YES," SHOULD IT?
YOU'RE LEARNING.

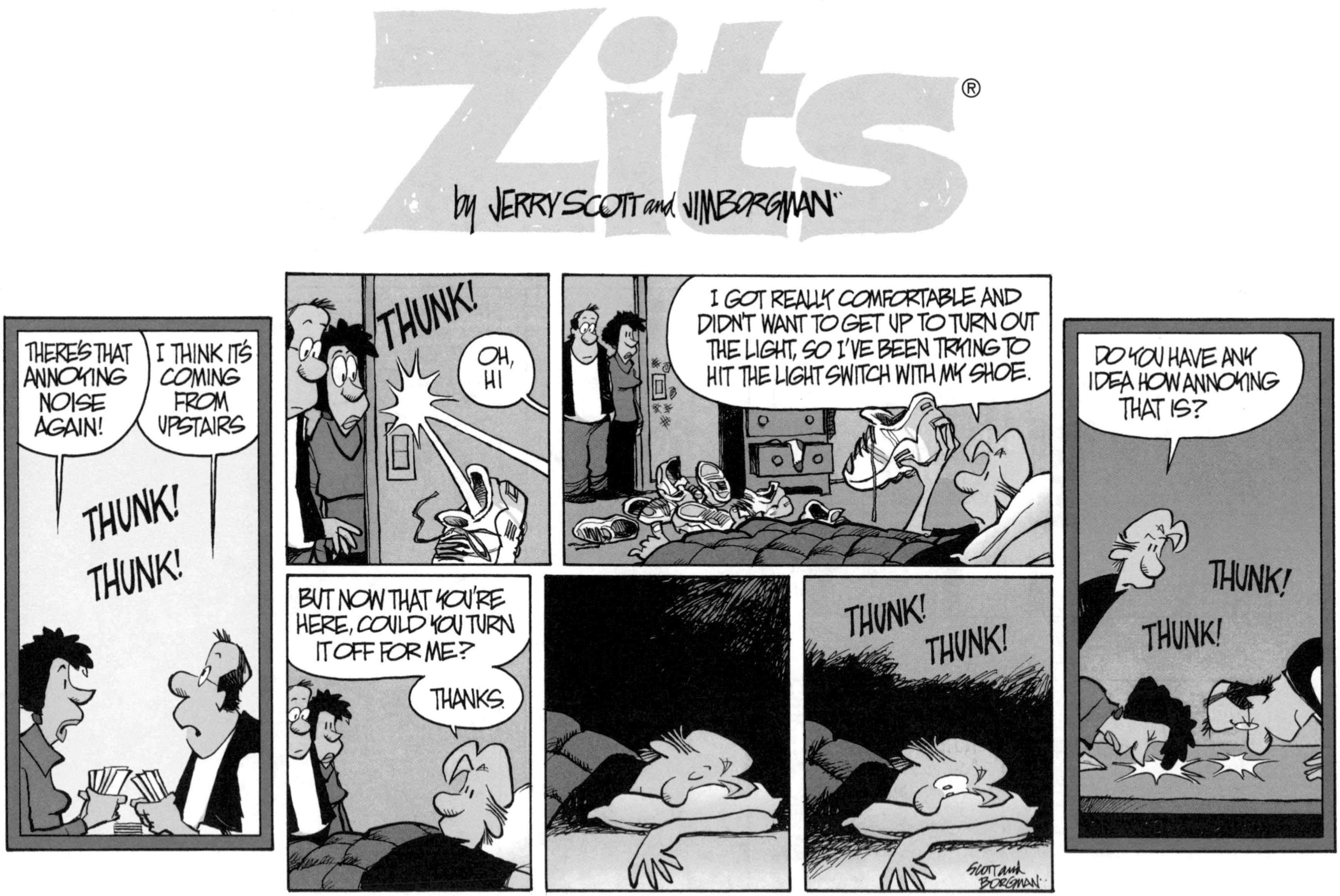
Zits®
by JERRY SCOTT and JIM BORGMAN
THERE'S THAT ANNOYING NOISE AGAIN!
I THINK IT'S COMING FROM UPSTAIRS
THUNK!
THUNK!
THUNK!
OH, HI
I GOT REALLY COMFORTABLE AND DIDN'T WANT TO GET UP TO TURN OUT THE LIGHT, SO I'VE BEEN TRYING TO HIT THE LIGHT SWITCH WITH MY SHOE.
BUT NOW THAT YOU'RE HERE, COULD YOU TURN IT OFF FOR ME?
THANKS.
THUNK!
THUNK!
SCOTT and BORGMAN
DO YOU HAVE ANY IDEA HOW ANNOYING THAT IS?
THUNK!
THUNK!

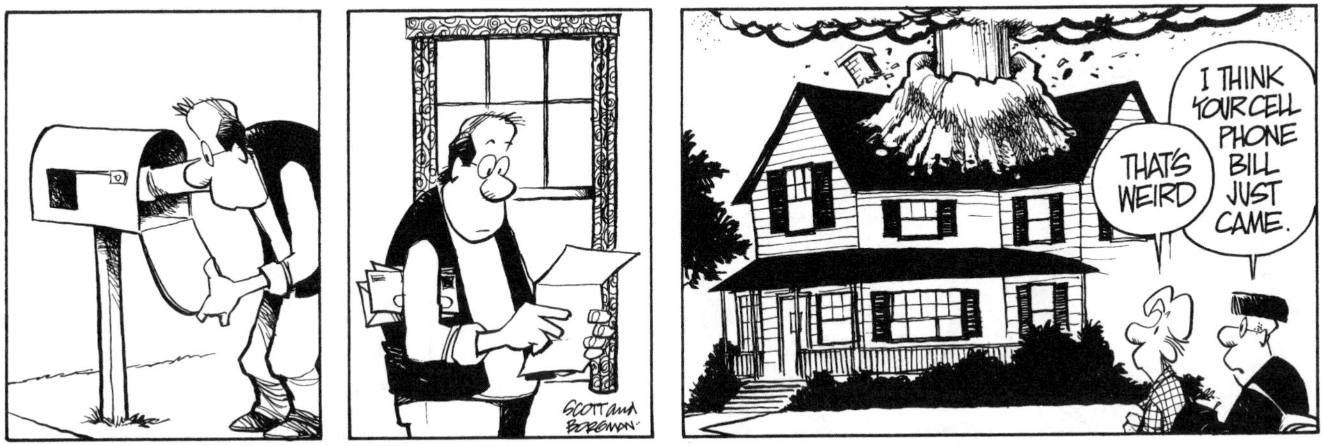
THAT'S WEIRD
I THINK YOUR CELL PHONE BILL JUST CAME.

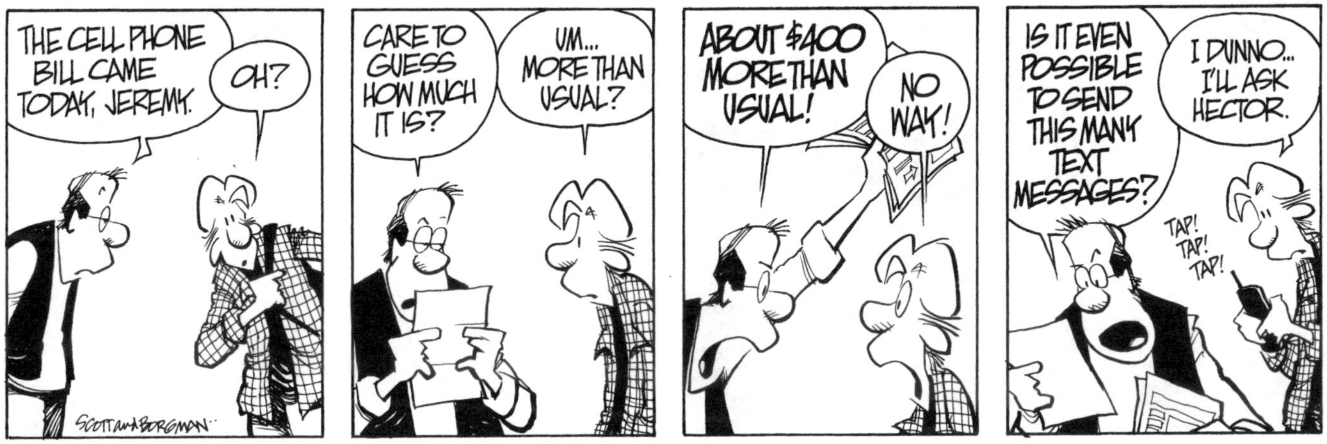
THE CELL PHONE BILL CAME TODAY, JEREMY.
OH?
CARE TO GUESS HOW MUCH IT IS?
UM... MORE THAN USUAL?
ABOUT $400 MORE THAN USUAL!
NO WAY!
IS IT EVEN POSSIBLE TO SEND THIS MANY TEXT MESSAGES?
I DUNNO... I'LL ASK HECTOR.
TAP! TAP! TAP!

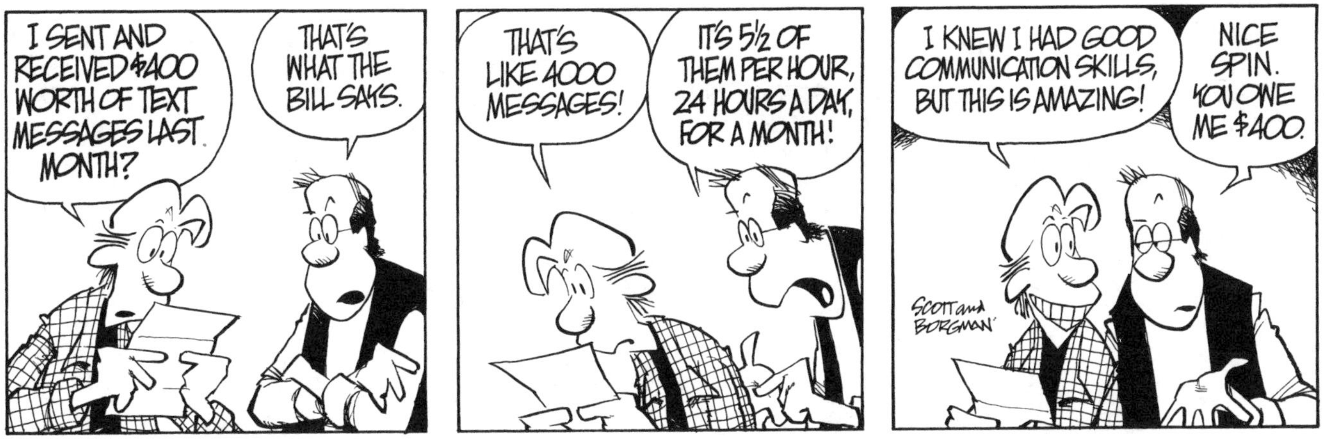
I SENT AND RECEIVED $400 WORTH OF TEXT MESSAGES LAST MONTH?
THAT'S WHAT THE BILL SAYS.
THAT'S LIKE 4000 MESSAGES!
IT'S 5½ OF THEM PER HOUR, 24 HOURS A DAY, FOR A MONTH!
I KNEW I HAD GOOD COMMUNICATION SKILLS, BUT THIS IS AMAZING!
NICE SPIN. YOU OWE ME $400.

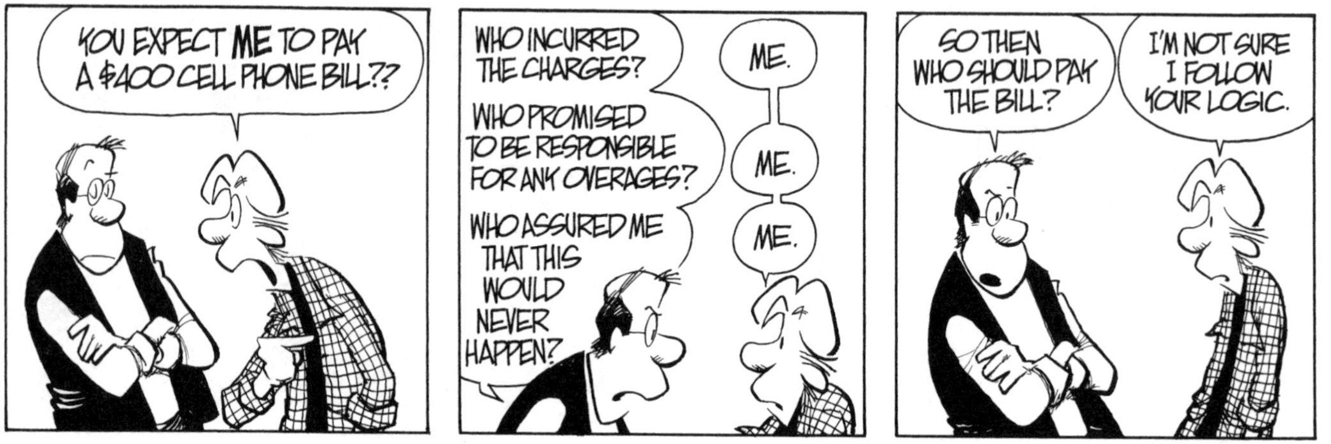

YOU EXPECT **ME** TO PAY A $400 CELL PHONE BILL??
WHO INCURRED THE CHARGES?
ME.
WHO PROMISED TO BE RESPONSIBLE FOR ANY OVERAGES?
ME.
WHO ASSURED ME THAT THIS WOULD NEVER HAPPEN?
ME.
SO THEN WHO SHOULD PAY THE BILL?
I'M NOT SURE I FOLLOW YOUR LOGIC.

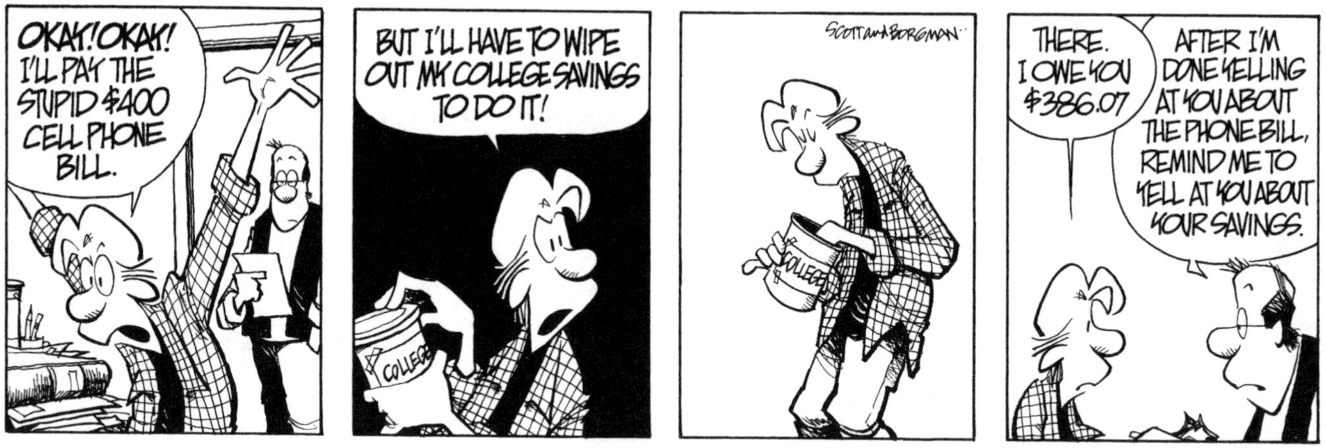

OKAY! OKAY! I'LL PAY THE STUPID $400 CELL PHONE BILL.
BUT I'LL HAVE TO WIPE OUT MY COLLEGE SAVINGS TO DO IT!
COLLEGE
THERE. I OWE YOU $386.07
AFTER I'M DONE YELLING AT YOU ABOUT THE PHONE BILL, REMIND ME TO YELL AT YOU ABOUT YOUR SAVINGS.

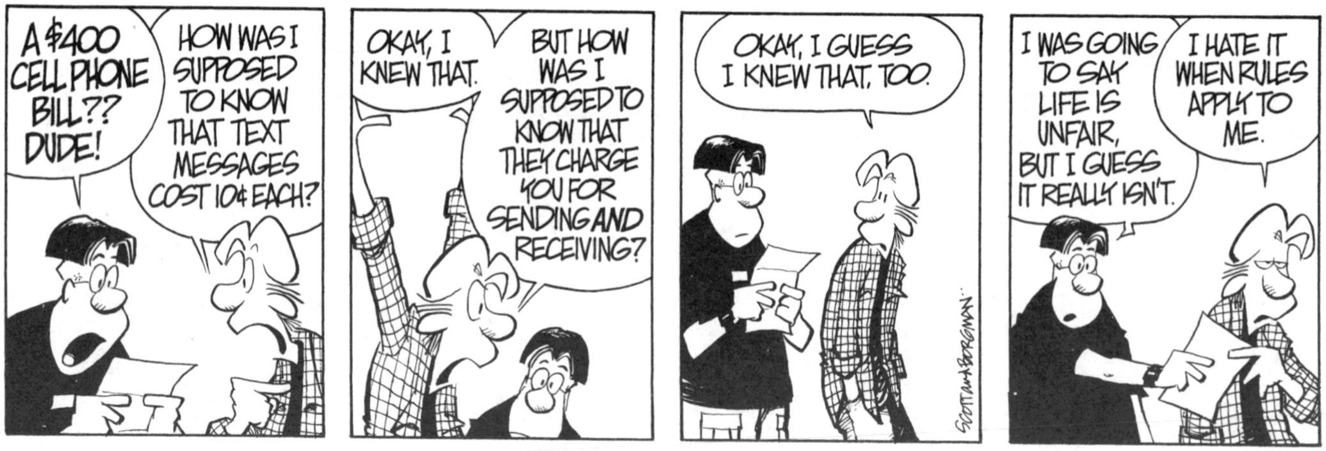

A $400 CELL PHONE BILL?? DUDE!
HOW WAS I SUPPOSED TO KNOW THAT TEXT MESSAGES COST 10¢ EACH?
OKAY, I KNEW THAT.
BUT HOW WAS I SUPPOSED TO KNOW THAT THEY CHARGE YOU FOR SENDING **AND** RECEIVING?
OKAY, I GUESS I KNEW THAT, TOO.
I WAS GOING TO SAY LIFE IS UNFAIR, BUT I GUESS IT REALLY ISN'T.
I HATE IT WHEN RULES APPLY TO ME.

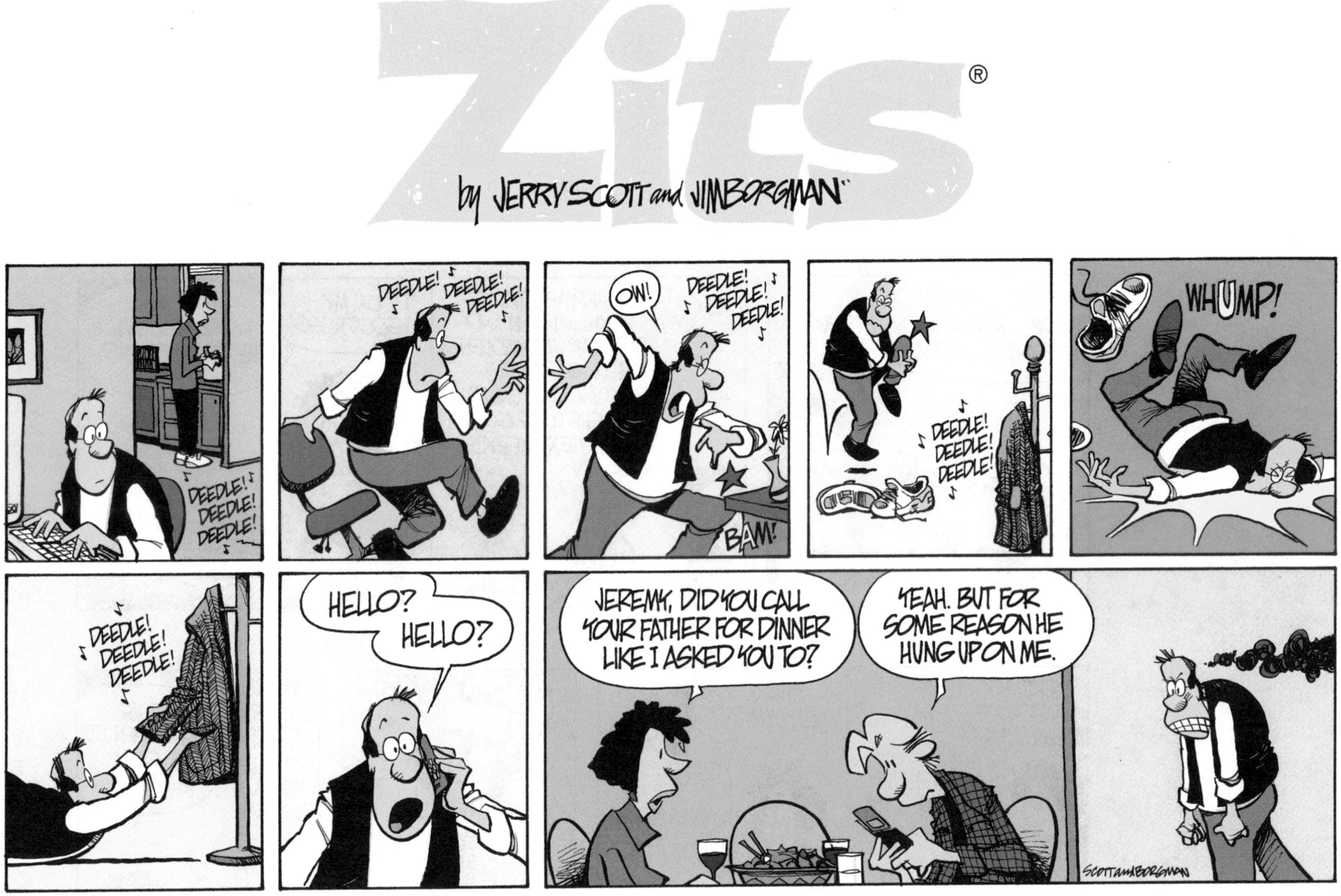
Zits®
by JERRY SCOTT and JIM BORGMAN
DEEDLE! DEEDLE! DEEDLE!
DEEDLE! DEEDLE! DEEDLE!
OW!
DEEDLE! DEEDLE! DEEDLE!
BAM!
DEEDLE! DEEDLE! DEEDLE!
WHUMP!
DEEDLE! DEEDLE! DEEDLE!
HELLO? HELLO?
JEREMY, DID YOU CALL YOUR FATHER FOR DINNER LIKE I ASKED YOU TO?
YEAH. BUT FOR SOME REASON HE HUNG UP ON ME.
SCOTT and BORGMAN

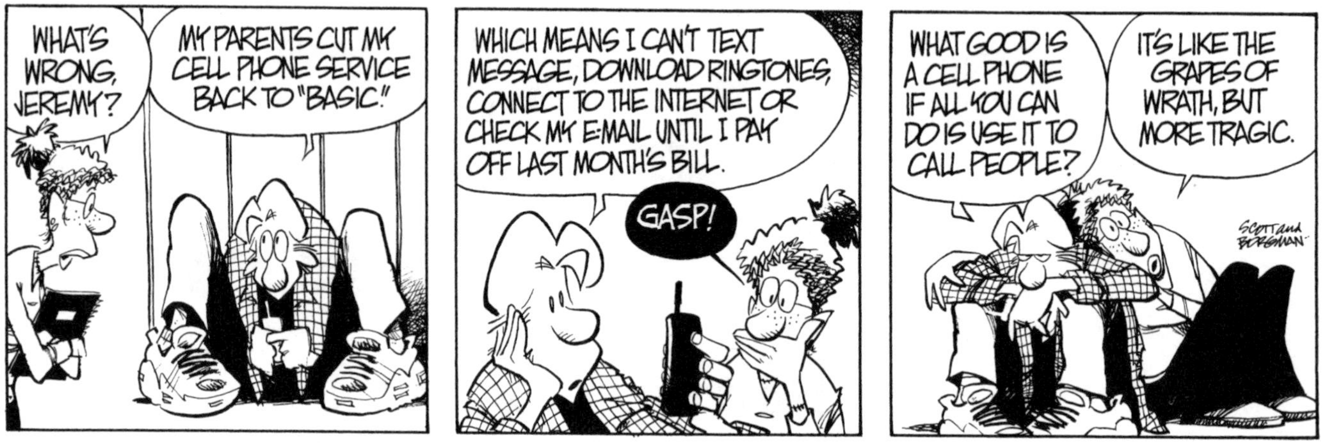
WHAT'S WRONG, JEREMY?
MY PARENTS CUT MY CELL PHONE SERVICE BACK TO "BASIC."
WHICH MEANS I CAN'T TEXT MESSAGE, DOWNLOAD RINGTONES, CONNECT TO THE INTERNET OR CHECK MY E-MAIL UNTIL I PAY OFF LAST MONTH'S BILL.
GASP!
WHAT GOOD IS A CELL PHONE IF ALL YOU CAN DO IS USE IT TO CALL PEOPLE?
IT'S LIKE THE GRAPES OF WRATH, BUT MORE TRAGIC.
SCOTT and BORGMAN

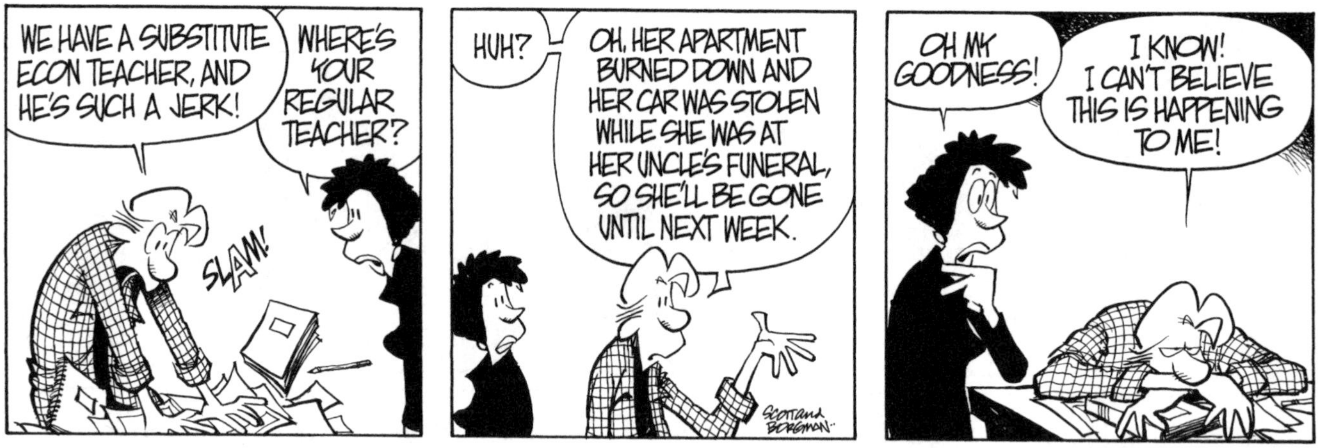
WE HAVE A SUBSTITUTE ECON TEACHER, AND HE'S SUCH A JERK!
WHERE'S YOUR REGULAR TEACHER?
SLAM!
HUH?
OH, HER APARTMENT BURNED DOWN AND HER CAR WAS STOLEN WHILE SHE WAS AT HER UNCLE'S FUNERAL, SO SHE'LL BE GONE UNTIL NEXT WEEK.
SCOTT and BORGMAN
OH MY GOODNESS!
I KNOW! I CAN'T BELIEVE THIS IS HAPPENING TO ME!

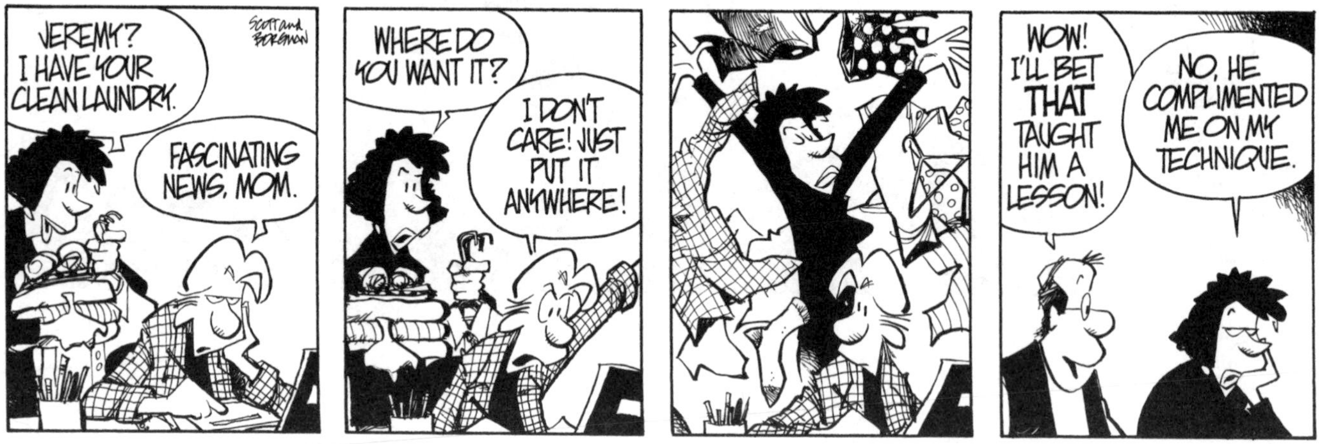
JEREMY? I HAVE YOUR CLEAN LAUNDRY.
SCOTT and BORGMAN
FASCINATING NEWS, MOM.
WHERE DO YOU WANT IT?
I DON'T CARE! JUST PUT IT ANYWHERE!
WOW! I'LL BET THAT TAUGHT HIM A LESSON!
NO, HE COMPLIMENTED ME ON MY TECHNIQUE.

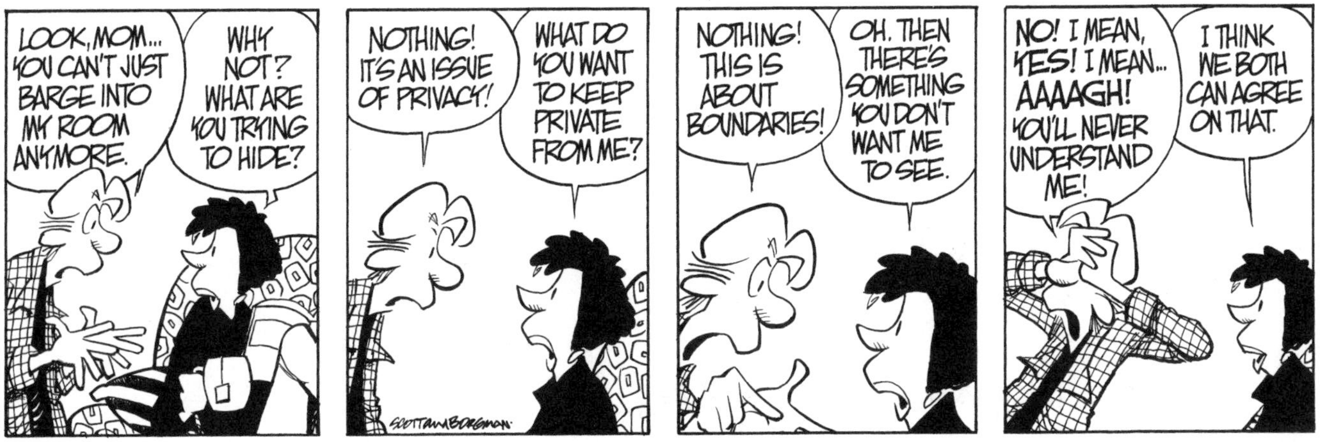
LOOK, MOM... YOU CAN'T JUST BARGE INTO MY ROOM ANYMORE.
WHY NOT? WHAT ARE YOU TRYING TO HIDE?
NOTHING! IT'S AN ISSUE OF PRIVACY!
WHAT DO YOU WANT TO KEEP PRIVATE FROM ME?
NOTHING! THIS IS ABOUT BOUNDARIES!
OH. THEN THERE'S SOMETHING YOU DON'T WANT ME TO SEE.
NO! I MEAN, YES! I MEAN... AAAAGH! YOU'LL NEVER UNDERSTAND ME!
I THINK WE BOTH CAN AGREE ON THAT.

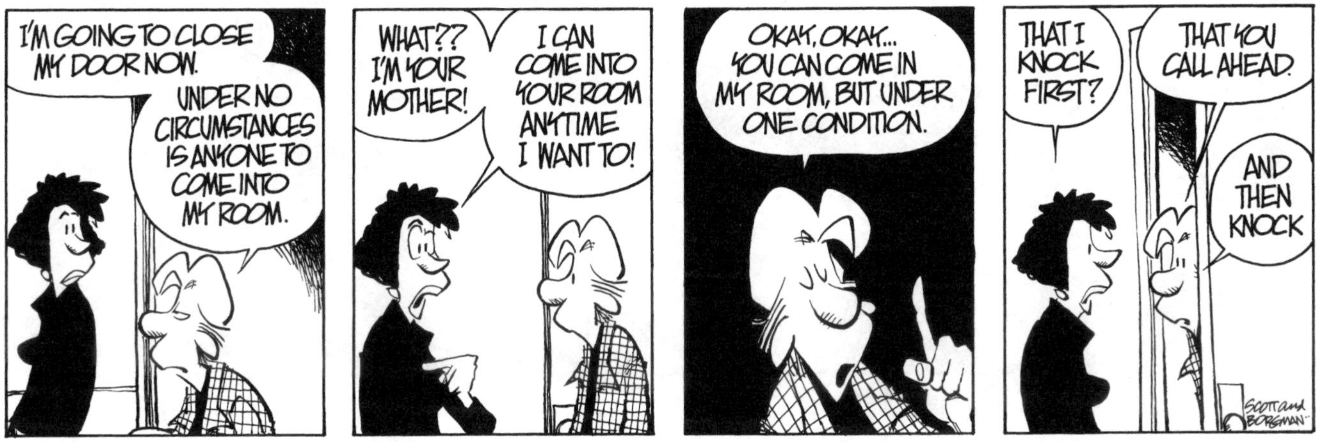
I'M GOING TO CLOSE MY DOOR NOW.
UNDER NO CIRCUMSTANCES IS ANYONE TO COME INTO MY ROOM.
WHAT?? I'M YOUR MOTHER!
I CAN COME INTO YOUR ROOM ANYTIME I WANT TO!
OKAY, OKAY... YOU CAN COME IN MY ROOM, BUT UNDER ONE CONDITION.
THAT I KNOCK FIRST?
THAT YOU CALL AHEAD.
AND THEN KNOCK

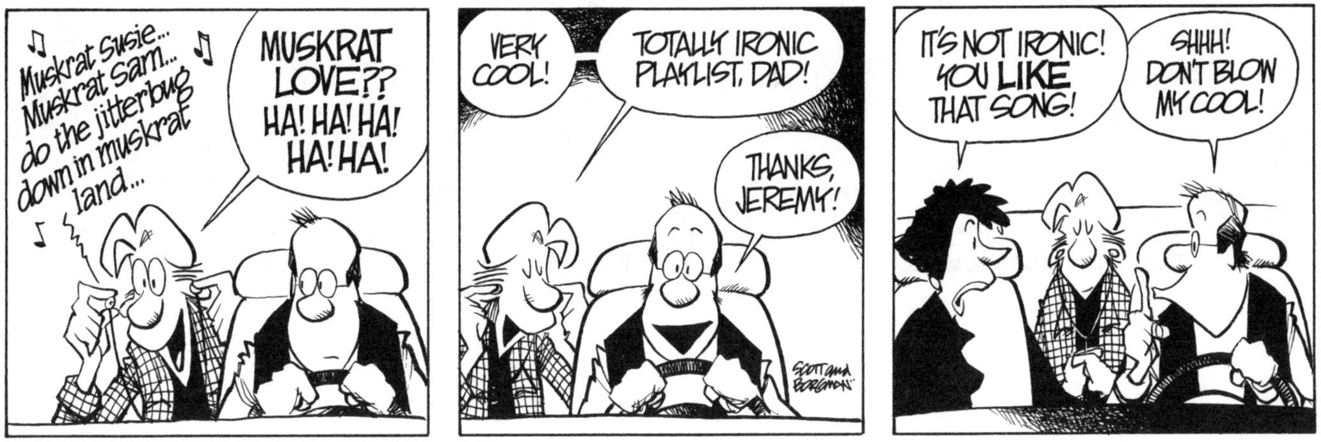
Muskrat Susie... Muskrat Sam... do the jitterbug down in muskrat land...
MUSKRAT LOVE?? HA! HA! HA! HA! HA!
VERY COOL!
TOTALLY IRONIC PLAYLIST, DAD!
THANKS, JEREMY!
IT'S NOT IRONIC! YOU LIKE THAT SONG!
SHHH! DON'T BLOW MY COOL!

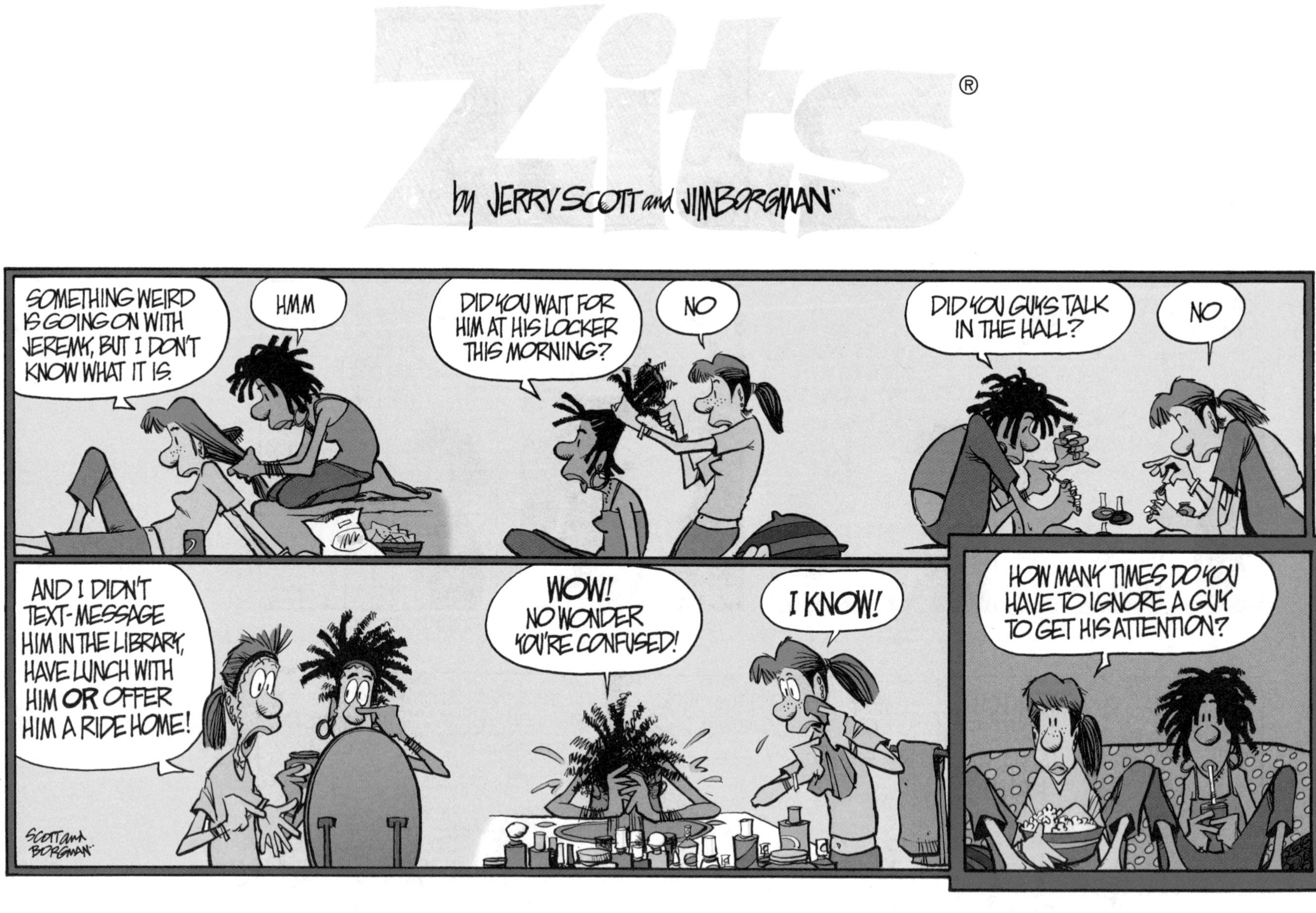
Zits®
by JERRY SCOTT and JIM BORGMAN
SOMETHING WEIRD IS GOING ON WITH JEREMY, BUT I DON'T KNOW WHAT IT IS.
HMM
DID YOU WAIT FOR HIM AT HIS LOCKER THIS MORNING?
NO
DID YOU GUYS TALK IN THE HALL?
NO
AND I DIDN'T TEXT-MESSAGE HIM IN THE LIBRARY, HAVE LUNCH WITH HIM OR OFFER HIM A RIDE HOME!
WOW! NO WONDER YOU'RE CONFUSED!
I KNOW!
HOW MANY TIMES DO YOU HAVE TO IGNORE A GUY TO GET HIS ATTENTION?
SCOTT and BORGMAN

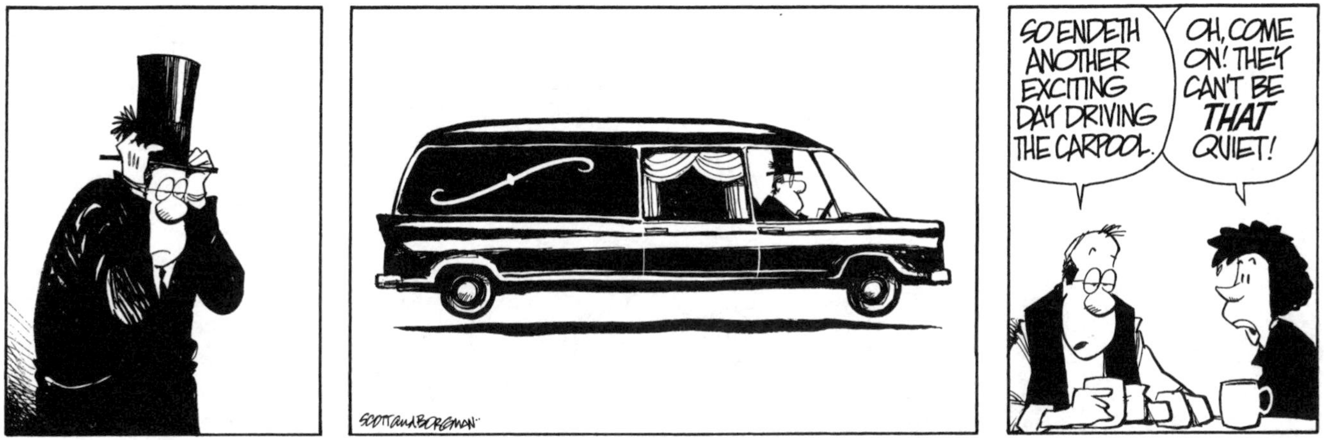
SO ENDETH ANOTHER EXCITING DAY DRIVING THE CARPOOL.
OH, COME ON! THEY CAN'T BE *THAT* QUIET!

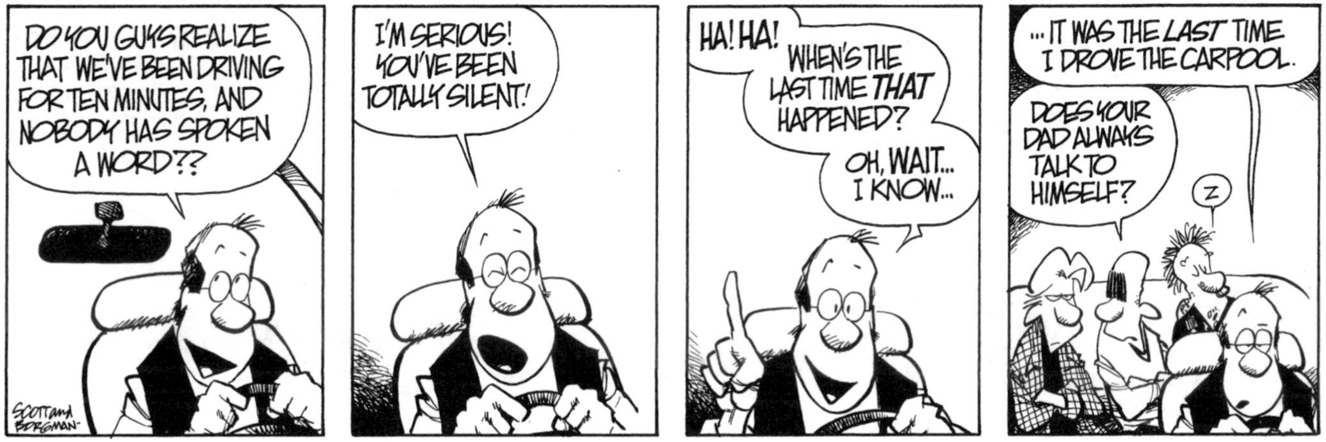
DO YOU GUYS REALIZE THAT WE'VE BEEN DRIVING FOR TEN MINUTES, AND NOBODY HAS SPOKEN A WORD??
I'M SERIOUS! YOU'VE BEEN TOTALLY SILENT!
HA! HA!
WHEN'S THE LAST TIME *THAT* HAPPENED?
OH, WAIT... I KNOW...
... IT WAS THE *LAST* TIME I DROVE THE CARPOOL.
DOES YOUR DAD ALWAYS TALK TO HIMSELF?
Z

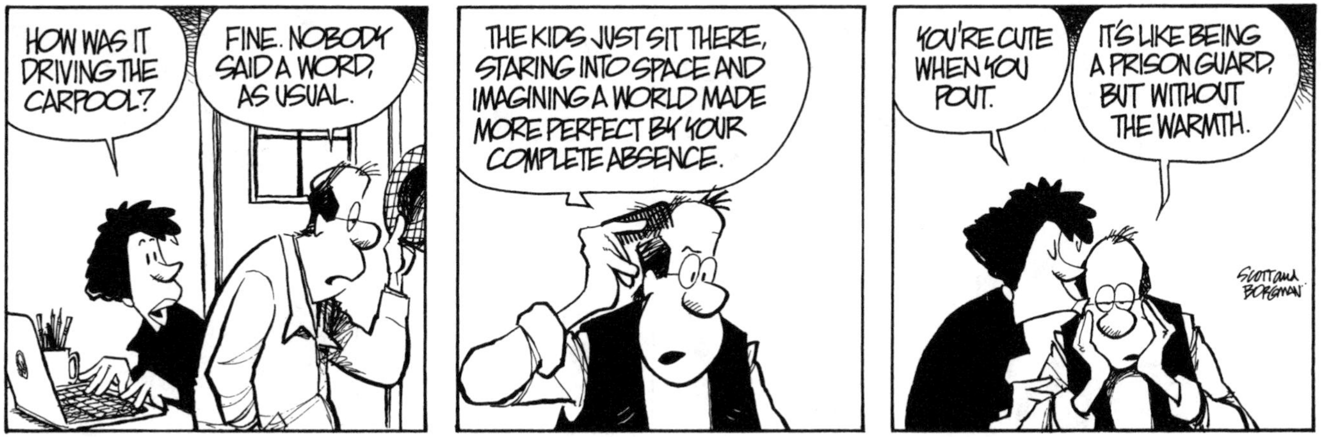
HOW WAS IT DRIVING THE CARPOOL?
FINE. NOBODY SAID A WORD, AS USUAL.
THE KIDS JUST SIT THERE, STARING INTO SPACE AND IMAGINING A WORLD MADE MORE PERFECT BY YOUR COMPLETE ABSENCE.
YOU'RE CUTE WHEN YOU POUT.
IT'S LIKE BEING A PRISON GUARD, BUT WITHOUT THE WARMTH.

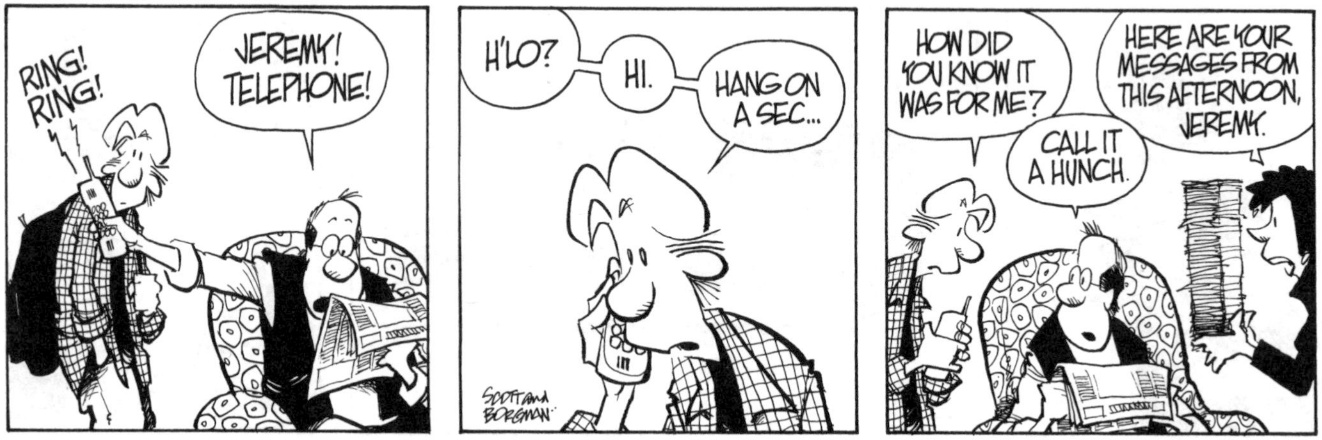
RING! RING!
JEREMY! TELEPHONE!
H'LO?
HI.
HANG ON A SEC...
SCOTT AND BORGMAN
HOW DID YOU KNOW IT WAS FOR ME?
CALL IT A HUNCH.
HERE ARE YOUR MESSAGES FROM THIS AFTERNOON, JEREMY.

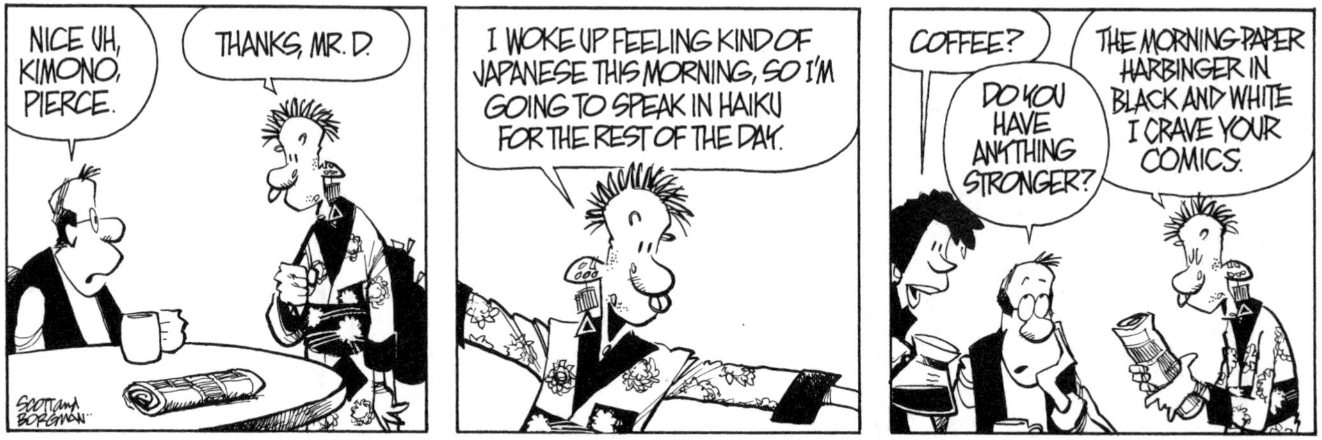
NICE UH, KIMONO, PIERCE.
THANKS, MR. D.
SCOTT AND BORGMAN
I WOKE UP FEELING KIND OF JAPANESE THIS MORNING, SO I'M GOING TO SPEAK IN HAIKU FOR THE REST OF THE DAY.
COFFEE?
DO YOU HAVE ANYTHING STRONGER?
THE MORNING PAPER HARBINGER IN BLACK AND WHITE I CRAVE YOUR COMICS.

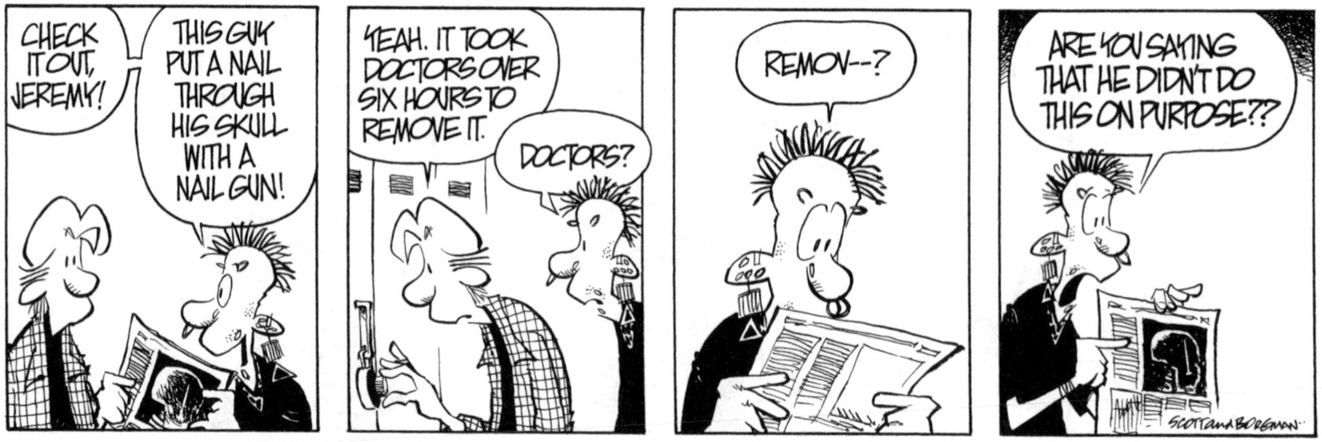
CHECK IT OUT, JEREMY!
THIS GUY PUT A NAIL THROUGH HIS SKULL WITH A NAIL GUN!
YEAH. IT TOOK DOCTORS OVER SIX HOURS TO REMOVE IT.
DOCTORS?
REMOV--?
ARE YOU SAYING THAT HE DIDN'T DO THIS ON PURPOSE??
SCOTT AND BORGMAN

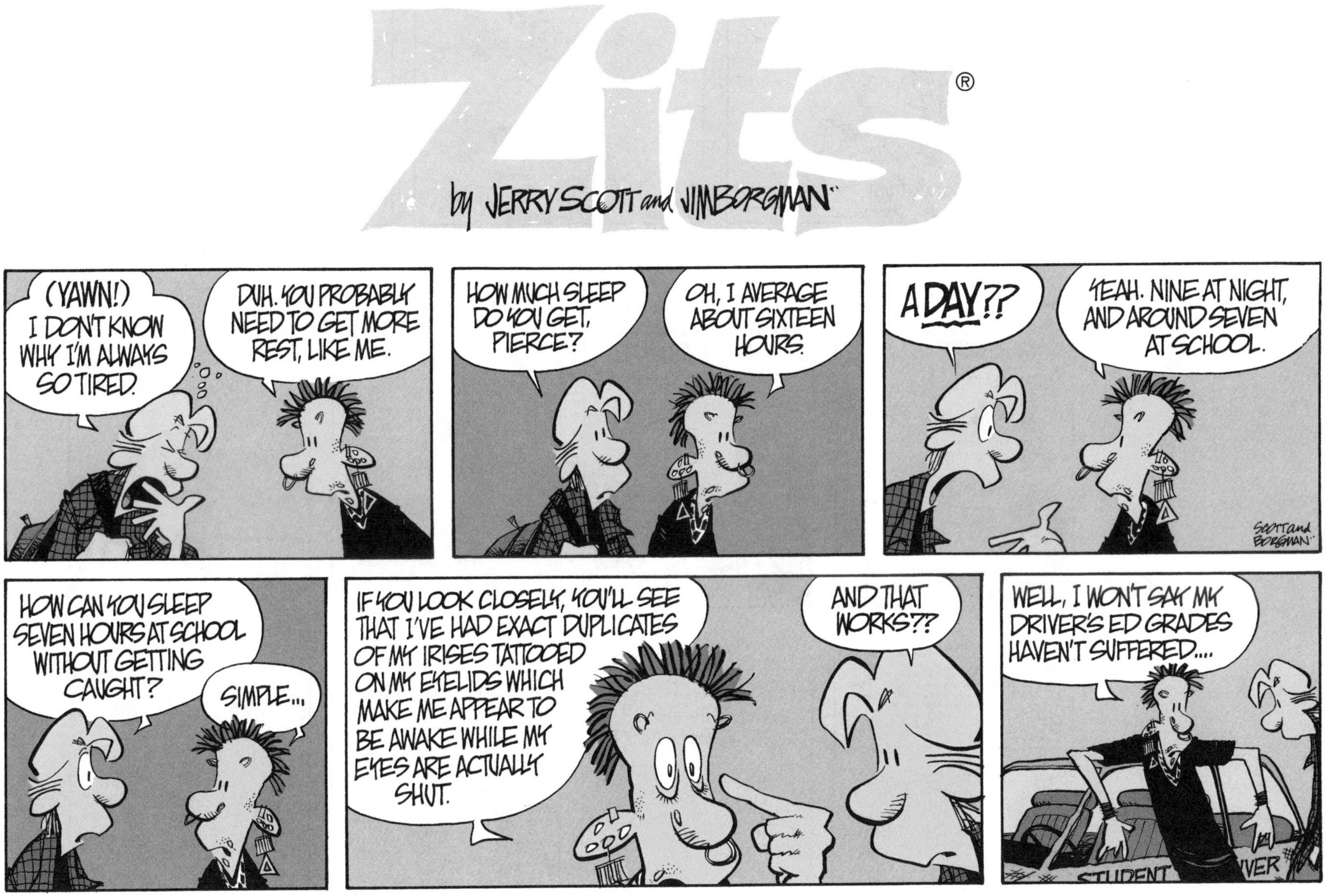
Zits®
by JERRY SCOTT and JIM BORGMAN
(YAWN!) I DON'T KNOW WHY I'M ALWAYS SO TIRED.
DUH. YOU PROBABLY NEED TO GET MORE REST, LIKE ME.
HOW MUCH SLEEP DO YOU GET, PIERCE?
OH, I AVERAGE ABOUT SIXTEEN HOURS.
A DAY??
YEAH. NINE AT NIGHT, AND AROUND SEVEN AT SCHOOL.
SCOTT and BORGMAN
HOW CAN YOU SLEEP SEVEN HOURS AT SCHOOL WITHOUT GETTING CAUGHT?
SIMPLE...
IF YOU LOOK CLOSELY, YOU'LL SEE THAT I'VE HAD EXACT DUPLICATES OF MY IRISES TATTOOED ON MY EYELIDS WHICH MAKE ME APPEAR TO BE AWAKE WHILE MY EYES ARE ACTUALLY SHUT.
AND THAT WORKS??
WELL, I WON'T SAY MY DRIVER'S ED GRADES HAVEN'T SUFFERED....
STUDENT
VER

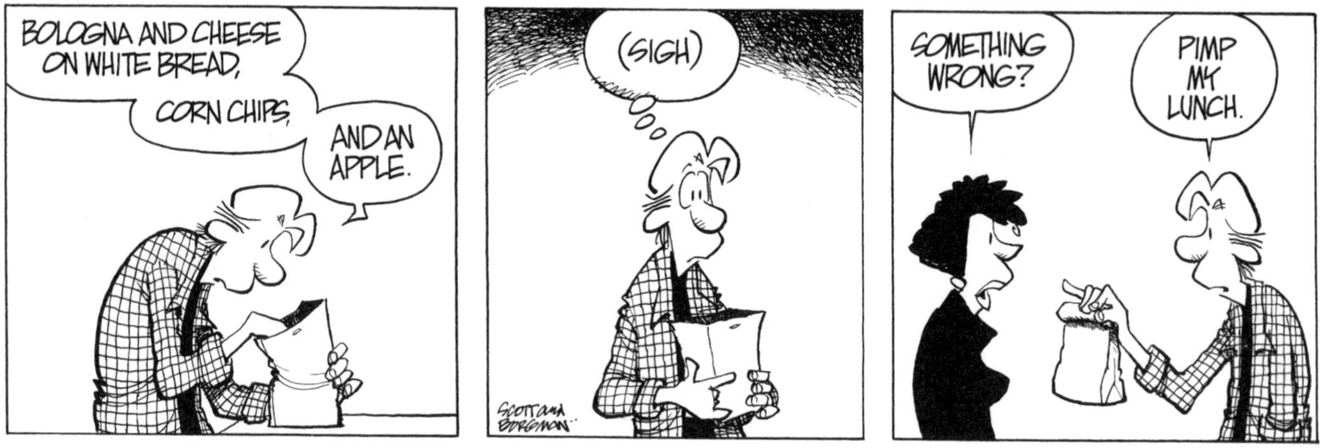
BOLOGNA AND CHEESE ON WHITE BREAD,
CORN CHIPS,
AND AN APPLE.
(SIGH)
SOMETHING WRONG?
PIMP MY LUNCH.

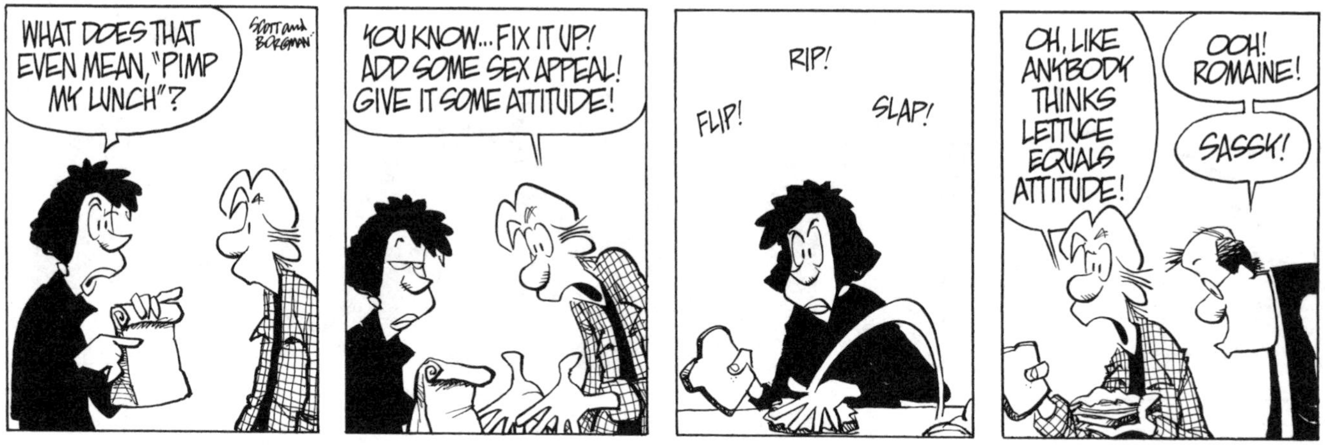
WHAT DOES THAT EVEN MEAN, "PIMP MY LUNCH"?
YOU KNOW... FIX IT UP! ADD SOME SEX APPEAL! GIVE IT SOME ATTITUDE!
RIP!
FLIP!
SLAP!
OH, LIKE ANYBODY THINKS LETTUCE EQUALS ATTITUDE!
OOH! ROMAINE!
SASSY!

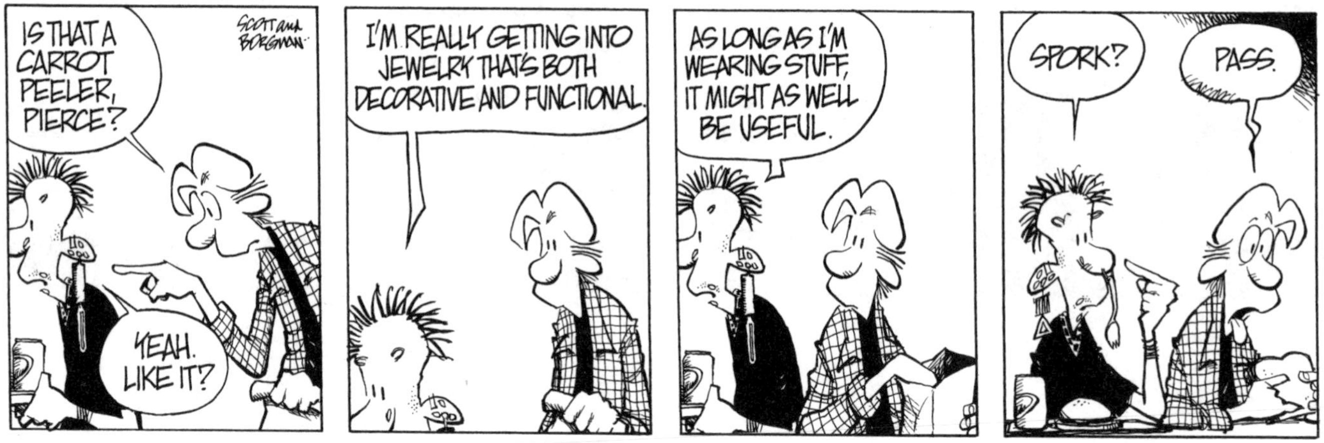
IS THAT A CARROT PEELER, PIERCE?
YEAH. LIKE IT?
I'M REALLY GETTING INTO JEWELRY THAT'S BOTH DECORATIVE AND FUNCTIONAL.
AS LONG AS I'M WEARING STUFF, IT MIGHT AS WELL BE USEFUL.
SPORK?
PASS.

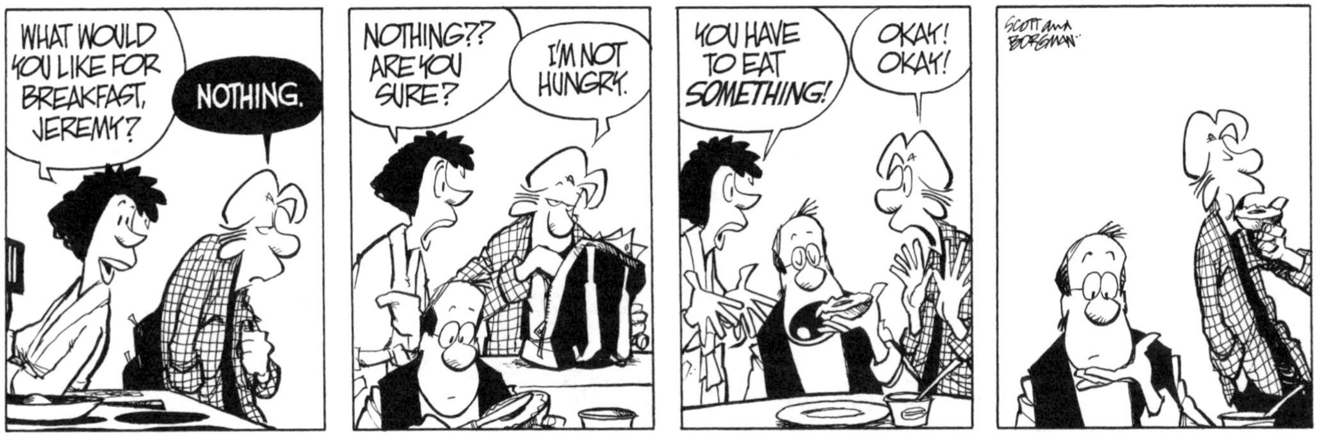
WHAT WOULD YOU LIKE FOR BREAKFAST, JEREMY?
NOTHING.
NOTHING?? ARE YOU SURE?
I'M NOT HUNGRY.
YOU HAVE TO EAT *SOMETHING!*
OKAY! OKAY!

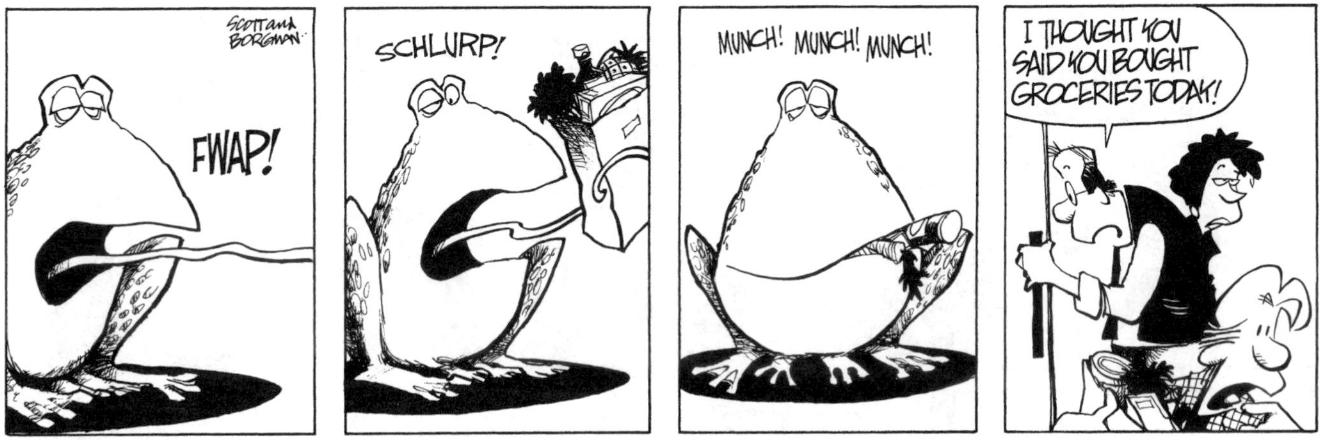
FWAP!
SCHLURP!
MUNCH! MUNCH! MUNCH!
I THOUGHT YOU SAID YOU BOUGHT GROCERIES TODAY!

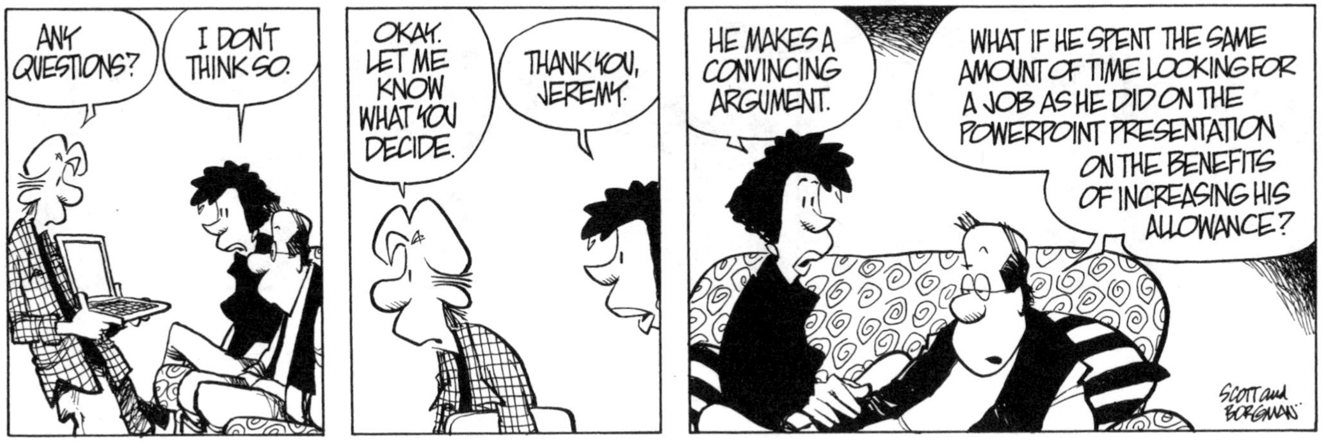
ANY QUESTIONS?
I DON'T THINK SO.
OKAY. LET ME KNOW WHAT YOU DECIDE.
THANK YOU, JEREMY.
HE MAKES A CONVINCING ARGUMENT.
WHAT IF HE SPENT THE SAME AMOUNT OF TIME LOOKING FOR A JOB AS HE DID ON THE POWERPOINT PRESENTATION ON THE BENEFITS OF INCREASING HIS ALLOWANCE?

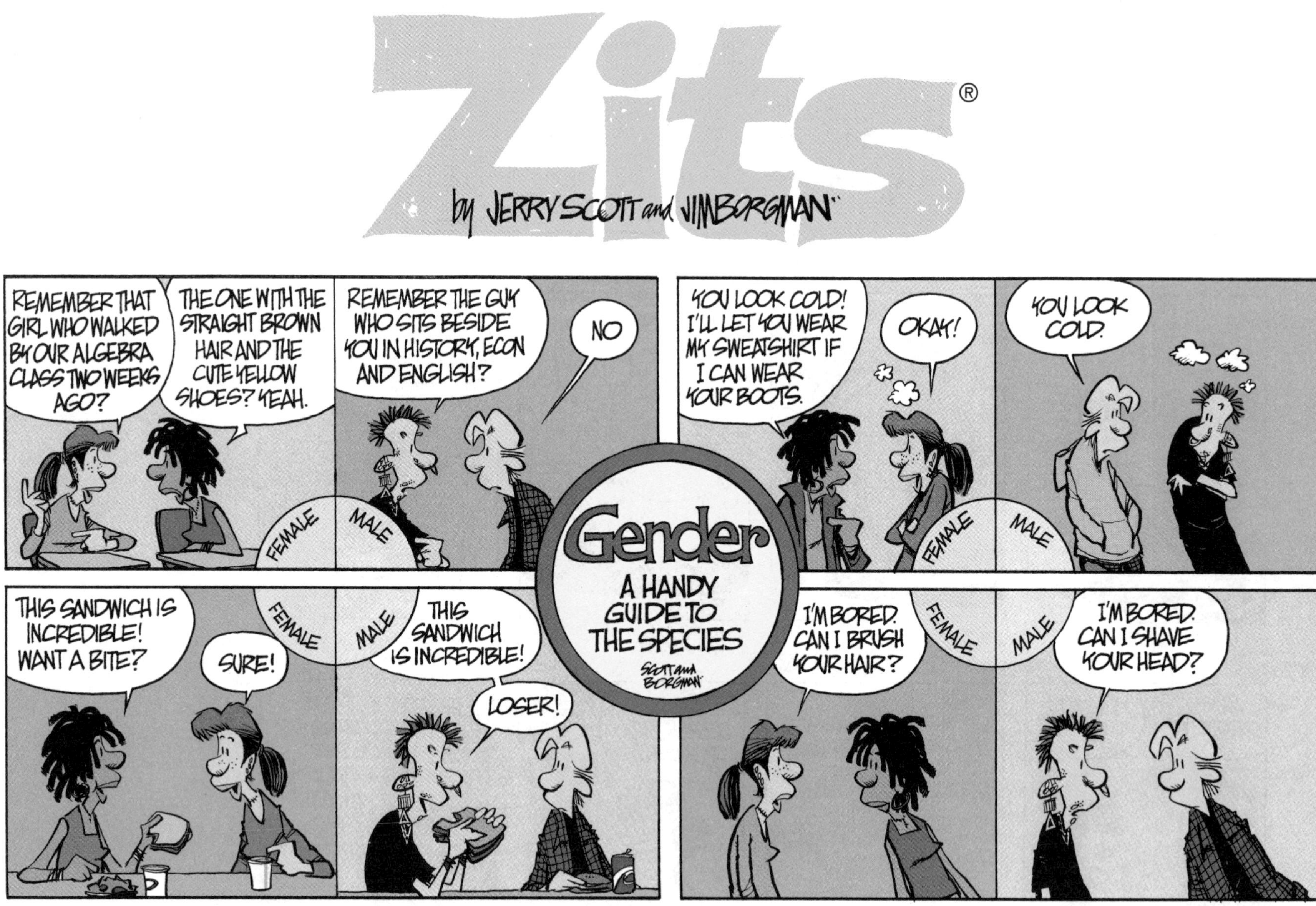

Zits®
by JERRY SCOTT and JIM BORGMAN
REMEMBER THAT GIRL WHO WALKED BY OUR ALGEBRA CLASS TWO WEEKS AGO?
THE ONE WITH THE STRAIGHT BROWN HAIR AND THE CUTE YELLOW SHOES? YEAH.
REMEMBER THE GUY WHO SITS BESIDE YOU IN HISTORY, ECON AND ENGLISH?
NO
YOU LOOK COLD! I'LL LET YOU WEAR MY SWEATSHIRT IF I CAN WEAR YOUR BOOTS.
OKAY!
YOU LOOK COLD.
FEMALE
MALE
Gender
A HANDY GUIDE TO THE SPECIES
SCOTT and BORGMAN
THIS SANDWICH IS INCREDIBLE! WANT A BITE?
SURE!
THIS SANDWICH IS INCREDIBLE!
LOSER!
I'M BORED. CAN I BRUSH YOUR HAIR?
I'M BORED. CAN I SHAVE YOUR HEAD?

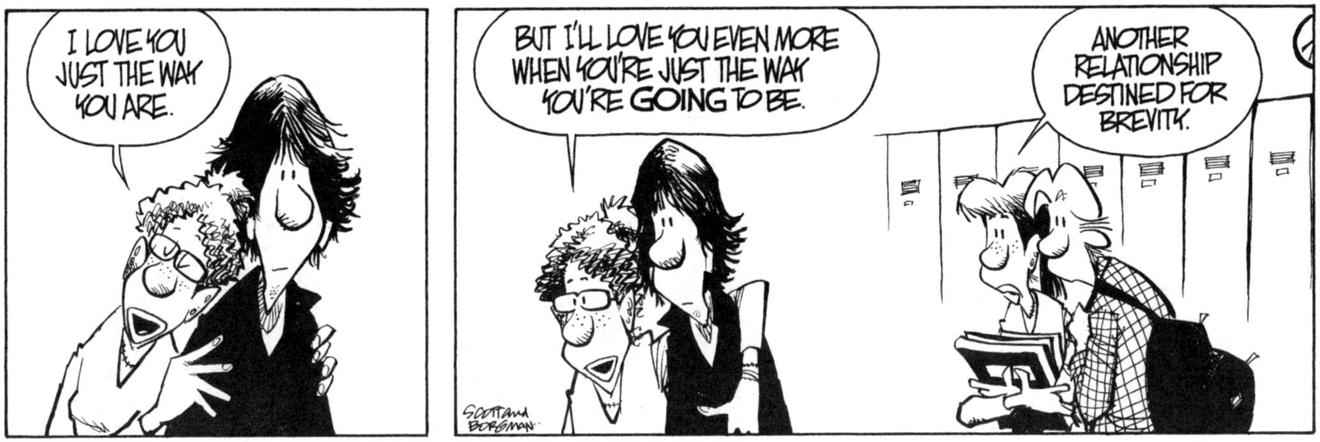
I LOVE YOU JUST THE WAY YOU ARE.
BUT I'LL LOVE YOU EVEN MORE WHEN YOU'RE JUST THE WAY YOU'RE GOING TO BE.
ANOTHER RELATIONSHIP DESTINED FOR BREVITY.

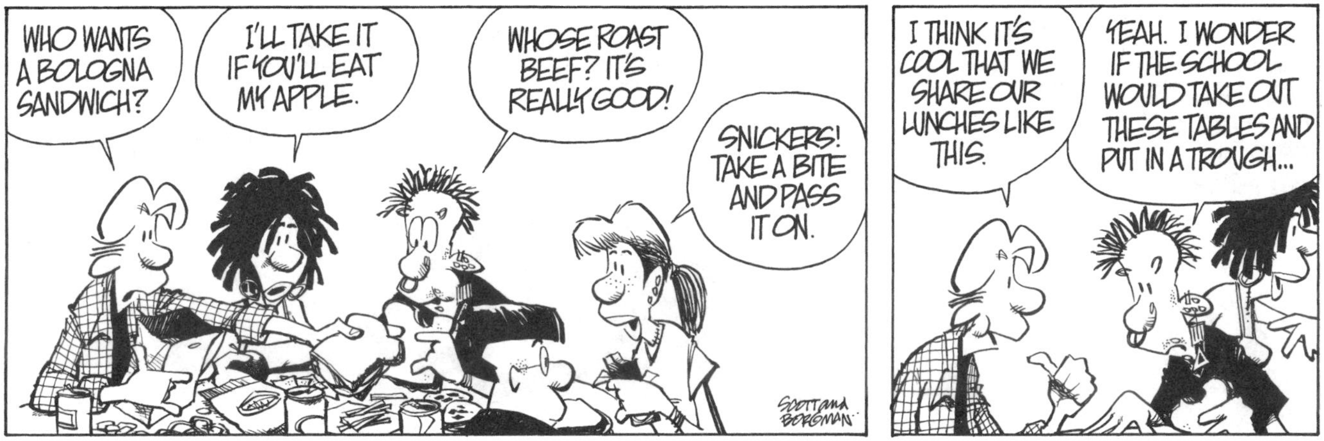
WHO WANTS A BOLOGNA SANDWICH?
I'LL TAKE IT IF YOU'LL EAT MY APPLE.
WHOSE ROAST BEEF? IT'S REALLY GOOD!
SNICKERS! TAKE A BITE AND PASS IT ON.
I THINK IT'S COOL THAT WE SHARE OUR LUNCHES LIKE THIS.
YEAH. I WONDER IF THE SCHOOL WOULD TAKE OUT THESE TABLES AND PUT IN A TROUGH...

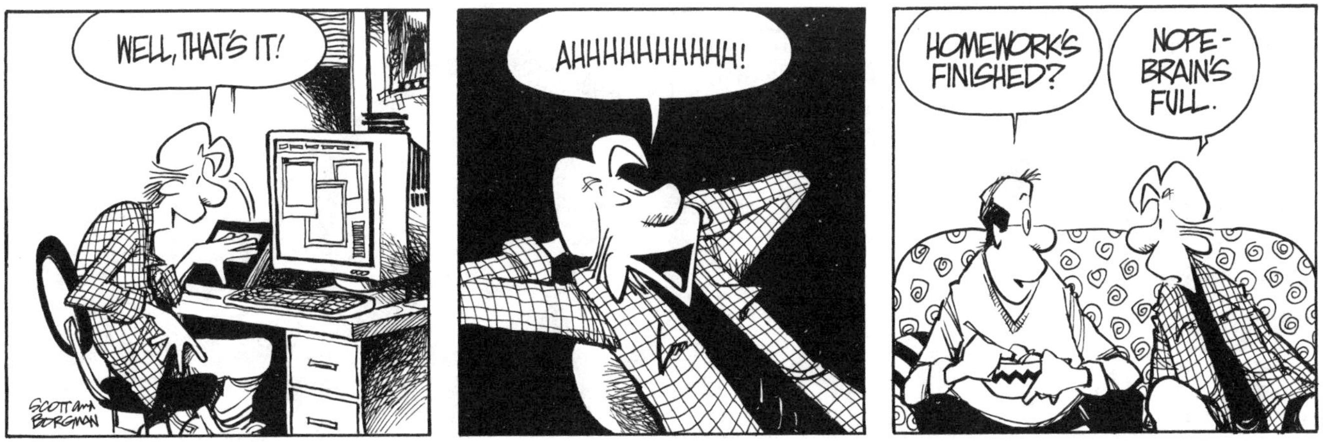
WELL, THAT'S IT!
AHHHHHHHHHH!
HOMEWORK'S FINISHED?
NOPE-BRAIN'S FULL.

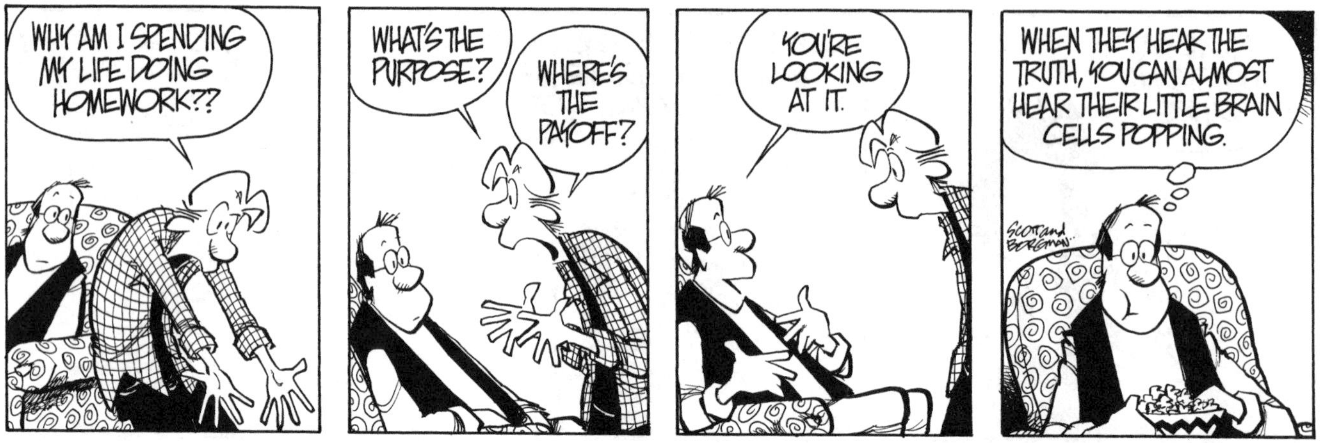
WHY AM I SPENDING MY LIFE DOING HOMEWORK??
WHAT'S THE PURPOSE?
WHERE'S THE PAYOFF?
YOU'RE LOOKING AT IT.
WHEN THEY HEAR THE TRUTH, YOU CAN ALMOST HEAR THEIR LITTLE BRAIN CELLS POPPING.

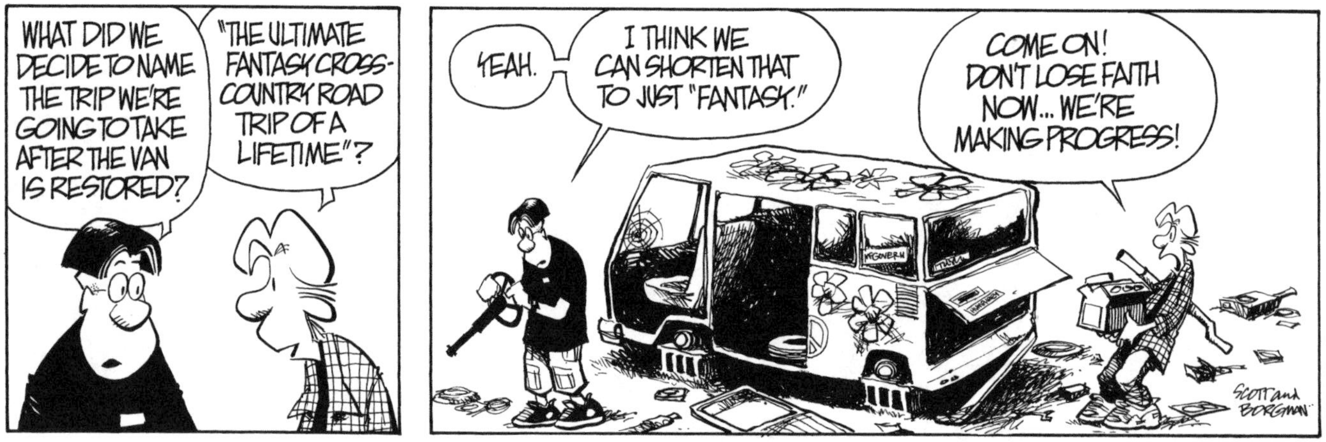
WHAT DID WE DECIDE TO NAME THE TRIP WE'RE GOING TO TAKE AFTER THE VAN IS RESTORED?
"THE ULTIMATE FANTASY CROSS-COUNTRY ROAD TRIP OF A LIFETIME"?
YEAH.
I THINK WE CAN SHORTEN THAT TO JUST "FANTASY."
COME ON! DON'T LOSE FAITH NOW... WE'RE MAKING PROGRESS!

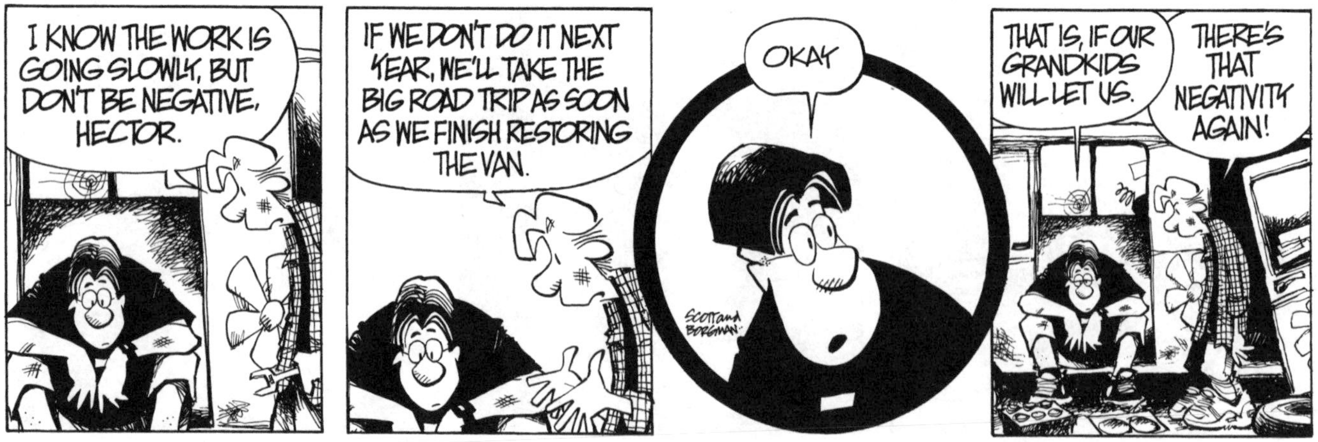
I KNOW THE WORK IS GOING SLOWLY, BUT DON'T BE NEGATIVE, HECTOR.
IF WE DON'T DO IT NEXT YEAR, WE'LL TAKE THE BIG ROAD TRIP AS SOON AS WE FINISH RESTORING THE VAN.
OKAY
THAT IS, IF OUR GRANDKIDS WILL LET US.
THERE'S THAT NEGATIVITY AGAIN!

Zits®

by JERRY SCOTT and JIM BORGMAN

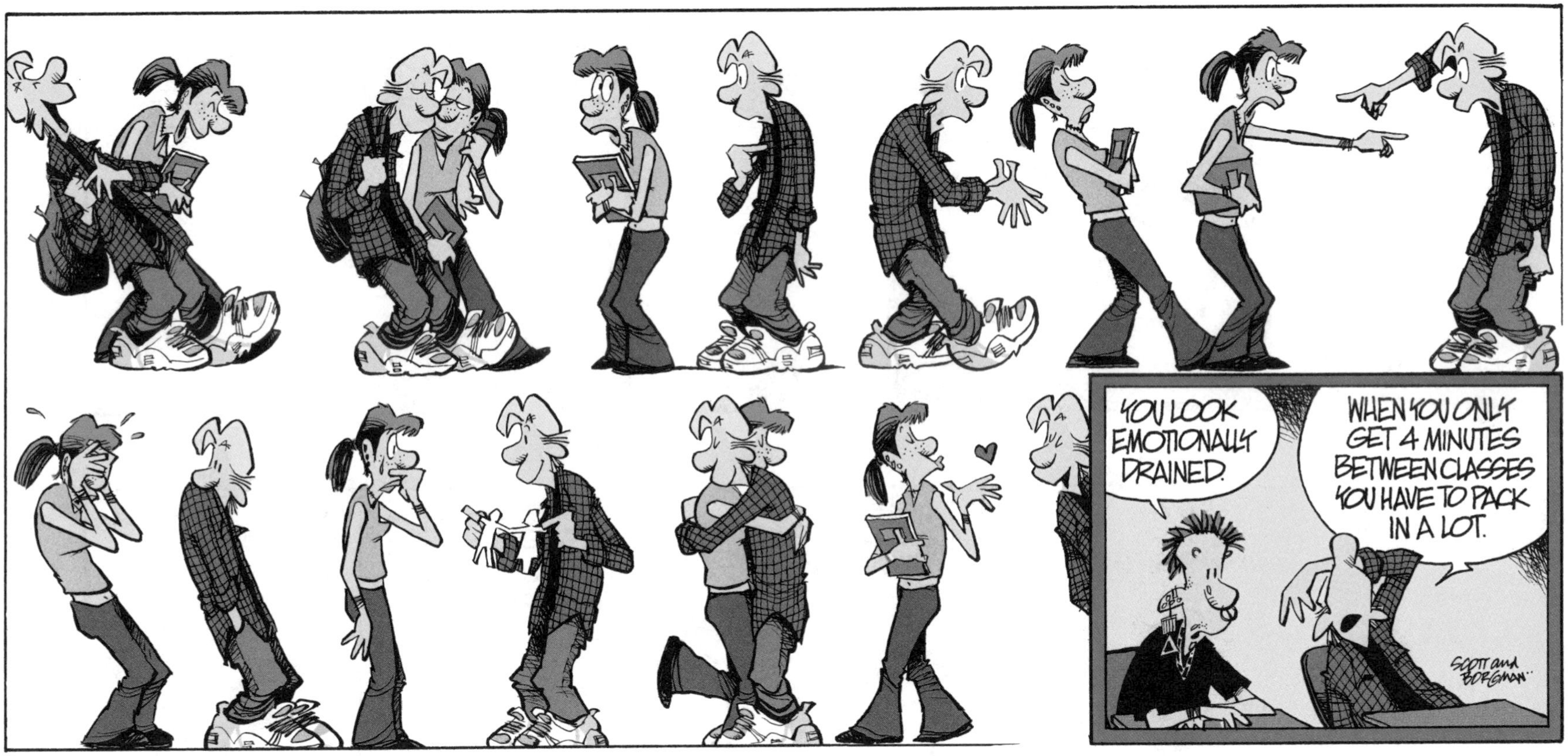
YOU LOOK EMOTIONALLY DRAINED.
WHEN YOU ONLY GET 4 MINUTES BETWEEN CLASSES YOU HAVE TO PACK IN A LOT.
SCOTT and BORGMAN

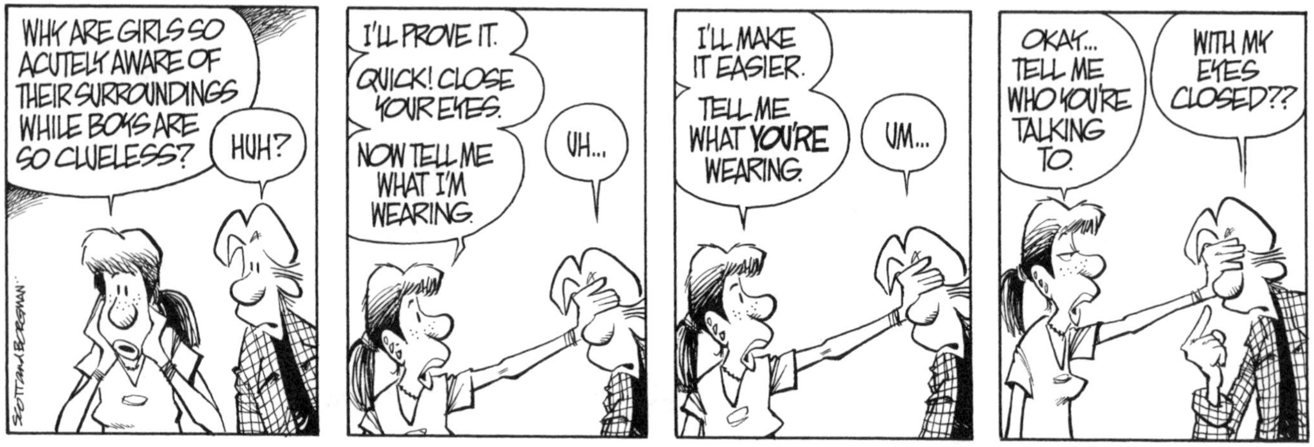
WHY ARE GIRLS SO ACUTELY AWARE OF THEIR SURROUNDINGS WHILE BOYS ARE SO CLUELESS?
HUH?
I'LL PROVE IT.
QUICK! CLOSE YOUR EYES.
NOW TELL ME WHAT I'M WEARING.
UH...
I'LL MAKE IT EASIER.
TELL ME WHAT **YOU'RE** WEARING.
UM...
OKAY... TELL ME WHO YOU'RE TALKING TO.
WITH MY EYES CLOSED??

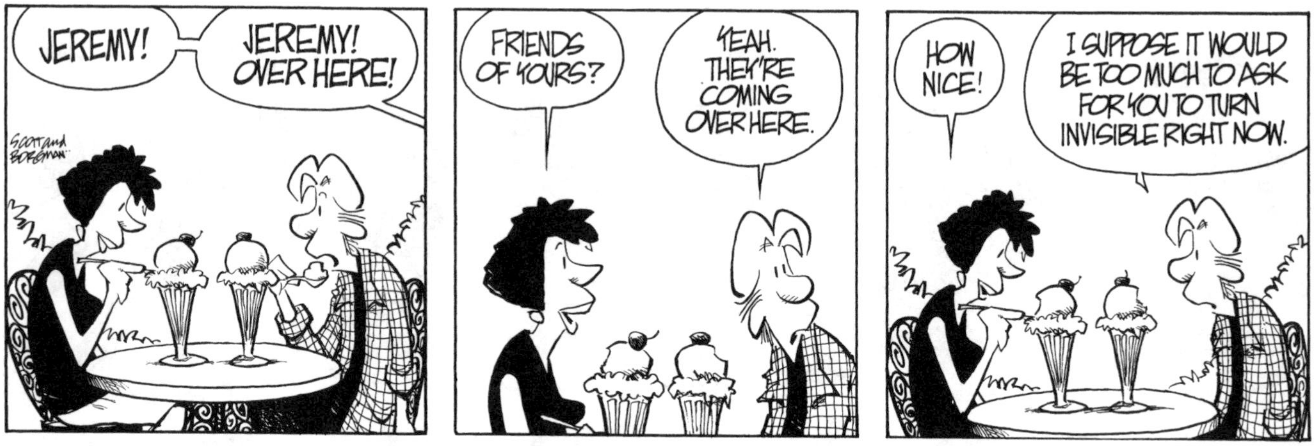
JEREMY!
JEREMY! OVER HERE!
FRIENDS OF YOURS?
YEAH. THEY'RE COMING OVER HERE.
HOW NICE!
I SUPPOSE IT WOULD BE TOO MUCH TO ASK FOR YOU TO TURN INVISIBLE RIGHT NOW.

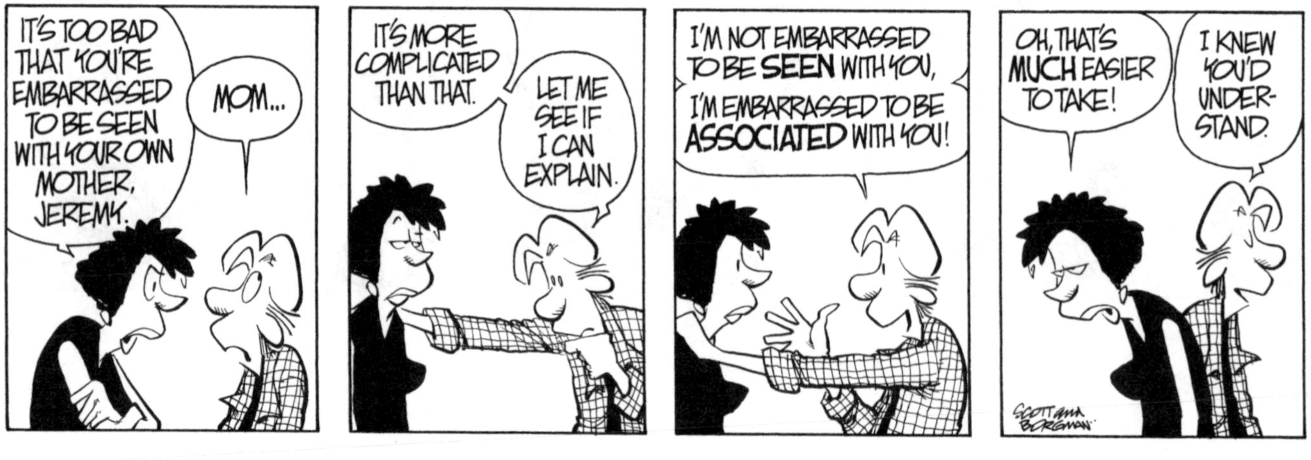
IT'S TOO BAD THAT YOU'RE EMBARRASSED TO BE SEEN WITH YOUR OWN MOTHER, JEREMY.
MOM...
IT'S MORE COMPLICATED THAN THAT.
LET ME SEE IF I CAN EXPLAIN.
I'M NOT EMBARRASSED TO BE **SEEN** WITH YOU,
I'M EMBARRASSED TO BE **ASSOCIATED** WITH YOU!
OH, THAT'S **MUCH** EASIER TO TAKE!
I KNEW YOU'D UNDER-STAND.

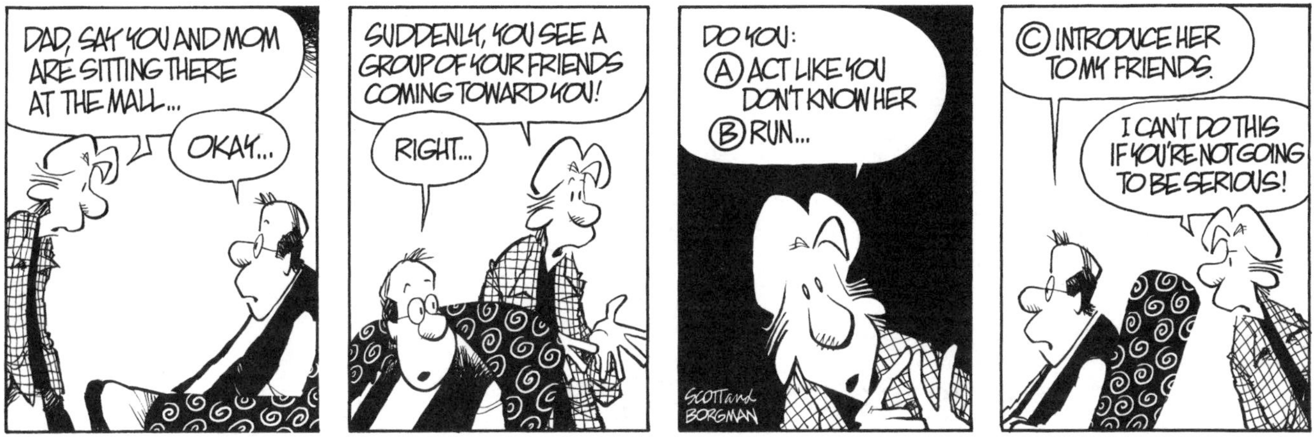
DAD, SAY YOU AND MOM ARE SITTING THERE AT THE MALL...
OKAY...
SUDDENLY, YOU SEE A GROUP OF YOUR FRIENDS COMING TOWARD YOU!
RIGHT...
DO YOU: (A) ACT LIKE YOU DON'T KNOW HER (B) RUN...
SCOTT and BORGMAN
(C) INTRODUCE HER TO MY FRIENDS.
I CAN'T DO THIS IF YOU'RE NOT GOING TO BE SERIOUS!

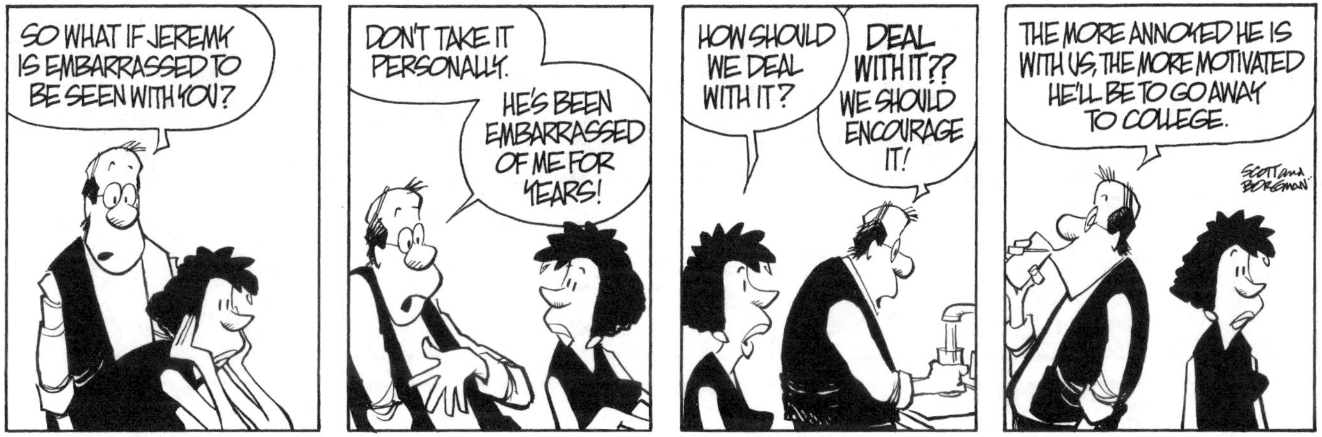
SO WHAT IF JEREMY IS EMBARRASSED TO BE SEEN WITH YOU?
DON'T TAKE IT PERSONALLY.
HE'S BEEN EMBARRASSED OF ME FOR YEARS!
HOW SHOULD WE DEAL WITH IT?
DEAL WITH IT?? WE SHOULD ENCOURAGE IT!
THE MORE ANNOYED HE IS WITH US, THE MORE MOTIVATED HE'LL BE TO GO AWAY TO COLLEGE.
SCOTT and BORGMAN

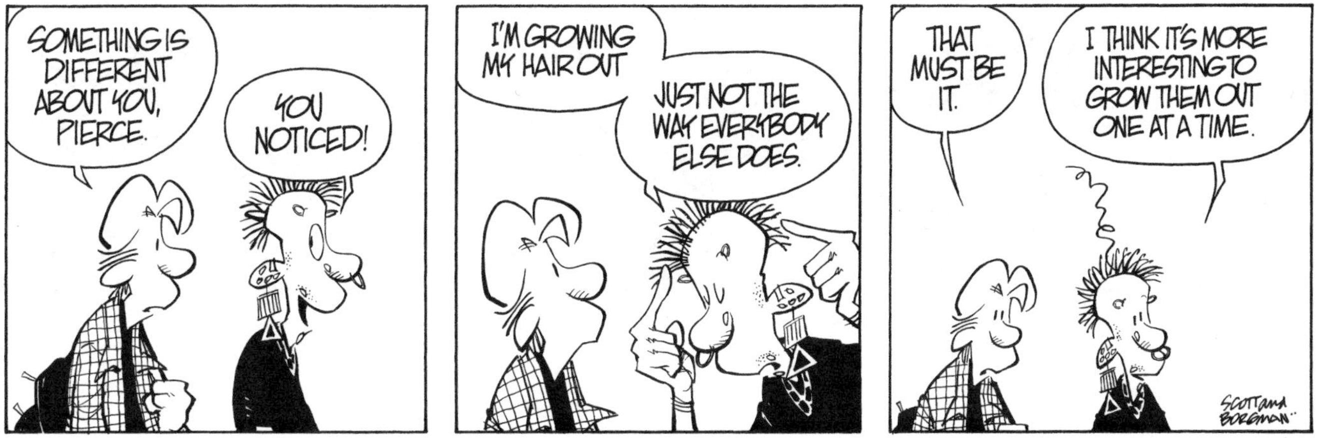
SOMETHING IS DIFFERENT ABOUT YOU, PIERCE.
YOU NOTICED!
I'M GROWING MY HAIR OUT
JUST NOT THE WAY EVERYBODY ELSE DOES.
THAT MUST BE IT.
I THINK IT'S MORE INTERESTING TO GROW THEM OUT ONE AT A TIME.
SCOTT and BORGMAN

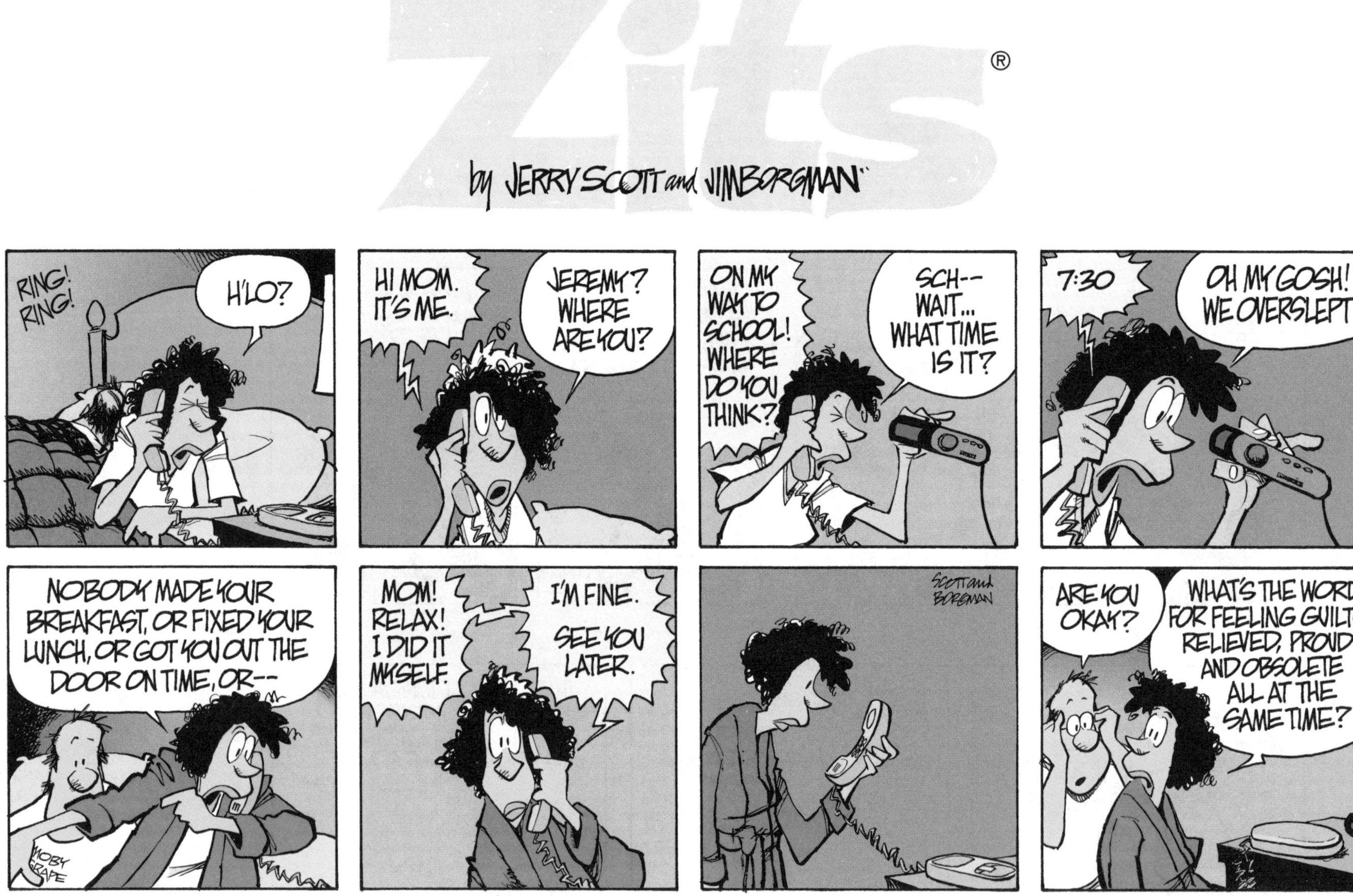
Zits®
by JERRY SCOTT and JIM BORGMAN
RING! RING!
H'LO?
HI MOM. IT'S ME.
JEREMY? WHERE ARE YOU?
ON MY WAY TO SCHOOL! WHERE DO YOU THINK?
SCH-- WAIT... WHAT TIME IS IT?
7:30
OH MY GOSH! WE OVERSLEPT!
NOBODY MADE YOUR BREAKFAST, OR FIXED YOUR LUNCH, OR GOT YOU OUT THE DOOR ON TIME, OR--
MOBY GRAPE
MOM! RELAX! I DID IT MYSELF.
I'M FINE.
SEE YOU LATER.
SCOTT and BORGMAN
ARE YOU OKAY?
WHAT'S THE WORD FOR FEELING GUILTY, RELIEVED, PROUD AND OBSOLETE ALL AT THE SAME TIME?

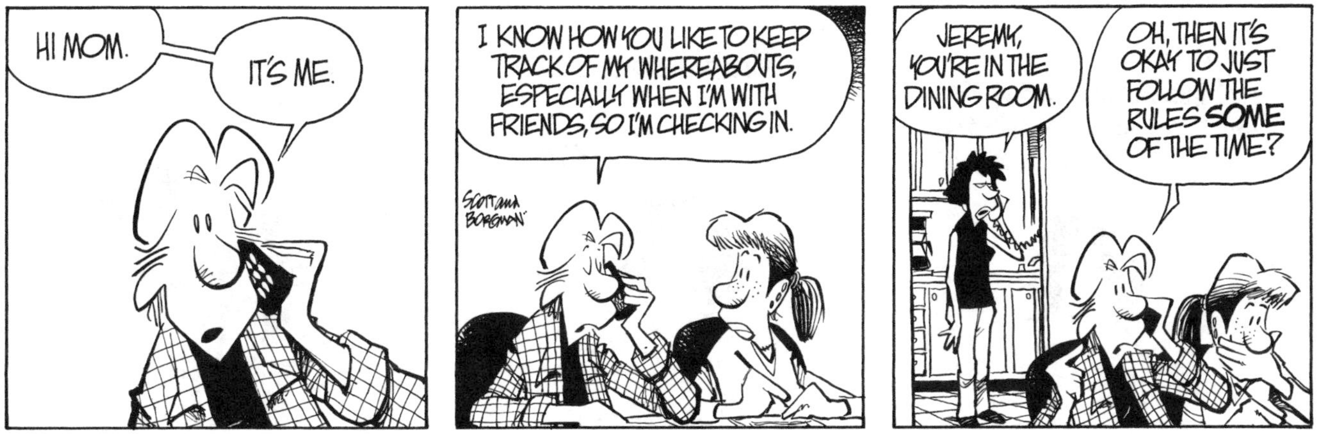
HI MOM.
IT'S ME.
I KNOW HOW YOU LIKE TO KEEP TRACK OF MY WHEREABOUTS, ESPECIALLY WHEN I'M WITH FRIENDS, SO I'M CHECKING IN.
JEREMY, YOU'RE IN THE DINING ROOM.
OH, THEN IT'S OKAY TO JUST FOLLOW THE RULES **SOME** OF THE TIME?

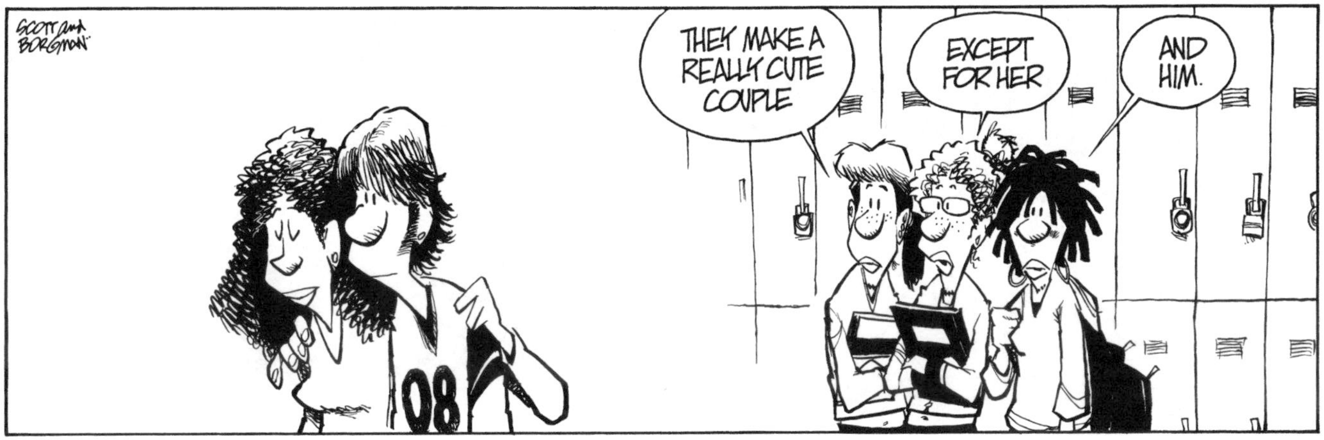
THEY MAKE A REALLY CUTE COUPLE
EXCEPT FOR HER
AND HIM.
08

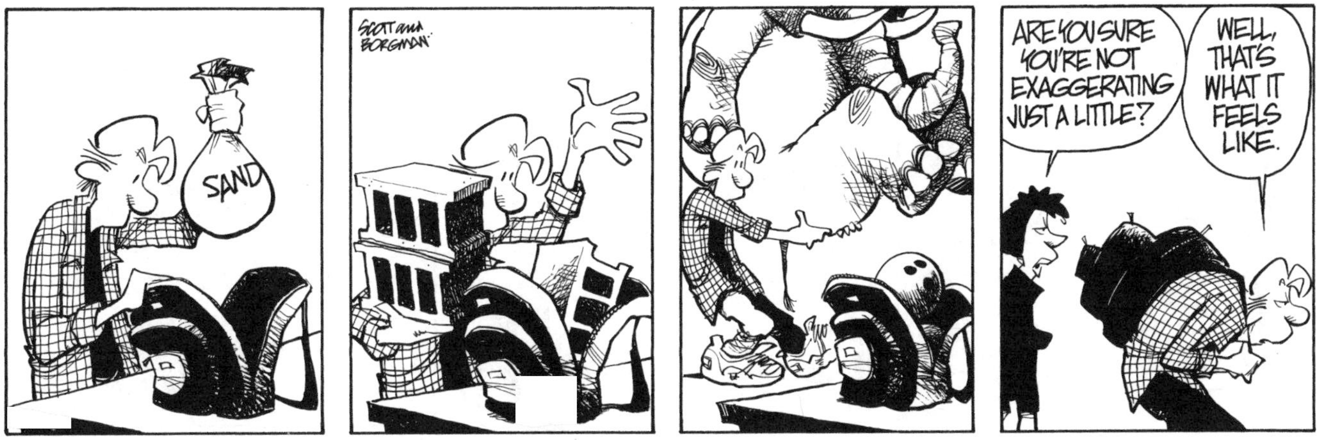
SAND
ARE YOU SURE YOU'RE NOT EXAGGERATING JUST A LITTLE?
WELL, THAT'S WHAT IT FEELS LIKE.

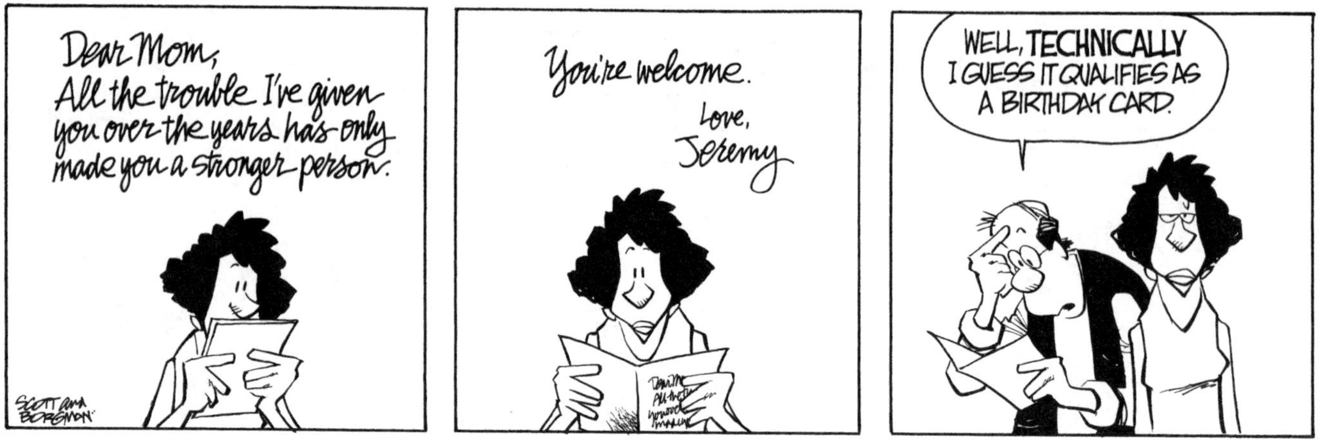
Dear Mom,
All the trouble I've given you over the years has only made you a stronger person.
SCOTT and BORGMAN
You're welcome.
Love, Jeremy
WELL, TECHNICALLY I GUESS IT QUALIFIES AS A BIRTHDAY CARD.

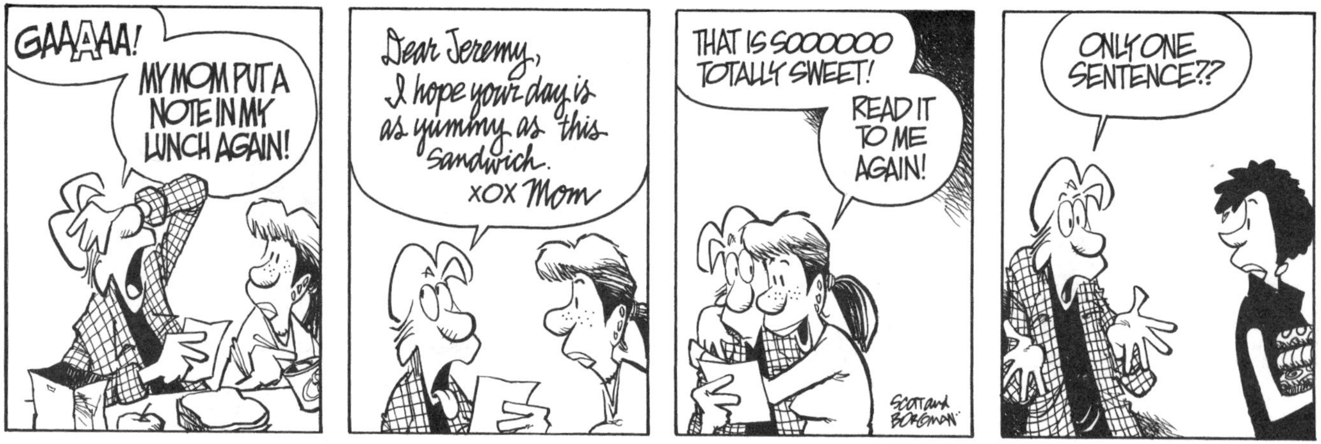
GAAAAA!
MY MOM PUT A NOTE IN MY LUNCH AGAIN!
Dear Jeremy,
I hope your day is as yummy as this sandwich.
XOX Mom
THAT IS SOOOOOO TOTALLY SWEET!
READ IT TO ME AGAIN!
SCOTT and BORGMAN
ONLY ONE SENTENCE??

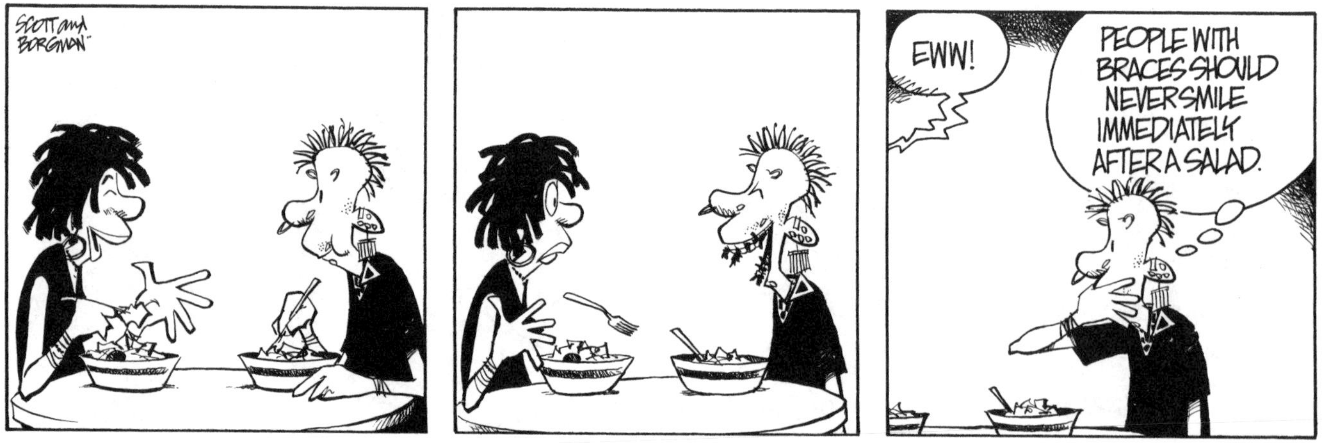
SCOTT and BORGMAN
EWW!
PEOPLE WITH BRACES SHOULD NEVER SMILE IMMEDIATELY AFTER A SALAD.

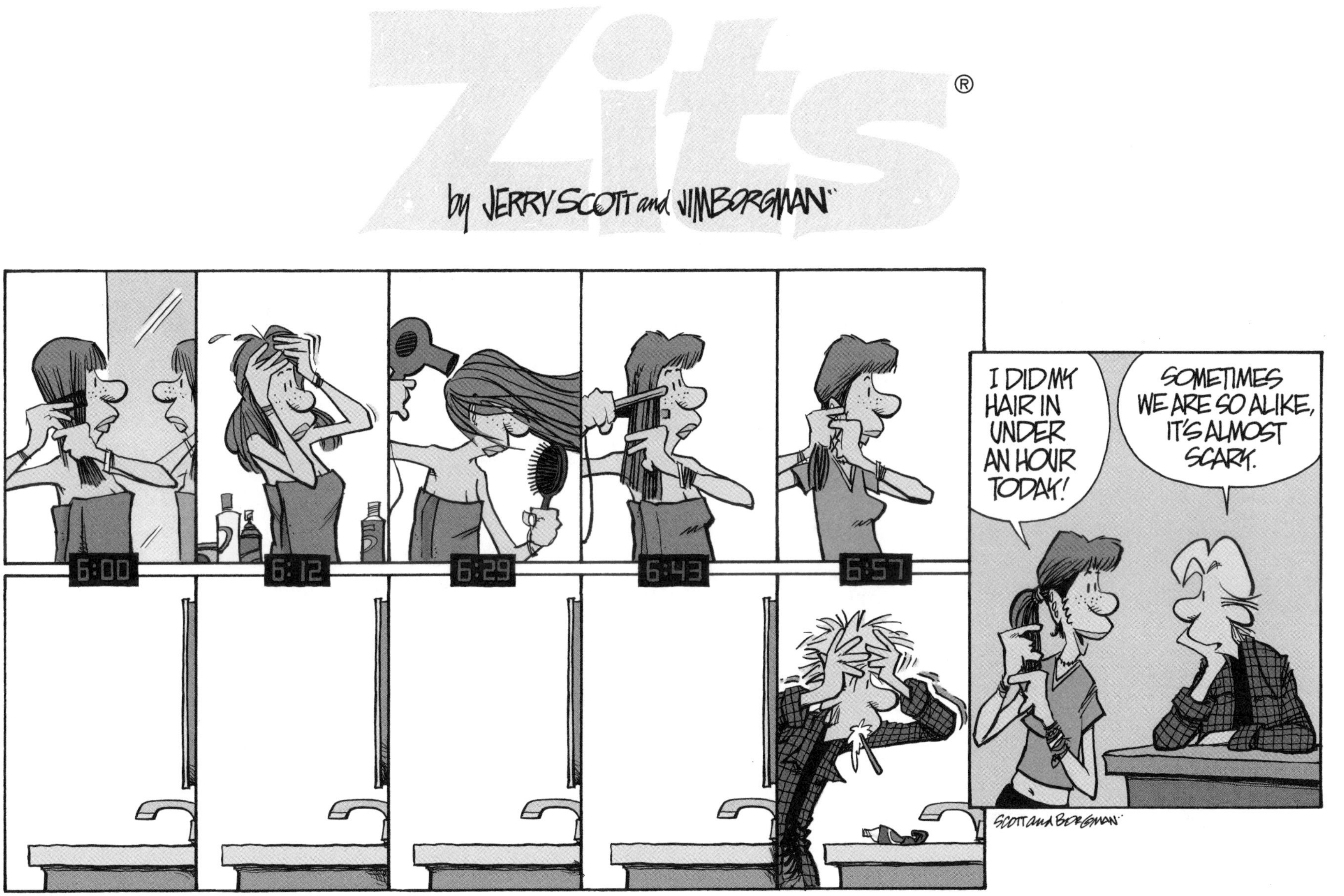
Zits®
by JERRY SCOTT and JIM BORGMAN
6:00
6:12
6:29
6:43
6:57
I DID MY HAIR IN UNDER AN HOUR TODAY!
SOMETIMES WE ARE SO ALIKE, IT'S ALMOST SCARY.
SCOTT and BORGMAN

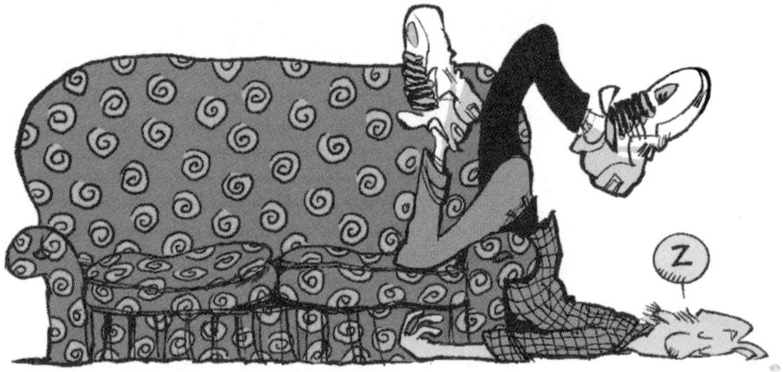
Z